Sources of State Practice in International Law

Sources of State Practice in International Law

Second Revised Edition

Edited by

Ralph F. Gaebler
Alison A. Shea

BRILL
NIJHOFF

LEIDEN | BOSTON

First published as loose leaf publication *Sources of State Practice in International Law*, edited by Ralph Gaebler and Maria Smolka-Day, Transnational Publishers 2001.

Library of Congress Cataloging-in-Publication Data
Sources of state practice in international law / edited by Ralph F. Gaebler, Alison A. Shea. -- Second Revised Edition.
pages cm
Includes bibliographical references and index.
ISBN 978-90-04-17886-1 (hardback : alk. paper) -- ISBN 978-90-04-27222-4 (e-book : alk. paper)
1. International law--Sources. 2. International law--Bibliography. I. Gaebler, Ralph, editor of compilation. II. Shea, Alison A., editor of compilation.
KZ64.S67 2014
016.341--dc23

2014013062

This publication has been typeset in the multilingual "Brill" typeface. With over 5,100 characters covering Latin, IPA, Greek, and Cyrillic, this typeface is especially suitable for use in the humanities.
For more information, please see www.brill.com/brill-typeface.

ISBN 978-90-04-17886-1 (hardback)
ISBN 978-90-04-27222-4 (e-book)

This book is printed on acid-free paper.

FSC www.fsc.org MIX Paper from responsible sources FSC® C109576

Printed by Printforce, the Netherlands

Contents

List of Contributors

Jennifer Allison (*Germany*)

Jennifer Allison is a Librarian for Foreign, Comparative, and International Law at the Harvard Law School Library, specializing in German-language jurisdictions. She earned her B.A. in English and German from Pacific Lutheran University in 1994, and taught English at the Wilhelm Busch Gymnasium in Stadthagen, Germany as a Fulbright grant recipient during the 1995–96 academic year. After working for several years as a technical writer, she earned her J.D. from Pepperdine Law School in 2007, and her M.L.I.S. from San Jose State University in 2010. During law school, she was an exchange student at the Juristische Faklutät at the University of Augsburg in Germany, where her German-language coursework included international civil procedure, international criminal law, and legal theory and philosophy.

Martin Bouda (*Czech Republic*)

Martin was born in Prague, Czech Republic. He earned a B.A. *summa cum laude*, Phi Beta Kappa, at the University of Pennsylvania in 2008, an M.E.Sc. at the Yale School of Forestry and Environmental Studies in 2010, and is currently a doctoral candidate in Environmental Science at Yale University. During his time at the University of Pennsylvania, he worked as an Assistant Reference Librarian in the Foreign and International Law section of the Biddle Law Library. He also repeatedly held the position of Librarian in the Philomathean Society of the University of Pennsylvania, in which capacity he compiled a catalogue of the Society's collections. Throughout his foray into natural science, he maintains an active interest in legal research and he collected much of the information in his chapter at the Faculty of Law of Charles University in Prague.

Rob Britt (*Japan*)

Rob Britt is the Coordinator of East Asian Library Services at the Marian Gould Gallagher Law Library in the University of Washington School of Law, where he has worked for 26 years. His focus is on Japanese and East Asian legal resources. Rob holds a Master of Arts in International Studies from the University of Washington.

Talia Einhorn (*Israel*)

Talia Einhorn is a Full Professor (Ordinaria) at Ariel University Department of Economics and Business Management and Visiting Senior Research Fellow at Tel-Aviv University Faculty of Management, having earned the degrees of

B.Sc. (math-physics) (*cum laude*), Hebrew University of Jerusalem; LL.B., LL.M. (*magna cum laude*), Tel-Aviv University; and Dr.iur. (*magna cum laude*), University of Hamburg. She has taught and lectured widely at Israeli, European and American universities and is the author of a number of books, including PRIVATE INTERNATIONAL LAW IN ISRAEL, 2nd ed. (Kluwer Law International, 2012), and numerous articles in international, European and Israeli law journals and scientific publications. She was founder and Editor-in-Chief of *European Business Organization Law Review* (*EBOR*) (2000–2002), and a member of the Advisory Board (2003–2013). Ms. Einhorn is a member of various international organizations including the International Academy of Comparative Law; the Scientific Board of the Interdisciplinary Association of Comparative and Private International Law (IACPIL); the German Society of International Law; the American Society of International Law ILA International Arbitration Committee; and the Israeli Bar Association.

Victor Essien (*Ghana, Kenya*)

Victor Essien holds LL.B. (Hons), LL.M. (Ghana), LL.M. (Int'l), and J.S.D. (NYU) degrees. He is International Law Librarian and Adjunct Associate Professor of Law at Fordham Law School, where he teaches International Oil and Gas Law, International Investment Law, Multinational Corporations, Law Advanced Legal Research in International Humanitarian Law and International and Comparative Law. He was formerly Law Lecturer (on National Service) at the University of Ghana, Legon and the University of Jos, Nigeria. He was also a Consultant to the UNCTC in New York and a Legal Assistant to the Iran-US Claims Tribunal at The Hague, the Netherlands. He was admitted to the Ghana Bar in 1977. He is currently a Member of the Bars of Ghana, New York State, United States District Court, Southern and Eastern Districts of New York and The United States Court of Appeals, Second and Third Circuits. He has written extensively in learned journals on international and comparative law.

Gabriela Femenia (*Belgium*)

Gabriela Femenia has been Foreign and International Law Librarian at the University of Pennsylvania Law School's Biddle Law Library since 2009. She received her M.L.I.S. from the University of Washington in 2009 and her J.D. from the University of Pennsylvania in 2000. In addition, she holds degrees in History from the University of California - Berkeley and Harvard University.

Ralph F. Gaebler (*Co-Editor; Austria, Belgium, Canada, Germany, South Africa, Switzerland*)

Ralph F. Gaebler is International & Foreign Law Librarian at the Maurer School of Law, Indiana University-Bloomington. He earned his A.B. from Brown University

(1981), and J.D. (1984), M.L.S. (1985), and M.A. in philosophy (2008) from Indiana University-Bloomington. He has published in the areas of comparative law, legal bibliography, and philosophy, and teaches advanced legal research.

Susan Gualtier (Italy)

Susan Gualtier is a Foreign, Comparative, and International Law Librarian at the Paul M. Hebert Law Center at Louisiana State University. She obtained her J.D. from the Georgetown University Law Center, her M.L.I.S. from the University of Wisconsin, Milwaukee, and her B.A. in history from Yale University. Prior to obtaining her M.L.I.S., she practiced law in New York, NY, and Washington, DC, and worked as an intern and independent contract attorney for an in-house legal department in Florence, Italy. Her academic interests include legal history, women's human rights, customary and religious laws, and mixed legal systems.

Ryan Harrington (Spain)

Ryan Harrington is the Head of Reference at the Yale Law Library, where he has worked since 2008. He is also a Lecturer in Legal Research at the Yale Law School and teaches a specialized legal research course in foreign and international law. Mr. Harrington has served as a Corresponding Editor for International Legal Materials since April 2011. He holds a B.A. in History from Arizona State, an M.L.S. from the University of Arizona, and a J.D. from the Georgetown University Law Center.

Carole L. Hinchcliff (Australia)

Carole L. Hinchcliff has been the Law Librarian at the University of Melbourne's Law School Library since 2008. She received her B.A. and L.L.B. degrees from The University of Melbourne, Australia and her M.L.S. degree from the University of Wisconsin, Madison. From 1984–2007 she held various positions at The Ohio State University's Moritz Law Library including Associate Director from 1996–2007. Ms. Hinchcliff is the current convenor of The Australian & New Zealand Academic & College Law Librarians Group (ANZACLL) and was convenor of the 2013 Joint Study Institute for law librarians, which was sponsored by AALL, ALLA, BIALL, CALL/ACBD and NZLLA and hosted by Melbourne Law School. She has held leadership positions in the American Association of Law Libraries, including chair of the Academic Special Interest Section and has written and presented on a variety of law library topics during her career in law librarianship.

Marci Hoffman (United States)

Marci Hoffman is the Associate Director and International & Foreign Law Librarian at the University of California, Berkeley Law School. Ms. Hoffman received her B.A. in Political Science from the University of California, Davis and her M.L.I.S. from the University of California, Berkeley. She served as the foreign, comparative, and international law librarian at the University of Minnesota Law Library from 1993 to 1999 and was the international and foreign law librarian at Georgetown University Law Library until she returned to Berkeley Law in fall 2003. Ms. Hoffman has done extensive work and written widely on international and foreign legal research, including *International and Foreign Legal Research: A Coursebook* (2d ed. 2012) with Mary Rumsey. Ms. Hoffman is also the General Editor of the *Index to Foreign Legal Periodicals* (IFLP) and the *Foreign Law Guide*.

Vera Korzun (Belarus)

Vera Korzun is an Adjunct Professor of Law, a doctoral fellow and an S.J.D. candidate at Fordham University School of Law. Her research primarily involves international and European law, antitrust, and international arbitration. She previously taught law courses, including international business law, contracts law, and private international law, at the Universities in Belarus and the Netherlands. She also interned for the European Commission in Brussels and the United Nations in New York. Ms. Korzun received her LL.M. degrees from the University of Michigan Law School, the University of Hamburg, and Central European University. She earned her Candidate of Law Sciences – a post-graduate scientific degree – from Belarusian State University, where she also obtained her first degree in law.

Jootaek "Juice" Lee (Korea)

Jootaek (Juice) Lee is a senior law librarian (the Research Librarian for Foreign, Comparative & International Law) and affiliated faculty of the Program of Human Rights and Global Economy at the Northeastern University School of Law. He received a B.A. from Korea University where he also received an LL.M. in international law. Jootaek completed his J.D. at Florida State University, where he was also awarded his M.L.S. He used to work as a law librarian assistant professor at the University of Miami School of Law. He is currently teaching international and foreign legal research and advanced legal research. He has published articles relating to legal informatics, legal pedagogy, and East Asian legal resources in a law review, Law Library Journal, International Journal of Legal Information, Globalex by NYU, SSRN, etc. Furthermore, he has presented at national conferences several times. Finally, he actively participates in the American Association of Law Libraries (AALL) and the American Society of International Law (ASIL).

Joseph Luke (Russia)

Joseph Luke earned his J.D. at the University of Michigan, his M.L.I.S. at the University of North Carolina Greensboro and his M.A. in Slavic Linguistics at the University of Washington. He practiced law in Hawaii, North Carolina and Kazakhstan. In addition he spent several years in Central Asia administering foreign assistance projects, among which were those focused on rule of law and legal education. Most recently he joined KIMEP University, an American style university in Almaty, first as reference librarian, then as Library Director and Head of Learning Resources. He presently is the acting dean of its school of law. He teaches classes in Legal Research and Writing and International Business Transactions for the LLM program.

Evelyn Ma (*Singapore*)

Evelyn Ma is currently Asian Law Reference Librarian and Lecturer of Legal Research at the Lillian Goldman Law Library at Yale Law School. Ms. Ma earned her B.A. degree from the University of Hong Kong, her M.L.S. from the State University of New York at Buffalo, and her J.D. from Santa Clara University. She has been Chair of the Asian Law Interest Group in the Foreign, Comparative, and International Law Special Interest Section of the American Association of Law Libraries, since 2012.

Teresa M. Miguel-Stearns (*Argentina, Mexico*)

Teresa M. Miguel-Stearns is the Associate Director and oversees the Foreign and International Law collection at the Lillian Goldman Law Library at Yale Law School. She is the Latin American Bibliographer, and a Lecturer in Law and Legal Research. She received a J.D. from the University of Richmond School of Law, an M.A. in Information Resources and Library Science from the University of Arizona, a B.A. from the University of Wisconsin-Madison, and a Diploma de Español como Lengua Extranjera from the Escuela Oficial de Idiomas, Salamanca, Spain. Ms. Miguel-Stearns has authored a chapter and several articles and web guides on foreign and international law and legal research, and has served as moderator, speaker, and panelist in continuing education programs at the annual meetings of the American Association of Law Libraries, the American Library Association, the International Federation of Law Libraries, and the Seminar on the Acquisition of Latin American Library Materials.

Dana Neacsu (*Romania*)

Dana Neacsu is Librarian and Lecturer-in-Law at Columbia Law School, Arthur W. Diamond Law Library, in New York City. She holds a Ph.D. in Philosophy from Rutgers University, a library degree from CUNY, and various law degrees, including an LL.M from Harvard Law School. Since she immigrated to the United States, Ms. Neacsu has practiced law as a junior associate in a private law firm and then for the New York City Law Department, and librarianship at

Columbia Law School. Since 2003 she also co-teaches in the Barnard College-Environmental Studies Department as an adjunct professor. She wrote the introductory legal research book for LL.M students (Transnational, 2005). In 2011, Ms. Neacsu updated and published it on Columbia University's Academic Commons, where most of her published work can be freely accessed. Dana actively promotes free-of-charge legal research through http://legalresearch.wikischolars.columbia.edu/. In her spare time she writes political satire for ThePothole View.com.

Kara Phillips (*China*)

Kara Phillips is the Collection Development Librarian and Associate Director at Seattle University Law Library. She is coauthor of the book, REAL PROPERTY LAW IN CHINA: A GUIDE TO FOREIGN INVESTMENT (American Bar Association 2011) (with Amy L. Sommers). Recipient of a Blakemore Fellowship, she studied Mandarin Chinese at the Stanford Center in Taipei, Taiwan. Ms. Phillips was also a visiting scholar at the Shanghai Jiaotong University School of Law. She serves on the Executive Board of the Chinese-American Forum on Legal Information and Law Libraries: http://cafllnet.org/. Ms. Phillips holds an M.A.I.S. (China Studies), M.L.S., and J.D. (with honors) from the University of Washington.

Sunil Rao (*India*)

Sunil Rao is the Foreign and International Law Librarian at the University of Wisconsin Law Library. He earned a J.D. from Marquette University Law School in 1995, an M.L.S. from the University of Wisconsin (2000) and an M.F.A. from Warren Wilson College (2008). His professional interests include foreign, comparative, and international legal research; writing; and scholarship concerning law and spirituality.

Mary Rumsey (*Nigeria*)

Mary Rumsey is Foreign, Comparative, and International Law Librarian at the University of Minnesota Law Library. She holds a B.A. from the University of Wisconsin in philosophy and political science, a J.D. from the University of Chicago, and an M.L.I.S. from Dominican University. Among her publications are contributions to *Law Library Journal, Legal References Services Quarterly,* the EISIL project of the American Society of International Law, and other periodicals. With Marci Hoffman, she wrote *International and Foreign Legal Research: A Coursebook* (2d ed. Brill 2012). With David Weissbrodt, she recently edited the book *Vulnerable and Marginalised Groups and Human Rights* (Edward Elgar, 2011), and is editing a forthcoming volume from Ashgate, *The Development of International Human Rights Law.*

Alison A. Shea (Co-Editor; Ireland)
Alison A. Shea is Reference Librarian/Foreign & International Specialist at Fordham Law School Library. She received a B.A. from Boston University, and a J.D. and M.S.L.S. from Catholic University of America in Washington, D.C. At Fordham, Ms. Shea teaches a number of sections of both basic and advanced legal research courses on a variety of topics, including administrative law, US legal research for LLMs, and foreign and international law. She has authored a number of articles for a variety of publications, and was a co-editor for African jurisdictions on the ABA's recent publication *Essentials of Merger Review* (2013). She is an active member of the American Association of Law Libraries, the British and Irish Association of Law Librarians, and the International Association of Law Libraries.

Maria I. Smolka-Day (United Kingdom)
Maria I. Smolka-Day was formerly Associate Director for Foreign and International Law and Lecturer at the Biddle Law Library, University of Pennsylvania Law School. She earned an LL.M. there in 1983 and an M.L.S. at Drexel University in 1985. Before moving to the United States, she earned an S.J.D. from Marie Curie-Sklodowska University in Lublin, Poland, where she was an Assistant Professor of Law for several years. With a background in both law and library science, she has published legal and bibliographic articles in both Poland and the United States.

Suzanne Thorpe (Denmark, Norway, Sweden)
Suzanne Thorpe is Associate Director for Faculty, Research, and Instructional Services at the University of Minnesota Law Library and Professor of Legal Research Instruction. Professor Thorpe earned B.A. and M.A. degrees from the University of Wisconsin, Madison. She received her J.D. degree from the University of Minnesota. She worked at Hamline University Law Library for nine years before becoming the Public Services Librarian for Hennepin County Law Library in Minneapolis. Professor Thorpe joined the University of Minnesota Law School Library faculty as a reference librarian in 1987. She has been President of the Minnesota Association of Law Libraries and is active in the American Association of Law Libraries, currently serving as a member of the AALL Executive Board.

Beatrice A. Tice (France)
Beatrice A. Tice is Associate Dean, Law Library and Research Professor of Law at the University of California – Irvine School of Law. Prior to joining the University of California, she served as Chief Law Librarian at the Bora Laskin

Law Library, University of Toronto Faculty of Law as well as Foreign and Comparative Law Librarian and Adjunct Instructor of Law at the University of Michigan Law School. Before turning to law librarianship, she practiced for over eight years as a commercial litigator with several major law firms in southern California. Ms. Tice holds a B.A. magna cum laude in modern European languages from Pomona College; an M.A. in linguistics from Yale University; a J.D. with distinction from Stanford Law School; and an M.L.I.S. with a Special Certificate in Law Librarianship from the University of Washington.

Introduction to the Second Edition

Ralph F. Gaebler and Alison A. Shea

The current edition of Sources of State Practice in International Law is essentially an update to the first edition, published in 2001, and supplemented in 2005. Like that edition, this revised second edition is principally a descriptive bibliography of sources of treaties and diplomatic documents, useful to those engaged in research in international law and international relations. In addition, it continues to include a narrative section for each jurisdiction, discussing issues related to treaty succession, the law of ratification within the municipal law of the jurisdiction, and the current state of official treaty publication. This information was included in the first edition because it was difficult to locate elsewhere. Other sources now make at least some of this information available for some jurisdictions, but it continues to be a body of information that is difficult to locate in a comprehensive way. All URLs were functional as of March 2014.

There are several other ways in which the current edition continues the plan of the first. For example, it continues to be collegial in authorship, relying on the expertise of many to provide comprehensive access to information on multiple jurisdictions. Therefore, it continues also to forsake the goal of uniformity, preferring to leave it up to individual contributors to determine such matters as the relative space given to narrative and bibliographic sections.

Despite continuity between the two editions, there are some differences. In the Introduction to the first edition, we referred to the fact that we were, at the time, in a "transitional period," in which electronic sources on the Internet were beginning to come into their own. Nevertheless, emphasis was placed on printed sources, with references to electronic sources segregated in a separate section at the end of each jurisdictional chapter. Today we are still in a transitional period, and our prediction that the Internet would become a "comprehensive venue for the publication of treaties" remains unfulfilled. However, the penetration of the Internet has proceeded apace, and today the availability of treaty and diplomatic documents on the Internet is far greater than it was even when the 2005 supplement was completed. Therefore, we have chosen in this new edition to integrate bibliographic description of electronic sources into the main body of each chapter, dispensing with separate sections on electronic sources.

Of even greater importance, the new edition greatly expands the number of jurisdictions covered. The first edition was a "down payment," containing

 | DOI 10.1163/9789004272224_002

chapters on a selection of countries in North America and Europe. In comparison, this new edition moves well beyond these limitations, adding chapters on many important Asian jurisdictions, in particular.

As in the case of the first edition, the editors wish to thank those librarians and scholars who have generously contributed their time and expertise to make this bibliography a reality. With the addition of so many new jurisdictions, our indebtedness to them has only increased. In particular, the editors would like to thank Maria I. Smolka-Day, co-editor of the first edition and contributor to the second. Maria is an exceptional scholar, a dear friend, and an example of graciousness and good humor to all who know her. In fact, it was the opportunity to work with Maria that motivated the first edition, and it is the chance to keep her work before the eyes of the younger generation of librarians that comprises one of the pleasures of working on the second.

March 2014

Introduction to the First Edition

Ralph F. Gaebler and Maria I. Smolka-Day

It is a truism today that international law is growing at a tremendous rate of speed. The digital communications revolution of the past decade, together with the advent of global economic, environmental, and political inter-dependance, have led to an explosion of international regulation affecting every aspect of life. *Sources of State Practice in International Law* is an attempt to impose some sort of bibliographic order on the mass and variety of sources that have arisen to document this great body of supra-national law.

It is interesting to note that our work is by no means the first to attempt this task. In fact, the vast body of international law has always challenged researchers, and has brought forth various efforts in the past to document its sources. Each of these efforts faced particular obstacles and accomplished important goals. The editors of the present work are mindful of the achievements of those who have gone before them, seeking to add to, rather than to replace, the substance of their work.

In particular, we would like to draw attention to two earlier bibliographies of treaty sources. The first is the *Manual of Collections of Treaties and of Collections Relating to Treaties*, by Denys Peter Myers (Cambridge: Harvard University Press, 1922). As Librarian of the World Peace Foundation, Myers worked ten years to amass his bibliography of sources containing the texts of treaties concluded down to the outbreak of World War I. As the first to attempt such a comprehensive bibliography, Myers remains the most important bibliographer of treaty sources. Moreover, his book is still an indispensable guide to older materials. The researcher of today can only marvel at the thoroughness of Myers' work, especially knowing that it was accomplished long before the advent of word processing simplified the task of cut-and-paste. Because the *Manual of Collections of Treaties* is such a superb work, the editors have not felt any need in the current bibliography to document sources before the modern era of treaty-making. While the time frame of the modern era is flexible and differs from country to country, it generally means that sources listed here do not precede the mid-nineteenth century.

A second important bibliography of treaties is the *List of Treaty Collections* (New York: United Nations, 1956, reprinted in 1981 by the Symposia Press). This bibliography resulted from General Assembly Resolution 686 (VII), of December 5, 1952, authorizing the Secretary General to undertake such a project. As a result of discussions in the Sixth Committee, the U.N. bibliography

 | DOI 10.1163/9789004272224_003

was undertaken not so much as a supplement to Myer's very scholarly work, but as an aid to the legal practitioner. Therefore, it omitted references to official gazettes, reviews of international law, and to any other sources that might contain the texts of treaties, but which were not treaty collections per se. Nevertheless, the *List of Treaty Collections* was important because it contained references to treaty sources for some seventy countries, including internationally significant ones that either did not exist (*e.g.*, India) or had only recently come into existence (*e.g.*, Soviet Union) at the time Myers completed his work. In fact, the *List* remained so important that it was reprinted in 1981, despite the fact that it was by then woefully out-of-date.

The challenge to any new effort is, once again, not so much to update a previous effort, but to provide a useful snapshot of sources currently available. The particular obstacles this time around include not only the much greater number of countries whose sources of practice must be documented (now over 180), but the multiple formats in which those sources exist. In particular, we now find ourselves in the midst of a transitional, digital era, in which the Internet is of ever-increasing importance. It is safe to assume at this point that the Internet will ultimately provide a comprehensive venue for the publication of treaties, especially for international agencies and those newer and less developed countries that have never achieved consistent publication of treaties in printed form. Without the advent of the Internet as a venue for the widespread distribution of information, it is difficult to imagine treaties ever being comprehensively available, given the number of countries that now exist. Thus, the Internet will ultimately prove to be a great friend to international legal researchers. However, in this transitional period, web sites come and go, evolve and mutate, sometimes provide information in an authoritative and usefully organized fashion, sometimes in a great mess that defies logic. How is one therefore to document with confidence what is now available on the Internet, while at the same time continuing to describe in traditional bibliographic terms what is available in printed form? Comprehensiveness of coverage seems to be an ever more elusive goal.

Given this background, the editors hope that the current work will prove to be a down payment on what will eventually become a comprehensive guide to both electronic and printed sources of state practice in international law. In order to launch *Sources of State Practice in International Law* on this trajectory, we have begun with countries in North America and Europe, many of which have been active in international affairs for hundreds of years and which have well developed printed sources of state practice. In addition, many of these countries (the United States in particular) have begun to exploit the Internet as well, as a source of both official and commercial publication. Thus, *Sources of State Practice* takes the form of a traditional bibliography, while beginning the task of capturing information about sources that are available electronically. As more countries and sources are added, *Sources of State Practice* will perhaps look less like a traditional bibliography, and more like a guide to electronic sources. There is still much work to be done in determining how best to describe such sources; hopefully our effort will both benefit from and contribute to it.

Given the great mass and variety of sources that exist today, we have departed from the approach of previous bibliographies in several respects. First, we have chosen a collegial approach, recognizing that the job of documenting sources of state practice has become too large for one or two individuals. Second, we have forsaken the goal of uniformity. We have left it up to the individual contributors to determine how selective or comprehensive they wish to be, whether to describe archival sources or only printed sources, and so on. In a world of transition, this seems to be the best approach.

We have also departed from previous practice to expand our coverage. In addition to treaty sources, *Sources of State Practice* also provides references to sources of diplomatic documentation, on the theory that they contain useful information about customary state practice in international law, and other information that will be of use to those engaged in international relations research. For the same reasons, we have chosen to include information about yearbooks and digests of state practice. Finally, we have also included for each country information about issues related to treaty succession and a summary of the process of treaty ratification and implementation since this information is not readily available elsewhere.

The value of the work lies primarily in its description of sources that have become available in the last fifty years, since these are not described elsewhere. In addition, many printed sources of treaties that have been listed before acquire here a full bibliographic description for the first time. Indeed, we have tried to provide more detailed descriptions than either Myers or the U.N. *List* were able to do. We are aided in this by the availability of bibliographic utilities, such as OCLC and RLIN, and by the increasing availability of library catalogs on the Internet. As far as possible, authors have inspected the items included; however, where this was not possible, bibliographic utilities and electronic catalogs have still permitted fairly detailed bibliographic description in many cases.

The editors wish to thank those who have contributed their time and expertise to this publication. Librarians and other information professionals are busier and more committed to projects of various kinds today than ever before. We hope that the community of international legal researchers will find their efforts useful.

December 2001

Argentina

Teresa M. Miguel-Stearns[1]

Issues of Treaty Succession

La República de Argentina[2] is the successor State of Spain in the Southeastern portion of the former Spanish empire in the Americas. At the time of independence, first declared in the Viceroyalty of Buenos Aires in 1810, the territory included present-day Argentina, Uruguay, Paraguay, and Bolivia. The region became known as the United Provinces of the Rio de la Plata. The territory was administered by the government in Buenos Aires. The Congress of Tucumán issued a formal Declaration of Independence in 1816. Shortly thereafter, Uruguay, Paraguay, and Bolivia established independent nations and the remaining territory formed Argentina.[3]

When the nations of the Americas declared independence from Spain and Portugal in the early 19th century, they adhered to the concept of *uti possidetis* first articulated by Spain and Portugal in the *Treaty of Madrid*[4] in order to maintain the status quo regarding national territorial limits.[5] *Uti possidetis* in

1 The author is grateful to the work of several predecessors whose publications contributed significantly to the research she has done into the historical treaty and diplomatic collections. They include: Denys Peter Myers, MANUAL OF COLLECTIONS OF TREATIES AND OF COLLECTIONS RELATING TO TREATIES (Cambridge, Harvard Univ. Press 1922). Wholly available on Google Books at: http://books.google.com/books?id=HlQUAAAAIAAJ; and Edwin M. Borchard, GUIDE TO THE LAW AND LEGAL LITERATURE OF ARGENTINA, BRAZIL AND CHILE (Washington D.C., Library of Congress 1917). Wholly available on Google Books at: http://books.google.com/books?id=KVYbAQAAMAAJ.

2 Derived from the Latin, *argentum*, meaning *silver*; in Spanish, *plata*.

3 *See, generally* MARCELA TERNAVASIO, HISTORIA DE LA ARGENTINA, 1806–1852 (2009); VICENTE D. SIERRA, HISTORIA DE LA ARGENTINA, 1492–1852 (1967).

4 Treaty of Madrid, Spain-Portugal, Jan. 13, 1750, 38 C.T.S. 357.

5 SUZANNE LALONDE, DETERMINING BOUNDARIES IN A CONFLICTED WORLD: THE ROLE OF UTI POSSIDETIS 24–5 (2002). The concept of *uti possidetis*, also found in Roman law, was utilized in the Americas to require countries to maintain their territorial status quo at a certain point in time. In addition to imputing *uti possidetis*, Spain and Portugal also agreed to use the best know landmarks, such as rivers and mountains, to demarcate states, provinces, and viceroyalties. The Treaty of Madrid was annulled in 1761. In 1777, the Treaty of San Ildefonso granted the Amazon basin to Portugal and the Rio de la Plata territory (including present-day Uruguay) to Spain.

 | DOI 10.1163/9789004272224_004

Spain's view was based on rightful possession not actual occupation of land.[6] In maintaining the colonial status quo at the time of independence, South American countries defined their national territory using colonial administrative divisions in effect in 1810. Treaties and international agreements that followed excluded further European colonization and prevented expansion, conquest, and occupation of the newly established republics.[7]

The Argentine Constitution[8] is one of the oldest in the Americas. It has undergone several reforms over the years, most significantly and recently in 1994 when the Constitution was reorganized and renumbered. At that time, several *Disposiciones Transitorias* were made concerning Argentine territory. The first declares that Argentina is the proper owner of the *Islas Malvinas* (Falkland Islands (U.K.)), the South Georgian and South Sandwich Islands (U.K.), and the corresponding maritime territories.[9] Argentina has claimed the *Islas Malvinas* since the early days of independence as a matter of state succession.[10]

The *Islas Malvinas*/Falkland Islands have long been a point of contention in British – Argentine relations. Argentina traces Spanish claims to the islands going back to the papal bull of 1493 dividing all new world territories between Spain and Portugal according to certain lines of latitude and longitude.[11] The

---

6 Id. at 31–2. In the early 19th century, Spain argued that so much of the Americas was still unexplored such that possession would have been an impossible requirement thus favoring title based on rightful possession (*uti possidetis de jure*). Nonetheless, Portugal and later Brazil favored an interpretation of actual possession (*uti possidetis de facto*).

7 Id. at 28–30. The *Monroe Doctrine* also viewed efforts of further European conquest and expansion in the Americas to be acts of aggression. See, Monroe Doctrine, 41 Annals of Cong. 13–4 (1823) (Gales and Seaton., 1856).

8 CONSTITUCIÓN NACIONAL [CONST. NAC.](Arg.) (1853), *available in English at* http://www.senado.gov.ar/deInteresEnglish.

9 CONST. NAC. "Disposiciones Transitorias". RICARDO LEANDRO DE ZAVALÍA, CONSTITUCIÓN DE LA NACIÓN ARGENTINA 48 (2004).

10 RAPHAEL PERL, THE FALKLAND ISLANDS DISPUTE IN INTERNATIONAL LAW AND POLITICS: A DOCUMENTARY SOURCEBOOK 24 (1983).

11 The Bull *Inter Caetera* (Alexander VI), May 4, 1493, Francis G. Davenport, EUROPEAN TREATIES TO 1648 (Vol. I) 56 (1917). *See also*, LALONDE, *supra* note 5, at 24–5 (emphasis added): "...all lands discovered and to be discovered to the west and south of a line drawn, from the North to the South Pole, 100 leagues west and south of the Azores and Cape Verde Islands, *and not in actual possession of any Christian power*, should belong exclusively to Spain". *See also*, FRANCISCO CENTENO, TRATADOS, CONVENCIONES, PROTOCOLOS, ACTOS Y ACUERDOS INTERNACIONALES. PUBLICACIÓN OFICIAL (11 Vols.) 11:11–16 (Buenos Aires, Imp. J.A. Alsina 1911).

Treaty of Tordesillas (1494) confirmed such possession.[12] Argentina attributes discovery of the *Islas Malvinas* to Magellan's expedition of 1520; old Spanish cartographic maps show the *Islas Malvinas* as early as 1522. The British maintain that Captain John Strong made the first landing in 1690 and simultaneously named the islands after Viscount Falkland, Treasurer of the English Navy.[13]

It is disputed by the British that Spain possessed a valid legal claim to the *Islas Malvinas* in the early 19th century. Argentina contends that the second *Treaty of Utrecht* (1713) between Great Britain and Spain assured no further interference from the British on Spanish territories in the Americas.[14] The *Saint Lawrence Convention* (1790) further prohibited both Spain and Great Britain from claiming new territories off the coast of South America.[15] Prior to the *Saint Lawrence Convention*, in 1766, the British established a small colony of about 400 people in West Falkland at Port Egmont. In 1767, the French ceded Port Louis on the eastern island (established by the French in 1764) to the Spanish who renamed it Puerto Soledad. The Spanish forced the British to leave in 1770 and both sides agreed in a formal, written declaration that Spain was the legal possessor of the islands. Spain then allowed the British to reestablish the colony in 1771, which lasted until 1774 when the British departed for economic reasons, leaving behind a plaque declaring the land to be British.[16]

---

12 Treaty of Tordesillas, Spain-Portugal, June 7, 1494, Supp. I Recueil de Traites 372, 389; Davenport, *supra*, at 84. Portugal and Spain partitioned South America by a meridian defined in the treaty: 370 leagues west of the Cape Verde Islands. VICTOR PRESCOTT AND GILLIAN D. TRIGGS, INTERNATIONAL FRONTIERS AND BOUNDARIES: LAW, POLITICS AND GEOGRAPHY 245–7 (2008). *See also*, CENTENO *supra* at 11:17–36.

13 PERL, *supra* note 10, at 4.

14 Id. at 22; Treaty of Peace and Friendship between Great Britain and Spain (Second Treaty of Utrect), Art. VIII., Jul. 13, 1713, 28 C.T.S. 295, 325, 328–9.

15 Id. at 22–3; Convention between Great Britain and Spain (Saint Lawrence Convention), Oct. 28, 1790, 51 C.T.S. 67, 69.

16 Id. at 5. *See also*, Transaction between the Kings of Spain and England regarding certain Hostile Acts on the Islas Malvinas, Jan. 22, 1771, CARLOS CALVO, COLECCIÓN COMPLETA DE LOS TRATADOS, CONVENCIONES, CAPITULACIONES, ARMISTICIOS, Y OTROS ACTOS DIPLOMÁTICOS DE TODOS LOS ESTADOS DE LA AMÉRICA LATINA COMPRENDIDOS ENTRE EL GOLFO DE MÉJICO Y EL CABO DE HORNOS, DESDE EL AÑO DE 1493 HASTA NUESTROS DÍAS, PRECEDIDOS DE UNA MEMORIA SOBRE EL ESTADO ACTUAL DE LA AMÉRICA, DE CUADROS ESTADÍSTICOS, DE UN DICCIONARIO DIPLOMÁTICO, Y DE UNA NOTICIA HISTÓRICA SOBRE CADA UNO DE LOS TRATADOS MÁS IMPORTANTES (6 Vols.) Vol. II, 391–396 (Madrid, Carlos Bailly-Bailliere 1864), *available at* http://babel.hathitrust.org/cgi/pt?id=ucm.5319480563;view=1up;seq=401.

The Spanish then peacefully and uninterruptedly occupied and governed the *Islas Malvinas* from 1774 until Argentine independence in 1810. When Spanish subjects abandoned the islands in 1811 for economic reasons due to Spain's diminishing wealth and power in the Americas, they left behind a plaque claiming the territory. Shortly after declaring independence from Spain, the government of Buenos Aires sent an official to the vacant islands and established a community in the former Spanish town of Puerto Soledad. The Argentines enforced sovereignty three times against fishing vessels during which time Argentine title to the islands was never challenged even though its actions were contested. In response to Argentina asserting its sovereignty over the islands, the U.S.-backed British invaded the islands in 1833 and displaced the Argentine governor and its citizens. In 1844, the Falkland Islands officially became a crown Colony.[17] The British have remained on the islands despite repeated claims by the Argentine government that Argentina is the rightful owner of the islands.[18]

Argentina has and continues to have boundary disputes with its neighbors, especially Chile, but such disputes arise more from previously-unclear demarcations rather than from issues of treaty succession. Incomplete and imperfect maps at the time of independence, changing rivers and other landmarks, and international conflict has all given rise to confusing territorial limits.[19]

Treaty Ratification and Implementation

The Argentine Constitution provides authority and establishes the role of the Federal Government, specifically both the Executive Power and the Congress, in the treaty-making process. The Constitution obligates the federal

---

17 PERL, *supra* note 10, at 6–8. For the official Argentine position, *see* PERL at 21–27. *See also*, REPÚBLICA ARGENTINA, LA CUESTIÓN MALVINAS: UNA HISTORIA DE COLONIALISMO. UNA CAUSA DE LA NACIONES UNIDAS (Ministerio de Relaciones Exteriores y Culto, 2012), *available at* http://www.mrecic.gov.ar/es/la-cuestion-de-las-islas-malvinas and http://www.mrecic.gov.ar/es/question-malvinas-islands-0. For the British position, *see* PERL at 28–30. Perl concludes that given Britain's affirmative actions and duration of occupation, "the case appears strong but not conclusive that British title to the Falklands vested". Id. at 35. He also notes that Argentina was in the process of establishing sovereign rights to the exclusion of other nations but due to British invasion and expulsion was "prevented from doing so and thus from practically perfecting her claim". Id. at 36.

18 Id. at 24.

19 Victor Prescott and Gillian D. Triggs, INTERNATIONAL FRONTIERS AND BOUNDARIES: LAW, POLITICS AND GEOGRAPHY 245–61 (2008).

government to establish treaties of peace and of commerce with foreign powers according to the principles of public law established in the Argentine Constitution.[20] The President has the general power to conclude and sign treaties, concordats, and other negotiable instruments in order to maintain good relations with international organizations and foreign countries, as well as the power to receive foreign ministers and admit foreign consuls.[21] Argentine legal scholars agree that 'conclude' means negotiate and sign treaties.[22]

After signing a bilateral or multilateral treaty, the President submits the treaty to Congress, to both the Senate and the Chamber of Deputies, for approval. Prior to the 1994 Constitutional amendments, there was no Constitutional provision or existing law setting forth how Congress was to approve the treaty. Therefore, each chamber passed a law by normal, ordinary means approving the treaty or rejecting it.[23] Provisions created by the 1994 Amendments now distinguish between two types of treaties: human rights treaties and other treaties. Congress has the power to approve or reject treaties with other nations or international organizations, and concordats with the Holy See, and all treaties and concordats enjoy a status higher than laws but below the Constitution in Argentine legal hierarchy. A human rights treaty may be further elevated in the hierarchy after a separate vote whereby by a two-thirds majority of each chamber of Congress approves giving the treaty the highest status possible, that is, equal to the Argentine Constitution.[24] Withdrawal from or denouncement of one of these treaties requires the

---

20 Zavalía, *supra* note 9, at 14, *citing*, Art. 27, Const. Nac.

21 Id. at 38, *citing*, Art. 99, Const. Nac. This paragraph is significantly different than the pre-1994-reform Article 86 that narrowly specified the types of treaties the President could conclude: peace, commerce, navigation, alliance, boundaries, and neutrality.

22 José María Ruda, *The Role of the Argentine Congress in the Treaty-Making Process* in Parliamentary Participation in the Making and Operation of Treaties 177–185 (S.A. Riesenfeld and F.M. Abbott eds., 1994).

23 Id. at 181.

24 Art. 75, Const. Nac. The ten human rights treaties enumerated in Article 75, para. 22 are the following: the American Declaration of the Rights and Duties of Man; the Universal Declaration of Human Rights; the American Convention on Human Rights; the International Convention on Economic, Social and Cultural Rights; the International Convention on Civil and Political Rights and its empowering Protocol; the Convention on the Prevention and Punishment of Genocide; the International Convention on the Elimination of all Forms of Racial Discrimination; the Convention on the Elimination of all Forms of Discrimination against Woman; the Convention against Torture and other Cruel, Inhumane or Degrading Treatments or Punishments; the Convention on the Rights of the Child.

approval of the President after a two-thirds vote in each chamber of Congress denouncing the treaty.[25]

Treaties of integration that confer power and jurisdiction to supranational organizations (such as MERCOSUR) under conditions of reciprocity and equality and that respect democracy and human rights are superior to ordinary federal laws (second only to the Constitution and certain human rights treaties). Approval of treaties with other Latin American States must be made by an absolute majority of all members of each chamber of Congress. For all other treaties, Congress, with the approval of an absolute majority of those members present in each chamber, declares its intent to approve a treaty; but the treaty will only pass if an absolute majority of the total representatives of each chamber approves the treaty within 120 days of the initial declaration. The withdrawal of treaties previously ratified under this section also requires the absolute majority of the total members of each chamber of Congress.[26]

There is a difference of opinion among scholars as to whether Congress can modify the treaty. Modification has occurred in the past but not since the late 19th century when Congress modified a boundary treaty with Bolivia; it was thereafter renegotiated, signed, approved again by Congress, promulgated, published, and ratified some 10 years after initial negotiations began.[27] One influential scholar, Jorge R.A. Vanossi, contends that if Congress attempts to modify a bilateral treaty, it must be sent back for renegotiation. If Congress modifies a multilateral treaty, it can be ratified without further negotiations if the President agrees with the modification; the modification then becomes a formal reservation.[28]

Once a treaty is approved by both chambers of Congress, it is published in *Diario de Sesiones*, the official bulletin of the National Congress, and is sent back to the President for ratification and promulgation. The President promulgates the new treaty by issuing a decree and publishing the treaty in the *Boletín Oficial*, Argentina's national gazette. Shortly thereafter, instruments of ratification are exchanged and/or deposited, and the treaty enters into force.[29]

---

25 Zavalía, *supra* note 9, at 28–9. Art. 75, para. 22, Const. Nac.

26 Id. at 29. Art. 75, para. 24, Const. Nac.

27 Ruda, *supra* note 22, at 183.

28 Id. See also, Jorge Reinaldo A. Vanossi and Alberto Ricardo Dalla Via, Régimen Constitucional de los Tratados, 179–183 (Buenos Aires, Abeledo-Perrot, 2nd ed., 2000). For a discussion of 'reservations' generally, *see*, Anthony Aust, Modern Treaty Law and Practice, 125–61 (2nd ed., 2007).

29 Ruda, *supra* note 22, at 181.

At different times in the 20th century, Argentina was ruled by a *de facto* government as a result of *coups d'etat*. The question arose as to whether treaties entered into by these provisional governments were valid. The Supreme Court in the first half of the 20th century said they were valid as long as Congress approved them once Congress was formed.[30] In the latter half of the 20th century, the Court moved away from the rule of subsequent approval by Congress and held merely that treaties entered into by *de facto* governments were valid and in force.[31]

The Argentine Constitution grants provinces the power to celebrate *convenios internacionales* or international conventions (which in final form are indistinguishable from treaties) that are not incompatible with the foreign relations of the Nation, and that do not affect the powers delegated to the federal government nor the public credit (or debt) of the Nation. The National Congress must be made aware of such conventions by the provinces.[32]

Further, provinces are permitted to conclude *tratados parciales* or partial treaties to aid in the administration of justice, for economic interests, and for the common good. Again, the national Congress must be aware of such partial treaty negotiations.[33] Partial treaties, the definition of which is the subject of much scholarship, are generally understood to be agreements between provinces.[34] On the other hand, provinces are explicitly prohibited from exercising powers granted to the federal government, including entering into partial treaties of a political nature.[35]

---

30 Id. at 184, *citing, Municipalidad de la Ciudad de Buenos Aires c. Carlos M. Mayer,* 201 Fallos 249 (1945).

31 Id. at 184–5, *citing, Egido Ziella v. Smiriglio Hermanos*, 209 Fallos 26 (1947).

32 Zavalía, *supra* note 9, at 46. Art. 124, Const. Nac.

33 Id. Art. 125, Const. Nac. According to Article 125, the provinces may also specifically promote, by way of local laws and their own financial means, industry, immigration, construction of railways and navigable waterways, the colonization of territory, the introduction and establishment of new industries, the importation of foreign capital, and the exploration of their own rivers. This section of Article 125 remains relatively unchanged since first written in 1853.

34 Ruda, *supra* note 22, at 178–9. Ruda highlights that Article 125 is written with positive language and Article 126 in negative form; he contends that Article 126 powers are specifically reserved for the Federal Government.

35 Zavalía, *supra* note 9, at 47. Art. 126, Const. Nac. Article 126 also restricts the provinces from creating laws related to commerce, navigation, customs, printing money, establishing banks, and dictating legal codes without the consent of the federal government. Provinces may not pass laws related to citizenship and naturalization, bankruptcy, counterfeiting money and documents, weights, arms, and armies except in emergency

Evidence of State Practice

Argentine international relations fall under the jurisdiction of the Executive Power, specifically the President[36] and his or her cabinet.[37] Policies and practices related to foreign affairs can be found on the website of the *Ministerio de Relaciones Exteriores y Culto*,[38] and include reference documents such as the Ministry's general objectives, strategies, and plans, as well as its objectives pertaining to international cooperation and economic relations. There are subsections that explore the history of bilateral relations, specifically pertaining to territorial limits, between Argentina and each of its neighbors: Bolivia, Brazil, Chile, Paraguay, and Uruguay. Naturally, there are documents available on the website in both English and Spanish regarding the question of the *Islas Malvinas*/Falkland Islands. There is also an open-access *Digital Library of Treaties*.[39] This searchable database contains not only treaties but also historical national and international documents, and documents exchanged between the minister and other Argentine institutions. The search results provide the title of the document plus the dates of signature and entry into force. It also flags treaties and agreements that are no longer in force. The full-text of each document is available as a pdf which is a scan of the original, official, authenticated document.

The *Ministerio de Relaciones Exteriores y Culto* has published *Memoria*, an annual report of the Ministry of Foreign Affairs and Culture, since 1860. The Ministry's Foreign Office published a *Boletín* containing reports of consular and diplomatic officers at the end of the 19th century and during first quarter of the 20th century.

Both houses of Congress maintain webpages and publish their daily proceedings online and in their respective *boletines*, including full-text laws passed and treaties approved.[40] The national government also publishes a daily *Boletín Oficial* wherein all laws, ratified treaties, and other legal documents of interest are published.[41]

---

instances of foreign invasion or other imminent danger. Provinces may not name or receive foreign diplomats. This provision remains relatively unchanged since first established in 1853.

36 Art. 99, CONST. NAC.

37 Art. 100, CONST. NAC.

38 Ministerio de Relaciones Exteriores y Culto: http://www.mrecic.gov.ar/.

39 Biblioteca Digital de Tratados: http://tratados.cancilleria.gob.ar/index.php.

40 Senado de la Nación Argentina: http://www.senado.gov.ar/. Honorable Cámara de Diputados de la Nación: http://www.diputados.gov.ar/.

41 Boletín Oficial de la República Argentina: http://www.boletinoficial.gov.ar/Inicio/Index.castle.

Annotated Bibliography of Sources

General Treaty Collections

1 COLECCIÓN DE TRATADOS CELEBRADOS POR LA REPÚBLICA ARGENTINA CON LA NACIONES ESTRANJERAS

(Buenos Aires, Bernheim y Boneo 1863; La Nacion 1877). 2 vols.

Summary: Vol. I contains treaties concluded from 1811–1863. It is wholly available on Hathi Trust: http://hdl.handle.net/2027/hvd.32044080444342. Vol. II contains treaties concluded from 1865–1877. It is wholly available on Google Books: http://books.google.com/books?id=Pk4CAAAAYAAJ.

Index: The back of each volume contains an index of the treaties reprinted in the volume in chronological order.

2 COLECCIÓN DE TRATADOS CELEBRADOS POR LA REPÚBLICA ARGENTINA CON LA NACIONES EXTRANGERAS

Juan A. Alsina and Mariano A. Pelliza and Cuberto Shoolbred (Buenos Aires, Imp. Juan A. Alsina 1884). 3 vols.

Summary: This three-volume set supersedes the previous set (above) and includes treaties omitted in the old set. These volumes are available free on the Hathi Trust:

Vol. 1 (1811–1860):
http://hdl.handle.net/2027/mdp.35112104629813;
Vol. 2 (1863–1875): http://hdl.handle.net/2027/njp.32101060433370;
Vol. 3 (1876–1884): http://hdl.handle.net/2027/njp.32101060433388.

Index: The index at the end of each volume is a list of treaties for that volume, organized chronologically by signature date.
At the end of the index in the third volume is a list of treaties, mostly boundary, signed by Spain in relation to the Americas (1492–1778).

3 TRATADOS, CONVENCIONES, PROTOCOLOS, Y DEMÁS ACTOS INTERNACIONALES VIGENTES CELEBRADOS POR LA REPÚBLICA ARGENTINA

(Buenos Aires: Imp. de "La Nación", 1901–5). 3 vols.

Summary: This comprehensive set publishes official version of treaties, conventions, protocols and other international documents where Argentina is a party. It is wholly available in Google Books:

Vol. 1: http://books.google.com/books?id=K6BBAAAAYAAJ;
Vol. 2: http://books.google.com/books?id=6RrwAAAAMAAJ;
Vol. 3: http://books.google.com/books?id=100CAAAAYAAJ.

Index: There are three indices in the back of each volume allowing the researcher to find documents chronologically, alphabetically by country, or alphabetically by subject matter. Vol. 2 contains a dual index for Vols. 1 and 2.

4 COLECCIÓN COMPLETA DE LOS TRATADOS, CONVENCIONES, CAPITULACIONES, ARMISTICIOS, Y OTROS ACTOS DIPLOMÁTICOS DE TODOS LOS ESTADOS DE LA AMÉRICA LATINA COMPRENDIDOS ENTRE EL GOLFO DE MÉJICO Y EL CABO DE HORNOS, DESDE EL AÑO DE 1493 HASTA NUESTROS DÍAS, PRECEDIDOS DE UNA MEMORIA SOBRE EL ESTADO ACTUAL DE LA AMÉRICA, DE CUADROS ESTADÍSTICOS, DE UN DICCIONARIO DIPLOMÁTICO, Y DE UNA NOTICIA HISTÓRICA SOBRE CADA UNO DE LOS TRATADOS MÁS IMPORTANTES

Carlos Calvo (Madrid: Carlos Bailly-Bailliere, 1864). 6 vols.

Summary: A collection of full-text treaties and agreements for all of Latin America. Relevant to Argentina are Vols. I and II. Vol. I begins with the Papal Bull of 1493; Vol. 2 ends with the declaration of 1771 between Spain and England concerning *Gran Malvina*/Falkand's Island.

Index: The Index in the back of each volume lists each document in that volume in chronological order.

5 TRATADOS, CONVENCIONES, PROTOCOLOS, ACTOS Y ACUERDOS INTERNACIONALES

Francisco Centeno (Buenos Aires: Imp. J.A. Alsina, 1911). 11 vols.

Summary: A collection of full-text bilateral and multilateral treaties organized alphabetically by country and subject (for example: Alemania (Germany) followed by Alianzas (Alliances) followed by Armisticios (Armistices), Austria-Hungary, Belgium, and so on). Further organized chronologically within each country or subject from 1810 to the present. Vol. 10 includes intra-provincial agreements. Vol. 11 includes treaties from the Spanish colonial era (1493–1810).

Index: There are three indices in the back of each of the first nine volume allowing the researcher to find documents chronologically, alphabetically by country, or alphabetically by subject matter. Vol. 10 contains an appendix with intra-provincial agreements. Vol. 11 contains an index of all eleven volumes.

6 EDICIÓN PROVISIONAL DE TRATADOS

Ministerio de Relaciones Exteriores y Culto, Oficina de Derecho Internacional y Legislación Extranjera (Buenos Aires, 1922).

Summary: This is a provisional edition of bilateral treaties from 1825–1920; some have been verified by the foreign government involved, but not all. The treaties are organized by subject within which they are listed alphabetically by country, then by date within each country.

7 TRATADOS Y CONVENCIONES VIGENTES EN LA NACIÓN ARGENTINA
Ministerio de Relaciones Exteriores y Culto, (Buenos Aires: Imp. Coni, 1925). 2 vols.

Summary: Vol. I contains first a list of Presidents from 1810 (Independence) to the present, followed by another list of Ministers of the Office of Foreign Affairs from 1822, the year it was established, to the present. Vol. I then reprints all bilateral treaties organized alphabetically by country and then chronologically within that country. The bilateral treaties with non-Spanish language countries are bilingual side-by-side. Vol. II reprints all multilateral treaties chronologically from 1863–1921.

Index: The index in back of each volume organizes the treaties alphabetically by subject, followed by a chronological index.

8 REGISTRO DIPLOMÁTICO DEL GOBIERNO DE BUENOS-AIRES
(Buenos Aires: Imp. del Estado, 1835).

Summary: Treaties are organized chronologically from 1810 (a treaty between Buenos Aires and Paraguay) to 1831 (a treaty amongst the western provinces). Wholly available on Google Books: http://books.google.com/books?id=geovAAAAYAAJ.

Index: Contains a general index of treaties concluded by the national government, and by the government of Buenos Aires with other provinces or with foreign states.

9 TRATADOS DE LOS ESTADOS DEL RIO DE LA PLATA Y CONSTITUCIONES DE LAS REPÚBLICAS SUD-AMERICANAS : COLECCIÓN FORMADA POR LAS PUBLICACIONES OFICIALES HECHAS EN LOS ESTADOS RESPECTIVOS, CON LOS TEXTOS EN INGLES, FRANCES, ITALIANO Y PORTUGUES, EN FRENTE DEL TEXTO ESPAÑOL, EN LOS TRATADOS CONCLUIDOS CON POTENCIAS ESTRANJERAS
Florencia Varela (Montevideo, 1847–48).

Summary: Treaties are organized by country (República Argentina, Provincia Oriental, and República Oriental del Uruguay) and chronologically within each country, beginning in 1811. This volume also reprints current constitutions for countries, provinces, and regions. Wholly available on HathiTrust: http://hdl.handle.net/2027/uc1.31822009491432; and Google Books: http://books.google.com/books?id=cMUrAQAAMAAJ.

Index: The index lists treaties as they are organized in this volume: by country (República Argentina, Provincia Oriental, and República Oriental del Uruguay) and chronologically within each country, beginning in 1811. This index also lists the current constitutions for countries, provinces, and regions.

10 BOLETÍN OFICIAL DE LA REPÚBLICA ARGENTINA
(Buenos Aires, 1893 –).
URL: http://www.boletinoficial.gov.ar/.

Summary: Daily government publication that contains original version of all treaties approved by Congress and the President. Full coverage from 1895 to the present; legislation (not comprehensive) back to 1853.

Topical and Selected Treaty Publications

Commerce

13 TRATADOS DE COMERCIO CONCLUIDOS POR LA REPÚBLICA ARGENTINA: POLÍTICA CONTRACTUAL ARGENTINA DE CARÁCTER INTERNACIONAL EN MATERIA COMERCIAL, ECONÓMICA Y DE NAVEGACIÓN, 1812–1942
Carlos Torres Gigena (Buenos Aires: Ediciones Centurión, 1943).

Summary: A detailed and informative list of bilateral treaties concluded between Argentina and foreign States from the time of independence from Spain (1810). Not a full-text compilation. Generally contains the title, signatories on both sides, signature location and date, date of Congressional approval, date and place of exchange of instruments of ratification if applicable, current status, publications, if any, to find full-text, reservations, and some relevant articles from the more recent treaties.

Index: A helpful index of treaties organized alphabetically by foreign country and chronologically.

14 ESTUDIO DE LOS TRATADOS DE COMERCIO DE LA REPÚBLICA ARGENTINA
Alejandro Guesalaga (Buenos Aires: Lajouane, 1898).

Summary: Contains a discussion of individual treaties signed with various nations, as well as an explanation of *most favored nation* status and of the need for treaty reform. Wholly available on Google Books at: http://books.google.com/books?id=mxosAAAAYAAJ.

Private International Law

15 TRATADOS SANCIONADOS POR EL CONGRESO SUD-AMERICANO DE DERECHO INTERNACIONAL PRIVADO INSTALADO EN MONTEVIDEO EL 25 DE AGOSTO DE 1888 Y CLAUSURADO EL 18 DE FEBRERO DE 1889
(Buenos Aires: Imp. J.A. Alsina, 1889).

Summary: A collection of treaties pertaining to private international law (trade, criminal law, intellectual property, procedure, etc.) written and endorsed by a group government officials, foreign diplomats, and legal scholars throughout South America.

16 ACTAS DE LAS SESIONES DEL CONGRESO SUD-AMERICANO DE DERECHO INTERNACIONAL PRIVADO: INSTALADO EN MONTEVIDEO EL 25 DE AGOSTO DE 1888 Y CLAUSURADO EL 18 DE FEBRERO DE 1889
(Buenos Aires: Imp. J.A. Alsina, 1889).

Summary: A collection of documents that lead up to this first South American conference on private International law as well as the *actas* or proceedings of the individual sessions during the course of the conference.

17 ACTAS DE LAS SESIONES DEL CONGRESO SUD-AMERICANO DE DERECHO INTERNACIONAL PRIVADO: INSTALADO EN MONTEVIDEO EL 25 DE AGOSTO DE 1888 Y CLAUSURADO EL 18 DE FEBRERO DE 1889
(Buenos Aires: Tip. de la Penitenciaría Nacional, 1889).

Summary: A collection of documents that lead up to this first South American conference on private International law as well as the *actas* or proceedings of the individual sessions during the course of the conference. This second edition contains two additions: the first is an introductory note authorizing this second edition; the second is the Argentine law No. 3.192 (1894) that approved the treaties concluded by Argentina during the conference signed by the Secretary of the Senate and the Secretary of the House of Deputies (p. 655).

18 EL DERECHO INTERNACIONAL PRIVADO Y EL CONGRESO SUD-AMERICANO DE MONTEVIDEO
Lisandro Segovia (Buenos Aires: Imp. Lit. y Enc. Mariano Moreno, 1889).

Summary: This volume contains an extensive analysis by the autor of the state of private international law in South America. The Appendix at the end of the volume reproduces all of the treaties approved and concluded at the conference.

19 ACTAS Y TRATADOS DEL CONGRESO SUD-AMERICANO DE DERECHO INTERNACIONAL PRIVADO (MONTEVIDEO 1888–1889): COMPLETADOS CON NUEVOS DOCUMENTOS Y COMPILADOS SISTEMÁTICAMENTE
Ernesto Restelli (Buenos Aires: Cámara de Diputados, 1928).

Summary: This single volume publishes the proceedings and negotiations of the conference as well as the final model treaties. This update includes the national legislation implemented by each participating country in ratifying the various treaties.

20 SEGUNDO CONGRESO SUDAMERICANO DE DERECHO INTERNACIONAL PRIVADO, DE MONTEVIDEO, 1939–40
Ministerio de Relaciones Exteriores y Culto, Division de Asunto Juridicos (Buenos Aires: Tip. de M. Durrity, 1940).

Summary: A collection of documents pertaining to the second South American conference of private international law, some 50 years after the first. Includes reports of countries, comparative analyses of the treaties from the first conference with proposed treaties of the second conference, proceedings of the plenary sessions, and texts of the final treaties agreed upon by the nations present.

21 J. IRIZARRY Y PUENTE AND GWLADYS L. WILLIAMS (TRANS.), TREATIES ON PRIVATE INTERNATIONAL LAW SIGNED AT THE SECOND SOUTH AMERICAN CONGRESS ON PRIVATE INTERNATIONAL LAW, MONTEVIDEO, 1939–1940 WITH TREATIES OF THE FIRST CONGRESS HELD AT MONTEVIDEO, 1888–1889, WHICH HAVE NOT BEEN REVISED, 37 AMERICAN JOURNAL OF INTERNATIONAL LAW (1943).

Summary: This publication provides an English translation of the treaties concluded at the Second South American Congress on Private International Law. The Introduction provides context.

22 INTER-AMERICAN SPECIALIZED CONFERENCE ON PRIVATE INTERNATIONAL LAW: CIDIP-I (1975) THROUGH VII (2002)
URL: http://www.oas.org/dil/private_international_law.htm.

Summary: Argentina participated in all of the CIDIP conferences. Reports, drafts, and final treaties can be found on the website of the Organization of American States. Treaty information includes whether and when a country signed and ratified the various treaties resulting from these conferences.

23 ACTA FINAL: CONFERENCIA ESPECIALIZADA INTERAMERICANA SOBRE DERECHO INTERNACIONAL PRIVADO
Department of Legal Affairs, Division of Legal Codification and Integration, (Washington, D.C.: Secretary General of the Organization of American States, 1975).

Summary: This official OAS multilingual publication provides the procedural documents that bring to close CIDIP I, including a list of the six treaties that were concluded in Panama, and calls for the convening of CIDIP II. It provides background information with citations to OAS documents as well as a brief summary of the CIDIP I conference proceedings.

24 CONFERENCIA ESPECIALIZADA DE DERECHO INTERNACIONAL PRIVADO: ANALYSIS Y SIGNIFICADO DE LAS CONVENCIONES APROBADAS EN PANAMA, 1975
Tatiana B. De Maekelt (Caracas, 1979).

Summary: In addition to a concise history of private international law in the Americas, and the author's analysis of each conference leading up to CIDIP I, the author also provides a bibliography, index of treaties, laws, documents, and jurisprudence, and appendix containing the reproduction of treaties concluded in 1975.

25 MANUEL A. VIEIRA, DIDIER OPERTTI, AND E. GONZALEZ LAPEYRE, CONVENCIONES DE PANAMA (1975), 1 CUADERNO DE DERECHO INTERNACIONAL PRIVADO 9 (1977).

Summary: This publication first reproduces the six treaties concluded in CIDIP I in Panama. In the second section, the authors provide commentary regarding the treaties.

26 ACTAS Y DOCUMENTOS SEGUNDA CONFERENCIA ESPECIALIZADA INTERAMERICANA SOBRE DERECHO INTERNACIONAL PRIVADO (CIDIP II: MONTEVIDEO, REPUBLICA ORIENTAL DEL URUGUAY, 23 DE ABRIL A 8 DE MAYO DE 1979.
Inter-American Specialized Conference on Private International Law (Washington, D.C.: Organization of American States Secretariat for Legal Affairs, 1980). 3 Vols.

Summary: Contains the acts and reports of the plenary sessions, *proyectos* (draft conventions), and final text of the eight conventions approved by CIDIP-II along with the list of participants to each convention. Vols. II and III contain the acts of the sessions of the Commission, *proyectos* presented by the commission to various delegations, and the final text of those the Commission approved.

Note: One year after this conference in Uruguay, the General Secretariat of the Organization of American States (OAS) hosted the *First Meeting of Experts on Private International Law*, April 9–15, 1980, in Washington, D.C. A publication of the same title memorializes the continued efforts to formulate norms begun at the CIDIP-I and II. The result was a *Draft Additional Protocol to the Inter-American Convention on the Taking of Evidence Abroad,* and a second document pertaining to international jurisdiction. *First Meeting of Experts on Private International Law: Final Report, April 9–15, 1980, Washington, D.C.* (OAS, Washington, DC) (1980).

Bilateral Treaty Collections

27 ARGENTINA-ESTADOS UNIDOS: ACUERDOS BILATERALES: 1853–2000

Consejo Argentino para las Relaciones Internacionales (CARI) (Buenos Aires: CARI, 2000).

Summary: A collection of 207 treaties, agreements, declarations, and memoranda between Argentina and the United States organized chronologically. Each treaty has an introductory note with useful information such as classification or subject, summary, signatories, and signature and entry-into-force dates.

28 ARGENTINA-ESPAÑA: ACUERDOS BILATERALES: 1857–2000

Consejo Argentino para las Relaciones Internacionales (CARI) (Buenos Aires: CARI, 2000).

Summary: A collection of 207 treaties, agreements, declarations, and memoranda between Argentina and Spain organized chronologically. Each treaty has an introductory note with useful information such as classification or subject, summary, signatories, and signature and entry-into-force dates.

29 ARGENTINA-MÉXICO: ACUERDOS BILATERALES, 1912–2000

Consejo Argentino para las Relaciones Internacionales (CARI) (Buenos Aires: CARI, 2002).

Summary: Publication of bilateral treaties, agreements, declarations, acts, and memoranda of understanding between Mexico and Argentina. There is a helpful introduction detailing the history of bilateral agreements between the two countries.

Index: There are two indices: the first lists the treaties chronologically by date of signature; the second organizes the agreements topically. The treaties and agreements are reprinted in full in chronological order beginning with their first in 1912.

Diplomatic Documents

30 BOLETÍN

Ministerio de Relaciones Exteriores (Buenos Aires, 1903–1916).

Summary: This publication's name varies slightly over time. 45 vols. published. Monthly publication includes reports of foreign affairs including treaty negotiations and ratifications.

31 MEMORIA

Ministerio de Relaciones Exteriores (Buenos Aires, 1860–).

Summary: Annual report. Throughout the late 19th and early 20th centuries, there were a multitude of *Memorias* published with varying titles. An excellent compilation of these publications can be found in: Denys Peter Myers, Manual of Collections of Treaties and of Collections Relating to Treaties (Cambridge, Harvard Univ. Press 1922).

32 DIGESTO DE RELACIONES EXTERIORES, 1810–1913

Francisco Centeno (Buenos Aires, Est. Grafico "Centenario" 1913).

Summary: A collection of important documents concerning the Ministry of Foreign Affairs from the time of Independence. Includes a few treaties and many documents relating to treaties; policies for conducting foreign affairs; laws establishing the Ministry and the diplomatic corps; etc.

Index: There is a topical, alphabetical index in the back of the volume.

Australia

Carole L. Hinchcliff

Issues of Treaty Succession

Australia's status as a country responsible for its own international relations, including treaty-making, evolved slowly over time in a series of significant historical developments.[1] When the first British settlers established a penal colony in Sydney, New South Wales in 1788, they brought with them English law.[2] Despite the existence of the indigenous people, the British considered Australia to be "terra nullius" (empty land) because the Aborigines did not hold and use land following European views of property ownership. Unlike British colonies such as Canada, Australia was "settled" rather than conquered, which according to Sir William Blackstone meant that:

> [i]t hath been held, that if an uninhabited country be discovered and planted by English subjects, all the English laws then in being, which are the birthright of every subject, are immediately there in force. But this must be understood with very many and very great restrictions. Such colonists carry with them only so much of the English Law, as is applicable to their own situation and the condition of an infant colony...[3]

The author wishes to thank Cate Read for her assistance in the editing of this chapter.

1 For a history of the development of international relations and treaty making in Australia, see Anne Twomey, Federal Parliament's Changing Role in Treaty Making and External Affairs (Research Paper No. 15 1999–2000, Information and Research Services, Department of the Parliamentary Library, 2000), *available at:* http://www.aph.gov.au/About_Parliament/Parliamentary_Departments/Parliamentary_Library/pubs/rp/rp9900/2000RP15 and as a chapter in G Lindell and R Bennett eds., Parliament: The Vision in Hindsight (2001).

2 For an overview of the development of common law in Australia, see Catriona Cook et al., *Chapter 3: The Common Law System in Australia* in Laying Down the Law (8th ed. 2011). For more detailed accounts of the prominence of English law in Australian legal history, *see* Alex C. Castles, *The Reception and Status of English Law in Australia*, 2 Adelaide L. Rev. 1–31 (1963), *available at*: http://www.austlii.edu.au/au/journals/AdelLawRw/1963/1.html, and D.P. O'Connell, *Evolution of the British Empire and Commonwealth in* 1 State Succession in Municipal Law and International Law 36–49 (1967).

3 William Blackstone, 1 Commentaries on the Laws of England 108 (1978 reprint of the 1783 edition printed for W. Strahan & T. Cadell, London & D. Prince, Oxford).

 | DOI 10.1163/9789004272224_005

New South Wales began operation as a penal colony largely under military rule, and confusion about the applicability of English common law needed was removed by the passage of the Australian Courts Act 1828,[4] which provided that all laws and statutes in force in England on July 25, 1828 applied in New South Wales and Van Dieman's land, (now Tasmania, which had separated from New South Wales in 1825).

Australia became a nation on January 1, 1901 when federation brought together the six British colonies established between 1788 and 1850. The Australian federal government was established by the Australian Constitution, which is Section 9 of the Commonwealth of Australia Constitution Act, 1900 (Imp),[5] an act of the British Parliament. The Australian Constitution does not specifically address treaty-making and details relating to the executive and legislative responsibilities for this function. Despite federation, given Australia's colonial status, it was simply assumed that Britain would dictate Australia's involvement in international affairs, which included entering into treaties on behalf of Australia. Therefore, when Great Britain declared war on Germany in 1914 Australia, as a member of the British Empire, was also at war.[6] Until 1919, the relationship between the United Kingdom and the Dominions was such that:

> [t]he United Kingdom continued to enter as the sole contracting party into international agreements, the subject matter of which was not within the legislative competence of the Dominions and Colonies, but which affected them, and these agreements were binding on the whole of the British Empire.[7]

Australia first became active internationally in 1919 when the Treaty of Versailles was signed on behalf of the British Empire. It was also signed by representatives of the Dominions, being Australia, Canada, New Zealand and South Africa. The Dominions also became separate members of the League of Nations and The International Labor Organization at that time. The treaty-making powers of the Dominions were discussed extensively at the Imperial Conference in 1923, leading to The Balfour Declaration at the Imperial

4 Australian Courts Act, 1828, 9 Geo. 4, c. 83 (Imp).

5 Commonwealth of Australia Constitution Act, 1900, 63 & 64 Vict., c. 12, § 9 (Imp).

6 Cook et al., *supra* note 2, at 49.

7 Department of External Affairs, List of International Agreements (Treaties, Conventions, Etc.) to Which Australia is a Party, or which Affect Australia, Together With Prefatory Note 5 (1935).

Conference of 1926.[8] In describing the status and relationship of Great Britain and the dominions, the Balfour Declaration gave the Dominions responsibility for their foreign affairs independent from the British government, including the right to make treaties. Further, the Royal Commission on the Australian Constitution in 1929 confirmed that the Commonwealth government had the right to enter into treaties with foreign governments.

While Australia was gaining some measure of independence from Great Britain in conducting its foreign relations, on the domestic legal front the Commonwealth and the states were still closely linked to Great Britain. The Statute of Westminster 1931 (Imp)[9] provided in Section 3 that only at the Dominions' request and consent would the British Parliament pass legislation affecting any of the Dominions, and in Section 4 permitted the Dominions to make laws of extra-territorial application. The Australian Parliament's eventual passage of this legislation via the *Statute of Westminster Adoption Act 1942* (Cth), gave Australia legislative independence from Britain and more autonomy in acting on its own behalf in foreign affairs.[10] The *Statute of Westminster Adoption Act 1942* was given retrospective effect to the beginning of the Second World War on September 3, 1939. During the Second World War Australia first made independent declarations of war[11] and the first Australian Embassy was established in Washington in 1946.[12] Events such as these signified Australia's new autonomy in the international arena.

---

8 See Anne Twomey, *International Law and the Executive*, *in* INTERNATIONAL LAW AND AUSTRALIAN FEDERALISM 72–73 (Brian R. Opeskin & Donald R. Rothwell eds., 1997) for various commentator's interpretations of The Balfour Declaration.

9 Statute of Westminster, 1931, 22 Geo. 5, c. 4 (Imp).

10 The Australian states chose not to be covered by the *Statute of Westminster Adoption Act 1942* (Cth) and retained their constitutional links with Britain. One aspect of this was that the states were still subject to the repugnancy doctrine in the Colonial Laws Validity Act, 1865, 28 & 29 Vict., c. 63 (Imp), which meant that they could not legislate repugnantly to Imperial statutes that applied to them. Legal ties to the British government existed until March 3, 1986 when each of the Australian state parliaments, the Australian federal government and the British Parliament passed the "Australia Acts," the effect of which finally ended the British Parliament's legislative authority to create Australian law and the colonial status of the state parliaments. For a more comprehensive analysis of the Australia Acts see ANNE TWOMEY, THE AUSTRALIA ACTS 1986: AUSTRALIA'S STATUTES OF INDEPENDENCE (2010).

11 Twomey, *supra* note 8, at 74–75 outlining how, during the Second World War, the Labor government proceeded in making declarations of war.

12 Australia began having some diplomatic relations overseas during the 1930s and 1940s. See id. at 75–76.

Since the Second World War, Australia has become a party to an ever increasing number of treaties and international agreements in addition to the treaties that were gained by virtue of "inheritance" from Britain before Australia independently entered into treaties in its own right. In 1999, it was not known precisely how many treaties were currently in force in Australia since there were a number of treaties that remained in force although they had no practical effect. It was speculated that approximately one thousand "head treaties" were formally in force. A call for an audit of treaties was one of the recommendations in the 1995 Australian Senate Report on Australian treaty-making practices. The audit was proposed to determine a list of treaties to which Australia is currently a party, a list of departments that administer such treaties, and information indicating whether the currently in-force treaties were implemented by executive action or legislation. If implemented by legislation, the legislation was to be noted.[13] The Australian Government Department of Foreign Affairs and Trade launched the Australian Treaties Database on August 20, 2002. The database can be searched to find basic information about treaties to which Australia is a signatory, or where Australia has taken other treaty action. Entries include links to treaties provided by the Australian Treaties Library.[14]

Treaty Ratification and Implementation

The Australian Parliament can implement treaties pursuant to any of its powers as enumerated in Section 51 of Australia's constitution. For example, defence treaties can be implemented pursuant to the defence power set out in Section 51(vi), and international trade treaties pursuant to Section 51(i).

---

13 *See Introduction* to AUSTRALIAN TREATY LIST (as at 31 December 1999) in AUSTRALIAN TREATY SERIES 1999 No. 38 at (vi)–(vii). Not knowing the number of treaties in force in Australia is a long-standing issue, which has also been noted in the introductory notes to prior versions of the AUSTRALIAN TREATY LIST. D.P. O'CONNELL, in 2 STATE SUCCESSION IN MUNICIPAL LAW AND INTERNATIONAL LAW 122 (1967), states in footnote 1 that "the treaty lists of other countries are inconsistent with respect to the inclusion of British treaties under the names of Australia, New Zealand and Canada. The U.S. *Treaties in Force*, 1966, exhibits some inconsistencies, and there are five in the French list in the case of Australia, and one in the case of New Zealand." *See* SENATE LEGAL AND CONSTITUTIONAL REFERENCES COMMITTEE, TRICK OR TREATY? COMMONWEALTH POWER TO MAKE AND IMPLEMENT TREATIES 8 and 175–184 (1995). Also available via AustLII at: http://www.austlii.edu.au/au/other/dfat/reports/tortcon.html (see references to Chapter 11).

14 *Available at:* http://www.austlii.edu.au/au/other/dfat/.

Although treaty-making is not explicitly mentioned in Section 51,[15] it is considered to be encompassed by the external affairs' power as first established in *R v Burgess; Ex Parte Henry* in 1936.[16] It is well established by the Australian High Court that under the external affairs' power, the Australian federal government may legislate to give effect to a treaty, whether or not the subject normally falls under the legislative power of the states. The Australian High Court clearly established this interpretation of the external affairs' power in *Koowarta v Bjelke-Peterson*,[17] the *Tasmanian Dam* Case[18] and subsequent cases. Federal statutes implementing treaties often include the relevant treaties or international agreements as schedules to the statutes.[19]

Interestingly, the only section of the Australian Constitution that specifically mentions the word "treaties" is Section 75, which confers original jurisdiction on the Australian High Court in matters (i) "arising under any treaty" and (ii) "affecting consuls or other representatives of other countries."

In many other countries, including the United States, treaties and other instruments are self-executing in that they become the law of the country

---

15 For a discussion of the wording and meaning of the External Affairs' power as it was drafted at the Australasian Federal Conventions during the 1890s, see Peter M. McDermott, *External Affairs and Treaties: The Founding Fathers' Perspective*, 16 U. QUEENSLAND L.J. 123–136 (1990). In the original Federation Bill of 1891 drafted at the Sydney Convention, Section 51 was drafted to read "External Affairs and Treaties." The phrase "and treaties" was dropped because treaty-making authority was considered to rest with the Imperial government, although it was acknowledged that "there is nothing to prevent the Crown from delegating to the Commonwealth the power of negotiating treaties, on behalf of the Empire, to any extent which may be deemed advisable." See JOHN QUICK & ROBERT RANDOLPH GARRAN, THE ANNOTATED CONSTITUTION OF THE AUSTRALIAN COMMONWEALTH 768 (1976) *available at:* http://adc.library.usyd.edu.au/data-2/fed0014.pdf (pages 752–753 of 1137).

16 *R v Burgess; Ex Parte Henry* (1936) 55 CLR 608. Beginning with *Burgess; Ex Parte Henry*, the High Court of Australia has interpreted Section 51(xxix) of the Australian Constitution to mean that the external affairs' power extends to the implementation of treaties and other international agreements to which Australia is a party.

17 *Koowarta v Bjelke-Peterson* (1982) 153 CLR 168.

18 *Commonwealth v Tasmania* (1983) 158 CLR 1.

19 There are many examples of Commonwealth statutes that include treaties and international agreements in their schedules including well known acts such as the *Racial Discrimination Act 1975*, which includes the International Convention of the Elimination of All Forms of Racial Discrimination; the *Sex Discrimination Act 1984*, which includes the Convention on the Elimination of All Forms of Discrimination Against Women; and, the *World Heritage Properties Conservation Act 1983*, which includes the Convention for the Protection of the World Cultural and Natural Heritage.

without action by the legislature, and they become directly enforceable by the courts of the country upon ratification by that country. Following the Westminster model, except for treaties relating to peace, war and the cession of territory, which are the prerogative of the Crown and therefore do not require legislative action, treaties are not viewed by courts as Australian law unless they have been implemented by statute. This was expressly stated in the *Dietrich* case in which the High Court of Australia stated the effect of the International Covenant on Civil and Political Rights 1966 in Australian law.[20] The rule means that if there is no existing legislation in place, the Australian Parliament must pass legislation to give effect to the obligations in treaties or other international agreements, which create rights in or impose obligations on Australian citizens and residents.[21] If the treaty obligations are stated in a form suitable for immediate incorporation into domestic law, the legislation may declare that the treaty provisions have the force of law in Australia. Even if the statutory language makes no specific reference to the treaty, it should be apparent from the legislation that the treaty is being implemented. Including a treaty (in whole or in part) in the schedule to the implementing act, does not alone, give the treaty force of law in Australia.[22]

Federal legislation implementing treaties may override existing federal and state legislation. However, given that the Executive branch of government can independently sign and ratify treaties, it is possible to have Australia become a party to a treaty without there being domestic legislation to give effect to the treaty obligations. This happened when the World Heritage Convention was ratified on August 22, 1974 before the enactment of the *World Heritage*

20 Mason C.J. and McHugh J. in *Dietrich v The Queen* (1992) 177 CLR 292 at 305. "Ratification of the I.C.C.P.R. as an executive act has no direct legal effect upon domestic law; the rights and obligations contained in the I.C.C.P.R. are not incorporated into Australian law unless and until specific legislation is passed implementing the provisions."

21 Australia is not alone in this approach. A judicial colloquium investigating the domestic application of international human rights principles was hosted by the former Chief Justice of India, PN Bhagwati in Bangalore, India, in February 1988. "The (resulting) Bangalore Principles acknowledged that in most of the countries of the common law world such international rules are not directly enforceable unless expressly incorporated into domestic law by legislation." See Glen Cranwell, *The Bangalore Principles and the Internationalisation of Australian Law*, 32 AIAL Forum 1 (March 2002).

22 See generally Rosalie Balkin, *International Law and Domestic Law* in Public International Law: An Australian Perspective 125–131 (Sam Blay et al. eds., 2nd ed. 2005), and Bill Campbell, *The Implementation of Treaties in Australia, in* Opeskin, *supra* note 8, at 144–152 for more detailed information about legislative methods of implementing treaties in Australia.

Properties Conservation Act 1983. This also occurred in the *Teoh* case in which the High Court of Australia held that ratifying a treaty (in this case the International Convention on the Rights of the Child) gives rise to a legitimate expectation that the administrative decision makers will take into consideration the terms of the treaty.[23] It has also happened on a number of occasions that Australia has entered into a treaty when the domestic laws conflict with the terms of the treaty.[24] Critics of this anomalous situation have called for parliamentary approval for the ratification of treaties.[25] For some treaties, the Australian government considers the relevant Australian legislation to be in conformance with the obligations of a proposed treaty, and therefore does not consider specific implementation legislation to be necessary. A simple statement to that effect is included in the National Interest Analysis (NIA) for the treaty.[26] For other treaties, the NIA provides a more detailed summary of legislative and regulatory amendments required to implement a treaty.[27]

Public international law has had increasing influence on many areas of Australian domestic law in recent years, especially since the early 1970s when

---

23 *Minister for Immigration and Ethnic Affairs v Teoh* (1995) 183 CLR 273. For further discussion of *Teoh, see* Glen Cranwell, *Treaties and Australian Law – Administrative Discretions, Statutes and the Common Law*, 1 QUEENSLAND U OF TECH. L & JUST. J. 49 (2001), and Gavan Griffith & Carolyn Evans, *Teoh and Visions of International Law*, 21 AUST. Y.B. INT'L L. 75 (2001). *See also* Wendy Lacey, *A Prelude to the Demise of Teoh: The High Court Decision in Re Minister for Immigration and Multicultural Affairs; Ex parte Lam*, 26 SYDNEY L. REV. 131 (2004) in which the author dissects the obiter comments in the *Lam* case at (2003) 214 CLR 1, which challenge the doctrine that ratification of a treaty creates a legitimate expectation that administrative decision-makers will follow the terms of a treaty.

24 *See* Twomey, *supra* note 8, at 85–86 in which the author gives a number of examples.

25 Glen Cranwell, *The Case for Parliamentary Approval of Treaties in Australia*, 8 E-LAW, 18 (December 2001), *available at:* http://worldlii.austlii.edu.au/au/journals/MurUEJL/2001/25.html. This issue of Parliamentary approval of treaties was examined in SENATE LEGAL CONSTITUTIONAL REFERENCES COMMITTEE, *supra* note 13, at 18–19 and 269–299, and raises issues relating to whether having Parliamentary approval of treaties would violate the constitutional separation of powers.

26 *See*, e.g. Section 21 of the NIA drafted for the World Health Organisation Framework Convention on Tobacco Control, under the heading "Implementation," which states: "It is not anticipated that any legislative or administrative action will be required by either the Commonwealth or State and Territory Governments to implement the Convention at the domestic level": World Health Organisation Framework Convention on Tobacco Control, May 21, 2003, ATNIF 23, which can be accessed on AustLII via the database containing the Australian Treaty National Interest Analyses, *available at:* http://www.austlii.edu.au/cgi-bin/sinodisp/au/other/dfat/ATNIA/2004/7.html?stem=0&synonyms=0&query=ATNIF%20tobacco.

27 Australia-United States of America Free Trade Agreement, Feb. 8, 2004, ATNIF 5, *available at:* http://www.austlii.edu.au/au/other/dfat/nia/2004/5.html.

Australia entered into a number of treaties and other international agreements relating to areas such as human rights and the environment. There are some interesting issues relating to this development and alleged violations of Australia's treaty obligations. In Toonen v Australia, an application brought by a Tasmanian gay rights' activist, the UN Human Rights Committee upheld Toonen's claim that his right to privacy as set out in the First Optional Protocol to the International Covenant on Civil and Political Rights (ICCPR) was infringed by the provisions of the *Criminal Code Act 1924* (Tas), which prohibited male homosexual acts.[28] Toonen was allowed to take his complaint to the UN Human Rights Committee because Australia had acceded to the First Optional Protocol, which provides Australians with this avenue of complaint. The finding of the UN Human Rights Committee and the reluctance of the Tasmanian government to change its laws resulted in the Australian Parliament enacting the *Human Rights (Sexual Conduct) Act 1994* (Cth). Tasmania subsequently repealed the offending provisions of the Tasmanian Criminal Code in the wake of the High Court of Australia judgment in *Croome v Tasmania*.[29] One controversial issue in this case was that the involvement of an international committee commenting on Australian domestic law was viewed as a threat to Australian sovereignty. Consequently, subsequent Australian federal governments have not attempted to implement the recommendations of the UN Human Rights Committee through legislative changes that might be seen as imposing international will on the states.

In the landmark indigenous land rights' case, *Mabo v Queensland*,[30] the Australian High Court held that Australian common law recognized the native title of Australia's indigenous inhabitants thereby overturning the common law doctrine of *terra nullius*. In recognizing native title, Justice Brennan acknowledged that "international law is a legitimate and important influence on the development of the common law, especially when international law declares the existence of universal human rights."[31] *Mabo* also involved the application of the *Racial Discrimination Act 1975* (Cth), which gives effect to the International Convention on the Elimination of All Forms of Racial Discrimination. There is a presumption that Parliament does not curtail an individual's rights and freedoms unless that is unambiguously stated in

---

28 Toonen v. Australia, UN Human Rights Committee, UN Doc. CCPR/C/50/D/488/1992 (4 April 1994). Also available via the University of Minnesota Human Rights Library at: http://www1.umn.edu/humanrts/undocs/html/vws488.htm

29 (1997) 191 CLR 119.

30 *Mabo v Queensland (No. 2)* (1992) 175 CLR 1.

31 Id. at 42.

legislation. While this principle of legality has been applied in interpreting statutes with reference to common law rights and freedoms, in cases such as *Plaintiff S157/2002*,[32] there is uncertainty as to how broadly statutes should be interpreted to conform with international law. There is a view that common law rights includes "fundamental rights," and interpretation of legislation by reference to international human rights standards should be embraced.[33] In *Al-Kateb v Godwin*, Kirby J strongly advocated that an "interpretative principle" be applied in construing the Australian Constitution with reference to international law;[34] a minority view that was decried by McHugh J.[35] The continuing internationalization[36] of Australian law has caused Australian courts to increasingly refer to treaties, and to draw upon principles of customary or general international law in interpreting statutes and developing the common law. Interest in treaties has also gained prominence due to the number of Australian High Court cases involving the interpretation of the Australian Constitution's external affairs' power and the resulting impact on federal and state government relations. In the wake of a number of controversial, high profile cases in the High Court of Australia especially during the 1980s and 1990s, the increase in treaty activity, and challenges to Australia's participation in some treaties, there were growing concerns that the Australian Parliament and the public should be better informed about and be more involved in the treaty-making process before the Federal Executive Council approves a treaty and it is signed or ratified by the Prime Minister or the Minister for Foreign Affairs.

There was great concern that the Australian Parliament was at best only tangentially involved in treaty-making through the treaty implementation process, and at other times quite uninvolved. This is inconsistent with the tenets of democratic government. In 1961, the then Prime Minister, Sir Robert Menzies introduced a modified version of the British Parliament's Ponsonby rule.[37] This rule provided that treaties (other than those that needed to be implemented

---

32 *Plaintiff S157/2002 v Commonwealth* (2003) 211 CLR 476, 492, 29–30.

33 Hilary Charlesworth et al., *Deep Anxieties: Australia and the International Legal Order*, 25 SYDNEY LAW REVIEW 423 (2003).

34 (2004) 219 CLR 562, 622–624 (Kirby J).

35 Id. at 589–592 (McHugh J). *See also* Luke Beck, *What is Kirby's Interpretive Principle Really About?* 87 AUST. L.J. 200, 209 (2013), in which the author states that the interpretive principle "reflects Kirby's belief in the inevitability and desirability of the internationalisation of law in that it provides a means by which that can be achieved in constitutional law."

36 For an examination of how the Australian federal government's executive, legislature and judiciary have responded to the increasing influence of international law on Australian law. *See* e.g. Charlesworth, et al., *supra* note 33.

37 *See* Twomey, *supra* note 1, at 29.

by legislation) were to be tabled in both Houses of Parliament. According to the rule, the Federal Executive would not proceed to ratification or accession unless that treaty had been tabled for at least 12 sitting days. However by the late 1970s, adherence to this rule lapsed, resulting in many treaties being tabled after they had been ratified. Even when they were tabled, treaties were often tabled in large batches with little or no time available for Parliamentary debate.[38]

The Senate Legal and Constitutional References Committee began a detailed review of treaty-making practice and procedures in December 1994, which resulted in a report containing eleven recommendations being tabled in November 1995.[39] On May 2, 1996, the Australian government implemented five significant reforms based on the report's recommendations. The first change was that treaties are to be tabled in both the House of Representatives and the Senate at least 15 sitting days before the government takes definitive treaty action. Fifteen sitting days may translate into 30–100 calendar days depending on the parliamentary calendar. This applies if the government proposes to terminate or denounce a treaty, or accept amendments or create new reservations to an existing treaty. The only exception to this is that the federal government reserves the right to table the treaty after ratification if the treaty is sensitive or requires urgent and immediate implementation.[40]

Secondly, every treaty tabled in Parliament is to be accompanied by a National Interest Analysis (NIA) prepared by the department or agency sponsoring the treaty in consultation with the Department of Foreign Affairs and Trade, and made available to the state and territory governments and the public. Each NIA includes a treaty impact statement and analyzes the provisions of the treaty in terms of the impact of the treaty on Australia including the economic, environmental, social and cultural effects, the obligations imposed by the treaty, the treaty's direct financial costs, how the treaty will be implemented, what consultation has occurred in relation to the treaty and whether the treaty provides for withdrawal or denunciation.

---

38 An examination of the procedure of tabling treaties revealed that approximately two-thirds of treaties had been ratified or acceded to before being tabled in Parliament. *See* Brian Galligan & Ben Rimmer, *The Political Dimensions of International Law in Australia* in OPESKIN, *supra* note 8, at 310, and Twomey, *supra* note 1, at 29.

39 SENATE LEGAL AND CONSTITUTIONAL REFERENCES COMMITTEE, *supra* note 13.

40 Examples of urgent treaties are the 1994 Bougainville Peace Keeping Treaty and the 1996 Subsidiary Agreement with Japan on Tuna Long-Line Fishing cited in Glen Cranwell, *The Treaty Making Process in Australia: A Report Card on Recent Reforms*, (2001) AUST. INT'L L.J. 177, 191.

Thirdly, the Joint Standing Committee on Treaties (JSCOT), was established on May 30, 1996 as an advisory committee to the Federal Parliament, and comprises 16 members from all political parties in both the House and Senate. The role of this parliamentary committee is to scrutinize current and prospective treaties that Australia contemplates entering into and whether reservations or declarations should be made upon ratification. JSCOT holds public hearings in which information is gathered and used in the writing of its reports. After JSCOT reports are tabled, they are available at their website.[41]

The fourth reform established the Treaties Council and the Commonwealth-State and Territories Standing Committee on Treaties (SCOT). SCOT now provides a forum for the states and territories to advise the federal government on treaty matters that concern them. The Treaties Council was established by the Council of Australian Governments on June 14, 1996 and comprises the Prime Minister, all the state premiers and the Chief Ministers. To date, it appears to have met once in 1997.[42]

For researchers and people interested in access to government information, a significant recommendation was that a database be established containing the full text of treaties to which Australia is a party along with explanatory material such as national interest analyses (NIAs)[43] for all tabled treaties, lists of multilateral treaties under negotiation and treaties signed by, but not yet in force, for Australia. Furthermore, the Committee recommended that the database be accessible free of charge via the Internet.

Although in its report the Senate Legal and Constitutional References Committee recommended that there should be legislation implementing its recommendation on the tabling of treaties, former Prime Minister John Howard's government implemented this recommendation by way of administrative procedures.[44]

In 1998, as promised, the federal government reviewed the reforms two years after they were implemented.[45] The resulting report stated that the

---

41 *See* Joint Standing Committee on Treaties' website at: http://www.aph.gov.au/Parliamentary_Business/Committees/House_of_Representatives_Committees?url=jsct/index.htm.

42 *See* http://www.coag.gov.au/treaties_council

43 National Interest Analyses from 1996 are found at: http://www.austlii.edu.au/au/other/dfat/nia/.

44 Cranwell, *supra* note 40, at 189–190.

45 *See* Commonwealth of Australia, Review of the Treaty Making Process §1.4 and §3 on "The Review Process" (1999). A copy of this document is available at: http://www.austlii.edu.au/au/other/dfat/reports/review_treaty_making.html.

reforms were working well and that no further changes were needed. However, in 2000, in response to the increase in public submissions to the Joint Standing Committee on Treaties (JSCOT), it was announced that about one-third of treaty actions, "those of major political, economic or social significance which are likely to attract considerable public interest and debate" would now be tabled for 20 days.[46] This change and reference to these treaties as "Category 1" treaties affects approximately one-third of treaty actions. The 15-day sitting period continues to apply to the remaining two-thirds of "Category 2" treaties.[47]

The Department of Foreign Affairs and Trade, which is responsible for the conclusion of treaties and other forms of international agreement between Australia and other international entities, has outlined the stages in the development and implementation of bilateral and multilateral treaties.[48] As a result of the reforms, bilateral treaties are now implemented in a two-stage process rather than simply entering into force on signature without being tabled in Parliament, as had occurred to avoid breaching confidentiality surrounding their negotiation and content. Now, after signature, bilateral treaties are tabled in Parliament for at least 15 days, after which there is an exchange of notes signifying that the constitutional processes of the parties are complete. The publication *Signed, Sealed and Delivered: Treaties and Treaty Making: An Official's Handbook* is a publication that provided practical information for Australian government employees who dealt with treaties, and covered in detail the steps in the treaty making process in Australia.[49] More general publications prepared by The Australian Department of Foreign Affairs and Trade,

---

46 The Hon. Alexander Downer, MP, Federal Minister for Foreign Affairs, Treaties and Community Debate: Towards Informed Consent, Speech at the Launch of the Australian Treaties Database Canberra (August 20, 2002). A copy of this speech is available at: http://www.foreignminister.gov.au/speeches/2002/020820_fa_treaties.html. For information on tabling, *see* TABLING OF TREATY ACTIONS ON PARLIAMENT at: http://www.dfat.gov.au/treaties/making/tabling-of-treaty-actions-in-parliament.html.

47 For an explanation of the shortcomings of the treaty reforms, *see* Madelaine Chiam, *Evaluating Australia's Treaty-Making Process*, 15 PUB. L. REV. 265–269 (2004).

48 *See* http://www.dfat.gov.au/treaties/making/.

49 DEPARTMENT OF FOREIGN AFFAIRS AND TRADE, SIGNED, SEALED AND DELIVERED: TREATIES AND TREATY MAKING: AN OFFICIALS' HANDBOOK (2nd ed. Undated). A copy of this document is available in pdf format at: http://web.archive.org/web/20030608072051/http:/www.dfat.gov.au/treaties/making/treaties_handbook.pdf. It was retrieved from the Department of Foreign Affairs and Trade website at http://dfat.gov.au/treaties, by way of The Wayback Machine, on June 14, 2013.

Australia and International Treaty Making Information Kit and *Australian and International Treaty Making* (Plain English Guide), are available on the Austlii web site.[50]

Evidence of State Practice

At this time, the Australian federal government alone represents Australia in international law matters and signs, ratifies or accedes to a treaty as determined by the terms of the treaty.

Section 61 of the Australian Constitution vests the Executive power of the Commonwealth in the Crown and sets out that the power, extending "to the execution and maintenance of this Constitution, and of the laws of the Commonwealth," is exercisable by the Governor-General as the Crown's representative.[51] Although Section 61 does not specifically mention treaties, following the precedent of English law whereby the sovereign acted on the advice of British ministers, the Australian practice has been that "the federal executive, through the Crown's representative, possesses exclusive and unfettered treaty-making power."[52]

The section of the Australian Constitution, which covers the Australian federal government's executive and legislative responsibilities for treaty-making, is the "external affairs" power; namely, section 51(xxix). It states that "The Parliament shall, subject to this Constitution, have power to make laws for the peace, order, and good government of the Commonwealth with respect to: ... External Affairs." The external affairs' power is located in Section 51, which sets out 40 areas in which the Australian federal government has legislative competence; if a power is not listed, the assumption is that it is under the purview of the states. It is exercised by the Federal Executive Council, comprising the Prime Minister and Ministers of the Australian Government pursuant to Section 62 of the Constitution,[53] and administered according to Section 64[54]

---

50 *See* http://www.austlii.edu.au/au/other/dfat/reports/.

51 Commonwealth of Australia Constitution Act, 1900, 63 & 64 Vict., c. 12, § 61 (Imp).

52 Stephen J. in *Koowarta v. Bjelke-Peterson* (1982) 153 CLR 168, 215.

53 *See* The Commonwealth of Australia Constitution Act, Section 62, which sets out that the Governor-General selects the members of the Federal Executive Council who advise in the government of the Commonwealth. The current version of The Constitution can be found at: http://www.comlaw.gov.au/Details/C2005Q00193

54 *See* The Commonwealth of Australia Constitution Act, Section 64, which provides the constitutional basis for the Governor-General appointing officers to administer such departments of State of the Commonwealth as the Governor-General in Council may establish.

by the Minister of Foreign Affairs who oversees the Department of Foreign Affairs and Trade.

Annotated Bibliography of Sources

General Treaty Collections

Prior to 1948 when the *Australian Treaty Series* commenced publication, the United Kingdom's control over Australia's external affairs was reflected in the publication of Australian treaties. From 1901, treaties to which Australia became a party were not systematically published by the Australian federal government. In cases where texts were ordered to be printed by the Australian Parliament, they were published as Parliamentary Papers. At other times, the full text of a treaty or other international agreement was published in the *Commonwealth Gazette.* With the exception of some agreements relating to postal matters, all international agreements entered into by Australia were printed as *British Parliamentary Papers* (*Treaty Series*). All agreements entered into by Australia were registered with the then League of Nations under Article 18 of the Covenant of the League and then published in the *League Treaty Series.*[55]

1 AUSTRALIAN TREATY SERIES (ATS)
(Canberra: Australian Government Publication Service, 1948–).

Summary: A series of volumes prepared by the Department of Foreign Affairs and Trade, which provides in chronological order, the full text of all treaties to which Australia is a party. Available electronically, 1901–.[56] (see No. 2 below).

Index: The subject index to the *Australian Treaty List* (see Nos. 3–6 below) can be used to find treaties in the *Australian Treaty Series.*

Note: Title varies. Known as *Treaty Series* from No. 1, 1948–No. 44, 1988. ISSN: 0729–6525 before title was changed to *Australian Treaty Series.*

Note: Author varies. Issued by Department of External Affairs, No. 1, 1948 – No, 9, 1970; Department of Foreign Affairs, No. 10, 1970–No. 9, 1987; Department of Foreign Affairs and Trade, no. 10, 1987–.

Note: Treaties in the *Australian Treaty Series* are commonly cited by year and their sequential number; e.g. Aust. TS 2002 No. 4, which refers to the fourth treaty in the 2002 volume of the Australian Treaty Series.

---

55 *See* DEPARTMENT OF EXTERNAL AFFAIRS, *supra* note 7, at 8.

56 *See* http://www.austlii.edu.au/au/other/dfat/treaties/.

2 AUSTRALIAN TREATIES LIBRARY 1901–

URL: http://www.austlii.edu.au/au/other/dfat/

Summary: Current and historical Australian treaty information is available at the Australian Treaties Library, which is hosted at this Austlii web site. The treaty information and accompanying explanatory information is provided by the Department of Foreign Affairs and Trade as a result of the 1996 treaty reforms, and reflects the Commonwealth government's commitment to wider dissemination of information about Australian treaties and the treaty-making process to all interested parties and the general public. Features of the web site include:

Australian Treaty Action – Monthly Updates: Monthly updates on bilateral and multilateral treaty actions. Available from 1999–.

Australian Treaty Series (*ATS*): The full text of all treaties to which Australia is a party from 1901 to present is found at the above site.

Australian Minor Treaty Actions – Explanatory Statements (*AMTAES*): From 2012– information is now available relating to minor treaty actions. Amendments to existing treaties, which have negligible legal, financial or practical effect on Australia, are referred directly to the Joint Standing Committee On Treaties[57] (rather than tabled in Parliament) and are accompanied by a one-page Explanatory Statement, instead of a National Interest Analysis;[58] such amendments generally enter into force automatically.

Australian Treaties Not Yet In Force (*ATNIF*): 1992– (except for 1996). Coverage for the 1980s is for selected years only: 1983, 1988, and 1989. Contains current signed treaties, not yet in force for Australia. These include bilateral treaties or other treaties that are not sensitive in nature. Once the treaties enter into force, they appear under the *Australian Treaty Series* heading.

Joint Standing Committee on Treaties (*JSCOT*) *Reports*: A table showing JSCOT reports in pdf and html formats from 38th Parliament (May 1996 – August 1998) onwards.

Select Documents on International Affairs (*ATSD*): Issues from 1996–1999 are available at http://www.austlii.edu.au/au/other/dfat/seldoc/ (see No. 14 below).

Australian Treaty National Interest Analyses (*ATNIA*): Prepared by the responsible government department in consultation with the Department of Foreign Affairs and Trade from 1996–.

List of Multilateral Treaty Actions Under Negotiation or Consideration: The most recent list of multilateral treaty actions – current or expected within the next year to be under negotiation, consideration or review by the Australian government – is publicly available. The list is tabled in both Houses of the

57 *Available at:* http://www.austlii.edu.au/au/other/jscot/.

58 *Available at:* http://www.austlii.edu.au/au/other/dfat/nia/.

Australian Parliament. Each entry is accompanied by the name and contact information for the responsible government official, and also contains notes regarding past, current and prospective activity.

Status Lists for Multilateral Treaties: Multilateral Treaties for which Australia is the depository available at http://www.austlii.edu.au/au/other/dfat/treaty_list/depository/.

Treaty Law Resources:[59] Provides two reports: *Australia's Report Under The International Covenant on Economic, Social and Cultural Rights*; and, *Tenth, Eleventh and Twelfth Periodic Report of the Government of Australia Under Article 9 of the International Convention on the Elimination of All Forms of Racial Discrimination (1 July 1992 – 30 June 1998)*. Also includes explanatory information: *Australia and International Treaty Making* (Plain English Guide); *Australia and International Treaty Making Information Kit* (DFAT, July 2000); and, the influential report, *Trick or Treaty? Commonwealth Power to Make and Implement* Treaties (Australian Senate Legal and Constitutional References Committee Report, November 1995).

Note: The most recent versions of the Bilateral Treaty List and the Multilateral Treaty List replace the lists in the most recent print, consolidated version of the *Australian Treaty List* found in the *Australian Treaty Series* 1999 No. 38 (see No. 3 below). *Note:* Since 2000, the *Australian Treaty List* now provides references to the texts of many amendments to multilateral treaties to which Australia is a party, but which have not previously appeared in the *Australian Treaty Series* or *Select Documents in International Affairs.* This change makes these amendments, which tend to deal with technical amendments to texts or annexed material, more readily available.

Treaty Indexes

3 AUSTRALIAN TREATY LIST, AUSTRALIAN TREATY SERIES, NO. 38, 1999
Part I, Bilateral Treaty List, 360 pp. Part II, Multilateral Treaty List, 405 pp.

Summary: Published as part of the *Australian Treaty Series* (see No. 1 above). The various versions (1921, 1956, 1971, 1989, and 1999) of the *Australian Treaty List* provide an official list of Australian treaties in force at various points in time together with brief descriptive information about the treaties. The introduction to the 1970 electronic version of the *Australian Treaty List,* which is available on AustLII,[60] includes an "Historic Summary of Australian Treaty Relationships."

---

59 *Available at:* http://www.austlii.edu.au/au/other/dfat/reports/

60 *Available at:* http://www.austlii.edu.au/cgi-bin/sinodisp/au/other/dfat/treaties/ATS/1971/1.html?stem=0&synonyms=0&query=%22australian%20treaty%20list%20as%20at%22.

Index: The various versions of the *Australian Treaty List* serve as indexes for the *Australian Treaty Series.* The 1999 list includes a chronological list of all treaties published in *Select Documents on International Affairs* from 1966–1998. Prospective bilateral treaties are not included, since the unsigned texts are usually confidential. The 1999 list also includes a numerical list of treaties and a keyword index, in addition to the subject index.

Note: This most recent version of *Australian Treaty List* replaces *Australian Treaty List* 1989, No. 38, which lists treaties effective as at December 31, 1989.

Note: Current to December 31, 1999. Part I lists treaties chronologically by country, arranged alphabetically. Part II provides separate, chronological lists of multilateral treaties and agreements with international organizations. As a result of the 1996 treaty reforms, the 1999 list now provides, in Part II, references to multilateral treaties to which the Australian government is considering becoming a party.

4 AUSTRALIAN TREATY LIST, AUSTRALIAN TREATY SERIES, NO. 38, 1989
739 pp.

Summary: Current to December 31, 1989. Supplement I updates the 1989 list from January 1, 1990 to December 31, 1994. Since 1995, annual updates to the 1989 list were printed as "Treaty Action," No. 1, in the 1995–1999 volumes of the *Australian Treaty Series.*[61]

Index: The 1989 list comprises 2018 entries.

Note: Prior to 1989, the *Australian Treaty Series* was known as the *Treaty Series.*

5 AUSTRALIAN TREATY LIST, AUSTRALIAN TREATY SERIES, NO. 1, 1971

Summary: Current to December 31, 1970. The 1971 list comprises 1268 entries, and its accompanying supplements provide separate lists of agreements made between Australia and international organizations.

Note: Following 1971, the *Australian Treaty List* was updated annually in the first issue of the *Treaty Series* under the sections: "Cumulative Supplement" (1972–1974), and "Treaty Action" (1975–1999).

6 AUSTRALIAN TREATY LIST, AUSTRALIAN TREATY SERIES, NO. 1, 1956
266 pp.

Summary: Current to December 31, 1955. The 1955 list comprises 879 entries, and its accompanying supplements provide separate lists of agreements made

---

61 For further details, *see* http://www.austlii.edu.au/au/other/dfat/treaties/ATS/

between Australia and international organizations. Section A lists bilateral treaties, Section B lists multilateral and general treaties, and Section C lists agreements with international organizations. Information for each entry is found under the columns labeled Date and Place of Signature, Description and Notes, and References to Printed Text. Index: pp. 219–266.

Note: The 1955 list was updated by: "Supplement (No. 1)," *Treaty Series*, 1959, No. 30, as at December 31, 1959; "Cumulative Supplement (No. 2)," *Treaty Series*, 1962, No. 18, as at December 31, 1962; and, finally, "Cumulative Supplement (No. 3)," *Treaty Series*, 1966, No. 21, as at December 31, 1966.

7 LIST OF INTERNATIONAL AGREEMENTS (TREATIES, CONVENTIONS, ETC.) TO WHICH AUSTRALIA IS A PARTY, OR WHICH AFFECT AUSTRALIA, TOGETHER WITH PREFATORY NOTE, 15TH AUGUST, 1935
Commonwealth of Australia, Department of External Affairs.
(Canberra: L.F. Johnson, 1935). 50 pp.

Summary: This 1935 list of 308 entries is described as the only other printed list preceding the beginning of the *Australian Treaty Series* in 1948. Australia was held up as leading the world in producing a "*Treaty List.*" The composition of the list raised the thorny question of which British treaties continued to apply to Australia, or which covered Australia by implication.[62] A seven-page prefatory note outlines information about the history of treaty-making as it related to Australia. "List A," entitled "Bilateral International Agreements," lists the treaties and agreements first in alphabetical order by the countries with which they are concluded, and then chronologically. The second list, "List B," entitled "General and Multilateral International Agreements" is arranged chronologically. For each entry, both lists offer information regarding date and place of signature, a brief description, where printed, and brief explanatory notes.

Index: There are separate subject indexes for each list.

Note: The 1935 list is also found in *Parliamentary Papers* 1934–1937, Vol. III, p. 237.

Note: A supplementary list to the 1935 list was published by the then Department of External Affairs in 1 *Current Notes on International Affairs*, No. 3, 15 May 1936, pp. 66–70. The author of this chapter on Australian treaties examined annual issues of the *Report of the Department of External Affairs* for each year ending 31 December between 1936–1940, and found appendices

62 *See* D.P. O'CONNELL, *The Evolution of Australia's International Personality in* INTERNATIONAL LAW IN AUSTRALIA 23–24 (1965).

listing Australian treaty actions affecting bilateral and multilateral treaties for the year on the report.

8 LIST OF TREATIES, ETC., AS TO WHICH THE COMMONWEALTH GOVERNMENT HAS BEEN CONSULTED, TO WHICH THE COMMONWEALTH IS A PARTY OR HAS ACCEDED…TO 30TH JUNE 1921
Prime Minister's Department, Foreign Section (Pacific).
(Melbourne: Government Printer, 1921). 42 pp.

Summary: According to the Introduction to *Australian Treaty List (to 31 December 1989)*, the first Australian treaty list was printed by the Prime Minister's Department listing 198 treaties as of June 30, 1921. The list was for internal use only.

Diplomatic Documents

9 AUSTRALIAN DEPARTMENT OF FOREIGN AFFAIRS AND TRADE (DFAT)
URL: http://www.dfat.gov.au/

Summary: The official web site of the Australian Department of Foreign Affairs and Trade. Includes the Australian Treaties Database at: http://www.dfat.gov.au/treaties/ which has a full-text search option, or which can be browsed to find treaties by subject, agreement type and/or country, the date a treaty was concluded, and the status (signed, acceded to and entered in force) of different types of treaties. The database also links to the "Status lists for multilateral treaties for which Australia is a depository" on AustLII, and the list of links to multilateral treaty status sites provided by DFAT at: http://www.info.dfat.gov.au/Info/Treaties/Treaties.nsf/LinksPage?OpenForm.

Also provides information about the variety of department activities including recent media releases,[63] and recent speeches about treaties at: http://www.dfat.gov.au/treaties/workshops/.

10 DOCUMENTS ON AUSTRALIAN INTERNATIONAL AFFAIRS 1901–1918
Gordon Greenwood and Charles Grimshaw, eds., (West Melbourne: Thomas Nelson (Australia) Limited, in association with The Australian Institute of International Affairs and The Royal Institute of International Affairs, 1997). 779 pp.

Summary: A collection of official and unofficial documents relating to Australian foreign affairs from the time of federation in 1901 to the end of World War One.

Index: Includes a detailed table of contents and an index.

---

63 *Available at:* http://www.dfat.gov.au/media/

11 DOCUMENTS ON AUSTRALIAN FOREIGN POLICY 1937–1949
R.G. Neale, ed. (Canberra: Department of Foreign Affairs, Australian Government Publishing Service, 1975–1998).

Summary: A 16-volume set, which officially published in chronological order diplomatic documents from the Department of External Affairs and documents relating to foreign affairs from other departments dating from the 1937 Imperial Conference through World War Two to 1949. Documents were selected by the editors and their inclusion was finally approved by a Committee of Review consisting of the Prime Minister, the Minister for Foreign Affairs, and the Leader of the Opposition political party. Documents are arranged in most volumes in chronological order. Documents include cablegrams, dispatches and records of conversation from officers of the United Kingdom government and other documents from British diplomatic sources. Australian sources are drawn from the files of the Department of External Affairs, the archives of other departments, and collections of papers from ministers and officials who made and implemented Australian foreign policy. Footnotes and editorial notes are included to summarize material that is not published in full, and to otherwise assist the reader without offering historical interpretations.

Index: Most volumes include a subject list of documents, a chronological list of documents, an index of persons, and a subject index.

Note: The years covered by each volume are as follows: Vol. 1: 1937–1938; Vol. II: 1939; Vol. III: January–June 1940; Vol. IV: July 1940–June 1941; Vol. V: July 1941–June 1942; Vol. VI: July 1942–December 1943; Vol. VII: 1944; Vol. VIII: 1945; Vol. IX: January–June 1946; Vol. X: July–December 1946; Vol. XI: 1947–Documents relating to Indonesian independence; Vol. XII: 1947–Documents appearing in this volume are arranged by subject rather than chronologically; Vol. XIII: 1948–Documents relating to Indonesia; Vol. XIV: 1948–1949–Documents relating to the Commonwealth, Asia and the Pacific; Vol. XV: Documents relating to Indonesia; and Vol. XVI: 1948–1949–Australia and the Post World War: Beyond the Region.

Note: Vols. XI, XIII and XV are also published separately under the title *Australia and Indonesia's Independence.*

Note: Various editors for different volumes.

12 DOCUMENTS ON AUSTRALIAN FOREIGN POLICY (SECOND SERIES)
Department of Foreign Affairs
(Canberra: Australian Government Publishing Service, 1997–).

Summary: Titles in this series consist of selections of Australian government documents relating to themes in Australian international relations. Titles to date are *The Australia-Japan Agreement on Commerce 1957,* (1997); *Australia and the Indonesian Incorporation of Portuguese Timor, 1974–1976* (2000); *Australia and the Formation of Malaysia: 1961–1966* (2000); *The ANZUS Treaty 1951* (2001); *Australia and Recognition of the People's Republic of China* (2002); *The Negotiation of the Australia New Zealand Closer Economic Relations Trade Agreement 1983* (2003); *The Negotiation of the Australia New Zealand Closer Economic Relations Trade Agreement 1983* (2003); and, *Australia and the Colombo Plan: 1949–1957* (2004).

Note: See the web pages for the Historical Documents Unit of the Australian Department of Foreign Affairs and Trade,[64] which publishes foreign policy historical material and provides access to the records of the department.

13 AUSTRALIAN FOREIGN AFFAIRS AND TRADE: THE MONTHLY RECORD
(Canberra: Overseas Information Branch, Department of Foreign Affairs and Trade, 1997–2000). ISSN: 1033-5722.

Summary: A monthly periodical, which was an official publication of the Department of Foreign Affairs and Trade. Included items such as ministerial statements, information about diplomatic representation and international agreements to which Australia is a party, Australian commentary on international issues, and served as a journal of record in summarizing events affecting Australian international relations. Over the years this title served as a method of updating the *Australian Treaty List.*

Index: Includes index for each volume. Indexed from 1962 by Australian Public Affairs Information Service (APAIS).

Note: Formerly known as *Current Notes on International Affairs* (1936–1972), *Australian Foreign Affairs Record* (1973–1988). See also *Backgrounder,* (1975–1992) which merged with *Australian Foreign Affairs and Trade Record* (1989–1992) to form *Insight: Australian Foreign Affairs and Trade Issues* (1992–1996).

Note: Formerly known as *Current Notes on International Affairs* from 1936–1972. For an article outlining developments in the 36-year history of *Current Notes* in its role as the journal of record for the then Department of Foreign Affairs, see 43 *Current Note on International Affairs*, pp. 599–602 (1972).

14 SELECT DOCUMENTS ON INTERNATIONAL AFFAIRS
(Canberra: Department of Foreign Affairs and Trade, 1963–). ISSN: 0519-5950.

Summary: Published twice per year, 1963–1967, and annually thereafter. As explained in the brief introduction to each issue, this title offers the texts of international treaties and conventions, in the preparation of which Australia participated at conferences, but to which Australia did not become a party

64 *Available at:* http://www.dfat.gov.au/historical/index.html.

during that year. Since No. 10 1966, treaties have been published in this series prior to their ratification. The Australian government began this practice on the recommendation of the Joint Select Committee on Parliamentary and Government Publications (*Hansard*, House of Representatives, 25 August 1966, p. 414). Amendments to existing treaties, which are not published in the *Australian Treaty Series*, are also found in *Select Documents on International Affairs*. Some issues include texts from prior years that were received after publication of the volume, or for public information purposes. If a treaty appearing in *Select Documents* enters into force for Australia, the text will then appear in both the print and Internet versions of the *Australian Treaty Series*.

Index: For a list of issues in this series and brief descriptions of their contents, consult the table in the introduction of the most recent issue available, No. 47. Some numbered issues in the series consist of two physical volumes. Also, a chronological list of documents in the series is found in the *Australian Treaty List* (see Nos. 3–6 above).

Note: 1963 – Nos. 1–2 of 1963, 1–2 of 1964, and 1–2 of 1965 were re-numbered Nos. 1–6.

Note: Imprint varies. Published by Department of External Affairs (1963–1969), Department of Foreign Affairs (1970–1985), Department of Foreign Affairs and Trade (1986–).

Note: Subtitle varies. Nos. 10, 12, 14–15, 17, 19, 21–39 have subtitle "International Treaties and Conventions," 1966–1991; Nos. 40–43: "Texts of International Treaties and Conventions," 1992–1995; and, Nos. 44– "Texts of International Treaties."

Note: Issues from 1996–1999 are available at the Australian Treaties Library at: http://www.austlii.edu.au/au/other/dfat/seldoc/

15 NATIONAL ARCHIVES OF AUSTRALIA
URL: http://www.naa.gov.au/

Summary: The official site of the National Archives of Australia, which houses Australian official documents. Records, including the papers of Governors-General, Prime Ministers, Ministers, Cabinet documents and departmental records are available to the public.

Yearbooks and Digests of State Practice

16 AUSTRALIAN YEARBOOK OF INTERNATIONAL LAW: BEING AN ANNUAL SURVEY OF CURRENT PROBLEMS OF PUBLIC AND PRIVATE INTERNATIONAL LAW WITH A DIGEST OF AUSTRALIAN PRACTICE
(Canberra: Faculty of Law, Australian National University, 1965–).
ISSN: 0084-7658.

Summary: Published annually. Provides articles and commentary on cases, legislation and practice in Australian international law. A regular section entitled "Australian Practice in International Law" began with Vol. 11.

Index: Indexed from inception by *Index to Legal Periodicals and Books.* Also indexed by *Current Law Index* which began publication in 1980 and its online format called *LegalTrac.*

Note: Various editors, beginning with J.G. Starke for the 1965 volume. Vols. 21 and 22 comprise a festschrift in honor of longtime editor and co-editor D.W. Greig.

Note: 1966 volume covers events in 1965–1966. Some volumes cover more than one year: Vol. 4 covers 1968–1969; Vol. 5 covers 1970–1973; Vol. 6 covers 1974–1975; Vol. 7 covers 1976–1977; Vol. 8 covers 1978–1980; Vol. 10 covers 1981–1983; Vol. 11 covers 1984–1987. Vol. 9 comprises a collection of papers on "The Protection of the Human Being in Armed Conflicts" from a seminar on international humanitarian law held in Canberra in 1983 for participants from countries in the Asia and Pacific regions.

Note: Imprint varies. Vols. 1–3 published by Butterworths; Vols. 3–5 published by Butterworths under the auspices of Monash Law School; and, Vol. 6 1978– published by the Faculty of Law at The Australian National University.

Note: Beginning with Vol. 14 for 1992, Treaty Action for the year on the volume is reprinted as it appears in the *Australian Treaty Series.*

Note: Vols. 1 (1965) – 28 (2009) are available in electronic format to subscribers of *HeinOnline,* and from 1965–2009 are provided by AustLII at http://www.austlii.edu.au/au/journals/AUYrBkIntLaw/.

Austria

Ralph F. Gaebler

Issues of Treaty Succession

The history of Austria is principally the history of the Habsburg dynasty, which governed a vast territory in central Europe, including present-day Austria, from 1292 until the abdication of Emperor Charles I on November 11, 1918. During this period of 626 years, the territories contained within this empire continually changed with fluctuations in Habsburg fortunes, as did the ethnic nationalities comprising its population. At the time of its collapse, the empire contained no less than ten significant ethnic-linguistic groups. Thus, Austria is best viewed throughout the great majority of its history not as a single nation, but as an agglomeration of peoples unified only by the personal authority of the Habsburgs and by the administrative state that depended upon them.

Against this background, it is a somewhat arbitrary matter to date the beginning of "modern" Austria. A strong argument could be made that it did not emerge until the wreckage of the Habsburg dynasty was swept away by the First World War. However, the first important printed sources of information regarding Austria's practice in international law date from the mid-19th century, a time when the Habsburg empire was enjoying both gradual industrialization of the economy and the development of modern administration. It was at this time also that Austria achieved the constitutional shape it was to retain until its demise.

Reform of the state at mid-century was necessitated fundamentally by the rise of ethnic and liberal nationalism, but the immediate trigger was Austria's disastrous defeat at the hands of Prussia in the Seven Weeks War (1866). Several statutes followed, collectively known as the "December Constitution," which transformed the empire into the so-called "dual monarchy" of Austria-Hungary, and placed it on a more republican footing. Equally important was the *Ausgleich*, or compromise, of 1867, which established relations between Hungary and the Emperor, Franz Josef I.[1] According to this compromise,

1 The *Ausgleich* was consummated for the Austrian lands by the so-called *Delegationsgesetz*, approved by the Reichsrat (Reichsgesetzblatt 146), and by Law XII/1867, approved by the Hungarian parliament. These statutes are reprinted in various sources, including Heinz Fischer and Gerhard Silvestri, Texte zur Österreichischen Vefassungs-Geschichte: von der Pragmatischen Sanktion zur Bundesverfassun (1713–1966) 87–101 (1970).

 | DOI 10.1163/9789004272224_006

Hungary was restored to complete independence within the empire, subject only to several unitary institutions. As a result, the dual monarchy was actually a three-part administration: it included Hungary, with its own parliament and government, the rest of the Habsburg lands (known until 1915 as the "*im Reichsrat vertretenen Königreiche und Länder*," or "kingdoms and lands represented in the Reichsrat," and thereafter as Austria), which continued under the authority of the existing Reichsrat and government, and the unified institutions, encompassing the foreign ministry, the war ministry, the finance ministry and a customs union. The latter were responsible to the emperor, but he was prevented from acting unilaterally without their cooperation.[2]

As a result of the constitutional reforms, treaty-making became a somewhat complex issue. The emperor retained his prerogative power to conclude treaties as long as they did not pertain to affairs of the joint monarchy. The Reichsrat now had authority to approve treaties that affected the entire state and its population. Additionally, the Reichsrat and the Hungarian parliament were required to enter a treaty every ten years, which governed division of costs for maintaining joint institutions.

The *Ausgleich* and other constitutional reforms of 1867 represented a fundamental change in the structure of the state, rather than the establishment of a new state. Therefore, they do not raise any question of state succession. The issue of succession for modern Austria arose only at the end of World War I, after the Habsburg empire had virtually evaporated in the face of military annihilation and internal ethnic conflict. On November 11, 1918, the emperor abdicated, and on the following day the German members of the Reichsrat,

---

Legislative history of the statutes is contained in BARBARA HAIDER, DIE PROTOKOLLE DES VERFASSUNGSAUSSCHUSSES DES REICHRATES VOM JAHRE 1867 (1997). The Austrian statute is reprinted in English in WALTER FAIRLEIGH DODD, MODERN CONSTITUTIONS: A COLLECTION OF THE FUNDAMENTAL LAWS OF TWENTY-TWO OF THE MOST IMPORTANT COUNTRIES OF THE WORLD (1909, reprinted by Hein in 2003). The 1909 edition is available in Google Books, at: http://books.google.com/books?id=vthAAAAAIAAJ&pg=PA113&lpg=PA113&dq=ausgleich++Law+XII/1867&source=bl&ots=zQNsa5RwjP&sig=NThlBURblkvSVx3vyhFZg9cYNe4&hl=en&sa=X&ei=jGPkUJLILMvvoQGo44GoDA&ved=0CE4Q6AEwBQ#v=onepage&q=ausgleich%20%20Law%20XII%2F1867&f=false.

2 The *Staatsgrundgesetz über die Ausübung der Regierungs – und Vollzugsgewalt* (Reichsgesetzblatt 145) required the counter-signature of the corresponding ministers for any actions undertaken by the emperor in the areas of foreign policy, finance, and war. It also required the ministers to act in accordance with the law. *See* MODERN CONSTITUTIONS, *supra* at 97–98. The *Gesetz über die Ministerverantwortlichkeit* (Reichsgesetzblatt 101) gave each house of the Reichsrat a cause of action to prevent the ministers for finance, war, and foreign affairs from acting contrary to law.

who had formed a rump national assembly for Austria, declared *Deutsch-Österreich*, or German-Austria, a "democratic republic."

With respect to treaty succession, the first question therefore is whether the war extinguished Austria-Hungary's treaty commitments towards fellow belligerents. If so, there no longer existed any such commitments to which *Deutsch-Österreich* could succeed. It has been asserted, with much qualification, that "[t]oday the majority view seems to approve the general applicability of peacetime law during war in regard to certain types of peacetime treaties.[3] This would imply that at least some pre-war treaties continued in force at the time *Deutsch-Österreich* came into existence. However, it is argued by some that *Deutsch-Österreich* was not a successor state, but a completely new nation without ties to the old Austro-Hungarian Empire.[4] This conclusion seems to flow from the observation that the Reichsrat, meeting as a "provisional national assembly" in October 1918, claimed to represent the sovereign will of the people of German-speaking Austria, and manifestly did not wish to be associated with a continuation of the now defunct Empire.[5]

Whether or not the Republic of Austria ought to be regarded as a successor state, the issue of treaty succession was settled by the Treaty of St. Germain en Laye, concluded between Austria and the Allied and Associated Powers in September 1919 (ratified on September 10, 1919, in force July 16, 1920).[6] By the

---

3 *See* S. Vöneky, *Armed Conflict, Effect on Treaties, in The Max Planck Encyclopedia of Public International Law*, Oxford University Press, 2008–, online edition, [www.mpepil.com]. Despite the fact that the International Law Commission in 2008 adopted "Draft Articles on Effects of Armed Conflicts on Treaties" (UN Doc A/CN.4/L.727/Rev.1.), Vöneky nevertheless considers "the question of the effect of an armed conflict on treaties...one of the most unsettled and complicated topics in international law."

4 This was the view taken by A. Merkl, in *Die Verfassung der Republik Deutschösterreich: ein Kritisch-Sytematischer Grundriss* (Vienna: F. Deuticke, 1919), cited in WILHELM BRAUNEDER ÖSTERREICHISCHE VERFASSUNGSGESCHICHTE 189–90 (7th ed., 1998). This was also the view of Hans Kelsen, in ÖSTERREICHISCHES STAATSRECHT: EIN GRUNDRISS, ENTWICKLUNGSGESCHICHTLICH DARGESTELLT (2nd ed., 1923).

5 In order to avoid any appearance of continuity with the past, the Reichsrat adjourned, and moved from its national parliamentary building to the state parliamentary building before reconstituting itself as the provisional national assembly. *See* BRAUNEDER, *supra* note 4, p. 190.

6 Treaty of Peace Between the Allied and Associated Powers and Austria, Sept. 10, 1919, art. 241, 11 *Nouveau Recueil Général de Traités*, vol. 3, p. 692. The treaty is also reprinted in 14 *American Journal of International Law.*, Supp. 1, p. 1. The Austrian official version of the treaty, published in the Australian Treaty Series, 1920 no.3, is available electronically in Austlii, at: http://www.austlii.edu.au/au/other/dfat/treaties/1920/3.html. The treaty is discussed in D.P. O'CONNELL, 2 STATE SUCCESSION IN MUNICIPAL LAW AND INTERNATIONAL LAW 178–82 (1967), and A.D. MCNAIR, THE LAW OF TREATIES 723–27 (1961). The United States did not sign

terms of this treaty, Austria was held jointly responsible for World War I, and treated as a successor to Austria-Hungary.[7] Under Articles 232–240, Austria agreed to adhere to certain, specified multilateral treaties, and under Article 241, the Allied and Associated Powers were granted a six-month period in which to renew any bilateral treaties they chose to.[8] The researcher will find acknowledgment of all such renewals published in the *Bundesgesetzblatt für den Bundesstaat Österreich.* (See entry no. 5, below)

Succession issues next arose in conjunction with the "*Anschluss*," or annexation of Austria by Germany in 1938.[9] According to the generally recognized rule, absorption leads to extinction of the absorbed state.[10] This was the view advocated by Germany, and by most of the international community at the time of the *Anschluss*, including France, Great Britain and the United States.[11] Moreover, the effect of absorption was regarded by these countries as leading to termination of the treaties concluded by Austria. For example, the United States informed Germany that the Treaty of Friendship, Commerce and Consular Rights between the United States and Austria was extinguished, and

---

the Treaty of St. Germain, but concluded a separate treaty with Austria on August 24, 1921 (Bundesgesetzblatt. 643) (42 Stat. 1946 (1921), T.S. 659). BRAUNEDER, *supra* note 4, regards the Treaty of Saint Germain not as a peace treaty, but as a state-creating treaty, since it established the boundaries of the new republic (arts. 22–35), specified certain constitutional, minority rights that must be guaranteed (arts. 62–69), and forbade unification with Germany (art. 88). It also changed the name of *Deutsch-Österreich* to *Republik Österreich* (Republic of Austria).

7 Treaty of St. Germain, art. 177.

8 The only limitation imposed by Article 241 was that any bilateral treaties renewed must conform to the terms of the Treaty of St. Germain. It is interesting to note that the right enjoyed by the Allied and Associated Powers to pick and choose among the treaties they wished to renew implies that all such treaties were thought to have survived the state of war (or else would not have been available for renewal with a successor state). Article 241 granted the right of choice to all Allied and Associated Powers, not only to those who had been in a state of war with Austria-Hungary. Under Article 242, Austria engaged to recognize all treaties concluded with other central powers before 1914. *See* MCNAIR, *supra* note 6, at 724.

9 German troops entered Austria on 12 March 1938. The following day the Austrian government adopted legislation proclaiming Austria a German state (Bundesgesetzblatt 75). The German government likewise adopted legislation to the same effect (Reichsgesetzblatt I S.237).

10 *See, e.g.,* SIR R. JENNINGS AND SIR A. WATTS, OPPENHEIM'S INTERNATIONAL LAW 210–11 (9th ed., 1992).

11 See BRAUNEDER, *supra* note 4, at 248. The United States formally recognized Austria's absorption into Germany on April 6, 1938. The text of the note according recognition appears in the *New York Times,* April 7, 1938.

therefore did not entitle Germany to the lower import duties Austrian goods had enjoyed.[12] However, termination of Austria's treaty obligations did not necessarily lead to extension of German treaties to include Austria's former territory.[13]

The advent of World War II prompted a change of attitude. In the Moscow Declaration of 1 November, 1943, the United States, the United Kingdom and the Soviet Union held the *Anschluss* "null and void."[14]

At the conclusion of World War II, Austria was divided into administrative zones and occupied by the allied powers, just as was Germany. However, unlike the case of Germany, a guarantee of military neutrality by Austria permitted the conclusion of a peace treaty in 1955, which terminated the occupation regime and re-established Austria's status as an independent, democratic state.[15] The treaty was silent on the question of whether existing treaties survived the war and the re-establishment of Austria. Obviously, all prior agreements inconsistent with the provisions of the peace settlement were void. However, the researcher who is interested in the fate of a consistent prior agreement must determine through research whether or not the treaty was terminated by the war. State practice seems to have varied. For example, the United States took the position that treaties concluded before the Nazi *Anschluss* were automatically revived. Thus, the Treaty of Friendship, Commerce and Consular Rights (signed June 19, 1928, entered into force May 27, 1931) was revived, and is still in force.[16] Similarly, the extradition treaty (signed January 31, 1930, entered into force September 11, 1930) remained in force until superseded in 1998 by a new extradition treaty.[17]

---

12 The US position is stated in a note, reprinted in 5 Hackworth Digest § 512, at 371 (1943). The letter from the US President to the Secretary of the Treasury, directing the latter to revoke the tariff reduction for the area of Germany formerly comprising Austria, is reprinted in the *New York Times,* April 8, 1938. Austria was party to six bilateral treaties with the United States at the time of its absorption. These treaties are listed in James Wilford Garner, "Questions of State Succession Raised By the German Annexation of Austria," 32 Am. J. Int'l L. 431, footnote 24 (1938).

13 The effect of Austria's annexation is discussed in O'Connell, *supra* note 6, pp. 38–39, and in Jennings and Watts, *supra* note 10, pp. 192–93.

14 The declaration is reprinted in 161 British and Foreign State Papers 288 (1954), and is available electronically in ibiblio at: http://www.ibiblio.org/pha/policy/1943/431000a.html. This position was reaffirmed by the Allied powers in a Joint Declaration on Austria, made at the Tripartite Meeting of Foreign Ministers held in London in May 1950.

15 6 UST 2369, 217 UNTS 223.

16 47 Stat. 1876 (1931), amended by a supplemental agreement, 47 Stat. 1899 (1931).

17 The 1930 treaty is located at 46 Stat. 2779 (1930), amended by supplementing agreement, 49 Stat. 2710 (1934).

Treaty Ratification and Implementation

Treaty implementation is governed principally by Article 50 of the *Bundesverfassungsgesetz* (federal constitutional statute), which was completely redrafted, and significantly altered, in 2008.[18] All treaties are concluded by the federal President, but under Article 50 special implementation requirements apply to certain important categories of treaties. These include political treaties, treaties that modify or complement existing law, and treaties that alter the foundational treaties forming the European Union. Political treaties are those that "directly affect the existence of [the] state, its territorial integrity, its independence, its position among states, its political influence on other states, or the order within the community of states."[19] Modifying and complementing treaties are those whose transposition into municipal law would require a regulation by means of law.[20]

Treaties within the purview of Article 50 must be approved by the *Nationalrat* (National Council), i.e. the democratically elected lower house of Parliament, before they can be ratified. At the time of approval, the National Council may also decide whether implementation requires the adoption municipal legislation. All resolutions of approval and any accompanying legislation must be adopted according to the normal procedures outlined in Article 42. Prior to the 2008 amendment, implementing legislation had to be identified as simple or

---

18 BGBl No. 1/1930, as last amended by BGBl. I No. 65/2012. A full description of the treaty implementation process is found in LUDWIG K. ADAMOVICH AND BERND-CHRISTIAN FUNK, ÖSTERREICHISCHES VERFASSUNGSRECHT 151–158 (3rd ed. 1985). See also HEINZ MAYER, ÖSTERREICHISCHE BUNDES-VERFASSUNGSRECHT 236–239 (4th ed. 2007), and the chapter on Austria in NATIONAL TREATY LAW AND PRACTICE 55–90 (Duncan B. Hollis et al. eds., 2005). Unfortunately, there is a dearth of commentary on the *Bundesverfassungsgesetz* incorporating the 2008 amendment of the provisions on treaty implementation. A more up-to-date discussion is found in MANFRED STELZER, THE CONSTITUTION OF THE REPUBLIC OF AUSTRIA: A CONTEXTUAL ANALYSIS 134–136 (2011). An up-to-date text of the *Bundesverfassungsgesetz* is available in German in GEORG LIENBACHER, ÖSTERREICHISCHE VERFASSUNGS – UND VERWALTUNGSGESETZE (1992–), as well as electronically in English in HeinOnline's *World Constitutions Illustrated* and in German at the web site of the Austrian Federal Chancellery (see no. 7, *infra*) at: http://www.ris.bka.gv.at/Ergebnis.wxe?Abfrage=Bundesnormen&Kundmachungsorgan=&Index=&Titel=Bundes-Verfassungsgesetz&Gesetzesnummer=&VonArtikel=&BisArtikel=&VonParagraf=&BisParagraf=&VonAnlage=&BisAnlage=&Typ=&Kundmachungsnummer=&Unterzeichnungsdatum=&FassungVom=02.01.2013&NormabschnittnummerKombination=Und&ImRisSeit=Undefined&ResultPageSize=100&Suchworte=&Position=1.

19 *See* STELZER, *supra* note 18, at 135.

20 Id.

constitutional in nature. Now all such legislation is regarded as non-constitutional in nature.

Additional requirements apply to treaties altering the foundational treaties of the European Union (and, under Article 3 of the *Bundesverfassungsgesetz*, to those affecting the boundaries of the Austrian Republic). In these cases, resolutions of approval must be adopted by both the *Nationalrat* and *Bundesrat*, and in each case at least half the membership must be present with at least two thirds voting for approval. In the case of treaties altering foundational EU treaties, either the *Nationalrat* or *Bundesrat* can further require a national referendum under Article 44(3) of the *Bundesverfassungsgesetz*, if one third of either body demands it.

The *Bundesrat*, or upper house of Parliament, has an additional important role to play in the Article 50 treaty implementation process. Representing the B*undesländer*, or states, the upper house can veto resolutions granting consent or condition consent upon further, internal legislation, if such commitments would alter the competence of the states or add to their burdens.

Treaties that do not fall under Article 50 are also concluded by the federal President. However, in a decision of 1920, the President limited himself to acting on his own only in those cases where the agreement to be entered is not expressly referred to as a treaty, and where there is no exchange of ratification instruments.[21] In addition, Article 66, paragraph 2, of the *Bundesverfassungsgesetz* permits the federal President to delegate his authority to conclude non-Article 50 treaties to the federal government in most cases. Hence non-Article 50 treaties fall into two categories, those concluded by the federal president acting alone, and those concluded by the Chancellor and his Cabinet. The latter category includes treaties styled as inter-governmental or inter-departmental agreements. Like the National Council in the case of Article 50 treaties, both the federal President and the Chancellor and his Cabinet can condition implementation upon the adoption of corresponding municipal legislation.

Even in the absence of an express condition of this type, a ratified treaty that would otherwise be self-executing might lose this effect on the ground that it is not sufficiently specific with respect to the rights or duties it creates or the persons to whom they are directed. Thus, Austria is somewhat dualist on the question of incorporation.

As noted, the federal government may conclude treaties that fall within the subject matter jurisdiction of the *Bundesländer*. However, the *Bundesländer* also have a role to play in treaty-making. Since 1974, it has been possible for the federal government and the states to conclude so-called *Gliedsstaatsverträge*

21 Decision of Dec. 31, 1920, Bundesgesetzblatt 1921/49.

between themselves, under Article 15a of the *Bundesverfassungsgesetz*. Under Article 16, paragraph 1, states have enjoyed the right since 1988 to conclude treaties on their own with neighboring states and regions in areas that fall within their jurisdiction.[22] However, this right is subject to federal control in various ways, and in fact no such treaties have yet been concluded.[23]

Finally, Article 50 requires the federal executive to notify both the *Nationalrat* and *Bundesrat* at the beginning of negotiations of any treaty covered by Article 50(1). However, this notification requirement is viewed as a formality, since it is impractical for the legislative branch to be involved in treaty negotiations. Moreover, in a parliamentary system it is extremely unlikely that the legislature would fail to approve any treaty concluded by the government in any case.[24]

All treaties adopted under Article 50 of the federal constitutional statute must appear in the official gazette, unless this is precluded by technical difficulties, such as the necessity of including maps.[25] Thus, border treaties may frequently not be found in this source. Non-Article 50 treaties are also to be published in the official gazette, unless they are directed exclusively at administrative agencies. Self-executing treaties that are published in the official gazette become binding the day after their appearance, unless the effective date is altered by terms of the treaty itself.

As of 2004, the official gazette is no longer published in paper. It is now published only electronically, and made available through the web site of the Federal Chancellery. (See no. 7, below.) Older issues of the federal gazette are available electronically through the National Library web site (see no. 4, below).

Annotated Bibliography of Sources

General Treaty Collections

1 REICHSGESETZBLATT FÜR DIE IM REICHSRATE VERTRETENEN KÖNIGREICHE UND LÄNDER
(Vienna: Staatsdrückerei, 1870–1918).

---

22 *See* BRAUNEDER, *supra* note 4, p. 272.

23 *See* STELZER, *supra* note 18, p. 166.

24 Id. at 136.

25 Publication and date of entry into force of treaties are governed by Article 5 of the *Bundesgesetzblattgesetz*, BGBl. I 2003/100, and by Article 49 of the *Bundesverfassungsgesetz*.

Summary: In 50 volumes. Official gazette of the dual monarchy. Includes the text of treaties. Bilateral treaties are printed in German. Multilateral treaties are printed in the original language, and in German translation. Each year's volume includes chronologically arranged table of contents and subject index, where treaties are listed under the heading *"Staatsverträge."* References are to item number and page number.

2 RECUEIL DES TRAITES ET CONVENTIONS. CONCLUS PAR L'AUTRICHE AVEC LES PUISSANCES ETRANGÈRES, DEPUIS 1763 JUSQU'A NOS JOURS
Leopold Neumann (Leipzig: FA. Brockhaus, 1855–1859).

Summary: Six volumes, covering the period 1718–1856. Treaties are printed in their original language, with titles in French translation as needed, together with a brief note indicating the source of the text. Treaties are arranged chronologically, and each volume includes a chronological table of treaties.

Index: Vol. VI includes all six chronological tables, as well as a table organized alphabetically by country of opposite party and a subject index. (See also no. 3, below.)

3 RECUEIL DES TRAITES ET CONVENTIONS. CONCLUS PAR L'AUTRICHE-HONGRIE AVEC LES PUISSANCES ETRANGÈRES, DEPUIS 1763 JUSQU'A NOS JOURS. NOUVELLE SUITE
(Vienna: Imprimerie de la Cour I R de Carl Fromme, éditeur, 1877–1912).

Summary: 26 volumes, covering the period 1851–1912. Each volume includes a chronological table. Treaties are printed in their original language. Titles are in French and German.

Index: Vol. VII includes a general index to the first series and the first six volumes of the new series. The general table reproduces the chronological tables from all 12 volumes. It also includes an alphabetical table organized by country of opposite party, and a subject index. Vol. XIII includes an alphabetical index of states and subjects, covering vols. X–XIII. Vol. XXII includes a similar index for vols. XIV–XXII. Beginning with vol. XXIII, each volume includes a chronological table, as well as an alphabetical index of countries and subjects. (See also no. 2, above.)

Note: Title varies. Vols. I–XII have the title *Recueil des Traités et Conventions Conclus par l'Autriche avec les Puissances Etrangères.*

Note: Imprint varies. I. Et R. De la Cour et de l'Etat (vols. I–VIII); Imprimerie Steyremühl (vols. IX–XI).

Note: Each volume has an added title page on which volume numeration continues that of the first series, i.e., vols. I–XXVI numbered as vols. VII–XXXII.

Note: Author varies. Vols. I–XII compiled by Leopold Neumann and Adolf de Plason de la Woestyne. Vols. XIII–XXVI compiled by Adolf de Plason de la Woestyne.

Note: Reprinted under the imprint: Nendeln, Liechtenstein: Kraus Reprint, 1971.

4 ALEX: HISTORISCHE RECHTS – UND GESETZETEXTE ONLINE. ÖSTERREICHISCHE NATIONALBIBLIOTHEK
URL: http://alex.onb.ac.at/index.htm.

Summary: ALEX is an historical database of Austrian law dating back to 1740. Of particular relevance to treaty research are the *Reichsgesetzblatt*, 1849–1918, and *Bundesggesetzblatt*, 1918–1938. Both are searchable and displayable in PDF. Keyword searching permits the user to search by subject across any combination of sources and years in the database. ALEX is highly integrated with the RIS (see no. 7, below). In German only.

5 BUNDESGESETZBLATT FÜR DEN BUNDESSTAAT ÖSTERREICH
(Vienna: Staatsdrückerei, 1918–1938).

Summary: Official gazette of the Republic of Austria, established after World War I.

Note: Title varies: *Staatsgesetzblatt für den Staat Deutschösterreich, 1918–1919; Staatsgesetzblatt für die Republik Österreich, 1919–1920; Bundesgesetzblatt für die Republik Österreich, 1920–1934.*

Note: Superseded by the *Gesetzblatt für das Land Österreich,* after the *Anschluss.*

6. BUNDESGESETZBLATT FÜR DIE REPUBLIK ÖSTERREICH
(Vienna: Staatsdrückerei, 1945–2003).

Summary: Official gazette of the Republic of Austria, established after World War II. Part III contains the text of treaties. Includes a cumulative index.

Note: Prior to 1997, treaties were published in Part II.

Note: Title Varies: *Staatsgesetzblatt Für Die Reublik Österreich,* 5 January 1945–18 December 1945.

Note: As of 2004, the *Bundesgesetzblatt* is no longer published in paper. It is now published in electronic format only, and available through the web site of the Federal Chancellery. (See no. 7, below.)

7. RECHTSINFORMATIONSYSTEM (RIS). BUNDESKANZLERAMT ÖSTERREICH
[Legal Information System of the Federal Chancellery]
URL: http://www.ris.bka.gv.at/.

Summary: The Federal Chancellery web site provides access to the *Bundesgestezblatt* (see no. 6, above), which has been published only in electronic format since the beginning of 2004. Treaty information is available in several different databases: (1) issues of the *Bundesgesetzblatt* published since the end of 2003, which are legally authentic; (2) issues of the *Bundesgesetzblatt* from 1945–2003, which are not legally authentic; (3) issues of the *Bundesgesetzblatt* from 1848–1940, which are also not legally authentic; (4) a consolidated collection of currently applicable federal law, including currently applicable treaties. Treaties in all four databases are accessible in various formats, including HTML and PDF. All four databases use the same search interface, which permits the user to search by keyword, short title, document number, type, date and *Bundesgesetzblatt* part. By limiting the search to *Bundesgesetzblatt* Part III, or to "other documents, in particular treaties," the researcher can obtain a complete list of treaties concluded over any desired span of time since 1945. (Treaties were published in Part II prior to 1997, but are not retrievable by searching Part II; to retrieve them one must search for "other documents, in particular treaties.") In addition, there is also a systematic subject index of legislation covering 1945–present, which the researcher can use to search for treaties by topic. These databases, and their search interfaces are in German only, though there is also a small collection of legislation (including treaties) translated unofficially into English.

The Legal Information System also provides access to collections of current legislation and the official gazettes of the *Bundesländer*. This includes treaties concluded by the states under Articles 15a and 16b of the federal constitutional statute. (See introductory section on treaty implementation.) The electronic gazettes are retrospective in most cases only to 2000 or 2001, except in the case of Tirol (1995), Oberösterreich (1947), Steiermark (1989), and Vienna (1955, plus pre-1955 laws still in force). The search interface permits the researcher to search individual *Bundesländer* or all of them at once, and there is a systematic subject index as well. It is also possible to search current consolidated laws only, or all laws individually, whether or not currently in force.

Note: The RIS is authorized by the *Bundesgesetzblattgesetz*, BGBl I 2003/100, Article 6.

8 AUSSENMINISTERIUM [MINISTRY OF FOREIGN AFFAIRS]
URL: http://www.bmaa.gv.at/view.php3?f_id=1413&LNG=de&version=.

Summary: The Foreign Ministry web site maintains a database of bilateral treaties currently in force. Treaties are searchable by title keyword or by subject heading. Treaties are also listed in chronological order by country of opposite party. Each entry includes title, place of signature, date of signature and of coming into force, citation to the *Bundesgestezblatt* (see no. 6, above), and subject heading.

Titles of superseded or amended treaties provide links to entries for superseding and amending treaties. *Bundesgesetzblatt* citations provide links to text files containing the full text in the RIS database (see no. 7, above). There are also links from protocols, administrative agreements, etc., to the treaties to which they are attached. In German only.

Treaty Indexes

9 CHRONOLOGISCHES VERZEICHNIS DER ÖSTERREICHISCHEN STAATSVERTRÄGE

Ludwig Bittner (Vienna: A. Holzhausen, 1903–1917).

Summary: Four volumes, covering the years 1526–1911. Includes 5,459 chronologically arranged entries. Intended as an index to a series that would publish, country by country, the full text of treaties concluded between Austria and other nations. Each treaty annotation includes the date and place of signature, names of the parties, location of printed text and a brief description of the contents of the treaty. Entries are in German. Each volume includes an alphabetical index by country of opposite party, with individual entries listed chronologically under their respective country headings.

Index: Vol. IV comprises a cumulative subject index.

Note: Series title: *Veröffentlichungen der Kommission für neuere Geschichte Österreichs*, vols. 1, 8, 13, 15.

Note: Reprinted under the imprint: Nendeln, Liechtenstein: Kraus, 1970.

10 ÜBERSICHT DER VERTRÄGE ÖSTERREICHS MIT DEN AUSWÄRTIGEN STAATEN, MIT DEM REGIERUNGS-ANTRITTE MARIA THERESIA'S ANGEFANGEN BIS AUF DIE NEUESTE ZEIT, 2ND ED.

Johann Evangelist Vesque von Püttlingen (Vienna: C. Gerold, 1869).

Summary: Contains list of treaties concluded by Austria from 1740–[1869], organized by country of opposite party. Includes table of contents. In German.

Note: First edition published in 1854.

Note: Same author compiled similar work in 1847, entitled *Chronologische Übersicht der Verträge Österreichs mit den deutschen Staaten.* Part I includes treaties concluded with Prussia, Bavaria, and Saxony up to 1846. Part II includes treaties concluded with other German states up to 1846. Reprinted from *Österreichische Zeitschrift für Rechts – und Staatswissenschaft* (Vienna: Drück und Verlag von V.P. Sollinger, 1846–1849), vols. 1847–I and 1847–II. Vols. 1848–II and 1849–I include respectively a list of treaties concluded with Savoy from 1630–1815 and a list of treaties concluded with Turkey from 1533–1847.

11 INDEX: SYSTEMATISCHES VERZEICHNIS DES GELTENDEN BUNDESRECHTS
Bundeskanzleramt (Verlag der Österreichischen Staatsdrückerei, 1985–).

Summary: Annual index of laws currently in effect, systematically arranged by topical areas. Each topical area includes a section on treaties, which lists international agreements by sub-topic. Within each sub-topic, treaties are organized in groups of bilateral and multilateral instruments, and within each group by date. Each entry is identified by a unique reference number, and provides a brief description of the instrument together with a citation to the official gazette. Multilateral treaties are accompanied by a list of parties and a list of related protocols, annexes, etc. Treaties are removed from the index only when they have been officially abrogated or circumstances make clear that they have been materially abrogated. Volume includes a topical index, chronological index, and index by treaty number.

12 BGBI-INDEX: "WEGWEISER" DURCH ÖSTERREICHS BUNDESGESETZGEBUNG
(Vienna: Manz, 1948–).

Summary: Annual index to laws in force. Part 1 (2), entitled *Internationale Abkommen und andere ausgewählte Angelegenheiten*, is divided into ten sections, each listing international agreements binding on Austria of a particular type, as follows: United Nations; European Communities; Council of Europe; EFTA; European Coal and Steel Community; European Economic Community; other multilateral treaties; bilateral treaties; development assistance agreements; documents related to diplomatic and consular affairs. Within each section, documents are listed by subject, and a citation is provided for the year and page number of publication in the official gazette. (See no. 6, above.) Part 2 includes a list of laws, treaties, etc., voided since 1945, either by repeal or extinction. Documents are listed by date and page of publication in the official gazette, permitting the user to look up any treaty found in Part 1 to determine whether it continues in effect.

Note: Imprint varies: 1948–1994 (vols. 1–44) published by Ried im Innkreis: Landesverlag; 1995–? by Wien: Manz; ?-present, by Linz: Trauner Verlag.

Note: Title varies: ?-present, BGBl-Index.

13 INDEX ZUM ÖSTERREICHISCHEN REICHS-, STAATS – UND BUNDESGESETZBLATT: ZUSAMMENGESTELLT AUS AMTLICHEN QUELLEN
Bundeskanzleramt der Republik Österreich, per Karl Sinabell, ed. (Vienna: Verlag Österreich, Österreichische Staatsdrückerei, 1976–2003).

Summary: Annual loose-leaf index to laws recorded in the official gazette. (See no. 6, above.) Includes references to treaties.

Topical and Selected Treaty Collections

14 THE SECRET TREATIES OF AUSTRIA-HUNGARY, 1879–1914
Alfred Franzis Pribram and Archibald Cary Coolidge, eds., English ed. (Cambridge: Harvard University Press, 1920–1921). Vol. 1, 308 pp. ; Vol. 2, 271 pp.

Summary: In two volumes, covering the period from 1879–1913. Treaty texts are contained in vol. 1, in German or French together with English translation. Contains 28 treaties, including the five treaties comprising the "Triple Alliance." Most, if not all, of the texts contained in this set were unknown until publication during World War I in the original German edition. Each treaty includes information about the date and place of signature. Vol. 2 contains the negotiations leading up to the Triple Alliance, together with a documentary appendix.

Index: Each volume includes a table of contents and a name index.

Note: Translations are by Denys P. Myers and J.G. D'Arcy Paul.

Note: Originally published as *Die politischen Geheimverträge Österreich-Ungarns, 1879–1914, nach den Akten des Wiener Staatsarchivs* (Vienna; Leipzig: W. Braumuller, 1920), with texts in their original language, together with titles and other data in German. Also translated into French, as *Les Traités Politiques Secrets de l'Autriche-Hongrie, 1879–1914, d'après les Documents des Archives d'Etat de Vienne.* (Camille Jordan, trans. Paris: Alfred Costes, 1923)

15 ZWISCHENSTAATLICHES JUSTIZRECHT: INTERNATIONALE ABKOMMEN AUF DEM GEBIET DES ZIVIL – UND ZIVILPROZESSRECHTS, HANDELS – UND WIRTSCHAFTSRECHTS, STRAF – UND STRAFPROZESSRECHTS
Ena-Marlis Bajons. (Vienna: Wirtschaftsverlag Orac, 1981–1983).

Summary: In two looseleaf volumes, covering the years 1526–1847. Includes the text of treaties in the areas of civil law and procedure, trade and commerce, criminal law and criminal procedure.

Note: Vol. 2 has imprint: Vienna: A. Holzhausen.

16 ÖSTERREICHISCHE STAATSVERTRÄGE. ENGLAND
Alfred Francis Pribram, ed. (Innsbrück: Wagner, 1907 [1913]).

Summary: In two volumes. Contains 96 treaties, organized in chronological order from 1701–1847. Treaties are published in their original language (primarily French and Latin, but also some documents in English or German). Includes all treaties concluded with England during the period by any member of the German Habsburg line acting as sovereign of all or part of the Habsburg territories. Does not include treaties concluded by a Habsburg monarch acting exclusively in his capacity as Holy Roman Emperor. Each treaty is accompanied by a lengthy and detailed essay summarizing the diplomatic circumstances that led to the treaty in question. Vol. 1 also includes a long introduction (209 pages) summarizing Austrian-English relations from 1339–1700, and many treaties are appended from this time period. Vol. 2 includes a detailed, cumulative subject index.

Index: See no. 9, above.

Note: Imprint varies: Vol. 2 has the imprint: Vienna; Leipzig: Adolf Holzhausen; Wilhelm Engelmann.

Note: Series title: *Österreichische Staatsverträge: Veröffentlichungen der Kommission für Neuere Geschichte Österreichs*, vols. 3, 12. The series was not continued after World War I.

17 ÖSTERREICHISCHE STAATSVERTRÄGE: NIEDERLANDE. ERSTER BAND
HEINRICH RITTER VON SRBIK, ED. (VIENNA, LEIPZIG: ADOLF HOLZHAUSEN, WILHELM ENGELMANN, 1912).

Summary: Contains 48 treaties concluded by Austria with the Netherlands between 1672 and 1712.

Index: See no. 9, above.

Note: Series title: *Österreichische Staatsverträge: Veröffentlichungen der Kommission für Neuere Geschichte Östereichs*, vol. 10. The series was not continued after World War I.

18 ÖSTERREICHISCHE STAATSVERTRÄGE: FÜRSTENTUM SIEBENBÜRGEN (1526–1690)
Roderich Gooss, ed. (Vienna, Leipzig: Adolf Holzhausen, Wilhelm Engelmann, 1911).

Summary: Contains 94 treaties concluded by Austria with Siebenbürgen between 1527 and 1690.

Index: See no. 9, above.

Note: Series title: *Veröffentlichungen der Kommission für Neuere Geschichte*, vol. 9. The series was not continued after World War I.

19 AUSSENMINISTERIUM
URL: http://www.bmaa.gv.at/view.php3?f_id=6215&LNG=de&version=.

Summary: The Foreign Ministry web site maintains a page devoted to the five multilateral treaties, for which Austria acts as depositary. These treaties are the Alpine Convention, the Convention on the Establishment and

Operation of the International Centre for Migratory Policy Development, the Convention on the Establishment of the Joint Vienna Institute, treaty on the Establishment of the International Anti-Corruption Academy as an International Organization (IACA), and treaty on the Establishment of the King Abdullah bin Abdulaziz International Centre for Interreligious and Intercultural Dialogue. For each treaty there is a chart listing the parties, dates of signature and coming into force, and information regarding declarations and reservations.

Diplomatic Documents

20 DIE VÖLKERRECHTLICHE PRAXIS DER DONAUMONARCHIE VON 1859 BIS 1918: EINE AUSWAHL VON DOKUMENTEN

Stephan Verosta and Ignaz Seidl-Hohenveldern (Vienna: Österreichische Akademie der Wissenschaften, 1996).

Summary: In two volumes, containing 740 documents selected for their value in illustrating the international legal practice of Austria-Hungary from 1859–1918. Documents are organized by topic, and within each topic by date. Each entry includes background information, as well as extracts from the document concerned. All documents are from the archives of the foreign ministry, and information is provided regarding the precise archival location of each. Vol. 1 includes a comprehensive, detailed table of contents, and vol. 2 includes both name and subject indexes.

Note: Series titles: *Sitzungsberichte / Österreichische Akademie der Wissenschaften, Philosophisch-historische Klasse,* vol. 631; *Veröffentlichungen der Kommission für Völkerrecht und Internationale Beziehungen,* vol. 2.

Note: An additional 2,300 foreign ministry documents related to Austria-Hungary's practice in international law were reviewed by the editors, and made available at the Archiv der Republik (1030 Wien, Nottendorfergasse 2).

21 ACTENSTÜCKE AUS DEN CORRESPONDENZEN DES KAISERLICHEN UND KÖNIGLICHEN GEMEINSAMEN MINISTERIUMS DES ÄUSSERN ÜBER ORIENTALISCHE ANGELEGENHEITEN

Ministerium des K. Und K. Hauses und des Äussern (Vienna: Drück und Verlag der K.K. Hof – und Staatsdrückerei, 1878–1881).

Summary: In four volumes. Contains diplomatic correspondence related to the Balkan question and the Russo-Turkish War of 1877–1878. Covers the period from May 1873–August 1881 (vol. 1, 16 May 1873 to 31 May 1877; vol. 2, 7 April, 1877 to 3 November 1878; vol. 3, 13 July 1878 to 12 October 1880; vol. 4, 2 October 1880 to 30 August 1881). Contains very brief table of contents and no index.

22 ÖSTERREICH-UNGARNS AUSSENPOLITIK VON DER BOSNISCHEN KRISE 1908 BIS ZUM KRIGESAUSBRUCH 1914
Diplomatische Aktenstücke des Österreichisch-Ungarischen Ministeriums des Äussern.
Ludwig Bittner and Hans Uebersberger, eds. (Vienna: Österreichischer Bundesverlag, 1930).

Summary: Nine-volume set, containing over 11,000 diplomatic documents covering the time period from the Bosnian crisis of 1908 until the announcement of Russian mobilization on 31 July 1914. Documents are selected from among those held by the Political Archive of the Austro-Hungarian foreign ministry. More selective for earlier years, less so for the two years preceding the outbreak of war. Emphasis is placed on documents that explain political developments during the relevant time period, but documents of an international legal nature are included when they relate to political questions, such as the pan-Serbian movement. Documents are arranged in chronological order. Each is preceded by a brief title entry, noting the type, date and form of the document (e.g., original, decoded copy, summary of conversation, etc.), and including a brief description, with names of corresponding individuals and agencies.

Index: Vol. 9 comprises a detailed index of personal names.

Note: Series title: *Veröffentlichungen der Kommission für Neuere Geschichte Österreichs*, vols. 19–27.

Note: Also reprinted in facsimile form (Nendeln, Liechtenstein: Kraus, 1972).

23 AUSSENPOLITISCHE DOKUMENTE DER REPUBLIK ÖSTERREICH, 1918–1938 (ADÖ)
Arnold Suppan, Klaus Kloch, and Walter Rauscher, eds. (Vienna: Verlag für Geschichte und Politik; Munich: Verlag für Geschichte und Politik; R. Oldenbourg, 1993–).

Summary: Semi-official collection of foreign policy documents, prepared under the auspices of the Östrereichisches Ost – und Sudosteuropa-Institut. Currently in eight volumes, entitled *Selbstbestimmung der Republik* (vol. 1), *Im Schatten von Saint-Germain* (vol. 2), *Österreich im System der Nachfolgestaaten* (vol. 3), *Österreich zwischen Staatsbankrott und Genfer Sanierung* (vol. 4), *Unter der Finanzkontrolle des Völkerbundes* (vol. 5), *Jahre der Souveränität* (vol. 6), *Das Österreichisch-Deutsche Zollunionsprojekt* (vol. 7), and *Österreich im Zentrum der Mitteleuropapläne* (vol. 8). Contains diplomatic correspondence, and parliamentary documents related to the conduct of international relations. When complete, the set will cover the complete inter-war period. Currently covers the period from 1918–February 1933. Documents are numbered and ordered chronologically. Each document is accompanied by a detailed heading, providing information regarding the correspondents, their locales, the type of document concerned, degree of secrecy to be used by the recipient (when written on original), date and place of composition and archival location of the original. Also includes an essay on the organization of the Austrian foreign office during this period and an essay on the goals of Austrian foreign policy. Principally in German, with some material in English and French. Each volume contains an index of people, places and subjects, and a detailed table of contents, including summaries of document headings and subject headings.

Note: Series title: *Fontes Rerum Austriacarum = Österreichische Geschichtsquellen. Zweite Abteilung, Diplomataria et acta, 94 Bd.*

24 PROTOKOLLE DES MINISTERRATES DER ERSTEN REPUBLIK, 1918–1938
Gertrude Enderle-Burcel and Rudolf Neck (Vienna: Österreich, 1979–).

Summary: This series is published under the auspices of the *Österreichische Gesellschaft für historische Quellenstudien.* It contains the minutes of government cabinet meetings. Many of the Cabinet discussions recorded by the minutes revolve around questions of foreign policy. The series currently comprises 21 volumes. Since 1994, the *Österreichische Gesellschaft* has also publishes two similar titles related to the second republic, as follows: *Protokolle des Kabinettsrates der Provisorischen Regierung Karl Renners 1945* (Vienna: Österreich, 1995–2003), complete in three volumes, and *Protokolle des Ministerrates der Regierung Figl 1* (Vienna: Österreich, 2004–). Six volumes have been published in this series to date, running through September, 1947, but this title will eventually cover the years 1945–1949.

Note: Publisher of the *Protokolle des Ministerrates der ersten Republik*, varies. Formerly published by the Österreichische Staatsdrückerei.

Note: The Österreichische Gesellschaft für historische Quellenstudien maintains a web site at http://www.oegq.at/. Here the researcher can find a list of all planned titles and volumes in the series of published cabinet minutes.

25 ÖSTERREICH UND DIE GROSSMÄCHTE: DOKUMENTATION ZUR ÖSTERREICHISCHEN AUSSENPOLITIK 1945–1955
Alfons Schilcher (Vienna: Geyer Edition, 1980).

Summary: Collection of 104 documents from the archives of the foreign ministry, detailing the international relations of Austria during the period of occupation following World War II, and leading up to the treaty of reunification and Austria's declaration of neutrality. Documents are arranged by topic, and accompanied by an index of names. Documents are primarily in German. Includes topically arranged table of contents.

Note: Series title: *Materialien zur Zeitgeschichte*, vol. 2.

26 DER WEG ZU FREIHEIT UND NEUTRALITÄT: DOKUMENTATION ZUR ÖSTERREICHISCHEN AUSSENPOLITIK 1945–1955
Eva-Marie Csaky (Vienna: Österreichische Gesellschaft für Aussenpolitik und Internationale Beziehungen; Braumüller, 1980).

Summary: Contains 193 diplomatic documents. All documents are reproduced in their original language, with German translations as needed, and in full, unless the document relates to Austrian foreign policy only in part. Each document is accompanied by a descriptive heading, which includes both the document date and source of original publication. Includes subject and name indexes.

Note: Series title: *Schriftenreihe der Österreichischen Gesellschaft für Aussenpolitik und Internationale Beziehungen*, vol. 10.

27 ZWANZIG JAHRE ÖSTERREICHISCHE NEUTRALITÄTS – UND EUROPAPOLITIK (1955–1975): DOKUMENTATION
Hans Mayrzedt and Waldemar Hummer. (Vienna: W. Braumüller, 1976).

Summary: In two volumes. Contains documents from a variety of sources, including the foreign ministry, related to Austria's conduct of international relations, 1955–1975. Documents are organized topically, into the following areas: neutrality, participation in multilateral treaty regimes, bilateral relations and approach to east-west cooperation. Documents are primarily in German, but some are in other languages as well, depending on source. Vols. I and II each include a comprehensive table of contents for the set, and vol. II also includes a complete list of documents and a name index.

Note: Series title: *Schriftenreihe der Österreichischen Gesellschaft für Aussenpolitik und Internationale Beziehungen*, vol. 9.

28 AUSSEN – UND EUROPAPOLITISCHER BERICHT [AUSTRIAN FOREIGN POLICY YEARBOOK]
Aussenministerium. Austrian Federal Ministry for Foreign Affairs. (Vienna: Federal Ministry for Foreign Affairs, 1988–).

Summary: Contains a brief survey of world events for the year, including a survey of Austria's activities in international relations. Includes a table of contents. Beginning in 2000, the Yearbook is available from the web site of the Austrian Federal Ministry, at http://www.bmeia.gv.at/aussenministerium/

aussenpolitik/aussen-und-europapolitischer-bericht.html. Available in English at http://www.bmeia.gv.at/en/foreign-ministry/foreign-policy/foreign-and-european-policy-report.html, with several years' delay.

29 AUSSENPOLITISCHE DOKUMENTATION
Bundesministerium für Auswärtige Angelegenheiten (Vienna: Bundesministerium, 1990–2000).

Summary: Bimonthly collection of diplomatic documents, many excerpted, mostly in German.

Note: Title varies. 1990–1998 published as *Österreichische Aussenpolitische Dokumentation.*

Note: Jugoslawische Krise, Österreichisce Aussenpolitische Dokumentation Sonderdrück, published as special issue, 1992. Contains 204 documents tracing Austria's diplomataic reaction to the Yugoslavian crisis, 1989–1992. Many documents are excerpted. Includes chronological index and a chronology of the Yugoslavian crisis.

Yearbooks and Digests of State Practice

30 AUSTRIAN REVIEW OF INTERNATIONAL AND EUROPEAN LAW
(The Hague: Kluwer Law International, 1996–).

Summary: Annual publication includes a digest of Austrian state practice in international law. Divided into two parts. Part I includes Austrian judicial decisions involving questions of public international law. Part II includes documents relating Austrian diplomatic practice in international law. Commentary is in English. Documents are in German, with English translations in most cases. Material is organized topically according to a classification scheme set out at the beginning of the issue.

Note: Published four times per year, 1996–1998.

31 NEWSLETTER DER ÖSTERREICHISCHEN GESELLSCHAFT FÜR AUSSENPOLITIK UND DER VEREINTEN NATIONEN
(Wien: Österreichische Gesellschaft für Außenpolitik und die Vereinten Nationen, 2009–).
URL: http://www.oegavn.org/index.php?option=com_content&task=view&id=52.

Summary: Bimonthly newsletter of the semi-official Austrian Society for Foreign Policy and the United Nations. Chronicles current Austrian diplomatic activity at the United Nations, as well as in the areas of multilateral and bilateral treaty relations. Available electronically at the Society's web site.

Note: Supersedes *Chronik zur Aussenpolitik*, 2003–2008, available at the Society's web site, *Österreichisches Jahrbuch für Internationale Politik* 1984 – 2002, and the *Österreichische Zeitschrift für Aussenpolitik*, 1960–1983. The latter two titles included a *Chronik zur Österreichischen Aussenpolitik* as a regular feature.

Note: Complete table of contents of the *Jahrbuch für Internationale Politik* available at the Society's web site.

Belarus

Vera Korzun

Historical Background

The country has been officially called the "Republic of Belarus" (short version – "Belarus") only since the independence of the former Byelorussian Soviet Socialist Republic (BSSR) from the Soviet Union in 1991. Although the term "Belarus" (from "Belai͡a Rus′," translated into English as "White Rus′," or "White Russia") is believed to originate in the 12th century, it did not apply to the territories of modern Belarus. Instead, over time it was used to refer to various territories of Russia and even Ukraine, and only since the 14th century – also to some eastern parts of present-day Belarus (especially the region of Mahili͡oŭ). After the territories of Belarus consolidated into the Grand Duchy of Lithuania around the mid-13th century, the country was called "Litva" and its population – the "litsviny" (or "litviny"). Thus, the entire territory of Belarus was known as Litva for over 500 years (until the end of the 18th century, when the Belarusian territories were annexed to the Russian Empire as a result of the three partitions of 1772, 1793, and 1795 of the Polish-Lithuanian Commonwealth between Russia, Prussia, and Austria). Forty-five years later, in 1840, the Russian tsar Nicholas I banned the use of the terms "Litva" and "Belarus′" in official papers and instead ordered the territories of Belarus to be called the "Northwestern Region." Under this name Belarus existed until the formation of the BSSR in January 1919 (apart from the short period of existence of an independent Belarusian state called the "Belarusian National Republic," which was declared in Minsk on 25 March 1918, but ceased to exist with the proclamation of the BSSR).[1]

Issues of Treaty Succession

The first record of the people who lived on the territory of present-day Belarus dates back to the fifth century BC.[2] Already in the Current Era, around the fifth century AD, the early East Slavic tribes of the *Kryvichy*, the *Drygavichy*, and the

1 *See* 1 I.A. I͡Ukho, *Historyi͡a dzi͡arzhavy i prava Belarusi; u 2-kh chastkakh* 47–63 (2000). *See also* Jan Zaprudnik, Historical Dictionary of Belarus 44–45 (1998).

2 *See* 1 I.A. I͡Ukho, *Historyi͡a dzi͡arzhavy i prava Belarusi; u 2-kh chastkakh* 48 (2000).

 | DOI 10.1163/9789004272224_007

Radzimichy began moving to the territory of contemporary Belarus, which by then had been settled by Baltic people.[3] Among other towns, such as Vitsebsk and Vilnius, the *Kryvichy* founded the city of Polatsk – one of the ancient cities of Belarus first mentioned by the Primary Chronicle in the year 862 AD.[4] By the 11th century, it became the powerful center of the Duchy of Polatsk, which spread over the northern half of present-day Belarus and competed with Novgorod and Kiev.[5] Meanwhile, in the southern part of Belarus, the *Drygavichy* founded the city of Turaŭ, first mentioned in the year 980 AD as a center of the Turaŭ Duchy,[6] and the *Radzimichy* established the city of Homel′,[7] which became the second largest city of modern Belarus.

From 1230s to 1795, the territory of present-day Belarus formed the Grand Duchy of Lithuania, Rus′ and Samogitia – one of the most influential states of the medieval Europe with the capital first in Navahrudak, and from 1323 – in Vil′ni͡a (Vilnius).[8] Around the mid-15th century, when the Grand Duchy achieved its territorial peak becoming the largest state in Europe, it stretched from the Baltic coast to the Black Sea. Its territory at that time included all of Belarus and Lithuania, a big part of Ukraine, and some parts of Russia.[9] In 1468, the Grand Duchy of Lithuania provided Europe with one of the first codifications of legislation in the form of *Sudzebnik* – a written criminal code – of Casimir IV, a Grand Duke of Lithuania from 1440, and also a King of Poland from 1447 until his death in 1492.[10]

In 1529, Sudzebnik was superseded by the First Statute of the Grand Duchy of Lithuania, which became one of the first in Europe systematic collection of legal norms of various branches of law.[11] The First Statute originally consisted of 13 chapters of a total of 244 articles of feudal and customary law and judicial and official decisions, which set the foundations of the civil and political systems of

3 *See* ZAPRUDNIK, *supra* note 1 at 104–5.

4 Id. at 172.

5 Id. at 172–3.

6 Id. at 207.

7 Id. at 120.

8 Id. at 113.

9 Id.

10 *See* FRANCIS DVORNIK, THE SLAVS IN EUROPEAN HISTORY AND CIVILIZATION 345 (1962). For further reading on *Sudzebnik*, *see* 1 I.A. I͡Ukho, *Historyi͡a dzi͡arzhavy i prava Belarusi; u 2-kh chastkakh* 202 (2000).

11 *See* ZAPRUDNIK, *supra* note 1 at 82–83. For further reading on three editions of the Statute, see Aleksandras Plateris, *Codification of the Law in the Grand Duchy of Lithuania*, 11 LITUANUS: LITHUANIAN Q.J. ARTS & SCI. (1965), http://www.lituanus.org/1965/65_2_03_Plateris.html.

the Grand Duchy, its social relationships, as well as procedures for forming administrative and legal bodies of the state.[12] The second edition of the Statute of 1566 further limited the power of the sovereign (Grand Duke), separated the courts from the governing and administrative bodies, and increased the rights of *shli͡akhta* (gentry) over their subjects.[13] Notably, the Belarusian language was declared to be the state language and the Statute required all court proceedings and documentation to be conducted in Belarusian.[14]

The third edition of the Statute – the 1588 Statute of the Grand Duchy of Lithuania – presented in the systematic form the norms of the state (constitutional), administrative, military law, rules on the court structure and procedure, norms of the family, trusteeship, civil, forestry and hunting, and criminal laws.[15] Significantly expanded and revised, the Third Statute consisted of 14 chapters of a total of 488 articles.[16] It was written in the old Belarusian language using Cyrillic characters and was published in the printing press of the brothers Mamonichi in Vil′ni͡a (Vilnius).[17] The 1588 Statute was translated into Polish in 1614,[18] and Russian – in 1811.[19] It continued to be used on the territory of present-day Belarus until 1840,[20] first within the Polish-Lithuanian Commonwealth formed under the Union of Lublin of 1569,[21] and then – after gradual acquisition of the Belarusian territories in 1772, 1793, and 1795 by the Russian Empire under the reign of Catherine II. The application of the 1588 Statute on the Belarusian territories was discontinued only in 1840 by a special Decree of the Governing Senate of 25 June 1840, which replaced the Statute with the laws of the Russian Empire.[22]

During the period of 1795 until the October revolution in the Russian Empire in November 1917, the territory of Belarus developed as a part of the Russian Empire. After the October revolution in response to the partitioning of Belarus

12 *See* 1 I.A. I͡Ukho, *Historyi͡a dzi͡arzhavy i prava Belarusi; u 2-kh chastkakh* 204-5 (2000).

13 *See* Jan Zaprudnik, Historical Dictionary of Belarus 82 (1998).

14 *See* 1 I.A. I͡Ukho, *Historyi͡a dzi͡arzhavy i prava Belarusi; u 2-kh chastkakh* 210 (2000).

15 Id. at 215. For further reading, *see, e.g.*, Ivan I. Lappo, *Litovskiĭ Statut" 1588 Goda* (1934–38).

16 *See* I.I. Lappo, *1588 Metų Lietuvos Statutas. Litovskiĭ Statut" 1588 Goda* 483 (1936).

17 Id. at 273.

18 Id. at 414.

19 Id. at 472.

20 Id. at 5.

21 The Union of Lublin of 1569 between the Grand Duchy of Lithuania and the Kingdom of Poland that created a federated state – the Commonwealth. *See* Zaprudnik, *supra* note 1 at 210.

22 *See* I.I. Lappo, *1588 Metų Lietuvos Statutas. Litovskiĭ Statut" 1588 Goda* 483 (1936).

under the 1918 Treaty of Brest-Litovsk,[23] on 25 March 1918, an independent Belarusian state – the Belarusian National Republic – was created "within the borders of the numerical majority of the Belarusan people."[24] The state was recognized by the governments of several foreign states, but ceased to exist after the proclamation of the Byelorussian Soviet Socialist Republic (BSSR) on 1 January 1919.[25]

On 27 February 1919, shortly after the BSSR was created, it was merged together with the Lithuanian SSR into a single Lithuanian-Byelorussian Soviet Socialist Republic (LBSSR), also known as Litbel. The capital was initially established in Vilnius, but moved to Minsk in April 1919 after Vilnius was seized by the Polish Army. Litbel was then liquidated on 17 July 1919 in the hopes to start peace negotiations with Poland. In the midst of the Soviet-Polish war (February 1919–March 1921), the last resistance to the occupation by the Soviet Army of the Belarusian territories was organized by the representatives of the Belarusian National Republic. In November-December 1920, it led to the Slutsk uprising of 1920 – a military action against Bolsheviks fought in Belarus in the region of town of Slutsk by the 10,000-member Slutsk brigade.[26] The resistance was unsuccessful and the Soviet Army soon regained control over the Belarusian territories.

The peace negotiations between the Soviets and Poland began in the late 1920 and were concluded on 18 March 1921 with the signing of the Treaty of Riga,[27] which completed the Soviet-Polish War.[28] The Treaty divided Belarus between the Russian Soviet Federated Socialist Republic and Poland. West Belarus was transferred to the Polish State without any autonomous status. The Byelorussian SSR was formed only on the small territory on the eastern side of the new border (20,000 square miles of the former Minsk gubernia with the population of 1.5 million).[29] Eastern territories of Belarus were transferred

---

23 Peace treaty signed on 3 March 1918 between, on one side, the Soviet Russia, and, on the other side, Germany, Austro-Hungary, Bulgaria, and Turkey, by which Russia withdrew from WWI. *See* ZAPRUDNIK, *supra* note 1 at 205.

24 *See* ZAPRUDNIK, *supra* note 1 at 51.

25 In 1919–1920, the Belarusian National Republic was recognized *de jure* or *de facto* by Bulgaria, Czecho-Slovakia, Estonia, Finland, Germany, Latvia, Lithuania, Turkey, as well as the Ukrainian National Republic. *See* 2 I.A. I͡Ukho, *Historyi͡a dzi͡arzhavy i prava Belarusi; u 2-kh chastkakh* 29 (2003).

26 *See* 2 I.A. I͡Ukho, *Historyi͡a dzi͡arzhavy i prava Belarusi; u 2-kh chastkakh* 66–8 (2003). *See also* ZAPRUDNIK, *supra* note 1 at 197.

27 Treaty of Peace between Poland, Russia, and Ukraine, March 18, 1921, 6 L.N.T.S. 52 (1921).

28 JAN ZAPRUDNIK, BELARUS. AT A CROSSROADS IN HISTORY 70–1 (1993).

29 Id.

to the Russian Federation, but returned to the BSSR on 3 March 1924 and additionally on 6 December 1926.[30] The partitioning of Belarus was undone only 18 years later, on 17 September 1939, when the Soviet troops crossed the Polish border and occupied West Belarus (a territory of nearly 39,000 square miles with the population of 4.5 million) and West Ukraine in accordance with the then-secret Soviet-German Nonaggression Pact of 23 August 1939, which divided the sphere of influence between two countries.[31] Further, under the Soviet-Lithuanian Mutual Assistance Treaty of 10 October 1939,[32] the Vil'ni͡a (Vilnius) region of 2,750 square miles in size and a population of 457,500 was transferred by the Soviet government from West Belarus to Lithuania in exchange for the right to establish military bases on the Lithuanian territory.[33] Thus, Belarus was deprived of its historical city and a capital of the medieval Grand Duchy of Lithuania. The capital of the BSSR was proclaimed to be Minsk.

After WWII, although at the time a part of the Soviet Union and not recognized as a sovereign state, Belarus (under the name of the Byelorussian Soviet Socialist Republic) was admitted to the United Nations as a full member together with the USSR and the Ukrainian SSR. The delegation of the BSSR signed the UN Charter on 25 June 1945. It was ratified by the Presidium of the Supreme Soviet of the BSSR on 30 August 1945.[34] Such membership of two individual Soviet republics in the United Nations was granted in consideration of the sufferings endured by Belarus and Ukraine during WWII. Consequently, until its dissolution in 1991, the Soviet Union was represented in the United Nations by three seats, including that of Belarus.

The process of eventual independence of Belarus from the USSR began with the Declaration of State Sovereignty, adopted by the Supreme Soviet of the BSSR, then the legislative body of the country, on 27 July 1990.[35] In particular,

---

30 Id. at 70.

31 Id. at 88–89.

32 Treaty on the Transfer of the City of Vilno and Vilno Province to the Lithuanian Republic and on Mutual Assistance Between the Soviet Union and Lithuania, Oct. 10, 1939, 2(4) AM. Q. ON THE SOVIET UNION 53–55 (April 1940).

33 *See* JAN ZAPRUDNIK, BELARUS. AT A CROSSROADS IN HISTORY 89–90 (1993).

34 *See generally* 2 I.A. I͡Ukho, *Historyi͡a dzi͡arz͡havy i prava Belarusi; u 2-kh chastkakh* 180 (2003).

35 Deklarat͡siі͡a Verkhovnogo Soveta Respubliki Belarus′ ot 27 ii͡uli͡a 1990 g. No. 193–XII "O Gosudarstvennom Suverenitete Respubliki Belarus′" [Declaration of the Supreme Soviet of the Republic of Belarus of July 27, 1990 No. 193–XII "On the State Sovereignty of the Republic of Belarus"], VEDAMASTSI VI͡ARKHOŬNAHA SAVETA RĖSPUBLIKI BELARUS′ [VVS RB] [Bulletin of the Supreme Soviet of the Republic of Belarus] 1991, No. 31, Item 536. For an English translation of the Declaration, *see* THE INT'L INST. FOR DEMOCRACY (ED.), TRANSITION TO DEMOCRACY. CONSTITUTIONS OF THE NEW INDEPENDENT STATES AND MONGOLIA 105–08 (1997).

the Declaration proclaimed supremacy, independence and indivisibility of the power of the Republic on its territory, set the aim of the Republic to make its territory a nuclear-free zone and to become a neutral state, and proclaimed that the Republic shall independently exercise the right to enter into voluntary unions with other states, as well as to withdraw freely from such unions.[36] Almost a year later, on 25 August 1991, the Declaration of State Sovereignty received the status of a constitutional law, thus proclaiming independence of the BSSR from the Soviet Union.[37] On 19 September 1991, in accordance with the decision of the Supreme Soviet of the BSSR, the name of the country was changed to the Republic of Belarus (with a short version – Belarus).[38]

The dissolution of the Soviet Union was completed on 8 December 1991, when at the meeting at the residence of the Belarusian government in Viskuli, Brest region, leaders of Belarus, Russia, and Ukraine signed the Declaration by the Heads of State and the Agreement dissolving the Soviet Union and creating instead the Commonwealth of Independent States (CIS).[39] The new Constitution of the Republic of Belarus, which proclaimed Belarus a presidential republic, was adopted by the Supreme Soviet on 15 March 1994 and entered

36 Id. at 97.

37 Zakon Respubliki Belarus′ ot 25 avgusta 1991 g. No. 1017–XII "O Pridanii Statusa Konstitut͡sionnogo Zakona Deklarat͡sii Verkhovnogo Soveta Respubliki Belarus′ o Gosudarstvennom Suverenitete Respubliki Belarus′" [Law of the Rep. of Belarus of August 25, 1991 No. 1017–XII "On Giving the Status of a Constitutional Law to the Declaration of the Supreme Soviet of the Republic of Belarus on the State Sovereignty of the Republic of Belarus"], Vedamastsi Vi͡arkhoŭnaha Saveta Rėspubliki Belarus′ [VVS RB] [Bulletin of the Supreme Soviet of the Republic of Belarus] 1991, No. 28, Item 425.

38 Zakon BSSR ot 19 senti͡abri͡a 1991 g. No. 1085–XII "O Nazvanii Belorusskoĭ Sovetskoĭ Sot͡sialisticheskoĭ Respubliki i Vnesenii Izmeneniĭ v Deklarat͡sii͡u Verkhovnogo Soveta Belorusskoĭ Sovetskoĭ Sot͡sialisticheskoĭ Respubliki o Gosudarstvennom Suverenitete Belorusskoĭ Sovetskoĭ Sot͡sialisticheskoĭ Respubliki i Konstitut͡sii͡u (Osnovnoĭ Zakon) Belorusskoĭ SSR" [Law of the BSSR of Sep. 19, 1991 No. 1085–XII "On the Name of the Byelorussian Soviet Socialist Republic and Amendments to the Declaration of the Supreme Soviet of the Byelorussian Soviet Socialist Republic and to the Constitution (Supreme Law) of the Byelorussian SSR], Vedamastsi Vi͡arkhoŭnaha Saveta Rėspubliki Belarus′ [VVS RB] [Bulletin of the Supreme Soviet of the Republic of Belarus] 1991, No. 30, Item 490.

39 Declaration by the Heads of State of the Republic of Belarus, the RSFSR, and Ukraine of Dec. 8, 1991, 31 I.L.M. 142 (1992); UN Document A/46/771 of December 14, 1991; Agreement Establishing the Commonwealth of Independent States, Dec. 8, 1991, 31 I.L.M. 143–146 (1992); UN Document A/46/771 of December 14, 1991.

into force on 30 March 1994.[40] Further amendments to the text of the 1994 Constitution were introduced following the referendums of 1996 and 2004.[41]

After the dissolution of the Soviet Union in December 1991, the issues of the state succession with respect to treaties, assets and liabilities, and archives, were decided by the former Soviet republics differently based on various considerations. For international treaties, such considerations included previous membership in the treaty and its subject matter, which in practice could concern only a part of the former Soviet Union. Already in the Agreement Establishing the Commonwealth of Independent States,[42] the CIS countries agreed to ensure the fulfillment of all international obligations that derive for them from the treaties of the former USSR.[43] Further, on 6 July 1992, the CIS countries signed in Moscow the Memorandum of Understanding on the Issue of Succession in Respect of Treaties of the Former USSR of Mutual Interest.[44] The Memorandum noted that virtually all multilateral treaties of the former USSR were of mutual interest for the CIS countries. Such treaties, however, did not require mutual decisions or actions of the CIS countries. Instead, each CIS country would decide the issue of succession in respect of the treaties independently in line with the principles and norms of international law and

---

40 For a text of the original 1994 Constitution of the Republic of Belarus in Belarusian and Russian, as well as its official translation into the English, French and German languages, see KANSTYTUTSYI͡A RĖSPUBLIKI BELARUS′ = KONSTITUT͡SII͡A RESPUBLIKI BELARUS′ = CONSTITUTION OF THE REPUBLIC OF BELARUS = CONSTITUTION DE LA REPUBLIQUE DU BELARUS = VERFASSUNG DER REPUBLIK BELARUS (Minsk: Belarus′, 1994).

41 Konstitut͡sii͡a Respubliki Belarus′ 1994 goda (s izmenenii͡ami i dopolnenii͡ami, prini͡atymi na respublikanskikh referendumakh 24 noi͡abri͡a 1996 g. i 17 okti͡abri͡a 2004 g.) [Constitution of the Republic of Belarus of 1994 (with changes and additions adopted at the national referendums of 24 November 1996 and 17 October 2004)] (Minsk: Amalfei͡a, 2005).

42 Article 12, Agreement Establishing the Commonwealth of Independent States, Dec. 8, 1991, 31 I.L.M. 143–146 (1992); UN Document A/46/771 of December 14, 1991.

43 L.E. Astapovich et al. (comps.), *Sbornik Mezhdunarodnykh Dogovorov ob Izbezhanii Dvoĭnogo Nalogooblozhenii͡a. Mezhdunarodnye Soglashenii͡a Respubliki Belarus′* [COLLECTION OF INTERNATIONAL TREATIES ON AVOIDANCE OF DOUBLE TAXATION. INTERNATIONAL AGREEMENTS OF THE REPUBLIC OF BELARUS] 6 (1997).

44 Memorandum o Vzaimoponimanii po Voprosu Pravopreemstva v Otnoshenii Dogovorov Byvshego SSR, Predstavli͡ai͡ushchikh Vzaimnyĭ Interes, July 6, 1992. Text of the Memorandum is available in the *Uniform Register of the Legal Acts and Other Documents of the Commonwealth of Independent States* (EDINYĬ REESTR PRAVOVYKH AKTOV I DRUGIKH DOKUMENTOV SODRUZHESTVA NEZAVISIMYKH GOSUDARSTV), Registration No. 00128. *See also* W.E. BUTLER, THE LAW OF TREATIES IN RUSSIA AND THE COMMONWEALTH OF INDEPENDENT STATES. TEXT AND COMMENTARY 197 (2002) [hereinafter BUTLER, THE LAW OF TREATIES].

depending on the specifics of each individual case and the nature and contents of the treaty.[45] It was also observed that there were a number of bilateral treaties of the former Soviet Union that would affect the interests of two or more, but not all, CIS countries. For these treaties, joint actions or decisions of the respective CIS countries were required.[46] In addition, bilateral treaties of the former USSR that affected the interests of all CIS countries, such as treaties on the borders and their regime, would remain in force for the CIS countries with the relevant borders.[47] In practice, after the dissolution of the USSR, each state made a statement with respect to treaties of the former Soviet Union for which it considered itself a successor state.

Consequently, the practice on treaty succession for Belarus depended on whether the relevant treaty of the former Soviet Union was multilateral or bilateral. Being a founding member of the United Nations, Belarus preserved its membership in the UN and its specialized agencies. Hence, there was continuity with respect to the treaties it concluded as the BSSR along with the Ukrainian SSR and the USSR. Further, it continued to apply bilateral treaties of the USSR with foreign countries, if such treaties also concerned independent Belarus. Sometimes, the revision of the treaties between two countries was made to identify obsolete or expired bilateral treaties. For instance, the United States exchanged the notes with the former Soviet republics that included an annex with the treaties remaining in force between them.[48] Similarly, the United Kingdom informed the Soviet republics of the bilateral treaties of the Soviet Union that would continue to apply between them.[49]

The succession of the Republic of Belarus with respect to international treaties is now regulated by Article 24 of the 2008 Law on International Treaties, which provides that the Republic of Belarus may express its consent to be bound by the international treaty by means of succession in cases provided by international law.[50] In cases of succession with respect to international treaties of the former USSR, the Republic of Belarus is considered to be bound by obligations deriving from such international treaties as of 10 December 1991,

45 Id. at para. 1.

46 Id. at para. 2.

47 Id. at para. 3.

48 Anthony Aust, Modern Treaty Law and Practice 376 (2nd ed., 2007).

49 Id. at 377.

50 Zakon Respubliki Belarus′ ot 23 i͡uli͡a 2008 g. No. 421–3 "O Mezhdunarodnykh Dogovorakh Respubliki Belarus′" [Law of the Rep. of Belarus of July 23, 2008 No. 421–3 "On International Treaties of the Republic of Belarus"], Nat͡sional′nyĭ Reestr Pravovykh Aktov Respubliki Belarus′ [NRPA RB] [National Register of the Legal Acts of the Republic of Belarus] 2008, No. 184, 2/1518.

unless otherwise is provided by the international treaty or has been agreed by the parties.[51]

According to the 2008 Law on International Treaties, decisions on succession with respect to interstate and intergovernmental treaties that require ratification are made by the National Assembly of the Republic of Belarus in the form of a law. For treaties that do not require ratification, the decisions on succession are made for interstate treaties – by the President of the Republic of Belarus in the form of an edict, for intergovernmental treaties – by the Council of Ministers of the Republic of Belarus in the form of a regulation.[52]

Despite succession of Belarus to many treaties of the former USSR, the text and contents of some of these treaties are revised and updated over time. This may lead to the conclusion of new treaties in the same area between Belarus and a relevant foreign country. For instance, new treaties on the issues of taxation were concluded with Germany, Great Britain, and the Netherlands, although Belarus succeeded to the respective treaties on double taxation of the former Soviet Union.[53] Belarus also started signing new treaties with individual countries. To date, according to the Ministry of Foreign Affairs of Belarus, the country is a party to more than 3,600 international treaties, including over 2,000 bilateral and 1,550 multilateral treaties.[54]

Treaty Ratification and Implementation

Negotiation, entry into force, publication, registration, deposition, implementation, suspension and termination of the international treaties of Belarus are now regulated by the Law of the Republic of Belarus of 23 July 2008 No. 421–3 "On International Treaties of the Republic of Belarus" (the 2008 Law on International Treaties).[55] The 2008 version of the Law is the result of continuous improvement of the national legislation of Belarus in the area of international

51 Id.

52 Id.

53 For these treaties, see L.E. Astapovich et al. (comps.), *Sbornik Mezhdunarodnykh Dogovorov ob Izbezhanii Dvoĭnogo Nalogooblozhenii͡a. Mezhdunarodnye Soglasheniia͡ Respubliki Belarus′* (Minsk: Amalfei͡a, 1997).

54 Official web-site of the Ministry of Foreign Affairs of the Republic of Belarus, http://www.mfa.gov.by/en.

55 Zakon Respubliki Belarus′ ot 23 ii͡uli͡a 2008 g. No. 421–3 "O Mezhdunarodnykh Dogovorakh Respubliki Belarus′," *supra* note 50. For an English translation of the previous version of the Law on International Treaties (the 1991 Law on International Treaties, as amended in 1992 and 1998), *see* BUTLER, THE LAW OF TREATIES, *supra* note 44 at 271–84 (2002).

treaties. In the recent history of Belarus,[56] the first of such laws was adopted by the Supreme Soviet of the Republic of Belarus on 23 October 1991 as the Law "On the Procedure for the Conclusion, Execution, and Denunciation of International Treaties of the Republic of Belarus."[57] The Law evidenced independence and sovereignty of Belarus acquired following the dissolution of the Soviet Union, including the right of the country to independently enter into international treaties.[58] Subsequent amendments to the 1991 Law were introduced in 1992, 1998, 1999, 2000, 2004, and most recently – in 2008.[59]

---

56 Prior to the dissolution of the Soviet Union, the USSR applied the 1978 Law on the Procedure for the Conclusion, Execution, and Denunciation of International Treaties (17 ILM 1115–22 (1978)). For an English translation of this law, *see* W.E. Butler, Soviet Law 395–97 (2nd ed., 1988).

57 Zakon Respubliki Belarus′ ot 23 okti͡abri͡a 1991 g. "O Pori͡adke Zakli͡ucheniia͡, Ispolnenii͡a i Denonsat͡sii Mezhdunarodnykh Dogovorov Respubliki Belarus′" [Law of the Rep. of Belarus of Oct. 23, 1991 "On the Procedure for the Conclusion, Execution, and Denunciation of International Treaties of the Republic of Belarus"], Vedamastsi Vi͡arhoŭnaha Saveta Rėspubliki Belarus′ [VVS RB] [Bulletin of the Supreme Soviet of the Republic of Belarus] 1991, No. 32, Item 584.

58 L.V. Pavlova, *Osobennosti Zakonotvorchestva Respubliki Belarus′ v Oblasti Zakli͡ucheniia͡ Mezhdunarodnykh Dogovorov*, Aktual′nye Problemy Mezhdunarodnogo Publichnogo i Mezhdunarodnogo Chastnogo Prava. Sbornik Nauchnykh Trudov. Vypusk 1. 102, 102 (2009).

59 Zakon Respubliki Belarus′ ot 26 noi͡abri͡a 1992 g. [Law of the Rep. of Belarus of Nov. 26, 1992], Vedamastsi Vi͡arhoŭnaha Saveta Rėspubliki Belarus′ [VVS RB] [Bulletin of the Supreme Soviet of the Republic of Belarus] 1992, No. 32, Item 519; Zakon Respubliki Belarus′ ot 8 ii͡uli͡a 1998 g. [Law of the Rep. of Belarus of July 8, 1998], Vedamastsi Natsyi͡anal′naha Shodu Rėspubliki Belarus′ [VNS RB] [Bulletin of the National Assembly of the Republic of Belarus] 1998, Nos. 29–30, Item 469; Zakon Respubliki Belarus′ ot 14 ii͡uni͡a 1999 g. [Law of the Rep. of Belarus of June 14, 1999], Nat͡sional′nyĭ Reestr Pravovykh Aktov Respubliki Belarus′ [NRPA RB] [National Register of the Legal Acts of the Republic of Belarus] 1999, No. 47, 2/42; Zakon Respubliki Belarus′ ot 16 ii͡uni͡a 2000 g. [Law of the Rep. of Belarus of June 16, 2000], Nat͡sional′nyĭ Reestr Pravovykh Aktov Respubliki Belarus′ [NRPA RB] [National Register of the Legal Acts of the Republic of Belarus] 2000, No. 59, 2/176; Zakon Respubliki Belarus′ ot 15 noi͡abri͡a 2004 g. [Law of the Rep. of Belarus of Nov. 15, 2004], Nat͡sional′nyĭ Reestr Pravovykh Aktov Respubliki Belarus′ [NRPA RB] [National Register of the Legal Acts of the Republic of Belarus] 2004, No. 180, 2/1080; Zakon Respubliki Belarus′ ot 23 ii͡uli͡a 2008 g. No. 421–3 "O Mezhdunarodnykh Dogovorakh Respubliki Belarus′" [Law of the Rep. of Belarus of July 23, 2008 No. 421–3 "On International Treaties of the Republic of Belarus"], Nat͡sional′nyĭ Reestr Pravovykh Aktov Respubliki Belarus′ [NRPA RB] [National Register of the Legal Acts of the Republic of Belarus] 2008, No. 184, 2/1518.

The Republic of Belarus is a party to the 1969 Vienna Convention on the Law of Treaties.[60] The 1991 Law on International Treaties, as amended in 1992 and 1998, brought substantial changes to the text of the law, and among other things established that Belarus concludes and performs international treaties in accordance with the generally-recognized principles and norms of international law, including provisions of the 1969 Vienna Convention.[61]

Depending upon the representation of the parties to the treaty, the 2008 Law on International Treaties distinguishes three types of international treaties, i.e. interstate treaties, intergovernmental treaties, and international treaties of interdepartmental character. "Interstate treaty" is an international treaty concluded on behalf of the Republic of Belarus with a foreign state(s) and/or with an international organization(s).[62] "Intergovernmental treaty" is an international treaty concluded by the government of the Republic of Belarus with the government(s) of a foreign state(s) and/or an international organization(s), except of the international treaties concluded by the government of the Republic of Belarus on behalf of the Republic of Belarus.[63] "International treaty of interdepartmental character" is an international treaty concluded by the governmental body(-ies) of the Republic of Belarus, the department of a governmental body with respect to the issues in its/their competence, with a corresponding governmental body(-ies) of a foreign state(s) and/or international organization(s).[64]

Under Article 17 of the 2008 Law on International Treaties, the Republic of Belarus can express its consent to be bound by the international treaty by a number of ways. This includes signing of the international treaty, exchanging notes, letters or other instruments constituting the international treaty, ratification of the international treaty, confirmation (acceptance), accession, and succession to the international treaty.

The decisions expressing consent to be bound by interstate and intergovernmental treaties are taken by the President of the Republic of Belarus, National Assembly or the Council of Ministers of the Republic of Belarus in accordance with their competence as determined by the Constitution of the Republic of Belarus, the Law on International Treaties, and other legal acts of the Republic of Belarus.[65] With respect to international treaties of interdepart-

---

60 Vienna Convention on the Law of Treaties, May 23, 1969, 1155 U.N.T.S. 331.

61 Pavlova, *supra* note 58, at 103.

62 Article 1 of the 2008 Law on International Treaties (translation of the author).

63 Id.

64 Id.

65 Article 17 of the 2008 Law on International Treaties (translation of the author).

mental character, the decisions are taken by the Council of Ministers or heads of the governmental bodies of the Republic of Belarus, department of the governmental body, which conclude such international treaties in accordance with their competence as determined by the Law on International Treaties and other legislative acts.

In particular, under Article 19 of the 2008 Law on International Treaties, the following interstate and intergovernmental treaties are subject to ratification:

- international treaties which provide for their ratification as the only means of expressing consent to be bound by such treaties;
- international treaties that establish rules other than those provided in the laws of the Republic of Belarus, decrees and edicts of the President of the Republic of Belarus;
- international treaties with their subject matter being in exclusive scope of legislative regulation, but not yet regulated by the laws of the Republic of Belarus, decrees and edicts of the President of the Republic of Belarus;
- international treaties on territorial demarcation of the Republic of Belarus with other states; and
- international treaties with respect to participation of the Republic of Belarus in international organizations and interstate bodies.

With regard to the hierarchy of legal norms, including norms of the international treaties of the Republic of Belarus, the reference to international law was made already in the preamble of the 1990 Declaration of State Sovereignty of the Republic of Belarus. In particular, it was stated that while proclaiming the state sovereignty the Supreme Soviet acted "in conformity with the principles of the Universal Declaration of Human Rights and other universally recognized international legal instruments."[66]

Under Article 8 of the Constitution, the Republic of Belarus recognizes the priority of universally-acknowledged principles of international law and ensures that its legislation conforms to these principles.[67] However, part 3 of Article 8 prohibits the conclusion of international treaties which contradict to the Constitution of the Republic of Belarus.[68] Thus, in the hierarchy of legal norms of Belarus, the Constitution of the Republic of Belarus is ranked higher than its international treaties. Further, the Constitution establishes the prior-

66 Deklarat͡sii͡a Verkhovnogo Soveta Respubliki Belarus′ ot 27 ii͡uli͡a 1990 g. No. 193–XII "O Gosudarstvennom Suverenitete Respubliki Belarus′," *supra* note 35.

67 Konstitut͡sii͡a Respubliki Belarus′ 1994 goda, *supra* note 41.

68 Id.

ity of international treaties ratified by the Republic of Belarus over the laws of the Republic of Belarus, including the Codes. This follows from the provisions of Article 116 of the Constitution, which deals with the composition and powers of the Constitutional Court of the Republic of Belarus. In particular, part 4 of Article 116 grants to the Court the power to produce the rulings on the conformity of laws of the Republic of Belarus, decrees and edicts of the President, and regulations of the government to the Constitution and international treaties ratified by the Republic of Belarus.[69] Hence, the Constitution for the first time provided the Constitutional Court with the right to directly apply the norms of international law along with the norms of national law, and therefore included the norms of international law into the legal system of the Republic of Belarus.[70]

The relationship between international treaties and normative legal acts is also governed by the Law of the Republic of Belarus of 10 January 2000 No. 361–3 "On Normative Legal Acts of the Republic of Belarus," as amended[71] (the Law on Normative Legal Acts). Article 20 of the Law entitled "Correlation between International Treaties and Normative Legal Acts" reiterates the Constitutional provisions, according to which Belarus recognizes the priority of universally-acknowledged principles of international law and ensures that its legislation conforms to these principles. It further stipulates that legal norms contained in the international treaties of Belarus are considered to be a part of the legislation in force on the territory of the Republic of Belarus. Such legal norms are to be applied directly, except of the cases where it follows from the international treaty that a domestic normative legal act has to be adopted for their application. Further, legal norms of the international treaties have the force of a normative legal act by which the Republic of Belarus has expressed its consent to be bound by the international treaty.[72]

The rules of publication of the legal acts of the Republic of Belarus, including its international treaties, are now established by the Decree of the President of the Republic of Belarus of 24 February 2012 No. 3 "On Certain Issues of

---

69 Id.

70 Pavlova, *supra* note 58, at 103.

71 Zakon Respubliki Belarus′ ot 10 i͡anvari͡a 2000 g. No. 361–3 "O Normativnykh Pravovykh Aktakh Respubliki Belarus′" [Law of the Rep. of Belarus of Jan. 10, 2000 No. 361–3 "On Normative Legal Acts of the Republic of Belarus"], Nat͡sional′nyĭ Reestr Pravovykh Aktov Respubliki Belarus′ [NRPA RB] [National Register of the Legal Acts of the Republic of Belarus] 2000, No. 7, 2/136.

72 Id. For various ways of expressing such consent to the bindingness of international treaties for the Republic of Belarus, *see* Article 17 of the 2000 Law on Normative Legal Acts, as amended.

Publication and Entry into Force of the Legal Acts of the Republic of Belarus,"[73] and the Law on Normative Legal Acts, as amended. Under the Decree, as from 1 July 2012, the only method of official publication of the legal act to be included in the National Register of Legal Acts of the Republic of Belarus is publication of such legal act on the National Legal Internet Portal of the Republic of Belarus. The date of appearing of a legal act on the Internet Portal under the section "Official publication" is considered to be the date of its official publication.[74]

Further distribution of the legal acts (although now considered unofficial publication) is possible through their placement in the official periodic printing publications. For international treaties, such publications include: the print digest of legal acts entitled "Natsional′nyĭ Reestr Pravovykh Aktov Respubliki Belarus′" [National Register of Legal Acts of the Republic of Belarus] (for international treaties – Section 3 of the Register), the newspaper "Sovetskaia Belorussiia" [Soviet Belorussia] (for interstate and intergovernmental treaties for which the agreement on their binding effect for Belarus has been expressed in the form of an edict of the President or a regulation of the Council of Ministers of the Republic of Belarus), the newspaper "Zviazda" [The Star] (for international treaties in the Belarusian language for which the agreement on their binding effect for Belarus has been expressed in the form of a law, or resolution or decision of the Constitutional Court of the Republic of Belarus), the newspaper "Narodnaia Voliia" [The People's Will] (for international treaties in Russian for which the agreement on their binding effect for Belarus has been expressed in the form of a law, or resolution or decision of the Constitutional Court of the Republic of Belarus), the newspaper "Rėspublika" [The Republic] (for international treaties of interdepartmental character).[75]

---

73 Dekret Prezidenta Respubliki Belarus′ ot 24 fevraliia 2012 g. No. 3 "O Nekotorykh Voprosakh Opublikovaniia i Vstupleniia v Silu Pravovykh Aktov Respubliki Belarus′" [Decree of the President of the Republic of Belarus of Feb. 24, 2012 No. 3 "On Some Issues of Publication and Entry into Force of the Legal Acts of the Republic of Belarus"], Natsional′nyĭ Reestr Pravovykh Aktov Respubliki Belarus′ [NRPA RB] [National Register of the Legal Acts of the Republic of Belarus] 2012, No. 26, 1/13351. Note that the Decree will operate until entry into force of the new Law "On Legal Acts of the Republic of Belarus," the draft of which has been introduced by the Council of Ministers on 27 December 2011 and, as of June 2013, is in its first reading at the House of Representatives of the National Assembly of Belarus. The text of the draft law substantially repeats the text of the above Decree on the issue of official publication of legal acts.

74 Id., para. 1.1.

75 Id., para. 1.2.

Prior methods of official publication of international treaties included for treaties subject to ratification – publication in "VEDAMASTSI NATSYI͡ANAL′NAHA SKHODU RĖSPUBLIKI BELARUS′" = "VEDOMOSTI NAT͡SIONAL′NOGO SOBRANII͡A RESPUBLIKI BELARUS′" [Bulletin of the National Assembly of the Republic of Belarus], and for treaties not subject to ratification and which have entered into force – publication in an Annex to the "ZBOR DĖKRĖTAŬ, UKAZAŬ PRĖZIDĖNTA I PASTANOŬ URADA RĖSPUBLIKI BELARUS′" = "SOBRANIE DEKRETOV, UKAZOV PREZIDENTA I POSTANOVLENIĬ PRAVITEL′STVA RESPUBLIKI BELARUS′" [Collection of Decrees, Edicts of the President and Regulations of the Government of the Republic of Belarus].[76]

Provisions of certain laws still reflect the old rules of official publication. For instance, the 2008 Law on International Treaties provides in Article 28 that official publication of international treaties of the Republic of Belarus is made in the Belarusian and/or Russian languages in the periodic print publication of the National Register of Legal Acts of the Republic of Belarus, its electronic version and other official publications in accordance with the procedure established by the legal acts of the Republic of Belarus.[77] Further, official announcements of the Ministry of Foreign Affairs of the Republic of Belarus regarding entry into force of international treaties for the Republic of Belarus, as well as regarding suspension or termination of international treaties of the Republic of Belarus are published in the periodic print publication of the National Register of Legal Acts of the Republic of Belarus, its electronic version.[78] This will be amended following the introduction of the Law "On Legal Acts of the Republic of Belarus."[79]

Evidence of State Practice

Following the dissolution of the Soviet Union, adoption of the new Constitution of the Republic of Belarus in 1994 and then amendments to the Constitution after the 1996 and 2004 referendums, the Republic of Belarus

76 *See* Article 20 of the previous version of the 1991 Law on International Treaties (as amended in 1992 and 1998), reproduced in English in BUTLER, THE LAW OF TREATIES, *supra* note 44 at 271–84 (2002).

77 Zakon Respubliki Belarus′ ot 23 ii͡uli͡a 2008 g. No. 421–3 "O Mezhdunarodnykh Dogovorakh Respubliki Belarus′," *supra* note 50.

78 Id.

79 Dekret Prezidenta Respubliki Belarus′ ot 24 fevrali͡a 2012 g. No. 3 "O Nekotorykh Voprosakh Opublikovanii͡a i Vstuplenii͡a v Silu Pravovykh Aktov Respubliki Belarus′," *supra* note 73.

became a presidential republic. Its major organs for conducting diplomatic relations thus include the President, the National Assembly (parliament), the Council of Ministers (government) – all of them received relevant powers under the Constitution of an independent Belarus.[80]

Based on a type of the treaty – an interstate, intergovernmental, or an international treaty of interdepartmental character – different procedures of negotiating and concluding of international treaties have to be observed. For interstate and intergovernmental treaties, such procedures and the role in the process of state bodies and their departments, including the President, the National Assembly, the Council of Ministers, the Ministry of Foreign Affairs, and the Ministry of Justice of the Republic of Belarus, are thoroughly addressed by Articles 5–8 of the 2008 Law on International Treaties.[81] Similarly, for international treaties of interdepartmental character, the procedure is outlined in Articles 9–13 of the Law.[82] Within the government, the Ministry of Foreign Affairs of the Republic of Belarus coordinates and controls the process of concluding of international treaties, their entry into force and implementation, and, within its competence, prepares drafts of the international treaties of the Republic of Belarus.

Modern treaty practice of Belarus is also determined by the memberships of the Republic of Belarus in various international organizations, unions and interstate formations. Belarus is a founding member of the United Nations. After the collapse of the USSR, it continued its membership in the UN and has since then entered into new international treaties in the framework of the United Nations. It also continued applying and confirmed treaty succession for international treaties of the former BSSR.

On the regional level, Belarus is a full member of the CIS and a party to numerous treaties concluded within the CIS region.[83] The Executive Committee of the CIS – a permanent executive, administrative and coordinating body of the CIS – has its headquarters in Minsk, Belarus. Also located in Minsk is the Economic Court of the CIS, which has the competence to interpret agreements and other legal acts of the CIS on economic issues, and (where a

80 *See*, in particular, Articles 79, 84, 97 and 107 of the 1994 Constitution, as amended. Konstitut͡sii͡a Respubliki Belarus′ 1994 goda, *supra* note 41.

81 Zakon Respubliki Belarus′ ot 23 ii͡uli͡a 2008 g. No. 421–3 "O Mezhdunarodnykh Dogovorakh Respubliki Belarus′," *supra* note 50.

82 Id.

83 For further reading on international treaties of the Republic of Belarus in the framework of the CIS, *see, e.g.*, I͡U.P. Brovka, *Dogovory s Uchastiem Respubliki Belarus′ v Ramkakh SNG,* in L.V. Pavlova (ed.), Implementat͡sii͡a Norm Mezhdunarodnogo Prava vo Vnutrigosudarstvennoe Pravo 74 (2001).

jurisdictional reservation to this effect is made in the agreement)[84] can resolve other disputes related to the implementation of the agreements and other acts of the CIS adopted on their basis.

Belarus is also a member state of the Eurasian Economic Community (EAEC or EurAsEC) – a regional intergovernmental organization with the goals of forming common external customs borders and developing common foreign economic policies, tariffs and other components of the common market. The Treaty on the Establishment of the Eurasian Economic Community was signed by the presidents of Belarus, Kazakhstan, Kyrgyzstan, Russia, and Tajikistan on 10 October 2000 in Astana.[85] In December 2003, the EAEC was invited to participate in the sessions and work of the UN General Assembly in the capacity of observer.[86] One of the main bodies of the EAEC – the Court of the Eurasian Economic Community – began operating in Minsk on 1 January 2012. The Court operates in accordance with the relevant provisions of the Treaty on the Establishment of the Eurasian Economic Community and the Statute of the Court of 5 July 2010.[87]

Following the creation of the EAEC, the work on the formation of the customs union was continued within the framework of the EAEC. On 6 October 2007, Belarus, Russia, and Kazakhstan signed the Treaty on the Establishment of Common Customs Territory and Formation of the Customs Union.[88] The Customs Union between these countries began working fully in July 2010 (on July 1 – between Russia and Kazakhstan, and on July 6 – also for Belarus)

---

84 For a current list of 37 international agreements which contain such jurisdictional reservation, see the web-site of the Economic Court of the CIS for the *List of Documents which Contain a Reservation on the Recognition of the Jurisdiction of the Economic Court*, http://sudsng.org/download_files/docs/iz11s007w_2013.pdf.

85 *See Dogovor ob Uchrezhdenii Evraziĭskogo Ėkonomicheskogo Soobshchestva* [Treaty on the Establishment of the Eurasian Economic Community], Oct. 10, 2000, as amended on January 25, 2006 and October 6, 2007. English version is available on the web-site of the Eurasian Economic Community at http://evrazes.com/docs/view/95.

86 Observer Status for the Eurasian Economic Community in the General Assembly, G.A. Res. 58/84, U.N. Doc. A/RES/58/84 (Dec. 9, 2003).

87 *See Statut Suda Evraziĭskogo Ėkonomicheskogo Soobshchestva* [Statute of the Court of the Eurasian Economic Community], July 5, 2010, http://sudevrazes.org/ru/main.aspx?guid=19121. English translation of the Statute is available on the web-site of the Eurasian Economic Community at http://www.evrazes.com/docs/view/111.

88 See *Dogovor o Sozdanii Edinoĭ Tamozhennoĭ Territorii i Formirovanii Tamozhennogo Soi͡uza* [Treaty on the Establishment of Common Customs Territory and Formation of the Customs Union], Oct. 6, 2007, http://evrazes.com/docs/view/75. For an English translation, see the web-site of the Eurasian Economic Community at http://evrazes.com/docs/view/163.

after the Customs Code of the Customs Union came into effect. Further, during 2010–2011, a package of 20 international treaties establishing the Common Economic Space – a single market for goods, services, capital and labor – was signed in December 2010 and then ratified by Belarus, Kazakhstan, and Russia.[89] The Common Economic Space began operating on the territories of these three countries on 1 January 2012. A permanent supranational body of the Customs Union and the Common Economic Space – the Eurasian Economic Commission – began working in Moscow as from 2 February 2012 on the basis of the Treaty of 18 November 2011 on the Eurasian Economic Commission[90] and the Regulations of the Eurasian Economic Commission.[91] As a final goal of the Eurasian economic integration, by 1 January 2015, Belarus, Kazakhstan and Russia aim to complete codification of international treaties of the Customs Union and the Common Economic Space and on their basis create the Eurasian Economic Union.[92] Meanwhile, on 18 October 2011, Belarus also signed the CIS Free Trade Agreement (CISFTA) with seven other CIS countries (Russia, Ukraine, Kazakhstan, Kyrgyzstan, Tajikistan, Moldova, and Armenia).[93]

On a bilateral level, Belarus continues its close relations with Russia. Together the states created a supranational entity – the Union State of Russia and Belarus.[94] To this effect, Belarus concluded a number of bilateral treaties with Russia starting from the 1995 Treaty on the Friendship, Good

---

89 For texts of the founding treaties of the Common Economic Space, see the web-site of the Eurasian Economic Commission, under "Documents," http://www.eurasiancommission.org.

90 See *Dogovor o Evraziĭskoĭ Ėkonomicheskoĭ Komissii* [Treaty on the Eurasian Economic Commission], Nov. 18, 2011, http://www.tsouz.ru/MGS/18-11-11/Documents/Договоро ЕЭК.pdf.

91 *See Reglament Raboty Evraziĭskoĭ Ėkonomicheskoĭ Komissii* [The Regulations of the Work of the Eurasian Economic Commission], approved by the Decision of 18 November 2011 No. 1 of the Interstate Council of the Eurasian Economic Community, http://www.economy.gov.by/dadvfiles/002104_614455_Reglament.pdf.

92 *See Deklarat͡sii͡a o Evraziĭskoĭ Ėkonomicheskoĭ Integrat͡sii* [Declaration on the Eurasian Economic Integration], Nov. 18, 2011, http://sudevrazes.org/en/main.aspx?guid=19471.

93 *See Dogovor o Zone Svobodnoĭ Torgovli* [Agreement on the Creation of a Free Trade Area], Oct. 18, 2011, http://cis.minsk.by/reestr/ru/printPreview/text?id=3183&serverUrl=http://cis.minsk.by/reestr/ru. Note that as of June 2013, the agreement is in force for Armenia, Belarus, Kazakhstan, Moldova, Russia, and Ukraine. In addition, on 31 May 2013, Uzbekistan was admitted to the CIS free trade agreement.

94 *See Dogovor o Sozdanii Soi͡uznogo Gosudarstva* [The Treaty on the Creation of a Union State of Russia and Belarus], Dec. 9, 1999, http://www.soyuz.by/about/docs/dogovor5/. For further reading on the Union State of Russia and Belarus, *see, e.g.*, Audrius Žulys, *Towards a Union State of Russia and Belarus*, 15–16 Lithuanian Foreign Pol'y Rev. 148 (2005).

Neighbourhood and Co-operation between the Russian Federation and the Republic of Belarus.[95]

Annotated Bibliography of Sources

General Treaty Collections

1 NATIONAL LEGAL INTERNET PORTAL OF THE REPUBLIC OF BELARUS
URL: http://www.law.by (English)
URL: http://www.pravo.by (Russian)

Summary: The main Internet resource for the legal information of the Republic of Belarus with the links to three major electronic legal resources – (1) the *National Register of Legal Acts of the Republic of Belarus* (see a separate entry below), (2) section of the Internet Portal "*Official Publication*," which contains full texts of the legal acts as they are being published (current and archived as from June 2011) and, as from 1 July 2012, represents the only means of the official publication of the legal acts of the Republic of Belarus, including its international treaties, and (3) the *Belarus Legislation Databank "ĖTALON-ONLINE"* (see a separate entry below). The web-site also contains information about the legal system of Belarus, state system of legal information, legislative process, state bodies, legal acts and international treaties.

Note: On the English version of the web-site, under *International Treaties*, there are lists of countries that have concluded international treaties with Belarus on mutual protection of investments, double taxation, legal assistance and legal relations in civil, criminal and other matters, non-visa trips of citizens, and international road carriage of passengers and cargo international road relations.

2 NAT͡SIONALʹNYĬ REESTR PRAVOVYKH AKTOV RESPUBLIKI BELARUSʹ [THE NATIONAL REGISTER OF LEGAL ACTS OF THE REPUBLIC OF BELARUS]
URL: http://pravo.by/main.aspx?guid=10691.

Summary: A comprehensive system of registration of the legal acts of the Republic of Belarus. Created on 1 January 1999 in accordance with the Edict of the President of the Republic of Belarus of 20 July 1998 No. 369 "On the National

95 *Dogovor o Druzhbe, Dobrososedstve i Sotrudnichestve Mezhdu Rossiĭskoĭ Federat͡sieĭ i Respublikoĭ Belarusʹ* [Treaty on the Friendship, Good Neighbourhood and Co-operation between the Russian Federation and the Republic of Belarus], Feb. 21, 1995, http://www.soyuz.by/about/docs/dogovor1/.

Register of Legal Acts of the Republic of Belarus".[96] Managed by the National Center of Legal Information of the Republic of Belarus. Electronically available through the National Legal Internet Portal. Includes a search service that allows locating legal acts by their title, date of adoption or registration, etc. (in Russian). International treaties are included in Section 3 of the Register – "International treaties."

Note: Legal acts to be included into the National Register of Legal Acts are to be officially published by means of reproduction of their texts on the *National Legal Internet Portal of the Republic of Belarus* (under section "*Official Publication*"). After such official publication on the Internet Portal, legal acts can be further distributed in the print digest of legal acts with the same title "NATS͡IONAL′NYĬ REESTR PRAVOVYKH AKTOV RESPUBLIKI BELARUS′" [National Register of Legal Acts of the Republic of Belarus] or other periodic publications according to the rules of publication of the legal acts.

3 NATS͡IONAL′NYĬ REESTR PRAVOVYKH AKTOV RESPUBLIKI BELARUS′ [NATIONAL REGISTER OF LEGAL ACTS OF THE REPUBLIC OF BELARUS]

Summary: Digest of the legal acts of the Republic of Belarus. Represents a print version of the National Register of Legal Acts – a comprehensive system of registration of the legal acts of Belarus. Consists of ten sections, each section contains legal acts of a specified type. International treaties are included in Section 3 of the Digest. Four issues per month.

Note: Publication of the legal acts in the print digest is not considered official publication. As from 1 July 2012, the only method of official publication of the legal acts in Belarus is their reproduction on the National Legal Internet Portal of the Republic of Belarus.

4 NATIONAL CENTER OF LEGAL INFORMATION OF THE REPUBLIC OF BELARUS

URL: http://www.ncpi.gov.by.

Summary: Web-site of the National Center of Legal Information of the Republic of Belarus – a scientific and practical state institution responsible for the operation and development of the state system of legal information.

96 Ukaz Prezidenta Respubliki Belarus′ ot 20 ii͡uli͡a 1998 No. 369 "O Nats͡ional′nom Reestre Pravovykh Aktov Respubliki Belarus′," as amended [Edict of the President of the Republic of Belarus of 20 July 1998 "On the National Register of Legal Acts of the Republic of Belarus, as amended], NATS͡IONAL′NYĬ REESTR PRAVOVYKH AKTOV RESPUBLIKI BELARUS′ [NRPA RB] [National Register of the Legal Acts of the Republic of Belarus] 1999, No. 1, 1/1.

Among other functions, it manages the *National Register of Legal Acts*, runs databanks of legal information (e.g., the comprehensive legal databank *"ĖTALON"* and its electronic version *"ĖTALON-ONLINE,"* including updated twice a week databank "International Treaties" with over 8,000 documents – international treaties of the Republic of Belarus, legal acts adopted within the CIS and in the framework of the Union State), publishes the print digest "NAT͡SIONAL′NYĬ REESTR PRAVOVYKH AKTOV RESPUBLIKI BELARUS′" [National Register of Legal Acts of the Republic of Belarus]. The web-site contains further information on the functions, services and products of the National Center.

Note: Primarily in Russian and Belarusian.

Note: Access to the databanks of legal information requires subscription.

5 BELARUS LEGISLATION DATABANK "ĖTALON"
URL: http://law.by/main.aspx?guid=4251.

Summary: Databank of legal information with a comprehensive full-text search service. Major state informational and legal resource with the most complete information on the national and municipal legal acts of the Republic of Belarus and its international treaties. Databank *"ĖTALON"* requires installation, its online version *"ĖTALON-ONLINE"* is available through the Internet and accessible through the National Legal Internet Portal of the Republic of Belarus.

Note: Access to the databanks of legal information requires subscription.

6 DATABANK "KONSUL′TANT PLI͡US: BELARUS′"

Summary: A system of legal information with various databases available for subscription. Developed and distributed by the Russian company which produces the databank *"Konsul′tantPli͡us"* – the largest informational legal resource and search service of the Russian Federation. For Belarus, information on the offered services and subscription packages can be found at http://www.urspectr.info.

Note: Many of the international treaties of Belarus and legal acts adopted within the international organizations can be found through the online non-commercial (base) version of *Konsul′tantPli͡us* for the Russian Federation accessible through http://www.consultant.ru/online. Although it focuses on the Russian law, the database allows searching texts of the treaties by participating countries, including Belarus.

7 VEDAMASTSI NATSYI͡ANAL′NAHA SKHODU RĖSPUBLIKI BELARUS′ = VEDOMOSTI NAT͡SIONAL′NOGO SOBRANII͡A RESPUBLIKI BELARUS′
[Bulletin of the National Assembly of the Republic of Belarus]

Summary: Bulletin of the National Assembly (parliament) of the Republic of Belarus. Under the 1991 Law on International Treaties (as amended in 1992 and 1998), ratified international treaties were to be published in the Bulletin.[97] Bulletin was published in 1990–2000 (since 1997 – under the above name with three issues per month).

Note: In Belarusian and Russian.

8 MEZHDUNARODNYE DOGOVORY RESPUBLIKI BELARUS′ [INTERNATIONAL TREATIES OF THE REPUBLIC OF BELARUS]. ANNEX TO ZBOR DĖKRĖTAŬ, UKAZAŬ PRĖZIDĖNTA I PASTANOŬ URADA RĖSPUBLIKI BELARUS′ = SOBRANIE DEKRETOV, UKAZOV PREZIDENTA I POSTANOVLENIĬ PRAVITEL′STVA RESPUBLIKI BELARUS′ [COLLECTION OF DECREES, EDICTS OF THE PRESIDENT AND REGULATIONS OF THE GOVERNMENT OF THE REPUBLIC OF BELARUS]
(Minsk: Izd. Administrat͡sii Prezidenta i Pravitel'stva Respubliki Belarus', 1997–1998).

Summary: Journal of international treaties of Belarus published by the Administration of the President and the Government of the Republic of Belarus as an annex to the Collection of Decrees, Edicts of the President and Regulations of the Government of the Republic of Belarus. Under the 1991 Law on International Treaties (as amended in 1992 and 1998), treaties which were not subject to ratification and which had entered into force, were to be published in the Annex.[98] Collection was published in 1996–2000, the Annex on international treaties – in 1997–1998 with four issues per year.

Note: In Belarusian and Russian.

Topical and Selected Treaty Publications

9 MEZHDUNARODNYE DOGOVORY RESPUBLIKI BELARUS′, PRIMENI͡AEMYE V KHOZI͡AĬSTVENNOĬ (PREDPRINIMATEL′SKOĬ) DEI͡ATEL′NOSTI [INTERNATIONAL TREATIES OF THE REPUBLIC OF BELARUS USED IN ECONOMIC (BUSINESS) PRACTICE]
V.S. Kamenkov et al. (Minsk: Amalfei͡a, 2002).

Summary: A comprehensive collection of international treaties of the Republic of Belarus which are used in economic (business) practice. Treaties

---

97 *See* Article 20 of the previous version of the 1991 Law on International Treaties (as amended in 1992 and 1998), reproduced in English in W.E. Butler, *The Law of Treaties in Russia and the Commonwealth of Independent States. Text and Commentary* 271–84 (2002).

98 Id.

accompanied by information on their status and documents of ratification, accession, or succession by Belarus. Treaties and other legal acts presented in groups based on their topic: Part 1 includes legislation of the Republic of Belarus on international treaties, Part 2 – treaties related to the regulation of foreign economic activity, Part 3 – treaties on customs relations, Part 4 – treaties on tax relations, Part 5 – treaties on investments, Part 6 – treaties on exchange of legal information, Part 7 – treaties on international legal assistance.

10 PRAVA CHELOVEKA: SBORNIK MEZHDUNARODNO-PRAVOVYKH DOKUMENTOV [HUMAN RIGHTS: COLLECTION OF INTERNATIONAL LAW DOCUMENTS]
V. Shcherbov & A. Selivanov (Minsk: Belfrans, 1999).

Summary: Collection of 167 international law documents, including treaties of the Republic of Belarus which regulate various aspects of human rights. Includes conventions and resolutions of the United Nations on a variety of topics (such as rights of women and children, elimination and prevention of discrimination, and international humanitarian law), as well as documents of the Organization for Security and Co-operation in Europe (OSCE) and the Council of Europe. Contains an Annex on participation of Belarus in international treaties on human rights.

11 SBORNIK DOKUMENTOV PO MEZHGOSUDARSTVENNOMU OBMENU NAUCHNO-TEKHNICHESKOĬ INFORMAT͡SIEĬ GOSUDARSTV SNG [COLLECTION OF DOCUMENTS ON INTERSTATE EXCHANGE OF SCIENTIFIC AND TECHNICAL INFORMATION OF THE CIS COUNTRIES]
V.I. Fedorov et al. (Minsk: Belisa, 2001).

Summary: Collection of documents adopted in the framework of the CIS that regulate interstate exchange of scientific and technical information of the CIS countries.

12 SBORNIK DOKUMENTOV PO MIROTVORCHESKOĬ DEI͡ATEL′NOSTI, PRINI͡ATYKH V RAMKAKH SODRUZHESTVA NEZAVISIMYKH GOSUDARSTV [COLLECTION OF DOCUMENTS ON PEACEKEEPING ACTIVITIES ADOPTED IN THE FRAMEWORK OF THE COMMONWEALTH OF INDEPENDENT STATES]
I͡U.F. I͡Arov, ed. (Minsk: CIS Executive Committee, 2001).

Summary: Collection of documents adopted within the Commonwealth of Independent States which regulate the peacekeeping activities. Published in Minsk, Belarus by the CIS Executive Committee.

13 SBORNIK NORMATIVNYKH AKTOV, REGULIRUI͡USHCHIKH VZAIMODEĬSTVIE GOSUDARSTV-UCHASTNIKOV SODRUZHESTVA NEZAVISIMYKH GOSUDARSTV V BORʹBE S PRESTUPNOSTʹIU. VYPUSK 1 [COLLECTION OF NORMATIVE ACTS THAT REGULATE INTERACTION OF THE MEMBER STATES OF THE COMMONWEALTH OF INDEPENDENT STATES IN THE AREA OF FIGHT AGAINST CRIME. ISSUE 1] (Minsk: CIS Executive Committee, 1998).

Summary: Collection of normative acts of the CIS countries, including international agreements and treaties of the Republic of Belarus which regulate interaction of the CIS member states in the area of fight against crime. Published in Minsk, Belarus by the CIS Executive Committee.

14 SBORNIK NORMATIVNYKH AKTOV, REGULIRUI͡USHCHIKH VZAIMODEĬSTVIE GOSUDARSTV-UCHASTNIKOV SODRUZHESTVA NEZAVISIMYKH GOSUDARSTV V BORʹBE S PRESTUPNOSTʹI͡U. VYPUSK 2 [COLLECTION OF NORMATIVE ACTS THAT REGULATE INTERACTION OF THE MEMBER STATES OF THE COMMONWEALTH OF INDEPENDENT STATES IN THE AREA OF FIGHT AGAINST CRIME. ISSUE 2] (Minsk: CIS Executive Committee, 2000.)

Summary: Collection of normative acts of the CIS countries, including international agreements and treaties of the Republic of Belarus which regulate interaction between the CIS member states in the area of fight against crime. Published in Minsk, Belarus by the CIS Executive Committee.

Note: Second issue, follows the first issue of 1998.

15 SBORNIK MEZHDUNARODNO-PRAVOVYKH DOKUMENTOV I NAT͡SIONALʹNYKH ZAKONODATELʹNYKH AKTOV PO VOPROSAM BEZHENT͡SEV [COLLECTION OF INTERNATIONAL LAW DOCUMENTS AND NATIONAL LEGISLATIVE ACTS ON THE ISSUES OF REFUGEES] I͡U.L. Sarashevskiĭ & A.V. Selivanov (Minsk: Teseĭ, 2000).

Summary: Contains international treaties and other documents of the League of Nations and the United Nations, as well as regional international agreements on refugees, including conventions, resolutions, and documents of the Commonwealth of Independent States, the European Union, and the Council of Europe. Documents in the collection are not specific to Belarus, but rather thoroughly address the issues of refugees' protection in the world. Belarus has adhere to some of the international treaties on refugees provided in the publication, in particular, those listed in the UN and the CIS parts of the book.

16 SBORNIK MEZHDUNARODNO-PRAVOVYKH DOKUMENTOV I NAT͡SIONAL′NYKH NORMATIVNYKH PRAVOVYKH AKTOV PO VOPROSAM OPERATIVNO-ROZYSKNOĬ DEI͡ATEL′NOSTI [COLLECTION OF INTERNATIONAL LAW DOCUMENTS AND NATIONAL NORMATIVE LEGAL ACTS ON THE ISSUES OF OPERATIONS AND SEARCH PRACTICE]
V.V. Bachila et al. (Minsk: Registr, 2001).

Summary: Collection of excerpts of international law documents and national normative legal acts of the Republic of Belarus that regulate operations and search activity. In particular, Part I of this publication contains excerpts of the international agreements and conventions concluded within the United Nations, the Council of Europe, and the Commonwealth of Independent States, as well as bilateral international treaties of Belarus, which regulate various aspects of operations and search practice (such as treaties on cooperation and legal assistance on civil, family, and criminal matters, and treaties on cooperation against international organized crime and international terrorism).

17 SBORNIK MEZHDUNARODNYKH DOGOVOROV [COLLECTION OF INTERNATIONAL TREATIES]
A.A. Abakshina & M.L. Chudaeva (Minsk: Akademii͡a Upravlenii͡a pri Prezidente Respubliki Belarus′, 2006).

Summary: Collection of international treaties of Belarus with a focus on the issues of international family law. Includes the 1956 New York Convention on the Recovery Abroad of Maintenance, the 1989 UN Convention on the Rights of the Child, the 1993 Hague Convention on Protection of Children and Co-operation in Respect of Intercountry Adoption, the 1980 Hague Convention on the Civil Aspects of International Child Abduction, and international treaties concluded within the CIS region, such as the 1993 Minsk Convention on Legal Assistance and Legal Relations on Civil, Family and Criminal Matters and the 2002 Kishinev Convention on Legal Assistance and Legal Relations on Civil, Family and Criminal Matters.

18 SBORNIK MEZHDUNARODNYKH DOGOVOROV. MEZHDUNARODNAI͡A TORGOVLI͡A. MEZHDUNARODNYĬ GRAZHDANSKIĬ PROT͡SESS [COLLECTION OF INTERNATIONAL TREATIES. INTERNATIONAL TRADE. INTERNATIONAL CIVIL PROCEDURE]
I.V. Fisenko (Minsk: Amalfei͡a, 1999).

Summary: Collection contains full texts of the international treaties on the issues of international trade and international civil procedure, such as the 1980 UN Convention on Contracts for the International Sale of Goods, the 1930 Geneva Conventions on Bills of Exchange and Promissory Notes, the 1995 UN Convention on Independent Guarantees and Stand-by Letters of Credit.

19 SBORNIK MEZHDUNARODNYKH DOGOVOROV OB IZBEZHANII DVOĬNOGO NALOGOOBLOZHENII͡A. MEZHDUNARODNYE SOGLASHENII͡A RESPUBLIKI BELARUSʹ [COLLECTION OF INTERNATIONAL TREATIES ON AVOIDANCE OF DOUBLE TAXATION. INTERNATIONAL AGREEMENTS OF THE REPUBLIC OF BELARUS]
L.E. Astapovich et al. (Minsk: Amalfei͡a, 1997).

Summary: Collection contains 39 international agreements of Belarus that cover the issues of double taxation. Two types of agreements are included: agreements that have been concluded by the Republic of Belarus since its independence from the Soviet Union in 1991, and the agreements of the former USSR, to which Belarus succeeded following the dissolution of the Soviet Union. For the countries which concluded new agreements with Belarus to replace the old USSR treaties, such as Bulgaria, Great Britain, and the Netherlands, both the old and the new versions of the agreements are provided. In addition, there is a text of the 1992 Agreement on the Agreed Principles of the Tax Policy, concluded between the governments of the CIS countries on 13 March 1992.

20 SBORNIK MEZHDUNARODNYKH SOGLASHENIĬ (KONVENT͡SIĬ) I NAT͡SIONALʹNYKH NORMATIVNYKH PRAVOVYKH AKTOV PO VOPROSAM MEZHDUNARODNOGO SOTRUDNICHESTVA V BORʹBE S PRESTUPNOSTʹI͡U [COLLECTION OF INTERNATIONAL AGREEMENTS (CONVENTIONS) AND NATIONAL NORMATIVE LEGAL ACTS ON THE ISSUES OF INTERNATIONAL COOPERATION IN THE FIGHT AGAINST CRIME]
S.I. Mukashev & I.I. Poletilo (Minsk: Akademii͡a MVD Respubliki Belarusʹ, 2005).

Summary: A 2-volume collection of international treaties and national legal acts regulating international cooperation against crime.

Note: Includes conventions (or their excerpts) of the United Nations and the Council of Europe, such as the 1963 the Convention on Offences and Certain Other Acts Committed on Board Aircraft, the 1979 International Convention Against the Taking of Hostages, the 1980 Hague Convention on the Civil Aspects of International Child Abduction, the 1988 UN Convention Against Illicit Traffic in Narcotic Drugs and Psychotropic Substances, the 1997 International Convention for the Suppression of Terrorist Bombings, and the 2000 UN Convention Against Transnational Organized Crime.

21 SBORNIK NORMATIVNYKH DOKUMENTOV PO KONSUL′SKIM VOPROSAM: S KOMMENTARII͡AMI [COLLECTION OF NORMATIVE DOCUMENTS ON CONSULAR ISSUES: WITH COMMENTARIES]
L.V. Pavlova, ed. (Minsk: Teseĭ, 2004).

Summary: Collection of texts and excerpts of normative documents on the issues of consular affairs. Includes international agreements of Belarus. Accompanied by commentaries.

22 SBORNIK OSNOVNYKH MEZHDUNARODNYKH DOGOVOROV RESPUBLIKI BELARUS′ V DEI͡ATEL′NOSTI OBSHCHIKH I KHOZI͡AĬSTVENNYKH SUDOV [COLLECTION OF MAIN INTERNATIONAL TREATIES OF THE REPUBLIC OF BELARUS IN THE PRACTICE OF GENERAL AND ECONOMIC COURTS]
V.S. Kamenkov et al. (Minsk: Informpress, 1999).

Summary: Collection of 18 main international treaties of the Republic of Belarus used in practice of general and economic courts, accompanied by the acts of ratification, accession, or succession to such treaties by Belarus.

Note: The publication includes texts of multilateral treaties (such as the 1965 Hague Convention on the Service Abroad of Judicial and Extrajudicial Documents in Civil or Commercial Matters and the 1968 European Convention on Information on Foreign Law), bilateral agreements of Belarus on legal assistance on civil, family and criminal matters (with Finland, China, Poland, Latvia, Lithuania), as well as treaties within the CIS countries (such as the 1992 Kiev Agreement on Procedure of Settlement of Disputes Connected to Economic Activity and the 1993 Minsk Convention on Legal Assistance and Legal Relations on Civil, Family and Criminal Matters).

23 TRANSPORTNAYA DEI͡ATEL′NOST′: SBORNIK ZAKONODATEL′NYKH AKTOV RESPUBLIKI BELARUS′ I MEZHDUNARODNYKH DOGOVOROV [TRANSPORT ACTIVITY: COLLECTION OF THE LEGISLATIVE ACTS OF THE REPUBLIC OF BELARUS AND INTERNATIONAL TREATIES]
V.G. Gavrilenko (Minsk, Pravo i Ėkonomika, 2007).

Summary: Collection of the legislative acts of the Republic of Belarus, as well as its international treaties regulating various aspects of transport activity and practice.

Note: Includes close to 30 international agreements, conventions and declarations, such as those regulating road traffic (e.g., the 1968 Vienna Convention on Road Traffic, the 1971 Convention on the Law Applicable to Traffic Accidents), transportation of oil and gas (e.g., the 1999 Umbrella Agreement on the Institutional Framework for the Establishment of Interstate Oil and Gas Transportation Systems), and bilateral agreements of Belarus on road transport (e.g., those with Azerbaijan, Lithuania, Moldova, Poland, Ukraine, and Uzbekistan) and agreements on principles of cooperation and relations in the field of transport (e.g., agreements with Kazakhstan and Turkmenistan).

24 VOENNAI͡A STRATEGII͡A. MEZHDUNARODNYE DOGOVORY I SOGLASHENII͡A V OBLASTI RAZORUZHENII͡A I KONTROLI͡A NAD VOORUZHENII͡AMI: SPRAVOCHNIK [MILITARY STRATEGY: INTERNATIONAL TREATIES AND AGREEMENTS IN THE AREA OF DISARMAMENT AND ARMS CONTROL: REFERENCE BOOK]
V.D. Seregov (Minsk: Military Academy of the Republic of Belarus, 2007).

Summary: Reference book on international treaties and agreements of the Republic of Belarus in the area of disarmament and arms control. Also provides a list of normative legal acts of Belarus of 39 items that deal with the implementation of international treaties of Belarus on the issues of disarmament and arms control.

25 UNITED NATIONS IN BELARUS
URL: http://un.by.

Summary: The official web-site of the United Nations in Belarus. The English version of the web-site provides information on various international documents relevant to the work of the United Nations in Belarus. This includes texts of the Conventions (e.g., the 1989 Convention on the Rights of the Child), agreements and memorandums (such as the Agreement of 15 May 1992 between the United Nations and the Government of the

Republic of Belarus relating to the Establishment of the United Nations Interim Office in Minsk, the Agreement of 24 September 1992 between the Government of the Republic of Belarus and the United Nations Development Programme, and the Memorandum of Cooperation between the Government of Belarus and UNESCO), and documents relating to the United Nations Development Assistance Framework (UNDAF) for the Republic of Belarus for 2011–2015.

Note: The web-site contains information both in Belarusian/Russian and English.

26 EXECUTIVE COMMITTEE OF THE COMMONWEALTH OF INDEPENDENT STATES (CIS)
URL: http://www.cis.minsk.by.

Summary: The web-site of the CIS Executive Committee. Among other information on the CIS, contains a databank entitled the *Uniform Register of the Legal Acts and Other Documents of the Commonwealth of Independent States* (EDINYĬ REESTR PRAVOVYKH AKTOV I DRUGIKH DOKUMENTOV SODRUZHESTVA NEZAVISIMYKH GOSUDARSTV), accompanied by a search engine. With regard to international treaties, under the tab "Reports," there is an option to generate current reports on international treaties which require ratification (including the total number of such treaties, their status, and dates of entry into force for individual CIS countries) and reports on the completion of intra-state procedures in the CIS countries with respect to international treaties. The databank allows saving documents in .pdf or .doc format, and printing them.

Note: In Russian.

27 ECONOMIC COURT OF THE COMMONWEALTH OF INDEPENDENT STATES (CIS)
URL: http://www.sudsng.org.

Summary: Official web-site of the Economic Court of the CIS. Contains databanks of the Court's judicial acts (decisions, advisory opinions, findings, resolutions of the Plenum), abstracts of the decisions of the Court for 1992–2012, normative information and other documents (including selective CIS agreements), resolutions of the Plenum of the Court for 1994–2013, and review of the court practice with regard to interpretation of international agreements (agreements establishing the CIS, the status and competence of the CIS organs and organizations, the CIS free trade area, as well as the agreements that ensure social and economic rights of citizens of the CIS member states, and agreements on pensions concluded within the CIS).

28 EURASIAN ECONOMIC COMMUNITY

URL: http://www.evrazes.com.

Summary: Official web-site of the Eurasian Economic Community (EAEC). The Russian version of the web-site, under the tab "Documents," contains documents of the EAEC, including international treaties concluded between its member states and agreements of the bodies of the EAEC with other organizations. There is a search engine with the options to perform basic or advanced search by term and date.

Note: The English version of the web-site contains the so-called "basic documents collection" (http://evrazes.com/en/docs/base), with the full texts of the relevant treaties, such as the Treaty of 10 October 2000 on the Establishment of the Eurasian Economic Community (EAEC), Treaty of 28 April 1998 on the legal status of citizens of one state permanently residing in the territory of another state, Agreement of 25 January 2008 on export duties with regard to third countries, etc.

Note: In addition, the English version of the web-site contains a list of 110 international treaties and protocols concluded within the EAEC as of December 2008, with the dates of their entry into force, as applicable (available at http://www.evrazes.com/docs/view/148).

29 EURASIAN ECONOMIC COMMISSION

URL: http://www.eurasiancommission.org (current site)

URL: http://www.tsouz.ru (old archived web-site)

Summary: Official web-site of the Eurasian Economic Commission – a permanent supranational body of the Customs Union and the Common Economic Space that functions as from 2 February 2012. Under "Documents," contains comprehensive database and a search service for documents related to the EAEC, including international agreements and decisions of the Court of the Eurasian Economic Community (as of June 2013, a total of 2,990 documents).

Note: The old (archived) web-site of the Eurasian Economic Commission contains the list of 67 international treaties regulating the formation and work of the EurAsEC, Customs Union, and Common Economic Space at http://www.tsouz.ru/Docs/IntAgrmnts/Pages/Perechenangl.aspx (unofficial translation in English, last visited June 1, 2013). The list is broken into three sections. Section 1 contains the list of international treaties constituting the legal framework of the Customs Union (as of 1 July 2010). Section 2 contains the list of the international treaties stipulated by the Plan of Actions on implementation of the Customs Code of the Customs Union (19 treaties). Section 3 contains other international treaties of the Customs Union.

Note: The Russian version of the archived web-site contains a more current list of 94 international treaties and protocols (in force or applied provisionally), as well as the texts of most of these treaties and protocols available through http://www.tsouz.ru/Docs/IntAgrmnts/Pages/Perechen_MDTS.aspx.

30 INFORMATION ANALYSIS PORTAL OF THE UNION STATE
URL: http://www.soyuz.by.

Summary: Official Internet portal of the Union State of Russia and Belarus with the information analysis related to the Union State. On its Russian version, under "Documents of the Union," contains texts of founding treaties of the Union State, such as the 1995 Treaty on the Friendship, Good Neighbourhood and Co-operation between the Russian Federation and the Republic of Belarus, the 1996 Treaty establishing the Commonwealth of Russia and Belarus (no longer in force), the 1997 Treaty on the Union between Belarus and Russia and the Charter to the Treaty (no longer in force), the 1998 Declaration Regarding the Further Unification of Russia and Belarus, and the 1999 Treaty on the Creation of a Union State of Russia and Belarus.

Historical Treaty Collections – USSR

For an extensive list of sources relevant to the time period when Belarus was a part of the USSR (1922–1991), see chapter on the Russian Federation in the current edition of this book, pp. 422–451.

31 BELORUSSKAI͡A SSR V MEZHDUNARODNYKH OTNOSHENII͡AKH: MEZHDUNARODNYE DOGOVORY, KONVENT͡SII I SOGLASHENII͡A BELORUSSKOĬ SSR S INOSTRANNYMI GOSUDARSTVAMI, 1944–1959 [BYELORUSSIAN SSR IN INTERNATIONAL RELATIONS: INTERNATIONAL TREATIES, CONVENTIONS AND AGREEMENTS OF THE BYELORUSSIAN SSR WITH FOREIGN COUNTRIES, 1944–1959]
K.V. Kiselev, S.P. Margunskiĭ & A.S. Zaĭt͡sev (Minsk: Izd-vo Akademii Nauk Belorusskoĭ SSR, 1960).

Summary: Collection contains treaties of the BSSR for the period of 1944–1959. Treaties presented in groups based on the covered issues, i.e. treaties on political issues (e.g., peace treaties with individual countries – Bulgaria, Italy, Romania, Hungary, and Finland), legal issues (e.g., Convention on the Privileges and Immunities of the United Nations, Convention on the Nationality of Married Women, Convention on the High Seas), the issues of labor regulation and social security (e.g., the Charter of the International Labour Organization), healthcare issues (e.g., the Charter (Constitution) of the World Health Organization), the peaceful use of nuclear energy (e.g., the Charter of the

International Agency on Atomic Energy), communication (e.g., the European Convention of Broadcasting), meteorology (e.g., the Convention of the World Meteorological Organization), education, science and culture (e.g., Constitution of the United Nations Educational, Scientific and Cultural Organisation), and improvement of fate of war victims (e.g., the 1949 Geneva Conventions).

32 BELORUSSKAI͡A SSR V MEZHDUNARODNYKH OTNOSHENII͡AKH: MNOGOSTORONNIE MEZHDUNARODNYE DOGOVORY, KONVENT͡SII I SOGLASHENII͡A BSSR, 1960–1980 [BYELORUSSIAN SSR IN INTERNATIONAL RELATIONS: MULTILATERAL INTERNATIONAL TREATIES, CONVENTIONS AND AGREEMENTS OF THE BSSR, 1960–1980] Ministerstvo inostrannykh del Belorusskoĭ SSR [Ministry of Foreign Affairs of the Byelorussian SSR], A.A. Zarit͡skiĭ, ed. (Minsk: Belarus′, 1983).

Summary: Contains treaties of the BSSR for the period 1960–1980 divided into several groups based on the covered issues, i.e. issues of disarmament (e.g., the 1963 Treaty Banning Nuclear Weapon Tests in the Atmosphere, in Outer Space and under Water, the 1976 Convention on the Prohibition of Military or Any Other Hostile Use of Environmental Modification Techniques), legal issues (e.g., the Vienna Convention on Diplomatic Relations and the International Convention on the Elimination of All Forms of Racial Discrimination), economic relations (e.g., the 1961 European Convention on International Commercial Arbitration), the issues of labor regulation (e.g., the Convention concerning Minimum Age for Admission to Employment (No. 138)), cultural relations (e.g., the Convention concerning the International Exchange of Publications), healthcare and environment (e.g., the 1961 Single Convention on Narcotic Drugs, the Convention on Long-range Transboundary Air Pollution), and the issues of transport (e.g., the 1968 Vienna Convention on Road Traffic, and the 1972 Customs Convention on Containers).

Historical Treaty Collections – Imperial Russia

For a list of sources relevant to this period of history of Belarus (end of the 18th century-1917), see chapter on the Russian Federation in the current edition of this book.

Yearbooks and Digests of State Practice

33 MINISTRY OF FOREIGN AFFAIRS OF THE REPUBLIC OF BELARUS URL: http://www.mfa.gov.by.

Summary: Official web-site of the Ministry of Foreign Affairs of Belarus. Includes press releases on the issues of foreign policy issued by the Ministry of

Foreign Affairs, statements and speeches made by the Minister of Foreign Affairs, Deputy Foreign Minister, delegations of the Republic of Belarus to the international organizations, such as the United Nations and the Organization for Security and Co-operation in Europe (OSCE), its ambassadors, and publications of the Ministry of Foreign Affairs (e.g., contains archive of *The Foreign Economic Review* for 2007–2009).

Note: A keyword search service is available.

Note: In Belarusian/Russian and English.

34 MINISTRY OF JUSTICE OF THE REPUBLIC OF BELARUS

URL: http://www.minjust.by.

Summary: Official web-site of the Ministry of Justice of the Republic of Belarus. The Ministry implements international treaties of Belarus on legal assistance related to the activities of the courts, the public notary, and registration of acts of civil status. Under section "*International Cooperation*," the web-site contains the lists of multilateral treaties of Belarus in the legal field and bilateral treaties on legal assistance in civil matters. As of June 2013, the first list includes 9 multilateral treaties with the notes on their place and date of signing and the date of entry into force for Belarus, as well as information on the functions performed by the Ministry of Justice of the Republic of Belarus with regard to such treaties. The second list contains information on 12 bilateral treaties concluded by Belarus, their date and place of signing, date of entry into force for Belarus, and information on the functions performed by the Ministry of Justice with regard to such treaties. These lists are on the Russian version of the web-site.

Note: In the area of international humanitarian law, the web-site provides information on the work of the Commission on the Implementation of the International Humanitarian Law. It also lists international treaties of Belarus on international humanitarian law issues. This list is available both on the Russian and English versions of the web-site.

35 NATIONAL CENTRE OF LEGISLATION AND LEGAL RESEARCH OF THE REPUBLIC OF BELARUS

URL: http://center.gov.by.

Summary: Official web-site of the National Centre of Legislation and Legal Research of the Republic of Belarus – a scientific and practical state institution which prepares drafts of normative legal acts, provides general guidance in the area of rule-making, and conducts research on the issues of law. In the area of international relations and foreign policy, the Russian version of the web-site provides comprehensive lists of the legislation and international agreements of Belarus on various topics (from general issues of international relations and foreign policy to human rights, international humanitarian law, economic cooperation, customs activity, energy, transport, telecommunications, standardization, intellectual property, etc.).

Note: Information is in Belarusian and Russian, partly also in English and German.

36 NATIONAL CENTER OF INTELLECTUAL PROPERTY

URL: http://www.belgospatent.org.by.

Summary: Official web-site of the National Center of Intellectual Property. Contains a list of treaties of the Republic of Belarus on intellectual property. As of June 2013, this includes 16 multilateral treaties concluded under the auspices of the World Intellectual Property Organization (WIPO) with references to the legal acts of accession of the Republic of Belarus to these treaties and the dates of entry into force of each treaty for Belarus, as well as the links to the texts of such treaties in Russian, the reference to the 1952 Universal Copyright Convention developed by UNESCO to which Belarus is a party, a list of six multilateral agreements concluded within the Commonwealth of Independent States (CIS) on the issues of intellectual property (with the links to the texts of most of these treaties in Russian), a reference to the 2010 Agreement on the Uniform Principles of Regulation in the Area of Protection and Enforcement of Intellectual Property Rights Concluded Within the Single Economic Area of the Republic of Belarus, the Russian Federation, and the Republic of Kazakhstan, references to five treaties on cooperation between Belarus and the WIPO, a list of bilateral intergovernmental treaties on cooperation in protection of intellectual property, and a list of bilateral treaties of interdepartmental character.

Note: Information and texts of the treaties are mostly in Russian.

Note: Texts of the relevant WIPO treaties in English can be found through the WIPO web-site.

Belgium

Ralph F. Gaebler and Gabriela Femenia

Issues of Treaty Succession

Modern Belgium dates from the Revolution of 1830, when the provinces that constitute roughly the present country separated from The Netherlands. Following the defeat of Napoleon, the two had been combined by the Congress of Vienna in order to contain French ambition in the north. At first, The Netherlands did not accept the result of the Belgian Revolution, but Belgium's independence was confirmed by the Treaty of London, of 15 November 1831, and eventually recognized by The Netherlands in 1839.[1]

Commentators disagree on the question of whether Belgium started life as a completely new legal entity (with The Netherlands retaining the legal personality of the former state), or as a successor state.[2] In addition to this question, there are a few other minor questions in Belgian history relating to the

1 Traité pour la séparation définitif de la Belgique d'avec la Hollande [Treaty for the Definitive Separation of Belgium from Holland between Austria, France, Great Britain, Prussia and Russia, and Belgium], Nov. 15, 1831, 82 Consol. T.S. 255, and Traité de paix (Traité de séparation) entre la Belgique et les Pays-Bas [Treaty between Belgium and the Netherlands relative to the Separation of their Respective Territories (Treaty of London)], April 19, 1839, 88 Consol. T.S. 427.

2 In Article 7 of the treaty of 1831, Belgium was declared "an independent state and perpetually neutral." Various other treaty articles and protocols of the London Conference assigned to Belgium obligations arising under earlier treaties. For example, Article 9 of the treaty required Belgium to accept Articles 108–117 of the General Act of the Congress of Vienna, concerning free use of navigable waterways separating or traversing the territories of Belgium and The Netherlands. Moreover, despite its enforced neutrality, Belgium was required to maintain fortresses along the French border formerly maintained by The Netherlands. *See* D.P. O'Connell, 2 State Succession in Municipal Law and International Law 263–364 (1967). In other regards, Belgium was a "blank slate," without any obligations respecting treaties to which The Netherlands was already a party. However, Paul Pradier-Fodéré expresses the view that the former Netherlands was extinguished and superseded by two successor states in 1831, at 1 Traité de Droit International Public Européen et Américain 251 (1885). His view is shared by Paul Fauchille, in Traité de Droit International Public 380 (8th rev. ed. 1921–22). Neither author infers from this any conclusions concerning the continuing effect of treaties in Belgium, but it should be noted that at least in two cases, in 1840 and 1842, the *Cour de Cassation* applied pre-1830 treaties reciprocally abolishing the right of escheat. O'Connell, *supra* at 96, 341–42.

 | doi 10.1163/9789004272224_008

possible extinction of treaties due to state succession.[3] Several of these questions arose from Belgium's decision to convert the Belgian Congo into a colony in 1908. According to Masquelin, this resulted in (1) the extinction of treaties between Belgium and the formerly independent Congo; (2) the succession of Belgium to the rights and obligations of treaties concluded prior to 1908 between the independent Congo and third states; and (3) the extension to the Belgian Congo of treaties concluded prior to 1908 by Belgium and third states. With the exception of treaties involving public debt or political questions, Belgian law regarded the Republic of Congo, when it achieved independence, as bound by treaties concluded by Belgium during the period of its colonial status.[4]

As in the case of many other European nations, additional succession issues arose from the unifications of Germany and Italy in the 19th century, as well as from the disruption of diplomatic relations caused by both world wars in the 20th. With respect to the unification of Germany and Italy, Belgian law regarded as still in effect treaties concluded by Belgium and the former states from which Germany and Italy were constituted.[5] Following World War I, the resumption of bilateral treaty rights and obligations between Belgium and the central powers was governed by the Treaty of Versailles. Resumption of multilateral treaty rights and obligations between Belgium and the former central powers was determined by the same treaty, as well as by separate peace treaties concluded in 1919 and 1920. Following World War II, resumption of bilateral treaty rights was governed by individual peace treaties, while the resumption of multilateral treaty rights was not specifically addressed.[6]

Treaty Ratification and Implementation

Constitutional reform, culminating in 1993, has converted Belgium from a unitary to a federal state, separated into three regions. Under this new

3 These questions are discussed in Jean Masquelin, Le Droit des Traités dans l'Ordre Juridique et dans la Pratique Diplomatique Belges (Bruxelles: Bruylant, 1980). A fairly lengthy bibliography of commentary on treaties in Belgian law can be found in 14 Répertoire Pratique du Droit Belge 733 (1953).

4 *See* Masquelin, *supra* note 3, at 599–601.

5 *See* Masquelin, *supra* note 3, at 600–01.

6 *See* Masquelin, *supra* note 3, at 618–19, for citation to applicable treaty articles, as well as to notifications of treaty resumptions in the Moniteur Belge.

arrangement, the national government retains jurisdiction only over matters granted to it in the Constitution (Article 35). While the regions retain jurisdiction over all matters not otherwise granted expressly to the national government, this plenary power does not extend to the power to make treaties. By the terms of Article 127, Section 1, the regions have power to conclude treaties only in matters relating to culture and some aspects of education. In addition to treaties that fall exclusively within the competence of the national government, and those that fall likewise within the jurisdiction of the regional governments, there are also mixed treaties that concern both.

National treaties are signed by either the prime minister or the minister of foreign affairs, pursuant to a royal decree granted by the king, who technically holds the "*jus tractati*." In the case of regional treaties, the regional head of government holds the *jus tractati*; he may himself sign the treaty, or confer authority to do so on another person. Ratification of national treaties requires that they be approved by both the Chamber of Deputies and the Senate in the form of an act of approval. Regional treaties must similarly be approved by the regional parliaments, and mixed treaties must be approved by both the national and regional legislative bodies. Ratification of all treaties also requires signature by the king, following which treaties are published in the MONITEUR BELGE. [7]

Inclusion of self-executing treaties in Belgian law requires no special act of parliament. Once ratified, a self-executing treaty is automatically a part of the domestic legal order. In fact, under a 1971 Supreme Court judgment the provisions of a self-executing treaty take precedence over any conflicting statute, regardless of whether the conflicting statute was adopted before or after ratification of the treaty.[8]

---

7 For a concise explanation of the Belgian treaty process, *see Conclusion of Treaties*, KINGDOM OF BELGIUM, FOREIGN AFFAIRS, FOREIGN TRADE AND DEVELOPMENT COOPERATION, http://diplomatie.belgium.be/en/treaties/conclusion_of_treaties.

8 Etat Belge v. S.A. Fromagerie Franco-Suisse Le Ski, Cour de Cassation [Cass.] [Court of Cassation], 1er ch. May 27, 1971, PAS. 1971, I, 886 ; 86 JT 460 (1971), 2 COMM. MKT. REP. ¶8141 (1971). *See also* Case Note, *Conflicts between Treaties and Subsequently Enacted Statutes in Belgium: Etat Belge v. S.A. Fromagerie Franco-Suisse Le Ski*, 72 MICH. L. REV. 118 (1973–1974). A useful monograph on the implementation of Belgian treaties is Godelieve Craenen, DE STAATSRECHTELIJKE REGELING VAN AANVAARDING EN INVOERING VAN VERDRAGEN IN BELGIË (1996). This is an up-to-date treatment that includes information on the introduction into Belgian law of federal, regional and mixed treaties.

Annotated Bibliography of Sources

General Treaty Collections

1 MONITEUR BELGE—BELGISCH STAATSBLAD
(Bruxelles: Moniteur Belge, 1845–).
URL: http://justice.belgium.be/fr/service_public_federal_justice/organisation/moniteur_belge (French);
http://justitie.belgium.be/nl/overheidsdienst_justitie/organisatie/belgisch_staatsblad/ (Dutch)

Summary: Official record of Belgium's treaties, laws, subsidiary legislation and other binding legal texts. Published daily since 1898, with Dutch and French versions placed in columns side by side.[9] In 2003, print publication was stopped in favor of online publication, with the exception of a limited number of copies for use in local libraries.

Index: Includes annual subject and name indexes. There is also a commercially published monthly subject index and chronological list, entitled *TABLES LEGISLATIVES MENSUELLES, INDIQUANT LA DATE ET LA PAGE DU MONITEUR BELGE DE TOUTES LES DISPOSITIONS LÉGISLATIVES ET COMMUNICATIONS D'INTÉRÊT GÉNÉRAL ÉDICTÉES AU COURS DE L'ANNÉE* (Bruxelles: Maison Larcier, 1950–). Also, ACTU LBU published fortnightly (Digem: Kluwer Editions Juridiques Belgique; Story-Scientia, 1986–), summarizes enactments appearing in the MONITEUR BELGE. Organized by topic, it also includes a cumulative *Tableau Récapitulatif*, which indexes amendments to existing law, including treaties.

Note: Treaty texts usually appear within ten days to two weeks of ratification. However, according to C.F. Verbeke, approximately one third of Belgium's treaties are never published.[10]

---

9 For a fuller description of the MONITEUR BELGE, *see* Gloria Westfall, *Belgium*, 2 OFFICIAL PUBLICATIONS OF WESTERN EUROPE 28–29 (Eve Johansson ed., 1988).

10 *See* Christian F. Verbeke, BELGIAN LAW: AN ANNOTATED BIBLIOGRAPHIC GUIDE TO REFERENCE MATERIALS, 1803–1993, at 31 (1994). See also Jean Masquelin, *supra* note 3, at 324–42. Masquelin notes that there is no general requirement in Belgian law that treaties be published. Article 129 of the Belgian Constitution has been interpreted to require publication of self-executing treaties, i.e., treaties that have direct effect on individuals. Moreover, the Conseil d'Etat has issued a number of decisions requiring publication in certain instances: when treaties modify a treaty of general interest to the citizenry or have effects of general interest to the citizenry; when treaties replace earlier, published treaties; when treaties are referred to in other, published treaties. Finally, publication may be required by statutes governing certain categories of treaties, or even particular individual treaties, or by ratifying statutes. In practice, the Belgian government publishes all treaties which are subject to ratification, or which it deems to be of sufficient interest. However,

Note: The link labeled "La publication Moniteur belge" provides access to the official gazette beginning with June 1, 1997. A multi-field advanced search engine permits phrase and keyword queries of full text and document segments, such as title, date, document type, etc. in French, Dutch and German. Treaties can also be searched, using the link labeled "Les banques de données (législation consolidée)." The Justel consolidated legislation database provides the text of treaties published in the *MONITEUR BELGE* from 1870 to the present from 1870 forward. At a minimum, index records can be found for treaties back to 1839. Treaties in this database may be displayed only in text format, not in PDF.

Note: Available in microfiche, from Bruxelles: Credoc; New York: Clearwater Publishing Co., 1985?–. Microfilm edition of earlier issues (1944–1983) available from the New York Public Library.

Note: Succeeds the JOURNAL OFFICIEL DU GOUVERNEMENT DE LA BELGIQUE (1814–1815), JOURNAL OFFICIEL DU ROYAUME DES PAYS-BAS (1816–1830) (Bruxelles: Imprimeur du Roi, 1814–1830) and the BULLETIN OFFICIEL DES LOIS ET ARRÊTÉS ROYAUX DE LA BELGIQUE-STAATSBLAD DER WETTEN EN KONINKLYJKE BESLUITEN VAN BELGIË (1830–1845) (Bruxelles: Imprimeur de Weissenbruch, 1830–1844).

Note: Interrupted during World War I, and superseded by GESETZ – UND VERORDNUNGSBLATT FÜR DIE OKKUPIERTEN GEBIETE BELGIENS-BULLETIN OFFICIEL DES LOIS ET ARRÊTÉS POUR LE TERRITOIRE BELGE OCCUPÉ-WET – EN VERORDENINGSBLAD VOOR DE BEZETTE STREKEN VAN BELGIË (Brüssel: Drückerei des Gesetz – und Verordnungsblattes) (1914–1917), and by GESETZ – UND VERORDNUNGSBLATT FÜR FLANDERN (in German and Flemish) and GESETZ – UND VERORDNUNGBLATT FÜR WALLONIEN (in German and French) (1918). Total of 429 issues. Republished in French and English in 17 volumes as GERMAN LEGISLATION FOR THE OCCUPIED TERRITORIES OF BELGIUM, OFFICIAL TEXTS (Charles Henry Huberich & Alexander Nicolas Speyer eds., 1915–1919).

Note: Companion publication, entitled RECUEIL DES LOIS, DÉCRETS, ORDONNANCES ET RÈGLEMENTS—VERSAMELING DER WETTER, DECRETEN,

---

very long treaties, or treaties of largely technical interest, may be published by insertion of a notice in the MONITEUR BELGE that the treaties in question may be consulted at the Ministry of Foreign Affairs. The only statute governing publication of treaties generally is concerned with the manner of publication, if publication is to take place. Loi relative à l'emploi des langues en matière législative, à la présentation, à la publication et à l'entrée en vigueur des textes légaux et réglementaires [Law Concerning the Use of Languages in Legislation] of May 31, 1961, art. 8, MONITEUR BELGE [M.B.] [Official gazette of Belgium], June 21, 1961, 5171.

ORDONNANTIES EN VERORDENINGEN (Bruxelles: Moniteur Belge, 1830–), provides a selective, weekly compilation of new legislation and treaties reprinted from the MONITEUR BELGE. Issues include chronological and alphabetical indexes, and there are cumulative indexes for 1830–1860, 1860–1870, and 1871–1880. Title varies: RECUEIL DES LOIS ET ARRÊTÉS ROYAUX DE BELGIQUE-VERZAMELING DER WETTEN EN KONINKLIJKE BESLUITEN VAN BELGIË (1845–1961), RECUEIL DES LOIS ET ARRÊTÉS-VERZAMELING DER WETTEN EN BESLUITEN (1962–1972), RECUEIL DES LOIS, DÉCRETS, ET ARRÊTÉS-VERZAMELING DER WETTEN DECRETEN EN BESLUITEN (1973–1991).

2 MINISTRY OF FOREIGN AFFAIRS, FOREIGN TRADE AND DEVELOPMENT COOPERATION TREATY DATABASE
URL: http://diplomatie.belgium.be/fr/traites/ (French)
http://diplomatie.belgium.be/nl/Verdragen/ (Dutch)

Summary: The French and Dutch language versions of the Ministry of Foreign Affairs, Foreign Trade and Development Cooperation web site includes an index of treaties concluded since 1987. The index permits searches by country of opposite party or international organization, or by thematic topic. Individual entries provide dates of signature, entry into force in international law and publication in the MONITEUR BELGE, where applicable. It is best to search the MONITEUR BELGE by combining the text source (Service Public Federal Affaires Etrangeres) with keywords from the title of the treaty, and not to search by date of publication, since there are some misprints of dates in the indexed entries.

Note: The Foreign Ministry web site enhances the consolidated legislation database at no. 1, above, because it permits the researcher to identify treaties by country of opposite party and by broad thematic category (though not both, unfortunately) before searching the MONITEUR.

3 RECUEIL DE LA LEGISLATION GENERALE EN VIGUEUR EN BELGIQUE
Publié par une Commission du Conseil de Législation Institué auprès du Ministère de la Justice
(Bruxelles: E. Bruylant, 1932–1959).

Summary: Edited by a legislative council of the Ministry of Justice, this set contains the text of treaties and law concluded or adopted from 1487–1921 and still in force at the time of publication.

Note: Vol. 1 contains all texts from 1487–1814. Texts are arranged chronologically. Treaties are contained in Section B.

4 RECUEIL DES TRAITES ET CONVENTIONS CONCERNANT LE ROYAUME DE BELGIQUE

Désiré de Garcia de la Véga and Alphonse de Busschere. (Bruxelles: J. Lebègue, 1850–1914).

Summary: Vol. I includes treaties concluded from 1831–1849, arranged chronologically. The treaties range over the following subject matter: politics, commerce, succession to property located in other countries, extradition, postal service and official communications concerning registration of agreements and collection of registration duties. Vol. 1 also includes a useful summary of diplomatic activity from 1831–1838, relating to the separation of Belgium and The Netherlands. Supplements 1 (1851) and 2 (1854) comprise vol. II. They contain treaties concluded during the intervening years, as well as additional treaties ranging back to 1816, and not included in Vol. I. Vols. III–XXI were published irregularly, covering the following periods: vol. III (1859), 1854–1859; vol. IV (1862), 1814–1862; vol. V (1864), 1861–1864; vol. VI (1866), 1862–1864; vol. VII, 1865–1868; vol. VIII (1870), 1866–1871; vol. IX (1875), 1872–1875; vol. X (1878), 1849–1878; vol. XI (1882), 1877–1881; vol. XII (1883), 1880–1882; vol. XIII, 1882–1886; vol. XIV, 1884–1889; vol. XV, 1888–1891; vol. XVI (1898), 1887–1896; vol. XVII (1901), 1851–1900; vol. XVIII (1904), 1867–1903; vol. XIX (1909), 1889–1909; vol. XX (1910), 1888–1910; vol. XXI (1914), 1905–1913. All texts are in French.

Set includes notices, extracted from the MONITEUR BELGE (see no. 1 above), of ratification, denunciation, etc., by all signatory nations, concerning the treaties reproduced. The RECUEIL also includes extracts of some acts, diplomatic documents, and decrees deemed relevant to application of the treaties. For example, vol. IV includes travaux préparatoires relating to the treaties that separated Belgium from The Netherlands. In addition, the RECUEIL includes a few pre-1814 treaties, all of which are listed in the chronological index in vol. XVIII. Finally, the RECUEIL includes a number of brief exposés, or commentaries, on aspects of Belgian diplomatic activity during the period covered.

Index: Vol. I includes topical and chronological indexes (the latter organized by country of opposite party). Vol. II includes a topically arranged table of treaties currently in force (as of 1854) and a cumulative index of treaties arranged by country and date. Vol. III includes a topical, cumulative index of treaties. Vols. IV and V include cumulative indexes of treaties and other documents organized by date and country. Vol. VI includes both a volume index, organized by date, and a cumulative index of treaties and other documents organized by date. Vols. VIII, IX, XI and XII include both volume indexes organized by date, and cumulative indexes, organized by type of document. Vol. X includes both a volume index organized by date, and a cumulative index of Vols. I–IX, organized by type of document. Vols. XVI and XVII include volume indexes organized by date. Vol. XVIII includes chronological volume and cumulative indexes. Vols. XIX, XX, and XXI include chronological volume indexes.

Note: Imprint varies. Vol. I, Bruxelles: C.-J.-A. Greuse; Supplement 1, Bruxelles: M. Hayez; Supplement 2, Bruxelles: F. Parent; Vols. III–VIII, Bruxelles: Aug. Decq; Vols. IX–XIV, Bruxelles: Librarie Polytechnique de Decq et Duhent; Vols. XV–XVI, Namur: Librarie Doufils, Victor Delvauz, successeur; Vols. XIII–XXI, Bruxelles: J. Lebègue et Cie.

Note: Editor varies: Désiré de Garcia de la Véga, Vols. I–XVI; Alphonse de Busschere, Vols. XVII–XXI.

5 CODES DES RELATIONS EXTERIEURES DE LA BELGIQUE

J.-B. Lanckman, ed. (Braine-Le-Comte: Zech & Fils, 1892).

Summary: Collection of in-force treaties divided into three parts. First part contains multilateral treaties. Second part contains bilateral treaties, organized by country. Third part contains laws related to the treaties reprinted in the first and second parts. Many texts are extracts, with references either to the MONITEUR BELGE (see no. 1, above) or to RECUEIL DES TRAITÉS (see no. 2, above). All texts are in French.

Index: Includes detailed subject index.

Note: Supersedes earlier work, entitled TRAITÉS DE COMMERCE ET DE NAVIGATION, CONVENTIONS RELATIVES AUX ATTRIBUTIONS CONSULAIRES AINSI QU'À LA PROPRIÉTÉ ARTISTIQUE, LITTÉRAIRE OU INDUSTRIELLE, ACTUELLEMENT EN VIGUEUR ENTRE LA BELGIQUE ET LES PAYS ETRANGERS (Bruxelles: au Bureau de la Revue Commerciale et Juridique, 1883, 558 pp.), which was supplemented twice, in 1885 (38 pp.) and in 1888.

6 CODE DE TRAITES ET ARRANGEMENTS INTERNATIONAUX INTERESSANT LA BELGIQUE

Complété 1° Par les Traités Conclus par l'Etat du Congo, 2° Par Divers Actes Internationaux Fixant des Règles de Droit Public International, 3° Par la Législation Relative aux Principales Matières Faisant l'Objet des Traités.

Alphonse De Busschere, ed. (Bruxelles: J. Lebègue & Cie, 1896–7).

Summary: The two-volume set contains 647 treaties and related texts of general interest, concluded from 1718–1897. Treaties are arranged in five parts, each corresponding to a particular subject area. Vol. 1 contains the first four parts, which cover (1) political treaties, especially those concerned with sovereignty, independence, and Belgian borders, (2) acts relative to the independent state of the Congo, (3) acts related to rail, post, telephone and telegraph and (4) extradition treaties, treaties related to suppression of certain criminal activities, and treaties related to forest and rural areas, hunting, and fishing. Vol. 2 contains consular treaties and those related to (5) commerce, customs duties and navigation, as well as miscellaneous treaties and (6) a supplementary part, containing information on modifications and denunciations, as well as a few additional treaties too recent for inclusion in Vol. 1. Each part is subdivided into multilateral treaties, bilateral treaties, and related Belgian laws. The texts are arranged chronologically within the sub-parts. All texts are in French; many are extracts only, but all are annotated and include references to where they appear in full-text in the MONITEUR BELGE (see no. 1, above).

Index: Each part begins with a detailed table of contents. Vol. 2 includes both a comprehensive chronological index, and a comprehensive, detailed subject index.

7 PASINOMIE

Collection Complète Des Lois, Décrets, Ordonnances, Arrêtes Et Règlements Généraux Qui Peuvent Etre Invoqués En Belgique (Bruxelles: Etablissements Emile Bruylant, 1833–).

Summary: Monthly compilation of laws and other binding legal instruments, including treaties. Each issue includes a table of contents, in which all newly ratified treaties are listed under the heading, "traités." Published in eight series: 1st series, 1788–1813 (16 vols.); 2nd series, 1814–1830 (9 vols.); 3rd series, 1831–1865 (35 vols.); 4th series, 1865–1908 (43 vols.); 5th series, 1909–1933 (24 vols.); 6th series, 1934–1951 (1 vol.); 7th series, 1951–1993 (2 vols.), 8th series, 1993–. All documents are in French.

Index: 1st series indexed by *Table Analytique et Raisonée*, in two volumes continuously paginated (Bruxelles: Société Typographique Belge, 1838). Cumulative indexes subsequently published covering the periods 1814–1830, 1831–1860, 1860–1870, and 1871–1880. Vol. for 1926 contains an index for the years 1921–1926.

Note: Unnumbered pre-volume published in 1851, entitled PASINOMIE: INTRODUCTION À LA PREMIÈRE SÉRIE, contains French acts adopted prior to 1789, and rendered obligatory in Belgium. Also includes "le texte des actes relatifs à la première invasion française, un exposé succinct de l'administration du pays du 25 octobre 1792 au 16 frimaire an V,…précédée de l'histoire des principes, des institutions et des lois, pendant la Révolution française."

Note: Edition published by Bruylant-Christophe et Cie (1860), numbered in consecutive volumes, from vol. 1–41, includes legislation back to 1539. Vol. 1 covers 1539–1789. Edition continues with 1861, numbered 3rd series, vol. 31.

Note: Title varies. Vols. for 1915–1918 contain a second part, entitled LOIS ET ARRÊTÉS DU GOUVERNEMENT GÉNÉRAL ALLEMAND EN BELGIQUE POUR LE TERRITORIE BELGE OCCUPÉ. Subtitle of 5th series, vols. 1–22, includes "*des lois, décrets et arrêtés de la colonie du Congo belge.*" From 1942–1944, during period of German occupation, issued together with BULLETIN USUEL DES LOIS ET ARRÊTÉS (see no. 7, below), to form BULLETIN USUEL DES LOIS ET ARRÊTÉS ET PASINOMIE REUNIS. Vols. for 1946–1974 have subtitle, COLLECTION COMPLÈTE DES LOIS, ARRÊTÉS ET RÈGLEMENTS GENÉRAUX.

Note: Publisher varies: Bruxelles: Administration Centrale de la Pasicrisie, 1860–1941.

8 BULLETIN USUEL DES LOIS ET ARRETES
(Bruxelles: Etablissements Emile Bruylant, 1851–).

Summary: Semi-monthly collection (20 issues per year) of statutes, decrees and treaties. Documents are arranged chronologically, and accessed via a cumulative annual subject index. All documents are in French. Current lag time between adoption and publication is approximately four years.

Note: From 1942–1944, during the period of German occupation, issued with PASINOMIE (see no. 6, above), to form BULLETIN USUEL DES LOIS ET ARRÊTÉS ET PASINOMIE REUNIS.

9 LEX BELGICA. RECUEIL PERMANENT DE LA LEGISLATION ET DE LA REGLEMENTATION GENERALE IN BELGIQUE—PERMANENTE VERZAMELING VAN DE WETGEVING EN DE ALGEMENE REGLEMENTERING DIE IN BELGIE VAN KRACHT IS
Victor Crabbe, general ed. (Bruxelles: Centre d'Administration et de Documentation; Heule: UGA, 1953–?).

Summary: Looseleaf collection of legislation (including treaties) currently in effect. In Dutch and French.

Treaty Indexes

10 REPERTOIRE DES TRAITES CONCLUS PAR LA BELGIQUE—REPERTORIUM VAN DE DOOR BELGIE GESLOTEN VERDRAGEN
Ignace de Troyer, ed. (Bruxelles: J. Goemaere, 1973–1988). 2 vols.

Summary: Contains comprehensive index of more than 6,300 treaties concluded by Belgium from 1830–1986. Main entries are arranged chronologically and provide the following information: title, parties, subject, place of signature, date of signature, date of ratifying statute (in cases submitted to Parliament for its approbation), date of exchange or deposit of instruments of ratification, date of entry into force, source of printed publication (e.g.,

MONITEUR BELGE, RECUEIL DES TRAITÉS, UNITED NATIONS TREATY SERIES, etc.), date of registration with the United Nations (where applicable) and date of cessation (where applicable). The latter case includes instances of denunciation, explicit or implicit abrogation by subsequent treaty, cessation due to fulfillment of purpose, and explicit or implicit termination due to extinction of one of the parties. Vol. 2 includes a list of treaties in force in 1988. Vol. 1 includes an annex listing the following: treaties concluded by the International Association of the Congo; treaties concluded by the Independent State of the Congo with countries other than Belgium, listed by country and date; treaties concluded by Belgium concerning the Congo (beginning in 1908) and Rwanda-Burundi (beginning in 1919), organized by country and date. Vol. 1 covers 1830–1940. Vol. 2 covers 1941–1986. Main entries are printed in both French and Dutch, in parallel columns.

Index: Each volume includes the following: an index of bilateral treaties, organized by country and date; an index of multilateral treaties, listed by date; a topical index, in which treaties are listed by subject and by date.

11 ALMANACH ROYAL OFFICIEL

Ministère de l'Interieur. (Bruxelles: Guyot, 1840–1939).

Summary: Annual almanac of government personnel, both in Belgium and in colonial offices abroad. Includes a list of treaties currently in force. Multilateral treaties are listed chronologically, followed by a subject index. Bilateral treaties are listed by country. Citations are to the MONITEUR BELGE.

Topical and Selected Treaty Collections

12 TRACTATEN EN TRACTAATSBEPALINGEN DE SCHELDE BETREFFENDE SINDS 1648

('s-Gravenhage: Gebrs. J.& H. van Langenhuysen, 1919).

Summary: Contains the text of 33 treaties or clauses excerpted from treaties, all dealing with the Scheide River, which provides access to Antwerp, but the mouth of which is in The Netherlands, and has been opened and closed to traffic at various periods in history, depending on relations between The Netherlands and Belgium. Treaties range from 1648 to 1912, and are arranged in chronological order. Most texts are in Dutch, but a few are in French. Includes an index arranging the treaties under eight broad subject areas: buoys and beacons, commerce and navigation in general, navigation on the Scheide, the Ghent Canal, pilotage, separation of Belgium and The Netherlands, customs and duties, and illumination.

Note: Many of the treaties are reprinted from Georg F. de Martens, RECUEIL DES PRINCIPAUX TRAITÉS (Göttingen: 1791–1801) and its various supplements and later editions.

Diplomatic Documents

13 DOCUMENTS DIPLOMATIQUE BELGE, 1920–1940: LA POLITIQUE DE SÉCURITÉ EXTÉRIEUR

Charles De Visscher and Fernand van Langenhove, eds. (Bruxelles: Palais des Académies, 1964–66). 5 vols.

Summary: Contains documents tracing the diplomatic activity of Belgium during the 20 years prior to World War II. Coverage is as follows:

vol. 1 (1920–1924); vol. 2 (1925–1931); vol. 3 (1931–1936); vol. 4 (1936–1937); vol. 5 (1938–1940).

Note: Published as first title in a monographic series, entitled DOCUMENTS RELATIFS AU STATUT INTERNATIONAL DE LA BELGIQUE DEPUIS 1830—BESCHEIDEN BETREFFENDE HET INTERNATIONAAL STATUUT VAN BELGIË SEDERT 1830, under the sponsorship of the Académie Royale de Belgique, Commission Royale d'Histoire—Koninklijke Academie van België, Koninklijke Commissie voor Geschiedenis.

14 LA POLITIQUE EXTERIEURE DE LA BELGIQUE EN [YEAR]

Unité des Relations Internationales, Département des Affaires Publiques et Internationales, Université Catholique de Louvain, under the direction of Christian Franck and Claude Roosens. (Louvain-la-Neuve: Academia, 1986–1991).

Summary: Annual survey of Belgian foreign relations. Includes *Chroniques*, which comprise brief articles organized by topic and global region; *Etudes*, which are longer articles that summarize developments and historical trends in more detail; and a *Chronologie*, which provides a detailed summary of all relevant government actions, organized by topic and date. Also includes a bibliography of books and articles published during the year, organized by topic. Series commences with coverage of 1984–1985.

Note: Title terminated with AUX TOURNANTS DE L'HISTOIRE: LA POLITIQUE EXTÉRIEURE DE LA BELGIQUE AU DÉBUT DE LA DÉCENNIE 90: SÉCURITÉ EUROPÉENNE NOUVELLE, CRISES AFRICAINES, TRAITÉ DE MAASTRICHT, GUERRE DU GOLFE (Bruxelles: De Boeck, 1993).

15 WEBSITE OF BELGIAN MINISTRY OF FOREIGN AFFAIRS, FOREIGN TRADE AND DEVELOPMENT COOPERATION — DOCUMENTATION

URL: http://diplomatie.belgium.be/fr/documentation/ (French)
http://diplomatie.belgium.be/nl/Documentatie/ (Dutch)

Summary: The French and Dutch versions of the Documentation portal of the Ministry's website contain the text of various foreign policy and development cooperation position papers and reports, as well as related laws. Some content is also available in German and English.

16 THE NEW GUIDE TO THE DIPLOMATIC ARCHIVES OF WESTERN EUROPE

Daniel M. Thomas and Lynn M. Case, eds. (Philadelphia: U. of Pennsylvania Press, 1975).

Summary: Chapter on Belgium appears at pp. 20–42. Describes the archive maintained by the Foreign Ministry, separate from the national Archives Générales du Royaume-Algemeen Rijksarchief. Includes information on the history and organization of the archive, classification of materials, and inventories and guides to locating items in the collection.

Yearbooks and Other Digests of Practice in International Law

17 REVUE BELGE DE DROIT INTERNATIONAL—BELGIAN REVIEW OF INTERNATIONAL LAW—BELGISCH TIJDSCHRIFT VOOR INTERNATIONAAL RECHT

Belgian Society of International Law, together with assistance from the Minister of Foreign Affairs, the Minister of Justice, the Minister of the French Community and the Minister of the Flemish Community. (Bruxelles: Bruylant, 1965–).

Summary: Semi-annual publication, which includes occasional, detailed summaries of Belgian practice in international law. Each summary covers a period of several years. Also includes periodic reports to the International Law Association (e.g., *Belgian Report to the International Law Association Committee on International Law in National Courts*, 29 REV. BELGE DROIT INT'L. 259 (1996).

Note: Author varies: Centre de Droit International et de Sociologie Appliquée au Droit International de l'Université Libre de Bruxelles, Centre de Droit International de l'Université Catholique de Louvain, 1965–1976.

Note: Publisher varies: Editions de l'Institut de Sociologie, 1965–1971; Editions de l'Université de Bruxelles, 1972–1976.

18 RECUEIL ANNUEL DE JURISPRUDENCE BELGE: CONTINANT LES SOMMAIRES DE TOUTE LA JURISPRUDENCE ET DE TOUS LES ARTICLES DE DOCTRINE PARUS EN BELGIQUE

Jacques, Christian, and Claude Lepaffe, eds. (Bruxelles: Ferdinand Larcier, 1949–2007).

Summary: Annual digest of Belgian court decisions and scholarly articles. Organized by topic, includes a section on "*Traités et Conventions Internationaux.*" Also includes cross-references to other topics.

Index: Each issue includes chronological, name, and alphabetical subject indexes. *Tables Decennales,* published in 1961 and 1972, cover the years 1949–1970.

Note: Author varies: Charles Van Reepinghen, together with Robert Pirson, Cyr Cambier and Jacques Lepaffe. Publication appears to have ceased in 2007.

19 TEXTES ET DOCUMENTS — TEKSTEN EN DOCUMENTEN
(Bruxelles: Ministère des Affaires Etrangères, du Commerce Extérieur et de la Coopération au Développement).

Summary: Monographic series published at irregular intervals and covering a wide range of subject matter. Many of the titles concern Belgian foreign policy, and include documentary appendices. For example, there is a series within the series, entitled LA POLITIQUE ETRANGÈRE DE LA BELGIQUE, in which, for example, no. 308 (1976, 405 pp.) covers the years 1973–1975 and no. 310 (1977, 204 pp.) the year 1976. Another series within the series, entitled DOCUMENTS D'HISTOIRE DE BELGIQUE (1977–1978, nos. 314 and 316), covers the history of Belgium to that point. Further examples of TEXTES ET DOCUMENTS concerned with foreign relations include no. 328 (1981, 100 pp.), entitled LA BELGIQUE ET LES DROITS DE L'HOMME, and no. 332 (1984, 167 pp.), entitled LA POLITIQUE AFRICAINE DE LA BELGIQUE. Published in six languages, in English under the series title, MEMO FROM BELGIUM. Described by one source as comprising "serious studies…for [Belgian foreign ministry] personnel abroad."[11]

---

11 *See* Westfall, *supra* note 7, at 32.

Canada

Ralph F. Gaebler

Issues of Treaty Succession

It has often been claimed that Canadian sovereignty "was acquired in the period between its separate signature of the Treaty of Versailles in 1919 and the Statute of Westminster, 1931."[1] The latter enacted into law the principle that Imperial statutes of the British Parliament could not extend to Canada without Canada's consent. It also abolished the prohibition on Canadian amendments to existing Imperial statutes, which derived from the Colonial Laws Validity Act of 1865.

Before the 1920s, Canada had no power to bind itself in international law. However, when it did acquire independence, there seems never to have been any question about the continuing force of treaty obligations contracted by Great Britain on behalf of Canada. In fact, the two book-length studies of Canadian treaty-making in English do not even mention the question of state succession.[2]

Without doubt, the assumption that independent Canada acceded to Empire treaties derives from the fact that it never broke the chain of legal authority extending back into its colonial past. Canada's path to independence was gradual, and its final separation from Great Britain was both peaceful and amicable. Therefore, it accepted not only treaty obligations but also the legislation adopted by both the British and colonial Parliaments. This entire body of law remained in force, subject to termination or alteration through repeal or amendment.

Despite the stability of Canada's history with respect to succession, an interesting speculative question is whether, and to what extent, an independent and sovereign Quebec would be bound by the existing body of

1 Supreme Court of Canada, Reference re Ownership of Mineral Rights, [1967] S.C.R. 792, 816, 65 D.L.R. 2d 353, 375. *See generally* Robert MacGregor Dawson, The Development of Dominion Status, 1900–1936 (1937).

2 A.E. Gotlieb, Canadian Treaty-making (1968), and A. Jacomy-Millette, Treaty Law in Canada (1975). *See also* Christian L. Wiktor, Canadian Bibliography of International Law (1984), for a list of articles concerning succession to treaties by Canada (p.156) and a list of articles on Canada's power to conclude treaties (pp. 150–54). For a more recent title, in French, *see* France Morrissette, Les Procédures Canadienne et Communautaure de Conclusion des Traités (Montréal: Wilson & Lafleur, 2008).

 | DOI 10.1163/9789004272224_009

Canadian treaty law. The process Quebec would have to follow in order to secede from Canada in a manner legally valid within the municipal law of Canada is laid out in an advisory opinion handed down by the Canadian Supreme Court, *Reference Re Secession of Quebec*.[3] This decision states that "[n]egotiations following a referendum vote in favour of seeking secession would inevitably address a wide range of issues, many of great import."[4] However, the decision does not address specifically the question of possible treaty succession.

In Bill 1, *An Act Respecting the Future of Quebec*, a 1995 provincial statute enacted by the Quebec National Assembly in anticipation of achieving sovereignty through a unilateral declaration of independence, the Quebec government indicated that all of Canada's treaties would continue in force for Quebec as well.[5] That Quebec would wish to succeed to all of Canada's treaties is understandable, considering that Canada is party to hundreds of multilateral treaties and more than 1,000 bilateral treaties. Canada has concluded 279 treaties with the United States alone. (See no. 7, below.) Succession to these treaties would instantly incorporate Quebec into the international community and obviate the necessity of expending enormous political resources to achieve the same result. Moreover, an independent Quebec would self-evidently benefit from continued participation in the North American Free Trade Agreement without having to re-negotiate the terms of its NAFTA membership.

Nevertheless, at least one commentator has argued that customary law would impose the "clean slate" doctrine on a newly independent Quebec, according to which it would, with some exceptions (including NAFTA), be free unilaterally to succeed, or not, to Canada's multilateral treaty obligations, but would have to reach agreement with countries of opposite party to ensure the survival of bilateral treaty commitments.[6]

---

3 [1998] 2 S.C.R. 217. The decision is summarized in Pierre Bienvenu, *Secession by Constitutional Means: the Decision of the Supreme Court of Canada in the Québec Secession Reference*, 23 Hamline J. Pub. L. & Pol'y 185 (2001).

4 [1998] 2 S.C.R. 217 at paragraph 96.

5 35th Leg., Québec, 1995, §15.

6 D.B. Majzub, *Does Secession Mean Succession? The International Law of Treaty Succession and an Independent Québec*, 24 Queen's L. J. 411 (1999). The argument is complex, but comes down to the claim that customary international law does not support the presumption of treaty continuity in cases of secession, despite the fact that article 34 of the Vienna Convention on Succession of States in Respect of Treaties does so; see Vienna Convention on Succession of States in Respect of Treaties art. 34, Aug. 23, 1978, 1946 U.N.T.S. 3.

Treaty Ratification and Implementation

Canada acquired international legal personality during the decade following the Versailles Conference of 1919, as part of its transition from dominion to independent state. Milestones along the way included Canada's separate signature on the Versailles Treaty, the Halibut Fisheries Convention,[7] which was the first treaty Canada negotiated and signed independently, and the 1926 Balfour Declaration, which endorsed the principle of equality of status within the Commonwealth for the purpose of signing and ratifying all bilateral treaties, regardless of subject.[8] By 1927 Canada was able to appoint a minister to the United States who was not attached to the British embassy, but to a separate mission.

Canadian treaty law is modeled on that of Great Britain. Therefore, treaties are not considered part of the municipal law of Canada absent a statute giving them this effect. Treaties that purport to affect the legal rights of individuals, and which therefore require some change in the internal law, can only be effected through the adoption of a statute that makes the requisite change, or through some act carried out by the executive. A certain complication derives from the fact that the only constitutional provision regarding treaty implementation occurs in the Constitution (British North America) Act, 1857, Section 132. Adopted long before Canada's independence, this provision states that "[t]he Parliament and Government of Canada shall have all Powers necessary or proper for performing the Obligations of Canada or of any Province thereof, as Part of the British Empire, towards Foreign Countries, arising under Treaties between the Empire and such Foreign Countries." Because Parliament's power is limited by this provision to implementation of Empire treaties, the Judicial Committee of the Privy Council held in the *Labour Conventions* case that it does not apply to treaty obligations undertaken by Canada acting independently.[9] Instead, it held that treaties requiring a change in statute law must be implemented by either the federal Parliament or the provincial Parliaments, depending on the subject matter. Therefore, one must look to the Constitution (British North America) Act, 1857, Sections 91 (federal jurisdiction) and 92 (provincial jurisdiction) to determine

7 Convention between United States of America and Canada for Preservation of Halibut Fisheries of the Northern Pacific Ocean, U.S.-Can., March 2, 1923, 43 Stat. 1841.

8 *Report of the Inter-Imperial Relations Committee of the Imperial Conference*, 1926. Cmd. 2768, reprinted in 21 AM. J. IN'TL L. SUPP. 21–38 (1927).

9 A.-G. Can. v. A.-G. Ont. (Labour Conventions) [1937] A.C. 326 (P.C.) (appeal taken from Can.).

which of these authorities has the responsibility for implementation in any given case.[10]

Under the Canadian Constitution, the conduct of international relations falls within the prerogative powers of the Crown. Therefore, Parliament plays no necessary role in the treaty-making process. Most international obligations are incurred simply through an exchange of notes with foreign states. However, if formal ratification is required, the Secretary of State for External Affairs will sign an instrument of ratification which certifies that the government of Canada has ratified the treaty. At one time the government submitted only about 25% of treaties to Parliament for its approval, but now follows a policy of tabling all treaties in the House of Commons for at least 21 sitting days, even those requiring provincial, rather than parliamentary, implementing legislation. However, it should be borne in mind that in most cases approval is given in the form of a resolution, rather than in the form of a statute, and therefore does not receive Royal assent. As mentioned above, legislation (federal or provincial) is required only when a treaty cannot be transposed into municipal law without altering or supplementing existing statutes or regulations.

Annotated Bibliography of Sources

General Treaty Collections

1 TREATY SERIES

Canada. Foreign Affairs and International Trade Canada. (Ottawa: F.A. Acland, 1929–).

At Head of Title: Dominion of Canada.

Summary: Coverage includes treaties, 1928–. The series is published as individual supplements, bound in annual volumes. Text is in English, 1928–, in French also, 1930–. Some multilateral treaties are also reproduced in other languages. Treaties are now available at the Government of Canada web site, at: http://www.treaty-accord.gc.ca/index.aspx. This collection is said to include "most treaties that apply to Canada..." Specifically, the database includes "bilateral treaties as soon as they enter into force and multilateral treaties if possible when the certified copy is received from

10 For commentary on the provincial role in treaty-making, see HUGO CYR, CANADIAN FEDERALISM AND TREATY POWERS: ORGANIC CONSTITUTIONALISM AT WORK (2009), AND ANNE MARIE JACOMY-MILLETTE ET AL., CANADIAN PROVINCES AND FOREIGN RELATIONS (1991).

the depositary of the treaty." Detailed entries include place and date of signature, date of coming into force, citation to publication in the Canada Treaty Series, and names of parties. The database does not include the text of all early treaties, including some that are still in force or partially in force. It is difficult to determine just how selective this database is, but it seems to vary by topic. For example, the texts of most extradition treaties and many boundary waters treaties are available, but far fewer environmental treaties and fisheries treaties are included. There is no indication that the Treaty Law Division plans to add currently missing treaties to the database, though one can probably presume that it is their intention to do so. The search interface permits one to search by date of signature, treaty publication number, and by keyword or subject, though it does not support multiple or combined keyword/subject searching. One can choose to search all treaties, or to limit the search to just bilateral or multilateral treaties. Bilateral treaty searching permits combination of subject/keyword and country-of-opposite party (which includes also international organizations). Interestingly, one may also search for "plurilateral treaties," defined as treaties "between one State and a group of States." Oddly, there is no link to this web site from the official web site of the Department of Foreign Affairs and International Trade. (See no. 16, below).

Index: Each volume contains an index by country. 1940, no. 16, includes index for 1928–1940. 1947, no. 1, includes an index for 1940–1945. 1960, no. 25, includes an index for 1946–1959. 1974, no. 1, includes an indexfor 1965–1974. Indexes are in English and French, with French on inverted pages. Indexes include lists of bilateral and multilateral treaties, and a subject list. There is also a cumulative list of treaties, 1979–, with each supplement.

Note: Imprint varies: J.P. Patenaude, 1934–1939; Edmond Cloutier, 1941–.

Note: Title varies: Canada Treaty Series, 1928 – ?

Note: Author varies: Department of External Affiars, 1929–1988. Department of External Affairs and International Trade Canada, 1989 – ?

Note: Also published in French, under the title, *Recueil Des Traités.* Index also published in French, under the title, *Index General: Recueil des Traités du Canada.*

Note: Canada Treaty Information web site (http://www.treaty-accord.gc.ca/procedures.aspx#tphp) includes a brief, but fairly detailed description of treaty negotiation and implementation procedures. See also *International Treaties: Canadian Practice,* prepared in 2000 by Daniel Dupras of the Law and Government Division, housed at the Government of Canada Publications web site: http://www.publications.gc.ca/Collection-R/LOPBdP/BP/prbøøø4-e

.htm#D.%c2%AOComing into Effect, Implementation and Ratification of a Treaty(txt).

2 TREATIES WITH CANADA
(Toronto: Carswell, ?–2001).

Summary: CD-ROM collection of more than 3,300 multilateral, bilateral and native treaties concluded by Canada or its predecessors since 1654. Includes some treaties never printed in the *Canada Treaty Series* (e.g., treaties creating the World Trade Organization and the World Intellectual Property Organization), as well as historical treaties predating the *Canada Treaty Series* (see no. 1, above). Additional, optional segments include some 150 land claims agreements between Canada and native peoples. Each treaty document may be viewed and printed in full text, and includes citations to Canadian, American, British and UN sources, as well as up-to-date signatory information. This title was updated semi-annually. Provides access via a variety of indexes.

Note: The title ceased publication with 2001, no.2.

Note: Runs under Adobe Acrobat software.

Note: Imprint varies: Lawthority, Inc., 1996–?.

Treaty Indexes

3 TREATIES IN FORCE FOR CANADA: A LIST OF TREATIES OF CANADA IN FORCE AS OF JANUARY 1, 1988
Canada. Department of External Affairs. Treaty Section (Ottawa: External Affairs Canada, 1988).

Summary: "This publication lists treaties of Canada on record in the Department of External Affairs on January 1, 1988 that had not expired by their terms or that had not been denounced by the parties, replaced or superseded by other agreements, or otherwise definitively terminated." Part I lists bilateral treaties by country and subject. Includes a number of treaties concluded by Great Britain on behalf of Canada, to which Canada became a party through state succession. Notifications received concerning succession to treaty rights and obligations, made by States, on attaining independence, are reproduced in whole or in part. Part II lists multilateral treaties by subject. Dates of signature (bold-faced type) and entry into force for Canada are given for all treaties, as well as citation to the *Canada Treaty Series.* (See no. 1, above.) Text is in English and French with French text on inverted pages.

Index: Subject index precedes Part I. Part I also includes index to countries and international organizations.

Note: Title on added title page: *Traités en Vigeur Pour le Canada.*

4 INDEX: CANADA TREATY SERIES

Canada. Foreign Affairs and International Trade Canada (Ottawa: Queen's Printer, 1928–).

Summary: Annual index to the *Canadian Treaty Series* (see no. 1, above), with cumulations issued irregularly. In English and French.

Note: Title varies slightly. French title: *Index: Recueil des Traités du Canada.*

Note: Formed by the union of *Index To Treaty Series* and *Index au Recueil des Traités.*

5 CANADA TREATY SERIES, 1928–1964

Canada. Department of Public Printing and Stationery. Documents Library (Ottawa: Queen's Printer, 1967). 388 pp.

Summary: This title is a chronological list of all treaties concluded by Canada from 1928 through 1964, and published in the *Canadian Treaty Series* (see no. 1, above).. Each entry includes date of signature, date of Canadian ratification, and date of entry into force. Also in French.

Index: A detailed alphabetical index provides references to subjects, places, and titles.

Series: Canadian Government Publications: Sectional Catalogue; no. 15.

Note: Compiled by M.-L. Myrand.

Note: French title: *Recueil des Traités du Canada, 1928–1964.*

6 CANADIAN TREATY CALENDAR, 1928–1978

Christian L. Wiktor (London; Rome: Oceana Publications, 1982).

Summary: In two volumes. Vol. 1 contains a chronological index and numerical list. This volume also includes a list of implementing legislation, a bilingual glossary of parties and subjects, and a section, entitled "Canadian Treaty Profiles." The latter includes tables showing the number of treaties Canada has concluded by party, subject, and form. Vol. 2 contains an index to bilateral treaties by country and subject, an index to multilateral treaties by subject, and a general subject index. Vol. 1 includes a lengthy introduction, and a section on the distribution of Canadian treaties. In English and French.

Note: French title: *Répertoire des Traités du Canada, 1928–1978.*

Note: Updated by *Index to Canadian Treaties/Index des Traités du Canada, 1979–2003.* Christian L. Wiktor (Ardsley, NY: Transnational Publishers, Inc., 2003), 393 pp.

Topical and Selected Treaty Collections

7 CANADO-AMERICAN TREATIES

Université de Montréal Faculté de Droit, Centre de Recherche en Droit Public. Canada. Foreign Affairs and International Trade Canada. Library of International Relations (Chicago-Kent College of Law, Illinois Institute of Technology).

URL is http://www.lexum.com/ca_us/index_en.html.

Summary: This database is part of the LexUM site, maintained by the University of Montreal Law Faculty. It provides access to the text of all bilateral treaties concluded between Canada and the United States from 1783–1997. The search engine supports full text searching, field searching, searches by citation, and searches by subject. Includes 279 treaties in all. Documents have been substantially reformatted for presentation in this database.

8 TREATIES AND AGREEMENTS AFFECTING CANADA IN FORCE BETWEEN HIS MAJESTY AND THE UNITED STATES OF AMERICA: WITH SUBSIDIARY DOCUMENTS, 1814–1925

Canada. Department of External Relations (Ottawa: F.A. Acland, 1927). 578 pp.

Summary: This title contains 82 treaties and related documents, covering the period 1814–1925, includes the Treaty of Ghent, together with declarations and decisions of commissions appointed under Articles 4, 5, 6, and 7. Treaties are arranged chronologically. An appendix includes extract of the International Telegraph Convention (1875), the Universal Postal Convention (1924), and Detailed Regulations for the Execution of the Universal Postal Convention.

Index: Table of contents and brief subject index.

Note: Earlier edition, including 34 treaties, covers 1814–1913. Also includes table of contents and brief subject index. Ottawa: J. de L. Taché, 1915. 301 pp.

9 TREATIES AND AGREEMENTS IN FORCE BETWEEN HIS MAJESTY AND THE UNITED STATES RELATING TO THE BOUNDARIES BETWEEN CANADA AND THE UNITED STATES AND TO WATERS CONTIGUOUS TO SUCH BOUNDARIES TOGETHER WITH VARIOUS SUBSIDIARY DOCUMENTS, 1814–1910. CANADA.

Department of External Relations (Ottawa: Government Printing Bureau, 1913). 136 pp.

Summary: This title contains 18 treaties and subsidiary documents, including the Treaty of Ghent (1814) and the Treaty respecting the Oregon Boundary (1846).

Index: Includes brief subject index.

10 PAPERS RELATING TO COMMERCIAL ARRANGEMENTS BETWEEN CANADA AND FOREIGN COUNTRIES

(Ottawa: Government Printing Office, 1910). 84 pp.

Summary: This title contains, inter alia, the commercial conventions with France and Germany (1910) and the convention between the United Kingdom and Japan (1906) affecting Canada.

Index: The title includes table of contents. It also includes a list of treaties of commerce and navigation between the United Kindgom and foreign powers, indicating whether they apply to Canada.

11 CANADA'S TAX TREATIES

A.B. McKie (Toronto: Butterworth's, 1981–).

Summary: Four volume looseleaf. Provides the texts of all tax treaties concluded by Canada. Also discusses the status of Canada's current treaty negotiations. Includes bibliographical references and an index.

Note: Author varies: Vern Krishna and A.B. McKie, 1981 – ?.

12 CANADA'S TAX TREATIES

(Toronto: Carswell, 1991–).

Summary: Includes the text of all Canadian tax treaties in force.

Note: Title varies: Originally published as Ward's Tax Treaties, 1991–1998.

13 TREATIES WITH CANADA. ENVIRONMENTAL

(Toronto: Carswell, 1999–2001).

Summary: This title is in CD-ROM format, and contains the text of environmental international agreements concluded by Canada. It also includes annexes, appendices, protocols and other additions, when available. Each text is accompanied by citations to printed sources, information about the treaty's history and signatory information drawn from printed sources. Updated twice yearly, in April and October. Subset of no. 2, above.

Index: Treaties can be searched by date, country of opposite party, or through one of 34 subject terms.

Note: Runs under Adobe Acrobat and Microsoft Windows or MacOS.

Note: Title varies: Environmental Treaties with Canada, 1997–1998.

Note: Imprint varies: Lawthority, 1997–1998.

14 CONSOLIDATED NATIVE LAW STATUTES, REGULATIONS AND TREATIES

Jack Woodward (Toronto Carswell, ? –).

Summary: This title is an annual compilation of treaties, which also includes the Indian Act and regulations, constitutional and imperial enactments, other federal legislation and regulations, and relevant proposed federal legislation.

Note: The title includes a master table of contents, as well as separate tables of contents for each legal instrument and a comprehensive keyword index.

Diplomatic Documents

15 DOCUMENTS ON CANADIAN EXTERNAL RELATIONS

Canada. Foreign Affairs and International Trade Canada (Ottawa: R. Duhamel, Queen's Printer; Hull, Québec: Canadian Government Publishing Center, 1967–).

Summary: Coverage begins with vol. 1 (1909–1918), and runs through vol. 27 (1960). The series contains documents "intended to illustrate the formulation and implementation of Canadian policy in the field of external relations." Preference is given to documents written by senior political appointees and, as between documents on the same subject, to those which are deemed most illuminating. Documents already in print are omitted, unless considered essential. Extracts of House of Commons speeches are included only when statements of government policy are otherwise unavailable. Documents are reprinted in their original language, with a minimum of commentary, and organized into chapters with particular themes. Each volume has a brief introduction, highlighting the policy concerns of the Canadian government during the period covered.

Index: Vol. 1 has a detailed, analytical subject index, permitting the user to trace issues through the entire nine-year period covered. Subsequent volumes, covering shorter periods of time, include much briefer subject indexes.

Note: Originally issued separately in French under the title, *Documents Relatifs aux Relations Exterieurs du Canada.* Now issued in one volume under both titles, with all documents in their original (almost exclusively English) language. Each document is preceded by a bilingual caption, indicating the document title, or the titles of the officials who sent and received the document. Recent volumes have individual, named editors.

Note: Imprint varies.

Note: Author varies: Department of External Affairs, 1967 – 1989; External Affairs and International Trade Canada, 1990–1991; Department of Foreign Affairs and International Trade, 1994–.

Note: Currently vols. 12–27, covering the years 1946–1960, are available online at the web site of the Department of Foreign Affairs and International Trade. The direct URL to these publications is http://www.international.gc.ca/department/history-histoire/dcer/browse-en.asp. The Department's History Section has produced a briefer, online history of the Department, available at: http://www.international.gc.ca/history-histoire/index.aspx?menu_id =8&menu =R&view=d.

16 DFAIT DIGITAL LIBRARY

Canada. Foreign Affairs and International Trade Canada.

URL: http://dfait-aeci.canadiana.ca/.

Summary: This database contains "over one million pages of departmental publications." This includes "material such as the Communiqués (1948–1995), Canadian Representation Abroad, CanadExport and other important works, in both official languages where possible." Unfortunately, the database is accompanied by no detailed description, including either a complete list of publications or dates of coverage.

17 STATEMENTS AND SPEECHES

Canada. Foreign Affairs and International Trade Canada.

(Ottawa: Department of Foreign Affairs and International Trade, 1946–).

Summary: Irregular. Each issue includes one speech or excerpt. There are no issues for 1992–1993. Speeches of selected years from 2004 onward, news releases from 2003 onward, and media advisories from 2004 onward, are available in electronic format at the web site of the Department of Foreign Affairs and International Trade. URL is http://www.international.gc.ca/media/archive-archives.aspx?view=d. Unfortunately, these documents are not indexed, so one must have a good idea of the subject and date of the document needed in order to retrieve anything relevant.

Index: Subject Index, 1946–1970, 1971–1976. Index to speakers, 1946–1981.

Note: Series title: Canadian Foreign Policy Series (1946–1991).

Note: Author varies: Department of External Affairs, 1946–1989; External Affairs and International Trade Canada, 1990–1991; Department of Foreign Affairs and International Trade, 1994–.

Note: Title varies: Statements and Speeches, 1946–1980; Statements and Speeches/External Affairs, Canada, 1980–198?.

Note: Imprint varies: Information Division, Department of External Affairs, 1946–1975; Information Services Division, 1976–1981; Public Affairs Branch, 1982–1984; Culture and Public Affairs Bureau, 1985; Communications and Culture Bureau, 1986–1991; Department of Foreign Affairs and International Trade, 1994–.

Note: Issued also in French, under the title *Declarations et Discours*.

18 ANNUAL REPORT

Canada. External Affairs and International Trade Canada (Ottawa: External Affairs and International Trade Canada, 1911–1991).

Summary: Coverage begins with 1910. Annual. Text in English and French with French text on inverted pages. Briefly summarizes the political and economic events of the year, and describes the organization, function and activities of each department branch. According to the Preface, "[m]ore detailed information can be found in Part III of the department's [year] Main Estimates."

Note: Title varies slightly: Annual Review, 1972(?)–1981.

Note: Author varies: Department of External Affairs, 1910–1987.

Note: Imprint varies: Department of External Affairs, 1910–1981(?); External Affairs Canada, 1982–1987.

Note: Also published in French, under the title *Rapport Annuel*.

Note: This title has been superseded by the annual Departmental Performance Report, which is available at the Department's web site, 2006– (http://www.international.gc.ca/about-a_propos/plans/index.aspx?lang=eng&view=d). Departmental Performance Reports, 1996 – , are archived at the web site of the Treasury Board of Canada Secretariat (http://www.tbs-sct.gc.ca/ems-sgd/esp-pbc/dpr-rmr-eng.asp).

19 DOCUMENTS ON THE KOREAN CRISIS
Canada. Department of External Affairs (Ottawa: E. Eloutier, King's Printer and Controller of Stationery, 1951). 37 pp.

Summary: This title includes 27 documents related to the Korean War, beginning with the Cairo Declaration of 1943. Most documents relate to Canada's involvement; many others are UN documents, mostly excerpted resolutions and draft resolutions of the General Assembly and Security Council. The title includes a table of contents.

Note: The title is published as supplement to a report, entitled *Documents on the Korean Crisis*, submitted by the Department of External Affairs, September 1, 1950.

20 DOCUMENTS ON CANADIAN FOREIGN POLICY, 1917–1939
Walter Alexander Riddell, ed. (Toronto: Oxford University Press, 1962). 806 pp.

Summary: Documents are topically arranged, each preceded by a heading indicating only date and author. Tables of abbreviations and sources at the end of the volume indicate the source for each document. The title also includes a bibliography, introduction, detailed table of contents and detailed subject index.

21 CANADIAN FOREIGN POLICY, [1945–1992]: SELECED SPEECHES AND DOCUMENTS
Arthur E. Blanchette, ed. (Ottawa: Carleton University Press, 1971–1994).

Summary: The title is in four volumes, covering the years 1945–1954, 1955–1965, 1966–1976, and 1977–1992. Each volume contains documents, speeches, etc., topically arranged. Entries are preceded by a brief note indicating the speaker/author, content and date of the document. Most entries are extracts. Each volume includes a table of contents, but no index.

Note: Imprint varies: Toronto: McClelland and Stewart (vol. 1); Toronto; Ottawa: McClelland and Stewart; Institute of Canadian Studies (vol. 2); Toronto: Gage Pubications in association with the Institute of Canadian Studies, Carleton University (vol. 3).

Note: Author varies: Robert A. MacKay, ed., vols. 1–3.

22 PEACEKEEPING & INTERNATIONAL RELATIONS
Canadian Institute of Strategic Studies (Ottawa: Peacekeeping & International Relations, 1949–2001).

Summary: As of 1990, this title became a monthly newsletter wholly independent of the Canadian government, and no longer containing official documentation of external affairs. From 1972, published bimonthly, first by the Department of External Affairs, then by a private publisher with government subsidy. The title included at various times, as a supplement from the Department, a "Reference Section," listing treaty information and publications of the Department, "For the Record," which included much the same information, and "International Canada." The latter included "For the Record," as well as more detailed information from the Department regarding treaty relations and policy.

Note: Author varies: Canada. Department of External Affairs, 1949–1971, joint author, 1972–1991.

Note: Title varies: *External Affairs: a Monthly Bulletin of the Department of External Affairs,* 1949–1971; *International Perspectives,* 1972–1991.

Note: Imprint varies: The Department, 1948–1980; International Perspectives, 1981–199?; Canadian Institute of Strategic Studies, 199?–.

23 CANADIAN BIBLIOGRAPHY OF INTERNATIONAL LAW
Christian L. Wiktor (Toronto: University of Toronto Press, 1984).

Summary: Part Two, I. International Relations, pp. 475–539, comprises a bibliography of articles and books written on various aspects of Canada's diplomatic history. The bibliography is organized both thematically and historically.

Yearbooks and Digests of State Practice

24 CANADIAN YEARBOOK OF INTERNATIONAL LAW

Canadian Branch, International Law Association, Canadian Council on International Law (Vancouver: University of British Columbia Press, 1962–).

Summary: Contains a section entitled Canadian Practice in International Law, including a summary of treaty actions taken by Canada during the year in question, and a section on Canadian case law. Each volume includes an analytical index and an index of cases. In French and English.

Index: The *Consolidated Index to The Canadian Yearbook of International Law* covers vols. I–XXV (1962–1987). It contains a combined analytical index of topics and cases.

Note: Published in French as *Annuaire Canadien de Droit International.*

China

Kara Phillips[1]

Issues of Treaty Succession

As early as the Spring and Autumn (772–476 BC) and the Warring States (476–221 BC) periods, ancient China engaged in interstate relations, diplomatic contacts, and treaty negotiation.[2] From the time China was unified under the Qin Dynasty (221 BC) until the end of the Qing Dynasty (1911), China conducted international relations by means of a tribute system.[3] Under the tribute system, China occupied a superior position in relation to surrounding subordinate nations. Foreign emissaries paid their respects to the Chinese emperor in the form of time-honored ceremonies of obeisance.[4]

Foreign trading companies introduced China to western international law concepts during trade negotiations in the 17th Century.[5] The Qing imperial government negotiated its first modern treaty with a western government (Russia) in 1689.[6] However, during the next two centuries, imperial China remained steadfast in its isolationist outlook and nonconformance to western

---

1 The author would like to thank the Professor Xu Xiaobing and the staff of the Shanghai Jiaotong University School of Law Library, librarian Bill McCloy and the staff of the University of Washington Gallagher Law Library, librarian Bob Menanteaux and the staff of the Seattle University Law Library, librarian Joan Liu of New York University School of Law Library Lani Cao, and Frances Chen for their assistance and support in writing this article. This bibliography is a selected bibliography for the P.R.C. For further research in the area of Chinese treaties, the author recommends: Xu Jialin & Tian Jianshe (徐佳林 田建设), *Guoji Tiaoyue de Jiansuo Dingyi yu Fangfa* (国际条约的检索定义与方法) [*Research Methods and Definitions for International Treaties*], *available at*: http://www.iolaw.org.cn/showNews.asp?id=14817 and LI YUMIN, LI CHUANBIN & LIU LIMIN (李育民, 李传斌, 刘利民) JINDAI ZHONGWAI TIAOYUE YANJIU ZONGSHU (近代中外条约研究综述) [SUMMARY OF MODERN CHINESE AND FOREIGN TREATY RESEARCH] (Changsha Shi: Hunan Renmin Chubanshe (长沙市: 湖南人民出版社) 2011).

2 Wang Tieya, *International Law in China: Historical and Contemporary Perspectives*, *in* 221 RECUEIL DES COURS: COLLECTED COURSES OF THE HAGUE ACADEMY OF INTERNATIONAL LAW 205–213 (1990).

3 Id. at 219–221.

4 JEROME ALAN COHEN & HUNGDAH CHIU, 1 PEOPLE'S CHINA AND INTERNATIONAL LAW: A DOCUMENTARY STUDY 4–5 (1974). The authors note that while there were some instances of more equal relations between China and other states, this was the exception rather than the rule.

5 Id. at 5.

6 GARY L. SCOTT, CHINESE TREATIES: THE POST-REVOLUTIONARY RESTORATION OF INTERNATIONAL LAW AND ORDER 18 (1975).

 | DOI 10.1163/9789004272224_010

style international relations, preventing the establishment of foreign diplomatic offices and requiring foreign representatives to adhere to the tribute system.[7] It was not until the late 19th Century and early 20th Century that Qing officials developed expertise in the theory and practice of international law. But by that time, Western nations had already imposed a series of "unequal treaties" on China from 1842–1860,[8] resulting in what has later been called China's "semi-colonization".[9] Under the "unequal treaties," 19 nations received several kinds of special privileges including extraterritoriality, tariff reduction, and territorial leases.[10]

In 1911, the Qing Dynasty was overthrown and the Republic of China (ROC) was formed under the leadership of Dr. Sun Yat-Sen.[11] Although the Republic of China continued to recognize treaties negotiated between the former Qing Dynasty and foreign governments,[12] the new government began to call for an end to the system of "unequal treaties".[13] From 1943 to 1947, China negotiated treaties with several Western nations, effectively ending the "unequal treaty" regime.[14] China was thrown into the turmoil of a civil war from 1945–1949 between the Kuomintang Party (KMT) and the Chinese Communist Party (CCP). In 1949, the People's Republic of China (PRC) was formally established under the auspices of the CCP.[15]

---

7 "A number of Western missions to China yielded to these demands and performed the humiliating traditional rites, including the series of abject prostrations before the emperor that have enriched our vocabulary with the word 'kowtow'". COHEN & CHIU, *supra* note 4, at 5–6. In 1908, Nepal sent the last tribute mission to China. Wang, *supra* note 2, at 225.

8 COHEN & CHIU, *supra* note 4, at 6–9.

9 Jacques deLisle, *China's Approach to International Law: A Historical Perspective*, 94 AM. SOC'Y OF INT'L L. PROC. 271 (2000).

10 Wang, *supra* note 2, at 252–253.

11 Xue Hanqin, *China's Open Policy and International Law*, 4 CHINESE J. OF INT'L L. 134 (2005).

12 Wei Wang, *Historical Evolution of National Treatment in China*, 39 INT'L LAW. 763 (2005).

13 Hungdah Chiu, *Comparison of the Nationalist and Communist Chinese Views of Unequal Treaties*, *in* CHINA'S PRACTICE IN INTERNATIONAL LAW: SOME CASE STUDIES 239–267 (Jerome A. Cohen ed., 1972).

14 Wang, *supra* note 2, at 262.

15 "On December 8, 1949, the ROC government, having lost the civil war to the Communist Chinese, was forced to move its government seat to Formosa [Taiwan]. Since then, the P.R.C. government, which controls China proper except Quemoy and Matsu islands, and the ROC government, which occupies Formosa, have coexisted". Y. Frank Chiang, *One-China Policy and Taiwan*, 28 FORDHAM INT'L L.J. 21 (2004). This relationship creates interesting and complex issues with regard to succession, diplomacy, and recognition.

Immediately after its founding, the PRC was faced with questions concerning succession and recognition.[16] China adopted the Common Program, a universal charter and forerunner to the constitution, on September 29, 1949 at the first session of the National Political Consultative Conference.[17] The Common Program stipulated that "[t]he Central People's Government of the People's Republic of China shall examine the treaties and agreements concluded between the Kuomintang and foreign governments, and shall recognize, abrogate, revise, or renegotiate them according to their respective contents".[18] This applied not only to treaties signed by the KMT,[19] but also to those executed by previous Chinese governments.[20]

While no standards were specified to determine the legitimacy of preexisting treaties,[21] the PRC government was very critical of treaties with adversary governments such as the United States and the KMT[22] and more favorable to treaties with the Soviet Union.[23] Preexisting bilateral treaties were annulled after renegotiation. Many boundary treaties remained intact.[24] The PRC continued to recognize certain multilateral agreements signed by previous Chinese governments and insisted on its rights to represent China in various international organizations.[25]

Since the founding of the PRC in 1949, the practice of international law can be divided into five stages: 1) from 1949–1952, China focused on its relations with the Soviet Union and other communist nations; 2) from 1953–1957, China concentrated on domestic industrialization and promoted "peaceful coexistence"; 3) from 1958–1965, China broke ties with the Soviet Union and actively

---

See Scott, *supra* note 6, at 81–85. For background on the PRC's early recognition practice, *see* James C. Hsiung, *China's Recognition Practice and Its Implications in International Law*, *in* China's Practice in International Law: Some Case Studies 14–56 (Jerome A. Cohen ed., 1972).

16 deLisle, *supra* note 9, at 272.

17 Xue Hanqin, Hu Zhiqiang & Fan Kun, *National Treaty Law and Practice: China*, *in* National Treaty Law and Practice 155 (Duncan B. Hollis, Merritt R. Blakeslee & L. Benjamin Ederington eds., 2005).

18 Cohen & Chiu, *supra* note 4, at 1122.

19 The KMT party held power in the late 1920's and early 1930's with its capital in Nanjing. At the same time, the CCP was consolidating power in Jiangxi.

20 Cohen & Chiu, *supra* note 4, at 1128; *see also* Scott, *supra* note 6, at 81.

21 Xue, Hu & Fan, *supra* note 17, at 155; Cohen & Chiu, *supra* note 4, at 214, 1124.

22 Wang, *supra* note 12, at 771.

23 Cohen & Chiu, *supra* note 4, at 1128.

24 Id. at 1127.

25 Id. at 268–313, 1124.

pursued diplomatic ties to third world countries in response to US and USSR hegemony; 4) from 1966–1969, China was occupied with the domestic turmoil of the Cultural Revolution and purged many international law scholars and officials; 5) from 1971 to current, China began to participate more fully in international organizations.[26] The first four stages are characterized by the PRC's continued alienation from the international order; while the last stage is characterized by the PRC's integration within the international order.[27]

The PRC's admittance to the United Nations in 1971 "became a symbol of China's reintegration into the international community".[28] Thereafter, China was invited, and in some instances, actively courted, to join a number of international organizations; however, China proceeded cautiously, carefully considering how issues of sovereignty and recognition of Taiwan were addressed within the organization. While its early interaction and participation in international organizations was focused on learning and observation, by the 1980s and 1990s, China's participation and experience in international organizations had expanded substantially.[29] Today, China operates with a high degree of "sophistication" in the international arena.[30]

---

26 Id. at 18–22. For a review of China's theories toward international law from 1977 to 1986, *see* Samuel S. Kim, *The Development of International Law in Post-Mao China: Change and Continuity*, 1 J. OF CHINESE L. 117–160 (1987). For a history of the study of international law in China during its first three decades, *see* Chen Tiqiang, *The People's Republic of China and Public International Law*, 8 DALHOUSIE L.J. 3–31 (1984).

27 ANN KENT, BEYOND COMPLIANCE: CHINA, INTERNATIONAL ORGANIZATIONS, AND GLOBAL SECURITY 33 (2007).

28 From 1949 to 1971, the ROC (Taiwan) held the "China" seat in the United Nations. Ann Kent, *China's International Socialization: the Role of International Organizations*, 8 GLOBAL GOVERNANCE 344 (2002). For a detailed discussion and analysis of China's entry and participation in the United Nations, *see* SAMUEL S. KIM, CHINA, THE UNITED NATIONS AND WORLD ORDER (1979).

29 KENT, *supra* note 27, at 50–54. For perspectives on China's involvement in the international order during this time, *see* James V. Feinerman, *Chinese Participation in the International Legal Order: Rogue Elephant or Team Player?*, 141 CHINA Q. 186–210 (1995); ELIZABETH ECONOMY & MICHAEL OKSENBERG, CHINA JOINS THE WORLD: PROGRESS AND PROSPECTS (1999).

30 KENT, *supra* note 27, at 54–55. *See also* Pitman B. Potter, *China and the International Legal System: Challenges of Participation*, 191 CHINA Q. 699–715 (2007); MARC LANTEIGNE, CHINA AND INTERNATIONAL INSTITUTIONS: ALTERNATE PATHS TO GLOBAL POWER (2005); WEIXING HU ET AL., CHINA'S INTERNATIONAL RELATIONS IN THE 21ST CENTURY: DYNAMICS OF PARADIGM SHIFTS (2000).

Treaty Ratification and Implementation

The treaty-making process is addressed within the Chinese constitution. As China has adopted four constitutions since its founding, the treaty implementation procedure has changed slightly with each successive constitution.[31] The first constitution approved in 1954 provided that the Standing Committee of the National People's Congress (NPC) had the power to ratify and abrogate treaties. The PRC president formally acted to ratify or abrogate treaties in accordance with the decisions of the NPC Standing Committee.[32] Two new constitutions were enacted during the 1970's, reflecting the political turbulence of the Cultural Revolution.[33] The 1975 constitution abolished the position of president and gave exclusive authority to the NPC Standing Committee for treaty ratification and abrogation.[34] Under the 1978 constitution, the NPC Standing Committee held the authority to ratify and abrogate treaties, and the formal act of ratification fell to the Chairman of the NPC Standing Committee in accordance to the decisions of the NPC Standing Committee.[35]

The fourth and current constitution was enacted in 1982 and stipulates that the NPC Standing Committee decides on ratification and abrogation of treaties and important agreements.[36] As with the 1954 Constitution, formal ratification of treaties and agreements occurs by act of the President in accordance with the NPC Standing Committee decision.[37] The President has no authority to challenge the NPC Standing Committee's decision on treaty ratification or abrogation.[38] Article 89 of the 1982 Constitution provides that the State Council conducts foreign affairs and concludes treaties and agreements.[39]

---

31 M. Ulric Killion, *China's Amended Constitution: Quest for Liberty and Independent Judicial Review*, 4 Wash. U. Global Stud. L. Rev. 43, 52–53 (2005).

32 Xue, Hu & Fan, *supra* note 17, at 156 n.2.

33 Killion, *supra* note 31, at 52.

34 Xue, Hu & Fan, *supra* note 14, at 156 n.2.

35 Id.

36 Treaties and important agreements involving politics, territories and boundaries, and extradition and judicial assistance require ratification. *See* Li Zhaojie, *Effect of Treaties in Domestic Law: Practice of the People's Republic of China*, 16 Dalhousie L.J. 69 (1993). The text, in English, of the 1982 Constitution and subsequent amendments is available at: http://www.npc.gov.cn/englishnpc/Constitution/node_2824.htm.

37 Xue, Hu & Fan, *supra* note 17, at 157.

38 Li Zhaojie, *supra* note 36, at 70 n.29.

39 Xue, Hu & Fan, *supra* note 17, at 157.

On December 28, 1990, China enacted the Law on Procedures for the Conclusion of Treaties (Treaty Procedures Law).[40] This landmark law covers both bilateral and multilateral treaty procedures including initiation and conclusion; appointment of representatives; ratification and approval; accession and acceptance of multilateral treaties; and publication, registration and amendment.[41] The Treaty Procedures Law provides that the NPC Standing Committee decides on the ratification and abrogation of treaties and important agreements; the PRC President ratifies and abrogates treaties in accordance with the NPC Standing Committee's decision; the State Council is responsible for concluding treaties and agreements; the Ministry of Foreign Affairs, under the State Council, administers treaty affairs.[42] In 1997, the PRC acceded to the Vienna Convention on the Law of Treaties.[43]

The return of Hong Kong to China in 1997 and Macao in 1999 has created complex issues with regard to treaty practice in these two Special Administrative Regions (SAR).[44] Prior to the return, there were extensive negotiations between the PRC and the United Kingdom and the PRC and Portugal on the recognition of multilateral treaties then in effect on Hong Kong and Macao, respectively.[45] Bilateral treaties concluded by the United Kingdom and applied to Hong Kong were no longer applicable after July 1, 1997. Likewise, after December 20, 1999, bilateral treaties signed by Portugal and applied to Macao were no longer applicable.[46] The PRC determines the application of international treaties to the SARs after soliciting input from the SAR governments.[47] Hong Kong and

---

40 Law on Procedures for the Conclusion of Treaties (promulgated by the Standing Comm. Nat'l People's Cong., Dec. 28, 1990, effective Dec. 28, 1990), *translated in* Xue, Hu & Fan, *supra* note 17, at 170–177, Annex B.

41 Id.

42 Id. art 3. For a discussion on the relationship between treaties and Chinese national law, *see* Xue Hanqin & Jin Qian, *International Treaties in the Chinese Domestic Legal System*, 8 CHINESE J. OF INT'L L. 299–322 (2009), *available at*: http://chinesejil.oxfordjournals.org/content/8/2/299.full.pdf.

43 Xue, Hu & Fan, *supra* note 17, at 158.

44 For a discussion of treaty practice in Hong Kong and Macau, *see* Xue, Hu & Fan, *supra* note 17, at 165–167.

45 Id.

46 Id. at 166.

47 Id. *See also*, the Basic Law of the Hong Kong Special Administrative Region of the People's Republic of China (promulgated by the Nat'l People's Cong., Apr. 4, 1990, effective July 1, 1997), ch. VII, *available at*: http://www.basiclaw.gov.hk/en/basiclawtext/chapter_7.html; Basic Law of the Macao Special Administrative Region of the People's Republic of China (promulgated by the Nat'l People's Cong., Mar. 31, 1993, effective Dec. 20, 1999), ch.VII *available at*: http://www.imprensa.macau.gov.mo/bo/i/1999/leibasica/index_uk.asp#c7.

Macao SAR governments have the authority to conclude agreements with foreign nations on certain matters such as economic, trade, finance, shipping, communications, tourism, culture, and sports and may participate in international organizations and conferences.[48]

Annotated Bibliography of Sources

General Treaty Collections

1 ZHONGHUA RENMIN GONGHEGUO WAIJIAOBU (中华人民共和国外交部) [MINISTRY OF FOREIGN AFFAIRS WEB SITE]
URL: http://www.mfa.gov.cn/chn.

Summary: The official web site of the People's Republic of China Ministry of Foreign Affairs offers information about the Ministry's activities including recent policies, speeches, communiqués, agendas, press releases, and statistics. Under the tab Material (资料), find text of selected treaties and agreements and status of recent multilateral and bilateral treaties.

Note: In Chinese. Selected information (news, speeches, communiqués) is available on the English portion of the web site.

2 ZHONGHUA RENMIN GONGHEGUO TIAOYUE JI (中华人民共和国条約集) [TREATY COLLECTION OF THE PEOPLE'S REPUBLIC OF CHINA]
Zhonghua Renmin Gongheguo Waijiaobu (中华人民共和国外交部) (Beijing: Falü Chubanshe (北京: 法律出版社), 1957–).

Summary: This multi-volume set is the annual, official compilation of treaties and agreements of the People's Republic of China, prepared by the Ministry of Foreign Affairs. Contains full text of bilateral and multilateral agreements from 1949 to current. Vol. 1 (1949–1951) to vol. 31 (1984) includes table of contents by topic. Vol. 32 (1985) to current includes table of contents with bilateral treaties organized by region, then individual country and multilateral treaties by date. In Chinese.

Index: Vol. 1 (1949–1951) to vol. 31 (1984) contain lists of agreements by date. Vol. 11 (1962) contains index by country and then date covering vol. 1 (1949–1951) to vol. 10 (1961). Vol. 21 (1974) contains index by country and then date

---

48 Xue, Hu & Fan, *supra* note 17, at 167. *See also*, the Basic Law of the Hong Kong Special Administrative Region of the People's Republic of China, *supra* note 47, ch.VII and the Basic Law of the Macao Special Administrative Region of the People's Republic of China, *supra* note 47, ch.VII.

covering vol. 11 (1962) to vol. 20 (1973). Vol. 31 (1984) contains index by country and then date covering vol. 21 (1974) to vol. 30 (1983). A free standing index was published in 1971 entitled *Zhonghua Renmin Gongheguo Tiaoyue Suoyin: 1949–1961* (中華人民共和國條約索引: 1949–1961) [People's Republic of China Treaty Index: 1949–1961] by Zhonghua Renmin Gongheguo Waijiaobu (中華人民共和國外交部). The index is organized by country and then date and provides volume and page number reference to *Zhonghua Renmin Gongheguo Tiaoyue Ji* (中华人民共和国条約集) [Treaty Collection of the People's Republic of China].

Note: Starting with vol. 29 (1982) to current, most volumes contain an Appendix listing treaties and agreements signed but not received for publication.

Note: Imprint varies: Vols. 1–10 have imprint: Falü Chubanshe (法律出版社); Vols. 11–14 and 22 to current: Shijie Zhishi Chubanshe (世界知识出版社); Vols. 15–21: Renmin Chubanshe (人民出版社).

3 QUANGUO RENMIN DAIBIAO DAHUI (全国人民代表大会) [NATIONAL PEOPLE'S CONGRESS WEB SITE]
URL: http://www.npc.gov.cn.

Summary: The official web site of the People's Republic of China National People's Congress offers text of treaties, conventions, and agreements from 1949 to current under the tab Literature (文献资料): http://www.npc.gov.cn/npc/xinwen/newwxzl.htm.

Note: In Chinese.

4 ZHONGHUA RENMIN GONGHEGUO QUANGUO RENMIN DAIBIAO DAHUI CHANGWU WEIYUANHUI GONGBAO (中华人民共和国全国人民代表大会常务委員会公报) [GAZETTE OF THE STANDING COMMITTEE OF THE NATIONAL PEOPLE'S CONGRESS]
Quanguo Renmin Daibiao Dahui Changwu Weiyuanhui (全国人民代表大会 常务委员会)
(Beijing: Zhonghua Renmin Gongheguo Quanguo Renmin Daibiao Dahui Changwu Weiyuanhui Bangongting (北京:中华人民共和国全国人民代表大会常务委员会办公厅), 1957–).

Summary: Text of treaties and agreements as approved by the Standing Committee of the National People's Congress, roughly arranged in chronological order by date of issuance. Published several times per year. In Chinese. Includes table of contents in rough chronological order. Beginning in 1997, table of contents also published in English. Beginning in 1992, includes annual index in Chinese and English in last issue.

Note: In Chinese.

Note: Available in full text in CNKI's China Academic Journals Database: www.eastview.com.

Note: Also available from 1957 to current on the National People's Congress web site: http://www.npc.gov.cn under link for Standing Committee Gazette (常委会公报).

5 ZHONGHUA RENMIN GONGHEGUO GUOWUYUAN GONGBAO (中华人民共和国国务院公报) [GAZETTE OF THE STATE COUNCIL]
Zhonghua Renmin Gongheguo Guowuyuan (中华人民共和国国务院) (Beijing: Zhonghua Renmin Gongheguo Guowuyuan Mishuting (北京: 中华人民共和国国务院秘书厅), 1954–).

Summary: Text of treaty ratification decisions, joint communiqués, joint statements, decrees, letters, speeches, roughly arranged in chronological order. Published several times per year. Includes table of contents in rough chronological order. Later issues contain table of contents in English and an annual index in Chinese and English in the last issue.

Index: Cumulative index issued as separate volume covers 1954–1990. Entries are in topical order and then by date.

Note: In Chinese.

Note: Available in full text in CNKI's China Academic Journals Database: www.eastview.com. In Chinese. Available online at: http://www.gov.cn/gongbao/2014/issue_4001.htm. In Chinese. Selected tables of contents are available online at: http://english.gov.cn/documents/gazettes/index.htm. In English.

6 ZHONGHUA RENMIN GONGHEGUO FALÜ QUANSHU (中华人民共和国法律全书) [COLLECTION OF LAWS OF THE PEOPLE'S REPUBLIC OF CHINA]
Wang Huai'an, ed. (王怀安) (Changchun Shi: Jilin Renmin Chubanshe (长春市: 吉林人民出版社), 1989–).

Summary: Multivolume collection of Chinese laws and regulations covering 1949 to current. A regular section on international laws is included in most volumes and contains the text of multilateral treaties as well as the approval decision by the Standing Committee of the National People's Congress. Includes chronological table of contents and index.

Note: In Chinese. Vols. 1–9 include chronological table of contents in English.

Note: Vol. 1 (1949–89) contains text of international agreements signed from 1945–1975.

7 CHINALAWINFO

URL: http://www.chinalawinfo.com.

Summary: A subscription database with bilateral and multilateral treaties and agreements. Search by title, country, promulgating department, date, and topic. The majority of the treaties are classified under the topics: foreign relations, trade, culture, and science/technology.

Note: In Chinese.

Note: Selected tax treaties are translated into English at: http://www.lawinfochina.com.

8 WESTLAW CHINA

URL: http://www.westlawchina.com.

Summary: A subscription database with bilateral and multilateral treaties and agreements. There are a few historical multilateral treaties from the late 1800s. Search by title, document number, text, validity status, and date.

Note: In English and Chinese.

Treaty Indexes

9 AGREEMENTS OF THE PEOPLE'S REPUBLIC OF CHINA, 1949–1967: A CALENDAR

Douglas M. Johnston & Hungdah Chiu (Cambridge: Harvard University Press, 1968).

Summary: Contains calendar of over 2,000 "official and semi-official exchanges of commitments" (including treaties, agreements, accords, protocols, statutes, contracts, arrangements, exchanges of letters and notes, joint statements and communiqués, declarations) from 1949–1967. Entries are organized chronologically by the date of signing or issuance and include effective date, place of signature or issuance, parties, type of document, subject matter, and citation to the original source. A notation next to the original source indicates whether the original source contains the full or partial text of the agreement or contains a summary or reference only.

Index: Includes an index of bilateral and trilateral treaties organized by country and then date and a topical index by subject and then date.

10 AGREEMENTS OF THE PEOPLE'S REPUBLIC OF CHINA: A CALENDAR OF EVENTS, 1966–1980

Hungdah Chiu (New York: Praeger, 1981).

Summary: Contains a calendar of over 1,500 "official and semi-official exchanges of commitments" (including treaties, agreements, accords, protocols, statutes, contracts, arrangements, exchanges of letters and notes, joint statements and communiqués, declarations) from 1966 – 1980. Entries are organized chronologically by date of signing or issuance and include effective date, place of signature or issuance, parties, subject matter, type of document, and citation to the original source. A notation next to the original source indicates whether the original source contains the full or partial text of the agreement or contains a summary or reference only. Bilateral and multilateral treaties are listed in separate sections. Includes an index of bilateral and trilateral treaties by country and then date; an index of bilateral agreements with international organizations alphabetically by organization and then date; and an index by subject and then date.

Note: Continues *Agreements of the People's Republic of China, 1949–1967: a Calendar* and includes additional treaty information from 1966 and 1967 not originally covered.

11 THE AGREEMENTS OF THE PEOPLE'S REPUBLIC OF CHINA WITH FOREIGN COUNTRIES, 1949–1990

Wolfgang Bartke (München; New York: K.G. Saur, 1992).

Summary: Contains index of treaties and agreements from 1949–1990. Bilateral agreements are arranged in alphabetical order by country and then date. Agreements with international organizations are arranged in alphabetical order by organization and then by date. Main entries provide the following information: date, title, type of agreement, and footnotes to the original source.

Note: 2nd revised and enlarged edition; 1st edition, *The Agreements of the PR China*, covers 1949–1975.

12 CHINA LAW REPORTER

(Chicago: Section of International Law of the American Bar Association, 1980–1999).

Summary: Checklist of bilateral and multilateral agreements and treaties covering 1985–1992, compiled by Constance A. Johnson and published in the *China Law Reporter*. Entries are generally arranged alphabetically by country and then by date. Listings include country, date, topic, and source.

Note: The years covered in each issue are as follows: 4 *China Law Reporter* 41–62: 1985–1986; 5 *China Law Reporter* 35–40: 1987; 7 *China Law Reporter* 207–230: 1989–1992.

Note: Lacks coverage for 1988.

13 GUOJI TIAOYUE ZAI ZHONGGUO TEBIE XINGZHENGQU DE SHIYONG (国际条约在中国特别行政区的适用) [INTERNATIONAL TREATIES AND THEIR APPLICATION TO THE SPECIAL ADMINISTRATIVE REGIONS OF CHINA]

Wang Xi'an (王西安) (Guangzhou: Guangdong Renmin Chubanshe (广州: 广东人民出版社), 2006).

Summary: Appendices contain lists of multilateral treaties and conventions applied to the Hong Kong Special Administrative Region and the Macau Special Administrative Region after their return to China.

Note: In Chinese.

14 ZHONGWAI TIAOYUE XIEDING SUOYIN, 1662–1980 (中外条约协定索引, 1662–1980)
[Index to the Treaties and Agreements with and Concerning China, 1662–1980]
Chen Chilou, ed. (陈尺楼) (Beijing: Zhongguo Duiwai Fanyi Chuban Gongsi (北京: 中国对外翻译出版公司), 1989).

Summary: Contains index of 3,838 treaties and agreements, some of which were never recognized, approved, or effectuated, concerning China from 1662–1980. Entries are arranged in chronological order and provide the following information: date, country, title of agreement, reference to original source, and language of original text.

Index: Includes alphabetical index (in English) by subject and then country as well as an alphabetical index (in English) by country and then by date.

Note: In English and Chinese.

Topical and Selected Treaty Publications

Historical Treaty Collections

15 GUOJI TIAOYUE DAQUAN (國際條約大全) [INTERNATIONAL TREATIES COLLECTION]
(Shanghai: Shangwu Yinshuguan (上海: 商務印書館), 1928).

Summary: Text of over 100 bilateral and multilateral treaties and agreements from the 1800's to the 1920's arranged by country. Part 1 focuses on multilateral agreements worldwide, parts 2 and 3 cover multilateral agreements for smaller regions, and parts 4–10 cover bilateral agreements. Includes table of contents by country and table of contents by topic.

Note: In Chinese.

16 QING CHAO TIAOYUE QUANJI (清朝条约全集) [THE COMPLETE WORKS OF QING DYNASTY TREATIES]
Tian Tao (田涛) (Ha'erbin: Heilongjiang Renmin Chubanshe (哈爾滨: 黑龙江人民出版社), 1999).

Summary: This 3 volume set contains the text of 200 treaties and agreements involving 50 countries during the Qing Dynasty, covering the years 1689–1911.

Index: Volume 1 contains an index in chronological order and an index by country and then by date.

Note: In Chinese.

17 TREATIES AND AGREEMENTS WITH AND CONCERNING CHINA, 1894–1919: A COLLECTION OF STATE PAPERS, PRIVATE AGREEMENTS AND OTHER DOCUMENTS, IN REFERENCE TO THE RIGHTS AND OBLIGATIONS OF THE CHINESE GOVERNMENT IN RELATION TO FOREIGN POWERS, AND IN REFERENCE TO THE INTERRELATION OF THOSE POWERS IN RESPECT TO CHINA, DURING THE PERIOD FROM THE SINO-JAPANESE WAR TO THE CONCLUSION OF THE WORLD WAR OF 1914–1919

John V.A. MacMurray (New York: Oxford University Press, 1921).

Summary: This 2 volume set contains the text of over 500 treaties and agreements, arranged in chronological order. Vol. 1 includes a comprehensive table of contents listing treaties chronologically for both volumes. Vol. 2 contains an index of agreements organized alphabetically by nation and then date as well as an index by topic covering both volumes. The years covered by each volume are as follows: vol. 1: 1894–1911 Manchu Period; vol. 2: 1912–1919 Republican Period.

Note: Series title: *Publications of the Carnegie Endowment for International Peace, Division of International Law.*

Note: A subsequent work, entitled *Treaties and Agreements with and Concerning China, 1919–1929* was compiled by the Carnegie Endowment for International Peace.

18 TREATIES AND AGREEMENTS WITH AND CONCERNING CHINA, 1919–1929 (WASHINGTON: CARNEGIE ENDOWMENT FOR INTERNATIONAL PEACE, 1929).

Summary: A continuation of John Van Antwerp MacMurray's *Treaties and Agreements with and concerning China* containing the text of over 90 treaties and agreements, arranged in chronological order. Footnotes provide references to the original source and other historical information. Table of contents lists document date, signatories, and document title.

Note: Pamphlet series of the *Carnegie Endowment for International Peace*, no. 50.

19 DIE VERTRÄGE DER VOLKSREPUBLIK CHINA MIT ANDEREN STAATEN

Institut für Asienkunde (Frankfurt: A. Metzner, 1962).

Summary: This 11 volume set contains the text of several hundred Chinese bilateral and multilateral treaties and agreements from 1949–1975. Vols. 1–5 cover specific regions as follows: vol. 1 covers South and East Asian regions from 1950–1961; vol. 2 covers the Orient and Africa 1950–1969; vol. 3 covers

Non-Communist States of Europe and the Americas (including Cuba) 1949–1964; vol. 4 is a supplement to vols. 1–3 covering 1961–1967; vol. 5 covers Communist States from 1949–1967. Vols. 6–11 cover all regions including Africa, Americas, Asia, Europe, Australia during specified time periods as follows: vol. 6 covers 1970–1971; vol. 7 covers 1968–1969; vol. 8 covers 1972; vol. 9 covers 1966–1967; vol. 10 covers 1965; vol. 11 covers 1973–1975. Treaties are generally organized by region and country. Each volume contains table of contents.

Note: In German.

Note: Vols. 4–10 contain imprint Wiesbaden: O. Harrassowitz.

Note: Vol. 4 includes table of contents to vols. 1–3. Vol. 8 includes index for 1966–1972.

Note: A related volume was published in 1957 called *Die Verträge der Volksrepublik China mit anderen Staaten* (Frankfurt: A. Metzner) covering treaties between China and other nations from 1949–1956.

20 ZHONGHUA RENMIN GONGHEGUO DUOBIAN TIAOYUE JI (中华人民共和国多边条约集) [MULTILATERAL TREATIES OF THE PEOPLE'S REPUBLIC OF CHINA]
Zhonghua Renmin Gongheguo Waijiaobu Tiaoyue Falü Si (中华人民共和国外交部条约法律司) (Beijing: Falü Chubanshe (北京:法律出版社), 1987).

Summary: This 7 volume set contains the text of over 240 multilateral treaties from 1875–1998 in which China participated. Organized in chronological order. Each volume includes table of contents in chronological order. Contents of each volume are as follows: vol. 1 covers 1875–1965; vol. 2 covers 1966–1974 (lacks 1975); vol. 3 covers 1976–1979; vol. 4 covers 1980–1984; vol. 5 covers 1985–1986; vol. 6 covers 1987–1992; vol. 7 covers 1993–1998.

Note: In Chinese. Vol. 6 includes a table of contents in English.

Note: Vol. 6, Appendix 1 contains chronological table of contents (in Chinese) for vols. 1–5. Vol. 6, Appendix 2 contains list of treaty texts in which China participated, but which were not received for publication in vols. 1–6. Entries (in Chinese) include name of treaty and dates of signing and approval.

Note: Vol. 7, Appendix 1 lists treaty titles in English. Vol. 7, Appendix 2 contains chronological table of contents (in Chinese) for vols. 1–6.

21 ZHONGWAI JIUYUE ZHANG HUIBIAN (中外舊約章彙編) [COMPILATION OF OLD TREATIES BETWEEN CHINA AND FOREIGN STATES]
Wang Tieya (王铁崖) (Beijing: Shenghuo, Dushu, Xinzhi Sanlian Shudian: Xinhua Shudian Faxing (北京:生活,讀書,新知 三联 书店:新华 书店 发行), 1957–1962 (1982 printing)).

Summary: Edited by Wang Tieya, a leading scholar on Chinese international and treaty law, this 3 volume set contains the text of approximately 1,200 treaties and agreements from 1689–1949. (International conventions are not generally included). Vol. 1 covers 1689–1901, vol. 2 covers 1901–1919, vol. 3 covers 1919–1949. Each volume contains a chronological table of contents.

Index: Each volume contains an index by country and then date.

Note: In Chinese.

22 ZHONGWAI TIAOYUE HUIBIAN (中外條約彙編) [CHINESE AND FOREIGN TREATY COMPILATION]
Huang Yuebo, Yu Nengmo & Bao Liren (黄月波, 于能模, 鮑釐人) (Shanghai: Shangwu Yinshuguan (上海: 商務印書館), 1935).

Summary: Text of over 250 multilateral and bilateral agreements from the 1800's until the 1930's, arranged by country and then date. Includes detailed table of contents for each country.

Index: Includes index in Chinese character stroke order by topic.

Note: In Chinese.

23 ZHONGWAI YUEZHANG HUIYAO, 1689–1949 (中外约章汇要, 1689–1949) [COLLECTION OF TREATIES BETWEEN CHINA AND FOREIGN STATES, 1689–1949]
Chu Dexin & Liang De (褚德新, 梁德) (Ha'erbin Shi: Heilongjiang Renmin Chubanshe (哈尔滨市: 黑龙江人民出版社), 1991).

Summary: Contains 120 treaties and agreements from 1689–1949 which had a significant impact on China's foreign relations and on Chinese society, politics, economics, and culture. Includes table of contents in chronological order.

Index: Includes Chinese character stroke order index by name of agreement.

Note: In Chinese.

Specialized Treaty Collections

24 CHINA'S BOUNDARY TREATIES AND FRONTIER DISPUTES
Luke T. Chang (London; New York: Oceana Publications, 1982).

Summary: Appendices 2–4 contain the text of over 50 treaties and agreements regarding China's boundaries with Burma, Nepal, Afghanistan, India, and Russia from 1689–1964. Each chapter contains substantive commentary on China's boundary disputes and treaties in the above regions. Organized by region and then date.

25 HERTSLET'S CHINA TREATIES: TREATIES, &C. BETWEEN GREAT BRITAIN AND CHINA AND BETWEEN CHINA AND FOREIGN POWERS; AND ORDERS IN COUNCIL, RULES, REGULATIONS, ACTS OF PARLIAMENT, DECREES, &C. AFFECTING BRITISH INTERESTS IN CHINA IN FORCE ON THE 1ST JANUARY, 1908

Edward Hertslet, Godfrey Edward Proctor Hertslet & Edward Parkes (London: Harrison and Sons, 1908).

Summary: This 2 volume set contains the text of 122 treaties and agreements between China and Great Britain and other countries from 1689–1907. Divided into five parts: vol. 1, part 1 contains treaties between Great Britain and China from 1942–1907; vol. 1, part 2 contains treaties between China and foreign powers from 1689–1907; vol. 1, part 3 contains treaties between foreign powers and between Great Britain and foreign powers relating to China from 1896–1907; vol. 2, part 4 contains Acts of Parliament, Orders in Council, rules and regulations affecting British interests in China from 1855–1907; vol. 2, part 5 contains miscellaneous documents such as protocols, circulars, ordinances, regulations, memorials, decrees, and notes relating to China from 1877–1907. Each part is preceded by a table of contents.

Index: Includes a comprehensive index arranged alphabetically by topic in vol. 2.

26 TREATIES BETWEEN THE EMPIRE OF CHINA AND FOREIGN POWERS: TOGETHER WITH REGULATIONS FOR THE CONDUCT OF FOREIGN TRADE, ETC.

William Frederick Mayers, ed. (Taipei: Ch'eng-Wen Publishing, 1966).

Summary: Contains the text of over 50 treaties and agreements regarding trade and foreign relations, organized by country and then date. Includes table of contents, organized by country and then date and listing type of document, place of signature, and date.

Index: Includes index by subject.

Note; In English, French, and Spanish.

Note: Reprint. Originally published: Shanghai: Broadhurst Tootal 1877.

27 TREATIES OF THE PEOPLE'S REPUBLIC OF CHINA, 1949–1978: AN ANNOTATED COMPILATION

Grant F. Rhode & Reid E. Whitlock (Boulder: Westview Press, 1980).

Summary: Contains text of approximately 50 treaties and agreements regarding friendship, boundary, commerce, consular, and dual nationality as well as selected agreements with the United States and Japan from 1949–1978. Treaties are organized according to the above topics and each topic is preceded by a substantive essay. Includes table of contents, organized by topic and then by country.

Note: Series title: *Westview Special Studies on China and East Asia.*

28 ZHONGGONG SHUANGBIAN TOUZI BAOZHANG XIEDING ZHI YANJIU (中共雙邊投資保障協定之研究) [STUDY OF COMMUNIST CHINA BILATERAL INVESTMENT PROTECTION AGREEMENTS]
Li Mengfen, Lin Derui & Xiao Wensheng (李孟玢, 林德瑞, 蕭文生) (Taibei Shi: Xingzhengyuan Dalu Weiyuanhui (台北市: 行政院大陸委員會), 1998).

Summary: Approximately 30 bilateral investment agreements, protocols, and exchange of notes from 1980–1988.

Note: In Chinese, English, and French.

29 ZHONGGUO DIJIE HE QIANSHU DE GUOJI HUANJING TIAOYUE JI (中国缔结和签署的国际环境条约集) [SET OF INTERNATIONAL ENVIRONMENTAL TREATIES CONCLUDED AND SIGNED BY CHINA]
Guojia Huanjing Baohu Zongju, Zhengce Faguisi. (国家环境保护总局, 政策法规司) (Beijing Shi: Xueyuan Chubanshe (北京市: 学苑出版社), 1999).

Summary: Approximately 50 international environmental treaties from 1946–1998 organized by topic and 25 bilateral treaties from 1980–1999 organized chronologically.

Note: In Chinese.

30 ZHONGGUO JINDAI BU PINGDENG TIAOYUE HUIYAO (中国近代不平等条约汇要) [COLLECTION OF UNEQUAL TREATIES IN MODERN CHINA]
Quanguo Renda Changweihui Bangongting Yanjiushi Bianxie (全国人大常委会办公厅研究室编写) (Beijing Shi: Zhongguo Minzhu Fazhi Chubanshe (北京市: 中国民主法制出版社), 1996).

Summary: Contains text of approximately 30 unequal treaties from 1842–1915. Treaties are organized in chronological order.

Note: In Chinese.

Note: Available as ebook at: http://www.chaoxing.com/.

31 ZHONGHUA RENMIN GONGHEGUO SIFA XIEZHU TIAOYUE JI (中华人民共和国司法协助条约集) [THE PEOPLE'S REPUBLIC OF CHINA JUDICIAL ASSISTANCE TREATY COLLECTION]
Waijiaobu, Tiaoyue Falüsi (外交部, 条约法律司) Beijing: Shijie Zhishi Chubanshe (北京: 世界知识出版社), 1998).

Summary: Contains text of approximately 50 judicial assistance treaties and agreements, including multilateral treaties from 1948–1988 and bilateral treaties from 1987–1998.

Note: In Chinese.

32 ZHONGWAI SIFA XIEZHU YU YINDU TIAOYUE JI (中外司法协助与引渡条约集) [CHINESE AND FOREIGN JUDICIAL ASSISTANCE AND EXTRADITION TREATIES SET]
Zuigao Renmin Jianchayuan Xingshi Jianchating Bian (最高人民检察院刑事检察厅编) (Beijing: Zhongguo Renmin Gongan Daxue Chubanshe (北京: 中国人民公安大学出版社), 1997).

Summary: Over 30 foreign judicial assistance and extradition treaties from 1987–1997.

Note: In Chinese.

Diplomatic Documents

33 CHUNGGUK NAMGYŎNG KUNGMIN CHŎNGBU OEGYOBU KONGBO, 1928-YŎN 5-WŎL-1949-YŎN 6-WŎL (中國南京國民政府外交部公報, 1928年 5月-1949年 6月) [THE FOREIGN AFFAIRS GAZETTE OF THE NANJING PEOPLE'S GOVERNMENT OF CHINA]
Shi Yuanhua & Yi Po-on (石源華, 李輔溫) (Sŏul: Koguryŏ (서울: 高句麗) 1995).

Summary: This 2 volume set contains text of selected diplomatic exchanges, correspondence, minutes, transmittals, surveys, and statistics between China and foreign nations, especially Korea from 1928–1949. Includes table of contents by date.

Note: In Chinese and Korean.

34 A DOCUMENTARY CHRONICLE OF SINO-WESTERN RELATIONS (1644–1820)
Lo-Shu Fu (Tuscon: University of Arizona Press, 1966).

Summary: Contains the text of over 640 official and unofficial documents and accounts chronicling Chinese-foreign relations from 1644–1820. Organized by emperor's reign and then in rough chronological order. References to original sources are included. Volume 2 contains detailed footnotes, topical index in alphabetical order, and bibliography of Chinese and English language sources.

Index: Topical index included in Volume 2

35 DOCUMENTS ON CHINA'S RELATIONS WITH SOUTH AND SOUTH-EAST ASIA, 1949–1962
G.V. Ambekar & V.D. Divekar (New York: Allied Publishers, 1964).

Summary: Contains the text of 179 selected foreign policy documents on China's relations with South and Southeast Asian countries including letters, communiqués, protocols, statements, memoranda, press releases, proclamations, cables, exchanges, and agreements. Includes detailed table of contents by topic and country.

Index: Includes index by country.

36 WAIJIAO DA CIDIAN (外交大辭典) [DIPLOMATIC DICTIONARY]
Wang Zhuoran & Liu Daren (王卓然, 劉達人) (Taibei: Wenhai Chubanshe, (台北: 文海出版社), 1965).

Summary: Over 2,100 entries concerning Chinese and international diplomatic affairs. Includes table of contents (in Chinese) by topic in Chinese character stroke order.

Index: Includes index (in English) by subject.

Note: In Chinese.

Note: Appendix 1 contains chronological table of important international diplomatic events from 1516–1936. Appendix 2 contains chronological table of treaties between China and foreign nations from 1689–1937.

Note: Facsimile reproduction of 1937 edition published by Zhonghua Shuju (中華書局).

37 WAIJIAO WENDU (外交文牘) [FOREIGN RELATIONS DOCUMENTS]
Waijiaobu; Quanguo Tushuguan Wenxian Suowei Fuzhi Zhongxin; Jiang Yasha (外交部; 全國圖書館文獻縮微復制中心; 姜亚沙) (Beijing: Quanguo Tushuguan Wenxian Suowei Fuzhi Zhongxin (北京: 全國圖書館文獻縮微復制中心), 2004).

Summary: This 7 volume set contains text of selected diplomatic exchanges, correspondence, minutes, transmittals between China and foreign nations from 1917–1927.

Index: Includes comprehensive index to entire set in vol. 1 by topic.

Note: In English, Chinese, French, and German.

38 ZHONGGUO DUIWAI TIAOYUE CIDIAN, 1689–1949 (中国对外条约辞典, 1689–1949) [DICTIONARY OF CHINA'S FOREIGN RELATIONS TREATIES, 1689–1949]
Zhu Huan & Wang Hengwei (朱寰, 王恒伟) (Changchun Shi: Jilin Jiaoyu Chubanshe (长春市: 吉林教育出版社), 1994).

Summary: Contains summaries and definitions regarding Chinese and international diplomatic affairs, treaties, people, and events from 1689–1949.

Index: Includes indexes by topic in Chinese character stroke order, by treaty in chronological order, and by country.

Note: In Chinese.

39 ZHONGHUA RENMIN GONGHEGUO DUIWAI GUANXI WENJIAN JI (中華人民共和国對外关系文件集) [PEOPLE'S REPUBLIC OF CHINA FOREIGN RELATIONS DOCUMENTS COLLECTION]
(Beijing: Shijie Zhishi Chubanshe (北京: 世界知識出版社), 1957–1963).

Summary: This 10 volume set contains text of selected diplomatic exchanges, correspondence, letters, and transmittals between China and foreign nations from 1949–1963. Includes table of contents organized by topic for each volume. Contents of each volume are as follows: vol. 1 covers 1949–1950; vol. 2 covers 1951–1953; vol. 3 covers 1954–1955; vol. 4 covers 1956–1957; vol. 5 covers 1958; vol. 6 covers 1959; vol. 7 covers 1960; vol. 8 covers 1961; vol. 9 covers 1962; vol. 10 covers 1963.

Note: In Chinese.

Yearbooks and Digests of State Practice

40 ZHONGGUO FALÜ NIANJIAN (中国法律年鉴) [CHINA LAW YEARBOOK]
Zhongguo Falü Nianjian Bianjibu (中国法律年鉴编辑部) (Beijing: Falü Chubanshe (北京: 法律出版社), 1987–).

Summary: Annual publication summarizing legal developments and statistics in China. Includes annual lists of important bilateral treaties and multilateral treaties in chronological order. Starting in 2005, includes commentary on China's involvement with the United Nations, international human rights, international environment, law of the sea, boundaries, and mutual legal assistance. Each volume contains table of contents in topical order and index by topic.

Note: In Chinese.

Note: Starting in 2002, an English version, *Law Yearbook of China*, has been published. Beginning with vol. 2003–2004, includes chapter on international treaties and related work in China with commentary on bilateral and multilateral treaties, China's involvement with the United Nations, international human rights, international environment, law of the sea, boundaries, mutual legal assistance, etc. Includes table of contents by topic.

Note: Available in full text online on Chinalawinfo: http://www.chinalawinfo.com (in Chinese) and LawinfoChina: http://www.lawinfochina.com (in English). Also available in full text in CNKI's China Yearbooks database: www.eastview.com.

41 ZHONGGUO GUOJI SIFA YU BIJIAO FA NIANKAN (中国国际私法与比较法年刊) [CHINESE YEARBOOK OF PRIVATE INTERNATIONAL LAW AND COMPARATIVE LAW]
Zhongguo Guoji Sifa Xuehui Zhuban (中国国际私法学会主办) (Beijing Shi: Falü Chubanshe (北京市: 法律出版社), 1982–).

Summary: Annual publication containing articles and commentary on international law from a Chinese perspective, academic activities, and international conferences. A regular section entitled *Documents and Materials* (1982–1989; 1994; 1996–1997) contains text (in Chinese) of selected international agreements, statements, and speeches. Includes a bibliography (in Chinese) of Chinese sources on international law (1986; 1988–1992).

Note: In Chinese. Each volume includes a detailed table of contents in English and Chinese.

Note: Title varies. From 1982–1997, published under the title *Zhongguo Guoji Fa Niankan* (中国国际法年刊) [Chinese Yearbook of International Law]. From 1998 to current, published under the title *Zhongguo Guoji Sifa yu Bijiao Fa Niankan* (中国国际私法与比较法年刊) [Chinese Yearbook of Private International Law and Comparative Law].

Note: Imprint varies: Some volumes published as Zhongguo Duiwai Fanyi Chuban Gongsi (中国对外翻译出版公司) (1982–1986; 1991–1995). Some volumes published as Falü Chubanshe (法律出版社) (1987–1990; 1996 to current).

42 ZHONGGUO WAIJIAO (中国外交) [CHINA'S FOREIGN AFFAIRS]
Zhonghua Renmin Gongheguo Waijiaobu, Zhengce Yanjiushi (中华人民共和国外交部, 政策研究室) (Beijing: Shijie Zhishi Chubanshe (北京: 世界知识出版社), 1996–).

Summary: Annual publication summarizing diplomatic activities and foreign policies. Of note are chapters covering: China's relations with foreign countries (with countries listed in alphabetical order), China's participation in international and regional organizations, and China's involvement in multilateral treaties. Also included is an annual chronicle of China's diplomatic activities and documents. Each volume contains a table of contents by topic.

Note: In Chinese.

Note: Title varies. An earlier version was published as *Zhongguo Waijiao Gailan* (中国外交概览) [China's Foreign Affairs Overview] (1987–1995).

Note: In 2003, an English version, *China's Foreign Affairs*, has been published. Includes table of contents by topic.

Czech Republic

Martin Bouda

Issues of Treaty Succession

Modern Czech statehood is a product of the early twentieth century, when it came into being in its Czechoslovak incarnation. The Czech Republic purports to have its roots in the mediaeval state known as the Lands of the Bohemian Crown. First united in 995, the duchy and later kingdom of Bohemia served as the nucleus of this state, which was established in 1348 as a largely autonomous part of the Holy Roman Empire. This autonomy, most importantly the right of the estates to elect the sovereign, was progressively eroded by kings of the Hapsburg dynasty, who ruled Bohemia after 1526. When Bohemian deputies in the Austrian Parliament made demands for federalism or independence, they often couched these in terms of a re-assertion of rights of the Bohemian Crown.[1] Even the founders and first government members of the modern Czechoslovak state expressed this thought in their Washington Declaration of Independence of 1918 and argued that the Hapsburg dynasty had overreached its mandate by violating the Bohemian constitution and had thus disqualified itself from further rule.[2] But though this political claim and legal fiction of continuity served to legitimise Czechoslovak sovereignty and the rejection of Austro-Hungarian supremacy, it had few practical implications.

When, in the course of the First World War, Czechoslovakia became a sovereign state, and to what extent it succeeded Austria-Hungary, are both questions of some ambiguity. The Czechoslovak National Council was recognised by and signed treaties with Allied Powers prior to the date of legal sovereignty of the Czech National Committee in Prague.[3] These treaties recognised the National Council not only as sovereign but also at war with Austria-Hungary. This speaks against the newly formed Czechoslovak state being a successor to the monarchy. Indeed, the new state was not expected to honour war-time treaties and commitments made by its opponent – Austria-Hungary, as

1 Zdenka Münzer et al., We Were and We Shall Be; the Czechoslovak spirit throughout the centuries. 112 (1941).

2 Id. at 133–135.

3 Bohuš Tomsa, Právo Mezinárodní: Díl Prvý, Část všeobecná. Subjekty mezinárodního práva. Stát a jeho orgány 149–151 (1930).

 | DOI 10.1163/9789004272224_011

expressed later by the Treaty of St. Germain-en-Laye[4] and the Treaty of Trianon.[5] For example the Austro-Hungarian debts that Czechoslovakia was to take upon herself (as discussed below) were limited to those incurred before the beginning of the war.

This conclusion is further supported by certain portions of the Treaties of St. Germain-en-Laye and of Trianon. While these documents treated Austria and Hungary as successors to Austria-Hungary, they implied no such succession by the newly established states, including Czechoslovakia. Unlike Austria and Hungary, these states did not carry responsibility for the damages arising from the war. Most importantly, while Austria and Hungary were compelled to adhere to treaties made by Austria-Hungary that were either specified or revived by notification procedures contained in the peace treaties,[6] these Austro-Hungarian treaties were not made binding on the other newly formed states, including Czechoslovakia. Instead, article 20 and Annex I of the separate treaty with Czechoslovakia[7] specified new treaties that the Czechoslovak state was to be bound by.

On the other hand, there are parts of the treaties of St. Germain and Trianon that counteract the tendency not to think of Czechoslovakia as a successor state: she was held to pay a proportional part of the Austro-Hungarian debt[8] and the Czechoslovak government took over leftover property of the former monarchy.[9] Also, Czechoslovakia signed treaties with Austria in Rome in 1922 and in Vienna in 1923 agreeing to pay out pensions owed by the former monarchy to its citizens.[10] These facts, and especially the succession to Austro-Hungarian debts due to the peace treaties, led certain prominent

---

4 Treaty of Peace Between the Principal Allied and Associated Powers [including Czechoslovakia] and Austria, Sep. 10, 1919, 226 Consol. T.S. 9. [hereinafter Treaty of St. Germain].

5 Treaty of Peace Between the Principal Allied and Associated Powers and Hungary, June 4, 1920. 6 Wiktor's Unperfected Treaties of the United States of America 172. [hereinafter Treaty of Trianon].

6 *See* articles 234 and 241 of the St. Germain Treaty, *supra* note 4, concerning Austria and articles 217 and 224 of the Treaty of Trianon, *supra* note 5, concerning Hungary.

7 Treaty Between the Principal Allied and Associated Powers and Czechoslovakia, Sep. 10, 1919, 226 Consol. T.S. 170.

8 Articles 203, 205 and 206 of the Treaty of St. Germain, *supra* note 4, and 186, 188 and 189 of the Treaty of Trianon, *supra* note 5, executed by laws č. 52/1928, 216/1924 and 237/1923 Sb. (*see infra* note 68 for explanation of references to Czechoslovak and Czech laws).

9 Articles 208 of the Treaty of St. Germain, *supra* note 4, and 191 of the Treaty of Trianon, *supra* note 5, executed by law č. 354/1921 Sb.

10 Items č. 194/1926 Sb. and 195/1926 Sb., both contain the original and authentic French text.

Czechoslovak legal scholars to believe Czechoslovakia to be a successor state to Austria-Hungary at least in part.[11]

As concerns municipal law, the new Czechoslovak legal order adopted all previous Austro-Hungarian laws that it did not explicitly repudiate and much of the early legislation amends or refers to statutes from the Austro-Hungarian period. This implies that the provisions of certain Austro-Hungarian treaties were applied by Czechoslovakia, as they were promulgated in previous municipal laws. But Austro-Hungarian treaties themselves were not referred to as binding upon Czechoslovakia and their provisions were disregarded in amending municipal law.[12] The Czechoslovak state thus did not, in general, succeed to Austro-Hungarian treaties, only certain debts, mentioned above.[13]

Issues of treaty succession next arose with respect to the period 1938–1945, after the signing of the Munich Agreement[14] by Britain, France, Germany and Italy, which (despite her not being party to the agreement) deprived Czechoslovakia of parts of her territory and ultimately led to her break-up and the German occupation of Bohemia and Moravia in the prelude to the Second World War. Once again, the theory of continuity of the Czechoslovak state prevailed, side-stepping the Czecho-Slovak Republic established shortly after the implementation of the agreement as well as the Protectorate of Bohemia and Moravia and the Slovak State established by the occupying forces of Nazi Germany. This approach favoured the London Government-in-Exile, which took over in Prague in 1945. According to Article 1 of the 3 August 1944 presi-

11 Tomsa, *supra* note 3, at 190–192.

12 An early reference to such treaties (§ 2 of ordinance č. 379/1919 Sb.) is that if customs laws derogate old treaty provisions allowing for local trans-boundary commerce, the latter provisions may be applied provided that they do not obstruct the execution of laws on border-checks and import or export as such. Even here, the legal text refers to specific provisions rather than binding treaties and the treaty provisions are only applicable because they are confirmed as such by this law (i.e. they had previously been overridden by law č. 97/1919 Sb. which regulated customs in general) and again only subject to their general conformity with the principles underlying Czechoslovak customs laws. It can thus hardly be said that such treaties were viewed as binding.

13 According to *Succession of States in respect of bilateral treaties: study prepared by the secretariat*, U.N. Secretariat, at 22, UN Doc. A/CN.4/229 (1970), *reprinted in* [1970] 2 Y.B. of Int'l L. Comm'n 124, U.N. Doc. A/CN.4/SER.A/1970/Add.1, "the suggestion of non-continuity is largely supported by practice." The study provides examples from German and Swiss courts' practice vis-à-vis Czechoslovakia.

14 Agreement concerning the Sudeten German Territory, Sep. 29, 1938, Vol. 8 Hudson's International Legislation 131 [hereinafter Munich Agreement].

dential edict of the exile government[15] all legal acts promulgated up to and including 29 September 1938 were rooted in the free will of the Czechoslovak people and are thus valid, while all legal acts from 30 September 1938[16] until a further date set by law (later set to be 4 May 1945)[17] were invalid as the Czechoslovak people were not free to exercise their own will during that period. Article 2 of the edict specified that certain legal acts from this period could be used during a transitional period insofar as they did not contradict the democratic nature of the state.[18] Article 5 established that all edicts and regulations of the (exiled) President of the Republic from this period were exempt from this nullity, though they required subsequent approval of the relevant constitutional authorities (ratihabition)[19] and were subject to special provisions with regard to their validity.

The legal continuity of the Czechoslovak state throughout this period is established by Czech as well as international legal practice. That the Czech Republic considers Czechoslovakia legally continuous between 1938–1945 is clear from the Constitutional Court's ruling sp. zn. Pl. ÚS. 14/94 of 8 March 1995 (republished as č. 55/1995 Sb.), which addresses the legal status of the decrees of the President of the Republic, from this period.[20] The same principles as are detailed in the ruling (i.e. the nullity of the Munich Agreement, the continuity of the Czechoslovak state via the government in exile and so on) are part of a number of international documents relating to the question.

---

15 *Ústavní Dekret Presidenta Republiky o obnovení právního pořádku* [Constiutional Edict of the President of the Republic on the renewal of legal order] (č. 11/1944 Úř. věst. čsl.), published and implemented after the war in the *Vyhláška ministra vnitra o platnosti ústavního dekretu presidenta republiky o obnovení právního pořádku* [Ordinance of the Minister of the Interior on the Validity of the Constitutional Decree of the President of the Republic on the Renewal of Legal Order] č. 30/1945 Sb., of the 27 July 1945.

16 The day when the content of the Munich Agreement became known in Czechoslovakia.

17 By Section 1 of the *Vládní nařízení jímž se stanoví konec doby nesvobody pro obor předpisů o obnovení právního pořádku* [Governmental Ordinance Setting the End of the Period of Subjection for the Purposes of Legal Acts on the Renewal of Legal Order] č. 31/1945 Sb.

18 This and subsequent articles establish the conditions for the application of such acts and establish that no acts in the sphere of criminal law, procedural criminal law, personal law and family law whatsoever may be applied.

19 This was achieved by article 1 of the *Ústavní zákon, kterým se schvalují a prohlašují za zákon dekrety presidenta republiky* [Constitutional law, by which are approved and declared law the decrees of the President of the Republic] č. 57/1946 Sb., of the 28 March 1946.

20 English version is linked from the browsable chronological list of selected decisions at http://www.usoud.cz/en/decisions/. See this ruling for the full argumentation in favour of legal continuity of Czechoslovakia as represented by the exile government.

A clear example is provided by the treaties on neighbourly relations between the Federal Republic of Germany and Czechoslovakia.[21]

It is clear, then, that post-war Czechoslovakia was not the successor to any Protectorate (i.e. German Reich) treaties or obligations and was instead the same entity as before the second world war, as well as that entity which participated in such war-time actions as the Declaration by the United Nations and whose armed forces actively participated in the war effort against the Axis Powers.

The one major difference between the two incarnations of Czechoslovakia was territorial. After demands from both the Soviets and local Ruthenian assemblies organised by them, the Czechoslovak government transferred its territory of Sub-Carpathian Ruthenia to Soviet Ukraine.[22] Post-war Czechoslovakia thus presumably did not succeed to obligations that previously arose for it from the federal union of Ruthenia with pre-war Czechoslovakia, particularly those of articles 10–13 of the 1919 treaty between the Allied and Associated Powers and Czechoslovakia.[23, 24]

The various constitutional and name changes that Czechoslovakia underwent between 1946 and the beginning of 1992 never created new subjects of international law and issues of succession thus did not arise. One notable change, from our perspective here, was the federalisation of Czechoslovakia, beginning with the establishment of the Czech and Slovak Socialist Republics,[25]

---

21 *See* Treaty on Mutual Relations Between the Federal Republic of Germany and the Czechoslovak Socialist Republic, art. 1 and 2 (1), Dec. 11, 1973, 951 UNTS 355 (English text begins on 366) and Treaty Between The Czech and Slovak Federal Republic and the Federal Republic of Germany on Goodneighbourliness and Friendly Cooperation, preamb. 8 and 9, Feb. 27, 1992, 1900 UNTS 27 (English text begins on 69).

22 Treaty (with Protocol) Concerning the Trans-Carpathian Ukraine, June 29, 1945, 504 UNTS 300 (English translation starts on p. 310). Approved and implemented by *Ústavný zákon o Zakarpatskej Ukrajine a úprave štátných hranic so Sväzom sovietskych socialistických republik* [Constitutional Law on Trans-Carpathian Ukraine and the Adjustment of State Boundaries with the Union of Soviet Socialist Republics] č. 2/1946 Sb., of the 22 November 1945 (this law is published in the authentic Slovak version).

23 *Supra*, note 7.

24 Other territorial changes from the post-war period include border adjustments with Hungary (č. 171/1947 Sb.), Poland (č. 62/1958, 74/1975, 143/1975, 43/1988, 49/1988 and 169/1988 Sb.), Austria (č. 30/1974, 41/1974 and 66/1974 Sb.) and Germany (č. 121/1981 and 37/1982 Sb.); all of these are minor adjustments, though, and do not entail major cessions of entire administrative units or changes of obligations under treaty law.

25 The entities were set up as federal entities within Czechoslovakia in the aftermath of the Soviet occupation of Czechoslovakia after the reform period of the Prague Spring in 1968 by the *Ústavní zákon o československé federaci* [Constitutional Law on Czechoslovak

and continuing after the fall of the Communist regime with further devolution of federal powers to the republics[26] as well as the name changes of the federation expressing an ever-increasing decentralising tendency.[27]

The year 1992, on the other hand, led to the dissolution of Czechoslovakia and establishment of the Czech Republic and the Slovak Republic as independent states. The Slovak National Council first passed a declaration of sovereignty of the Slovak Republic on 17 July and then a new constitution of the Slovak Republic on 1 September,[28] making the Slovak Republic an independent state capable of concluding international treaties, declaring war and so on.

In November of the same year, the Federal Assembly passed two constitutional laws facilitating the breakup of Czechoslovakia. The first of these allowed for the division of federal property between the republics[29] and the second for the final extinction of the federal state.[30] Both were published and entered into force on 8 December.[31] The former established the principles

---

Federation] č. 143/1968 Sb. of the 27 October 1968, which entered into effect on the 1 January 1969.

26 Items č. 159/1990, 295/1990 and importantly 556/1990 Sb., as well as the subsequent item č. 493/1992 Sb.

27 Constitutional statute č. 81/1990 Sb., which led to a brief period in which the federation essentially had two names: Czechoslovak Federal Republic for Czechs and Czecho-Slovak Federal Republic for Slovaks, a cause of much controversy between the two, and č. 101/1990 Sb., which finally settled the issue by re-naming the federation the Czech and Slovak Federal Republic.

28 Declaration of 17 July 1992 found as an appendix in *Uznesenie Slovenskej národnej rady o Deklarácii Slovenskej národnej rady o zvrchovanosti Slovenskej republiky* [Resolution of the Slovak National Council on the Declaration of the Slovak National Council on the Sovereignty of Slovak Republic] (this item is published in the authentic Slovak version) in issue 83 of the 1992 volume of the Sbírka Zákonů between items č. 424/1992 and 425/1992 Sb. The constitution of October 1 is *Ústava Slovenskej Republiky* [Constitution of the Slovak Republic] č. 460/1992 Sb. (this item is published in the authentic Slovak version), English translation in Gisbert H. Flanz *The Slovak Republic, in* Release 93–4, CONSTITUTIONS OF THE COUNTRIES OF THE WORLD: HISTORIC BINDERS 63–103 (A.P. Blaustein & G.H. Flanz, eds, 1971-).

29 *Ústavní zákon o dělení majetku České a Slovenské Federativní Republiky mezi Českou republiku a Slovenskou republiku a jeho přechodu na Českou republiku a Slovenskou republiku* [Constitutional Statute Regarding the Division and Transfer of Federal Property to the Czech and Slovak Republics] č. 541/1992 Sb., of the 13 November.

30 *Ústavní zákon o zániku České a Slovenské Federativní Republiky* [Constitutional Statute on the Extinction of the Czech and Slovak Federal Republic] č. 542/1992 Sb., of the 25 November.

31 For a description of the proceedings in English, *see* ERIC STEIN, CZECHO/SLOVAKIA: ETHNIC CONFLICT, CONSTITUTIONAL FISSURE, NEGOTIATED BREAKUP (1997).

according to which the property and obligations of the Federation were to be divided amongst the republics. Article 3 stated that rights or obligations relevant only to the territory of one federal republic would be inherited by that republic; it further stated that property (as defined by article 2 to include property rights and obligations) was to be divided according to two principles: either they were to be inherited by the republic on whose territory they were located or they were to be divided according to number of citizens, i.e. according to the ratio 2:1, between the Czech and Slovak republics, where the first principle could not be applied. Articles 4 and 5 regulate the treatment of obligations of Czechoslovakia to International Organisations[32] and debts, respectively. The law further presumed one or more treaties to be concluded between the republics to deal with the details.

In fact, such treaties had been in the process of negotiation since the early autumn,[33] despite the fact that the Federal order did not allow for such treaties until the entry into force of constitutional statute č. 542/1992 Sb.[34] The latter law allowed the two federal republics to conclude treaties with one another (article 7) as well as third parties (article 8), where such treaties could not enter into force before the 1 January 1993 (the day after the extinction of the Czech and Slovak Federal Republic). The treaties concluded between the federal republics on this basis formed the legal foundations for the subsequent break-up of the federation. It also provided for the devolution of remaining powers to the republics and by article 1 the extinction of the Czech and Slovak Federal Republic with the elapsing of 31 December 1992. The same article established that the successor states of the Czech and Slovak Federal Republic are the Czech Republic and the Slovak Republic. Both new states took this provision up and are indeed the successor states of Czechoslovakia.

It can be concluded from these two laws as well as from Czech practice[35] that international obligations of Czechoslovakia, both as concerns treaties and

---

32 For a brief treatment of membership in International Organisations after the dissolution of Czechoslovakia, *see* Konrad Bühler, State Succession and Membership in International Organizations: Legal Theories versus Political Pragmatism 273–283 (2001).

33 Vladimír Mikule, Mezinárodní smlouvy mezi Českou republikou a Slovesnkou Republikou (1995).

34 *Supra*, note 30.

35 For a general description of this practice, *see* Vladimír Mikulka, *The Dissolution of Czechoslovakia and Succession in Respect of Treaties*, *in* Succession of States 109–125

otherwise, were in general transferred to the Czech republic unless they were of a specific nature affecting only Slovak territory. One such exceptional case is the 1977 Gabčíkovo-Nagymaros Project treaty between Czechoslovakia and Hungary[36] and the eponymous case before the ICJ.[37] The treaty was meant to encourage cooperation between the two states concerning a dam project on the Danube, which touches no part of the territory of the Czech Republic. For this reason, the Czech parliament passed a resolution in 1993, in which it explicitly states the Czech Republic did not succeed to that treaty.[38] When Hungary and Slovakia submitted a dispute over the project to the ICJ, they agreed that they consider Slovakia the sole successor to the 1977 treaty.[39]

Treaty Ratification and Implementation

The method of implementation of international treaty law into Czech municipal law, as well as the relationship between the two, has relatively recently undergone radical reform after almost a century of uniform practice. Many treaties in force for the Czech Republic today were ratified under the old system and the implementation into Czech municipal law of those that do not fulfil certain criteria is by default governed by the old rules. Furthermore, the recent history of iterative changes has given rise to diverging interpretations of the system within the legal profession, creating the potential for confusion. For this reason, it will be useful to first describe the implementation process of the Czech Republic as of 1993 and touch upon its history, and only then restate the contemporary system succinctly.

(Mojmir Mrak (ed.), 1999). For a more detailed breakdown of succession to specific multi- and bi-lateral treaties with particular parties, *see State Succession in Respect of Treaties: Czech Republic (National Report)*, *in* STATE PRACTICE REGARDING STATE SUCCESSION AND ISSUES OF RECOGNITION 400–470 (Klabbers, Jan et al. (eds.), 1999).

36 Treaty concerning the construction and operation of the Gabcikovo-Nagymaros system of locks, Sep. 16, 1977, 1109 UNTS 211.

37 Case Concerning the Gabcikovo-Nagymaros Project (Hung./Slovk.), 1997 I.C.J. 7.

38 *Usnesení Poslanecké Sněmovny k vládnímu návrhu dalšího postupu České republiky ve věci Soustavy vodních děl Gabčíkovo-Nagymaros* [Resolution of the Chamber of Deputies to the Cabinet Proposal of Further Action of the Czech Republic in the Matter of the System of Waterworks Gabcikovo-Nagymaros], known as resolution č. 32/1993 Sb. of the 23 February 1993.

39 Special Agreement for submission to the International Court of Justice of the differences concerning the Gabcikovo-Nagymaros Project, April 7, 1993, 1725 UNTS 225.

The old system was established after the break-up of Austria-Hungary. The 1920 constitution of Czechoslovakia (constitutional statute č. 121/1920 Sb.) did not mention the relation of municipal to international law. The jurisprudence of the Czechoslovak courts established that international treaties do not by themselves constitute domestic law, but their provisions must always be promulgated in a special act.[40] This founded eighty years of Czechoslovak dualist practice with respect to international treaties.

Under this practice, treaty provisions were only implemented into domestic law if the particular law regulating the same issue included a section stating that the provisions of treaties had priority over the law. In this case, the treaty had the status of *lex specialis* vis-à-vis that particular law and its provisions had the same place and force in the overall legal system as the law before which it had priority.[41]

The first sign of change to this system came with a constitutional law passed in January 1991.[42] Section 2 of this law was a general reference to treaties about human rights and basic freedoms ratified and duly published, making them generally binding in the Czech and Slovak Federal Republic and giving them priority over laws. A constitutional law from February of the same year[43] established a Constitutional Court with the power to decide on the nonconformity of laws with these treaties (as per article 2 b of the law), rendering such laws or their provisions void (article 3 (1)). These changes were themselves partially formulated in the spirit of the dualistic system, but were the basis for the later move to monism.

The 1992 Constitution of the Czech Republic in principle continued the old system,[44] with one important exception, discussed below. Article 63 (1) b)

40 Jiří Malenovský, Poměr mezinárodního a vnitrostátního práva: obecně a v českém právu zvláště 59 (1st Ed., 2000).

41 Id., at 72–73.

42 *Ústavní zákon, kterým se uvozuje LISTINA ZÁKLADNÍCH PRÁV A SVOBOD jako ústavní zákon Federálního shromáždění České a Slovenské Federativní Republiky* [Constitutional Statute, which establishes the CHARTER OF FUNDAMENTAL RIGHTS AND FREEDOMS as a Constitutional Statute of the Federal Assembly of the Czech and Slovak Federal Republic] č. 23/1991 Sb., of the 9 January 1991.

43 *Ústavní zákon o Ústavním soudu České a Slovenské Federativní Republiky* [Constitutional Statute on the Constitutional Court of the Czech and Slovak Federal Republic] č. 91/1991 Sb., of the 27 February 1991.

44 Ústavní zákon č. 1/1993 Sb., Ústava České Republiky [Constitution of the Czech Republic], of the 16 December 1992; English version can be found in Gisbert Flanz, *Czech Republic, in* Release 93–4, Constitutions of the Countries of the World: Historic Binders 117–149 (A.P. Blaustein & G.H. Flanz, eds, 1971-).

and (3) states that negotiation and ratification of international treaties is one of the powers of the president, which requires the co-signature of the prime minister or one of the members of his government in order to be valid. Article 63 (1) b) also allows the president to transfer the power of negotiation of treaties to the government or its individual members.

President Václav Havel did indeed transfer the power to negotiate treaties that do not require the approval of parliament for their ratification to the government or, in the case of treaties that deal with competences belonging exclusively to one agency of government, to that member of the government in whose competence it is.[45] The President retains the possibility of taking back the power of negotiation in individual cases.

The types of treaties that require parliamentary approval for their ratification are spelled out in article 49 of the constitution.[46] They are treaties regarding human rights and basic freedoms, political treaties, treaties of a general economic nature as well as all treaties whose implementation requires a law.

By implication, the treaties that do not require parliamentary approval and whose negotiation was transferred to the government or its members are all other treaties. These latter treaties are binding on the government and its components as per section 25 of the law dealing with establishing ministries and other administrative institutions,[47] which makes the ministries responsible for the obligations that such treaties place on the Czech Republic.

The major innovation of the 1992 Constitution was its article 10, which made international treaties concerning human rights and basic freedoms, to which the Czech Republic is a party, directly binding and gave them priority over statutes. Ratification of such treaties required a three-fifths vote of approval in each chamber of parliament (article 39 (4)). Such a treaty has to be officially published[48] and be binding on the Czech Republic (according to international law) to become a part of the municipal legal order. That a treaty relates to human rights is established by the Parliament when it approves the treaty under the

45 *Rozhodnutí prezidenta republiky o sjednávání mezinárodních smluv* [Decision of the President of the Republic on the negotiation of international treaties] č. 144/93 Sb., of the 28 April 1993.

46 *Supra*, note 44.

47 *Zákon o zřízení ministerstev a jiných ústředních orgánů státní správy České republiky* [Statute on the Establishment of Ministries and Other Central Organs of State Administration of the Czech Republic] č. 69/1993 Sb., of the 15 February 1993.

48 This means published in the Sbirka Zakonu (later Sbirka Mezinarodnich Smluv) in both Czech and an authentic language of the treaty. For certain treaties concerning only small groups of citizens, publication consists of a notice by the Ministry of Foreign affairs as to where the text of the treaty may be found; Mikule, *supra* note 33, at 6.

three-fifths procedure rather than simple majority. For treaties ratified before the entry into force of this constitution, the decision as to whether or not the treaty relates to human rights rests with the constitutional court.[49]

All other treaties approved by the parliament required, as before, a mention in law in order to be made part of the municipal law. Parliamentary approval did not constitute ratification (done later by the president) or the treaty's acceptance as law.[50] These treaties were either implemented on the basis of a specific law that articulated particular provisions for the interpretation of the treaty's general ones (for example the Oslo convention on anti-personnel mines,[51] is thus implemented by law č. 305/1999 Sb.)[52] or a law that simply referred to a given treaty or set of treaties and gave it priority over relevant laws (see for example section 1 of law č. 151/1930 Sb.[53]), or sections in relevant laws referring to published, binding treaties in general as having priority over their provisions (see for example section 318 of law č. 13/1993 Sb.[54]).[55] Treaties signed and ratified but without any reference in municipal law were not part of the legal order and were not applied (for example the Antarctic treaty[56] had no enacting law for a full 42 years and its provisions were not enforced on Czech nationals, although it was binding on the Czech Republic).[57]

This system underwent significant changes with a 2001 constitutional amendment, which came into force on June 1 2002.[58] Article 49 of the Constitution was amended such that treaties requiring parliamentary approval are now those defining the rights and responsibilities of persons, alliance, peace and other political treaties, those which confer on the Czech Republic membership in international organisations, economic treaties of a general nature,

---

49 Malenovský, *supra* note 40, at 69–71.

50 Id., at 61.

51 Convention on the Prohibition of Use, Stockpiling, Production and Transfer of Anti-Personnel Mines and on their Destruction, Sep. 18, 1997, 2056 UNTS 211.

52 Jiří Malenovský, Mezinárodní právo veřejné: jeho obecná část a poměr k vnitrostátnímu právu, zvláště k právu českému 444 (4th Ed., 2004)

53 *Zákon o úpravě právních a hospodářských poměrů v pohraničních územích* [Law on the adjustment of legal and economic conditions in border territories] č. 151/1930 Sb., of the 10. October 1930; still in force at the time of publication of his volume.

54 Celní Zákon [Customs law] č. 13/1993 Sb., of the 15 December 1992.

55 Vladimír Týč, Právo mezinárodních smluv 109 (1995).

56 The Antarctic Treaty, Dec. 1, 1959. 402 UNTS 71; 12 UST 794.

57 Malenovský, *supra* note 52, at 444–445.

58 *Ústavní zákon, kterým se mění ústavní zákon České národní rady č. 1/1993 Sb., Ústava České republiky, ve znění pozdějších předpisů* [Constitutional Statute, which changes the Constitutional Statute of the Czech national Council č. 1/1993 Sb., Constitution of the Czech Republic, as amended to date] č. 395/2001 Sb., of the 18 October 2001.

and other treaties concerning issues whose regulation requires the passage of a law. This is not so much a change as a better definition of the previous order.

Article 1(b) of the constitution newly declares that the Czech Republic fulfils obligations that bind it under international law. This includes international treaties, whose provisions are thus binding on the Czech state and its agencies, in relation to subjects of Czech law, based on this constitutional provision.[59]

The most significant change comes in article 10. The article no longer mentions treaties concerning human rights. Instead, it specifies that all promulgated[60] treaties, whose ratification was approved by the parliament, and which are binding on the Czech Republic are *part of the legal order*. In the case of a conflict between their provisions and those of a domestic law, the provisions of the treaty are to be applied. In other words, the treaties fulfilling these requirements are viewed monistically as part of Czech municipal law.[61]

Article 10 also newly allows a popular referendum to substitute the assent of parliament in the case of treaties that transfer competences from the Czech Republic to international organisations or institutions.

The details of this most recent amendment are laid out here because they all enter into play when considering the municipal implementation of a treaty. As noted above, the provisions of any treaty binding on the Czech Republic can be enforced on relevant agencies of the state under municipal law, thanks to article 1(b) of the constitution. Article 10 specifies which treaties are part of the legal order binding on subjects of Czech law and what this means. What it means is that provisions of the treaty will be used instead of other contradictory legal provisions. Article 95(1) of the constitution binds judges to decide according to the law as well as those treaties that are part of the legal order. Thus self-executing treaty provisions will be used instead of contradictory legislation, but it is also true that legislation contradicting more general, non-self-executing provisions of qualified treaties cannot be applied. The actual replacement of such invalidated legal provisions with provisions binding on subjects of Czech law other than agencies of the state requires a further implementing act.[62]

As for which treaties become part of the legal order in this way, the conditions named in article 10 of the constitution have generated confusion and

---

59 Jiří Malenovský, Mezinárodní právo veřejné: Jeho obecná část a poměr k jiným právním systémům, zvláště k právu českému (5th Ed., 2008).

60 That is, those which are duly published in the appropriate collection (but see below).

61 Jan Wintr, Principy českého ústavního práva (s dodatkem principů práva evropského a mezinárodního 16 (2006).

62 Petr Mlsna & Jan Kněžínek, Mezinárodní smlouvy v českém právu: Teoretická východiska, sjednávání, schvalování, ratifikace, vyhlašování a aplikace 307 (2009).

controversy in the scholarship as well as jurisprudence of relevant courts. The most important question is that of 'apparent retroactivity' of the amendment, that is, whether the amendment applies to treaties whose dates of ratification or entry into force preceded the date of entry into force of the amendment. After significant debate,[63] it is now generally accepted[64] that this is the case even though it took a ruling of the Constitutional court[65] overturning a previous ruling of the Supreme Administrative Court[66] to the contrary.

Nevertheless, ambiguities remain. First, in the cases where a referendum is substituted for the assent of the Parliament, it is theoretically unclear whether the treaty becomes part of the legal order or not. In practice this applies only to the Czech Republic's accession treaty to the EU[67] and the notion that this has become part of municipal law has gone unchallenged.

---

63 For one side of the argument, *see* Pavel Šturma, *Postavení mezinárodních smluv po novele Ústavy ČR*, 4 České Právo Životního Prostředí, 7, (2002), for the other, *see* J. Filip, *Parlament schválil návrh euronovely Ústavy ČR*, 11 Právní Zpravodaj 4, (2001). The most widely cited argument against apparent retroactivity would have limited the scope of retroactivity to treaties approved after 1993 (Václav Pavlíček, *O subjektech práv a svobod v Listině, o principech přirozeněprávních ve vztahu k ústavnímu zákonu č. 395/2001 Sb.*, *in* DESET LET LISTINY ZÁKLADNÍCH PRÁV A SVOBOD V PRÁVNÍM ŘÁDU ČR A SR 91–94 (Vojtěch Šimíček & Břetislav Dančák (eds.), 2001). It was based on the notion that "Parliament" is defined strictly elsewhere in the constitution and thus must be given this strict interpretation here as well, i.e. the treaties must have been approved by the Parliament of the Czech Republic and not previous Czechoslovak legislatures. This argument was roundly rejected on various grounds, however, the most important of which included the stated constitutional continuity between legislative bodies declared in the constitutional statute č. 5/1993 Sb. (Jan Kysela & Kuhn Zbyněk, *Aplikace mezinárodního práva po přijetí tzv. euronovely Ústavy ČR*, 7 Právní Rozhledy 305, (2002).

64 E.g. Mlsna & Kněžínek, *supra* note 62, or Malenovský, *supra* note 59.

65 *Nález Ústavního soudu* [Finding of the constitutional court] sp. zn. I. ÚS 520/06, from January 23 2008, published under the reference N 18/48 SbNU 195 in the *Sbírka nálezů a usnesení Ústavního soudu* [Collection of Decisions and Resolutions of the Constitutional Court].

66 Decision č.j. 3 Ads 21/2005 – 71 from May 18 2006.

67 Treaty Between the Kingdom of Belgium, the Kingdom of Denmark, the Federal Republic of Germany, the Hellenic Republic, the Kingdom of Spain, the French Republic, Ireland, the Italian Republic, the Grand Duchy of Luxembourg, the Kingdom of the Netherlands, the Republic of Austria, the Portuguese Republic, the Republic of Finland, the Kingdom of Sweden, the United Kingdom of Great Britain and Northern Ireland (Member States of the European Union) and the Czech Republic, the Republic of Estonia, the Republic of Cyprus, the Republic of Latvia, the Republic of Lithuania, the Republic of Hungary, the Republic of Malta, the Republic of Poland, the Republic of Slovenia, the Slovak Republic,

The second issue has significantly more practical importance. All treaties that bind the Czech Republic (or previously Czechoslovakia) are required by law to be published, and the validity of their provisions in municipal law is predicated on this publication. Until 1999, they were either published as a notice of the Ministry of Foreign Affairs in the *Sbírka Zákonů*,[68] or else such a notice announced the treaty's availability at the ministry. Since 2000, treaties are published separately from domestic acts in the *Sbírka Mezinárodních Smluv*.[69] Treaties must be published both in Czech and, if applicable, one of the authentic languages. Besides treaties, the Ministry of Foreign Affairs has also been bound to publish notices of withdrawals from treaties, treaty annulment and other important events pertaining to treaties.

Regrettably the publication of some treaties was significantly delayed, inadequate, or completely absent.[70] This was especially a problem in the years 1948–1989, when Czechoslovakia's publication practices were particularly lax. Thus, the publication of the text of some treaties was delayed for decades,[71] others remain unpublished to this day.[72] Other treaties were formally published merely through a notice of the availability of their text at the Foreign Ministry, but the text was never published in full. The publication of others still was limited to a simple statement of their entry into force. The latter category may be argued to have never been published even formally, since this mode of publication did not meet the legal requirements.[73] Since, however, due

---

concerning the accession of the Czech Republic, the Republic of Estonia, the Republic of Cyprus, the Republic of Latvia, the Republic of Lithuania, the Republic of Hungary, the Republic of Malta, the Republic of Poland, the Republic of Slovenia and the Slovak Republic to the European Union, Apr. 16 2003, 2003 O.J. (L 236).

68 *See infra* item number 1 in General Treaty Collections; references to this publication are in the form: item č. number/year sometimes Sb. (in earlier years sometimes Sb. z. a n.).

69 *See infra* item č. number 3 in General Treaty Collections; references to this publication are in the form: item number/year Sb. m. s.

70 For one article specifically on the subject, *see* Jan Kněžínek, *Nevyhlašování mezinárodních smluv, kterými je ČR vázána* 3(1) Právní Fórum 8 (2006).

71 An example noted by Mlsna & Kněžínek, *supra* note 62, is the Convention concerning Forced or Compulsory Labour, June 28, 1930, 39 UNTS 55, which entered into force for Czechoslovakia on October 30 1958 but was published only as *Úmluva o nucené nebo povinné práci* in item č. 506/1990 Sb.

72 An example noted by Malenovský, *supra* note 59, is the Convention for the Suppression of the Traffic in Persons and of the Exploitation of the Prostitution of Others, Dec. 2, 1949, U.N. Doc. A/RES/317, which entered into force for Czechoslovakia in 1958, for the Czech Republic in 1993 but which remains unpublished even at the time of publication of this volume.

73 According to Mlsna & Kněžínek, *supra* note 62, the treaties listed in item č. 40/1980 Sb. fall into this category, and their municipal validity is deeply questionable.

publication is a condition of the treaty's incorporation into the legal order, the provisions of no treaty that has not been duly published can be binding on subjects of Czech law. They can only be binding on the agencies of the state.[74]

Finally, the Constitutional Court holds the controversial view that ratified treaties on human rights are still part of the constitutional order and may therefore form the basis of its decisions to strike down legislation,[75] which the court has done on the grounds that even if these treaties are no longer mentioned in the constitution, the level of protection of individual rights and freedoms can only be increased, not decreased.[76]

In essence then, the contemporary system of implementing treaties is as follows. Any treaty in force for the Czech Republic binds all relevant agencies of the state to act according to its provisions. A treaty in force whose ratification has been approved by the Czech parliament or any previous Czechoslovak legislature, which is binding on the Czech Republic, and which has been duly published is part of the municipal legal order. It should not, however, be taken for granted that any treaty which binds the Czech Republic fulfils the other conditions. The provisions of such a treaty will be applied instead of contradictory provisions of municipal legislation. Treaties whose ratification was not approved by the parliament, but which were duly published and which are referred to in the provisions of individual legal acts, retain the status of *lex specialis* with regards to those acts. Finally, human rights treaties in force, ratified with the consent of parliament, duly published, and binding on the Czech Republic remain part of the constitutional order and may be used to strike down non-conforming legislation.

Annotated Bibliography of Sources

General Treaty Collections

1 SBÍRKA ZÁKONŮ ČESKÉ REPUBLIKY [CITED AS SB.]
(Břeclav: Moraviapress, a.s., 1918–).

Summary: Official Gazette of the Czech Republic. Includes the texts of treaties until the year 1999.[77] Treaties usually appear in Czech; frequently the original (multilateral) version or the version in the other party's language (bilateral)

74 Mlsna & Kněžínek, *supra* note 62, as well as Malenovský, *supra* note 59.

75 Wintr, *supra* note 61, at 16.

76 *See Nález Ústavního soudu* [Finding of the constitutional court] sp. zn. Pl. ÚS 36/01, published as č. 403/2002 Sb.

77 *See* discussion on publication of treaties, *supra.*

is also included. Some treaties are introduced with the date and place of signing, the date of entry into force and a notice of ratification. Each year's volume includes non-cumulative chronological and subject indices at the front. Since the year 2000, treaties are no longer published here (See no. 3 below).

Index: The years 1918 and 1919 are often bound as one volume. They have two separate indices, however, and the index for 1919 is located after the last issue of 1918 and is followed by the issues for 1919. The volumes for the years 1918–1951 have both a chronological index, which refers to the date, page and item number, and an alphabetical subject index, which refers to item number and the page number in the *Sbírka* itself (1918–1947) or, where applicable, its supplement (1948–1951), where the full text of the treaty may be found.

Index: The subject index for these years has the treaties organised as follows. For the years 1918–1919, treaties are listed under thematic subject headings. In the 1920–1922 volumes and 1945 (*doba svobody*), treaties are organised chronologically under the heading "Úmluvy státní" or under the thematic subject heading and bilateral treaties can be found under the name of the other party. In the 1923–1939 as well as the 1946–1951 volumes, bilateral treaties are organised under "Úmluvy státní" alphabetically according to the other party and multilateral treaties are listed chronologically under the sub-heading "s několika státy," at the end of that section; treaties can also be found under the thematic subject heading and bilateral ones under the name of the other party. In the 1940 volume all treaties are under the term "Německo" in the Czech-language index and under the term "Versicherungswesen" in the German-language one. In the 1941–1944 volumes and 1945 (*doba nesvobody*), all treaties and legal texts pertaining to treaties are listed under the headings "Protektorát" and "Říše" in the Czech version and under "Deutsches Reich" and "Protektorat Böhmen und Mähren" in the German version (1941–1943). Treaties are listed chronologically under these headings along with other legal texts.

Index: In the 1952–1957 volumes there is a chronological index which refers to the number of the legal text and the page in the *Sbírka* as well as an alphabetical subject index, which refers to the number of the text and, where applicable, the page in the supplement where the full text may be found. Bilateral treaties may be found under the name of the other party, treaties may also be found under thematic subject headings or the name of the international organisation they are concerned with. For the years 1952–1954, all treaties may be found under the heading "Úmluvy státní," organised alphabetically according to the other party or under the sub-heading "s několika státy" at the end of the section, if they are multilateral. In the 1955 volume, they are also organised under the heading "Úmluvy státní," but chronologically. In the

1956 volume, they are organised chronologically under "Úmluvy mezinárodní." In the 1957 volume, they are organised chronologically under "Mezinárodní smlouvy."

Index: In the 1958–1959 volumes, the chronological index refers to the item number, the issue and the page where it can be found. In the subject index, treaties may be found chronologically ordered under "Mezinárodní smlouvy," under the thematic subject heading or the name of the other party. The subject index refers to the item number and, where applicable, the page in the supplement where the full text of the treaty can be found.

Index: In the 1960–1964 volumes, there is only a subject index that refers to the item number and the page and issue where it can be found. In the 1960 volume, treaties can be found under the name of the other party, a thematic subject heading or the heading "Mezinárodní smlouvy," where they are chronologically ordered. In the 1961–1962 volumes, treaties may be found under the name of the other party, a thematic subject heading or the heading "Mezinárodní smlouvy dvoustranné" if they are bilateral and "Mezinárodní smlouvy vícestranné" if they are multilateral. They are chronologically ordered under each of the headings. In the 1963–1964 volumes, treaties may be found under the name of the other party, a thematic subject heading or the heading "Mezinárodní smlouvy dvoustranné" if they are bilateral and "Mezinárodní smlouvy mnohostranné" if they are multilateral. They are chronologically ordered under each of the headings.

Index: In the 1965–1968 volumes, there is a subject index that refers to the item number only. Treaties may be found under the heading "Mezinárodní organizace," if they concern international organisations or else the heading "Mezinárodní smlouvy, dohody, úmluvy" where they are further divided thematically under alphabetically organised subject headings.

Index: In the 1969–1999 volumes, there is a chronological index that refers to the item number and page number and a subject index that refers to the item number. Treaties may be found in the latter index under the heading "Mezinárodní smlouvy, dohody, úmluvy" where they are chronologically ordered. In the volumes 1969–1992, the chronological index is divided into three parts: part one for federal legal documents, part two for the legislation of the Czech Socialist Republic and part three for the legislation of the Slovak Socialist Republic. In the volumes 1977–1999 the subject index is immediately preceded by a list of subject headings.

Note: Title varies: *Sbírka zákonů a nařízení státu československého*, 1918–1937; *Sbírka zákonů a nařízení*, 1940–1944; *Sbírka zákonů Republiky Československé*, 1946–1959; *Sbírka zákonů Československé socialistické republiky*, 1960–1968; *Sbírka zákonů: Československá socialistická republika; Česká socialistická republika; Slovenská socialistická republika*, 1969–1989; *Sbírka zákonů České a Slovenské Federativní Republiky, České republiky, Slovenské republiky*, 1991–1992.

Note: Title varies in the year 1938: *Sbírka zákonů a nařízení státu československého*, issues 1–99 (i.e. items no. 1/1938–299/1938); *Sbírka zákonů a nařízení státu česko-slovenského*, issues 100–123 (nos. 300–393); the entire volume is bound under the latter title.

Note: Title varies in the year 1939: *Sbírka zákonů a nařízení republiky česko-slovenské*, issues 1–24 of Part I[78] (i.e. items no. 1/1939–59/1939); *Sbírka zákonů a nařízení*, issues 25–74 (i.e. nos. 60/1939–202/1939); *Sbírka zákonů a nařízení Protektorátu Čechy a Morava*, issues 75–113 (i.e. nos. 203/1939–331/1939); the title page and index for this year were published under the title *Sbírka zákonů a nařízení* and the entire year is usually bound as one volume under this title.

Note: The first title in 1939 has two parts. Part I contains legal documents in force for the entire territory of the Czecho-Slovak Republic. Part II contains those legal documents only enforced in the Czech and the Moravia-Silesian lands.[79] The index for part II is found at the end of the index issue for the year and the text of the laws was published in 10 issues that constitute part II and are found at the very end of the volume.

Note: The volumes for 1940–1943 are bound under the title *Sbírka zákonů a nařízení*, but the individual issues are entitled *Sbírka zákonů a nařízení Protektorátu Čechy a Morava*. These volumes are bilingual in German and Czech. The German title is *Sammlung der Gesetze und Verordnungen* for the volumes and *Sammlung der Gesetze und Verordnungen des Protektorates Böhmen und Mähren* for the issues. The German imprint is: Praag: Druckerei des Protektorates Böhmen und Mähren, 1940–1943. These volumes have two sets of indices, one German and one Czech. The volume for 1944 is equally bilingual and has the same titles, except the title page and index are only in Czech; it has no German imprint (see below).[80]

Note: The volume for 1945 was published in two parts under the title *Sbírka zákonů a nařízení*. The first part has the subtitle (*doba nesvobody*)[81] and the second (*doba svobody*).[82] The first part covers the laws and ordinances issued

---

78 *See infra* next *note*.

79 Administrative units at the time, these two forming together the Czech part of Czechoslovakia; the Slovak and Sub-Carpathian Ruthenian lands formed the Slovak part.

80 For an evaluation of the validity of laws published during this period, *see* "Issues of Treaty Succession," *supra*.

81 Transl.: Period of subjection.

82 Transl.: Period of freedom. This period officially began on the 4th of May 1945, as per the governmental ordinance č. 31/1945 Sb., of the 27th July 1945.

by the protectorate government in that part of 1945 that belongs to the period of occupation. The issues[83] are numbered 1–31 and the items 1/1945–47/1945, but for reasons of differentiation from part two later indices and other publications place an asterisk after the number of the laws in this part. The issues are bilingual in German and Czech, entitled *Sammlung der Gesetze und Verordnungen des Protektorates Böhmen und Mähren* and *Sbírka zákonů a nařízení Protektorátu Čechy a Morava.* The second part covers the laws and ordinances issued after the liberation of Czechoslovakia as well as some issued by the Government-in-Exile.[84] The numbering of these laws begins again from 1/1945, these are usually the laws designated by the simple number (without asterisk) in later publications. The issues of this part carry the following titles: *Sbírka zákonů státu československého,* issues 1–10 (items no. 1/1945–22/1945); *Sbírka zákonů republiky Československé,* issues 11–67 (nos. 23/1945–165/1945).[85] Each of the two parts has its own index published in Czech only and placed immediately before the first issue of the respective part. The two parts are usually bound together.

Note: Title varies in the year 1990: *Sbírka zákonů: Československá socialistická republika, Česká socialistická republika, Slovenská socialistická republika,* issues 1–12 (i.e. items no. 1/1990 – 52/1990); *Sbírka zákonů: Československá socialistická republika; Česká republika; Sloveská republika,* issues 13–18 (i.e. nos. 53/1990 – 80/1990); *Sbírka zákonů: Československá federativní republika; Česká republika; Slovenská republika,* issues 19–20 (i.e. nos. 81/1990 – 99/1990); *Sbírka Zákonů České a Slovenské Federativní Republiky, České Republiky, Slovenské Republiky,* issues 21–101 (i.e. nos. 100/1990 – 602/1990); the title page and index for this year were published under the final title and the entire year is usually bound as one volume under this title.

Note: Imprint varies: Praha: Státní Tiskárna, 1918–1938; Praha: Tiskárna Protektorátu Čechy a Morava, 1939–1943; Praha: Státní Tiskárna, 1945–1947; Praha: Státní Tiskárna, n. p., 1948–1952; Praha: Knihtisk, n.p., 1953–1965; Praha: Statistické a evidenční vydavatelství tiskopisů, n.p., 1966–1988; Praha: Statistické a evidenční vydavatelství tiskopisů, s.p., 1989–1992; Praha: SEVT, a.s., 1993–1995.

---

83 I use the word "issue" to refer to the Czech "částka," whereas "č." refers the specific number of the item itself, as per the official notation of acts (e.g. act č. 32/1994 Sb.).

84 The dates of publication of the first issues do not correspond to the official beginning of the period of freedom, despite the subtitle. The division into parts is according to the issuing authority rather than period.

85 This title change was made in accordance with the edict of the president of the republic č. 19/1945 Sb.

Note: The 1944 volume was published in 1945 by the State Press (i.e. Státní Tiskárna); the 1945 and 1946 volumes were also published a year late, and two volumes were published in 1947.

Note: The alphabetical order of Me- and Mě- varies: sometimes the two are counted as identical, sometimes Mě- is counted as later in the alphabet. The alphabetical order of headings such as "Měna" and "Mezinárodní…" may thus be inverted in certain years.

2 SAMMLUNG DER GESETZE UND VERORDNUNGEN DES ČECHOSLOVAKISCHEN STAATES
(Prag: Staatsdruckerei, 1918–1938).

Summary: German language version of the *Sbírka zákonů a nařízení státu československého*. Includes German language versions of all the texts. Each year's volume includes non-cumulative chronological and subject indices at the front.

Index: The chronological index refers to the date of adoption, number and page of publication of each item. For the years 1918–1919, treaties are listed under thematic subject headings. In the 1920–1922 volumes, treaties are organised chronologically under the heading "Staatsverträge" or under the thematic subject heading and bilateral treaties can be found under the name of the opposite party. In the 1923–1938 volumes, bilateral treaties are organised under "Staatsverträge" alphabetically according to the other party and multilateral treaties are listed chronologically under the subheading "mit mehreren Staaten," at the end of that section; treaties can also be found under the thematic subject heading and bilateral ones under the name of the other party.

3 SBÍRKA MEZINÁRODNÍCH SMLUV: ČESKÁ REPUBLIKA [CITED AS SB. M. S.]
(Břeclav: Moraviapress, a.s., 2000-).

Summary: Official gazette of international treaties of the Czech Republic since the year 2000. Includes the texts of treaties, notices of withdrawal from treaties, notices of end of validity, additions, amendments and other important documents pertaining to treaties as well as decisions of international organs and organisations by which the Czech republic is bound. Language of publication varies: multilateral treaties are often published in the authentic language and in Czech translation, bilateral treaties may be published in the Czech version only.

Index: In the 2000–2008 volumes, there are two non-cumulative indices at the beginning of each annual volume. The first (A) is chronological and refers to the item number, the issue and page in the volume where it was published.

The second (B) is an alphabetical subject index, preceded immediately by a list of subject headings. It refers to the item number only. Bilateral treaties are listed chronologically under the name of the opposite party; multilateral treaties are all listed chronologically at the end of the index under the heading "mnohostranné."

Index: Since 2009 the first index (A) has three parts. Part I is a chronological list of all items published in a given year. Part II is list of bilateral treaties, decisions of international organisations binding on the Czech Republic, and other acts relevant to their implementation, ordered alphabetically by the other party or name of the international institution. Part III is a list of multilateral treaties, decisions of international organisations binding on the Czech Republic, and other acts relevant to their implementation ordered chronologically. The alphabetical subject index (B), preceded immediately by a list of subject headings, no longer lists bilateral treaties alphabetically by the opposite party. Rather, it is an index of keywords and topics, listing each treaty under its subject area.

4 SBÍRKA ZÁKONŮ A SBÍRKA MEZINÁRODNÍCH SMLUV

URL: http://aplikace.mvcr.cz/sbirka-zakonu/.

Summary: Online version of the *Sbírka zákonů* and the *Sbírka mezinárdních smluv* on the website of the Ministry of Interior. This database includes PDF copies of all issues of both collections in the volumes since 1945. In the case of large docoments, the copy is available compressed into ZIP format. The current interface has three numbered parts.

Under part 1 the user first chooses (by toggling radio buttons) whether to search/browse the *Sbírka zákonů* (first option), the *Sbírka mezinárdních smluv* (second option), or both collections (third option). This step must be completed before the user proceeds, for the rest of the application to work. For searches, the user next chooses (by toggling radio buttons) whether to search by item number (first option), by issue number (second option), or by text in the item title (third option). Finally, a search can be performed in the field provided at the bottom of part 1 of the interface.

Under part 2 the user (having completed the first step in part 1) may browse the collections by year, using the drop-down menu of years and the "Zobrazit" button. Each year is returned with the relevant index linked in PDF format, followed by a table of issues in descending order. The entry in the table for each issue includes its number, the date of publication, the range of numbers of items included, a link to the PDF copy of the issue, and for each item included its number and title.

Under part 3, the user may use a trial version of a full-text search utility built on the Google search engine.

Index: The indices linked through the browsing results are described under 1. and 3. above. The indices for 1945 provided on the website at the time of this publication are only those for the early part of the year – i.e. *doba nesvobody* – from the time of occupation, although only the texts of the issues from the later part of the year – i.e. *doba svobody* – are available in PDF format. As the numbering restarted from 1 in the latter part of the year, the index provided refers to some of the same item numbers as are provided but is entirely useless as it gives corresponding titles of items from the early part of the year. Fortunately, the table in which the issues are organised on the website acts as a substitute index.

5 PORTÁL VEŘEJNÉ SPRÁVY: VYHLEDÁVÁNÍ V ZÁKONECH
URL: http://portal.gov.cz/app/zakony/?path=/portal/obcan/.

Summary: A database of all the items currently in force from the entire *Sbírka zákonů* since 1918, searchable from this website. In order, the possible search fields are: full-text references, item number (in standard format: item number/year Sb.), issue number, or text in the item title. The search returns the item number in standard format, the title of the item, links to a brief summary of important information about the item and to the full text in plain-text and PDF formats.

Note: The database does not include the *Sbírka mezinárodních smluv* and so can only be used to search for treaties published before the year 2000.

6 ÚŘEDNÍ VĚSTNÍK ČESKOSLOVENSKÝ [CITED AS ÚŘ. VĚST. ČSL.]
(Paris/London: 1940–1945?).

Summary: The author was not able to inspect this material. It is the official gazette of the Czechoslovak Government-in-Exile from World War II. It was published first in Paris from the 1 January 1940 to 29 May 1940 (nos. 1–9) and subsequently in London from 4 December 1940 (no. 10) to the end of the war.[86] Certain decrees of the President of the Republic were later re-published in the *Sbírka zákonů* as supplements to indiviual enacting laws, and all of the decrees were re-published as a special supplement to the 1947 volume. The re-publication of treaties that appeared in the *Úřední věstník* is doubtful, but they may be available in other historical materials.

---

86 James B. Childs, *Exiled Governments: Their Official Records* 35(6) American Political Science Review 1158.

Treaty Indexes

7 MINISTRY OF FOREIGN AFFAIRS WEBSITE: INDEX OF TREATIES IN FORCE WITH PARLIAMENTARY APPROVAL
URL: http://www.mzv.cz/jnp/cz/zahranicni_vztahy/mezinarodni_smlouvy/.

Summary: This website contains two separate treaty indices. The first is a PDF index of treaties in force assented to by the Parliament of the Czech Republic and binding for the Czech Republic. It is divided into two parts. Part (a) includes bilateral treaties sorted alphabetically by the name of the other party. Part (b) includes multilateral treaties sorted alphabetically by descriptive headings. Each entry includes the title of the treaty in Czech, the place and date of signature and the standard item number in the *Sbírka Zákonů* or *Sbírka Mezinárodních Smluv*. This index can be accessed from two separate links on the website. Both links are entitled "Seznam vyhlášených mezinárodních smluv" and are found in the main body of the site: one towards the top and one at the very bottom.

Note: This index is updated periodically, but not continuously. As of the time of publication, the most recent update to the list occurred on July 1 2013.

Note: As of the time of publication, neither link was functional in all internet browsers. Both worked in Internet Explorer 8. Neverthertheless, both links could be followed successfully in other browsers if the site itself was accessed using Google's "Translate this page" utility after entering the url into the Google search engine. In that case, the links read "List of promulgated treaties." Note that this leads to Google's (i.e. unofficial) translation of the PDF document, which may contain errors. It is unclear whether the ministry has plans to add cross-browser compatibility to its website.

8 MINISTRY OF FOREIGN AFFAIRS WEBSITE: DATABASE OF TREATIES IN FORCE
URL: http://www.mzv.cz/jnp/cz/zahranicni_vztahy/mezinarodni_smlouvy/.

Summary: This website contains two separate treaty indices. The second is a searchable database of the Ministry of Foreign Affairs' register of treaties in force and binding for the Czech Republic. The database can be accessed using the very first link in the main body of the website. The database can be searched by keyword. Search results can be limited by treaty type (i.e. bilateral vs. multilateral), opposite party, category (i.e. mode of ratification and implementation) and thematic area. A search can be executed with no keyword, resulting in a list of all treaties that fulfil the search limitation criteria. For each treaty, the search results show its Czech and foreign-language name, other party, thematic area, type (see above), category (see above), place and date of signature, date of entry into force, date of entry into force for the Czech Republic, and a reference to its publication in the relevant collection, as applicable.

9 PRÁVNÍ PŘEDPISY ČESKÉ REPUBLIKY (9.5.1945–31.12.1999): VĚCNÝ A CHRONOLOGICKÝ PŘEHLED VŠECH PLATNÝCH PRÁVNÍCH PŘEDPISŮ VYHLÁŠENÝCH VE SBÍRCE ZÁKONŮ

Pavel Mates and Miroslava Matoušová (Praha: Linde, 2000). 894 pp.

Summary: Index to the *Sbírka Zákonů* in two parts. Refers to the standard numbers of texts in the *Sbírka* in the format [item no.]/[year] Sb. (e.g. 31/1961 Sb.). Only lists documents in force at the time of publication. Part I is a subject index. Under the heading "Mezinárodní dokumenty" are listed secondary documents such as laws implementing treaties, but not treaties themselves. Bilateral treaties can be found listed under "Mezinárodní dokumenty dvoustranné," where they are further ordered alphabetically by the name of the second party (within each such subsection they are ordered chronologically). Multilateral treaties are listed alphabetically by keyword under "Mezinárodní dokumenty mnohostranné." There is a list of keywords at the beginning of the publication. Where appropriate, amendments or additions are listed under a given item. Other headings of potential interest are: "Mezinárodní finanční institutce," (International Financial Institutions) "Mezinárodní organizace," (International Organisations) and "Mezinárodní právo soukromé a procesní" (Private and Procedural International Law).

Note: There is a similar 1998 edition, which includes documents from 1945–1997 in force at the date of publication. It is published by the same authors under virtually the same title, only with different dates. The imprint is the same except for the date of publication.

Topical and Selected Treaty Collections

10 MEZINÁRODNÍ SMLOUVY MEZI ČESKOU REPUBLIKOU A SLOVENSKOU REPUBLIKOU

Vladimír Mikule et al. (Praha: Codex Bohemia, 1995). 335 pp.

Summary: A collection of treaties concluded between the Czech Republic and the Slovak Republic before the date of publication. The collection includes 32 treaties, their dates of ratification, publication and entry into force as well as commentary on each in both Czech and Slovak. The commentary explains the content of the treaties, often article by article, and the relevant national implementation measures; it is adapted in each case for a Czech or Slovak audience, according to the language in which it is written.

11 DVOUSTRANNÉ MEZINÁRODNÍ DOHODY

(Praha: Ministerstvo Životního Prostředí, 1998). 243 pp.

Summary: Collection of bilateral treaties pertaining to the environment, published by the Czech Ministry of the Environment. There are 20 documents, organised roughly by the opposite party, though in no particular order. The table of contents shows the title in Czech and the language of the other side or English, except for four treaties with either Poland or Slovakia, which are only given in Czech. Only the texts of the treaties are published.

12 MNOHOSTRANNÉ MEZINÁRODNÍ SMLOUVY
(Praha: Ministerstvo Životního Prostředí, 1997).

Summary: Four volumes of multilateral environmental treaties published by the Ministry of the Environment. They are thematically divided: the first two volumes contain treaties relating to air quality, the third volume contains treaties on waters and waste and the fourth volume contains treaties about nature preservation and landscape protection. The text of the treaties is included. In some cases, the dates of ratification by the Czech Republic and of entry into force are included. Some volumes are ordered chronologically, or by the authentic language. All four volumes include texts both in Czech and English. Volume three also has documents, authentic in German, both in Czech and German.

13 OBRANA, BEZPEČNOST A KRIZOVÉ STAVY: SOUHRN VYBRANÝCH PRÁVNÍCH PŘEDPISŮ ČR A MEZINÁRODNÍCH SMLUV
Právnická Fakulta UK, Karedra Ústavního Práva (Praha: Vodnář, 2004). 387 pp.

Summary: A collection of selected documents pertaining to defense, security and crisis situations, in three parts. Part I is constitutional, part II deals with external security and part III with internal security. Each one of parts II and III has sections A and B, where A consists of domestic legal instruments and B of international treaties. There are twelve treaties in part II and six in part III, chosen for their leading significance among the whole set of treaties. All texts are given in the Czech version only and some are abridged.

14 VÝZNAMNÉ MEZINÁRODNÍ DOKUMENTY K OCHRANĚ LIDSKÝCH PRÁV
Vladimír Flégl (Praha: C.H. Beck, 1998). 325 pp.

Summary: A collection of the 51 human rights treaties, most significant from the perspective of internal and international law, especially the original article 10 of the constitution of the Czech Republic č. 1/1993 Sb.[87] The documents are divided into sixteen thematic parts according to the rights they protect. Apart from the text of the treaties, the publication also includes their date of entry

87 Which has been amended since the work's publication in such a way as to affect the significance of these treaties. *See supra* "Treaty Implementation".

into force, their item number in the *Sbírka Zákonů*, whether the Czech Republic is a successor the the treaty, a summary of Czech reservations to the treaty and other details of the ratification process. There is a subject index at the rear of the book, which allows the researcher to search the treaties by keyword.

15 MEZINÁRODNÍ DOKUMENTY O LIDSKÝCH PRÁVECH ANGLICKY A ČESKY
Vladimír Adamus (Praha: Linde, 2000). 495 pp.
Summary: Collection of 34 international treaties dealing with human rights published in the *Sbírka Zákonů* by the 31st December 1999. Also includes the date of ratification, of entry into force for the Czech Republic and of publication in the *Sbírka Zákonů* (along with the item number) and a summary of the reservations. Provides both the authentic (English) text of the treaty – as was not done in the *Sbírka Zákonů* – and the official Czech translation.

16 MEZINÁRODNÍ ZDANĚNÍ PŘÍJMŮ: SMLOUVY O ZAMEZENÍ DVOJÍHO ZDANĚNÍ A ZÁKON O DANÍCH Z PŘÍJMŮ
Sojka, Vlastimil (Praha: ASPI, a.s., 2nd Ed. 2008). 326 pp.
Summary: A general introduction to law of taxation in an international context. Appendix 20 is an index of treaties preventing dual taxation, listed alphabetically by opposite party. The index gives the date of entry into force, the reference in Sbírka zákonů or Sbirka Mezinárodních Smluv, as appropriate, as well as a list of other relevant acts and notices (as references to the appropriate gazette) and the basic parameters of each treaty. The index includes treaties in force on January 1 2008.

Diplomatic Documents

17 ZAHRANIČNÍ POLITIKA ČESKÉ REPUBLIKY
(Praha: Odbor administrativy a zpracování informací, 1993–).
Summary: Periodical publication of the Ministry of Foreign Affairs, dealing with the foreign policies of the Czech Republic. It comes out in two separate parts. The first is published under the subtitle *Data*, and has the character of reports on the events in the past month as pertains to Czech diplomacy, including brief quotations of the chief actors. The second is published under the subtitle *Dokumenty* and includes official letters and notes, interviews, statements, press releases, speeches, government declarations, newspaper articles and so on by the various actors. The reports as well as the documents may pertain to diplomatic activity of Czech officials, reactions to foreign activity or statements, international treaties, their validity, material breach and

so on. Each issue is divided into sections according to the actor involved; in order, they are: the President, the Parliament (subdivided since 1996 into Chamber of Deputies and Senate), the Cabinet, the Ministry of Foreign Affairs and optionally other categories, recently often including Representatives of the Czech Republic to European Institutions. Within each section, the items are ordered chronologically.

Note: The publication is also available online, on the website of the Ministry of Foreign Affairs at http://www.mzv.cz/jnp/cz/o_ministerstvu/archivy/mesicnik_zahranicni_politika_ceske.html. The online archive includes both parts of the publication separately and goes back to the July-August 1999 issues. Each issue may be opened as a separate PDF document, although some of the links may appear broken depending on the internet browser employed.

Denmark

Suzanne Thorpe

Issues of Treaty Succession

Denmark has existed within its current borders since 1944. From the end of the 14th Century through the middle of the 20th Century, Denmark was continuously united with one or more of its Nordic neighbors. In 1380, Denmark began a union with the kingdom of Norway. Denmark-Norway subsequently joined with Sweden to form the Kalmar Union in 1397. This union lasted until 1523. As part of the Kalmar Union, Norway, Denmark, and Sweden maintained a common foreign policy and defense under the rule of the Danish monarch. Sweden left the union in 1523, but Denmark and Norway remained united under Danish rule for the next three centuries. In 1814, Denmark ceded Norway to Sweden under the Treaty of Kiel.[1] Iceland, Greenland, and the Faroe Islands, previously under Norwegian rule, were retained by Denmark. Although Iceland became a sovereign state in 1918, it remained in union with Denmark and continued to have a common foreign policy under the Danish monarch until the union dissolved in 1944.

Denmark's various unions with its neighbors are well documented by historians and legal scholars.[2] However, aside from probable discussions in unpublished diplomatic records, few writers have commented on the continuing force of the treaties concluded during these unions. A succession dispute arising out of the Treaty of Kiel has received brief attention.[3] Under Article 6 of this treaty, Denmark obligated Norway to pay a proportionate share of the entire national debt of the formerly united Norway-Denmark. The successor state, Norway-Sweden, disputed this obligation. In 1819, Norway-Sweden ultimately negotiated another treaty with Denmark that obligated Norway to pay a reduced portion of the amount agreed upon by Denmark in

1 Fredstractat mellom Danmark og Sverig, signed at Kiel 14 January 1814, 1 DANSKE TRACTATER EFTER 1800, 1.samling, 60–72 (1877).

2 *E.g.*, LESTER. B. ORFIELD, THE GROWTH OF SCANDINAVIAN LAW (1953); ARNOLD RÆSTAD, DANMARK, NORGE OG FOLKERETTEN (1933).

3 ERNEST H. FEILCHENFELD, PUBLIC DEBTS AND STATE SUCCESSION 142–44 (1931); DANIEL P. O'CONNELL, 1 STATE SUCCESSION IN MUNICIPAL LAW AND INTERNATIONAL LAW 396 (1967); THEODORE JORGENSEN, 1 NORWAY'S RELATION TO SCANDINAVIAN UNIONISM, 1815–1871, 389–400 (1935).

 | DOI 10.1163/9789004272224_012

the treaty.[4] Although the prior state practice held ceded territories proportionally liable for debts incurred before cession, this was the first instance in which a ceded territory was held liable for more than a local debt.

Treaty Ratification and Implementation[5]

Although the Danish Constitution (*Grundlov*)[6] does not generally define the relationship between public international law and Danish municipal law, Denmark adheres to the dualist approach to international law.[7] International treaties usually become a binding part of Danish municipal law through express legislative action of the Danish Parliament (*Folketing*).[8] Section 19, Subsection 1 of the *Grundlov* grants the King[9] the power to "act on behalf of the Kingdom in international affairs." However, this subsection further requires the *Folketing* to approve beforehand any international treaty obligation "that increases or decreases the area of the Kingdom, or…which is of major importance in some other way."

4 J.H.W. Verzijl, 7 International Law in Historical Perspective, Part 7, State Succession 230 (1974).

5 For an official government report on Danish treaty implementation practices, *see* Betænkning [nr. 682–1973] Betænkning om kundgørelse og opfyldlelse af traktater. [government report series] (Den.). For an academic dissertation covering Danish treaty making law and practice, *see* Ole Espersen, Indgåelse og Opfyldelse av Traktater (1970).

6 A current English language version of the Constitution is available online from the *Folketing* at http://www.thedanishparliament.dk/Publications/The_Constitutional_Act_of_Denmark .aspx (updated Aug. 27, 2013).

7 Frederik Harhoff, *Danemark Treaties*, *in* L'Intégration du Droit International et Communautaire dans l'Ordre Juridique National: Étude de la Pratique en Europe [The Integration of International and European Community Law into the National Legal Order: A Study of the Practice in Europe] 159 (1996). However, this author notes that the "classic dualist principle has been modified in particular by rules of interpretation, presumption and instruction. Thus, the prevailing view in legal theory today is more pragmatic on the position of international law which regards international law as a possible source of law…," at 164–64.

8 Betænkning [nr. 682–1973] *supra* note 5, at 12; Claus Gulmann, *The Position of International Law within the Danish Legal Order*, 52 Nordisk Tidsskrift for International Ret, no. 3–4, 1983, at 45.

9 Although the *Grundlov* uses the word, King, it is interpreted to mean the King in Council (with the cabinet). The *Udenrigsministeriet* generally negotiates and concludes treaties. Betænkning [nr. 682–1973] *supra* note 5, at 16.

The Ministry of Foreign Affairs (*Udenrigsministeriet*) confers closely with the *Folketing* while negotiating treaties.[10] Following the conclusion of a treaty, the *Udenrigsministeriet* introduces the adopted treaty to the *Folketing* for ratification and implementation.[11] The introduced treaty is referred to the Committee on Foreign Policy (*Udenrigspolitiske Nævn*). This committee issues a report on the treaty with a recommendation to the *Folketing* on ratification and implementation.[12]

Treaties are typically implemented in Denmark through two legislative methods: incorporation (*inkorporation*) and transformation. When *inkorporation* is used, the *Folketing* passes a law adopting the treaty text as Danish law. This is usually a very brief declaration that appears with other legislation in the official parliamentary gazette, *Folketingstidende*.[13] When transformation is used, the *Folketing* amends an existing law or enacts an entirely new law to mirror the provisions of the treaty. These proposed and adopted legislative changes also appear in the *Folketingstidende*.

Infrequently, a third method of implementation known in Denmark as "*konstatering af normharmoni*" (declaring norm harmony) is used. The *Udenrigspolitiske Nævn* issues a position statement indicating to the *Folketing* that the provisions of an adopted treaty already exist in Danish municipal law and do not require further ratification or implementation.[14] The treaty then becomes effective in Denmark. This method was employed in 1953 when the European Convention on Human Rights was declared to be in harmony with Danish municipal law.[15]

---

10 For a discussion of the role of the *Folketing* in treaty affairs, *see* ESPERSEN, *supra* note 5, at 65–92.

11 The treaty is introduced as a *forslag* (proposal) and is published with other legislative proposals from the *Regering* (Government) to the *Folketing* in the FOLKETINGSTIDENDE, TILLÆG A: FREMSATTE LOVFORSLAG (proposed bills). Since 2009, the FOLKETINGSTIDENDE is only available in electronic format. Volumes 2004/2005– can be accessed at http://www.folketingstidende.dk. Volumes from 1986/1987–2003/2004 can be accessed at http://webarkiv.ft.dk/doc.aspx?/samling/arkiv.htm.

12 These reports are published in the FOLKETINGSTIDENDE, TILLÆG B: UDVALGENES BETÆNKNINGER (reports of committees). For online availability, *see supra* text accompanying note 11.

13 The declaration appears as a "*folktingsbeslutning*" (parliamentary decision) in TILLÆG C: VEDTAGNE LOVFORSLAG OG BESLUTNINGER (resolutions and bills passed). For online availability *see supra* text accompanying note 11.

14 This statement usually appears in FOLKETINGSTIDENDE, TILLÆG A. *See* Betænkning [nr. 682–1973] *supra* note 5, at 22.

15 It was approved for ratification without implementing legislation, although eventually in 1992, the *Folketing* did formally incorporate this treaty into Danish municipal law.

Once ratified, treaties must be published in the Danish legal gazette, *Lovtidende for Kongeriget Danmark.*[16] Subsequently, treaties are published by the *Udenrigsministeriet* one or two years after ratification in part C of this gazette.

Because treaty provisions are carefully compared with existing Danish law throughout the treaty negotiation and ratification process, Danish municipal law generally conforms to the provisions of the international treaties concluded by Denmark. When rare conflicts arise after a treaty is in force, Danish courts and administrative agencies presume that the Danish municipal law is to be applied in conformity with the treaty.[17]

Annotated Bibliography of Sources

General Treaty Collections

1 LOVTIDENDE C
(Copenhagen: Civilstyrelse, 2008–).
URL: https://www.lovtidende.dk.

Summary: This work is searchable by popular title, document number, and year. It provides annual listings of bilateral treaties and multilateral treaties.

Note: Continues: *Lovtidende for Kongeriget Danmark. Afdeling C.*

2 LOVTIDENDE FOR KONGERIGET DANMARK, AFDELNING C: DANMARKS TRAKTATER
Denmark. Udenrigsministeriet (Copenhagen: J.H. Schultz, 1937–2007).

Summary: Contains treaties and other agreements concluded 1936–. Texts are arranged in chronological order. For each treaty, the title, dates of signature, ratification, and entry into force are given. Treaties appear in their

---

Søren Stenderup Jensen, The European Convention on Human Rights in Scandinavian Law: A Case Law Study 6, 31–33 (1992).

16 Betænkning [nr. 682–1973] *supra* note 5, at 25. Denmark does not have a provision in the *Grundlov* prescribing publication of treaties. Treaties are initially published in the Lovtidende, in accordance with the laws stipulating publication of Danish municipal laws and regulations. Electronic access to the full text of Danish treaties in the Lovtidende, starting in 1987, is now available from the *Folketing* at https://www.lovtidende.dk.

17 The rule is known as *fortolkningsreglen* (interpretation rule). See Søren Stenderup Jensen, *Folkretten som Retskilde i Dansk Ret*, 6 Ugeskirft for Retsvæsen, January 1990, at 1. *See also* Harhoff, *supra* note 6, at 161–62; Danish Law in a European Perspective 68–69 (Børge Dahl et al, eds., 2d ed. 2002) (additionally discussing the presumption rule and instruction rule, which similarly interpret official actions by the *Folketing* and the *Regering* as conforming to international obligations).

original languages with a Danish translation. Annual chronological and country indexes are provided.

Index: Cumulative chronological indexes: 1936–1940; 1936–1950; 1951–1960; 1961–1970; 1971–1980.

Note: Continues: *Danmarks Traktater.*

Note: Continued by: *Lovtidende C.*

3 DANMARKS TRAKTATER

Denmark. Udenrigsministeriet (Copenhagen: J.H. Schultz, 1929–1937). 15 vols.

Summary: Contains treaties and other agreements concluded 1921–1935. Each annual volume contains the treaties concluded during the year arranged in chronological order. The treaty title, place and dates of signature and ratification, and parties are given. Treaties appear in their original languages with a Danish translation. Each volume contains a list of treaties by party.

Index: Chronological list of treaties and subject index covering all 15 vols., published in 1937.

Note: Continued by: *Lovtidende for Kongeriget Danmark, Afdelning C.*

4 DANMARKS TRAKTATER OG AFTALER MED FREMMEDE MAGTER EFTER 1814

Denmark. Udenrigsministeriet (Copenhagen: Gyldendalske Boghandel; Nordisk Forlag, 1918–1951). 4 vols.

Summary: Contains treaties, declarations, and notes 1880–1920. For each treaty, title, date and place of signature, date of ratification, and entry into force are provided. Treaties appear in one or more of the official treaty languages. Bd. 4: 1880–1890; Bd. 5: 1891–1900; Bd. 6: 1901–1907; Bd. 7: 1908–1920. Each volume provides chronological and country lists of the treaties contained in it and an alphabetical subject index in Danish and French.

Note: Compilers: Bd. 4: Frank Le Sage de Fontenay; Bd. 5–7: Axel Heils.

Note: Bd. 1–3, containing treaties concluded 1814–1879, were never published.

5 DANSKE TRACTATER EFTER 1800

Denmark. Udenrigsministeriet (Copenhagen: J. Jørgensen, 1874–1885). 3 vols.

Summary: Bd. 1, 1. samling contains political treaties: 1800–1863; Bd. 1, 2. samling contains commercial and other treaties: 1800–1863; Bd. 2 contains political, commercial, and other treaties: 1863–1879. Treaties appear in each volume in chronological order in one or more of their official languages. The treaty title, place and date of signature are given for each treaty. Each volume provides a chronological list of the treaties included in it and an alphabetical list of the parties to these treaties.

Note: Imprint varies: Bd. 1, 1. samling: J.H. Schultz, 1877; Bd. 1, 2. samling: J.H. Schultz, 1874.

Note: Microfiche version filmed from the original held by Harvard Law School Library. Zug, Switzerland: Inter Documentation Co., 1987.

6 DANSKE TRACTATER, 1751–1800

Denmark. Udenigsministeriet (Copenhagen: J. Jørgensen, 1882). 463 pp.

Summary: Contains 71 treaties concluded 1751–1800. Treaty texts appear in chronological order in one of the official treaty languages. For each treaty, the title, place of signing, and date of signature and/or ratification are provided. A chronological list of treaties and an alphabetical list of parties appear at the end of the volume.

7 DANMARK-NORGES TRAKTATER, 1523–1750...MED DERTIL HØRENDE AKTSTYKKER

(Copenhagen: G.E.C. Gad, 1907–1949). 11 vols.

Summary: Although the title indicates treaty coverage through 1750, this work only contains treaties concluded by Denmark-Norway through 1700. Bd. 1: 1523–1560; Bd. 2: 1561–1588; Bd. 3: 1589–1625; Bd. 4:1626–1649; Bd. 5: 1651–1664; Bd. 6: 1665–1675; Bd. 7:1676–1682; Bd. 8: 1683–1689; Bd. 9: 1690–1693; Bd. 10: 1694–1698; Bd. 11: 1699–1700. Treaties are arranged in chronological order. Each entry provides the date of signature, the title, the place of signature, the treaty text in Danish, French, Latin, German, or Swedish. Each volume has a chronological list of treaties for each year covered in that volume, a country index in Danish and French, and a table of proper names in Danish.

Note: Head of title reads "Traités du Danemark et de la Norvège".

Note: Treaties concluded 1700–1750 were never published.

Note: Compilers vary: Bd. 1–9: Laurs Rasmus Laursen; Bd. 10–11: Carl S. Christiansen.

Note: Funded by the Carlsbergfondet.

Note: Microfiche version filmed from the original held by Harvard Law School Library. Zug, Switzerland: Inter Documentation Co., 1986.

8 RECUEIL DE TOUS LES TRAITÉS, CONVENTIONS, MÉMOIRES, ET NOTES CONCLUS ET PUBLIÉS PAR LA COURONNE DE DANNEMARC

Depuis l'avénément au Thrône du Roi Régnant Jusqu'à l'époque Actuelle, ou dès l'année 1766 Jusqu'en 1794 Inclusive (Berlin: J.F. Unger, 1796). xiv, 352 pp.

Summary: Contains the texts of 65 treaties concluded 1766–1794. Treaties are in French or German.

Note: Dedication signed: Henri Fredric Chretien Claussen.

Note: Microfilm version available from University Microforms International.

Treaty Indexes

9 GENERAL-REGISTER TIL DEN PAA UDENRIGSMINISTERIETS FORANSTALTNING UDGIVNE SAMLING DANSKE TRACTATER FRA 1761–1879

(Copenhagen: J.H. Schultz, 1901). 62 pp.

Summary: This index covers treaties concluded 1751–1879. An alphabetical country index lists treaties chronologically under each country. An alphabetical subject index lists treaties chronologically by country under each subject. A royal house index lists treaties chronologically under each dynasty. Country and subject lists are provided.

Note: Editor: C. Molke.

10 RÉPERTOIRE HISTORIQUE ET CHRONOLOGIQUE DES TRAITÉS CONCLUS PAR LA COURONNE DE DANNEMARC, DEPUIS CANUTE-LE-GRAND JUSQU'À 1800

(Gottingue: Dieterich, 1826). xxxiv, 242 pp.

Summary: This is an index of treaties concluded 1016–1800 by country and subject. A chronological list of treaties is provided. For each treaty, the parties, date of signature, the number of articles, the official languages used, and the names of the negotiators are given.

Note: Compiler: Holger Christian Reedtz.

11 INDEX CHRONOLOGICUS SISTENS FOEDERA PACIS, DEFENSIONIS, NAVIGATIONIS, COMMERCIORUM, SUBSIDIORUM, ET ALIA A REGIBUS DANIAE ET NORVEGIAE AC COMITIBUS HOL-SATIAE, INITA CUM GENTIBUS INTRA ET EXTRA EUROPAM, NEC NON CAPITULATIONES, LITERAS ET MERCATURAE PRIVILEGIA, AB ANNO 1200 USQVE AD 1789

(Gottingae: Dieterich, 1792). 148 pp.

Summary: This work is a chronological index of Danish peace, defense, navigation, and commercial treaties concluded between 1200 and 1789.

Note: Editor: Ivar Quistgaard.

Topical and Selected Treaty Collections

12 DANSKE HANDELSKONVENTIONER. DECEMBER 1911.

Denmark. Udenrigsministeriet (Copenhagen: F.E. Bording, 1911). 81 pp.

Summary: This work provides texts of Danish trade agreements that were in force on December 1, 1911. A list of treaties is provided.

Note: Prepared for use of the Ministry of Foreign Affairs.

13 DANMARKS HANDELS – OG SKIBSFARTSTRAKTATER

Denmark. Udenrigsministeriet (Copenhagen, J.H. Schultz, 1934). 610 pp.

Summary: This publication contains maritime and trade agreements concluded 1660–1933. Treaty titles are in Danish and French. Treaty texts are in the official language of the treaty as well as in Danish.

Note: Head of title reads "Les Traités de Commerce et de Navigation du Danemark".

14 DANSKE VOLDGIFTSKONVENTIONER

Denmark. Udenrigsministeriet (Copenhagen: J.H. Schultz, 1912). 57 pp.

Summary: This publication contains arbitration treaties concluded by Denmark 1904–1911. Treaties appear in chronological order in one of the official treaty languages and in Danish. For each treaty, the title, date and place of signature, and ratification dates are provided. References to implementing legislation are provided.

15 DANSKE UDLEVERINGS TRAKTATER

Denmark. Udenrigsministeriet (Copenhagen and Kristiania: Gyldendalske Boghandel, Nordisk Forlag, 1915–1929). 1 vol. and Supplement.

Summary: This publication includes extradition treaties concluded 1866–1923. Texts are in their original languages as well as in Danish.

Note: Printed for use of the Ministry of Foreign Affairs.

16 DE NORDISKE KONVENTIONER: ÆGTESKAB, ADOPTION OG VÆRGEMAAL, INDDRIVELSE AF UNDERHOLDSBIDRAG, ANERKENDELSE OG FULDBYRDELSE AF DOMME, KONKURS, ARV OG DØDSBOSKIFTE

(Copenhagen: Ejnar Munksgaard, 1947). 56 pp.

Summary: This title includes the Danish text of five treaties between the Nordic countries on marriage, adoption and guardianship, maintenance, recognition and enforcement of judgments, bankruptcy, and inheritance and succession. These treaties were concluded between 1931 and 1935.

17 SAMLING AF TRAKTATER M.M. AF SÆRLIG INTERESSE FOR FORSVARET

Denmark. Forsvarsministeriet (Copenhagen: Forsvarsministeriet, 1957).

Summary: This publication contains treaties of military interest.

Series: Love og Bestemmelser for Forsvaret: hefte 20.

18 SAMLING AF INTERNATIONALE KONVENTIONER M.M. VEDRØRENDE KRIGSFØRELSEN

Denmark. Forsvarsministeriet (Copenhagen, 1953). 206 pp.

Summary: This work contains 32 treaties and international agreements related to war arranged in chronological order. Texts are in official Danish translations. For each treaty, dates of ratification and entry into force are provided.

Series: Love og Bestemmelser for Forsvaret: hefte 13.

Diplomatic Documents

19 MINISTERIALTIDENDE

(Copenhagen: Civilstyrelsen, 1977–).

Summary: This official administrative gazette contains ministerial regulations and announcements. It includes information issued by the Udenrigsministeriet.

Index: Annual subject and chronological indexes.

Note: Continues: *Ministerialtidende for Kongeriget Danmark*, 1871–2008.

Note: Imprint varies: Copenhagen: J.H. Schultz, 1871–1977.

Note: Issued by Justisministeriet through 2004.

Note: Since 2008, this publication appears only in electronic format at http://www.ministerialtidende.dk. This online version is searchable by popular name, document number, and year. It provides an alphabetical list of keywords that will display results. It provides annual lists documents that can be sorted by ministry, title, and number. It provides lists by ministry, that can be sorted by year and types of documents.

Yearbooks and Digests of State Practice

20 DANISH FOREIGN POLICY YEARBOOK

(Copenhagen: Institut for Internationale Studier, 2002–).

Summary: This annual publication covers Denmark's position internationally and transnationally, both at the regional and global levels. It includes selected documents, statistics, and bibliographic references.

Note: Imprint varies: Copenhagen: Dansk Udenrigspolitisk Institut, 1997–2001.

Note: Condensed version of *Dansk Udenrigspolitisk Årbog*, 1997–2001.

Note: Continues *DUPIDOK: Dansk Udenrigspolitisk Dokumentation.*

Note: Since 2004, the yearbook is also available online at http://www.diis.dk.

21 DUPIDOK: DANSK UDENRIGSPOLITISK DOKUMENTATION

(Copenhagen: Dansk Udenrigspolitisk Institut, 1997–2001).

Summary: This is an annual review of Danish foreign relations. Each volume includes articles, documents, summaries of foreign policy actions in the Folketing, a bibliography of books and articles that have appeared during the year, and a subject index.

Note: Continues: *Dansk Udenrigspolitisk Årbog*, 1980–1995.

Note: Condensed English language version: *Danish Foreign Policy Yearbook*, 1997–.

22 DANSK UDENRIGSPOLITISK ÅRBOG

(Copenhagen: Dansk udenrigspolitisk institut: Samfundsvidenskabeligt forlag, 1979–1995).

Summary: This annual publication contains commentaries on Danish foreign policy, documents on foreign policy from the Folketing and government ministries, speeches, and opinion polls.

Note: Imprint varies: Copenhagen: Samfundsvidenskabeligt Forlag: 1980–1995.

Note: Continued by *DUPIDOK: Dansk Udenrigspolitisk Dokumentation,* 1997–2001.

23 NORDIC JOURNAL OF INTERNATIONAL LAW

(Leiden, Netherlands : Martinus Nijhoff, 2006–)

Summary: Volumes 69–70 and 72 contain articles that digest developments in Danish state practice for 1995, 1996, 1997, 1998, 1999, 2000, 2001/2002.

Imprint varies: Dordrecht: Kluwer Academic Publishers, 1986–2005.

Continues: Nordisk Tidsskrift for International Ret, 1930–1985.

France

Beatrice A. Tice

Issues of Treaty Succession

Since the time of its emergence as the first consolidated European nation state in the late 16th century, France has yet to find itself in the position of a successor state with respect to treaties. Accordingly, issues of treaty succession have not been raised with regard to France. On various occasions, France has considered succession issues involving another state wishing to succeed to an agreement to which France is a party. No general rule exists regarding this type of succession; instead, the French government decides these issues on a case-by-case basis. To date, it has not consulted with the Parliament in any of these matters.[1]

France's membership in the European Union and its predecessor organizations has raised succession issues of a different nature. Since 1951, when France became a founding member of the European Coal and Steel Community, France has transferred to the European Community institutions the competence to negotiate and conclude international treaties and agreements in all areas subject to Community control. Articles 88–1 and 88–2 of the French Constitution of 1958 specifically provide that France shall participate in the European Communities and the European Union, and, subject to reciprocity, will transfer all competencies necessary for the establishment of the Union.[2]

As is the case with all other member states of the European Union, France may not participate alone in any international agreement involving an area covered by one of the Community treaties. These areas include most economic and fiscal issues and many social issues. For example, the European Union has exclusive competence to conclude new commercial or partnership treaties with third countries. Such agreements substitute (completely or partially) for

1 *See* Pierre Michel Eisemann & Raphaële Rivier, *France*, *in* NATIONAL TREATY LAW AND PRACTICE 253, 274 (Duncan B. Hollis et al. eds., 2005).

2 These articles were added by Loi 92–554 du 25 juin 1992, ajoutant à la Constitution un titre "Des Communautés europées et de l'Union europeénne [Law 92–554 of June 25, 1992 adding to the Constitution the title "On the European Communities and the European Union], JOURNAL OFFICIEL DE LA RÉPUBLIQUE FRANÇAISE [J.O.] [OFFICIAL GAZETTE OF FRANCE], June 26, 1992, p. 8406, in connection with the constitutional problems raised by the Maastricht Treaty. *See infra* note 9.

 | DOI 10.1163/9789004272224_013

those previously existing between France and third countries. In addition, with rare exception, European Union law has replaced all bilateral commercial agreements previously in force between member states.[3]

Treaty Ratification and Implementation

Title VI of the French Constitution of 1958, entitled *Des traités et accords internationaux,* provides the legal and procedural basis for French treaty practice.[4] Although Title VI contains no definition of either 'treaty' or 'international agreement,' it distinguishes between them for purposes of ratification: Article 52 provides that treaties (*traités*) are to be negotiated and ratified by the President of the Republic, while international agreements (*accords internationaux*) are to be negotiated and approved (not ratified) by the French government. The Constitution does not enumerate which agreements must be submitted for ratification by the President and which may be approved by the Prime Minister. As a practical matter, the legal effect of both forms of authorization is identical. In fact, international agreements *not* subject to presidential ratification are the most common.[5]

Only the President and the Prime Minister (or their designees) have the authority to negotiate and enter into international agreements on behalf of France.[6] However, both may be required to seek the authorization of the French Parliament prior to ratification or approval of an agreement. Article 53 of the Constitution provides that peace treaties, trade treaties and treaties or agreements concerning international organizations, involving state finances, amending rules of a legislative nature, concerning individual status, or providing for the transfer, exchange or annexation of territory, must be submitted to the Parliament for approval. Such approval is limited to the granting or denial of

---

3 For a note on the effect of European Community regulation on French treaties and agreements, see Alexandre Carnelutti, *Incidence de l'appartenance de la France aux Communautés européenes sur sa compétence à nègocier et à conclure des traités et accords internationaux, in,* Liste des traités et accords de la France en vigueur au 1998 xxi (Ministère des Affaires étrangères ed., 1998). The brief notes here are intended only as a short introduction to this important area of the law.

4 For a critical discussion of Title VI, see Charles Rousseau, *La Constitution de 1958 et les traités internationaux, in* Hommage d'une génération de juristes au Président Basdevant 463 (1960).

5 Eisemann & Rivier, *supra* note 1, at 259–60.

6 Conseil constitutionnel [CC][Constitutional Court] decision No. 82–137DC, Feb. 25, 1982, Rec. 38 (Fr.).

authorization to enter into a treaty; the Parliament has no power to modify the treaty itself or cause its ratification. Indeed, once Parliamentary authorization has been secured, the President or the government must then ratify or approve the agreement in order for it to have legal effect. Since the Parliament's approval comes in the form of an authorization, rather than a mandate, the Executive's subsequent decision to ratify or approve the agreement is entirely discretionary.[7]

Article 53 sets forth the minimum requirements for parliamentary involvement in treaty approval. In practice, for political and other reasons, the President seeks the Parliament's approval more frequently than the Constitution requires.[8] In addition, members of Parliament have the right to submit written or oral questions to the Executive concerning international agreements under negotiation.

Agreements submitted for parliamentary authorization under Article 53 may also be subject to review by the Constitutional Council (*Conseil constitutionnel*). Article 54 provides that the President, the Prime Minister, the President of one of the houses of Parliament, or at least 60 members of Parliament may seek a determination of the constitutionality of a treaty or agreement. If the Council declares an international agreement to be in contravention of the Constitution, that agreement may not be entered into until the Constitution is appropriately revised.[9] In addition, Article 61 states that the

---

7 For a detailed discussion of the Parliament's role in French treaty practice, see François Luchaire, *The Participation of Parliament in the Elaboration and Application of Treaties*, *in* PARLIAMENTARY PARTICIPATION IN THE MAKING AND OPERATION OF TREATIES 45 (S. Riesenfeld & F. Abbott eds., 1994).

8 Nevertheless, the Executive retains complete discretion in construing Article 53. For example, of the 691 international agreements that came into effect between 1987 and 1993, only 176 were authorized by Parliament. Pierre Michel Eisemann & Catherine Kessedjian, *France*, *in* NATIONAL TREATY LAW AND PRACTICE 1, 7 (Monroe Leigh & Merritt R. Blakeslee eds., 1995). In 2003, Parliament authorized only 44 of the 103 conventions published that year. Eisemann & Rivier, *supra* note 1, at 260.

9 This occurred on June 23, 1992, when the Constitution was amended to allow ratification of the Maastricht Treaty, which created the European Union. Amendment was required after the *Conseil constitutionnel* held that the Maastricht Treaty was in contravention of the Constitution by providing for, among other things, the right of resident non-nationals to vote, the introduction of majority voting with respect to visa requirements for non-EU nationals and the creation of a single currency. Conseil constitutionnel [CC][Constitutional Court] decision No. 92–308DC, April 9, 1992, Rec. 55 (Fr.). *See generally* the series of articles by François Luchaire, *L'Union européenne et la constitution,* 108 REVUE DU DROIT PUBLIC ET DE LA SCIENCE POLITIQUE EN FRANCE ET À L'ÉTRANGER 589–616, 933–81, 1587–1624 (1992), 301–24 (1993).

statute by which the Parliament authorizes ratification or approval of an agreement may likewise be submitted to the Council for constitutional review.[10] Articles 54 and 61 provide the only manner in which the constitutionality of an international agreement may be reviewed; there is no basis in French law for the constitutional challenge of an agreement following its ratification or approval and promulgation.

In certain circumstances, the President may consult the French people regarding treaty ratification or approval through a referendum. Article 11 of the Constitution permits the President to submit to referendum any bill providing for approval of a treaty that is in harmony with the Constitution but may impact the functioning of existing institutions. The President has invoked this process three times since 1958, all with respect to treaties involving the European communities.[11]

Once a treaty or international agreement has been duly ratified or approved, it is automatically incorporated into French domestic law, provided it has been properly published. Article 55 of the Constitution further provides that such international law takes precedence over domestic law, subject only to a requirement that the opposite party(ies) apply the treaty provisions in a similar manner.[12] Treaties thus incorporated into domestic law cannot be abrogated, modified or suspended except in accordance with the rules of international law.[13] This principle applies to all international agreements, regardless of form (*traité* or *accord international*) or opposite party (bilateral or multilateral).

As previously mentioned, publication of a treaty determines its incorporation into domestic law. Pursuant to Article 55, an international agreement

---

10 The practical effect of this process is the same as that of Article 54, because without an authorizing statute, the Executive may neither ratify nor approve an international agreement subject to parliamentary review.

11 The first was on April 23, 1972, regarding the admission of the United Kingdom, Ireland and Denmark to the EEC; the second was on September 20, 1992, regarding the Maastricht Treaty; the third was on May 29, 2005, with regard to the proposed European Constitution.

12 Treaties and international agreements take precedence over both prior and subsequent national statutes. *See* Eisemann & Rivier, *supra* note 1, at 268–69. For a discussion of the relatively recent transformation of the French system of integration of treaties into domestic law, see Michel Fromont, *L'intégration du droit international au droit français*, *in* Jürgen F. Baur, et al. eds., EUROPARECHT, ENERGIERECHT, WIRTSCHAFTSRECHT: FESTSCHRIFT FÜR BODO BÖRNER ZUM 70. GEBURTSTAG 77 (1992).

13 See Article 28 of the Constitution of 1946: "The provisions of diplomatic treaties which have been properly ratified and published and which take precedence over internal laws, may only be revoked, amended or suspended after a proper denunciation, notified through diplomatic channels". (Translated in A.P. Blaustein & G.H. Flanz, eds., CONSTITUTIONS OF THE COUNTRIES OF THE WORLD (1971–).

takes effect as domestic law as of the date of its publication in the *Journal officiel de la République française*.[14] Publication is governed by French law, and not all treaties are published. The Minister of Foreign Affairs is only required to publish agreements whose implementation may affect the rights or duties of individuals. As a general rule, however, many more treaties are actually published. Notices of treaty termination must also be published.

The French rules regarding publication can cause a treaty to have different legal effects at the international and domestic levels. International agreements enter into force as a matter of international law as of the date of ratification or approval, or as of the date specified in the agreement; they are not dependent upon publication to take effect. Thus, an unpublished treaty has no binding force in domestic law, and may not be referred to before a domestic court, even though the treaty may have taken effect internationally. The Executive, which issues the decree ordering publication, may thus block application of an international agreement in domestic law by simply refusing to have it published.[15]

Annotated Bibliography of Sources

General Treaty Collections

1 JOURNAL OFFICIEL DE LA RÉPUBLIQUE FRANÇAISE: LOIS ET DÉCRETS (Paris: Direction des Journaux officiels, 1869–).

Summary: France's official gazette. This is the official source for the text of treaties and international agreements, authorizing statutes and notices of termination; all are found in the *Lois et décrets* section. Also includes the *travaux préparatoires* statutes authorizing treaty ratification. Published daily, except Monday.

Index: Includes monthly subject and chronological indexes, and a concordance table giving the inclusive page numbers found in each issue. Also includes cumulative annual indexes.

Note: Title and imprint vary.[16]

---

14 Publication in the *Journal officiel des communautés européenes* is the functional equivalent of publication in the *Journal officiel de la République française*.

15 Judges are required to raise the issue of publication on their own motion, if necessary; they are not permitted to ignore the effect of non-publication of a treaty of international agreement. *See* Conseil d'Etat (CE Sect.) (highest administrative court), decision No. 60,954, July 13, 1965, Rec. Lebon 422 (Fr.).

16 The publication now known as the *Journal officiel de la République française* has undergone variations in title and imprint too numerous to mention here.

2 JOURNAL-OFFICIEL.GOUV.FR

Direction de l'information légale et administrative.

URL: http://www.journal-officiel.gouv.fr.

Summary: Official web site of the Direction de l'information légale et administrative. Contains a link to the authenticated online version of the *Journal officiel,* available from June 2, 2004 to date. Also includes the current day's edition of the *Journal officiel* in PDF format. Not full-text searchable.

Note: Searchable database of major texts published in the *Lois et décrets* section of the *Journal officiel* from January 1, 1990 to date is available on *Legifrance,* the official web site of the French government, at http://www.legifrance.gouv.fr/. Documents are searchable on the date of publication, date of signature, document type or number, words from the title or text, or the originating institution. Includes link to authenticated version of the *Journal officiel.*

3 BASE DES TRAITÉS ET ACCORDS DE LA FRANCE

Ministère des Affaires étrangères.

URL: http://basedoc.diplomatie.gouv.fr/Traites/Accords_Traites.php.

Summary: Treaty database maintained by the Minister of Foreign Affairs. Includes all treaties and agreements concluded by France and presently in force, as well as pre-1915 treaties, agreements and related documents and objects maintained in the Ministry archives. Database is searchable on a number of terms, including title, date of signature, country of opposite party, number of decree and date of publication in the *Journal officiel.* Entries include title, date and place of signature, date of entry into force in France, date of decree, date of publication in the *Journal officiel* and citation to treaty source(s). Many treaty texts are available in full-text PDF format, as are digitized documents and other items from the archives.

4 RECUEIL DES TRAITÉS ET ACCORDS DE LA FRANCE

Ministère des Relations extérieures (Paris: Imprimerie des Journaux officiels, 1958–2004).

Summary: Compendium of bilateral and multilateral treaties, agreements, conventions and exchanges of letters published in the *Journal officiel.* Publication is irregular; generally appears in bimonthly fascicles and cumulated annual volumes.

Index: Annual volumes include alphabetical indexes by country and subject, and a chronological index.

Note: Author varies. Volume 1981, tome 2 issued jointly with the Ministère des Affaires étrangères.

Note: Imprint varies. Volumes 1958 through 1968 bear the imprint, Imprimerie nationale.

Note : Continued by Bases des Traités et Accords de la France (see no. 3).

5 RECUEIL GÉNÉRAL DES TRAITÉS DE LA FRANCE

R. Pinto and H. Rollet, eds. ([Paris]: Documentation française, 1976–1994). 10 vols, in 11.

Summary: Published in two series. The *1ère série* (*Accords bilatéraux publiés et non publiés au Journal officiel de la République française*) contains texts of bilateral agreements dating from 1564 to 1957 that were still in force as of June 30, 1972. This series, which includes both unpublished agreements and agreements published in the *Journal officiel*, appears in six volumes, arranged chronologically: vol. 1 (1564–1918), vol. 2 (1919–1928), vol. 3 (1929–1944), vol. 4 (1945–1949), vol. 5 (1950–1953) and vol. 6 (1954– 1957). The *2ème série* (*Accords bilatéraux non publiés*) contains texts of previously unpublished bilateral agreements concluded from 1958 through 1975 that were still in force at the time of publication of the series. It appears in four volumes: vol. 1 (1958–1964), vol. 2 (1965–1969), vol. 3 (1970–1972) and vol. 4 (1973–1975).

Index: Most volumes include a subject index.

Note: Series title: *Travaux et recherches de l'Université de Paris I, Laboratoire d'informatique de droit international.*

6 RECUEIL DES TRAITÉS DE LA FRANCE

Ministère des Affaires étrangères (Paris: A. Durand and Pedone-Lauriel, 1864–1917). 24 vols, in 23.

Summary: Chronological compendium of French treaties from 1713 through 1906. Reprints full and excerpted texts of treaties and related materials.

Index: Each volume contains a chronological index, an alphabetical index of treaties by country and a subject index.

Note: Editor varies. Vols. 1–13 (1864–1882) edited by A.J.H. de Clercq; vols. 14–16 (1883–1885) edited by A.J.H. de Clercq and J. de Clercq; vols. 17–23 (1886–1917) edited by J. de Clercq.

Note: Vols. 1 through 10 were reprinted in 1880.

Treaty Indexes

7 LISTE DES TRAITÉS ET ACCORDS DE LA FRANCE EN VIGUEUR AU...

Ministère des Affaires étrangères (Paris: Direction des Journaux officiels, 1976–).

Summary: Provides an "as complete as possible" list of bilateral and multilateral treaties and agreements to which France is a party. Treaty lists are presented in several sections: *'Traités et accords bilatéraux'* lists bilateral agreements organized alphabetically by country of opposite party; *'Traités et accords multilatéraux'* lists multilateral treaties, organized chronologically. *'Traités et accords spéciaux'* includes a list of treaties and agreements concluded with international organizations, also organized chronologically. *'Traités et accords résultant de l'appartenance de la France aux Communautés européennes,'* which lists agreements resulting from France's membership in the European Communities (beginning with the 1982 edition), is likewise organized chronologically. Various editions of this work include entries for signed agreements still in the process of ratification or approval, but omit confidential treaties whose publication would be contrary to public interest. Entries include date, title, place of signature, depository, date of entry into force for France, citation to treaty source(s) and list of parties. For agreements submitted to Parliament under Article 53 of the Constitution, entries also note the relevant authorization, approval, ratification or accession law. Introductory materials include selected excerpts from French domestic law related to treaties, and a note on the effect of European Community regulation on French treaties and agreements.

Index: Each edition includes a subject index.

Note: Continues *Liste des engagements bilatéraux et multilatéraux au 30 juin 1972* (see no. 8).

Note: Author varies. 1982 and 1985 editions issued by the Ministère des Relations extérieures.

Note: Editor varies. 1976 and 1978 editions edited by H. Rollet and J. Boudoy; 1980 edition edited by G. Meunier; 1982 edition edited by M. Surbiguet and D. Wibaux; 1985 editions edited by M. Surbiguet and P. Seigneurin; 1988 edition edited by M. Surbiguet and P. Vagogne.

Note: Imprint varies. 1976 and 1978 editions bear the imprint, Imprimerie nationale.

Note: Frequency varies. From 1976 through 1982 appeared biennially; thereafter appeared irregularly in 1985, 1988, 1993 and 1998.

8 LISTE DES ENGAGEMENTS BILATÉRAUX ET MULTILATÉRAUX AU 30 JUIN 1972: ACCORDS ET TRAITÉS SOUSCRITS PAR LA FRANCE

H. Rollet (Paris: A. Pedone, 1973). 571 pp.

Summary: Lists all bilateral and multilateral treaties and agreements in force as of June 30, 1972. Bilateral treaties are listed first, arranged alphabetically by country of opposite party and organized by date. Multilateral treaties are listed chronologically. Includes list of 'special treaties' with foreign or international organizations, arranged chronologically. Entries include date, title, citation to treaty source(s), and (for multilateral treaties) date of entry into force for France, list of parties, and references to other modifying, amending or completing agreements.

Index: Includes a subject index by international issue. Under each international issue heading, bilateral treaties appear first, arranged alphabetically by country and organized by date, followed by multilateral treaties, organized chronologically.

Note: Continues *Liste des engagements bilatéraux au 30 juin 1969* (see no. 9) and *Liste des engagements multilatéraux au 30 juin 1969* (see no. 10). Continued by *Liste des traités et accords de la France en vigueur au...* (see no. 7).

9 LISTE DES ENGAGEMENTS BILATÉRAUX AU 30 JUIN 1969: ACCORDS ET TRAITÉS SOUSCRITS PAR LA FRANCE

H. Rollet (Paris: A. Pedone, 1970). 207 pp.

Summary: Lists all bilateral treaties and agreements in force as of June 30, 1969 and provides citation to treaty source(s). Arranged alphabetically by country of opposite party and organized by date. Omits treaties that have been abrogated, fulfilled their objectives or ceased being applied over a long period of time. Includes a list of 'special treaties' with foreign or international organizations, arranged chronologically. Entries include date, title and citation to treaty source(s).

Note: Continued by *Liste des engagements bilatéraux et multilatéraux au 30 juin 1972* (see no. 8).

10 LISTE DES ENGAGEMENTS MULTILATÉRAUX AU 30 JUIN 1969: ACCORDS ET TRAITÉS SOUSCRITS PAR LA FRANCE

H. Rollet (Paris: A. Pedone, 1971). 364 pp.

Summary: Chronological list of multilateral treaties and agreements to which France was a party as of June 30, 1969. Entries include date and place of each agreement's opening for signature, depository, date of entry into force for France, citation to standard treaty source(s), list of parties and references to other modifying, amending or completing agreements.

Index: Includes a subject index by international issue that covers both multilateral treaties and bilateral treaties appearing in the companion volume, *Liste des engagements bilatéraux au 30 juin 1969* (see no. 9). Within each international issue heading, bilateral treaties appear first, arranged alphabetically by country and organized by date, followed by multilateral treaties, organized chronologically.

Note: Continued by *Liste des engagements bilatéraux et multilatéraux au 30 juin 1972* (see no. 8, above).

11 NOMENCLATURE DES TRAITÉS ET ACTES DIPLOMATIQUES DE LA FRANCE EN 1964

F. LeRoy and J. Saidenberg (Paris: Gauthier-Villars, 1967). 127 pp.

Summary: List of treaties, agreements, and 'diplomatic acts' (exchanges of letters, related legislation, etc.) from the year 1964, including unpublished agreements. Entries include title, date, parties and citation to standard treaty source(s); may also include excerpts or complete reprints of texts from relevant diplomatic documents. For unpublished agreements, includes citations to articles and other works referring to the agreement. Chapters 1 through 4 cover bilateral agreements, multilateral treaties, texts related to the European Communities and texts concerning the status of diplomats and international law in general. Chapter 5 provides a classification by subject of all international agreements concluded in 1964.

Index: Includes only a table of contents.

Note: Series title: *Publications de l'Institut d'études des relations internationales contemporaines,* t.1.

Note: An annual series was planned, but no additional volumes were ever published.

12 TRAITÉS ET ACCORDS EN VIGUEUR: LISTE DES ENGAGEMENTS BILATÉRAUX SOUSCRITS PAR LA FRANCE EN VIGUEUR AU 1ER JANVIER 1958

P. Duparc, ed. (Paris: A. Pedone, 1962). 112 pp.

Summary: Lists bilateral treaties in force as of January 1, 1958. Organized alphabetically by country of opposite party, and then by date. Entries include date, title, citation to treaty source(s) and, in some cases, a description of the treaty.

Note: For certain jurisdictions, such as the Federal Republic of Germany, the list of treaties is incomplete. Such instances are noted.

Topical And Selected Treaty Collections[17]

13 TRAITÉS ET CONVENTIONS EN VIGUEUR ENTRE LA FRANCE ET LES PUISSANCES ETRANGÈRES

J. Basdevant, ed. (Paris: Imprimerie nationale, 1918–1922). 4 vols.

Summary: Commonly known as '*Basdevant*,' after its editor. Reprints treaties in force for France at the beginning of World War I peace negotiations. Omits obsolete texts and any treaties limited only to the circumstances of the war. For bilateral treaties with allied and neutral powers, texts are those in force as

---

17 For a contextual overview of key treaties concluded by France from the Middle Ages through the formation of the European Union, see GÉRARD BLIER, CES TRAITÉS QUI ONT FAIT LA FRANCE (2010).

of the publication of the collection; for treaties with enemy powers, texts are those in force immediately prior to the beginning of hostilities. For multilateral treaties, texts are also those in force just prior to the war, but more recent accessions and denunciations are noted. Vols. 1–3 contain bilateral treaties in alphabetical order by country of opposite party (vol. 1: Allemagne-Equateur; vol. 2: Espagne-Italie; vol. 3: Japon-Vénézuéla). Vols. 3 and 4 contain multilateral treaties, arranged in chronological order. Entries include date of signature, title, ratification date, citation to treaty source(s), list of representatives, place of signature and relevant portions of the treaty text.

Index: Each volume has a table of contents arranged alphabetically by country and organized by date. Vol. 4 also includes an index table of multilateral treaties by alphabetical order of country, and a subject index for the entire work.

14 RECUEIL DE TEXTES USUELS DE DROIT INTERNATIONAL: NATIONALITE. ETRANGERS. CONFLITS DE LOIS. TRAITES DE LA FRANCE. PROJETS EUROPEENS ET PANAMERICAINS

J. Niboyet and P. Goulé, eds. (Paris: Librairie du Recueil Sirey, 1929). 2 vols.

Summary: A collection of international texts 'of which jurists who occupy themselves with questions of international law have the most need.' Includes texts of materials dating from 1629 to 1928. Presented in two parts: *Partie I: Lois, décrets et règlements français,* contains French laws arranged by subject, including citizenship and military service, condition of foreigners and conflicts of laws. *Partie II: Traités diplomatiques* contains the texts of treaties; bilateral treaties are presented first, arranged alphabetically by country of opposite party, followed by multilateral treaties, arranged by subject. Entries include citation to standard treaty source(s).

Index: Includes chronological indexes of *Lois et décrets,* bilateral treaties and multilateral treaties, as well as a table of bilateral treaties arranged alphabetically by country of opposite party and organized by date. Also includes a general subject index and a table of contents.

Note: Supplemented by *Supplément 1929* (Paris: Librairie du Recueil Sirey, 1930). 116 pp. Annual supplementations were planned, but no others were ever published.

15 RECUEIL DES TRAITÉS, CONVENTIONS, LOIS, DÉCRETS ET AUTRES ACTES RELATIFS A LA PAIX AVEC L'ALLEMAGNE

A. Villefort, ed. (Paris: Imprimerie nationale, 1872–1879). 5 vols.

Summary: Compilation of treaties and many other related documents concerning the Franco-Prussian War (1870–1871). Vol. 1 contains military and diplomatic treaties and conventions. Vol. 2 reprints 'complementary documents,' including legislative debates and other treaty-related commentaries. Vols. 3 and 4 include laws and other documents relating to changes resulting from the war. Vol. 5, entitled *Addenda,* includes later documents related to all four preceding volumes.

Index: Vols. 1–4 each include a chronological table of contents and a subject index. The indexes in vol. 5 cover all volumes and include chronological tables of all laws and decrees appearing in the collection.

Note: Another collection of treaties and certain other documents related to the Franco-Prussian war is *Traités de la France avec l'Allemagne, Janvier 1871 à Octobre 1873* (Imprimerie nationale, 1873). 295 pp. Includes chronological table of contents and subject index.

16 LES TRAITÉS DE COMMERCE
TEXTE DE TOUS LES TRAITÉS EN VIGUEUR NOTAMMENT DES TRAITÉS AVEC L'ANGLETERRE, LA BELGIQUE, LA PRUSSE (ZOLLVEREIN), ET L'ITALIE: AVEC UNE INTRODUCTION HISTORIQUE ET ÉCONOMIQUE DES RENSEIGNEMENTS SUR LES MONNAIES, LES MESURES, LES DOUANES, LES USAGES ET UN CATALOGUE ALPHABÉTIQUE DES PRINCIPAUX ARTICLES TARIFÉS DANS LES DIVERS PAYS DU MONDE
P. Boiteau d'Ambly, ed. (Paris: Guillaumin, 1863). 566 pp.

Summary: Compilation of all treaties relating to commerce in force as of December 1863, organized by geographic region of the country of opposite party (Europe, America, Africa and Asia). Includes an introduction with information about commercial practices in various parts of the world and an alphabetical list of goods subject to tariff.

Index: Includes a table of contents, organized by geographic region of the country of opposite party.

17 LE CONGRÈS DE VIENNE ET LES TRAITÉS DE 1815
Précedé et suivi des actes diplomatiques qui s'y rattachent
L. Chodzko, ed. (Paris: Amyot, 1864). 4 vols.

Summary: Complete collection of acts of the Congress of Vienna and the treaties of 1815, including relevant diplomatic documents. Includes documents dating from 1813 to 1861. Also includes an extensive historical introduction.

Index: Vol. 1 contains a chronological table of contents and subject index arranged alphabetically by country and organized by date; both tables cover the entire set, which is continuously paginated.

Note: The editor's pseudonym, Comte d'Angeberg, appears on the spine of the volumes.

Note: Various other works have reprinted these treaties and acts, including: *Congrès de Vienne: Acte principal et traités additionnels édition complète collationnée sur les documents officiels* (Paris: Gerdes, 1847). 144 pp.; *Les traités de 1815: Texte des traités et conventions diplomatiques de 1814, 1815, et 1818, entre la France et les puissances alliées* (Paris, A. Bourdilliat, 1859). 172 pp.; and *Recueil des traités et conventions entre la France et les puissances alliées, en 1814 et 1815: Suivi de l'acte du Congrès de Vienne* (Paris: L'Imprimerie royale, 1815). 196 pp.

18 TRAITÉS INTERNATIONAUX DE L'ANCIEN RÉGIME: EDITIONS ISOLÉES ET RECUEILS CONSERVÉS A LA BIBLIOTHÈQUE NATIONALE DE FRANCE: CATALOGUE

M. Rémy-Limousin, ed. (Paris: Bibliothèque nationale de France, 1997). 190 pp.

Summary: Chronological listing of treaties published prior to 1800, edited in the Roman alphabet. Presented in two parts: *Editions isolées* contains listings of individual editions of treaties; *Recueil de traités* lists treaty collections. Entries include date, title, place of signature, language, publisher, date and place of publication, format, pagination and (where applicable) a note regarding abridgment of treaty. The bibliographic description is followed by a brief contents description, classification number and supplementary notes.

Index: Individual treaties are indexed alphabetically by place of signature, signatory countries and subject. Treaty collections are indexed chronologically. Also includes indexes of authors, places of publication and printers, each of which cover both individual treaties and treaty collections.

Note: Another detailed bibliography of historical French treaties may be found in *Manual of Collections of Treaties and of Collections Relating to Treaties.* D. Myers, ed. (Cambridge, Mass: Harvard University Press, 1922). 685 pp. Series title, *Harvard Biblographies. Library Series,* vol. II. Also contains bibliographic information on legal bibliographies, diplomatic documents, memoirs, periodicals, etc. The section on French sources is found at pages 149–174.

19 DOCUMENTS DIPLOMATIQUES DU CONSULAT ET DE L'EMPIRE

M. Kerautret, ed. (Paris: Nouveau Monde: Fondation Napoléon, 2002–2004). 3 vols.

Summary: Collection of major treaty texts from the '*époque consulaire*' and '*l'empire*,' organized chronologically into three volumes: '*Les grands traités du consulat* (1795–1804),' '*Les grands traités de l'empire: de l'empire au grand empire* (1804–1810)' and '*Les grands traités de l'empire: la chute de l'empire et la restauration europeénne* (1811–1815).' Includes annotations, explanatory notes and bibliographic references.

Index: Each volume includes a table of contents and an index of treaties organized alphabetically by country of opposite party.

Note: Series title: *La bibliothèque Napoléon. Série 'Sources.'*

20 LES GRANDS TRAITÉS DU REGNE DE LOUIS XIV

H. Vast, ed. (Paris: A. Picard, 1893–99.) 3 vols, in 1.

Summary: Contains the texts of major treaties concluded during the reign of Louis XIV, from 1648 to 1714. Texts are in French or Latin, corrected and edited using the original sources. Entries include location of original and of principal copies. Also includes explanatory notes and bibliographic references. Vol. 1 contains *Traité du Münster, Ligue du Rhin,* and *Traité des Pyrénées* (1648–1659); vol. 2 contains *Traité d'Aix-la-Chapelle, Traités de Nimègue et Tréve de Ratisbonne,* and *Traités de Turin et de Ryswick* (1668–1697); vol. 3 contains *La succession d'Espagne* and *Traités d'Utrecht, de Rastadt* and *de Bade* (1713–1714).

Index: Includes table of contents, an alphabetical list of personal names and a geographic index of places.

Note: Series title: *Collection de textes pour servir à l'étude et à l'enseignement de l'histoire,* t. 15, 23, 28.

21 LES GRANDS TRAITÉS DE LA GUERRE DE CENT ANS

E. Cosneau, ed. (Paris: A. Picard, 1889). 187 pp.

Summary: Contains the texts of the six major treaties and truces negotiated by France and England during the Hundred Years' War. Includes the treaties of Brétigny (1360), Troyes (1420), Arras (1435) and the unratified treaty of London (1359). Also included are the truces of Paris (1396) and Tours (1444). Texts are in French or Latin, corrected and edited using the original sources. Includes explanatory notes and bibliographic references.

Index: Includes only a table of contents.

Note: Series title: *Collection de textes pour servir à l'étude et à l'enseignement de l'histoire, t.* 7.

22 THE TREATIES OF 1778 AND ALLIED DOCUMENTS

G. Chinard, ed. (Baltimore: Johns Hopkins Press, 1928). 70 pp.

Summary: Reprints in French and English both the Treaty of Alliance and the Treaty of Amity and Commerce, signed by France and the United States in 1778. Includes reprints of related materials drawn from original documents. Also includes an extensive historical introduction.

23 RECUEIL DES TRAITÉS CONCLUS PAR LA FRANCE EN EXTRÊME-ORIENT

L. de Reinach, ed. (Paris: E. Leroux, 1902–1907). 2 vols.

Summary: Chronological compilation of treaties concluded by France and Far East countries from 1684 to 1907. Vol. 1 contains treaties dating from 1684–1902; vol. 2 contains treaties from 1901–1907. Treaties concluded since 1873 are accompanied by various annexes, including excerpts from relevant diplomatic correspondence and notes on sources of parliamentary commission reports.

Index: Includes table of treaties arranged alphabetically by country of opposite party.

24 TRAITÉS DE DÉLIMITATION CONCERNANT L'AFRIQUE FRANÇAISE
E. Rouard de Card, ed. (Paris: A. Pedone, 1910). 198 pp.

Summary: Reprints treaties of delimitation dating from 1845 to 1908 between France and various countries, regarding 'French Africa.' Each treaty is followed by a set of explanatory notes; some also include a map. Includes an historical introduction.

Index: Includes detailed table of contents arranged alphabetically by country of opposite party.

Note: Supplemented by two later volumes: *Traités de délimitation concernant l'Afrique française: Supplement 1910–1913*. E. Rouard de Card, ed. (Paris: A. Pedone, 1913). 129 pp. and *Traités de délimitation concernant l'Afrique française: Supplement 1914–1925*. E. Rouard de Card, ed. (Paris: A. Pedone, 1926). 84 pp.

Diplomatic Documents

25 DOCUMENTS DIPLOMATIQUES
Ministère des Affaires étrangères (Paris: Imprimérie imperiale, 1861–1928). 240 vols.

Summary: This title, also known as the 'Yellow Books' (*'Livres jaunes'*), contains numerous documents related to major diplomatic affairs dating from 1860 through 1928. It was originally published in volumes numbered 1 through 13, covering 1860–1869, and in one unnumbered volume covering 1870–1873. Thereafter, all documents relating to individual diplomatic matters were collected and published in separate volumes, sub-titled by diplomatic matter.

Index: A separate index volume, covering 1869–1902, includes a chronological list of volumes and their contents, organized into the following series: *Série A, Affaires diplomatiques proprement dîtes* (relating to diplomatic matters such as delimitation of territories, diplomatic missions and peace negotiations); *Série B, Affaires commerciales* (customs regulations, railroad regulation, etc.); *Série C, Conférences internationales;* and *Série D, Conférences monétaires internationales.* Also includes a subject index.

Note: Documents in the volumes are individually numbered. Document nos. 1–213 are numbered as they appear in *Bibliographie des 'livres jaunes' à la date du 1er janvier, 1922: Extrait de la Revue des bibliothèques, 32e année, 1922*. R. Doré. (Paris: H. Champion, 1922). 28 pp.; document nos. 214 and following are assigned arbitrarily.

26 DOCUMENTS DIPLOMATIQUES FRANÇAIS (1954–)
Ministére des Affaires étrangères (Paris: Imprimérie nationale, 1987–).

Summary: Contains diplomatic documents, including documents from collections that have not previously been opened to the public. Series begins with 21 juillet 1954, and to date includes materials dating through 1969.

Index: Each volume includes an opening index, arranged by diplomatic matter and organized by date; also includes the type of document and information regarding the document's place of origin and intended recipient. Each volume also contains an alphabetical index of personal names.

Note: Some volumes include supplements entitled Annexes.

27 DOCUMENTS DIPLOMATIQUES FRANÇAIS (1932–1939): RELATIFS AUX ORIGINES DE LA GUERRE DE 1939–1945
Ministére des Affaires étrangères (Paris: Imprimérie nationale, 1964–1986). 32 vols.

Summary: Extensive chronological compilation of diplomatic documents concerning diplomatic relations leading up to World War II, drawn from many ministerial archives. Each volume contains from 300 to 500 documents, covering a period of three to four months, in a topical and geographic organization. Also included are cross-references and explanatory footnotes. Published in two series: *1ère série* (1932–1935) consists of 13 volumes; *2ème série* (1936–1939) consists of 19 volumes.

Index: Each volume includes an opening index, arranged by diplomatic matter and organized by date; also includes the type of document and information regarding the document's place of origin and intended recipient. Each volume also contains an alphabetical index of personal names and a subject index of international issues.

Note: Of related interest is a privately published compilation of similar documents related to Germany, France, Great Britain and Poland: *Des accords de Munich à la déclaration de guerre à l'Allemagne 29/09/1938–03/09/1939: III volumes: Documents diplomatiques relatifs à l'Allemagne, la France, la Grande-Bretagne et la Pologne*. T. Mage (Paris: Tristan Mage, auteur, editeur, diffuseur, 1991). 3 vols.

28 DOCUMENTS DIPLOMATIQUES FRANÇAIS 1871–1914: RELATIFS AUX ORIGINES DE LA GUERRE DE 1914

Ministére des Affaires étrangères (Paris: Imprimerie nationale, 1929–1960). 41 vols, in 43.

Summary: Chronological compilation of documents concerning diplomatic relations among France and other European powers leading up to World War I. Published in three series: *1ère série* (1871–1900) consists of 16 volumes; *2ème série* (1901–1911) consists of 14 volumes; *3ème série* (1911–1914) consists of 11 volumes.

Index: Each volume includes an opening index, arranged by diplomatic matter and organized by date; also includes the type of document and information regarding the document's place of origin and intended recipient. Each volume also includes an alphabetical index of personal names.

29 LES ORIGINES DIPLOMATIQUES DE LA GUERRE DE 1870–1871

Recueil de documents publié par le Ministère des Affaires étrangères (Paris: G. Ficker, Imprimerie nationale, 1910–1932). 29 vols.

Summary: Chronological compilation of diplomatic documents dating from 1863 to 1870, relating to the Franco-Prussian war.

Index: Each volume includes a detailed table of contents.

Note: Imprint varies. Vols. 11–29 bear the imprint, H. Charles-Lavauzelle; Imprimerie nationale.

30 ARCHIVES DIPLOMATIQUES: RECUEIL MENSUEL DE DIPLOMATIE ET D'HISTOIRE

Ministère des Affaires étrangères (Paris: Amyot; Leipzig: F.A. Brockhaus, 1861–1914). 193 vols.

Summary: Compendium of records and correspondence from the French diplomatic and consular services, from 1861 to May 1914. In French; correspondence originally in other languages has been translated. Published in four series: *1ère série* (1861–1879) includes vols. 1–62; *2ème série* (1880–1900) includes vols. 1–76; *3ème série* (1901–1913) includes vols. 77–129; *4ème série* (1914) includes vols. 130–131.

Note: Volumes also known and cited as *1.–4., année.*

Note: Subtitle varies. From 1861–1878, appeared under the subtitle *Recueil de diplomatie et d'histoire.*

Note: Frequency varies. 1861–1878 volumes appeared irregularly; 1879–1914 volumes published monthly or quarterly.

Note: Of related interest is *Les archives du Ministère des Relations extérieures depuis l'origine: Histoire et guide, suivi d'une étude des sources des affaires*

étrangères dans les dépôts parisiens et départementaux. Ministère des Affaires étrangères (Paris: Imprimerie nationale, 1984–1985). 2 vols. A history and guide to the archives of the Ministry of Foreign Relations. Includes a study of sources of diplomatic documents in Paris archives.

31 BULLETIN OFFICIEL DU MINISTÈRE DES AFFAIRES ETRANGÈRES (Paris: Imprimerie nationale, 1883–).

Summary: Quarterly foreign relations publication from the Ministry of Foreign Affairs. Includes information about treaties, new laws relating to foreign affairs, etc., as well as modifications of such documents.

Index: Includes table of contents organized alphabetically by country.

Note: Title varies: From 1983–1994, appeared as *Bulletin officiel (France. Ministère des Affaires étrangères);* from 1883–1983, appeared as *Bulletin officiel (France. Ministère des relations extérieures).*

32 LA POLITIQUE ETRANGÈRE DE LA FRANCE: TEXTES ET DOCUMENTS (Paris: Ministère des Affaires étrangères, Direction de la presse, de l'information et de la communication, 1966–2004).

Summary: Bimonthly publication presenting France's essential positions in foreign policy. Includes such items as official statements of government officials, exchanges of diplomatic correspondence, etc. Also includes answers of the Foreign Minister to written questions submitted by Parliament regarding treaties and foreign affairs. Texts arranged in chronological order. Some issues include annexes containing, among other items, a chronological list of agreements concluded by France during the period of the issue.

Index: Each volume includes a subject index, a country index, and a table of texts reproduced.

Note: Issued as *Notes et études documentaires,* 1966–1968.

Note: Publisher varies. Issued jointly by Ministère des Affaires étrangères and la Documentation française, 1966–1991.

Note: Frequency varies. Appeared as an annual in 1966; appeared semiannually 1967–1982.

33 FRANCE DIPLOMATIE

Ministère des Affaires étrangères.

URL: http://www.diplomatie.gouv.fr.

Summary: Official web site of the Ministry of Foreign Affairs. Contains information on French foreign policy. Also contains *Déclarations officielles et Points de presses,* a searchable database of all foreign policy statements since 1990 and most such statements from 1966 through 1989. Also includes press releases since 1983.

Yearbooks and Digests of State Practice

34 ANNUAIRE FRANÇAIS DE DROIT INTERNATIONAL

([Paris]: Centre nationale de la recherche scientifique, 1955–).

Summary: Annual publication relating to international law. Lists international conventions concluded by France, with citations to the *Journal officiel* (see no. 1) and the *Recueil des traités et accords de la France* (see no. 4). Other sections include summaries of French jurisprudence related to public international law and of French international law practice, and a chronology of international events of legal interest.

Index: Each volume includes an index of cited treaties and other texts, arranged chronologically, and an index of cited court decisions, also arranged chronologically. These indexes are cumulated into decennial tables volumes (1955–1964, 1965–1974, 1975–1984, 1985–1994, 1995–2004) and a quinquennial tables volume (1965–1969).

35 JOURNAL DU DROIT INTERNATIONAL (CLUNET)

J. Jacquet, ed. (Paris: Juris-Classeur, 1874–).

Summary: Commonly known and cited as *Clunet,* after its original editor. Includes information about, and reprints texts of, new treaties and agreements, and reprints texts of new treaties and agreements. Also includes international jurisprudence and articles on international law.

Index: Annual index volumes include an index of treaties by country.

Note: Title varies. From 1874–1914 appeared as *Journal du droit international privé et de la jurisprudence privée.*

Note: Editor varies. 1874–1922, edited by E. Clunet; 1923–1949, edited by A. Prudhomme; 1950–1993, edited by B. Goldman; 1994–2002, edited by P. Kahn.

Note: Frequency varies.

36 REVUE CRITIQUE DE DROIT INTERNATIONAL PRIVÉ

B. Ancel, ed. (Paris: Librairie du Recueil Sirey, 1905–).

Summary: Quarterly (irregular) publication including articles on international law, international jurisprudence and information on treaties and agreements. Some volumes include section *Traités nouveaux de la France,* which contains texts of new treaties.

Index: Separate cumulative index volumes were published for 1905–1924 and 1925–1950, including a detailed subject index and a chronological index of legislation. Thereafter, annual indexes published in the final issue for each year.

Note: Title varies. Vols. 1–17 (1905–1921) appeared as *Revue de droit international privé et de droit penal international;* vols. 18–28 (1922–1933) appeared as

Revue de droit international privé; vols. 29–35 (1934–1946) appeared as *Revue critique de droit international.*

Note: Editor varies. January 1905–September 1908, edited by A. Darras; 1909–1933, edited by A. de Lapradelle; 1934–1952, edited by J. Niboyet; 1953–1975, edited by H. Batiffol; 1976–1989, edited by H. Batiffol and P. Francescakis; 1990–1992, edited by P. Francescakis and P. Lagarde; 1993–2006, edited by P. Lagarde; 2007–2011, edited by P. Lagarde and B. Ancel.

Note: Imprint varies. Volumes from 1905–1921 appeared under the imprint, Librairie de la Société du Recueil J.B. Sirey & du Journal du palais.

Note: Frequency varies. Appeared bimonthly (irregular) January 1905–December 1909.

Note: Publication suspended 1940–1945.

37 REVUE GÉNÉRALE DE DROIT INTERNATIONAL PUBLIC

P. DuPuy and J. Queneudec, eds. (Paris: A. Pedone, 1894–).

Summary: Quarterly publication including articles on international law topics, international jurisprudence, and notes on current international matters. Most volumes include *Documents* section, containing texts of new treaties and international agreements.

Index: Final issue of each year contains annual table of contents and subject index.

Note: Vols. 26–33 also called *2ème série,* v. 1–8; vols. 34–80 also called *3ème série,* v. 1– [47].

Note: Editor varies. 1894–1903, edited by A. Pillet and P. Fauchille; 1904–1918, edited by P. Fauchille; 1919–1925, edited by P. Fauchille and A. Lapradelle; 1926, edited by A. Lapradelle and M. Sibert; 1927–1929, edited by C. Rousseau; 1930–1932, edited by C. Rousseau and R. Geret; 1933–1935, edited by R. Pelloux; 1936–1957, edited by M. Sibert; 1958–1975, edited by C. Rousseau; 1976–1989, edited by C. Rousseau and M. Virally; 1990–1993, edited by C. Rousseau.

Note: Frequency varies.

Germany

Ralph F. Gaebler and Jennifer Allison

Issues of Treaty Succession

Germany has undergone a variety of geographic and political transformations during the past several hundred years. During that time, it has participated actively in international diplomacy. Therefore, it presents a large number of interesting questions regarding treaty succession, as well as treaty survival in circumstances of war and political revolution.

Germany's modern incarnation is conventionally thought to date from the collapse of the Holy Roman Empire in 1806. At that time the Confederation of the Rhine[1] (*Rheinbund*, 1806 to approximately 1813[2]) was formed through a treaty concluded between France and several independent German states along the Rhine River. The treaty formally established something of a hybrid, according to which each of the German states retained its sovereign independence, yet joined together with the others in a joint assembly of political leaders.[3]

1 Hans A. Schmitt provides an informative English-language historical overview of the Confederation of the Rhein, from its initial establishment as an alliance between France and the original 17 German polities through its development into what became a 35-member confederation. *See* Hans A. Schmitt, *Germany Without Prussia: A Closer Look at the Confederation of the Rhein*, 6 German Stud. Rev. 9–39 (Feb. 1983).

2 It is difficult to date the termination of the Confederation of the Rhine. Generally, it is thought to be 1813, when Mecklenburg quit the Confederation, and sought protection from Austria-Hungary. Other members of the Confederation soon followed. A. Erler and E. Kaufmann, 1 Handwörterbuch zur Deutschen Rechtsgeschichte 687 (1971); 4 Handwörterbuch zur Deutschen Rechtsgeschichte 1010 (1990).

3 The Treaty of the Confederation of the Rhine, signed at Paris 12 June 1806, is printed in French in 58 Consol. T.S. 461. According to Article XXV, each state retained its sovereignty, and according to Article XXVI this comprised the powers of legislation, taxation, conscription or recruitment, jurisdiction and the police power. In addition to Schmitt, other scholars have discussed in detail how the sovereign powers granted to the German polities through this treaty were received by their citizens and exercised by their political leaders. *See* Schmitt, *supra* note 1; *see also* Katherine Aaslestad & Karen Hagemann, *1806 and Its Aftermath: Revisiting the Period of the Napoleonic Wars in German Central European Historiography*, 39 Central European History 547–579 (2006); Erwin Hölzle, *Das Napoleonische Staatssystem in Deutschland*, 148 Historische Zeitschrift 277–293 (1933); Eberhard Weis, *Bayern und Frankreich in der Zeit des Konsulats und des Ersten Empire* (1799–1815), 237 Historische Zeitschrift 559–595 (1983).

 | DOI 10.1163/9789004272224_014

In reality, the joint assembly never met.[4] Moreover, France became "protector"[5] of the Confederation under Article XII, effectively eliminating the possibility that the Confederation might have any real independence in the conduct of foreign relations or war. In fact, France reserved to itself the right to intervene in the internal affairs of the Confederation as well. Therefore, one can reasonably assert that the Confederation of the Rhine possessed international legal personality only as a formal matter.[6]

Following Napoleon's defeat and the Congress of Vienna, the Confederation of the Rhine was superseded by the Germanic Confederation (*Deutscher Bund*, 1815–1866), which was also a loose political association of virtually independent states. It had neither a central executive nor a common judiciary. However, formal structure once again conferred international legal personality. In fact, the Vienna system attempted explicitly to limit the sovereignty of states within the Confederation. Article II of the Constitution of the Germanic Confederation stated that "this confederation is composed internally of a community of self-sufficient states, independent among themselves, with equal rights relative to one another to conclude and perform treaty obligations, but in external matters is composed of a single political whole".[7] But despite this effort to

4 A good description of the constitutional situation of the Confederation of the Rhine is found in 1 E.R. Huber, Deutsche Verfassungsgeschichte Seit 1798 79–84 (Rev. 2nd ed. 1960).

5 Napoleon explained his position as a protector in a letter to Karl von Dalberg, reprinted in Ernst Rudolf Huber, Dokumente zur deutschen Verfassungsgeschichte, I: Deutsche Verfassungsdokumente 1803–1850 36 (1961).

6 According to Huber, "[t]he Rhine Confederation was one of the first modern European examples of an imperial state assuming sovereign control over foreign soil without formal annexation, and while concealing this fact behind the appearances of international law" (author's translation). Huber (1960), *supra* note 4, at 83.

7 Final Act of the Ministerial Conference to Complete and Consolidate the Organisation of the German Confederation, May 15, 1820, art. II, 71 Consol. T.S. 89, 92 (author's translation). This treaty was concluded as a follow-up to the Final Act of the Vienna Congress, June 9, 1815, 64 Consol. T.S. 453. The Act Relative to the Federal Constitution of Germany, June 8, 1815, 64 Consol. T.S. 443, and incorporated by reference in the Final Act of the Congress of Vienna, indicates that the individual state-members of the Confederation continued to retain sufficient sovereignty to conclude separate treaties with non-confederated states. Article XI of this agreement obligated state-members "not to contract any engagement that would harm the security of the Confederation or that of any of the states that compose it" (author's translation). This is the only limitation imposed on the member states, and implies that they were free to conclude agreements with outsiders that did not compromise those interests. For a similar interpretation of this language, *see* W. Grewe, *Auswartige Gewalt, in* 3 Handbuch des Staatsrechts der Bundesrepublik Deutschland 929 (J. Isensee and P. Kirchhof, 1987–). Comparing this clause to the more general statement in Art. II of the 1820 Final Act, one can

curtail their power, member states of the Confederation, and especially Prussia, did conclude treaties with non-confederation states on a regular basis. Many of these treaties related to extradition,[8] judicial assistance generally or to various measures that enabled the unimpeded growth of a commercial and industrial infrastructure throughout central Europe.[9] Thus, the German states continued to possess, and to exercise, international legal personality throughout this period.

Issues of succession first arise in conjunction with the foundation of the North German Federation (*Norddeutscher Bund*, 1866–1870)[10] and the German Empire, or *Deutsches Reich* (1871–1918). The former realized Bismarck's ambition to unify Germany under Prussian hegemony; the latter, following the Franco-Prussian War of 1870–1871, completed the process by adding the German states south of the Main River. Unlike their forebears, the new Federation and Empire enjoyed strong, central political authority, as well as other national institutions, such as courts and the military. In particular, the Constitution of the North German Federation conferred on the central government the power to engage treaty obligations. Specifically, it granted the power to conclude treaties to the Kaiser, and to the *Reichstag* and *Bundesrat* it gave the power of ratification in certain circumstances.[11] The Constitution of the

---

only conclude that the Vienna system did not address the issue of individual state sovereignty with any precision or finality.

8 For example, every German state at the time had one or more extradition-related treaties in place, which "have been recognized as inter-state definitions of citizenship[.]" Andreas K. Fahrmeir, *Nineteenth-Century German Citizenships: A Reconsideration*, 40 HIST. J. 721–752 (1997).

9 Treaty partners were not necessarily limited to European countries. For example, the United States entered into a bilateral commerce and navigation treaty with Prussia, as well as a multilateral extradition treaty with several states of the Germanic Confederation, during this period. Treaty of Commerce and Navigation, U.S.-Prussia, 8 Stat. 378 (1828); Proclamation of the President of the United States, June 16, 1852, 10 Stat. 964 (1852).

10 The formation of the Norddeutscher Bund was an important step toward the consolidation of individual German states to a more unified nation that is similar to modern Germany. Already at that point, the beginnings of a centralized German diplomatic power were beginning to take shape. *See* Richard Hudson, *The Formation of the North German Confederation*, 6 POL. SCI. Q. 424–438 (1891).

11 Article 11 conferred upon the Kaiser the power to make foreign policy. Specifically, he was entrusted to represent the Confederation in matters of public international law, to send and receive ambassadors, and to conclude treaties. The Kaiser's authority was limited only in two respects. First, in the event he declared war *in the name of the Confederation*, the *Bundesrat* must agree. Second, if a proposed treaty involved a subject within the jurisdiction of federal legislation, the *Bundesrat* must agree to its conclusion, and the *Reichstag*

German Empire was virtually the same, save for necessary editorial changes.[12] It is generally agreed that Germany assumed international legal personality during this period.[13]

Treaty succession issues raised by this political transformation involve the continuing effect of treaties concluded by state-members of the Germanic Confederation, as well as the continuing effect of treaties concluded by the Germanic Confederation itself. According to one commentator, "the sole test of the effect of federation on treaties is the compatibility of a treaty with the federal structure, and this incompatibility may not arise until the federal instrumentalities bring it about".[14] Relying on this principle, the researcher would conclude that pre-1866 state treaties "continued to bind the respective states through the Empire until terminated by an inconsistent exercise of federal legislative power".[15] With respect to treaties concluded by the Germanic Confederation itself, one would presumably apply the general principle that

must agree to give it effect. In fact, the Kaiser was limited much more by the requirement of Article 17 that the Chancellor co-sign agreements and be responsible for them. *See* 1867 Constitution of the North German Federation, BUNDES-GESETZBLATT DES NORDDEUTSCHEN BUNDES 1867 at 2. The Constitution of the North German Federation is reprinted in E.R. HUBER, DOKUMENTE ZUR DEUTSCHEN VERFASSUNGSGESCHICHTE 272–85 (3rd ed. 1978–). All of the limitations mentioned above were imposed in favor of other federal organs. The member states, in contrast, retained only the power to make treaties with respect to subjects left within their exclusive legislative jurisdiction, such as promotion of culture. *See* Grewe, *supra* note 7, at 931.

12 R. SCHRÖDER AND E. FREIHERR VON KÜNSSBERG, LEHRBUCH DER DEUTSCHEN RECHTSGESCHICHTE 1012 (6th ed. 1922). Constitution of the German Empire, Apr. 16, 1871, BUNDES-GESETZBLATT DES NORDDEUTSCHEN BUNDES 1871, no. 16 at 63. The minor alterations it included were enacted by the *Beschluss des Norddeutschen Bundesrats und Reichstags betreffend die Einführung der Bezeichnungen "Deutsches Reich" und "Deutscher Kaiser,"* of 10 December 1870, and published in the Verhandlungen des Norddeutschen Reichstags 1870, II. Ausserordentliche Session, p. 151. This resolution is reprinted in HUBER (1978–), *supra* note 11, at 352. The North German Federation and the Empire are considered by some to have been a single entity. *See, e.g.*, J. MERVYN JONES, BRITISH NATIONALITY LAW AND PRACTICE 365 (1947).

13 The diplomatic process and strategy by which the new boundary between France and Germany was established in 1871 is especially indicative of the emerging centralized control exercised by Germany's Prussian leadership over Germany's foreign diplomatic activities. *See* Richard Hartshorne, *The Franco-German Boundary of 1871*, 2 WORLD POL. 209–250 (1950).

14 2 D.P. O'CONNELL, STATE SUCCESSION IN MUNICIPAL LAW 57 (1967).

15 O'Connell cites a number of instances in which both German and foreign courts assumed the continued force of German state treaties after 1866, id. at 57–60.

successor states assume only those obligations that relate in some sense to the predecessor state's actual territory.[16]

Treaty issues arising from World War I and the demise of the German Empire were addressed directly in the Treaty of Versailles.[17] Articles 282 to 286 listed the multilateral treaty commitments revived by termination of the war, Article 290 abrogated all treaties concluded by the central powers among themselves, and most particularly, Article 289 granted to the allied and associated powers the right to notify Germany of those pre-war bilateral agreements each wished to revive. The United States, for example, chose to revive only the patent agreement of 1909.[18]

The rise of Nazi Germany and the war that it precipitated present their own set of questions with respect to treaty succession. Hitler was elected chancellor in 1933, and converted the Republic into a police state through means that superficially adhered to the requirements of the Weimar Constitution, even while subverting it.[19] According to the weight of contemporary doctrine, these purely internal, political changes did not cause an instance of succession to occur.[20] However, in 1934 Germany was converted from a federal into a unitary state, and the states into administrative districts without international legal personality. As a result, the German government declared that it succeeded only to state treaties that were non-political in nature. Nevertheless, in subsequent practice many foreign states have regarded their pre-1934 agreements

16 1 Sir Robert Jennings and Sir Arthur Watts, Oppenheim's International Law 211–13 (9th ed. 1992).

17 225 Consol. T.S. 188. The treaty also appears in the official gazettes of the states party, e.g., *Reichsgesetzblatt*, 1919, p. 688.

18 5 Hackworth Digest § 512, at 288 (1943). Article 289 provided only a six-month period in which to revive bilateral treaties, and notices of revival are printed in the *Reichsgesetzblatt*.

19 As chancellor in 1933 Hitler persuaded the *Reichstag* to pass the Enabling Act, which empowered the government to issue decrees independently of the *Reichstag* or President. The Enabling Act, March 24, 1933 RGBl I at 141, and is reprinted in 4 Huber (1960), *supra* note 4, at 665–66. While not involving a question of succession, it is worth noting that the Nazi regime concluded treaties during its time in power that arguably were void from the start as violative of international legal norms. An example would be the agreement with Vichy France which bound France to supply workers to the German armaments industry. *See* U. Hoenicke, Die Fortgeltung von Verträgen des Deutschen Reiches in der BRD und der DDR 5 (1972). Part I of this book includes a thorough discussion of illegal Nazi treaties.

20 *See* J. Frowein, *"Die Identität der Bundesrepublik Deutschland als Völkerrechtssubjekt,"* §196, *in* 8 Handbuch des Staatsrechts der Bundesrepublik Deutschland 478 (J. Isensee and P. Kirchhof, 1987–).

with the German states as still in force.[21] The researcher must consult a subject-country's list of treaties in force to determine which of these pre-1934 agreements are among them.

The outbreak of World War II must also be considered for the effect it had on Germany's treaty relations. The general view held today is that war does not by itself cancel all treaties concluded by the belligerants. War cancels only political treaties between belligerants that have not been concluded "for the purpose of setting up a permanent condition of things".[22] Non-political treaties may be suspended or cancelled, and multilateral treaties may be suspended as necessitated by the conditions of war. With respect to Germany in particular, this is also the view taken by Hoenicke.[23]

The end of World War II, and the unconditional surrender of Germany, ushered in an occupation regime under the governance of the Allied High Commission.[24] Occupation ended officially in 1955, when the Convention on Relations Between the Three Powers and the Federal Republic of Germany, together with the Protocol on the Termination of the Occupation Regime in the Federal Republic of Germany, came into force.[25] However, the allied

---

21 O'CONNELL, *supra* note 14, at 80.

22 2 H. LAUTERPACHT, OPPENHEIM'S INTERNATIONAL LAW 302 (7th ed. 1952). For example, Lauterpacht asserts that war does not cancel treaties estabishing proprietary rights of nationals; *see* id. at 304, footnote 1. *See also* J. Delbrück, *War, Effect on Treaties*, in 4 ENCYCLOPEDIA OF PUBLIC INTERNATIONAL LAW 1367–1373. . According to Delbrück, the law today is driven by the desire "to minimize the disruptive effects of war in the sphere of treaty law without overlooking the fact that in some areas of political and social relations between States, the continuing effectiveness of treaties is incompatible with a state of war". Hence, cases of treaty termination by war have become the exception, rather than the rule.

23 HOENICKE, *supra* note 19, at 59. As examples of treaties cancelled by the outbreak of war, Hoenicke cites the 1938 German-French declaration of peaceful and neighborly relations, and the 1939 German-Soviet non-aggression pact. Delbrück agrees that the category of treaties cancelled by the outbreak of war includes those whose continuing operation is incompatible with the outbreak of war. *See* Delbrück, *supra* note 22, at 1369.

24 Charter of the Allied High Commission for Germany, June 20, 1949, 128 U.N.T.S. 141. Germany forfeited its sovereignty in the Declaration Regarding the Defeat of Germany and the Assumption of Supreme Authority with Respect to Germany, June 5, 1945, 68 *UNTS* 189. The western powers then ended military rule and returned partial sovereignty to Germany subject to reserved rights in the Agreements on Germany, April 8, 1949, 140 U.N.T.S. 196. The Allied High Commission was established to exercise those reserved rights, which included the right to supervise Germany's foreign affairs. (See also 48, below.)

25 The former is located at 6 U.S.T. 4251, the latter at 6 U.S.T.4118. Despite the end of the occupation, the western powers retained the right to station troops in the Federal

powers retained certain rights, and did not officially terminate all aspects of the occupation until the Treaty on the Final Settlement with Respect to Germany came into force in 1991.[26] Under Article 7(1) of that treaty, the allies terminated their rights and responsibilities related to Germany and Berlin, and declared that "corresponding, related quadripartite agreements, decisions and practices are terminated and all related Four Power institutions are dissolved". Under Article 7(2), united Germany was accorded "full sovereignty over its internal and external affairs". Thus, Germany enjoyed a gradual reintroduction of sovereignty over the entire post-war period.

A significant question involves the effect of the occupation on pre-existing Empire and Weimar treaties. According to Hoenicke, Germany did not lose its international legal personality as a result of its defeat in World War II, nor by virtue of the occupation that followed.[27] Therefore, prior treaties other than those of an incompatible, political nature were not abrogated as of the date of Germany's surrender, although they may have been suspended in order to hinder Germany's war aims. In order to deal with this situation, the Allied High Command adopted a treaty resumption and renovation procedure in 1945. According to this procedure, the occupation government had the right to approve or disapprove the abrogation, introduction, resumption or implementation of all German treaties.[28] Moreover, in 1951 the Allied High Commission adopted a directive requiring the German government (and foreign governments) to apply to it for permission to resume pre-war treaties through a

---

Republic, the right to exercise political control over Berlin, the right to control of flights between the two Germanys and the right to be involved in any future process of unification of the two Germanys.

26 Vertrag über die abschließende Regelung in bezug auf Deutschland [Treaty on the Final Settlement With Respect to Germany], Sep. 12, 1990, BGBl. II at 1317. The Treaty on Final Settlement is also reprinted in English in 29 I.L.M. 1186 (1990).

27 Hoenicke, *supra* note 19, at 203–207. According to Michael Schweitzer, this represents the overwhelming opinion. *See* M. Schweitzer, *"Die Verträge Deutschlands mit den Siegermächten"* § 190, *in* 8 Handbuch des Staatsrechts der Bundesrepublik Deutschland 200 (J. Isensee and P. Kirchhof, 1987–).

28 This procedure was created by a proclamation of the Allied High Commission. See Proclamation No. 2, Parag. III, Sect. 6, *Official Journal of the Allied High Commission*, No. 5 (1945) p. 27. The relevant portion is also quoted in Hoenicke, *supra* note 19, at 79. Apparently, some commentators argue that this provision caused the abrogation of all treaties concluded between Germany and its former enemies. Id. *at* 79–80. However, Bleckemann makes the point that the procedure presupposed that pre-existing treaties had not been terminated by the war. *See* A. Bleckemann, *Die Wiederanwendung Deutscher Vorkriegsverträge*, 33 Zeitschrift für Ausländisches Öfentliches Recht und Völkerrecht 607–635 (1973).

resumption treaty.[29] The Federal Republic could revive suspended treaties only through the conclusion of a new agreement to that effect with the state of opposite party. Following this procedure, the Federal Republic embarked on a number of such agreements, through which it revived some 70 bilateral and 80 multilateral agreements. After concluding agreements with various east European countries in the 1970s, it was able to restore a number of treaties with these countries as well.

When the advent of the Cold War precluded reunification, and therefore final settlement, the three western allies decided to unify their occupation zones provisionally as the Federal Republic of Germany. The *Grundgesetz*, or Basic Law, established parliamentary government for the new Republic, and under Articles 32(1) and 73 conferred the power to conduct foreign affairs upon the central government.[30] The Basic Law also included a provision, in Article 23, through which the portion of Germany under Soviet control could join the Federal Republic.[31] Several years later, the Soviet Union granted limited sovereignty to the German Democratic Republic.[32] In 1991 the German Democratic Republic joined the Federal Republic through operation of Article 23 of the Basic Law.[33]

This final development, and the 42-year existence of separate, provisional governments prior to re-unification, raise several questions related to treaty succession.[34] First, there is the question of the fate of treaties related to the

---

29 Directive No. 6, 52 OFF, J. ALLIED HIGH COMM'N 846 (1951) (the so-called Petersburg Accord). Bleckemann argues that the obligation to conclude resumption treaties has no basis in international law, despite this precedent, and that the German resumption treaties should be looked upon as an expedient to clarify the scope and nature of the resumption. *See* Bleckemann, *supra* note 28, at 622–24.

30 Grundgesetz Für Die Bundesrepublik Deutschland [Grundgesetz] [Gg] [Basic Law], May 23, 1949, BGBL. I at 1.

31 Article 23, S.2, stated that "[i]t (the Basic Law) shall come into force in other parts of Germany upon their accession". This language was subsequently changed by Article 4 of the Unification Treaty. Id. at art. 23.

32 Agreement to Raise the Status of Missions to Embassies, Aug. 22, 1953, GDR-USSR, 1 E.G.D.A. 286

33 Vertrag zwischen der Bundesrepublik Deutschland und der Deutschen Demokratischen Republik über die Herstellung der Einheit Deutschlands Bundesgesetzblatt [Einigungsvertrag] [Unification Treaty], Aug. 31, 1990, BGBL. II at 889, 890, art. 3.

34 According to Jochen Frowein, none of these questions actually involves succession. In his view, Germany became a subject of international law with the establishment of the North German Federation in 1867 and has never lost that status since. Even the reunification, together with the extinction of the German Democratic Republic, did not involve an instance of succession because it was effected through operation of Article 23 (old) of the

occupation. Second, one must consider the fate of treaties concluded between the Federal Republic and the German Democratic Republic. Third, one must consider the fate of other treaties concluded by both the German Democratic Republic and the Federal Republic prior to extinction of the former through accession to the latter.

To begin first with the easiest category of treaties, those related to the occupation itself became defunct when the allied powers renounced any further rights or responsibilities in Germany. As for treaties concluded between the two Germanys during the occupation period, those concluded before 1990 are obsolete, and of no further effect.[35] The Unification Treaty is another matter. Although it caused the extinction of one of the parties, it remains binding federal law.

The fate of treaties concluded by the German Democratic Republic with third parties is governed by Aritcle 12 of the Treaty of Unification, according to which the continued effect of these treaties depends upon their conformity to the treaty obligations of the Federal Republic and their compatibility with "the principles of a free, democratic basic order governed by the rule of law".[36]

Basic Law of the Federal Republic of Germany. Thus, reunification did not constitute the merger of two sovereign states into a new entity, but the absorption of one by another, which retained the status first obtained by the North German Federation. See Frowein, *supra* note 20, at 478–82.

35 Although this is a relatively easy post-unification conclusion, during the height of the Cold War, the validity of treaties between the Federal Republic and any of the Eastern Bloc countries, including the German Democratic Republic, was an area of heightened interest for international law scholars. *See, e.g.*, Claus Arndt, *Legal Problems of German Eastern Treaties*, 74 AM. J. INT'L L. 122–133 (1980).

36 Not only by operation of this clause, but by the terms of the Warsaw Pact itself, East Germany's membership in that organization was terminated through reunification. *See* Treaty of Friendship, Co-operation, and Mutual Assistance, May 14, 1955, Article 7, 219 U.N.T.S. 3. According to Anthony Aust, consultations with over 135 nations resulted in agreement that most of the German Democratic Republic's bilateral treaties had lapsed. *See* ANTHONY AUST, MODERN TREATY LAW AND PRACTICE 311 (2000). Thus, notification of lapse for some 2,200 treaties may be found in the *Bundesgestzblatt*, Part II. Although Article 12 of the Unification Treaty, *supra* note 33, made no provision for consultation concerning the continuing effect of GDR multilateral treaties, it was found that the GDR had ratified only 35 multilateral conventions (excluding those sponsored by the Council for Mutual Economic Assistance) which the FRG had not, and the GDR's rights and obligations under most of these 35 terminated with the GDR itself. *See* Dieter Papenfuss, *The Fate of the International Treaties of the GDR within the Framework of German Unification,* 92 AM. J. INT'L L. 469–88 (1998). *See also* RALF WITTKOWSKI, DIE STAATENSUKZESSION IN VÖLKERRECHTLICHE VERTRÄGE UNTER BESONDERER BERÜCKSICHTIGUNG

By Article 11 of the Treaty of Unification, agreements concluded by the Federal Republic continue in effect, with the exception that certain ones scheduled in an annex of the Treaty are not extended to the territory of the former German Democratic Republic.

With respect to the German Democratic Republic, it is obvious that the continuing effect of pre-war treaties is irrelevant.[37] Pre-war treaties that would have fit the criteria for continuing effect set out in Article 12 of the Treaty of Reunification, were surely effective in the Federal Republic as well, and therefore are still in effect today, under the terms of Article ll.[38]

Treaty Ratification and Implementation

According to Article 32(1) of the Basic Law, the power to conduct foreign relations, and therefore to conclude treaties, resides in the federal executive. Under Article 59(1) the Federal President concludes and ratifies treaties in the name of the Federal Republic. However, under Article 65 the Chancellor and his cabinet are actually responsible for the conduct of foreign relations, and under Article 59(2) parliament must adopt a statute ratifying the actions of the government in certain cases. Depending on the subject matter of the treaty, the ratifying statute must be adopted by the lower house (*Bundestag*) alone, or by both the lower and the upper house (*Bundesrat*).

In addition to concluding treaties in the name of the Federal Republic (*Staatsverträge*), the federal executive also enters inter-governmental agreements (*Regierungsabkommen*) and inter-ministerial agreements (*Ressortabkommen*). These latter categories of agreement are mentioned in Article 59(2),

---

der Herstellung der staatlichen Einheit Deutschlands (1992.); Dieter Papenfuss, Die Behandlung der Völkerrechtlichen Verträge der DDR im Zuge der Herstellung der Einheit Deutschlands: ein Beitrag zur Frage der Staatennachfolge in völkerrechtlichen Verträge (1997.); Gregor Dornbusch, Das Schicksal der Völkerrechtlichen Verträge der DDR nach der Herstellung der Einheit Deutschlands (1997).

37 As a matter of historical interest, the status of pre-World War II multilateral treaties in the German Democratic Republic is the subject of Volker Hausmann, Die Wiederan-Wendungserklärungen der DDR zu multilateralen Verträgen des Deutschen Reiches (1976) (D.Jur. thesis, Philipps-Universität zu Marburg).

38 According to the summary of the Political Archive of the Foreign Ministry, found at the Foreign Ministry web site, there are now over 100 pre-World War II bilateral and multilateral treaties currently in force.

which specifies that they are governed by administrative regulations. Typically, inter-governmental and inter-ministerial agreements become effective upon signature or exchange of notes.

Treaties requiring parliamentary consent include those that touch upon "areas of federal legislative jurisdiction", or which "regulate the Republic's political relations". The *Bundesverfassungsgericht*, or Federal Constitutional Court, was called upon early in the history of the Republic to interpret this provision, in a case that challenged the constitutionality of the government's failure to submit a commercial and payments agreement with France to the *Bundestag*.[39] The court held that a treaty is political only if it affects "the existence of the state, its territorial integrity, its independence, its position or its weight in the international community".[40]

When necessary, parliamentary approval is expressed in the form of a federal statute. However, according to Section 82 of the Rules of Procedure of the Federal Parliament, approval may not amend the treaty, nor may it be granted conditionally. This is compatible with the rule that Parliament controls the government, but does not itself conduct foreign relations. If the treaty in question not only requires parliamentary approval, but also a change in existing law, that change will be carried out in a separate statute. In accordance with their differing functions, approval statutes are published in Part II of the *Bundesgesetzblatt* (where treaties are published), while statutes changing existing law to conform to treaty obligations appear in Part I.

Since the consent of Parliament is expressed in terms of a statute, the role of the upper house parallels that which it plays in the adoption of legislation generally. Depending on the subject matter of legislation, the upper house must either participate in adoption of the proposed matter, or exercise a power of objection. The latter is a procedure governed by Article 77 of the Basic Law, and comprehends both a right to consult and ultimately a defeasible power to veto an action of the lower house.

Perhaps the most unusual aspect of German treaty law relates to the states (*Länder*), which exercise a qualified right to participate in the treaty-making process. In this respect, the Federal Republic differs from most other democratic republics. Under Article 32(2), each state enjoys a right to be heard when a proposed treaty would have a special impact on that state, typically because it would affect its geographic situation or economic interests. However, the right to be heard does not imply any right to share in the decision-making process. Potentially far more important, Article 32(3) grants the states the right

39 Decision of 29 July 1952, 1 Entscheidungen des Bundesverfassungsgerichts [BverfGE] 372.

40 Id. at 381 (author's translation).

to conclude treaties of their own with the approval of the federal government. This power extends not only to areas within the exclusive jurisdiction of the states, such as culture, but also to areas of jurisdiction shared concurrently by the states and the federal government, subject to preemption by federal treaties. Finally, because Article 32(3) is limited by its terms to treaties with foreign countries, states have come to enjoy the right to conclude treaties with the Holy See without federal supervision.

It should also be noted that the states' treaty-making power does not bar the federal government from concluding treaties as well that touch upon areas within the exclusive jurisdiction of the states. However, potential clashes are not governed in this case by a simple rule of federal preemption, as they are in the case of concurrent jurisdiction. In fact, no theoretical demarcation of power has ever gained currency. Instead, a political compromise was worked out in 1957, which assures the states effective participation in the conclusion of federal treaties that impinge on their exclusive jurisdiction or otherwise affect their interests.[41]

Annotated Bibliography of Sources

For the purposes of organization, sources that apply exclusively to the Federal Republic of Germany or the German Democratic Republic are included as subsections to the type of source under which they fall.

General Treaty Collections

Federal Republic of Germany

1 VERTRÄGE DER BUNDESREPUBLIK DEUTSCHLAND

Series A, Multilaterale Verträge. Auswärtiges Amt. (Bonn: Heymann, 1955–1996).

Summary: Biweekly compilation of multilateral treaties, printed in their official languages (usually English and French), together with official German

41 The procedures to be followed by the federal and state governments when the federal government concludes international agreements in areas of state jurisdiction are set out in the Lindau Arrangement, reprinted in English *in* NATIONAL TREATY LAW AND PRACTICE 337–338 (D.B. Hollis, M.R. Blakeslee, and L.B. Ederington eds., 2005). The original German version is reprinted in 20 *Zeitschrift für Ausländisches Öffentliches Recht und Völkerrecht* 116 (1959–1960). The power of the *Länder* to conclude treaties under Article 32(3) is the subject of PETER SEIDEL, DIE ZUSTIMMUNG DER BUNDESREGIERUNG ZU VERTRÄGEN DER BUNDESLÄNDER MIT AUSWÄRTIGEN STAATEN GEMÄSS ART. 32 III (1975).

translations. In German only, if an official language. Published in annual bound volumes. Terminated with vol. 74.

Index: Includes *Ergänzungsband: Verzeichnis und Stand der Verträge, 1960–.* See no. 5, below.

Note: Series B, covering bilateral treaties, has never been issued.

Note: A selection of important bilateral and multilateral treaties concluded by the Federal Republic since 1949 is available at the web site of the Foreign Ministry. (See no. 56, below.) Most of these treaties are available in full text, but some comprise excerpts only.

2 BUNDESGESETZBLATT

Bundesministerium der Justiz (Bonn: Bundesanzeiger-Verlag, 1949–).

Summary: Part II includes treaties and other international agreements. Text of international treaties in German, English and French. Text of bilateral treaties in German and language of opposite party. This is the only current official source for the text of bilateral and multilateral treaties.

Index: Annual chronological and subject indexes.

Note: Available in microfiche from München: C.H. Beck, Bonn: Bundesanzeiger-Verlag. Distributed in the U.S. by Clearwater Publishing.

3 REICHSGESETZBLATT

Reichsministerium des Innern (Berlin: Reichsdrückerei, 1871–1945).

Summary: Includes treaties and other international agreements concluded by Germany from its unification until the end of World War II. Published annually in bound volumes. Beginning in 1918, published in two parts, with treaties included in Part II. Accompanied by annual and periodic cumulative subject indexes (e.g., 1897–1906). All treaties are listed in the index under the heading *Staatsverträge,* and further grouped by subheading.

Index: Separate index published under the title, *Systematische Übersicht über 78 Jahrgänge Reichsgesetzblatt (1867–1944), das geltende alte und neue Reichsrecht und das Recht der Reichsverteidigung, 22nd edition.* Alfred Dehlinger (Stuttgart: W. Kohlhammer, 1945).

Note: Indexes also include references to the *Bundesgesetzblatt des Norddeutschen Bundes,* 1867–1870, the official gazette of the North German Confederation, which preceeded the empire.

German Democratic Republic

4 GESETZBLATT DER DEUTSCHEN DEMOKRATISCHEN REPUBLIK

Büro des Präsidiums des Ministerrates der Deutschen Demokratischen Republik (Berlin: Deutscher Zentralverlag, 1949–1990).

Summary: Treaties appear in Part I in German and other official languages. The first treaty listed is the Treaty on Relations Between the GDR and the Soviet Union, 18 December 1955 (no. 107, p. 918). Beginning in 1973, treaties appear in Part II. Treaties are listed in the annual cumulative index by title.[42]

Treaty Indexes

Federal Republic of Germany

5 VERTRÄGE DER BUNDESREPUBLIK DEUTSCHLAND

Series A. Multilaterale Verträge. Ergänzanzungsband. Verzeichnis und Stand der Verträge (Bonn: Carl Heymanns Verlag, 1959–1988).

Summary: Looseleaf index to multilateral treaties published in *Verträge der Bundesrepublik Deutschland. Series A. Multilaterale Verträge.* (See no. 1, above.) In four volumes. Vol. 1 includes a chronological index and an index by title and subject. Each entry includes the following information: date and place of signing; date treaty came into effect; date treaty came into effect for Germany; list of parties; full text of all declarations and reservations, in the original language and German translation. Entries are arranged by unique treaty number, which refers to order of publication, not to chronological order.

Note: Ceased publication with 13th update, November 1988.

6 DIE MULTILATERALEN VERTRÄGE DER BUNDESREPUBLIK DEUTSCHLAND

Ergänzung zum Fundstellennachweis über die Bundesgesetzgebung. H.J. Glaesner and G. Langer (Bonn: Bundesanzeiger-Verlag, 1958).

Summary: Chronological and subject index of treaties concluded by the Federal Republic of Germany, 1949–1958. Supplement to *Fundstellennachweis über die Bundesgesetzgebung,* which indexed legislation during the same period, in seven volumes.

---

42 According to Dieter Papenfuss, the GDR concluded over 2,600 treaties with 137 states, in an effort to gain international recognition. Of this staggering number, only about 5% were published in the *Gesetzblatt.* Some treaties were unregistered, others not deemed to qualify as treaties in negotiations under Article 12. In fact, "[i]t is not possible to make a definitive statement on the total number of international treaties actually concluded by the GDR, since the documentation is incomplete". *See* Papenfuss, *supra* note 36, at 484.

7 FUNDSTELLENNACHWEIS. B

Völkerrechtliche Vereinbarungen, Verträge Zur Vorbereitung Und Herstellung Der Einheit Deutschlands (Bonn: Bundesministerium Der Justiz, 1959–).

Summary: Annual supplement to the *Bundesgesetzblatt.* (See no. 2, above.) Includes information about every treaty in force for the Federal Republic, published in the *Bundesgesetzblatt* or its predecessors. The bilateral treaty section is divided into two parts. In Part I, treaty entries are arranged alphabetically by country of opposite party, and chronologically within each country heading. Part II includes treaties concluded with international organizations, similarly arranged. A separate section was included for treaties with the German Democratic Republic before it ceased to exist. For each bilateral treaty, information is provided on the date of signature, date of commencement, date of parliamentary concurrence, citation to publication of parliamentary concurrence in the *Bundesgesetzblatt* and citation to publication in the *League of Nations Treaty Series* or the *United Nations Treaty Series.* Information is also provided in each entry on any amending provisions, or provisions listed elsewhere that are closely related. Multilateral treaties are listed separately in chronological order. Similar information is provided, together with a listing of other parties, and dates of signature and commencement for each. There is also a separate chronological overview of multilateral treaties. Finally, there is a listing of "declarations," dealing with such matters as fishing zones, coastal waters and the continental shelf. In addition to a table of contents, there are both subject and topical indexes.

Note: Title varies: *Fundstellennachweis. B. Völkerrechtliche Vereinbarungen,* 1968–1971, *Fundstellennachweis, B. Völkerrechtliche Vereinbarungen und Verträge mit der DDR,* 1972–1990.

Note: Title succeeded *Fundstellennachweis der Sammlung des Bundesrechts,* published in eight volumes from 1960–1967. This title varied as well: *Fundstellen der Bundesgesetzgebung und Fortschreibung der Sammlung des Bundesrechts,* 1960–1965.

Note: Separate title, *Fundstellen der Bundesgesetzgebung: Fortschreibung der Sammlung des Bundesrechts,* published in 1959.

8 VÖLKERRECHTLICHE VEREINBARUNGEN DER BUNDESREPUBLIK DEUTSCHLAND AUF DEM GEBIETE DES UMWELTSCHUTZES

S. Lohse (Berlin: Umweltsbundesamt, 1989).

Summary: Index of environmental treaties concluded by the Federal Republic of Germany and its predecessor states, and still in force as of July 1, 1989. Treaty entries are arranged by broad subject categories, and chronologically within each category. Entries include date of commencement for

Germany, citation to publication in the *Bundesgesetzblatt* or one of its predecessors, list of state parties, and place of signature. A separate annex includes a listing of environmental treaties concluded with the German Democratic Republic, organized into the same broad subject categories. Includes chronological index, as well as indexes by party and place of signature.

German Democratic Republic

9 VÖLKERRECHTLICHE VEREINBARUNGEN DER DEUTSCHEN DEMOKRATISCHEN REPUBLIK

eine Zusammenstellung der Internationalen Verträge, Abkommen und sonstigen Vereinbarungen der Regierung der Deutschen Demokratischen Republik, ihrer Organisationen und Institutionen Seit 1949.

Gesamtdeutsches Institut. (Bonn: Bundesanstalt für Gesamtdeutsche Aufgaben, 1973–?). Looseleaf.

Summary: Comprehensive index of multilateral and bilateral treaties concluded by the GDR, 1949–1972. Multilateral treaties are listed chronologically, with earliest entry being for 29 September 1950. Each entry provides the title and source of publication, as well as information on duration of treaty, if limited, and its date of coming into force. Bilateral treaties are listed by country of opposite party and within country by date. According to the introduction, annual updates were planned. Includes a table of contents.

10 ZUSAMMENSTELLUNG DER VON DER "DEUTSCHEN DEMOKRATISCHEN REPUBLIK" SEIT DEREN GRUNDUNG ABGESCHLOSSENEN INTERNATIONALEN VERTRÄGE UND VEREINBARUNGEN, 5TH ED

L. Kapsa, Archiv für Gesamtdeutsche Fragen, ed. (Bonn: 1967). 232 pp.

Summary: Cumulative chronological list of treaties concluded by the German Democratic Republic, 1949–November 1967. Divided into two sections, corresponding to multilateral and bilateral treaties. The latter section is subdivided by country of opposite party.

Note: Ergänzungsband, published in 1970, updates the index through 1969.

Topical and Selected Treaty Publications

Treaties Between the Allied Powers and the Federal Republic Relating to Termination of the Occupation Regime

11 PARISER UND BONNER VERTRÄGE

(München: Beck, 1955). 295 pp.

Summary: Includes the *Protokoll über die Beendigung des Besatzungsregimes in der Bundesrepublik Deutschland* (Protocol on the Termination of the

Occupation Regime in the Federal Republic of Germany), the *Vertrag über die Beziehungen zwischen der Bundesrepublik Deutschland und den Drei Mächten* (Convention on Relations Between the Three Powers and the Federal Republic of Germany) and the *Vertrag über die Rechte und Pflichten Ausländischer Streitkräfte* (Treaty on the Rights and Obligations of Foreign Forces and Their Members in the Federal Republic of Germany), together with side treaties, supplementary documents and implementing legislation. Includes subject index. In German.

Note: At the time that the post-war occupation was officially brought to an end, a number of publishers and government agencies published the relevant treaties. There are several additional titles available in German. *Bonner Vertrag: Vertrag Über Die Beziehungen Zwischen Der Bundesrepublik Und Den Drei Mächten ...* (Hans Kutscher, ed., München: Beck, 1952, 309 pp.) includes the *Vertrag über die Beziehungen zwischen der Bundesrepublik Deutschland und den Drei Mächten*, together with related treaties and exchanges of letters. Includes an index. *Die Pariser Verträge* (Heinrich Brandweiner, ed., Berlin: Akademie Vergag, 1955, 363 pp.) contains the text of the *Vertrag über die Beziehungen zwischen der Bundesrepublik Deutschland und den Drei Mächten* and the *Protokoll über die Beendigung des Besatzungsregimes in der Bundesrepublik Deutschland*, together with related treaties and documents. Includes table of contents, but no index. Reprinted in 1956, together with English and French translations.

12 THE BONN AGREEMENTS OF 1952 AS AMENDED BY THE PARIS PROTOCOL OF 1954

Four-Power Conference (Washington, D.C.: U.S. Government Printing Office, 1955). 144 pp.

Summary: Includes the *Convention on Relations Between the three Powers and the Federal Republic of Germany*, together with the *Protocol on the Termination of the Occupation Regime in the Federal Republic of Germany.* Also includes the text of several executive agreements related to the status of allied forces stationed in the Federal Republic and the settlement of matters arising out of the war and occupation.

Note: 84th Congress, 1st Session, Senate. Document No. 11.

Note: Termination of the Occupation Regime in the Federal Republic of Germany ... (Washington, D.C.: U.S. Government Printing Office, 1956, 1571 pp.) contains the text of the *Protocol on the Termination of the Occupation Regime in the Federal Republic*, together with related documents. It was originally published as T.I.A.S. No. 3425.

Berlin Treaties

13 THE QUADRIPARTITE AGREEMENT ON BERLIN

Presse- und Informationsamt (Bonn: The Office, 1971). 119 pp.

Summary: Contains the *Quadripartite Agreement on Berlin*, of September 3, 1971, signed by the four allied powers.

Note: Of related interest is *3 Juni 1972: Das Viermächtnis-Abkommen in Kraft* (Berlin: Presse- und Informationsamt des Landes Berlin, 1972). This title includes the Final Act of the Quadripartite Agreement on Berlin, signed 3 June 1972, which brought the Agreement into effect. Also includes declarations of the four-power foreign ministers, the German Chancellor, and the Mayor of Berlin, as well as the text of the Quadripartite Agreement itself.

14 DOKUMENTE ZUR BERLIN-FRAGE 1944–1962

Heidelmeyer, W. (München, R. Oldenbourg, 1962), 622 pp.

DOKUMENTE ZUR BERLIN-FRAGE 1967–1986

Mahnke, H.H. (München : R. Oldenbourg, 1987), 700 pp.

Summary: These two volumes contain reprinted diplomatic documents from much of forty years between 1944 and 1986 related to the resolution of the "Berlin question". In German.

Treaties Between the Federal Republic of Germany and the German Democratic Republic

15 DER GRUNDVERTRAG: VERTRAG ÜBER DIE GRUNDLAGEN DER BEZIEHUNGEN ZWISCHEN DER BUNDESREPUBLIK DEUTSCHLAND UND DER DEUTSCHEN DEMOKRATISCHEN REPUBLIK VOM 21 DEZEMBER 1972 …

(Hamburg: Hoffmann und Campe Verlag, 1973). 224 pp.

Summary: Includes the text of the *Vertrag über die Grundlagen der Beziehungen zwischen der Bundesrepublik Deutsehland und der Deutschen Demokratischen Republik* (Treaty on the Basis of Relations between the Federal Republic of Germany and the German Democratic Republic), the so-called Grundvertrag or Grundlagenvertrag, of 1972, normalizing relations between the Federal Republic of Germany and the German Democratic Republic, as well as the treaty of 1972 relating to cross-border traffic between the two countries. Also includes a large selection of supplementary official documents, and the 1973 decision of the German Constitutional Court upholding the Grundvertrag. In German.

16 GRUNDVERTRAG ZWISCHEN DER BUNDESREPUBLIK DEUTSCHLAND UND DER DEUTSCHEN DEMOKRATISCHEN REPUBLIK, MIT BUNDESVERFASSUNGSGERICHTS-URTEIL, VERKERHRSVERTRAG, VIERMÄCHTE-ABKOMMEN ÜBER BERLIN, TRANSITVERTRAG UND WEITEREN DOKUMENTEN ZUR VÖLKERRECHTSLAGE DEUTSCHLANDS
(München: C.H. Beck'sche Verlag, 1973). 192 pp.

Summary: Includes the same treaties as no. 15, above, as well as the *Viermächte Abkommen* (1971), the *Abkommen ... über den Transitverkehr* (1971), the *Vereinbarung ... über Erleichterungen und Verbesserungen des Reise- und Besucherverkehrs* (1971), and a variety of post-war treaties of 1944 and 1945, including the London Protocol and the Convention on Relations between the Federal Republic and the Three Powers. In German.

17 VERTRÄGE BUNDESREPUBLIK DEUTSCHLAND-DDR
R. Ehlers, comp. (Berlin; New York: De Gruyter, 1973). 181 pp.

Summary: Contains 6 treaties concluded by the Federal Republic and the German Democratic Republic between 1960 and 1972. Includes the Grundvertrag. Also includes declarations, letters and other official documents related to relations between the Federal Republic and the German Democratic Republic. Table of contents, but no index.

Note: Series title: *Aktuelle Dokumente.*

18 DOCUMENTATION RELATING TO THE FEDERAL GOVERNMENT'S POLICY OF DÉTENTE
Press and Information Office of the Government of the Federal Republic of Germany (Bonn: The Office, 1974). 142 pp.

Summary: Contains the text of several important treaties and agreements concluded between the Federal Republic and east European states in the early 1970s, together with related notes, protocol notes, information and statements. Includes the *Treaty on the Basis of Relations between the Federal Republic of Germany and the German Democratic Republic* (1972), and the *Quadripartite Agreement on Berlin* (1971). Also includes the *Agreement between the Federal Republic of Germany and the German Democratic Republic on Transit Traffic of Civilian Persons and Goods Between the Federal Republic of Germany and Berlin (West)* (1971), and the *Arrangement Between the Senat and the Government of the German Democratic Republic Concerning the Facilitation and Improvement of Travel and Visitor Traffic* (1971), both of which were concluded under the auspices of the Quadripartite Agreement.

19 VERTRÄGE, ABKOMMEN UND VEREINBARUNGEN ZWISCHEN DER BUNDESREPUBLIK DEUTSCHLAND UND DER DEUTSCHEN DEMOKRATISCHEN REPUBLIK
(Stuttgart: Kohlhammer, 1973). 411 pp.

Summary: Contains treaties, exchanges of letters, declarations, explanations, memoranda, etc., concluded by the Federal Republic and the German Democratic Republic. Divided into two sections, covering the regulation of relations between the Federal Republic and the German Democratic Republic, and agreements supplementing the Quadripartite Agreement. Also includes an appendix of related documents. Includes table of contents, but no index.

20 GERMAN CONSTITUTIONAL DOCUMENTS SINCE 1871: SELECTED TEXTS AND COMMENTARY
L.W. Holborn, et al., eds. (New York: Praeger Publishers, 1970). 243 pp.

Summary: Part I, entitled *International Status and Establishment of the Two Germanys*, includes excerpts of a variety of international instruments related to the establishment of the two post-war Germanys.

Treaties Related to Reunification

Titles listed in this section reprint the various agreements related to the reunification of Germany. In the annotations these agreements are referred to by their common short titles. The official titles, and their abbreviated form, are as follows: *Vertrag zwischen der Bundesrepublik Deutschland und der DDR über die Herstellung der Einheit Deutschlands* (Einigungsvertrag, or Unification Treaty); *Vertrag über die Schaffung einer Wahrungs-, Wirtschafts-, und Sozialunion zwischen der Bundesrepublik Deutschland und der DDR* (Staatsvertrag, or Treaty on Economic, Social, and Monetary Union); *Vertrag über die abschliessende Regelung in Bezug auf Deutschland* (*Zwei-plus-Vier-Vertrag*, or Two Plus Four Agreement); *Vertrag über die Vorbereitung und Durchführung der ersten gseamtdeutschen Wahl des Deutschen Bundestages zwischen der Bundesrepublik Deutschland und der Deutschen Demokratischen Republik* (Wahlvertrag, or Election Treaty).

The Unification Treaty is published officially in the *Bundesgesetzblatt*, August 31, 1990, Pt. II, p. 889. The Treaty on Economic Social, and Monetary Union is published in the issue for May 18, 1990, Pt. II, p. 537. The Two Plus Four Agreement is published in the issue for October 13, 1990, Pt. II, p. 1318. The Election Treaty appears in the issue for September 1, 1990, Pt. II, p. 822.

21 EINIGUNGSVERTRAG: TEXTAUSGABE MIT EINFÜHRUNG
E. Bülow, ed. (Regensburg: Walhalla u. Praetoria Verlag, 1990). 438 pp.

Summary: Includes the text of the Unification Treaty and annexes, as well as the text of the statute implementing the treaty. Also includes a brief, but useful introduction, detailed table of contents, and indexes arranged by statute and topic.

Note: Of related interest are *Deutschland Ist Eins: der Einigungsvertrag* (Presse- und Informationsamt, Bonn: Das Amt, 1990, series title *Reihe Politik-Information*), *Vertrag zwischen der Bundesrepublik Deutschland und der Deutschen Demokratischen Republik über die Herstellung der Einheit Deutschlands* (Bonn: Das Amt, 1990, series title *Reihe Berichte und Dokumentationen*), and *Der Einigungsvertrag ...* 3rd ed. (München: Goldmann, 1990, series title *Goldmann Sachbuch*). None are indexed.

22 EINIGUNGSVERTRAG MIT AMTLICHEN ERLÄUTERUNGEN, 4TH ED
(Baden-Baden: Nomos Verlag, 1992). 1060 pp.

Summary: Contains the Unification Treaty, additional protocol and annexes, together with implementing and related legislation. Includes subject index to the treaty and annexes.

Note: Offprinted from *Sammlung Das Deutsche Bundesrecht*, 4th ed., 1992.

23 DER EINIGUNGSVERTRAG, 2ND ED
(Wiesbaden: MediConsult, 1990). 673 pp.

Summary: Contains the Unification Treaty, together with implementing legislation. Part I reprints the legal texts. Part II includes all annexes. Part III includes an index of laws and subjects.

24 TREATY BETWEEN THE FEDERAL REPUBLIC OF GERMANY AND THE GERMAN DEMOCRATIC REPUBLIC ON THE ESTABLISHMENT OF GERMAN UNITY
(New York: German Information Center, 1990). 29 pp.

Summary: Contains English version of the text of the Unification Treaty.

25 VERTRÄGE UND RECHTSAKTE ZUR DEUTSCHEN EINHEIT
K. Stern and B. Schmidt-Bleibtreu, eds. (München: Beck, 1990–1991).
Vol. 1, 371 pp.; Vol. 2, 1096 pp.; Vol. 3, 693 pp.

Summary: In three volumes. Vol. 1, entitled *Staatsvertrag zur Wahrungs, Wirtschafts-, und Sozialunion*, includes the text of the Treaty Establishing a Monetary, Economic, and Social Union, as well as indexes. Vol. 2, entitled *Einigungsvertrag und Wahlvertrag*, includes the text of the Unification Treaty and the Election Treaty. Also includes implementing legislation and indexes. Vol. 3, entitled *Zwei-plus-Vier Vertrag*, includes the Two Plus Four Agreement, and the various other treaties between Germany and East European countries and Germany and the European Communities. Also includes indexes. This is the standard unofficial source for the reunification treaties.

26 DIE VERTRÄGE ZUR EINHEIT DEUTSCHLANDS
I. von Munch, ed. (München: Deutscher Taschenbuch Verlag, 1992). 625 pp.

Summary: Contains the Treaty on Monetary, Economic, and Social Union; the Unification Treaty, together with annexes; the Election Treaty; and the Two Plus Four Agreement. Also includes the text of various statutes passed by the *Bundestag* to accompany reunification, relating to the former German Democratic Republic, with respect to investment, the settlement of property rights, the establishment of a single currency, and the establishment of church taxes. Includes subject index.

Note: First edition published in 1991. 647 pp.

27 STAATSVERTRAG: VERTRAG ÜBER DIE SCHAFFUNG EINER WAHRUNGS-, WIRTSCHAFTS-, UND SOZIALUNION ZWISCHEN DER BUNDESREPUBLIK DEUTSCHLAND UND DER DEUTSCHEN DEMOKRATISCHEN REPUBLIK
(Regensburg: Walhalla u. Praetoria Verlag, 1990). 104 pp.

Summary: Contains the text of the Treaty on Monetary, Economic, and Social Union, together with other documents related to its signing. Also includes the *Gemeinsame Erklärung der Regierungen der Bundesrepublk Deutschland und der Deutschen Demokratischen Republik* (Joint Declaration of the Governments of the Federal Republic of Germany and the German Democratic Republic on the Settlement of Questions Relating to Property Rights).

28 VERTRAG ÜBER DIE SCHAFFUNG EINER WAHRUNGS-, WIRTSCHAFTS-, UND SOZIALUNION: ZWISCHEN DER BUNDESREPUBLIK DEUTSCHLAND UND DER DEUTSCHEN DEMOKRATISCHEN REPUBLIK: ERKLÄRUNGEN UND DOKUMENTATION
Presse- und Informationsamt der Bundesregierung (Bonn: Das Amt, 1990). Unpaginated.

Summary: Includes the text of the Treaty on Monetary, Economic, and Social Union. Also includes the *Gemeinsame Erklärung der Regierungen der Bundesrepublk Deutschland und der Deutschen Demokratischen Republik* (Joint Declaration of the Governments of the Federal Republic of

Germany and the German Democratic Republic on the Settlement of Questions Relating to Property Rights), and the *Entschliessung von Bundestag und Volkskammer zur deutsch-polnischen Grenze* (Resolution of the *Bundestag* and the *Volkskammer* concerning the German-Polish Border). Also includes signing statements of the respective heads of government, as well as related speeches and declarations made in the *Bundestag* and *Bundesrat.*

29 TREATY BETWEEN THE FEDERAL REPUBLIC OF GERMANY AND THE GERMAN DEMOCRATIC REPUBLIC ESTABLISHING A MONETARY, ECONOMIC AND SOCIAL UNION
(New York: German Information Center, 1990). 24 pp.

Summary: Contains the official English translation of the treaty named in the title, including Annexes I–LX.

Treaties Between the Federal Republic of Germany and Other East European Nations

30 OSTVERTRÄGE
I. von Munch (Berlin; New York: De Gruyter, 1971–1973).

Summary: In three volumes. Vol. 1 contains German-Soviet treaties dating back to 1918. Includes treaties concluded between the German Democratic Republic and the Soviet Union. Vol. 2 contains German-Polish treaties dating back to 1919. Includes treaties between the German Democratic Republic and Poland. Vol. 3 contains German-Czech treaties.

Note: Series title: *Aktuelle Dokumente.*

Note: Die Ostverträge: Die Verträge von Moskau, Warschau, Prag, der Berlin-Abkommen und die Verträge mit der DDR (B. Zündorf, ed., München: Beck, 1979) contains an article-by-article commentary on the 1970 treaty with the Soviet Union, the 1970 treaty with Poland and the 1973 treaty with Czechoslovakia, among others.

31 DOKUMENTATION ZUR OSTPOLITIK DER BUNDESREGIERUNG: VERTRÄGE, VEREINBARUNGEN UND ERKLÄRUNGEN, 13TH ED
Presse- und Informationsamt der Bundesregierung (Bonn: Das Amt, 1990). 352 pp.

Summary: Part A contains a variety of treaties concluded by the Federal Republic with east European nations together with related documents, organized by country of opposite party. Part C includes a variety of agreements concluded between the Federal Republic and the German Democratic Republic related to Berlin, and such matters as travel and territorial exchanges, as well as the *Vier-Mächte-Abkommen* of 1971 (Four Power Agreement).

Note: Series title: *Reihe Berichte und Dokumentationen.*

32 DIE VERTRÄGE DER BUNDESREPUBLIK DEUTSCHLAND...
Presse- und Informationsamt der Bundesregierung (Bonn: Das Amt, 1971). 318 pp.

Summary: Contains the *Vertrag zwischen der Bundesrepublik Deutschland und der Union der Sozialistischen Sowjetrepubliken,* concluded by the Federal Republic and the Soviet Union, on 12 August 1970, and the *Vertrag zwischen der Bundesrepublik Deutschland und der Volksrepublik Polen über die Grundlagen der Normalisierung ihrer gegenseitigen Beziehungen,* concluded by the Federal Republic and the People's Republic of Poland, on 7 December 1970. Also includes a variety of diplomatic documents, including transcripts of press conferences and televised appearances, related to the conclusion of the treaties. Finally, each treaty is accompanied by a "Chronology and Documentation," which reprints a large amount of diplomatic prehistory. (See also no. 56, below.)

Note: The treaty between the Federal Republic and the Soviet Union was also published separately by the Presse- und Informationsamt in 1970.

Note: The treaty with the People's Republic of Poland was published by the Presse- und Informationsamt in English, 1971.

33 DEUTSCH-POLNISCHE NACHBARSCHAFT: DIE VERTRÄGE ÜBER GRENZEN UND GUTE NACHBARSCHAFT: GRUNDLAGE FÜR EIN KONSRUKTIVES VERHÄLTNIS ZWISCHEN DEUTSCHLAND UND POLEN
Walter Poeggel (Leipzig: Rosa-Luxembourg-Verein, 1993). 74 pp.

Summary: Contains the text of the treaties concluded between reunified Germany and Poland, namely the 1990 *Vertrag zwischen der Bundesrepublik Deutschland und der Republik Polen über die Bestätigung der zwischen ihnen bestehenden Grenze* (Treaty Confirming the German-Polish Border), the 1990 *Vertrag zwischen der Bundesrepublik Deutschland und der Republik Polen über gute Nachbarschaft und freundschaftliche Zusammenarbiet* (Treaty Establishing Friendly Relations) and the 1993 *Abkommen zwischen der Regierung der Bundesrepublik Deutschland und der Regierung der Republik Polen über die Zusammenarbiet hinsichtlich der Auswirkungen von Wanderungsbewegungen* (Treaty of Cooperation Concerning the Consequences of Population Movements). Also includes an introductory essay on issues involved in the German-Polish relationship. (See also no. 55, below.)

Note: Series title: *Texte zur Politischen Bildung, heft 6.*

Note: For a book-length discussion of Germany's treaty relations with east Europe, and Poland in particular, see Seiffert, Wolfgang, *Die Verträge zwischen Deutschland und seinen östlichen Nachbarn: unter dem Gesichtspunkt des Selbstbestimmungsrechts der Völker sowie des Fehlens gemeinsamer eindeutiger Willensbekundungen in den Vertragstexten* (Köln: Verlag Wissenschaft und Politik, 1994).

German Democratic Republic

34 DER INTERNATIONALE RECHTSVERKEHR DER DEUTSCHEN DEMOKRATISCHEN REPUBLIK IN ZIVIL-, FAMILIEN-, UND STRAFSACHEN, 3RD ED

Ministerium der Justiz (Berlin: Staatsverlag der Deutschen Demokratischen Republik, 1987).

Summary: Collection of treaties in the area of civil procedure, family law and criminal law. Divided into two parts. Part I contains bilateral treaties organized alphabetically by country of opposite party. Part II contains multilateral treaties, including the Hague Convention on Civil Procedure of 1905, a 1924 Protocol to the same and the decision of the German Democratic Republic to recognize them as in effect. Each treaty document is accompanied by a citation to the *Gesetzblatt*, and annotations to alterations, dates of commencement, etc. Annexes contain a list of consular treaties and a list of treaties concluded on the topic of dual citizenship. Includes detailed subject index, citing to individual treaty articles, paragraphs and clauses.

Note: First edition, entitled *Der Internationale Rechtsverkehr Der Deutschen Demokratischen Republik in Zivil-, Familien-, und Strafsachen: Sammlung von Texten der Abkommen über den internationalen Rechtsverkehr sowie wichtiger Inlandvorschriften mit Anmerkungen und Sachregister* (1969), reprints various regulations concerning the status of foreign missions in the German Democratic Republic and the conduct of relations with them, and also includes a list of 39 multilateral treaties, dating back to 1869, declared in effect for the German Democratic Republic. Reprinted from (1959) *Gesetzblatt* Pt. I p. 505 (Declaration of April 4, 1959).

35 BEISTANDS- UND KOOPERATIONSVERTRÄGE DHER DDR

H.-H. Mahnke, ed. (Köln: Verlag Wissenschaft und Politik, 1982). 167 pp.

Summary: Includes a collection of 23 mutual assistance and cooperation treaties concluded by the German Democratic Republic. Also includes a table showing for each treaty the date of signature, date of commencement, and citation to official publication in the *Gesetzblatt*.

36 SOZIALISTISCHE INTERNATIONALE BEZIEHUNGEN: GRUNDSATZDOKUMENTE

C. Büchner and J. Krüger, eds. (Potsdam-Babelsberg: Akademie für Staats- und Rechtswissenschaft der DDR, 1985). 78 pp.

Summary: Includes collection of 24 multilateral agreements, mostly between the German Democratic Republic and other socialist nations.

Note: Series title: *Aktuelle Beitrage der Staats- und Rechtswissenschaft, heft 316.*

37 DIE RECHTSHILFABKOMMEN DHER DDR

F. Majoros, ed. (Berlin: Berlin Verlag A. Spitz, 1982). 280 pp.

Summary: Contains the text of ten treaties of judicial assistance concluded by the German Democratic Republic, as amended through 1981 (Hungary, Rumania, Yugoslavia, Iraq, Algeria, Soviet Union, Cuba, United Kingdom, Austria, Viet Nam). Includes a list of all 25 such treaties concluded by the GDR, as of 1982 (pp. 91–92.) Also includes an analysis of GDR treaties of judicial assistance, together with a brief subject index.

Note: Series title: *Quellen zur Rechtsvergleichung. Verträge Sozialistischer Staaten, Bd. 3.*

38 DIE KONSULARABKOMMEN DHER DDR

F. Majoros (Berlin: Berlin Verlag A. Spitz, 1984). 318 pp.

Summary: Contains a selection of 12 treaties on diplomatic and consular service concluded by the German Democratic Republic (withYugoslavia, Soviet Union, Poland, Austria, U.S.A., Viet Nam, Mali, Belgium, Afghanistan, Cuba, Greece, and Colombia). Includes a list (pp. 9–10) of all 40 such treaties concluded by the GDR as of the end of 1983, together with citations to their publication in the *Gesetzblatt.* Also includes an analysis of GDR consular treaties and a brief subject index.

Note: Series title: *Quellen zur Rechtsvergleichung. Verträge Sozialistischer Staaten, Bd. 4.*

Topical Collections

39 VÖLKERRECHTLICHE VEREINBARUNGEN DER BUNDESREPUBLIK DEUTSCHLAND AUF DEM GEBIETE DES UMWELTSCHUTZES: FUNDSTELLEN IM BUNDESGESETZBLATT II

S. Lohse, ed. (Berlin: Umweltsamt, 1992). 214 pp.

Summary: Contains a detailed list of environmental treaties concluded by Germany from 1848 to 1988, and in force on 1 June 1992. Each entry includes the title, date of entry into force, date of entry into force for Germany, list of parties, citation to location of publication in the *Bundesgesetzblatt* and a list of any amendments, including citations. Treaties are organized into groups by topic, and chronologically within each group. Includes an appendix, listing environmental treaties concluded between the Federal Republic and the German Democratic Republic. Also includes chronological and party indexes, as well as an index by place of signing.

40 SAMMLUNG DER INTERNATIONALEN VEREINBARUNGEN DER LÄNDER DER BUNDESREPUBLIK DEUTSCHLAND

U. Beyerlin and Y. Lejeune, eds. (Berlin; New York: Springer, 1994). 345 pp.

Summary: Includes the text of international agreements concluded by states of the Federal Republic, as well as related documents. Documents are numbered consecutively and organized by state, with the states arranged alphabetically. Within each state, documents are organized under 11 headings, which are as follows: general cooperation; management of economic relations with nearby regions; hunting and fishing; watercourses, hydroelectric plants, and dams; traffic; parks; environmental protection; science and culture; public health; taxation; and police matters. A detailed table of contents lists the documents by topic, and within topic by state. Each entry lists the document title, entity or entities of opposite party, date and place of signature and document number within the collection. Cross-references are included both in the table of contents and in the body of the text. There is no index.

41 RECHTSTELLUNG DEUTSCHLANDS: VÖLKERRECHTLICHE VERTRÄGE UND ANDERE RECHTSGESTALTENDE AKTE, 2ND ED

D. Rauschning, ed. (München: Deutsche Taschenbuch Verlag, 1989). 240 pp.

Summary: Contains 35 treaties and other documents related to the legal status of Germany after the Second World War. Divided into six, topically arranged sections. In order, they cover: acts of the allied powers related to Germany; documents related to the Federal Republic; documents related to Berlin; treaties between the Federal Republic and the Soviet Union, Poland and Czechoslovakia; documents establishing the relationship between the Federal Republic and the German Democratic Republic; documents related to the legal status of the German Democratic Republic. Includes subject index.

42 DIE UMSIEDLUNGSVERTRÄGE DES DEUTSCHEN REICHES WÄHREND DES ZWEITEN WELTKRIEGS

H. Haker (Berlin; Frankfurt am Main: Alfred Metzner Verlag, 1971). 223 pp.

Summary: Of historical interest only, this volume includes the text of resettlement treaties concluded between Nazi Germany and various east European and Baltic States during the Second World War.

Note: Series title: *Werkhefte der Forschungsinstitut fur Völkerrecht und ausländisches öffentliches Recht der Univrsität Hamburg, No. 17.*

43 INTERNATIONALE ZIVILPROZESSRECHT AUF GRUND DER STAATSVERTRÄGE DES DEUTSCHEN REICHES UNTER BERÜCKSICHTIGUNG DER PRAXIS DER JUSTIZVERWALTUNG UND UNTER BEIGABE DER VERTRAGSTEXTE

v. Normann, A. (Berlin, G. Stilke, 1923), 188 pp. Part of a series: *Stilkes Rechtsbibliothek.*

Summary: This book discusses international civil procedure law during the period of the German Reich, as it was shaped by the following: (1) foreign treaties, and (2) the practice of the Reich's justice administration. It includes the texts of treaties that Germany entered into with other European nations pursuant to the requirements of the Hague Convention. In German.

44 STAATSVERTRÄGE IM INTERNATIONALEN STEUERRECHT

Weber-Fas, R. (Tübingen : J.C.B. Mohr, 1982), 146 pp.

Summary: This book discusses the operation of treaties in international tax law, focusing specifically on Germany's double-taxation treaties with other nations during the second half of the twentieth century. In German.

45 GERMANY AS A DEPOSITARY OF MULTILATERAL TREATIES

URL: http://www.auswaertiges-amt.de/EN/Aussenpolitik/InternatRecht/Vertraege/Verwahrer_node.html.

Summary: This section of the Federal Foreign Ministry's website provides links to status information about and the text of the multilateral treaties of which Germany is a depositary. In English.

Historical Treaty Sources of Germany and the Germanic States Prior to the Twentieth Century

The sources in this section provide historical information about treaties with foreign entities entered into by Germany and the various Germanic states prior to the twentieth century. This time period pre-dates the creation of the modern state of Germany; however, researching this era may still be important for understanding the historical development of German foreign relations.

46 STAATSVERTRÄGE DES KURFÜRSTENTUMS BAYERN 1745–1764

Schmidt, A. (München : C.H. Beck'sche Verlagsbuchhandlung, 1991), 129 pp. Volume 95 of the series *Schriftenreihe zur bayerischen Landesgeschichte.*

Summary: This volume describes the treaties entered into by the electorate of Bavaria between 1745 and 1764. In German.

47 PREUSSENS STAATSVERTRÄGE AUS DER REGIERUNGSZEIT KÖNIG FRIEDRICH WILHELMS I

Loewe, V. (Leipzig: S. Hirzel, 1923), 123 pp. From the series *Publicationen aus den k. preussischen Staatsarchiven.*

Summary: This volume is an index of the treaties entered into by the state of Prussia during the rule of King Friedrich Wilhelm I, who was in power during the early 18th century. In German.

48 DIE STAATSVERTRÄGE WÜRTTEMBERGS MIT NICHTDEUTSCHEN STAATEN

Elben, O. (Berlin, F. Dümmler, 1926), 127 pp. From the series *Völkerrechtsfragen; eine Sammlung von vorträgen und Studien.*

Summary: This volume is a collection of treaty documents between the kingdom of Württemberg and non-German states. These treaties pre-date the entrance of Württemberg into the German nation, which took place in 1918. In German.

49 KURBRANDENBURGS STAATSVERTRÄGE VON 1601–1700

v. Morner, T. (Berlin, de Gruyter, 1965), 864 pp.

Summary: This volume is a collection of treaties entered into by the Electorate of Brandenberg between 1601 and 1700. In German.

50 FINDBUCH ZUM BESTAND HANNOVER 10: HANNOVERSCHE STAATSVERTRÄGE, 1690–1866

Gieschen, C. (Hannover : Kommissionsverlag Hahnsche Buchhandlung, 1991), 450 pp. + Index. Book 2 of the series *Veröffentlichungen der Niedersächsischen Archivverwaltung, Inventare und kleinere Schriften des Hauptstaatsarchivs in Hannover.*

Summary: Finding aid for treaties entered into by the various governmental entities of Hannover between 1690 and 1866 (prior to the time in which Hannover became part of Prussia). In German.

51 DIE STAATSVERTRÄGE DES DEUTSCHEN ORDENS IN PREUSSEN, 1230–1449: STUDIEN ZUR DIPLOMATIE EINES SPÄTMITTELALTERLICHEN DEUTSCHEN TERRITORIALSTAATES

Neitmann, K. (Köln : Böhlau, 1986), 692 pp. Volume 6 of the series *Neue Forschungen zur brandenburg-preussischen Geschichte.*

Summary: This book discusses the treaties entered into by the Germanic peoples of Prussia between 1230 and 1449. In German.

52 EXPLANATION OF THE DANISH QUESTION: WITH TRANSLATIONS OF THE CONSTITUTION OF NOVEMBER 19, 1863, AND OTHER STATE PAPERS

Foreign and Commonwealth Office (London: J. Bolton, 1864), 117 pp. Part of the *Foreign and Commonwealth Office Collection of Pamphlets.*

Summary: This pamphlet discusses the "Danish question," which largely focused on a dispute between Germany and Denmark regarding the territories of Holstein and Sleswick. It describes the historical development of and battle for sovereignty over these territories, and provides documentation related to efforts to mediate the dispute between the two countries. In English.

Diplomatic Documents

53 AKTEN ZUR AUSWÄRTIGEN POLITIK DER BUNDESREPUBLIK DEUTSCHLAND

Institut für Zeitgeschichte, Hans-Peter Schwarz, series ed. (München: R. Oldenbourg, 1989–). 1949/50, LXXXVI, 559 pp. (1997); 1951, LVIII, 816 pp. (1999); 1952, LVIII, 842 pp. (2000); 1953 (two volumes), LXXXI, 1254 pp. (2001); 1963 (three volumes), CXCV, 1813 pp. (1994); 1964 (two volumes), *CUM* 1676 pp. (1995); 1965 (three volumes), CCXXIII, 2090 pp. (1995); 1966 (two volumes), 1835p. (1997); 1967 (three volumes), CXCIV, 1826 pp. (1998); 1968 (two volumes), CLVIII, 1773 pp. (1999); 1969 (two volumes), LXXXIII, 1601 pp. (2000); 1970 (three volumes), CVII, 2494 pp. (2001); 1971 (three volumes), LXXXVIII, 2153 pp. (2002); 1972 (three volumes), LXXXLX, 2028 pp. (2003); 1973 (three volumes), LXXXV, 2215 pp. (2004); 1974 (two volumes), 1805 pp. (2005); 1975 (two volumes), 2008 pp. (2006); 1976 (two volumes), 1868 pp. (2007); 1977 (two volumes), 1968 pp. (2008); 1978 (two volumes), 2108 pp. (2009); 1979 (two volumes), 2128 pp. (2010); 1980 (two volumes), 2115 pp. (2011); 1981 (three volumes), 2250 pp. (2012); 1982 (two volumes), 2000 pp. (2013).

Summary: Contains the official history of Germany's diplomatic relations since 1951. Documents are arranged chronologically and annotated. Each volume includes name and subject indexes. Each part includes a detailed synopsis of all documents contained therein. First two volumes are in English, German and French.

Note: Author varies: Vols. 1 and 2 compiled by the Auswärtiges Amt.

Note: Detailed descriptions of all volume are available at the web site of the publisher, at http://www.degruyter.com

Note: Additional information available at the web site of the Institut für Zeitgeschichte, at http://www.ifz-muenchen.de

Note: Preface states that German diplomatic documents cannot be published for 30 years after their date of issue.

54 AKTEN ZUR AUSWÄRTIGEN POLITIK, 1918–1945

Auswärtiges Amt (Baden-Baden: Impr. Nationale, 1950–).

Summary: Divided into five series: Series A, 1918–1925 (vols. 1–14), Series B, 1925–1933 (vols. 1–21), Series C, 1933–1937 (vols. 1–6), Series D, 1937–1941 (vols. 1–13), Series E, 1941–1945 (vols. 1–8). Contains selected documents related to German diplomatic activity during the period covered, with an aim "to establish the record of German foreign policy preceding and during World War II". Documents are taken from the archives of the German Foreign Ministry, which were discovered by units of the United States First Army, scattered through various hiding places in the Harz Mountains in April 1945. The archives actually include files dating back to 1867. Selections for Series C and D made by a combined British and American editorial team, directed to proceed without government interference, "on the basis of the highest scholarly objectivity". The only criterion for inclusion was "their value for an understanding of German foreign policy". Individual volumes have descriptive titles. Volumes include separate indexes and appendices.

Index: Ergänzungsband zur Deutschen Auswartigen Politik, 1918–1945 (Göttingen: Vandenhoeck & Ruprecht, 1995). Includes index by name, pictures and dates of service.

Note: Imprint varies. Some volumes from Series A, B, D, and E have imprint, Göttingen: Vandenhoeck & Ruprecht. Some volumes from Series D have imprints, Baden-Baden: P. Keppler, Frankfurt am Main: P. Keppler, and Bonn: Gebr. Hermes.

Note: Volumes of Series C and D translated into English under the sponsorship of the US Department of State, the British Foreign Office and the French government. Published simultaneously with the German edition under the title, *Documents on German Foreign Policy, 1918–1945, From the Archives of the German Foreign Ministry* (Washington, D.C.: U.S. Government Printing Office, 1949–; London: H.M. Stationery Office, 1949–).

Note: Of interest in relation to this series is a monograph by Sacha Zala, entitled *Geschichte Unter der Schere Politischer Zensur: Amtliche Aktensammlungen*

im Internationalen Vergleich (München: Oldenbourg, 2001, 385 pp.). Focusing primarily on documents published in *Akten zur Auswartigen Politik*, the analysis considers the political uses made of official foreign office publications. Also considers the history of "war of documents," in which various nations attempted to exculpate themselves from blame for the First World War, as well as the "professionalization" of documentation in the *Foreign Relations of the United States* series.

55 DIE GROSSE POLITIK DER EUROPAISCHEN KABINETTE, 1871–1914: SAMMLUNG DER DIPLOMATISCHEN AKTEN DES AUSWÄRTIGEN AMTES
J. Lepsius, A. Mendelshon and F. Timme, comp. (Berlin: Deutsche Verlag für Politik und Geschichte, 1922–1927).

Summary: Magisterial, 54-volume compilation of approximately 15,000 documents, culled from the archives of the German foreign ministry, and covering the period 1871–1914. Work was sponsored by the German government, which was stung by Article 231 of the Versailles Treaty, blaming Germany for World War I, and by the alleged tendency of French writers to ascribe the origin of the war to Bismarck's drive toward European hegemony. In response, the German government opened its archives, including secret diplomatic correspondence, to scholars, whose assignment was to publish the most important documents, using strict objectivity in their selection. Altogether, the set includes about 10% of available documents, with the emphasis placed on those most related to the origins of World War I. Nevertheless, a great many documents deal with questions related to international law.

Index: A comprehensive subject index was planned, but never completed. Name indexes appear in approximately every twelfth volume.

Note: Documents are grouped by topic and secondarily by date. The topical chapters are themselves in roughly chronological order. Each document is preceded by a heading, indicating author and recipient, place and date of composition and provenance of the document (e.g., certified copy, summary or decoded message). Documents are also accompanied by detailed and very helpful contextual notes, and by separately numbered notes reproducing important marginalia inserted by the recipient. All documents are in their original language, mostly German, but also English and French. The set was of wide interest at the time of publication and helped to stimulate a boom in the publication of pre-war diplomatic documents. (See no. 60, below, for a complete description of contents.)

Note: Accompanying volume, entitled *Im Dienst der Wahrheit: Zum Abschluss der Aktenpublikation des Auswartigen Amtes, Die Grosse Politik der Europäischen Kabinette, 1871–1914* (Berlin: Arbeitsauschuss Deutscher Verbände, 1927), contains a description and history of the set, as well as various letters, plates and the certification of President Von Hinderburg that it includes whichever previously secret documents the compilers chose to include.

Note: Abridged, four-volume English edition published under the title, German Diplomatic Documents, 1871–1914, E.T.S. Dugdale, trans. (London: Methuen & Co., 1928–1931). Reprinted under the imprint, New York: Barnes & Noble, 1969.

Note: Microfiche version available under the imprint, Wooster, OH: Bell & Howell, Microphoto Division, 197?.

Note: Also of interest is Erwin Hölze, ed., *Quellen zur Enstehung des Ersten Weltkrieges: Internationale Dokumente, 1901–1914*, 2nd ed. (Darmstadt: Wissenschaftliche Buchgesellschaft, 1995). This title contains a selection of documents tracing the diplomatic sources of the First World War, culled from a wide variety of sources. It also includes a Foreword by Winfried Baumgart, summarizing recent research on the assignment of war guilt.

56 DAS POLITISCHE ARCHIV DES AUSWÄRTIGEN AMTS (2011)
URL: https://www.auswaertiges-amt.de/cae/servlet/contentblob/372522/publicationFile/173410/PolitischesArchiv.pdf.

Summary: This document describes the collection of the Federal Foreign Ministry's political archive, including these specific collections: Akten des Auswärtigen Amts des Deutschen Reiches (1867–1945); Akten der Auslandsvertretungen des Deutschen Reiches (bis 1945); Akten des Auswärtigen Amts der Bundesrepublik Deutschland (1949/51 ff.); Akten der Auslandsvertretungen der Bundesrepublik Deutschland (1950 ff.); Archiv des Ministeriums für Auswärtige Angelegenheiten der Deutschen Demokratischen Republik (MfAA); and Archiv der Völkerrechtlichen Vereinbarungen. In German.

57 PUBLIKATIONEN VON AKTEN DES AUSWÄRTIGEN AMTS
URL: http://www.auswaertiges-amt.de/DE/AAmt/Politisches Archiv/AkteneditionenPublikationvonAkten.html?nn=372850.

Summary: This page provides continuously-updated bibliographic information about publications of the activities of the Federal Foreign Ministry, including the following: Die Große Politik der Europäischen Kabinette 1871–1914; Die deutschen Dokumente zum Kriegsausbruch 1914; L'Allemagne et les problèmes de la paix pendant la première guerre mondiale; Akten zur deutschen auswärtigen Politik 1918–1945; Akten zur Auswärtigen Politik der Bundesrepublik Deutschland; Adenauer und die Hohen Kommissare (1949–1952); Akten zur Auswärtigen Politik der Bundesrepublik Deutschland (1949–1953 und 1962–1982). In German.

58 GERMAN MISSION IN THE UNITED STATES: FOREIGN POLICY AND STATE DOCUMENTS

URL: http://www.germany.info/Vertretung/usa/en/06__Foreign__Policy__State/00/__Home.html.

Summary: Includes information about U.S.-Germany relations, German foreign policy, Germany in the European Union, and Germany's Political System and Government. In English.

59 GERMAN COUNCIL ON FOREIGN RELATIONS: PUBLICATIONS

URL: https://dgap.org/en/think-tank/publications/all.

Summary: The German Council on Foreign Relations (German: Deutsche Gesellschaft für Auswärtige Politik) is a non-partisan organization that researches and informs the public on German public policy issues. Its English-language website offers a Publications database, which includes English-language reports on key German public policy topics. It also has a database of German-language documents.

Pre-World War I and World War I

60 QUELLEN ZUR DEUTSCHEN AUSSENPOLITIK IM ZEITLATER DES IMPERIALISMUS: 1890–1911

M. Behnen (Darmstadt: Wissenschaftliche Buchgesellschaft, 1977). LVI, 539 pp.

Summary: Contains 251 documents, telegrams, speeches, etc., relating to Germany's conduct of foreign affairs, 1890–1911, together with an introduction summarizing Germany's foreign policy. Documents are arranged chronologically, each with a brief descriptive title and source note. Footnotes provide background information, and indicate marginalia inscribed on originals. Includes documents relating to the Hague peace conferences. Chronological and name indexes are included, together with a brief subject index.

Note: Series title: *Ausgewählte Quellen zur deutschen Geschichte der Neuzeit*, vol. 26.

61 DIE DEUTSCHEN DOKUMENTE ZUM KRIEGESAUSBRUCH, 2ND ED

K. Kautsky, comp; M. Montgelas and W. Schücking, eds. (Berlin: Deutsche Verlagsgesellschaft für Politik und Geschichte, 1922).

Summary: In five volumes. Contains documents related to the outbreak of World War I. Vol. 5 contains a commentary on the documents written by B.W. von Bülow and Graf Max Montgelas.

Note: Translated into English by the Carnegie Endowment for International Peace, Division of International Law, under the title *Outbreak of the World War*

(New York: Oxford University Press, 1924, 688 pp.). Of related interest is *Official German Documents Relating to the World War*, translated under the supervision of the Carnegie Endowment for International Pece, Division of International Law (New York: Oxford University Press, 1923). Vol. II includes a substantial selection of diplomatic correspondence betwen Berlin and Washington, D.C., translated into English, and covering the period from April 11, 1916–February 15, 1917.

62 A PLACE IN THE TROPICAL SUN: THE GERMAN ACQUISITION OF THE CAROLINES, PALAU, AND THE MARIANA ISLANDS: SELECTED DOCUMENTS, 1885–1921

Ilona Stolken and Thomas Fitschen, eds. (Mangilao, Guam: Richard F. Taitano Micronesian Area Research Center, University of Guam, 1999). 179 pp.

Summary: Contains documents in English, French, German and Spanish. Includes introduction.

Note: MARC Working Papers, No. 75.

63 L'ALLEMAGNE ET LES PROBLEMES DE LA PALX PENDANT LA PREMIERE GUERRE MONDIALE

Documents Extraits de l'Office Allemand des Affaires Etrangères.

André Scherer and Jacques Grunewald, ed. (Paris: Presses Universitaires de France, 1962–1978). 4 vols.

Summary: Collection of German Foreign Ministry documents, dating from August 1914–October 1918. Volumes have separate titles, as follows: Vol. 1, *Des Origines à la Déclaration de la Guerre Sous-Marine à Outrance (Août 1914–31 Janvier 1917);* Vol. 2, *De la Guerre Sous-Marine à Outrance à la Révolution Soviétique (1er Fevrier 1917–7 Novembre 1917);* Vol. 3, *De la Révolution Soviétique à la Paix de Brest-Litovsk (9 Novembre 1917–Mars 1918);* Vol. 4, *De la Paix de Brest-Litovsk à la Demande d'Armistice (4 Mars–4 Octobre 1918).* Documents are in German, with editorial apparatus in French.

Note: Imprint varies: Vols. 3 and 4 have imprint: Paris: Publications de la Sorbonne.

Note: Series title: Vols. 1 and 2: *Publications de la Faculté des Lettres et Sciences Humaines de Paris. Série Textes et Documents, tome 3, 14;* also, *Travaux de l'Institut d'histoire des Relations Internationales.* Series title: Vols. 3 and 4: *Publications de la Sorbonne Série Documents, tome 26–27.*

64 DAS KAISERREICH AM ABGRUND ; DIE DAILY-TELEGRAPH-AFFÄRE UND DAS HALE-INTERVIEW VON 1908: DARSTELLUNG UND DOKUMENTATION

P. Winzen (Franz Steiner Verlag, 2002), 369 pp.

Summary: Collection and analysis of documents related to the German Kaiser's foreign relations crisis in 1908. The work is in German; however, the documents collected are in their original language.

65 DEUTSCHE GESCHICHTE 1918–1933: DOKUMENTE ZUR INNEN- UND AUSSENPOLITIK
W. Michalka and G. Niedhart, eds. (Fischer, 2002), 332 pp.
Summary: The focus of this book is on 1919–1923, 1924–1929, and 1930–1933 time periods, in which German foreign policy was impacted by the country's defeat in World War I and political rebuilding period, and the dissolution of the Weimar Republic. In German.

66 BRITISH ENVOYS TO GERMANY 1816–1866
German Historical Institute London (2000–2010), four volumes.
Summary: This is a collection of documents written by British envoys in Germany to the British Foreign Office during the nineteenth century. They present the envoys' observations of political, social, cultural, and economic views in Germany during this time period. Volume I : 1816–1829 ; Volume II : 1830–1847 ; Volume III : 1848–1850 ; Volume IV : 1851–1866.

Inter-War and World War II

67 QUELLEN ZUR DEUTSCHEN AUSSENPOLITIK 1933–1939
Friedrich Kiessling, ed. (Darmstadt: Wissenschaftliche Buchgesellschaft, 2000). XXXI, 318 pp.
Summary: Contains 118 documents arranged in chronological order, detailing the German-Soviet relationship from the assumption of power by the Nazi regime until the conclusion of the non-agression pact. Includes foreword by Gregor Schöllgen.
Note: Series title: *Ausgewählte Quellen zur deutschen Geschichte der Neuzeit*, vol. 34.

68 DEUTSCHE QUELLEN ZUR GESCHICHTE DES ZWEITEN WELTKRIEGES
Michael Salewski, ed. (Darmstadt: Wissenschaftliche Buchgesellschaft, 1998). (II)XXX, 318 pp.
Summary: Contains 175 documents, focusing on conduct of the war, especially the war at sea, as well as development of Nazi ideology and German war aims. Documents also trace German relations with the Soviet Union, allies, and neutral states. Includes chronological list of documents, a thematic index, list of published document sources, as well as a bibliography of secondary literature.

Note: Series title: *Ausgewählte Quellen zur deutschen Geschichte der Neuzeit*, vol. 34a.

69 DOCUMENTS AND MATERIALS RELATING TO THE EVE OF THE SECOND WORLD WAR

Auswärtiges Amt. (Salisbury, N.C: Documentary Publications, 1978).

Summary: Vol. 1 contains 44 secret documents from the archives of the German Ministry of Foreign Affairs, dated November 1937 to December 1938, captured by the Soviet Army in Berlin at the end of the World War II. Documents are organized in chronological order. Headings indicate the nature of each document, its date, whether the document was marked secret and whether it was a copy. Footnotes indicate the source and important marginal notations. Includes a table of contents and a name index.

Note: Originally published in 1948, by International Publishers, New York, and by the Foreign Language Publishing House, Moscow, in English, French and German. Republished as *Dokumente und Materialien aus der Vorgeschichte des Zweiten Weltkrieges, 1937–1939*, S. Ebel and L. Gurwitsch, trans. (Frankfurt am Main: Marxistische Blätter, 1983).

70 DOCUMENTS SECRETS DU MINISTERE DES AFFAIRES ETRANGERES D'ALLEMAGNE; LA POLITIQUE ALLEMANDE

Madeleine and Michel Eristov, trans. (Paris: P. Dupont, 1947).

Summary: Three volume set contains secret documents of the German foreign ministry. Organized by country and period. Vol. 1 covers relations with Turkey, 1941–1943. Vol. 2 covers relations with Hungary, 1937–1943. Vol. 3 covers Spain, 1936–1943. Documents are accompanied by descriptive headings, indicating the date and place of composition. Each volume incudes a list of documents and a name index.

Note: From documents captured by Russian soldiers, and translated from an original Russian publication.

71 NAZI-SOVIET RELATIONS, 1939–1941: DOCUMENTS FROM THE ARCHIVES OF THE GERMAN FOREIGN OFFICE

R.J. Sontag and J.S. Beddie, eds. (Honolulu : University Press of the Pacific, 2003), 362 pp.

Summary: In 1945 the American and British armies captured the archives of the German Foreign Office which had been evacuated from Berlin. This collection of the most significant documents bearing on German-Soviet relations during 1939–1941 was originally published by the U.S. Department of State in 1948.

72 DEUTSCHE GESCHICHTE 1933–1945: DOKUMENTE ZUR INNEN- UND AUSSENPOLITIK
W. Michalka, ed. (Fischer, 2002), 420 pp.

Summary: This book contains excerpts from speeches, letters, diaries, and other writings related to the foreign policy and war strategies of the Third Reich. In German.

German Democratic Republic

73 DOKUMENTE ZUR AUSSENPOLITIK DER DEUTSCHEN DEMOKRATISCHEN REPUBLIK
Deutsche Akademie für Staats- und Rechtswissenschaft, and Abteilung Rechts- und Vertragswesen, Ministerium für Auswärtige Angelegenheiten
(Berlin: Staatsverlag der Deutschen Demokratischen Republik, 1954–1988).

Summary: In 33 volumes. Vols. 14–28, 33, issued in two parts. Includes selected documents covering the period from the founding of the German Democratic Republic, on 7 October 1949, until the end of 1985. Vol. 1 covers the period, 1949–1954. Documents are grouped under the following headings: relations with socialist governments; relations with Asian, African, and Latin American countries; relations with capitalist countries and with Berlin; relations with international organizations and concerning participation in international conferences; and documents expressing the view of the government on fundamental questions of foreign relations. Each group includes a descriptive list of documents. Also included in each volume is a time line of events for the year under review, a descriptive list of treaties concluded, and a subject index. The first ten volumes include a table of contents and a detiled subject index.

Note: Title varies. First ten volumes published under the title *Dokumente zur Aussenpolitik der Regierung der Deutschen Demokratischen Republik.*

Note: Imprint varies. Vols. 1–10, 1954–1962, published under the imprint, Berlin: Rutten & Loening.

Note: Author varies. Vols. 1–10 issued by the Deutsches Institut für Zeitgeschichte. Vol. 11 issued by the same, together with the Institut für Internationale Beziehungen, and the Deutsche Akademie für Staats- und Rechtswissenschaft.

74 THE ANTI-IMPERIALIST LIBERATION STRUGGLE OF THE AFRO-ASIAN AND LATIN AMERICAN PEOPLES AND THE GERMAN DEMOCRATIC REPUBLIC
Ministerium fur Auswärtige Angelegenheiten (Dresden: Verlag Zeit im Bild, 1964). 120 pp.

Summary: Contains 76 documents relating to the foreign policy of the German Democratic Republic towards newly independent states and continuing colonial dependants. Documents are in chronological order, dating from 1949–1964. Some are extracts. All are in English translation. Includes table of contents, but no index.

75 BEZIEHUNGEN DDR-UDSSR 1949 BIS 1955: DOKUMENTSAMMLUNG
M.A. Charlamow, et al. (Berlin: Staatsverlag der Deutschen Demokratischen Republik, 1975). 1056 pp.

Summary: In two volumes. Contains 368 documents covering the relationship between the German Democratic Republic and the Soviet Union between 1949–1955. Translation of Russian edition, published in 1974. Includes a table of contents and an index of personal names. No subject index.

76 DDR-UDSSR, 30 JAHRE BEZIEHUNGEN, 1949–1979: DOKUMENTE UND MATERIALIEN
Ministerium für Auswärtige angelegenheiten der DDR, and the Foreign Ministry of the Soviet Union (Berlin: Staatsverlag der Deutschen Demokratischen Republik, 1982). 816 pp.

Summary: In two volumes, chronologically arranged. Contains 263 documents covering the relationship between the German Democratic Republic and the Soviet Union, 1949–1979. Includes treaties, joint declarations, communiqués, reports of proceedings, speeches, interviews, letters, telegrams, etc. Some documents are excerpted only. Many are from the archives of the Ministry of Foreign Affairs, and not published elsewhere. Each entry includes source note. Includes index of personal names. Issued also in Russian.

Federal Republic and Re-Unification

77 AUSSENPOLITIK DER BUNDESREPUBLIK DEUTSCHLAND: DOKUMENTE VON 1949–1994
R. Bettzüge and G. Gehlhoff, eds. (Köln: Verlag Wissenschaft und Politik, 1995). 1160 pp.

Summary: Contains a selection of 348 documents related to the conduct of West German foreign policy. Mostly diplomatic documents, but also includes some legal documents, such as statutes and treaties. From the preface: "Special weight [is] given to documents concerning recent events". Also includes a detailed time line, indicating important events forming the background of West German foreign policy, various other tables, maps and dia-garams. Table of contents and index of names and subjects. Compiled by the Auswärtiges Amt, in celebration of its 125th anniversary.

Note: Substantially reprints and updates two previous publications of the Auswartiges Amt: *Aussenpolitik Der Bundesrepublik Deutschland: vom Kalten Krieg zum Frieden in Europa* (Stuttgarat: Bonn Aktuell, 1990, 896 pp.), which contains selected documents related to the conduct of West German foreign policy, 1949–1989; and *40 Jahre Aussenpolitik Der Bundesrepublik Deutschland: eine Dokumentation* (Stuttgarat: Bonn Aktuell, 1989, 797 pp.), which also contains selected documents related to the conduct of West German foreign policy, 1949–1989. Both works include a subject index. Reprinted in part by *Die Auswartige Politik der Bundesrepublik Deutschland: Dokumente von 1949–1963* (Köln: Verlag Wissenschaft und Politik, 1999, 286 pp.).

78 WESTINTEGRATION, SICHERHEIT UND DEUTSCHE FRAGE: QUELLEN ZUR AUSSENPOLITIK IN DER ÄRA ADENAUER 1949–1963
K.A. Maier and B. Thoss (Darmstadt: Wissenschaftliche Buchgesellschaft, 1994). 331 pp.

Summary: 126 selected documents related to German integration and security during the Adenauer era. Chronologically arranged. Includes table of contents and index of names and subjects.

Note: Series title: *Ausgewählte Quellen zur Deutschen Geschichte der Neuzeit*, vol. 42.

Note: Also of interest in the same series are *Die Ära Adenauer* (Hans-Dieter Kreikamp, ed., vol. 11, 2003) and *Quellen zur Staatlichen Neuordnung Deutschlands 1945–1949* (Hand, Dieter Kreikamp, ed., vol. 35, 1994). Documents reprinted in these volumes trace the diplomatic and political activity that led to the founding of the Federal Republic.

79 THE GERMAN QUESTION SINCE 1919: AN ANALYSIS WITH KEY DOCUMENTS
Stefan Wolff (Wetport: Praeger, 2003).

Summary: Principally a monographic study of the diplomatic and political repercussions of various efforts to achieve German unification and contain German expansion since the 19th century. Also contains an *Appendix of Key Documents.* Many of the documents are readily available in English elsewhere (e.g., Treaty of Versailles and German Basic Law) but some are not (e.g., Potsdam Proposal on the Disposal of the German Navy and Merchant Marine, Letter on German Unity of 1970 and the Joint Communiqué of Erich Honecker and Helmut Kohl of 1987). Unfortunately, documents are heavily excerpted, and no source notes are provided for the researcher who would like to see the full-text, original version.

Note: Published as part of a series, entitled *Perspectives on the Twentieth Century.*

80 SICHERHEIT, KONTROLLE, SOUVERÄNITÄT
das Petersberger Abkommen vom 22 November 1949: eine Dokumentation. 568 pp.

Summary: Contains the text of the 1949 Petersburg Agreement, which secured to the Federal Republic the gradual resumption of responsibility for consular and commercial affairs. Also includes substantial section of more than 125 related documents, annotated and printed in their original English or German. Documents include diplomatic exchanges, instructions, memoranda, press conferences and interviews and court decisions. Includes index of names.

81 POLITICS AND GOVERNMENT IN GERMANY, 1944–1994: BASIC DOCUMENTS
C.-C. Schweitzer, et al., eds. (Providence; Oxford: Berghahn Books, 1995). 470 pp.

Summary: Chapter 2 contains documents related to the international status of Berlin. Chapter 3 contains documents related to relations between the Federal Republic and the German Democratic Republic. Chapter four contains documents related to the reunification of Germany. Chapter 5 contains documents related to West German foreign policy in the post-war era. Each chapter includes a short introduction, and each document includes a source note. Includes fairly detailed subject index.

82 DER AUSWÄRTIGE AUSSCHUSS DES DEUTSCHEN BUNDESTAGES: SITZUNGSPROTOKOLLE
Wolfgang Hölscher, ed. (Düsseldorf: Droste Verlag, 1998–).

Summary: Comprises 4 volumes to date. Vol. 1 (in two physical volumes, clxi, 1865 pp., 1998) covers the period 1949–1953, vol. 2 (in two physical volumes, clxi, 1846 p., 2002) covers the period 1953–1957), vol. 3 (in two physical volumes, clii, 1429 pp., 2003) covers the period 1957–1961 and vol. 4 (in two physical volumes, cxlv, 1440 pp., 2004) covers the period 1961–1965. Each volume contains the minutes of meetings of the foreign affairs committee of the Bundestag during the period covered. Vols. 3 and 4 also include a CD-ROM version of the edited minutes.

Note: Vol. 13 of the series *Quellen zur Geschichte des Parlamentarismus und der Politischen Parteien: Deutschland seit 1945.*

83 DEUTSCHE AUSSENPOLITIK NACH DER EINHEIT 1990–1993
eine Dokumentation. Auswärtiges Amt. (München: Bonn Aktuell, 1993). 492 pp.

Summary: Contains more than 100 treaties, speeches, communiqués, notes, press releases, etc., related to German diplomacy, 1990–1993. Some of the documents are previously unpublished. Includes a time-line, maps, and appendices (*"Informationsteil"*). Also includes a list of documents and a brief index of names and subjects.

84 DEUTSCHE EINHEIT: SONDEREDITION AUS DEN AKTEN DES BUNDESKANZLERAMTES 1989/90
Hanns Jürgen and Daniel Hofmann, eds. (München: R. Oldenbourg Verlag, 1998). 1668 pp.

Summary: Contains 430 well-annotated and previously unpublished documents from the archives of the Federal Chancellory, detailing the diplomatic and political events leading up to re-unification. Documents are arranged chronologically. Includes 215-page introduction, as well as personal name and subject indexes and a biographical index providing brief information on hundreds of people who figured in the events either politically or diplomatically. The subject index is particularly useful, since it includes treaty titles as entries followed by very detailed subheadings.

Note: Published as a special, unnumbered volume of the series, *Dokumente zur Deutschland-Politik.*

Note: Also published as a CD-ROM (Berlin: Directmedia, 2000).

Relations with Specific Nations and Socio-Cultural Groups

85 QUELLEN ZU DEN BEZIEHUNGEN DEUTSCHLANDS ZU SEINEN NACHBARN IM 19. UND 20. JAHRHUNDERT
Wilfried Baumgart, founding ed. (Darmstadt: Wissenschaftliche Buchgesellschaft, 1996–).

Summary: This series currently includes 11 volumes. The first three volumes are entitled *Quellen zu den Deutsch-Amerikanischen Beziehungen* (XLIV, 247 pp., 1996; LII, 283 pp., 1996; XXXVI, 266 pp., 1998), and cover the period from 1776–1990. Vol. 4 is entitled *Quellen zu den DeutschBritischen Beziehungen 1815–1914* (LXXXII, 229 pp., 1997). Vols. 5 and 6 are entitled *Quellen zu den Deutsch-Französischen Beziehungen* (XLVI, 258 pp., 1997; XXXVIII, 241 pp., 2003), and cover the period of 1815–1963. Vol. 7 is entitled *Quellen zu den Deutsch-Italienischen Beziehungen 1861–1963* (XXX, 290 pp., 2004). Vol. 8 is entitled *Quellen zu den Deutsch-Polnischen Beziehungen 1815–1991* (LVI, 267 pp., 2001). Vol. 9 is entitled *Quellen zu den Deutsch-Russischen Beziehungen 1801–1917*

(XXXII, 256 pp., 2001). Vols. 10 and 11 are entitled *Quellen zu den Deutsch-Sowjetischen Beziehungen*, covering the period 1917–1991 (XXVIII, 271 pp., 1998; XXX, 254 pp., 1999).

The volumes are highly selective. For example, vol. 2 contains only 86 documents. However, documents are included in full, are often quite lengthy, and accompanied by English language abstracts. Many documents are from diplomatic archives. However, documents are drawn from diverse sources in order to reflect political thinking broadly. Each volume includes a bibliography of primary and secondary sources, as well as subject and personal name indexes.

86 DIE BEZIEHUNGEN DER BUNDESREPUBLIK DEUTSCHLAND ZUM HEILIGEN STUHL, 1949–1966
aus den Vatikanakten des Auswartigen Amts. Eine Dokumentation. Michael F. Feldkamp, ed. (Köln: Böhlau, 2000). 541 pp.

Summary: Over 200 documents from the archives of the foreign office trace the relationship between the Federal Republic and the Vatican. Topics include Vatican assistance of post-war occupied Germany, negotiations over the continuing effect of the *Reichskonkordat*, and efforts to dissuade Pope John XXIII from taking actions that might lead to *de facto* recognition of East Germany.

87 BONN WARSCHAU, 1945–1991: DIE DEUTSCH-POLNISCHEN BEZIEHUNGEN: ANALYSE UND DOKUMENTATION
H.-A. Jacobsen and M. Tomala, eds. (Köln: Verlag Wissenschaft und politik, 1992). 655 pp.

Summary: Includes 149 documents relating to German-Polish diplomatic relations from the end of World War II until the normalization of relations in 1991. Each document is accompanied by a descriptive heading and a date. Also includes two introductory essays on the history of post-war German-Polish relations, and a chronology of events. A name index is provided, as well as a list of documents, but there is no subject index. Documents include the text of the 1990 *Vertrag zwischen der Bundesrepublik Deutschland und der Republik Polen über die Bestätigung der zwischen ihnen bestehenden Grenze* (Treaty Confirming the Existing German-polish Border), and the 1991 *Vertrag zwischen der Bundesrepublik Deutschland und der Republik Polen über gute Nachbarschaft und freundschaftliche Zusammenarbeit* (Treaty on Good Neighborliness and Freindly Cooperation Between the Two Countries). (See also no. 33, above.)

Note: See also *Polen und die Deutsche Wiedervereinigung*, by Mieczylaw Tomala (Warszawa: ELIPSA, 2004, 249 pp.). This title includes the treaties mentioned above, as well as an analysis of German-Polish relations during the German re-unification period. Published originally in Polish as *Zjednoczenie Niemiec: reakcje Polaków* (Warszawa: Polska Fundacja Spraw Miedzynarodowych, 2000).

88 DIE DEUTSCH-SOWJETISCHEN BEZIEHUNGEN: EINE AUSWAHL VON VERTRÄGEN, ERKLÄRUNGEN UND REDEN ROLF ELIAS (BERLIN: EDITION NEUE WEGE, 1979–1980)

Summary: In two volumes. Vol. 1 covers the period, 1917–1945, and includes the text of the 1917 peace treaty as well as the 1939 non-agression pact. Vol. 2 covers the period, 1945–1980. Documents are preceded by brief introductions. 114 documents in all. Each volume includes a table of contents.

Note: Also of interest is *Die UdSSR und die Deutsche Frage, 1941–1948: Dokumente aus dem Archiv für Aussenpolitik der Russischen Föderation*, Jochen P. Lauffer and G.P. Kynin, eds. (Berlin: Duncker & Humblot, 2004). This is a three-volume set. Vol. 1 covers the period 1941–1945, vol. 2 covers the period 1945–1946, vol. 3 covers the period 1946–1948. Includes indexes and bibliographical references. Issued also in Russian.

89 DEUTSCH-CHINESISCHE BEZIEHUNGEN 1928–1938: EINE AUSWERTUNG DEUTSCHER DIPLOMATISCHER AKTEN KUO HENG-YU (MÜNCHEN: MINERVA, 1988). 186 PP

Summary: Contains a descriptive summary of files in the Foreign Ministry relating to Sino-German relations, 1928–1938. Documents are described in chronological order. Includes a table of contents, name index, and a brief introduction summarizing Sino-German relations during the period.

Note: Series title: *Berliner China-Studien, No. 17.*

90 THE FEDERAL REPUBLIC OF GERMANY AND THE GERMAN DEMOCRATIC REPUBLIC IN INTERNATIONAL RELATIONS
G. Döker and J.A. Bruckner, with assistance from R. Freiberg. (Dobbs Ferry, NY: Oceana, 1979–1992). Vol. 1, 504 pp.; Vol. 2–3, 440 pp.; Second Series, Vol. 1–2, 504 pp.; Vol. 3, 440 pp.

Summary: Contains selected documents concerning relations between the Federal Republic and the German Democratic Republic. In two series. First series contains three volumes: *Confrontation and Cooperation* (vol. 1), and *The Federal Republic of Germany and the German Democratic Republic in*

International Relations and Organizations (vols. 2–3). Second series has three volumes also, entitled *From Cooperation to Unification* (vols. 1–2), and *The Unification Process of Divided Germany* (vol. 3). Each series includes a detailed table of contents, but no subject index.

91 DIE DEUTSCH-FRANZÖSISCHEN BEZIEHUNGEN SEIT 1963
A. Kimmel and P. Jardin, eds. (VS Verlag für Sozialwissenschaften, 2002). 541 pp.

Summary: This volume documents, through 2002, the France-Germany relationship since the Elyseé Treaty of January 22, 1963. It includes difficult-to-find texts and documents, including interviews, press conferences, speeches, and summaries of meeting and round-table discussions, related to France-Germany summit meetings that have taken place twice-yearly since 1963. In German.

92 AUSWÄRTIGES AMT WEBSITE: BILATERAL RELATIONS
URL: http://www.auswaertiges-amt.de/EN/Laenderinformationen/LaenderUebersicht_node.html.

Summary: The Federal Foreign Office's English-language website provides overview-level information about Germany's relations with the other nations of the world. Topics covered for each country include political, economic, cultural, and military relations. The German-language version of this site provides more detailed information (http://www.auswaertiges-amt.de/DE/Aussenpolitik/Laender/Laender_Uebersicht_node.html).

93 FEDERAL REPUBLIC OF GERMANY – REPUBLIC OF SOUTH AFRICA JOINT INSPECTION REPORT (2013)
URL: https://www.auswaertiges-amt.de/cae/servlet/contentblob/648058/publicationFile/181263/Antarktisbroschuere_EN.pdf.

Summary: This report outlines Germany's obligations toward the oversight of Antarctica under the Antarctic Treaty and the Protocol on Environmental Protection. It also discusses the findings of its 2013 inspection of the continent. In English.

94 DIALOGUE WITH THE ISLAMIC WORLD
URL: https://www.auswaertiges-amt.de/cae/servlet/contentblob/382906/publicationFile/4308/Islamdialog.pdf.

Summary: This report from Germany's Federal Foreign Office discusses several important diplomatic issues in Germany's relationship with Islamic countries and groups around the world, including political change in the Arab world, popular diplomacy, negotiating with extremists, and Islamic cultural identity. In English and German.

95 DEUTSCHLAND UND ISRAEL: EIN SYMPOSIUM (2005)
URL: https://www.auswaertiges-amt.de/cae/servlet/contentblob/382904/publicationFile/4307/Deutschland-Israel.pdf.

Summary: This publication of Germany's Federal Foreign Office discusses topics raised during a 2005 symposium on diplomatic relations between Germany and Israel. These topics focused mainly on the influence of memory and memorial on the past, present, and future relations between these two countries. In German.

Yearbooks and Digests of State Practice

96 GERMAN YEARBOOK OF INTERNATIONAL LAW
Institut für Internationales Recht an der Universität Kiel (Berlin: Duncker & Humblot, 1948–).

Summary: Text in English, French or German. Beginning with vol. 36 (1993), includes a section on current German legal developments in international law. Unfortunately, this section has proved to be only occasional. When included, reports analyze German court decisions of international legal significance. Annual.

Note: Title varies. Vols. 1–2 (1948–1949) entitled, *Jahrbuch für Internationales und Ausländisches Öffentliches Recht*, vols. 3–18 (1950–1976) entitled *Jahrbuch für Internationales Recht*, vols. 19–20 (1976–1978) carry the title *Jahrbuch für Internationales Recht = German Yearbook of International Law.*

Note: Publisher varies. Vols. 1–2 (1948–1949) carry imprint, Hamburg: Rechts- und Staatswissenschaftlicher Verlag, vols. 3–18 (1950–1975) carry imprint, Göttingen: Vandenhoeck & Ruprecht.

Ghana

Victor Essien

Historical Background

Present day Ghana came into being on March 6, 1957 when it attained independence from British colonial rule.[1] The United Kingdom's formal colonial relations with the erstwhile Gold Coast were preceded by a long period of European trade relations with the native kingdoms that inhabited the west coast of Africa.[2] The native Kingdoms included the Ashantis, the Fantes, the Gas, the Denkyeras, the Assins, and the Adansis.[3] The European adventurers and merchants included the Portuguese, the Danes, the Swedes and the Dutch.[4] In 1874, Britain was the only remaining European power and it made the Gold Coast a Protectorate.[5] During the period of multiple European presence in the Gold Coast, the various European merchants signed treaties of friendship, commerce and protection with the rulers of the different kingdoms.[6] Where the natives, particularly the Ashanti's, had waged war with the Europeans, the end of hostilities had been signaled with the signing of peace treaties.[7] Thus, treaty-making was common in the pre-colonial times. One of the best known treaties is the Bond of 1844 between eight Fante rulers and Captain Hill as governor of the British forts and settlements.[8] This Bond is credited with formalizing British jurisdiction over the native subjects.[9] John Mensah Sarbah, the first lawyer of Gold Coast origin, unofficially reproduced a number of these pre-colonial treaties in his scholarly

---

1 Ghana Independence Act, 1957, 5 & 6 Eliz. 2 (Eng.). For a colorful account of the history of Ghana's Independence, *see* Kwame Nkrumah, I Speak of Freedom 95 (London: Mercury Books, 1961).

2 John Mensah Sarbah, Fanti National Constitution 54 *et seq* (London: Clowes, 1906).

3 Id.

4 Id.

5 James L. McLaughlin and David Owusu-Ansah, *Historical Setting, in* Ghana Country Studies 16 (LaVerle Berry, ed., 3rd ed. 1994).

6 Sarbah, *supra* note 2 at 80.

7 Id.

8 John Mensah Sarbah, Fanti Customary Laws 281 (London: Clowes, 1897).

9 Kwame Frimpong, *Some Dark Spots in the Post-Independence Administration of Criminal Justice in Ghana in* Ghana Law Since Independence: History, Development and Prospects 219 (Henrietta J.A.N. Mensa-Bonsu et al, eds., 2007).

 | doi 10.1163/9789004272224_015

writings.[10] Official collections of these treaties can be located in the Records of the Colonial Office of the United Kingdom[11] and after 1921, in the British Foreign and State Papers.[12]

In 1901, the British Orders in Council defined the boundaries and declared the Gold Coast a colony by settlement, the Ashanti territory a colony by conquest and the Northern territory a British Protectorate.[13] From this time onwards, the native kingdoms lost their sovereignty and with it, their treaty-making power. The conduct of international relations during the colonial period was ceded to the colonial power, the United Kingdom.[14] The United Kingdom entered into treaties with other sovereign nations, some of which treaties applied to their colonial possessions, including the Gold Coast colony.[15]

Issues of Treaty Succession

On April 29, 1954, the Gold Coast colony received a measure of self-government.[16] On March 6, 1957, it gained independence as Ghana.[17] The attainment of independence raised issues of succession to treaties entered into by the United Kingdom and other States during Ghana's colonial period. On November 25, 1957, the Governments of Ghana and the United Kingdom, through an Exchange of Letters Constituting an Agreement entered into a devolution agreement or an inheritance agreement relative to the colonial treaties.[18] In clear terms the agreement stated as follows:

i. all obligations and responsibilities of the Government of the United Kingdom which arise from any valid international instrument shall henceforth, in so far as such instrument may be held to have application to Ghana, be assumed by the Government of Ghana;

---

10 SARBAH, *supra* note 2 at 153 *et seq.*

11 RECORDS OF THE COLONIAL OFFICE, COMMONWEALTH & FOREIGN OFFICES, EMPIRE MARKETING BOARD & RELATED BODIES, 1570–1990 (London: Colonial Office, 1860–).

12 BRITISH AND FOREIGN STATE PAPERS (London: H.M.S.O., 1815–).

13 The Gold Coast Order in Council, 1901, Statutory Instrument 1901/5002 (U.K.). *See also*, S.A. de Smith, *The Independence of Ghana*, 20 MOD. L. REV. 347, 348 (1957).

14 D.P. O'Connell, *Independence and Succession to Treaties*, 38 BRIT. Y.B. INT'L L. 85 *passim* (1962).

15 Id.

16 *The Gold Coast (Constitution) Order in Council, 1954* Statutory Instrument 1954/551 (U.K.).

17 *Supra* note 1.

18 O'Connell, *supra* note 14.

ii. the rights and benefits heretofore enjoyed by the Government of the United Kingdom in virtue of the application of any such international instrument to the Gold Coast shall henceforth be enjoyed by the Government of Ghana".[19]

What was not clear in the inheritance agreement was which of these treaties Ghana inherited from the United Kingdom.[20] The United States was not going to take such issues for granted. The United States, therefore, in addition to the general inheritance agreement through an Exchange of Notes Constituting an Agreement, entered into a separate treaty identifying which treaties applied as between the United States and Ghana.[21]

Treaty Ratification and Implementation

Article 75(1) of the 1992 Constitution of Ghana confers on the President of Ghana the authority to execute treaties in the name of Ghana.[22] All such treaties are subject to ratification by an Act of Parliament or a resolution of Parliament supported by the votes of more than one-half of all Members of Parliament.[23] A similar provision was contained in the 1979 Ghana Constitution[24] and the 1969 Ghana Constitution.[25] The 1957 Ghana Independence Constitution[26] and the 1960 First Ghana Republican Constitution[27] did not have any explicit provisions on treaty authority.

19 Exchange of Letters Constituting an Agreement Relative to the Inheritance of International Rights and obligations by the Government of Ghana. Accra, November 25, 1957, 287 *U.N.T.S.* 233 (1958).

20 *Supra* note 14. Also, Okon Udokang, "Succession to Treaties in New States" *8 Can Y.B. Int'l L.* 123 (1970), especially p. 136 for his response to O'Connell's criticism of the value and validity of the inheritance agreements.

21 Exchange of Notes Constituting an Agreement Relating to the Continued Application to Ghana of Certain Treaties and Agreements Concluded between the U.S.A and the U.K. Accra, September 4, and December 21, 1957 and February 12, 1958 442 *U.N.T.S.* 175 (1962).

22 *Constitution of the Republic of Ghana*, 1992 Art. 75(1) (Accra-Tema: Ghana Publishing Corporation, 1992).

23 Id., Article 75(2)

24 *Constitution of the Republic of Ghana, 1979* Art. 63 (Accra-Tema: Ghana Publishing Corporation, 1979).

25 *Constitution of the Republic of Ghana, 1969* Art. 59 (Accra-Tema: Ghana Publishing Corporation, 1969).

26 *The Ghana (Constitution) Order in Council*, Statutory Instrument 1957/277 (U.K.).

27 *Constitution of the Republic of Ghana*, Accra: Government Printing Department, 1961.

The Independence Constitution reflected the United Kingdom constitutional practice with its roots in parliamentary democracy.[28] The treaty practice at the time and also during the first republican constitution borrowed heavily from the British tradition of treaty power being the sole preserve of the executive branch and one requiring no legislative ratification.[29] In Ghana, as in the United Kingdom, dualism, as opposed to monism, is the theory behind the relationship between international law and municipal law.[30] Hence, most treaties signed and ratified by the executive branch still require Parliament to pass an enabling statute for them to apply in Ghana.[31] Dualism is still the order of the day and so even though the 1969, 1979 and 1992 Constitutions all require Parliament to ratify treaties executed by the President of the Republic, these treaties still need to be domesticated in order to apply in Ghana.[32] In other words, generally, international treaties are not self-executing in Ghana.

The pace of domestication of Ghana's international treaties has been rather slow.[33] In response to this, an inter-ministerial committee was established on February 5, 2008 to, among other things, provide guidelines for the domestic ratification of treaties.[34] On June 1, 2009 the committee's work-product was launched as *The Republic of Ghana Treaty Manual*.[35] A highlight of this manual is the section titled, "Guidelines for the domestic ratification of treaties/agreements/conventions under the dualist approach and for the transformation of treaties into national legislation".[36] The manual also contains a list of multilateral treaties deposited with the Secretary-General of the United Nations ratified by the Republic of Ghana, treaties adopted under the aegis of the African Union and the Economic Community of West African States ratified by the

28 De Smith, *supra* note 13 at 359.

29 Kwadwo Appiagyei-Atua, *Ghana at 50: The Place of International Human Rights Norms in the Courts, in* GHANA LAW SINCE INDEPENDENCE: HISTORY, DEVELOPMENT AND PROSPECTS 179–185 (Henrietta J.A.N. Mensa-Bonsu et al eds. 2007). Note, however, the role of the Ponsonby Rule of 1924 in the United Kingdom, requiring that treaties subject to executive ratification should be laid in Parliament for 21 days.

30 Appiagye-Atua, op cit.

31 THE REPUBLIC OF GHANA TREATY MANUAL 2 (Accra: Office of the Attorney-General and Ministry of Justice, 2009).

32 Id. at 3.

33 AFRICAN PEER REVIEW MECHANISM: COUNTRY REPORT OF THE REPUBLIC OF GHANA 15 (June 2005). *See also* OPEN SOCIETY INITIATIVE FOR WEST AFRICA, GHANA JUSTICE SECTOR AND THE RULE OF LAW: A DISCUSSION PAPER 3 (2007).

34 *The Republic of Ghana Treaty Manual*, *supra* note 31.

35 Id.

36 Id. at 3.

Republic of Ghana.[37] The guidelines contained in the treaty manual states that the sponsoring Government Ministry for the treaty, first has to prepare a Cabinet Memorandum for consideration of the Cabinet. The said memorandum should indicate what decision is required of Cabinet on the treaty.[38] The memorandum should explain the contents of the treaty and include relevant background information.[39] The memorandum should "further spell out the obligation of government, which is the financial and legal impact, if the treaty, agreement or convention was ratified and must state that the Attorney-General and Minister of Justice has been consulted".[40] The memorandum "should state whether an amendment to legislation is required or whether a new law is needed".[41] The memorandum should also specify whether there is the need for the Republic of Ghana to make any reservations and must include the text of the treaty under consideration.[42]

Cabinet shall convey its decision on the treaty to the sponsoring Ministry and depending on whether the treaty is to be ratified by an Act of Parliament or by a resolution of Parliament, different additional steps are to follow.[43] If ratification is by an Act of Parliament, the Secretary to Cabinet shall send the sponsoring Ministry a letter providing approval for the issuance of drafting instructions for the Attorney-General's department to prepare the law.[44] After the legislative drafting process, the draft Bill and explanatory memorandum is submitted to Cabinet for approval for the Bill to be laid in Parliament.[45] When Parliament passes the Bill by a simple majority, the Act is published in the Government Gazette.[46]

Where ratification is by a resolution of Parliament, Cabinet is required to send a letter to Parliament, with a copy to the sponsoring Ministry, authorizing a resolution to be adopted on the treaty, agreement or convention.[47] Before a resolution is adopted, the Business Committee of Parliament designates a day for the treaty to be laid in the House by the sponsoring Minister.[48] The Speaker of Parliament then orders the treaty to be referred to the relevant committee or

---

37 Id.
38 Id.
39 Id.
40 Id. at 4.
41 Id.
42 Id.
43 Id.
44 Id.
45 Id. at 5.
46 Id.
47 Id.
48 Id.

joint committee of the House for consideration.[49] Invariably, it is the Committee on Foreign Affairs that has responsibility for these matters but a second committee may be directed to participate in the consideration of the treaty.[50] The said committee prepares a report on its deliberations for the full House of Parliament.[51] The treaty is subsequently debated by the full House after which a resolution for adoption is put to Parliament by the Speaker on a voice vote.[52] If the resolution is adopted, the Clerk of Parliament prepares the resolution and forwards it to the Ministry of Foreign Affairs and Regional Integration for the appropriate instrument of ratification.[53] The instrument is then sent to the President for the signature and seal of the President.[54]

It appears that the responsibility for determining whether a treaty should be ratified by an Act of Parliament or a resolution is that of Cabinet. However, neither the Constitution nor the Guidelines is very clear on this point and none discusses the criteria for determining this.[55] The Constitutional Review Commission of Ghana, in its final report,[56] takes note of this failure and the failure of any direction as to which international agreements require legislative ratification and which do not.[57] The Commission has recommended that legislation should be passed to clarify these matters.[58]

Annotated Bibliography of Sources

General Treaty Collections

There is no official or unofficial publication of treaties to which Ghana is a party.[59] Due to the lack of a single resource for locating treaties to which Ghana

49 Id.

50 Id.

51 Id.

52 Id.

53 Id.

54 Id. at 6.

55 A thorough review of the 1992 constitutional provisions on the subject of the conduct of international relations and the text of the Republic of Ghana Treaty Manual reveals that they are both silent on this matter.

56 Constitutional Review Commission of Ghana, The Report of the Constitutional Review Commission. (2011).

57 Id. at p 801.

58 Id.

59 Ghana Justice Sector and the Rule of Law: A Discussion Paper, *supra* note 33 at 3. This paper points out that "it is surprisingly difficult to put together a complete list of Ghana's international treaty obligations".

is a party, a researcher may consider consulting one of the following organizations for assistance in locating a particular treaty.

Institute of Diplomatic Practice and Development Policies
Nyansapo House
Adjiringano Road
East Legon, Accra
Website: http://www.idpdp.com
Telephone number: +233 302 957977
Director: H.E. Nana Bema Kumi
Contact person: H.E. Nana Bema Kumi
Direct line: +233 248 895345
Email: nanabemakumi@gmail.com

Legon Centre of International Affairs and Diplomacy
University of Ghana
Legon, Accra
Website: http://www.ug.edu.gh/index1.php?linkid=666&sublinkid=524
Telephone number:+233 302 50 10 25
Director: Professor Henrietta J.A.N. Mensa-Bonsu
Contact person: Dr. Linda Darkwa
Email: lindark@hotmail.com & ldarkwa@ug.edu.gh

Ministry of Foreign Affairs and Regional Integration
P.O. Box M53
Accra
Telephone number: +233 302 664952
Email: ghmfaoo@ghana.co

Treaty Index

1 REPUBLIC OF GHANA TREATY MANUAL (2009)
URL: http://legal.un.org/avl/documents/scans/GhanaTreatyManual2009.pdf?teil=II&j.

Summary: The first attempt at publication of any national treaty finding tool is the Republic of Ghana Treaty Manual[60] published in 2009. It is dedicated to multilateral treaties deposited with the Secretary-General of the United Nations. Also included are ratified treaties adopted under the aegis of the African Union (AU) and the Economic Community of West African States (ECOWAS). The manual lists the AU and ECOWAS treaties as of May 12, 2008

60 *Supra* note 31.

and the treaties sourced from the United Nations Treaty Collection (UNTC) as of February 2, 2009. The manual has not been updated since its publication. The ECOWAS treaties are listed in chronological order of the date of ratification. The AU treaties are listed in some sort of partial alphabetical order. The treaties taken from the UNTC are arranged by subject-matter, using categories borrowed from the UNTC. The manual does not provide the citations to any of these treaties. At the minimum, there is the need for a more comprehensive, regularly up-dated index to Ghanaian treaties in force, both multilateral and bilateral. Meanwhile a researcher has to consult several multi-jurisdictional treaty databases and some national treaty sources as well as books to obtain information on Ghana's treaty obligations. These databases and books include the following:

Topical and Selected Treaty Publications

African Regional Treaties

2 AFRICAN UNION TREATIES

URL: http://www.au.int/en/treaties.

Summary: provides access to treaties, conventions, protocols and charters adopted under the auspices of the African Union (AU) and its predecessor organization, the organization of African Union (OAU). To determine if Ghana has signed a particular instrument, you have to click on the status list button.

3 ECONOMIC COMMUNITY OF WEST AFRICAN STATES TREATIES

URL: http://www.comm.ecowas.int/sec/index.php?id=treaty

Summary: provides access to treaties and protocols adopted under the auspices of the Economic Community of West African States (ECOWAS). The site does not provide a status link.

Colonial and Pre-colonial Treaties

4 BRITISH AND FOREIGN STATE PAPERS[61]

(London: H.M.S.O., 1815–).

Summary: Includes the text of treaties, diplomatic correspondence, foreign constitutions and laws pertaining mainly to international relations.

5 RECORDS OF THE COLONIAL OFFICE, COMMONWEALTH AND FOREIGN AND COMMONWEALTH OFFICES, EMPIRE MARKETING BOARD AND RELATED BODIES, 1570–1990

(London: Colonial Office, 1860–).

---

61 For more information on this resource, see chapter on "United Kingdom."

Summary: Includes text of 277 treaties made between British Officials and African rulers in Gambia, Sierra Leone, Gold Coast and Lagos between 1778 and 1891. The Gold Coast collection includes details of an agreement entered into by the Netherlands government in 1642 and renewed in 1844, 1846 and 1849. The Sierra Leone collection is indexed by name of ruler and place.

6 FANTI NATIONAL CONSTITUTION: A SHORT TREATISE ON THE CONSTITUTION AND GOVERNMENT OF THE FANTI, ASANTI, AND OTHER AKAN TRIBES OF WEST AFRICA
John Mensah Sarbah (London: Clowes, 1906).
Summary: Sarbah reproduces the text of four pre-colonial treaties on pages 153 to 160 of his book.

Diplomatic Documents

7 FOREIGN AFFAIRS: QUARTERLY BULLETIN OF THE MINISTRY OF FOREIGN AFFAIRS
(Accra-Tema, Ghana: Ministry of Foreign Affairs, 1974–)
Summary: Intended to be an official record of the foreign policy of Ghana. It ceased publication soon after it was launched.
Note: It was an attempt to revive an earlier experiment in the form of the *Ghana Foreign Affairs: A Monthly Bulletin of the Ministry of Foreign Affairs* (Accra: Ministry of Foreign Affairs, 1963–).
Note: Not widely held in North American libraries.

8 LEGON JOURNAL OF INTERNATIONAL AFFAIRS: LEJIA
(Legon, Ghana: Legon Centre for International Affairs, University of Ghana, 2004–)
Summary: This is an academic journal published by the Legon Centre for International Affairs and Diplomacy. The representative articles cover all areas of international affairs, including foreign policy. The journal does not contain diplomatic documents or treaties.
Note: It is a semi-annual published in May and November of each year. There was a break in publication after the 2009 issue. The Center has resumed publication under a new title, LEGON JOURNAL OF INTERNATIONAL AFFAIRS AND DIPLOMACY: LEGIAD, reflecting the name change of the Center. The May 2013 issue is expected to appear shortly.

India

Sunil Rao

Issues of Treaty Succession

The history of India is characterized by a rich tradition of highly developed legal and political systems. Before the British established themselves as the preeminent political force in the Subcontinent, 'India' consisted of innumerable local territories, loosely connected by a system of law known as *Dharmashastra*—later categorized as "Hindu Law."[1] *Dharmashastra* did not, however, function as unified legal system, nor contribute to any kind of political unification.[2] Even as these principalities fell under Mughal suzerainty in the 16th century, the regional rulers generally refrained from interfering with the day to day administration of their territories, leaving such work to the villages and other similar units.[3]

A unified administrative entity known as India began to take shape with the conquest of the Subcontinent by the British. Through its proxy, the East India Company, British influence rose gradually beginning in the late 17th century, at the same time that the Mughal Empire was beginning to disintegrate. By the late 19th century, the authority of the East India Company had faded, and the British government had assumed complete control. The Government of India Act of 1858[4] gave the British Crown official authority over the Subcontinent – directly, through administration over the regions commonly referred to as "British India"; and indirectly, via the Princely States, which were afforded a good deal of internal autonomy under British suzerainty.[5]

Because Indian law and legal institutions are steeped in the British legal system and legal discourse, for the researcher of international law issues

1 Devi Dayal Aggarwal, Jurisprudence in India Through the Ages 238–239 (2002).

2 Id. at 239.

3 The Republic of India: The Development of its Laws and Constitution 3 (2nd ed. 1964).

4 21 & 22 Vict. c. 106.

5 Often, the nature of authority to be divided between the Princely States and the British crown was spelled out in treaties. These treaties have been collected in a number of texts. *See, e.g.,* A Collection of Treaties and Engagements with the Native Prince and States of Asia Concluded on Behalf of the East India Company, by the British Governments in India, etc. (E. Cox and Son, 1812). Many of these texts can be found electronically via Google books.

 | DOI 10.1163/9789004272224_016

pertaining to contemporary India, the period of British influence is the most relevant. During colonial rule, and particularly in the early twentieth century, India came to be seen as having acquired a unique position within the British Commonwealth, and in some respects, was treated as an independent international legal personality.[6] India had, for example, become a member of the League of Nations and had been party to several prominent international acts and agreements, such as the Treaty of Versailles, the Statute of the Permanent Court of Justice, and the 1937 Geneva Convention for the Prevention and Punishment of Terrorism.[7] Nevertheless, British India was not a self-governing dominion, like Canada, Australia, New Zealand, etc.; rather, India's various roles as an international player, such as treaty ratification, were performed through various agencies of the British government.[8]

The Indian Independence Act of 1947[9] provided for the independence of the territory known as British India, and also for the creation of two independent states from that territory – the dominions of India and Pakistan. In the post-independence period, some of the scholarship devoted to the question of partition bears significance for issues of treaty succession. Did partition create two new states, or only one new state (Pakistan), with India continuing the international personality of British India?[10] The view of the UN Secretariat, reflected in a report submitted by the UN Assistant Secretary-General for Legal Affairs in 1946, is that India retained the same international status as "British India," while Pakistan became a totally new state.[11]

The majority of scholarship and case law addressing this issue have taken the Secretariat's position,[12] with the result that India, having continued the international personality of British India, would have automatically assumed its treaty rights and obligations, whereas Pakistan, as a new international

---

6 India and International Law 34 (Bimal N. Patel, ed., 2005).

7 Id.

8 H.O. Agarwal, State Succession: A Study of Indian Cases, 26–27 (1980).

9 10 & 11 Geo. 6, c. 30.

10 For a detailed discussion on competing views with respect to India's post-independence status as an international personality, *see* T.S.N. Sastry, State Succession in an Indian Context, 67–81 (2004).

11 Agarwal, *supra* note 8, at 37–38. (In note 58, Agarwal references [1962] 2 Y.B. Int'l L. Comm'n 199, as a source for the full text of the report).

12 *See, e.g.*, Sastry, *supra* note 10, at 78–80 (referring to Indian, Pakistani, and International Court of Justice cases that held the position that partition had not changed India's status as an international personality). *But see* Agarwal, *supra* note 8 (arguing the minority viewpoint that India and Pakistan both became new international personalities following partition, and are co-equal successor states to British India).

personality, would not have. In order to forestall such a situation,[13] the Governor-General promulgated the Indian Independence (international arrangements) Order of 1947[14] (hereinafter "Order"). Article 4 of the Order distributed rights, property and liabilities to the new dominions, including specific treaty rights and obligations.[15]

Treaty Ratification and Implementation

India is a federation, comprised of twenty-eight states and seven union territories.[16] As such, legislative, executive and judicial powers are divided between the national and state governments.[17] The consensus among legal authorities and scholars is that the Constitution gives the Executive—in particular, the President—the authority to conclude treaties, including the negotiation and ratification process.[18] No act of Parliament is required for ratification; the

---

13 *See generally* SASTRY, *supra* note 10 at 79–80; *and* PATEL, *supra* note 6 at 37 (suggesting that the Order's central purpose was to assign specific treaty rights and obligations to Pakistan, in order to respond to its claim as a co-successor state to India).

14 Before partition, many orders were promulgated by the Governor General of India in exercising powers conferred under the Independence Act of 1947, in order to pass on rights of British India to the two new dominions. These orders were separate from the Act itself, and acquired a character similar to law. (AGARWAL, *supra* note 8 at 40). One of these Orders was the Indian Independence (international arrangements) Order of 1947.

15 The Order gave effect to a report, accepted by the Partition Council, which classified all existing treaties, so that those of exclusive interest to Pakistan fell upon Pakistan alone; those of exclusive interest to India fell upon India alone; and those which were of common interest devolved on both of the dominions. *See* Agarwal, supra note 8, at 44–45; *see also* SASTRY, *supra* note 10 at 79, n. 39 (citing the PARTITION PROCEEDINGS 1948: Vol 3. Annexures V-VIII :217–76, as a full text source of the Order.).

16 Union territories are ruled directly by the President of India, via an Administrator or Lieutenant Governor. The states, on the other hand, have their own elected governments.

17 INDIA CONST. (hereinafter "Constitution") art. 246. As established in article 246, the powers of the central and state governments are set out in three lists—the Union List, the State List, and the Concurrent List—incorporated into the Seventh Schedule of the Constitution. List I, the Union List, includes those powers of national importance. Entry 14 in the Union List designates to the central government those powers dealing with "entering into treaties and agreements with foreign countries and implementation of treaties, agreements and conventions with foreign countries".

18 Article 53 of the Constitution vests the executive power in the President, while Article 73 holds that the executive power applies to all matters to which Parliament may make laws,

President, however, acts with the advice of the Council of Ministers—the ultimate decision making body headed by the Prime Minister—and is responsible to the Lok Sabha, the lower house of parliament.[19] The Constitution does not require that treaties be ratified in order to be entered into force. Whether a clause providing for approval or ratification is to be included in a treaty is a matter between India and the other party to the agreement.[20]

While the Executive holds the treaty making power, Parliament retains the power to pass legislation regulating it.[21] To date, Parliament has passed no such law. Parliament also has the authority to pass legislation implementing a treaty, if such legislation is called for.[22] The Executive, however, requires neither authorizing nor implementing legislation in order to conclude a treaty that comes into force.[23] Of course, many treaties will not be self-executing; the constitutional provision for Parliament to pass legislation implementing treaties is clearly an acknowledgement of this fact.[24]

---

and the "exercise of all powers that accrue to the Government of India from any International Treaty or Agreement." These two articles of the Constitution have been used to support the position that, as a rule, the power to conclude treaties is vested in the President. *See* C.G. Raghavan, *Treaty Making Power Under the Constitution of India, in* ESSAYS ON THE LAW OF TREATIES 221–22 (S.K. Agrawala ed., 1972) (discussing the treaty making power as an executive act under the Indian Constitution).

19 INDIA CONST. articles 74 and 75.

20 K. Thakore, *National Treaty Law and Practice: India,* in NATIONAL TREATY LAW AND PRACTICE: FRANCE, GERMANY, INDIA, SWITZERLAND, THAILAND, UNITED KINGDOM 86 (Monroe Leigh and Merritt R. Blakeslee, eds., 1995).

21 *See* T.S. Rama Rao, *Some Constitutional Aspects of Treaty-Making Power in India,* in ESSAYS ON THE LAW OF TREATIES, *supra* note 18, at 251 (noting that Entry 14 of the Union list of the Constitution gives Parliament the authority to pass a law regulating the treaty making power of the executive).

22 Article 246 of the Constitution gives Parliament exclusive power to legislate over matters falling into the Union List in the Seventh Schedule of the Constitution, which includes the matter of entering into treaties. Even more to the point, Article 253 specifically gives Union parliament the authority to make laws implementing treaties.

23 Article 73 of the Constitution gives the executive power over "matters with respect to which Parliament has power to make laws" and to "exercise of all powers that accrue to the Government of India from any International Treaty or Agreement". For further discussion of Article 73 as it relates to the executive's ability to enter into valid treaties without authorizing legislation from Parliament, *see generally* DURGA DAS BASU, CONSTITUTIONAL LAW OF INDIA 145 (6th ed. 1991); C.G. Raghavan, *supra* note 18, at 220–223; *and* Thakore, *supra* note 20, at 86–91.

24 Thakore, *supra* note 20, at 79. For further discussion on those situations in which enabling legislation from the Parliament of India might be necessary, *see generally* Thakore at 85; *and* AGARWAL, *supra* note 8 at 225.

There is no provision in the Constitution that explicitly gives treaties the force of law. If a treaty has been concluded and ratified, but no legislation has been passed to authorize or implement it, its enforceability in the courts as the "law of the land" is unclear. Traditionally, the weight of case law has seemed to suggest that, in the absence of implementing legislation, treaties are not enforceable by the courts.[25] However, recent decisions may be pointing to the opposite conclusion.[26]

Once a treaty has been concluded, ratified and implemented (whether through executive action or legislation), the question of publication arises. When required by a particular Act, a treaty will be published in the official gazette.[27] There is, however, no statutory requirement that as a rule, treaties must be published.[28] Nor is there is any current publication that serves as an official source for treaties and international agreements exclusively. A researcher looking for a resource that lists all treaties participated in by India in the current calendar year can consult the *Annual Report,* published by the Ministry of External Affairs.

There are several official publications in which treaties *may* be published. These are addressed in the bibliography below.

Evidence of State Practice

As noted earlier, the entire process for concluding a treaty—negotiation, signature, and ratification—falls to the executive.[29] While the Constitution does not define this process with any degree of specificity, in terms of practice, the Ministry of External Affairs (hereinafter MEA), including the Legal and Treaties Division, is the agency that is central to treaty making.[30] As a general rule, the MEA consults with the particular department or ministry concerned with the

25 *See* National Commission to Review the Working of the Constitution, *A Consultation Paper on Treaty-Making Power Under Our Constitution* (Jan. 8, 2001), *available at* http://lawmin.nic.in/ncrwc/finalreport/v2b2-3.htm; *see also* Narendra Kadoliya, *A Paradigm Shift In The Role Of Domestic Courts In Implementing International Treaty Provisions: An Indian Perspective* (Oct. 8, 2007), *available at* http://www.manupatrafast.com/articles/PopOpenArticle.aspx?ID=29c6ccdf-f94e-42e5-8bdd-64f58d2a962c&txtsearch=Subject:%20Miscellaneous.

26 Kadoliya, *supra* note 25.

27 Thakore, *supra* note 20, at 99.

28 Id.

29 INDIA CONST. articles 53 and 73, *supra* note 18.

30 Thakore, *supra* note 20, at 83.

subject matter to decide the form of the agreement to be concluded. The MEA then coordinates and directs the process of concluding the particular treaty or agreement.[31] There is often a distinction between government level agreements and agency or departmental level agreements; in the latter case, a formal concluding process is forgone unless the parties agree otherwise.[32]

The MEA's central role in the concluding process, and in diplomatic relations in general, makes its website[33] a logical repository for diplomatic documents, including treaties and agreements, press releases, and statements by the Ambassador of India, Minister of External Affairs, Prime Minister, and other high level officials.

It should be noted that India was not a party to the 1978 Vienna Convention, which provided in Article 16 that newly independent states were not bound to treaties that were in force for their predecessor states.[34] Some scholars have argued that the 1978 convention, which has few signatories and has only been in force since 1996, has not yet attained the status of customary international law, and reflects instead a progressive development of international law.[35] While India's position on this is unclear, in one case involving Pakistan that came before the International Court of Justice, India argued that, insofar as Article 16 of the 1978 Convention reflects customary international law, India can be seen "newly independent state," and therefore not bound to a treaty that was in force for British India at the time of independence.[36]

Annotated Bibliography of Sources

General Treaty Collections

As noted in Treaty Implementation, *supra*, there is no current[37] publication that serves as an official publication for treaties and international agreements

---

31 Id.

32 Id.

33 http://www.mea.gov.in/. For more information on the documents available on this site, *see infra* Diplomatic Documents.

34 Patel, *supra* note 6, at 37 (citing the 1978 Convention on the Succession of States in Respect of Treaties, art. 16, Aug. 23, 1978, 1946 UNTS 3) (hereinafter 1978 Convention).

35 *See e.g.*, Anthony Aust, Handbook on International Law, 394 (2005).

36 Patel, *supra* note 6, at 36, note 16 (citing the oral argument submitted by Professor Alain Pellet on behalf of India in the case concerning the Aerial Incident of 10 August 1999 (Pakistan v. India), (Jurisdiction), ICJ Reports 2000).

37 The *India Treaty Series*, discussed in this section, appears to have been an attempt at a general treaty collection.

exclusively. When required by statute, a treaty will be published in the official gazette.[38]

1 INDIA, BILATERAL TREATIES AND AGREEMENTS
Siba Exim. (New Delhi: Policy Planning and Research Division, Ministry of External Affairs, Govt. of India, New Delhi, 1994).

Summary: This ten volume set contains bilateral treaties and agreements involving India covering the period from 1947–1980. Each document contains the details regarding place and date of signing, the date of ratification and/or entry into force, and how the entry into force came into effect. The treaties are arranged chronologically by date of signature. The introduction notes that in the case where the agreement takes the form of an exchange of letters, "the date of the confirming letter is taken as the controlling date."

Index: Each volume has a detailed country index, further subdivided by topic, and a subject index, organized alphabetically by international issue, and further subdivided by country.

Note: The introduction to the first volume notes that the set would eventually cover up to 1990. The latest volume published so far is volume 10, covering up to 1980.

Note: The introduction to the first volume notes that every effort was made to include all important treaties and agreements, and that treaties located subsequently to the publishing of the first volume would be published in a supplement. No supplement has yet been published.

2 INDIA TREATY SERIES
(New Delhi: Legal and Treaties Division, Ministry of External Affairs, Govt. of India, 1980).

Summary: This is a two volume set of treaties and agreements involving India that came into force in the calendar year during which the volume was published. Part I contains bilateral treaties, and Part II contains multilateral treaties. The preface to Volume I notes that the series is intended to be comprehensive, covering the texts of all types of agreements – "political, cultural, economic, scientific, technical, financial, trade, and commercial."

Index: There is no index for this series. A table of contents is provided, arranged by first by type of treaty (bilateral or multilateral), then by the party that has entered into the agreement with India. Information for each entry includes title of the treaty, document number, and dates of signature and entry into force.

---

38 *See supra,* note 20, at 99.

Note: The forward to volume II states: "[A]part from continuation of the series from 1980 onwards, it is also proposed to publish the texts of treaties entered into in earlier years." However, the series was not continued. Both of these volumes are only concerned with treaties that came into force in 1980.

3 INDIAN TREATY SERIES

URL: http://www.liiofindia.org/in/other/treaties/INTSer/.

Summary: A web site maintained by the Legal Information Institute of India, a prominent, and free, source of legal information in India. The site offers the full text of treaties to which India is a party from 1947 to 1975, and selected subsequent bilateral treaties through 2009 (though the content may be updated in the future). Information is based on data obtained from the Ministry of External Affairs. The researcher can browse for treaties by date or by title.

4 FOREIGN AFFAIRS RECORD

India. External Publicity Division. (Ministry of External Affairs: External Affairs Division, Government of India, New Delhi, 1955–).

Summary: The annexes include treaties and agreements involving India, though coverage does not appear to be comprehensive. See no. 12 for additional information.

Treaty Indexes

There is at present no regular publication that comprehensively indexes treaties in force that India has entered into. However, the Annual Report, *infra,* provides access to a list of treaties and agreements that India has entered into for the current calendar year.

5 ANNUAL REPORT

India, Ministry of External Affairs. (Ministry of External Affairs, New Delhi, 1950-)

Summary: An annual chronicle of the activities, views, and statements of the government of India with respect to events around the world that have international consequences, particularly as they relate to India. The appendices to each *Annual Report* contain a list of treaties/conventions/agreements concluded by the Government of India, and entered into force during the current calendar year.

Note: From 1905–1997, the publication was known as *Report of the Ministry of External Affairs.*

Note: The Annual Reports are also available electronically via the Ministry of External Affairs website: http://mealib.nic.in/. The site contains reports in PDF from 1948/49 to the present.

6 INDIA TREATY MANUAL; CONTAINING INFORMATION ABOUT 1600 TREATIES AND RELATED DOCUMENTS CONCERNING INDIA
C.M. Samuel. (P.M. Kuruvilla at the Wesley Press, Mysore City, 1972).

Summary: This single volume work contains citations to over 1600 treaties binding India as of 1971. The book is divided into two sections. The "Numerical Section" contains a listing of treaties by League of Nations Treaty Series or United Nations Treaty Series cite, as the case may be. The "Chronological Section" organizes the treaties by date. It is unclear from the volume itself as to whether the date is the date of signature, ratification, or entry into force. Each entry lists the parties to the treaties, as wells as other details where relevant, such as references to later amendments, related treaties, and in some cases, explanatory commentary.

Note: This is a reissue of India Treaty Manual, 1966, covering the period from 1967–71.

Topical and Selected Treaty Publications

7 INDIA'S TRADE AGREEMENTS WITH OTHER COUNTRIES
(Controller of Publications, etc., Delhi, 1959–?)

Summary: This monograph contains the texts of agreements in force as of January 1st of the year of publication of the particular edition. The agreements are organized by country. Also included are exchanges of letters between diplomats that relate to current agreements in some way, or that expand on past agreements.

Note: There are several editions, beginning with 1949. The last edition published was 1976.

8 SECURITY AND DEFENCE RRELATED TREATIES OF INDIA. V.P. MALHOTRA
(Vij Books India, New Delhi, 2010).

Summary: A compilation of defense related treaties, agreements and other documents. The subjects dealt with include border disputes, maritime boundaries, river water, demographic issues, and other security related issues. The documents included relate to India and its neighbors– Pakistan, China, Tibet, Burma, and others. The preface to the 2010 edition notes that no analysis has been included. The preface also states that where full length treaties have not been included due to "reasons of space," summaries or extracts are included. The documents are arranged by region/topic, then chronologically.

Note: There is also a 2002 edition of this work.

Diplomatic Documents

9 ANNUAL REPORT

India, Ministry of External Affairs. (Ministry of External Affairs, New Delhi, 1950–)

See entry under Treaty Indexes, *supra*.

10 BILATERAL/MULTILATERAL DOCUMENTS

URL: http://www.liiofindia.org/in/other/treaties/INTSer/.

Summary: This site from the Ministry of External Affairs contains links to bilateral and multilateral diplomatic documents, including treaties and agreements, diplomatic joint statements and exchanges of notes, minutes, press statements, fact sheets, and more. It includes documents from 1947 to the present. Documents can be browsed by month and year. The site is also searchable, either globally, or by limiting to month and year.

11 DOCUMENTS ON INDIA'S FOREIGN POLICY

(Macmillan Co. of India, Delhi, 1972–)

Summary: This is an annual series prepared by the Diplomatic Studies of Division of the School of International Studies, Jawaharlal University, New Delhi. It includes official documents that cover India's relations with foreign countries during the year of the published volume. The documents are arranged first by region or category (e.g. India and World Affairs, India and the Subcontinent, India and Asia, etc.), then chronologically. Documents are collected from *Foreign Affairs Record,*[39] newspapers, periodicals, and various other governmental organizations.

Index: The annual volumes all contain indexes, but they may be organized differently depending on the volume. The indexes in some volumes are arranged alphabetically by country, and in others, by topic.

Note: Appears to have ceased publication after the 1974 volume.

12 FOREIGN AFFAIRS RECORD

India. External Publicity Division.

---

39 *See* no. 12, *infra*.

(Ministry of External Affairs: External Affairs Division, Government of India, New Delhi, 1955–).

Summary: A monthly periodical compiling selected official statements, speeches, press releases, and other documents pertaining to India's foreign affairs. The annexes also include treaties and other agreements between India and other nations, though it is not clear that these are covered comprehensively. Each monthly volume is organized by topic or country, depending on the particular case.

Note: Appears to have ceased publication with Vol. 48, January 2002.

Note: Also available from 1955–1999 via the Ministry of External Affairs website in PDF: http://mealib.nic.in/?2588?000. The online content appears to be the same as the print, MEA Library or elsewhere."

13 FOREIGN POLICY OF INDIA; TEXTS OF DOCUMENTS, 1947–1964
Parliament of India, House of the People.
(Lok Sabha Secretariat, New Delhi, 1966).

Summary: This monograph contains treaties, statements, and other documents issued or entered into by the government of India between the period of 1947 and 1964. The book is organized by type of document – Section I covering treaties; Section II covering Agreements; and Sections III-V covering other types of documents pertaining to the foreign policy of India. The entries are organized alphabetically by the country with which India has communicated or entered into an agreement with.

14 MINISTRY OF EXTERNAL AFFAIRS, BILATERAL/MULTILATERAL DOCUMENTS
URL: http://www.mea.gov.in/bilateral-documents.htm?53/Bilateral/Multilateral_Documents.

Summary: This site contains statements and declarations of government officials, lists of documents, and the full text of Memorandums of Understanding and other agreements to which India is a party. Coverage is from 1947 to the present.

15 OFFICIAL SPOKESMAN'S STATEMENTS AND PRESS RELEASES
India, Ministry of External Affairs. (Ministry of External Affairs, External Publicity Division, New Delhi, 1900s).

Summary: This quarterly publication contains press releases, statements from the official spokesperson for the Ministry of Affairs and from other ministers, texts of letters between heads of state and other high level governmental officials, and texts of or excerpts from other diplomatic documents.

Note: The latest issue published appears to be July-September, 2001.

16 WHITE PAPER

India. Ministry of External Affairs. (Ministry of External Affairs, New Delhi, 1959–?).

Summary: This irregular publication contains notes, memoranda, letters exchanged, and agreements signed between the governments of India and China.

Note: Begins with Vol.1, 1954. Latest volume published seems to be volume 14, 1967/1968.

Yearbooks and Digests of State Practice

17 INDIAN FOREIGN POLICY: ANNUAL SURVEY

Shri Ram Sharma. (Sterling Publishers; New Delhi : New York, 1971–2000).

Summary: This annual survey examines Indian foreign policy and the world political situation from India's perspective. Each of the volumes is written entirely by a single author, Shri Ram Sharma. Typical areas of focus include India's relations with her neighbors, and important treaties, international agreements and other interactions with nations of the world and international organizations such as the United Nations. Primary documents, such as treaties, are summarized and analyzed in a narrative format, and significant excerpts are usually not included. Volumes conclude with reflections on significant events in the international arena affecting India for that year. Each volume generally includes an appendix with a "Chronology of Major World Events."

Index: Each volume includes a subject index.

18 INDIAN YEARBOOK OF INTERNATIONAL AFFAIRS

University of Madras. Indian Study Group of International Affairs.
(Madras: University of Madras, 1952–).

Summary: Contains articles on comparative law and international affairs, surveys of Indian cases dealing with international law, and book reviews.

Index: Each volume contains a topical index.

Note: Irregular; appears to have ceased publication in 1986.

19 YEARBOOK ON INDIA'S FOREIGN POLICY
(New Delhi: Sage Publications, 1983–).

Summary: This is an annual publication, covering the period of July to June each year. It is divided into three sections. According the "Policy Statement" at the beginning of the book, the first section contains a comprehensive review of India's foreign policy over a twelve month period; the second section includes analytical essays written by journalists, scholars, diplomats, and other professionals, devoted to specific regions or countries that significantly affected India's foreign policy; and the third section contains important statistics and documents (or excerpts therefrom) relevant to India's foreign policy.

Ireland

Alison A. Shea

Historical Background

The present day Republic of Ireland, or *Éire*, has a rich and colorful history. Although an independent Irish government began acting on the global stage as early as 1919,[1] for purposes of this entry, the current Irish state came into being in 1922 following the Anglo-Irish Treaty[2] and the Irish Free State (Constitution) Act.[3] However, the 1922 Constitution did not specifically deal with international relations[4] and thus current Irish state practice is governed by the 1937 Constitution (*Bunreacht na hÉireann*).[5]

Issues of Treaty Succession

The issue of treaty succession in Ireland follows a similar course as many other former colonial territories of Great Britain.[6] The Irish Free State was admitted as a member of the League of Nations on September 10, 1923,[7] thus granting it "official" international status.[8] The Irish Free State was able to use its

1 John Doyle, Michael Kennedy, and Ben Tonra, *Theories, Concepts and Sources, in* Irish Foreign Policy 22–23 (Ben Tonra et al. eds., 2012).

2 Articles of Agreement for a Treaty Between Great Britain and Ireland (signed December 6, 1921), *in* 1 Documents on Irish Foreign Policy Sec. 4, NAI DE 2/304/1, *available at* http://www.difp.ie/documents/volume1/vol1_treaty.pdf.

3 13 Geo. 5 sess. 2, c. 1 (1922) (Eng).

4 Mahon Hayes and James Kingston, *Ireland in International Law: The Pursuit of Sovereignty and Independence, in* Irish Foreign Policy 71–72 (Ben Tonra et al. eds., 2012). This chapter, and indeed the entire book, provide a more in-depth discussion of many of the issues of state practice in Ireland and should be consulted in addition to this entry.

5 Irish Constitution (Bunreacht na hÉireann), *available at* https://www.constitution.ie/Documents/Bhunreacht_na_hEireann_web.pdf [hereinafter Ir. Const. (1937)].

6 For discussion on the acquisition of international legal personality by former colonial territories of Great Britain, including the Balfour Declaration, see chapters "Canada" and "South Africa".

7 4 L.N. OJ 1268 (1923).

8 For a more extensive discussion of the Irish Free State's admission to the League of Nations and its subsequent activities therein, *see* Michael Kennedy, Ireland and the League of Nations 1919–1946 (1996).

 | DOI 10.1163/9789004272224_017

membership to further assert its sovereignty when it registered the Anglo-Irish Treaty with the League as effectively being a treaty concluded between two internationally recognized persons.[9]

Following the creation of the Irish Free State, in 1925 the United States Department of State inquired whether the creation of the Free State had any effect on the applicability of a treaty to Ireland, who had previously been excluded from the treaty, signed in 1899, as it specifically contained a clause stating that it was not to be applicable to colonies or foreign possessions of Great Britain. The British Foreign Office replied that the creation of the Free State did not change the applicability of the 1899 treaty to Ireland.[10]

In 1933, the Irish Prime Minister, Éamon de Valera, declared that the position of the Irish Free State with regard to treaties and conventions concluded between Great Britain and other countries was:

> based upon the general international practice in the matter when a new State is established. When a new State comes into existence, which formerly formed part of an older State, its acceptance or otherwise of the treaty relationships of the older State is a matter for the new State to determine by express declaration, or by conduct (in the case of each individual treaty) as considerations of policy may require. The practice here has been to accept the position created by commercial and administrative treaties and conventions of the late United Kingdom, until such time as the individual treaties and conventions themselves are terminated or amended. Occasion has then been taken, where desirable, to conclude separate engagement with the States concerned.[11]

Further, unlike many other former territories of Great Britain, the Irish Free State was a "reluctant member" of the Commonwealth.[12] Neither the 1921 Treaty nor the 1922 Constitution contains any provision indicating that the

---

9 Constitution of the Free State, Ir.-Gr. Brit.,Dec. 6, 1921, 26 L.N.T.S. 10. *See also* Hayes and Kingston, *supra* note 4, at 73.

10 Treaties, 5 Hackworth Digest § 512, at 369–370 (1943).

11 Ceisteanna—Questions. Oral Answers. – The Saorstát and American Treaties (July 11, 1933), 48 Parliamentary Debates 2058–2059 *available at:* http://debates.oireachtas.ie/dail/1933/07/11/00004.asp.

12 Michael Kennedy, *The Foundation and Consolidation of Irish Foreign Policy: 1919–45, in* Irish Foreign Policy 24–25 (Ben Tonra et al. eds., 2012).

Irish Free State would be considered a Dominion[13] and Ireland officially severed its ties to the Dominion in 1949.[14]

Treaty Ratification and Implementation

International relations in Ireland are governed by Article 29 of the Irish Constitution.[15] Article 29.4 states that the execution of international agreements falls within the power of the executive.[16] In Irish treaty practice, the state must be in a position to meet the obligations under the terms of an international agreement to which it binds itself from the moment it enters into force.[17]

Article 29.5.1 provides that every international agreement to which the State becomes a party shall be laid before the lower house of the Irish parliament (*Dáil Éireann*). Agreements and conventions of a technical and administrative character are excluded from this requirement by article 29.5.3, it is the practice of the Irish Department of Foreign Affairs to lay such agreements also.[18]

Ireland is a dualist system in that international rules, including treaties, must be incorporated into domestic law before they have legal effect on the national level.[19] With specific reference to treaties, Article 29.6 of the Irish Constitution states that no international agreement may form part of the domestic law of the state, save for the determination of the Irish parliament (*Oireachtas*).[20] The necessity of incorporation of treaties into the Irish legal system was at the forefront of the legal argument made in the case *In re Ó Láighléis* where the litigant attempted to rely on the European Convention of Human Rights before it was incorporated into domestic law.[21] However, in

---

13 Extracts from the general preliminary memorandum by John J. Hearne for the Irish delegation to the Conference on the Operation of Dominion Legislation (July 15,1929), *in* 3 Documents on Irish Foreign Policy Doc. No. 241 (2002).

14 Ireland Act, 1949, 12, 13 & 14 Geo. 6, c. 41

15 Ir. Const. (1937), art. 29.

16 *See* "Evidence of State Practice", *infra*, for further discussion.

17 *Treaties – Meeting our Obligations*, Department of Foreign Affairs and Trade, https://www.dfa.ie/our-role-policies/international-priorities/international-law/treaties/.

18 *Treaties – Constitutional Requirements*, Department of Foreign Affairs and Trade, https://www.dfa.ie/our-role-policies/international-priorities/international-law/treaties/.

19 Raymond Byrne and J. Paul McCutcheon, The Irish Legal System 809–810 (5th ed. 2009).

20 Ir. Const. (1937), art. 29.6. *See also* J.M. Kelly, The Irish Constitution 547–549 (4th ed., 2003).

21 *In re Ó Láighléis* [1960] IR 93.

practice most treaties to which Ireland becomes a party are never incorporated because they relate solely to the state's rights and duties with respect to other states, or because they are human rights treaties where the rights are already protected in Irish law.[22]

A member of the European Union since 1973,[23] Ireland is bound by the legal framework governing all EU member states.[24] Articles 29.4.2 details the relationship between Ireland and international groups for purposes of international cooperation,[25] with specific reference to European maters in Articles 29.4.3–9.

Evidence of State Practice

Article 29.4.1 of the Irish Constitution states that power to conclude international agreements is the function of the executive of Ireland.[26] In practice, where an international agreement is concerned with a particular policy area, the Minister with primary responsibility for that area will undertake the relevant negotiations together with the Minister for Foreign Affairs and Trade.[27] Other parties may be authorized to undertake negotiations only under an Instrument of Full Powers executed under the seal and signature of one of the authorized office holders, but negotiations are most generally done by the Minister for Foreign Affairs and Trade.[28]

The Department of Foreign Affairs also has a legal division, whose principal functions are to provide advice and legal information, particularly on matters of public international law, human rights law and European Union law, to the Minister for Foreign Affairs; to represent Ireland in international legal proceedings including the European Court of Human Rights, and the International Court of Justice and in international fora such as the Sixth Committee of the

---

22 Byrne and McCutcheon, *supra* note 19.

23 Treaty of Accession of Denmark, Ireland and the United Kingdom, January 22, 1972, 1972 O.J. (L 73) 5.

24 For discussion on Ireland and the EU, *see, e.g.*, Ireland in the EU, Department of Foreign Affairs and Trade, https://www.dfa.ie/our-role-policies/ireland-in-the-eu/; David Fennelly, *Crotty's Long Shadow: the European Union, the United Nations and the Changing Framework of Ireland's International Relations, in* The Consitution of Ireland: Perspectives and Prospects (Eoin Carolan, ed., 2012).

25 Ir. Const. (1937), art. 29.4.2.

26 Ir. Const. (1937), art. 29.4.1.

27 *Treaties – Full Powers*, Department of Foreign Affairs and Trade, https://www.dfa.ie/our-role-policies/international-priorities/international-law/treaties/.

28 Id.

United Nations General Assembly, the Assembly of States Parties of the International Criminal Court, the bodies established under the UN Convention of the Law of the Sea and relevant Council of Europe and EU bodies; and to represent Ireland and to assist in negotiations concerned with international legal matters.[29] The Legal Division is also responsible for publication and registration of treaties.

For more information on the role of state practice in Ireland, including Ireland's experience with international legal issues as well as the relationship between Irish law and international law, researchers should consult the relevant chapters in *Biehler on International Law*.[30] Researchers wishing to extensively review primary sources relating to Irish foreign affairs will be able to do so at the National Archives of Ireland,[31] and should refer to an excellent explanatory guide found in Chapter 1 of *Irish Foreign Policy*.[32]

Annotated Bibliography of Sources

General Treaty Collections

1 TREATY SERIES
Department of External Affairs. (Dublin: The Stationary Office, 1930–2001).
URL: https://www.dfa.ie/our-role-policies/international-priorities/international-law/find-a-treaty/.

Summary: Issued as individual pamphlets. Print ceased in 2001 and is continued exclusively by PDFs issued online through the Department of Foreign Affairs website.

Note: All treaties published in the Irish Treaty Series since 2002 are available in PDF through the Irish Treaty Series Database. A limited number of selected treaties published in earlier years, including the full run from 1998–2002, are also available on this site. The search function allows searches by either title, party, or Irish Treaty Series number, as well as the ability to browse by year.

Note: At head of title, 1930–1937, no. 2: Saorstát Éireann; 1937, no. 3–1947: Éire

---

29 *International Law*, Department of Foreign Affairs and Trade, https://www.dfa.ie/our-role-policies/international-priorities/international-law/.

30 Roslyn Fuller, Biehler on International Law: An Irish Persective (2nd ed., 2013).

31 *See* http://www.nationalarchives.ie for further information.

32 Doyle, et. al, *supra* note 1, at 12–17.

Treaty Indexes

2 GENERAL INDEX TO THE TREATY SERIES

Minister for Foreign Affairs (Dublin: The Stationary Office, 1954–1994).

Summary: Issued as part of the Treaty Series in periodic updates: *General Index to the Treaty Series, 1930–1953*, I.T.S. No. 14/1954; *General Index to the Treaty Series 1954–1960 in continuation of Treaty Series No. 14 of 1954 and List of Treaties 1930–1960*, I.T.S. No. 4/1962; *General Index to the Treaty Series 1961–65 in continuation of Treaty Series Nos. 14 of 1954 and 4 of 1962 and List of Treaties 1961–65*, I.T.S. No. 10/1967; *General Index to the Treaty Series 1966–1970 in continuation of Treaty Series No. 4 of 1962*, I.T.S. No. 5/1975; *General Index to the Treaty Series 1971–1976 in continuation of Treaty Series 5 of 1975*, I.T.S. No. 2/1978; *General Index to the Treaty Series 1977–1994, in continuation of Treaty Series No. 2 of 1978*, I.T.S. No. 21/1994.

Note: A chronological index was also issued: *Chronological Index to the Treaty Series 1977–1986 in continuation of Treaty Series No. 2 of 1978*, I.T.S. No. 11/1986.

Note: Unfortunately, at this time none of these indexes are available electronically through the Irish Treaty Series Database.

3 IRISH TREATY SERIES DATABASE

URL: https://www.dfa.ie/our-role-policies/international-priorities/international-law/find-a-treaty/.

Summary: An itemized listing of every treaty published in the Irish Treaty Series is listed by year in this Database. The Database is also searchable by title of agreement, as well as by party or Irish Treaty Series number.

Topical and Selected Treaty Publications

4 TAX TREATIES

Office of the Revenue Commissioners.

URL: http://www.revenue.ie/en/practitioner/law/tax-treaties.html.

Summary: A listing of the 69 treaties on double taxation signed by Ireland with other countries, organized by country name. Information at the top of the page on recent developments helps assure currency of the documents below. Some treaties are included as a PDF document while others only exist as an HTML document.

Note: Site also provides some additional guidance on domestic and EU legal instruments that should be consulted when assessing issues of double taxation.

Note: Status table and corresponding Statutory Instrument number listing available at http://www.revenue.ie/en/practitioner/law/double/double-taxation-agreements.html.

5 IRISH TAX TREATIES

Susan Keegan, ed. (Dublin: Butterworths, 1996–).

Summary: Originally issued as a looseleaf, now issued annually as a stand-alone volume, includes interpretation agreements and commentary, constitutional and statutory basis for treaties, synoptic tables on treaties on income and capital, text of the treaties on income and capital limited tax treaties, treaties on inheritances and gifts, tax information exchange agreements, and EU and International Agreements.

Note: Coverage appears for about 50 countries and territories with whom Ireland has agreements.

Note: Now published by Bloomsbury Publishing (London); most recent volume issued was 2011–2012, edited by Mary Walsh, 2271 p.

Diplomatic Documents

6 DOCUMENTS ON IRISH FOREIGN POLICY

Ronan Fanning, ed. (Dublin: Royal Irish Academy, 1998–) 7 vols.

URL: http://www.difp.ie/browse-volumes/.

Summary: Extensive collection of documents selected by a team of editors from the Department of Foreign Affairs archives. Current content covers Volume 1, 1919–1922; Volume II 1923–1926; Volume III, 1926–1932; Volume IV, 1932–1936; Volume V, 1937–1939; Volume VI, 1939–1941; Volume VII, 1941–1945. Documents are presented in chronological order based on date of dispatch and are reproduced exactly as exactly as possible. Some documents may contain excisions due to current diplomatic negotiations.

Index: Electronic version is full-text searchable.

Note: The electronic version of the documents are re-formatted and thus do not appear as original PDFs.

Note: Anglo-Irish Treaty negotiations available in eBook format: http://www.difp.ie/ebook/default.asp.

7 IRELAND TODAY

Department of Foreign Affairs. (Dublin: Information Section, Dept. of Foreign Affairs, 1974–1989).

Summary: Semi-regular (weekly until 1963, then irregular) bulletin of the Department of Foreign Affairs which highlights recent developments in Irish foreign policy. Republishes selected speeches and statements relating to foreign policy, as well as details of meetings and foreign state visits.

Index: Cumulative yearly index issued irregularly.

Note: Continues "Ireland" (1949–1952), "Eire: Ireland" (1953–1973).

8 STATEMENTS BY IRELAND ON INTERNATIONAL LAW ISSUES
Department of Foreign Affairs.
URL: https://www.dfa.ie/our-role-policies/international-priorities/international-law/statements-by-ireland-on-international-law/.

Summary: This new sub-site of the Irish Department of Foreign Affairs website provides recent evidence of Irish state practice in various international fora. This site collects links to various locations where statements and other evidence can be found, including the Permanent Mission of Ireland to the United Nations, the UN's International Law Commission, other international organizations, as well as speeches made by the Minister of Foreign Affairs and Trade.

Yearbooks and Digest of State Practice

9 IRISH YEARBOOK OF INTERNATIONAL LAW
Jean Allain and Siobhán Mullally, eds. (Oxford: Hart, 2006–).

Summary: Annual publication includes scholarly articles on issues of international law generally. Includes Correspondents Reports on Irish practice in a variety of topical areas such as Ireland in International Law Abroad, Ireland in the European Union, and North-South Developments. Each volume also includes selected foreign policy documents such as speeches and statements, annual reports of the Department of Foreign Affairs, and official submissions to international organizations.

Note: A listing of all volume contents available at http://www.hartjournals.co.uk/iyil/contents.html.

Note: Title in Irish is *Bliainiris Éireannach an Dlí Idirnáisiúnta.*

Israel

Talia Einhorn

Historical Background

On 14 May 1948, upon the expiration of the British Mandate, the provisional State Council, the predecessor of the *Knesset* (Israel's Parliament), declared the establishment of Israel as a Jewish state in the Land of Israel.[1] The following exposition provides a concise history of the changes of sovereignty, with particular emphasis on the main pertinent events that have taken place since the beginning of the 20th Century, which are crucial to the discussion of State practice resulting from the changes of sovereignty, the practice regarding succession during the British Mandate, and Israel's practice regarding succession.

After the Jewish people had lost their sovereignty over the territory of Israel in 70 CE (Christian Era), the territory was governed in turn by the Romans and Byzantines (until 638 CE), Arab Moslems (638–1099 CE), Christian Crusaders (1099–1291 CE), Mamluks (1250–1516 CE) and Ottomans (1517–1917 CE). Following the demise of the Ottoman Empire, a British Mandate was envisaged for Palestine in the Treaty of Sèvres, signed by the Allies and the Ottoman Government on 20 August 1920. On 24 July 1922, the League of Nations decided upon the terms of the Palestine Mandate, and imposed on the Mandatory Power the responsibility for the establishment in Palestine of a national home for the Jewish People. Since Palestine was under Turkish rule, Turkey's consent was necessary. Turkey gave its consent in the Treaty of Lausanne of 23 July 1923. By Article 15, Turkey renounced rights to the territories outside its borders, as laid down in the Treaty, the future of these territories "being settled or to be settled by the parties concerned". Since the decision on Palestine had already been taken on 24 July 1922, with the final drafting of the Palestine Mandate by the League of Nations, the future of that territory had been settled.

The preamble of the Mandate confirmed that "recognition has thereby been given to the historical connection of the Jewish people with Palestine and to

1 1 *Official Gazette of the Provisional Government of Israel* 3, 14 May 1948. Following the Official Gazette, the term 'Land of Israel' is used hereinafter to describe the land occupied by the state of Israel.

 | DOI 10.1163/9789004272224_018

the grounds for reconstituting their national home in that country". Article 2 made the Mandatory "responsible for placing the country under such political, administrative and economic conditions as will secure the establishment of the Jewish national home, as laid down in the preamble, and the development of self-governing institutions, and also for safeguarding the civil and religious rights of all the inhabitants of Palestine, irrespective of race and religion". Article 6 required Great Britain to facilitate Jewish immigration to Palestine and encourage close settlement of the land, including State lands and waste lands not required for public purposes. Article 7 made Great Britain responsible for enacting a nationality law that would facilitate the acquisition of Palestinian citizenship by Jews who took up their permanent residence in Palestine. Originally, the Mandate extended to both banks of the Jordan River, however shortly prior to its ratification, Article 25 was added, empowering Great Britain, with the consent of the Council of the League of Nations, to postpone or withhold application of the Mandate provisions to the territories lying between the Jordan and the eastern Boundary of Palestine. Subsequently, Britain declared the provisions concerning the Jewish national home and the holy places inapplicable with respect to Trans-Jordan, i.e., the territory east of the Jordan River (almost 80% of the original Palestine Mandate territory). In 1928, Britain entered an autonomy agreement with respect to that area with the Emir of Transjordan. That territory remained under the Palestine Mandate until obtaining its independence on 22 March 1946, when the autonomous Emirate became the Kingdom of Jordan.

The Palestine Mandate was considered an 'A' Class Mandate, albeit with distinctive features, as it sought to establish a national Jewish home rather than independent statehood of the local population.[2] It was assumed that the territories of these 'A' Class Mandates were unaffected by Ottoman treaties and that the Mandatory had limited powers of treaty-making with respect to them.[3] Treaties concluded by the Mandatory prior to the establishment of the Mandate did not apply to the territory of the Mandate automatically, but required an act of extension by the Mandatory, emphasizing the fact that the Mandatory was not the sovereign, but just the holder of the land in trust. Article 8 of the Palestine Mandate provided that the capitulations formerly enjoyed in the Ottoman Empire no longer applied in Palestine, but that, to the

---

2 *Cf.* J. Stoyanovsky, The Mandate for Palestine 40–47 (London: Longmans, Green and Co 1928) (with further references).

3 O'Connell, 2 State Succession in Municipal Law and International Law 150 (Cambridge: Cambridge University Press, 1967),

extent that the Powers that enjoyed these privileges on 1 August 1914 had renounced their right to their re-establishment, or agreed to their temporary non-application, those privileges and immunities would be re-established immediately upon the expiration of the Mandate.[4]

Articles 10, 12, 18, 19 and 20 of the British Mandate conferred some degree of treaty-making power upon the Mandatory (i.e., His Britannic Majesty, according to the fourth recital of the Preamble to the Mandate) acting for Palestine (only in Article 18 a very limited treaty-making power regarding customs agreements was conferred upon the Administration of Palestine itself acting on the advice of the Mandatory).

Article 10 extended British extradition treaties to apply in the territory and authorized the Mandatory to conclude additional ones. Under Article 12, the Mandatory was entrusted with the control of the foreign relations of Palestine.[5] Two types of commercial agreements and treaties were concluded under Article 18: (1) agreements of general character concluded by the United Kingdom that were made applicable to Palestine; and (2) agreements concerning the particular problems of the relations between Palestine and other Middle Eastern States.[6] It has been noted that the Mandatory did not follow a uniform policy regarding the registration of the latter treaties with the Secretariat of the League of Nations.[7]

Article 19 required the Mandatory to adhere, on behalf of the Administration of Palestine, to any general international conventions already existing, or which may be concluded subsequently, with the approval of the League of Nations, respecting the slave traffic, the traffic in arms and ammunition, or the traffic in drugs, or relating to commercial equality, freedom of transit and navigation, aerial navigation and postal, telegraphic and wireless communication or literary, artistic or industrial property. Article 20 required the Mandatory to cooperate in the execution of any common policy adopted by the League of

---

4 This provision was required by the United States, which contended that its extraterritorial privileges in the former Ottoman territories continued until expressly renounced, as if those capitulations were a servitude attached permanently to the territory. Consequently, the Palestine Mandate, as well as the mandate of Syria, just suspended these capitulations for the period of the mandate. *Cf.* QUINCY WRIGHT, MANDATES UNDER THE LEAGUE OF NATIONS 483 (New York: Greenwood, 1968, a reprint of the 1930 edition).

5 A list of the treaties concluded under this provision is provided in "Law of Treaties"–Replies from Governments to Questionnaires of the International Law Commission, UN Doc A/CN.4/19, [1950] 2 Y.B. INT'L L. COMM'N. 206, 208a.

6 Id. at 208b.

7 Id.

Nations for preventing and combating disease, including diseases of plants and animals.[8]

The termination of the British Mandate was recommended, "as soon as possible but in any case not later than 1 August 1948", by UN General Assembly Resolution 181(II) of 29 November 1947.[9] The Resolution recommended the partition of the Land of Israel into two states, a Jewish state and an Arab one, linked in an economic union. The Partition Plan required each of the successor States to sign a declaration (Part I C of the Resolution) that, among other undertakings, it would be bound "by all international agreements and conventions, both general and special, to which Palestine has become a party. Subject to any right of denunciation provided for therein, such agreements and conditions shall be respected by the State throughout the period for which they were concluded".

On 21 January 1948, Great Britain declared that the Mandate would terminate on 15 May 1948, but stated that it would retain undivided control over the whole of Palestine until that date, rather than transfer control gradually, as planned by the United Nations. The Palestine Act, 1948,[10] provided for the end of British jurisdiction in Palestine on 15 May 1948, as well as the repeal of enactments referring to Palestine, and for the cessation of application to Palestine of any enactment. The Act underlined that their repeal would not affect the question of the continuity of the enactments concerned as part of the domestic law of Palestine.

Upon withdrawal of the British forces on 15 May 1948, shortly after Israel's Declaration of Independence, all four neighboring Arab States, as well as Iraq and Tunisia, invaded Israel. The Partition Resolution called upon the UN Security Council "to determine as a threat to the peace, breach of the peace or act of aggression, in accordance with Article 39 of the Charter, any attempt to alter by force the settlement envisaged by this resolution". But the Security Council considered that it had no power to enforce the implementation of the Assembly's recommendations. Consequently, the Resolution was never fully implemented and the Declaration (Part I C of the Resolution) was not made. The Mandate was terminated by Great Britain, without any arrangement

8 A list of treaties concluded under Articles 19 and 20 is provided in id. at 209–210, which refers further to a more detailed list provided in "A Survey of Palestine", prepared in December 1945–January 1946, by the Government of Palestine, vol. 2, pp. 963–966 and 751ff.

9 UN Doc A/516, resolving to adopt the report of the *ad hoc* committee contained in UN Doc A/AC 14/34.

10 11 & 12 Geo. VI, c. 27.

having been made for the disposal of the assets and liabilities of the Government of Great Britain. Israel came into existence by its own act, the Declaration of Independence, on 14 May 1948.[11]

Issues of Treaty Succession

With respect to the 'A' mandates, it was thought originally that the former mandated territories would be bound by international obligations undertaken by their mandatories during their 'infancy'.[12] The Permanent Mandates Commission considered that conventions to which the mandatories had acceded in accordance with the terms of the mandates themselves would remain in force after independence, but those extended incidentally to the mandated territories would lapse.[13] Lord Lugard, however, proposed that all treaties made by the Mandatory on behalf of the territory remain in force until denounced, by the new State, a proposal which was adopted by the Rapporteur.[14] The Commission drew up a memorandum "general conditions to be fulfilled before the mandate regime can be brought to an end in respect of a country placed under that regime".[15] One of the conditions was "maintenance in force for their respective duration and subject to the right of denunciation by the parties concerned of their international conventions, both general and special, to which, during the Mandate, the Mandatory Power acceded on behalf of the mandated territory".[16] In practice, however, since Syria and Lebanon became independent under abnormal conditions, at a time when the League was ineffective, supervision of treaty continuity was not possible.[17]

The Supreme Court of Palestine dealt with this matter in the case of *Abdalla Ibrahim Shehadeh v. Commissioner of Prisons, Jerusalem and Superintendent of Central Prisons, Acre*.[18] The case concerned an application for *habeas corpus* of a person whose extradition to Lebanon was requested. The applicant argued

11 O'Connell, *supra* n. 3, vol. II–International Relations, p. 155.

12 Angelo Piero Sereni, "La représentation en droit international", 73 Recueil des Cours 109 (1948).

13 League of Nations Permanent Mandates Commission, Minutes of Sessions 18–21, at 202 (1930–1931).

14 Id. at 208.

15 12 L.N. OJ 2055 (1931).

16 Id. at 2058; Annex, p. 2177, pt. II, para (g).

17 O'Connell, *supra* note 3 at 152.

18 14 PLR (1947) 461.

that the provisional agreement of 1921, between Syria and Palestine for the extradition of offenders, had lapsed because in Lebanon the Government was changed from a Mandatory to a Republic. The Supreme Court rejected the application on the ground that changes in the government, or in the constitution, of a state have no such effect on the continued validity of the state's international obligations. As long as the previous government was vested with legal sovereignty that enabled it to conclude the treaty, that treaty binds the successor government *unless the latter abrogates it* (emphasis added). The Court concluded that the treaty was therefore still effective between the Lebanese Republic and Palestine.

It has been pointed out that, in cases of violent disruption of the legal order, the categories of treaties that are not susceptible to succession are wider than those in the case of orderly transfer of sovereignty.[19]

The situation in the case of Palestine was complicated also by the lack of systematic publication in Palestine of the texts of the treaties whose application was extended by the Mandatory to Palestine. In the case of multilateral treaties, notice was given to the depositary Government, or to the Secretary-General of the League of Nations or the United Nations, as the case may be.[20] Even the official texts of treaties that were made especially for Palestine were not published in Palestine. Information regarding Israel's foreign relations was included in annual reports submitted by the Mandatory Government to the Council of the League of Nations on the Administration of Palestine and Transjordan, but it was not clear whether this information was complete. To the extent that these treaties required changes in Israeli domestic law, two alternative modes of implementation were used. First, such legislation could be enacted as an Imperial Statute by the Imperial Parliament at Westminster, usually containing a standard-form section enabling its provisions to be extended to British Colonies and other foreign territories. Orders extending such a statute to Palestine were usually published in the Palestine Gazette (e.g., the Carriage by Air (Parties to the Convention) Order, 1937). But, whether published or not, they became part of the law of Palestine, publication not being of the essence for their validity.[21] Second, an Ordinance could be enacted by the local legislative body (e.g., the Carriage of Goods by Sea Ordinance, 1926).

---

19 O'CONNELL, *supra* note 3; *Shabtai Rosenne*, "The Effect of Change of Sovereignty upon Municipal Law", 1950 BRIT. Y.B. INT'L L. 267, 272f.

20 "Law of Treaties"–Replies from Governments to Questionnaires of the International Law Commission, UN Doc A/CN.4/19, [1950] 2 Y.B. INT'L L. COMM'N. 206, 210.

21 *Jeanette Sara Benjamin v. Commissioner for Migration and Statistics*, 8 PLR (1941) 327.

After the Mandate had ended, the British Foreign Office furnished two lists of its own compilation, which contained altogether 140 items. Subsequently, the texts of the actual treaties were provided as well. However, establishing precisely to which treaties Palestine was actually a party turned out to be difficult.[22] Some treaties had undergone several amendments, without it being made clear which of those applied to Palestine. Sometimes the extension to Palestine was the result of an *ad hoc* arrangement, which might or might not have contained appropriate modifications in the terms of the treaty. Some treaties were applicable to Palestine by virtue of its being under British jurisdiction.

After a thorough, although inconclusive, examination of the treaty position of Palestine, the Government of Israel concluded that it could be said that, on the basis of generally recognized principles of international law, Israel was a new personality, not automatically bound by the treaties to which Palestine had been a party and that its future treaty relations with foreign powers would be regulated directly between Israel and the foreign states concerned.[23] In reaching this conclusion, the Government noted that Israel was not asked to make the Declaration contained in Resolution 181(II), and that, in accordance with General Assembly Resolution 273(III) of 11 May 1949, Israel was admitted as a Member of the United Nations without the said Declaration having been made.[24] On this basis, Israel conducted negotiations and established its international relations with the United Kingdom and with various foreign governments, following the termination of the British Mandate.

In line with this conclusion, the Government of Israel acceded *de novo* to a number of international treaties, regardless of whether or not Palestine had been a party to them.[25] One example concerns the General Agreement on Tariffs and Trade (GATT), which had been applied to Palestine provisionally at Geneva on 30 October 1947, when it was planned that Israel would conclude a customs union with the Arab state that would be established if Resolution 181(II) were implemented. The United Kingdom informed the United Nations Palestine Commission that it proposed to apply GATT provisionally to Palestine, and the Commission notified the United Kingdom that it had no objection to such action. Consequently, GATT was applied provisionally and the Customs Tariff and Exemption Ordinance No. 24, 1947, was amended to

---

22 "Law of Treaties"–Replies from Governments to Questionnaires of the International Law Commission, UN Doc A/CN.4/19, *Yearbook of the ILC* (1950), vol. II, pp. 206–218, at pp. 214–215.

23 Id. at 215, para. 23.

24 Id.

25 A list of such treaties is given id. at 216, para. 26.

conform to Palestine's GATT obligations.[26] Israel did not consider itself bound by these obligations and informed the Contracting Parties accordingly during the GATT Annecy Meeting in May 1949. Subsequently, Israel raised some of the customs tariffs which had been reduced in 1948.[27] Eventually, Israel became a Contracting Party to GATT in 1962.

The situation was different with respect to treaties that were implemented in Palestine by Order in Council or by the enactment of Ordinances. Section 11 of the Law and Administration Ordinance, 5708–1948,[28] the first Statute enacted by the Provisional State Council, established the principle that "The Law which existed in Palestine on . . . 14 May 1948 shall remain in force, so far as there is nothing therein repugnant to this Ordinance or to other laws which may be enacted by, or on behalf of, the Provisional Council of State, and subject to such modifications as may result from the establishment of the State and its authorities". Consequently, when Israel became independent, all these orders and ordinances remained in force until their operation was modified. Most of these orders and ordinances were not enabling acts relating to existing treaties, but were legislative acts implementing the treaties directly in Israeli domestic law.

There were however cases in which new treaties had to be made.[29] The operation of the Extradition Ordinance[30] depended upon the prior existence of an international arrangement between His Majesty and the foreign state requesting the extradition, as well as a proclamation of the High Commissioner in each case. Since Israel did not consider itself bound by the treaties to which Palestine was a party, the international arrangements that enabled the High Commissioner to issue the various proclamations had lapsed. Consequently, even though the Ordinance remained in force, these treaties became ineffective in practice. To an inquiry made by the United States, requesting clarification as to whether the Anglo-American Treaty of Extradition continued to apply between Israel and the United States, Israel responded in August 1949, that, "it is the view of the Government of Israel that, generally speaking, treaties to which Palestine was a party, or which the Mandatory Government had applied to Palestine, are not in force in relation to the Government of Israel".[31]

---

26 Palestine Gazette 1655, Supp. 2, p. 471 (25 March 1948).

27 *Cf.*, e.g., Order concerning Changes in Customs Tariff (No. 3), 5709–1949, issued by the Minister of Finance on 9 June 1949, Reshumot (Israel Gazette), Kovetz Ha-Takkanot (official compilation of regulations), 10 June 1949, p. 237.

28 Official Gazette of the Provisional Government of Israel, No. 2, 21 May 1948, Supp. 1, p. 1.

29 *Cf.* O'CONNELL, *supra* note 3 at 157, with further references.

30 DRAYTON, 1 LAWS OF PALESTINE 677 (1934).

31 Treaties, 2 Whiteman DIGEST §10 at 972.

Another example is provided by the various international copyright conventions, which the Mandatory Government made applicable to Palestine. Those included some special arrangements between the Government of the United Kingdom and the Government of the United States, even though the Government of the United States was not a party to all of those international conventions to which the United Kingdom was a party. The substantive law of Palestine was brought in line with these conventions. Upon termination of the Mandate, the United States insisted that it was necessary for Israel to enter a new agreement on copyright with itself, to replace the agreement that it had made with the Mandatory, which was made applicable to Palestine, regardless of the compatible Israeli domestic legislation.[32]

Israel not being a successor to the Mandatory notwithstanding, Israel's practice in matters of State succession is demonstrated in the following three examples treating, in turn, concessions granted by the sovereign before the establishment of the State of Israel, government pensions owed by the Mandatory to persons who had retired prior to the establishment of the State, and the case of the property owned in Israel by German citizens, domiciled in Israel, who were expelled by the British Mandatory during WWII:

(1) Concessions

Protocol XII annexed to the Treaty of Lausanne provided that all the concessions made before 29 October 1914 between the Ottoman Government or any local authority and nationals of the Contracting Parties were to be maintained (Art. 1). In addition, the successor States were to be fully "subrogated" as regards the rights and obligations of Turkey towards nationals of other States (Art. 9). Under Article 5, the concessions could be re-adapted to the new economic circumstances. Concessions that had not yet been put into operation could be dissolved "at the request of the concessionaire", subject to indemnification for expenses incurred (Art. 6).

Mavrommatis was the holder of two concessions to undertake public works, the Jerusalem and Jaffa Concessions. Relying on the Protocol, as well as on general principles of international law, the Greek Government brought a claim before the Permanent Court of International Justice, alleging that the British Government, as Mandatory of Palestine, was obliged to respect his

---

32 Law of Treaties – Replies from Governments to Questionnaires of the International Law Commission, UN Doc A/CN.4/19, *Yearbook of the ILC* (1950), vol. II, p. 212, para. 13. A list of treaties to which Israel acceded *de novo*, regardless of whether previously Palestine was formally party to them or whether their provisions had been made applicable to Palestine, is provided id. at para. 26.

concessions. Regarding the Jaffa concession, the PCIJ held that it had no jurisdiction, but pointed out that "If Protocol XII leaves intact the general principle of subrogation . . . the Administration of Palestine would be bound to recognize the Jaffa concessions, not in consequence of an obligation undertaken by the Mandatory, but in virtue of a general principle of international law to the application of which the obligations entered into by the Mandatory created no exception".[33] The Jerusalem Concession was decided on the merits, however the PCIJ denied the Greek Government's plea to supplement Protocol XII by 'principles taken from general international law', since the Protocol was complete in itself.[34] The Court held that, by granting a competitive concession, the fulfillment of the concession granted earlier to Mavrommatis had not been rendered impossible.[35]

When Israel was established, there were several concessions in force in Israeli territory: the Mavrommatis concessions, the Iraq-Petroleum Company concession of 1939, the Anglo-Iranian Oil Company concession of 1933, the Trans-Arabian Pipeline Company concession of 1946, and the Palestine Potash Ltd. concession.[36] Israel continued to respect existing concessionary rights, but opened negotiations with the concessionaires for their adaptation.

Of special interest is the case decided by the Israel Supreme Court in 1955, regarding a contract made in 1938 between the Palestine Railways and the appellants, who were granted a concession for newspaper kiosks and bookstalls at the Haifa Central Railway Station.[37] The contract was terminable on three months' notice in writing. In March 1948, the railway administration informed the concessionaire that the contract could not be regarded as binding any substitute for the Palestine Railways after the end of the Mandate. No notice of termination was given. The Israeli Ministry of Transport refused to recognize the contract. The parties agreed that Israel was not the successor of Palestine. However, the appellants alleged that the contract was recognized by the Law and Administration Ordinance, 5708–1948. The Supreme Court held that a distinction should be drawn between acts performed by the previous Government in its capacity as the Government, on the one hand, and transactions concluded by it in its capacity as owner of property, on the other. The new State should recognize activities of the first category, but is not required

33 *The Mavrommatis Palestine Concessions* (*Greece v. Britain*), (1927) PCIJ ser. A, no. 2, para. 69.

34 Id., no. 5, p. 27.

35 Id., p. 45.

36 Cf. O'Connell, *supra* n. 3, vol. I – Internal Relations, p. 337.

37 *Pales Ltd. v. Ministry of Transport*, 22 ILR 113 (17 March 1955), esp. at 121.

by logic to recognize transactions carried out by the State acting as *fiscus*, i.e., as 'the other party' in relation to a citizen. The Court concluded that, to be validated by the Ordinance, the term "concession" should be restricted to grants by the Mandatory authorities in their governmental capacity, e.g., the Palestine Electric Corporation and the Dead Sea Concession.

(2) Pensions

Under the Financial Agreement between Israel and the United Kingdom of 30 March 1950,[38] Israel was obliged to pay the pensions of former officials of the Mandatory Government resident in Israel, whether they had retired before 14 May 1948, or not, up to an amount not exceeding 200,000 Israeli pounds annually. Following the devaluation of the Israeli pound in 1953, the pensions paid by the State were substantially diminished in value. A claim brought by a pensioner failed on the grounds that the Financial Agreement had not been transformed into domestic law by implementing legislation. Therefore, it could not directly or indirectly form the basis of a claim in the domestic courts.[39]

(3) German Property in Israel: the Templar Mediation[40]

In 1939, the British Administration in Palestine enacted a Trading with the Enemy Ordinance, under which the Office of Custodian of Enemy Property was established, for vesting the property of enemy aliens in it. Since most of the property belonged to the members of a Christian Community–the Templar Society–the German assets in Palestine were named the Templar assets. The property remained vested in the Custodian until April 1948, when the vesting Orders were revoked. The revoking Orders were not published in Palestine before the termination of the Mandate, but were published and gazetted in London by instruction of the Palestine Attorney-General.

An amendment to the Law and Administration Ordinance excluded from continuity all laws and orders that had not been published in the Palestine Gazette.[41] Consequently, the revoking Orders had no effect in Israel and the German property remained in the hands of the Custodian. In 1950, Israel enacted a German Property Law, 5710–1950,[42] which created a Custodian of

38 86 UNTS 231 (1951).

39 *Richuk v. State of Israel*, 28 ILR 442 (27 March 1958).

40 Cf. O'Connell, *supra* note 3, vol. I, p. 193, 287–291.

41 Law and Administration Ordinance (Amendment) Law. 5709–1949, *Sefer Ha-Chukkim* (SH) No. 20, p. 159; 3 *Laws of the State of Israel* (LSI) 73 (1948–49).

42 German Property Law, 5710–1950, SH No. 312, p. 56; 4 LSI 142 (1949–50).

German Property, and vested in him the Templar assets, as security against settlement by Germany of claims of Israeli citizens against that country.

In the mediation that finally settled this dispute in May 1962, Germany argued that the United Kingdom did not expropriate German property, but just vested that property in the custodian as means of liquidating the property of Germans who wished to migrate permanently and could not individually dispose of their assets. Therefore, that property remained private at the date of Israel's establishment. Germany did not dispute the legality of the taking by the State of Israel, on the ground that the purpose of the Israeli law was to use the property as security. None the less, it contended that compensation should be calculated on the basis of full restitution, as per the decision of the PCIJ in the *Chorzów Factory* Case.[43] This was also the principle applicable to Jewish refugees under the Financial Agreement made between Germany and Israel on 10 September 1952.[44]

Israel, on the other hand, contended that, when Israel was established, the Templar assets were Palestine public property vested in the Palestine administration, and that its owners were divested of it. Since Israel was not the successor of the Palestine Administration, no obligation to compensate could have been inherited from the Mandatory. Furthermore, Israel was entitled to retain the property because Palestine had been involved in the war against Germany, and Germany had occasioned losses to European Jewry which involved the duty to compensate. The holding of the property could be regarded as a measure of reprisals or reparations. Since Israel received only a small proportion of the total value of Jewish loss under the indemnification provisions, it was not required to pay more than a similar proportion of the value of German property as compensation.

There is no reasoned award of the mediator. It has been reported that, following the mediator's proposals, Israel paid about half of the total value claimed by Germany.[45]

Treaty Ratification and Implementation

Israel does not have a formal, written constitution. The *Knesset* (Israel's parliament) was originally elected in 1949 as a Constituent Assembly but decided in the middle of 1950 not to proceed with the adoption of a constitution, but to

43 (1928) PCIJ, Ser. A, no. 17.

44 162 UNTS 205 (1953).

45 O'Connell, *supra* note 3, vol. I, p. 289.

focus on passing a number of basic laws which, in time, would become Israel's formal constitution. Accordingly, the *Knesset* has enacted a couple of basic laws concerning basic civil rights, i.e., Basic Law: Human Dignity and Liberty and Basic Law: Freedom of Occupation, as well as Basic Laws that define the respective roles of the *Knesset*, the Government, the Judiciary and the President. The Basic Laws address neither the relationship between international law and domestic law in general nor questions such as the status of customary international law, the law of the nations, or the treaty-making power.

The legal position with respect to the treaty-making power is essentially that included in a memorandum of 11 March 1951, submitted by the Government of Israel at the request of the Secretary General of the United Nations.[46] In the memorandum it is stated:

> 1. The situation in Israel is at present characterized by the absence of clear and specific provisions of a legislative character…
> 7. The authority which in this way is vested exclusively in the Government of Israel extends not only to negotiating and signing international treaties, whether or not they are subject to ratification. It also includes ratifying international treaties requiring ratification…
> 8. As far as concerns the manner in which the Government uses its powers, reference should be made to Section 2(d) of the Law and Administration Ordinance, 5708–1948, as read together with Section 12 of the Transition Law, 5709–1949. Decisions concerning the use of the treaty-making power are taken by the Cabinet as a whole, and the execution of these decisions is the responsibility of the Minister for Foreign Affairs. If the document to give effect to the Government's decision requires the signature of the President, such document has to bear the attesting signature of the Minister for Foreign Affairs.
> 9. The President's functions in connection with the exercise of the treaty-making power are governed by Section 6 of the Transition Law, 5709–1949, under which the President "shall sign treaties with foreign States which have been ratified by the *Knesset*".[47] This means that when in fact the *Knesset* has expressed its approval to the ratification of the

46 The memorandum is included in Laws and Practices concerning the Conclusion of Treaties, document ST/LEG/SER.B/3, at pp. 67ff. The volume includes authoritative information from 86 countries on their laws and practices concerning the conclusion of treaties.

47 Section 6 of the Transition Law was replaced in 1964 by the identical Section 11(a)(5) of the Basic Law: The President of the State.

> treaty, the act of ratification may be signed by the President. In other cases, the act of ratification may be signed by the President, or by the Foreign Minister... It is to be observed that this provision is one relating to the powers of the President. It does not import any modification in the general law about treaty-making or about the authority of the *Knesset* to ratify treaties. This aspect is not regulated by any law passed by the Israel Legislature and therefore remains as described above...

The position can therefore be summarized in the following way:

(a) The legal power to negotiate, sign and ratify international treaties on behalf of Israel is vested exclusively in the Government of Israel and is in charge of the Minister for Foreign Affairs;
(b) Where the *Knesset* has given its approval to the ratification of the treaty, the act of ratification is signed by the President of the State...

The memorandum bases these conclusions regarding the Government's exclusive power to conclude treaties on behalf of Israel, on two legislative instruments: the Law and Administrative Ordinance, 5708–1948, enacted upon the establishment of the State of Israel, and the Transition Law, 5709–1949.

Section 11 of the Law and Administration Ordinance establishes the principle that "The Law which existed in Palestine on ... 14 May 1948 shall remain in force, so far as there is nothing therein repugnant to this Ordinance or to other laws which may be enacted by, or on behalf of, the Provisional Council of State, and subject to such modifications as may result from the establishment of the State and its authorities".

According to Section 14(a) of the Law and Administration Ordinance, "any power vested under the law in the King of England or in any of his Secretaries of State, and any power vested under the law in the High Commissioner, the High Commissioner in Council, or the Government of Palestine, shall henceforth vest in the Provisional Government, unless such power has been vested in the Provisional Council of State by any of its Ordinances".[48]

Since no modifying enactment has been passed by the *Knesset*, the memorandum asserts that the treaty-making power in Israel is still that which existed during the League of Nations' British Mandate, subject to appropriate modifications because of the establishment of the sovereign State of Israel and its authorities.

48 Official Gazette No. 2 of 21.5.1948 (Law and Administration Ordinance, 5708–1948, 1 LSI 7, Sect. 15(a) (1948)) of the same Ordinance provides that "'Palestine', wherever appearing in the law, shall henceforth be used as 'Israel'".

Under Article 12 of the British Mandate, the Mandatory was entrusted with the control of the foreign relations of Palestine. During the British Mandate, the basic constitutional document was the Order-in-Council, 1922–1947, enacted by the British Mandatory to implement its international obligations imposed by the League of Nations' Mandate. The Order-in-Council did not contain rules regarding the treaty-making powers since the power was conferred upon the Mandatory itself rather than the High Commissioner, who was appointed by the British Sovereign to administer the Government of Palestine.

The memorandum concludes that the treaty-making power at the time of the Mandate vested exclusively in the British Sovereign or in the High Commissioner of Palestine, subject only to limitations imposed by the Mandate. Section 11 of the Law and Administration Ordinance maintained this legal situation, and Section 14 only provided for the devolution of powers from the various British authorities to the Provisional Government.

Following the first general elections, the first *Knesset* adopted the Transition Law, Section 12 of which provides that "the Government shall have all the powers vested by the law in the Provisional Government".[49] This language yields the conclusion that the legislature wanted to confer the powers of the British Crown, including its prerogative powers, upon the Israeli Government. These include the Crown's capacity, as a matter of prerogative, to conclude treaties.

By a Government decision taken in 1951, in accordance with Section 2(d) of the Law and Administration Ordinance, the Government delegated its powers to negotiate and sign treaties and international agreements to the Minister of Foreign Affairs, or to whoever he may appoint to that end.[50]

This state of affairs renders quite meaningless in practice the function of the President, mentioned in para. 9 of the memorandum. The memorandum based this rule on Section 6 of the Transition Law (replaced in 1964 by the identical Section 11(a)(5) of the Basic Law: The President of the State), which provided that "the President of the State shall sign treaties with foreign states which have been ratified by the *Knesset*".[51] It should be noted that the term "ratification" referred to in this Section is not the 'ratification' within the meaning of the Vienna Convention on the Law of the Treaties (Arts. 2(1)(b), 11 and 14), but rather the *domestic* procedure of establishing the state's consent to

49 Transition Law, 5709–1949, 3 LSI 3 (1949).

50 *Yalkut Ha-Pirsumim* (the Official Gazette: Government notices) 162, 5711–1951, p. 989.

51 Basic Law: The President of the State, 5724–1964, 18 LSI 111 (1964).

be bound by a treaty. In its landmark *Kamiar* case,[52] the Supreme Court held that it is neither appropriate nor necessary to fall back on interpretation of the corresponding powers vested in British or Mandatory authorities in the pre-State epoch and to construct some theory of succession from them. Rather, since in the constitutional position prevailing in Israel the Head of State is not the organ authorized to conclude international treaties, and in fact the treaties are concluded by the Government, then the Government is the organ qualified to ratify them.

The above legal situation notwithstanding, important instruments affecting Israel's foreign relations have been submitted for parliamentary approval, although not always prior to their being signed or ratified on the international level. These include the following:[53] Israel's accession to the UN Charter in 1948 was first approved by the Provisional State Council (the *Knesset*'s predecessor); the armistice agreements, 1949, were notified to the *Knesset* after having been signed;[54] The Convention on the Prevention and Punishment of the Crime of Genocide was approved by the *Knesset* and implemented by a domestic statute in 1950, prior to its ratification;[55] the disengagement of forces with Egypt in 1974 was approved by the *Knesset* prior to the conclusion of the Convention;[56] the disengagement of forces with Syria in 1974 was approved by the *Knesset* prior to concluding the Convention;[57] the Interim Agreement with Egypt in 1975 was approved by the *Knesset* prior to its conclusion;[58] the Camp David accords, 1978, were approved by the *Knesset* prior to their final conclusion and coming into

52 The leading case on this issue is *Kamiar v. The Attorney General of Israel*, Criminal Appeal 131/67, 22(2) PD 89 (1968); (1972) 44 ILR 197, where Kamiar argued that the Extradition Treaty between Israel and Switzerland was devoid of legal effect, since the procedure required by Israeli law, that a treaty subject to ratification should be ratified by the *Knesset*, rather than the Government, was not followed.

53 Shimon Shetreet, "The Role of the Knesset in the Conclusion of Treaties", 36 *Ha-Praklit* 349 (1985) (in Hebrew); Ruth Lapidoth, "The Authority to Conclude Treaties on behalf of the State of Israel", in *Studies in Public International Law in Memory of Sir Hersch Lauterpacht* (Nathan Feinberg [ed.]) (Jerusalem: Magnes 1961) (in Hebrew) 210, 237ff.

54 1 *Divrei Ha-Knesset* [hereinafter DK] (1949) 287; 2 DK (1949) 1095. However, the principles of the armistice agreement with Syria had first been approved by the *Knesset* Foreign Affairs and Security Committee, and the agreements with Egypt, Lebanon and Jordan were approved in principle by the Provisional State Council.

55 3 DK (1949) 315ff.

56 69 DK (1974) 10–60.

57 70 DK (1974) 1459ff.

58 74 DK (1975) 4080ff.

effect;[59] the 1979 peace treaty with Egypt was approved prior to its conclusion;[60] the agreement concerning the deployment of the multinational force in Sinai, 1981, was approved by the *Knesset* prior to its conclusion; the agreement Israel-Lebanon regarding Israel's retreat from Lebanon and the subsequent security arrangements, 1983, was likewise approved by the *Knesset*;[61] and the peace treaty with Jordan, 1994, was approved by the Knesset in 1994, prior to its conclusion.[62]

A different approach was adopted for Israel's economic agreements. The free trade agreement between Israel and the European Communities, 1975, was notified to the *Knesset* after its conclusion.[63] So was the free trade agreement between Israel and the US.[64] In both cases, MKs complained about the procedure used by the Government, which they considered inadequate.

It is noteworthy that even treaties approved by the *Knesset* were not subsequently signed by the President, as provided in Section 11(a)(5) of the Basic Law: the President of the State.[65] However, in view of the Government's declaration regarding its exclusive authority to conclude treaties, and the procedure adopted in Israel *de facto*, this disregard of the procedure stipulated by domestic law does not amount to a manifest disregard of an Israeli internal law of fundamental importance.[66]

In 1984, the Attorney General issued guidelines concerning the ratification of treaties.[67] According to the guidelines, every treaty which requires implementing legislation must be ratified by the Government. Ten copies of a treaty which is subject to ratification must be laid before the *Knesset*, together with a Hebrew translation of the text, at least 14 days prior to its ratification. The Minister in charge of the specific Treaty has to report to the Government any action taken by the *Knesset* regarding that treaty. However, the Minister of Foreign Affairs and the Minister of Defense may jointly decide to deviate from this procedure on the grounds of urgency or secrecy. In that case, the

59 83 DK (1978) 4058ff.

60 85 DK (1979) 1898ff.

61 96 DK (1983) 2188ff.

62 140 DK (1994) 752ff.

63 73 DK (1975) 2732ff.

64 101 DK (1985) 2350ff.

65 The Peace Treaty with Egypt, which was signed by the President, with the signature attested by the Minister of Foreign Affairs, was an exception, 25 *Kitvei Amana* [hereinafter KA] 868, p. 695, 758 (1978).

66 *Cf.* Vienna Convention on the Law of Treaties art. 46, May 5,1969, 1155 UNTS 331.

67 Attorney General Guidelines 64.000A–International Conventions: Ratification Process (1 January 1984).

Government alone will ratify the treaty. The Government may also decide that a certain treaty, because of its importance, should be approved by the *Knesset* prior to its ratification by the Government, as was done in the case of the Camp David Accords and the Peace Agreement with Egypt.

In 1999, a further legal development took place with respect to treaties that may determine or affect Israel's international borders. The *Knesset* enacted the Law and Administration (Cease of Application of the Law, Jurisdiction and Administration) Law, 5759–1999.[68] Section 2 of this law provides that a Government's Decision (by way of ratification of a treaty or an agreement or in any other way, including a future commitment and a conditional commitment), according to which the law, jurisdiction and administration of the State of Israel, shall no longer apply to a territory in which they apply at the time the Government decision is made, requires the approval of the *Knesset*, taken by a majority of its Members. This Law applies to any Government decision, even one taken unilaterally. Furthermore, Section 3 provides that the Government decision, approved by the *Knesset*, also requires approval in a referendum. Section 3 will only come into effect however once a law concerning a referendum is passed by the *Knesset* (§4). The *Knesset* has not yet enacted such a law.

The procedure adopted *de facto* by the Government with respect to the majority of important treaties has led some jurists to opine that a binding custom has developed whereby the Government must lay important treaties before the *Knesset* prior to their ratification.[69]

However, the texts of Israel's Agreements with the Palestine Liberation Organization (PLO) were not brought before the *Knesset* prior to their entering into effect. They remained secret and no debate took place regarding their content prior to signing the Oslo Agreements in Camp David and the Gaza-Jericho Agreement. Prior to the signing of the Oslo B Interim Agreements with the PLO, MK Shilansky, the Deputy Speaker of the *Knesset* petitioned the High Court of Justice to make an injunction forbidding the Government to sign the agreements without obtaining the prior approval of the *Knesset*.[70] MK Shilanksy argued that a

---

68 Law and Administration (Cease of Application of the Law, Jurisdiction and Administration) Law, 5759–1999, SH (*Sefer Ha-Chukkim*) no. 1703 p. 86.

69 *Cf.* Shetreet, *supra* note 59 at 360–366.

70 *MK Shilansky, Deputy Speaker of the Knesset v. Prime Minister Y. Rabin*, HCJ 5934/95 (Nevo electronic database). The Supreme Court reiterated its position that no constitutional convention had developed according to which the *Knesset*'s approval must be sought in advance in *Weiss v. The Prime Minister*, HCJ 5167/00, 55(2) PD 455. The dismissed petition concerned the Government's continuation of the negotiations with the Palestinians even after its resignation, at a period in which it was considered a transitional government, in office only until the next Government takes office and, since it had already resigned, the

binding custom had developed, according to which agreements of this kind require prior approval of the *Knesset*. The Supreme Court dismissed the petition, holding that no such custom had developed. Indeed, the Court pointed to the previous agreements with the PLO that had not been brought before the *Knesset* prior to their conclusion. A letter written by the Attorney General, dated July 30, 1995 (shortly before the submission of the petition), promising to lay the agreement before the *Knesset* for its approval, was held by the Supreme Court to be no more than a political commitment devoid of legal effect.

In Israel, treaties can be implemented in a number of ways. Some statutes, such as the following, were enacted with the specific purpose of implementing treaties to which Israel has become party:

(a) The Crime of Genocide (Prevention and Punishment) Law, 5710–1950, which implemented the Convention on the Prevention and Punishment of the Crime of Genocide;
(b) Carriage by Air of Goods by Air Law, 5740–1980, which implemented the Warsaw Convention for the Unification of Certain Rules Relating to International Carriage by Air, 1929, in its original form and as amended at The Hague, 1955. The Law states that effect will also be given to the supplementary Guadalajara Convention, 1961 (relating to international carriage by air performed by a person other than the contracting carrier), the Guatemala Protocol, 1971, and the further revision by the four Montreal Protocols;
(c) Sales (International Sale of Goods) Law, 5760–1999, which implemented the Vienna Convention on Contracts for the International Sale of Goods (CISG), 1980;
(d) The Arbitration Law, 5728–1968, applies to all arbitration proceedings, whether domestic or international. In 1974, the Law was amended in order to implement Israel's international obligations under the New York Convention on the Recognition and Enforcement of Foreign Arbitral Awards, 1958. Following the amendment, the Law contains rules which apply only to an arbitration to which "an international convention to which Israel is party applies" (§6), or to a "foreign arbitral award" (§29A).

Sometimes implementation is done via secondary legislation, i.e. regulations or administrative orders.[71] Treaties can also serve as a precondition to the

---

Knesset lost its power to compel the resignation of a Government that reaches an unacceptable agreement by a non-confidence vote.

71 Examples include significant aspects of Israel's international trade agreements which can be implemented in the domestic order through an administrative order made by the

application of Israeli statutes in areas of extradition[72] and recognition of foreign judgments.[73]

With regard to the doctrine of self-executing treaties, there is only very limited scope for this doctrine in Israeli law. The general rule is that, in order to have direct effect in the domestic domain, a treaty must be implemented by primary or secondary legislation. This rule was stated by the Supreme Court in the landmark case *Custodian of Absentee Property v. Samara*.[74] In that case, the claimant sought to rely on the Israel–Jordan Armistice Agreement (the Rhodes Agreement). The Supreme Court held that the Rhodes Agreement is a treaty between the State of Israel and another State, and only they acquire rights and undertake obligations towards each other. Such a treaty will become binding law in Israeli domestic law after being implemented in Israeli law. But, in that case, the courts apply the implementing legislation rather than the treaty itself. In another case, the National Labor Court stated that private parties cannot rely on the Treaty of Friendship, Commerce and Navigation between Israel and the United States of America,[75] which was not implemented in domestic legislation.[76]

Government, or by the Minister of Finance – *Cf.* Section 31 of the Purchase Tax Law (Goods and Services), 5712–1952; Section 232 of the Customs Ordinance (New Version), 5717–1957; and Section 3 of the Customs Tariff and Exemption Ordinance. The Tariff Order–a combined Customs and Purchase Tax Tariff–reflects Israel's commitments under the various international trade agreements. It is updated regularly to incorporate any change that takes place in these matters.

72 One of the preconditions for extradition by Israel of a person to another state is that an extradition treaty exist between Israel and the requesting state (§2A, Extradition Law, 5715–1954, as amended). In certain respects, such a treaty may even have primacy over conflicting rules of the Israeli Extradition Law (§21). The treaty may be bilateral or multilateral. Consequently, there is no need for special implementation of extradition treaties in Israeli law.

73 The Foreign Judgments Enforcement Law, 5718–1958, sets the following preconditions for the direct recognition of a foreign judgment (§11(a)): an agreement with a foreign state applies to it; Israel has undertaken by that agreement to recognize foreign judgments of the kind in question; the undertaking applies only to judgments capable of enforcement under law in Israel; and, it fulfils the conditions of the agreement *Cf.*, in detail, Talia Einhorn, *Private International Law in Israel*, 2nd ed. 419ff (Alphen aan den Rijn: Kluwer Law International 2012).

74 *Custodian of Absentee Property v. Samara*, Civil Appeal 25/55, (1955) 10 P. D. 1825

75 Treaty of Friendship, Commerce and Navigation between Israel and the United States of America, 2 KA 34 p. 15 (1951).

76 *Yehudith Schoenberger v. National Insurance Institute*, Labor Appeal 57/39–0, tak-National 97(3), 413 (1997).

However, provisions of treaties which codify customary law and are clear, unconditional, and no further implementing legislation is necessary to give them effect, and the treaty does not leave the implementing measures to the discretion of the contracting parties.[77]

If the *Knesset* passes a law which clearly contradicts an international norm, whether customary law or an obligation undertaken in a treaty, the Israeli statute will prevail.[78] However, the contradiction must be express. In a case which came before the District Court of Tel-Aviv, the claimant sought to recover damages in torts from the Egyptian Ambassador to Israel.[79] The claimant argued that the Civil Wrongs Ordinance [New Version] enumerated all defenses to claims in torts, and those did not include diplomatic immunity. The Court considered that the Ambassador was entitled to immunity under Article 13 of the Vienna Convention on Diplomatic Relations, 1961, for the duration of his office. The Convention was ratified by Israel but not implemented in Israeli domestic law. Yet, the Court held that the fact that the Civil Wrongs Ordinance did not mention the defense granted under international law could not be regarded as an implied contradiction to an international norm which is binding on Israel. This case can be viewed as an example of the rule of interpretation adopted by the Israeli courts.

As aforementioned, constitutive treaty provisions are not self-executing in Israel. This result is mitigated by two rules, each of which creates a presumption of compliance–a rule of interpretation and a rule of presumption. Furthermore, in numerous cases, the yardstick for judicial review has been the rule of proportionality, which substantially constrains the discretion of the Government.

According to the rule of interpretation, domestic law must be interpreted in compliance with international norms, provided that there is no Israeli legislation which expressly contradicts the international obligation. In applying this rule, the courts pay close attention to the international source and make an effort to interpret the convention autonomously, in order to attain a proper and unified application as much as possible. There are numerous cases in

---

77 For further details and references, *cf.* Talia Einhorn, "Israel", in *International Law and Domestic Legal Systems* 288, 303ff. (Dinah Shelton [ed.]), (Oxford: Oxford University Press 2011).

78 *Cf.*, two of the first cases in which the Supreme Court stated this rule – *Steinberg v. The Attorney General,* Criminal Appeal 5/51, 5 PD 1061; *Adolph Eichmann v. The Attorney General,* Criminal Appeal 336/61, 16 PD 2033.

79 *Shlomit Shalom v. The Attorney General, Shulman and Bassyounni,* Civil Appeal (Tel-Aviv) 4289/98, tak-District 99(3), 2.

which this rule has been followed. The Supreme Court has held that "Although our courts draw their judicial authorities from the laws of the State and not from the system of international law, . . . we have a well-established rule, following English law, that a court in Israel "will interpret a municipal statute, as long as its content does not dictate another interpretation, in accordance with the rules of public international law . . . ".[80] The courts will not construe the silence of the legislature as an implied intention to disregard international law.[81]

In deciding issues of Treaty Law, the courts turn to international sources in order to ascertain the proper interpretation of the treaty. A pertinent example is the Vienna Convention on the International Sale of Goods, 1980 (CISG), providing a set of unified substantive law rules on this subject, implemented by the Sales (International Sale of Goods) Law, 5760–1999, Annex 'A' of which reproduces the Treaty provisions. In interpreting the CISG, the Supreme Court turned to authoritative commentaries, as well as decisions of the Belgian, Austrian and German courts.[82]

Another example is the Hague Convention on Civil Aspects of International Child Abduction, 1980, which came into effect in Israel on 1 July 1991, implemented in Israeli law by the Hague Convention (Return of Abducted Children) Law, 5751–1991. The Convention has been applied rigorously by the courts and the defenses to returning abducted children have been construed narrowly, in line with its object and purpose.[83] In one rather complicated case,[84] in an effort to properly apply this Convention, the District Court checked a whole variety of international and comparative sources, among them: the text of the

80 *Sheikh Abu Hilu v. Government of Israel*, HCJ 302/72, 27(2) PD 169 (1973). *Cf.* also Lapidoth, "International Law within the Israel Legal System", 24 *Israel Law Review* (1990) 451, at p. 455, with further references. *Cf.*, also *Teichner v. Air France*, Further Hearing 36/84, 41(1) PD 589, in which the Supreme Court emphasized the importance of uniform interpretation of multilateral treaties with multiple contracting states (*in casu*, the Warsaw Convention for the Unification of Certain Rules Relating to International Carriage by Air, 1929).

81 *Cf. Shlomit Shalom v. The Attorney General, Shulman and Bassyounni*, Civil Appeal (Tel-Aviv) 4289/98, tak-District 99(3), 2.

82 *Pamesa Ceramica v. Israel Mendelson*, Civil Appeal 7388/06, tak-Supreme 2009(1) 4087.

83 *Cf.*, e.g., *plonit v. ploni*, Application Family Appeal 2338/09, tak-Supreme 2009(2), 2730, in which the Supreme Court referred to Elisa Pérez-Vera, "Explanatory Report on the 1980 Hague Child Abduction Convention", *Hague Conference on Private International Law, Acts and Documents of the Fourteenth Session* (Vol. III, 1980), p. 435, as well as to English case law.

84 *Sh.D. v. T.D.*, Appeal Family Matters (Tel-Aviv) 70/97, tak-District 98(4), 16182.

various pertinent provisions of the Child Abduction Convention; its preamble; the Pérez Vera Explanatory Report to the Convention; a lecture given by Mr. Hans van Loon, Secretary General of the Hague Conference on Private International Law (which was appended by the Court to its decision); foreign court decisions in similar matters, including American, Austrian, Australian, Canadian, English, French, German, Swedish and Swiss cases; other international conventions *in pari materia*, i.e., the UN Convention on the Rights of the Child (CRC), 1989, as well as the Hague Convention on Protection of Children and Co-operation in respect of Intercountry Adoption, 1993 (including the Parra-Aranguren Explanatory Report) and the Hague Convention on Jurisdiction, applicable Law, Recognition, Enforcement and Co-operation in respect of Parental Responsibility and Measures for the Protection of Children, 1996 (including the Lagarde Explanatory Report); and James D. Garbolino, *International Child Abduction: Guide to Handling Hague Convention cases in U.S. Courts* (1997).

According to the rule of presumption, which is a corollary of the rule of interpretation, the administrative and governmental authorities are presumed to be obliged to apply their discretion under the enabling legislation in a manner that conforms to international obligations, unless compelling public interests and considerations mandate disregard of them. Administrative regulations and orders, made in disregard of international obligations, may be set aside under this rule.[85]

Annotated Bibliography of Sources

General Treaty Collections

1 KITVEI AMANA [ISRAEL TREATY SERIES]
(Jerusalem: ha-Madpis ha-memshalti, 1949–).

Summary: All treaties binding on the State of Israel are published in *Kitvei Amana* (Israel Treaty Series). In practice, however, the treaty collection is not easily accessible. The treaties published are ordered neither according to the date of signature, nor to the date of ratification, nor to the date of their coming into effect.

Index: Each volume of *Kitvei Amana* has an index. There is also a consolidated index for volumes 1–36.

---

85 *Cf.*, e.g., the decisions in *The State of Israel v. Salon Tokyo*, Civil Appeal 544/88, 46(4) PD 226 (1992), per President of the Israel Supreme Court Justice Meir Shamgar, and in *Stessel v. The Customs Director*, Originating Summons 727/93 (District Court Haifa), tak-District 96(1) 423, per Judge Dan Bein.

Note: The accessibility has been made easier by the incorporation of the treaties into the Nevo electronic database (a private database, open to subscribers, providing access, in Hebrew, to case law, legislation, primary and secondary, administrative orders, and the treaties published in *Kitvei Amana*). Nevo electronic database allows access also by searching key words.

2 MINISTRY OF JUSTICE – TREATIES
URL: http://index.justice.gov.il/Units/TergomOmanotBimLeumi/Pages/Odot.aspx.

Summary: The Ministry of Justice has, on its webpage, a database of the treaties concluded by Israel. Treaties can be found by searching their title, their subject-matter, as well as the names of the contracting states or pertinent international organization.

Note: To access the collection, click on the blue-hyperlinked Hebrew characters.

3 MINISTRY OF FOREIGN AFFAIRS – TREATIES
URL: http://mfa.gov.il/MFA/AboutTheMinistry/LegalTreaties/Pages/default.aspx.

Summary: The Ministry of Foreign Affairs, too, has, on its webpage, a database of the treaties concluded by Israel. Database can be searched by title, subject, party, or date concluded/entered into force.

Note: Status table for a selection of multilateral agreements including the United Nations Treaty Series, Council of Europe, European Union, Hague Conference on Private International Law, International Civil Aviation Organization, International Committee of the Red Cross, International Labour Organization, International Maritime Organization, United Nations Educational, Scientific and Cultural Organization, World Health Conventions, World Intellectual Property Organization, World Trade Organization can be found here: http://mfa.gov.il/MFA/ForeignPolicy/MFADocuments/Pages/Treaties%20and%20Agreements.aspx.

Diplomatic Documents

4 SHNATON HA-MISMACHIM [DOCUMENTARY ANNUAL]
(Jerusalem: Ministry of Foreign Affairs, 1973–).

Summary: Covering the periods 1973–1979, 1993–2004. From 1973 till 1979 the Ministry of Foreign Affairs Department of History published annual reports on Israel's public policy, which included a list of pertinent documents of the respective years. The documents are given in Hebrew or in English, as the case may be. In 1993, the publication of the annuals was resumed, entitled *Shnaton Ha-Mismachim Ha-Rishmi'im* (Annual of Formal Documents).

Note: The last three volumes published in electronic format are those pertaining to 2002 (published in 2006), available at: http://mfa.gov.il/MFA/ForeignPolicy/MFADocuments/Yearbook2002/Pages/default.aspx; 2003 (published in 2009), available at: http://mfa.gov.il/MFA/ForeignPolicy/MFADocuments/Yearbook2003/Pages/default.aspx; and 2004 (published in 2012), available at: http://mfa.gov.il/MFA/ForeignPolicy/MFADocuments/Yearbook2004/Pages/default.aspx.

5 TE'UDOT LI-MEDINIYUT HA-HUTS SHEL MEDINAT YISRAEL [ISRAEL FOREIGN POLICY DOCUMENTS]
(Jersualem: Israel State Archives, 1981–) 14 vols.

Summary: A compilation of diplomatic documents currently covering the period 1947–1960. A list of the volumes can be found here: http://www.archives.gov.il/ArchiveGov_Eng/Publications/Documents/. Documents are published in original language of writing; summaries of the Hebrew documents, as well as a full translation of the notes, introduction and indexes are included in an English-language Companion Volume issued for each numbered volume.

Index: Available for each volume, English translation of each volume's index to be found in the English Companion Volume.

Note: Title in English, "Documents on the Foreign Policy of Israel."

6 ISRAEL'S FOREIGN RELATIONS: SELECTED DOCUMENTS
Meron Medzini, ed. (Jerusalem: Ministry of Foreign Affairs, 1981–2002) 18 vols.

Summary: 18 print volumes of documents covering the period 1947–2001. Includes short introductory editorial notes. Documents translated into English mainly by the English Publications Division of the Government Press Office. Continued by the Yearbook of Official Documents, covering the period 2002–2004.

Note: Now entirely available electronically from the Ministry of Foreign Affairs website with title "Israel's Foreign Policy - Historical Documents": http://www.mfa.gov.il/MFA/ForeignPolicy/MFADocuments/Pages/Documents_Foreign_Policy_Israel.aspx.

Collections of Documents on the Arab-Israeli Conflict

7 REFERENCE DOCUMENTS FOR THE ARAB-ISRAELI CONFLICT
URL: http://www.mfa.gov.il/MFA/ForeignPolicy/Peace/MFADocuments/Pages/Selected%20Reference%20Documents.aspx.

Summary: Reference documents on the Arab-Israeli Conflict are given on the webpage of the Ministry of Foreign Affairs (under "peace process").

8 ISRAEL-ARAB WORLD – COLLECTION OF RESOLUTIONS IN UN ORGANIZATIONS AND COMMITTEES
(Ministry of Foreign Affairs – Department of International Organizations, 1976–2001).

Summary: This collection of volumes, published annually by the Israeli Ministry of Foreign Affairs, Department of International Organizations, provides the full text (in English) of resolutions regarding the Arab conflict, made by UN organizations and committees from 1976 until 2001.

Note: An annex to each volume provides a summary of the resolutions and results of the votes.

9 THE ARAB-ISRAELI CONFLICT
John Norton Moore, ed. (Princeton, NJ: Princeton University Press 1974–1991). 4 vols.

Summary: Each volume contains a selected documentary compilation (full-text documents in English), a detailed table of contents arranged chronologically.

Index: Contains a subject-matter index.

Note: Vol. 3: Documents (1897–1974) vol. 4: Documents (1975–1988).

10 THE ARAB-ISRAEL CONFLICT AND ITS RESOLUTION: SELECTED DOCUMENTS
Ruth Lapidoth and Moshe Hirsch, eds. (Dordrecht: Martinus Nijhoff, 1991).

Summary: This volume contains the full-text of selected documents, in English origin or translated from Hebrew into English, with a detailed table of contents arranged chronologically.

Yearbooks and Digests of State Practice

11 ISRAEL YEARBOOK ON HUMAN RIGHTS
(Tel-Aviv: Tel-Aviv University, 1971–)

Summary: Annual publication produced under the auspices of the Faculty of Law of Tel Aviv University since 1971. In addition to scholarly articles on human rights in peace and war, with particular emphasis on problems relevant to the State of Israel and the Jewish people, the *Yearbook* incorporates also documentary materials relating to Israel and the Administered Areas which are not otherwise available in English (including summaries of judicial decisions, compilations of legislative enactments and military proclamations).

Italy

Susan Gualtier

Issues of Treaty Succession

The Italian Republic is a modern state. Prior to the *Risorgimento*, or unification, of the late 1800's, and the Sardinian king's assumption of the title of King of Italy in 1861, the geographical area now known as Italy existed as a number of separate kingdoms, republics, and other state entities, each with its own government, legal system, and laws, whose boundaries and governments were constantly shifting, merging, and disappearing.[1] To trace the legal history of Italy is to trace the history of this geographical region, describe its common legal developments, and attempt to identify any "national identity" that might have pre-dated Italy's unification.[2] While it is clear that for most of Italy's history, the various kingdoms, republics, and regions of the peninsula each acted as and considered themselves to be distinct sovereign nations, it is equally clear that in the area of law, there existed shared tendencies within the region, and that there existed an Italian cultural identity that was distinct from other European traditions.[3]

Based in part on the relative newness of the Italian state, as well as on the *Risorgimento* as a deliberate break from past institutions, Italian legal scholarship has been described as "ahistorical".[4] It tends toward a nonuse of history in

1 Mauro Capelletti, John Henry Merryman, & Joseph M. Perillo, The Italian Legal System: An Introduction 188 (Stanford University Press 1967).

2 Jeffrey S. Lena & Ugo Mattei, Introduction to Italian Law 1 (Kluwer Law International 2002).

3 Id. at 15.

4 Capelletti, *supra* note 1, at 186–89 (Stanford University Press 1967). Among the reasons for the Italians' "ahistorical attitude," Capelletti also cites the tendency to view Roman law not as one stage in the development of the modern law, but as a "completed legal system having contemporary legal validity"; the "dominance of a *jus commune* based heavily on these [same] assumptions about Roman law"; and the tendency toward a "dogmatic legal science" that does not make allowances for the type of sociological jurisprudence that would be necessary to study law with reference to its historical context. Id. At 187–91. Capelletti states, "Italian legal thought is … to the eye of a common lawyer, ahistorical. Although the suggestion that a legal system based in large part on Roman law, canon law, and the customs of medieval merchants lacks the historical dimension may seem bizarre, that is what is meant. Legal history of the sort so familiar to common lawyers through the work of the great Anglo-American

 | DOI 10.1163/9789004272224_019

discussing and explaining the development of legal institutions, and Italian books and legal treatises generally do not contain the "historical component" to which common lawyers are accustomed.[5] This tendency to refrain from legal historiography is evident in the area of international law, and Italian legal scholarship contains few references to specific problems or instances of treaty succession. Nonetheless, it is important to understand the most recent regime changes that have taken place on the Italian peninsula, as they will certainly raise questions of treaty succession.

The modern period in Italian history, which "carries the record of Italian public law to present times," and whose "now fully matured institutions ... dominate the civilized world," began with the French Revolution, "which placed public law on a new basis, furnished new aims and institutions, and spread its own principles wherever European civilization existed".[6] The revolutionary armies entered Italy in 1796,[7] after which the Italian kingdoms were transformed into makeshift republics.[8] The Italian states with pre-existing republican governments were maintained as such, albeit under the influence of French law.[9] Most of the new republics were unstable and full of unrest, and were unable to sustain themselves for more than a short time.[10] Only one – the Italian Republic, formed in 1802 through the Treaty of Campoformio by the uniting of Lombardian territory with the

legal historians hardly exists in Italy. The careful study of persons and events in relation to the growth, transformation, and decay of specific legal institutions ... is characteristic of contemporary Anglo-American legal history...In Italy...legal history is something quite different: it is a history of schools of legal thought, first and foremost, and historical persons and events are discussed primarily in relation to these schools". Id. at 186.

5 "[T]he more important evidence that Italian law is ahistorical lies in the prevailing non-use of history. Textbooks and treatises on the law do no contain the historical component common lawyers have been accustomed to finding in their own literature, and they seem lifeless and abstract by comparison". Id. at 186–87.

6 Carlo Calisse, A History Of Italian Law 198–99 (Layton B. Register, trans., Little, Brown & Company 1928).

7 Capelletti, *supra* note 1, at 41.

8 Calisse, *supra* note 6, at 200. "The republics that were formed on the French model usually copied the legislation of revolutionary France; they abolished feudal rights, the procedural privileges of the clergy and nobility, and most future interests in property; they confiscated a part of the ecclesiastical mortmain, introduced civil marriage, and lowered the age limits of majority. Even what was probably the most organic of the legislative enactments ... was but a revision of the corresponding French law". Cappelletti, *supra* note 1, at 42.

9 Calisse, *supra* note 6, at 200.

10 Id.

pre-existing Cisalpine Republic – was able to attain any remotely sustainable government organization, legal system, or military force.[11] Despite being marginally more stable than the other Italian states, the Italian Republic suffered from a constitution that was weak, opportunistic, and ultimately meant to be temporary.[12]

In 1805, the Italian Republic's own Council of State petitioned that the republic be transformed into a monarchy, with the president being made king.[13] The Kingdom of Italy was established, and Napoleon became king in 1805, a mere three years after the establishment of the Italian Republic.[14] The Kingdom grew in territory under Napoleon's reign. A new constitution was put in place to further the interests of the French Empire within the Kingdom, and French public law was applied throughout Italy, as it was throughout the rest of the Empire.[15] The Kingdom of Naples, in the southern peninsula, was established in 1806, and Napoleon's brother Joseph was named king.[16] Feudalism was abolished in the southern provinces, which was a victory, but no true constitutional government was put in place.[17] The French Civil Code was made applicable in both the Kingdom of Italy and the Kingdom of Naples in 1806, and was quickly followed by the Code of Civil Procedure, Commercial Code, and Penal Code; the Codes were also introduced in the smaller Italian states that had been formed under Napoleon's government.[18] Only Sicily and Sardinia, which remained refuges for the exiled Bourbons and Piedmontese kings, respectively, remained free of the umbrella of French rule.[19]

The French domination of Italy ended in 1815 with the Congress of Vienna, which restored Italy and most of Europe to its pre-Napoleonic conditions.[20] Kingdoms were reinstated, monarchs returned to their thrones, and pre-existing political structures were re-established.[21] Having been restored to their previous positions, monarchs sought to reinstate their kingdoms' old laws and customs, often without regard to the new liberties their peoples had been

---

11 Id.

12 Id. at 201.

13 Id.

14 Id.

15 Id.

16 Id. at 202.

17 Id. at 203.

18 CAPPELLETTI, *supra* note 1, at 42–43.

19 CALISSE, *supra* note 6, at 203.

20 Id. at 204.

21 Id.

given under the French rule.[22] Italy was once again splintered, which each territory facing its own complications as it struggled to re-establish itself as a sovereign nation. However, the French domination, though relatively brief and not entirely beneficial, had already planted deeply the seeds of modern Italian legal and political thought. Feudalism had been abolished, and the brief bringing together of Italy's many territories under one national government had raised, perhaps for the first time, a national consciousness and a new understanding of the values of liberty and equality.[23] Additionally, the benefits of political unity had become clear; the introduction of the Napoleonic Codes had convinced the Italian ruling class that unitary legislation "was a necessary condition for the material and moral development of the country" and that Italy's "fractured legal systems, the direct consequence of political disunity, constituted a serious impediment to the improvement of its standard of living".[24] Shortly after their restoration in 1815, most of the Italian monarchs authorized the drafting of new codes based on the Napoleonic model.[25]

Throughout the mid-19th century, support for a unified Italy grew. During this time, there developed the Italian conception of a "doctrine of nationalities," a doctrine of international law based upon the principles that every nation should be set up as a single unit, that every nation should be permitted to govern itself and to remain free of foreign domination, and that the government of every nation should be based on free democratic institutions.[26] The ideals of equality and independence between nations were critical to the

---

22 Id. For example, the king of Sardinia, having been restored to power, immediately issued an edict stating that all previous royal enactments should again be observed, an act that re-established trust-entails, abrogated the principle of equality, and abolished beneficial judicial and fiscal institutions. Id.

23 Id. at 203.

24 CAPPELLETTI, *supra* note 1, at 42–43.

25 Id. at 44. Capelletti suggests that, "The Napoleonic codification contained too many legal and technical virtues to be ignored in the changed ideological and political context of the time". Id. Discussing the political climate of the restoration, he goes on to state that, "Despite the conservative, if not reactionary, intentions of almost all of the restored monarchs, the Napoleonic experience left its mark on the Italian law of the restoration. It was not possible to reestablish the ancient feudal jurisdictions, municipal and noble privileges, and restrictions on the alienability of property. Indeed, the restored princes found many of the Napoleonic reforms congenial to their aims because they involved the suppression of privileges of the aristocracy, who, in the ancient régime, had set boundaries upon the central power of the monarch. Despite the repeal of some reform legislation, Italy's legal condition did not regress to its pre-Napoleonic state". Id. at 45.

26 ANGELO PIERO SERENI, THE ITALIAN CONCEPTION OF INTERNATIONAL LAW 158 (Columbia University Press 1943).

doctrine of nationalities, as was the principle of self-determination of the people, and the doctrine required that all laws, including treaties, should be set up or revised to further these principles and ideals.[27] Even without a detailed discussion, it is easy to see why the doctrine of nationalities would be appealing in the post-Napoleonic political climate, and why the principles and ideals on which it was based suggested the necessity of a unified and independent Italian nation.[28]

For Italy, the nineteenth century was one of uprisings, reforms, and foreign intervention, during which the conservative tendencies of many of the Italian states and their Austrian allies were distinctly at odds with the growing movement and increasing attempts toward the unification of Italy.[29] Despite efforts to suppress any liberal political activity on the peninsula, "the theory of nationalities exercised a practical influence on the method followed in the formation of the Kingdom of Italy," and many of the Italian states voted by plebiscite for annexation during this time.[30] After unsuccessful uprisings beginning in 1848, Lombardy, Venice, Modena, Parma, Piacenza, and Reggio voted for annexation to Sardinia.[31] In 1860, the peoples of Tuscany, Emilia, the Marches, Umbria, Naples, and Sicily all voted almost unanimously for annexation as well.[32] In 1961, the King of Sardinia officially assumed the title of King of Italy.[33] With the King's assumption of this new title, Italy's unification was almost complete. Five years later, in 1866, Austria ceded Venetia to Italy after another plebiscite vote.[34] As states were incorporated into the Kingdom of Italy, the old states were completely extinguished.[35] However, in practice, the Kingdom of Italy operated as a continuation of the Kingdom of Sardinia, and the Kingdom of Italy succeeded to all of the treaties that had been concluded by the Kingdom of Sardinia, with the exception of those that proved incompatible with the new political structure.[36] The treaties that remained in force

27 Id. at 163.

28 For a more detailed discussion of the development of the doctrine of nationalities, and the thinkers who supported and developed it, *see* Sereni, *supra* note 26, at 155–81.

29 Id. at 183.

30 Id. at 183–85.

31 Id. at 185.

32 Id. Other sources cite these votes as having taken place between 1859 and 1861. *See, e.g.*, Sir Augustus Oakes & R.B. Mowat, The Great European Treaties Of the Nineteenth Century 220–22 (Clarendon Press 1970).

33 Oakes, *supra* note 32, at 222.

34 Sereni, *supra* note 26, at 186.

35 Id.

36 Id.

were extended to all of the newly incorporated states, while any treaties that had previously been concluded by these states were considered to have been terminated.[37]

Italy's next regime change did not occur until 1922, when the Fascists gained control of Italy.[38] The Fascists asserted that Italy had a right to possess the regions of Dalmatia, Nice, Savoy, Corsica, and Malta, which had historically and ethnically been considered Italian, and also aspired to the acquisition of new colonies.[39] However, the Fascist government had no unique conception of international law and had little, if any, influence on the existing Italian doctrine.[40] As their government became more totalitarian, the Fascists consistently took advantage of and violated the contemporary international legal norms, all the while insisting that they were complying with traditional rules of international law.[41] They continued to do so until the fall of Fascism in 1945. In 1946, a referendum was called to determine whether Italy should remain a monarchy or become a republic, and in accordance with the vote, the Italian Republic was finally born.[42]

Italy was one of the founding members of the European Union in 1955.[43] Therefore, Italy's admission into the EU did not raise the same issues of treaty succession that have been raised in states that have joined the EU since its formation. Italy is of course bound to comply with EU law concerning the conclusion of international agreements.[44]

Treaty Ratification and Implementation

Each of Italy's government ministries has treaty-making power in relation to any matter falling within the scope of its administrative and technical competencies.[45] In most cases, a ministry's signature indicates Italy's intent to be bound by a treaty, and no additional constitutional ratification procedure must be

37 Id.

38 Id. at 269.

39 Id. at 270.

40 Id. at 273.

41 Id. at 309–311. For a detailed discussion of the incompatibilities between Fascist doctrine and international law written during the Fascist period in Italy, *see* id. at 269–78, 302–11.

42 Thomas Glyn Watkin, The Italian Legal Tradition 80 (Ashgate 1997).

43 Giuseppe Cataldi, *Italy*, *in* International Law and Domestic Legal Systems: Interpretation, Transformation, and Persuasion 328, 328 (Dinah Shelton ed., 2011).

44 Id. at 332.

45 Id. at 337.

followed in order for the treaty to become effective.[46] However, Article 80 of the Italian Constitution requires authorization by both Houses of the Italian Parliament (the Chamber of Deputies and the Senate of the Republic) prior to the ratification of international treaties that are of a political nature, call for arbitration or legal settlements, or that entail changes to the national territory, financial burdens, or changes to legislation".[47] Once the Houses authorize such a treaty, it must be ratified by the President of the Republic pursuant to Article 87 of the Constitution.[48] Article 89 of the Constitution then requires the proposing minister of the treaty to countersign the act of ratification before the treaty can become valid, thus providing a check to the President's ratification power.[49]

In practice, the Constitutional procedure for treaty ratification is frequently modified.[50] For example, in cases where Article 80 applies, the Italian government may conclude a treaty in a "simplified form," before asking the Houses to authorize ratification of the treaty. Such treaties are also known as 'executive agreements' and must be consistent with domestic law.[51]

Regardless of how they are concluded, treaties are incorporated into Italian domestic law only after implementing legislation has been adopted.[52] Implementing legislation can take one of two forms. It may consist of a few brief provisions implementing the treaty as a whole, or it may take the form of a new law that interprets and reformulates the treaty provisions, and that amends any pre-existing domestic legislation where necessary.[53] These two forms of implementing legislation are known as the 'special' method and 'ordinary' method, respectively.[54] For treaties falling under Article 80 of the Constitution, the 'special' method is preferred, and the implementing legislation is known as an 'execution order'.[55] Prior to the adoption of implementing legislation, the

---

46 Id.

47 Id. at 328; Art. 80 Costituzione [Cost.] (It.), English translation *available at* www.senato.it ("Parliament shall authorise by law the ratification of such international treaties as have a political nature, require arbitration or a legal settlement, entail change of borders, spending or new legislation".).

48 Cataldi, *supra* note 43, at 328; Art. 87 Cost. ("The President shall ... ratify international treaties which have, where required, been authorised by Parliament".).

49 Cataldi, *supra* note 43, at 329; Art. 89 Cost. ("A writ of the President of the Republic shall not be valid unless signed by the proposing Minister, who shall be accountable for it".).

50 Cataldi, *supra* note 43, at 329.

51 Id. at 329, 338.

52 Id. at 338.

53 Id.

54 Id.

55 Id.

only effect of a newly ratified treaty is that it can be used by domestic courts to interpret a domestic law that is already in force and that deals with the same matter of law.[56] Once implemented through domestic legislation, however, the treaty becomes fully incorporated into the domestic law.[57]

Once implementing legislation is passed, both the treaty and legislation are required by statute to be published in the *Raccolta ufficiale degli atti normattivi della Repubblica italiana* (the Official Collection Of the Legislation Of the Italian Republic), and to be communicated to the two Houses of Parliament.[58] The text of the treaty must also be published in a special quarterly supplement to the *Gazzetta ufficiale della Repubblica italiana*, Italy's Official Gazette, although history shows that publication may have occasionally been incomplete.[59]

Evidence of State Practice

Diplomatic relations in Italy are conducted primarily through the *Ministero degli Affari Esteri* (the Ministry of Foreign Affairs), which is responsible for international relations and for representing Italy in the European integration process. Although other ministries have treaty-making power and may be involved in international affairs, it is the responsibility of the Ministry of Foreign Affairs to ensure that the activities of the other ministries comply with Italy's international policy objectives.[60] Recent selected documents relating to the Ministry of Foreign Affairs, such as speeches, interviews, and press releases, are published on the Ministry's website, although publication is far from comprehensive.[61]

Article 10 of the Constitution provides for the automatic incorporation of international customary law into Italy's domestic law.[62] The provision does not

56 Id. 339.

57 Id.

58 Legge 1984 n. 839, art. 1.

59 Id. at art. 4; Giovanni Bognetti, *The Role of Italian Parliament In the Treaty-Making Process*, 67 Chi.-Kent L. Rev. 392, 406 (1991) ("It can be doubted ... that really *all* the agreements concluded after 1984 by the government have been published. Some concerning details of military matters may have remained secret".).

60 Ministry of Foreign Affairs, http://www.esteri.it/MAE/EN/Ministero/.

61 Ministry of Foreign Affairs: Minister, http://www.esteri.it/MAE/EN/Ministero/Ministro/.

62 Art. 10 Cost. ("The Italian legal system conforms to the generally recognised principles of international law".).

apply to treaties or to other international obligations.[63] Domestic laws that are in conflict with international customary law are considered unconstitutional.[64] Domestic courts have the autonomy to apply international customary law without deference to the government or legislature, and may take judicial notice of international customary law even if it is not raised by one of the parties to the litigation.[65] Nonetheless, a court's interpretation of international customary law applies only to the case at hand, and is not binding on any other court or tribunal.[66]

Annotated Bibliography of Sources

General Treaty Collections

1 GAZZETTA UFFICIALE DELLA REPUBBLICA ITALIANA [OFFICIAL GAZETTE OF THE ITALIAN REPUBLIC]
(Roma, Ministerio de grazia e giustizia, 1946–).
URL: http://www.gazzettaufficiale.it/.

Summary: Italy's official source of legal information and texts of the laws of Italy. It is published by the State Polygraphic Institute and Mint in collaboration with the Ministry of Justice, which oversees preparation of the text. The texts of international treaties are required by law to be published in the *Gazzetta ufficiale*, although publication has not always been comprehensive. The *Gazzetta ufficiale della Repubblica italiana* replaces the *Gazzetta ufficiale del regno d'Italia* (Torino, Roma, etc., 1861–1946).

Note: The *Gazzetta ufficiale* is available in print, and the daily releases for the past 60 days can be accessed free of charge on the Gazette's website.

Note: All information contained in the *Gazzetta ufficiale* is also available through the Normattiva database.

2 RACCOLTA UFFICIALE DEGLI ATTI NORMATTIVI DELLA REPUBBLICA ITALIANA [OFFICIAL COLLECTION OF THE LEGISLATION OF THE ITALIAN REPUBLIC]
(Roma, Libreria dello stato, 1987–).

Summary: Official compilation of laws that have originally been published in the Official Gazette. The *Raccolta ufficiale* is published in monthly volumes, and includes citations to the Gazette issue in which the laws originally appeared.

---

63 Cataldi, *supra* note 43, at 343.
64 Id. at 344.
65 Id. at 343.
66 Id. at 344.

The *Raccolta ufficiale* replaces the *Raccolta ufficiale delle leggi e dei decreti della Repubblica italiana* (Roma, Libreria dello stato, 1947–1986), *Raccolta ufficiale delle leggi e dei decriti del Regno d'Italia* (Roma, Istituto poligrafico dello stato, 1861–1946) (alternate title: *Leggi e decreti del Regno d'Italia*), and the *Raccolta degli atti del governo di Sua Maestà il Re di Sardegna* (Torino, Stamperia reale, 1814–1861) *available at* http://catalog.hathitrust.org/Record/010428071.

Index: Includes alphabetical and chronological indexes.

3 NORMATTIVA

URL: http://www.normattiva.it/.

Summary: Normattiva is an open-access, full-text database containing all of the laws that have been published in the *Gazzetta ufficiale della Repubblica italiana* since 1946, including those relating to international law. The database contains the original texts of the laws, as well as the current texts. It also includes a feature called "*multivulgenza*," which allows users to view the text of a law as it existed on any date between its promulgation and the present day.

Topical and Selected Treaty Publications

4 ITRA: ARCHIVIO DEI TRATTATI INTERNAZIONALI [DATABASE OF INTERNATIONAL TREATIES]

Ministero degli Affari Esteri (Ministry of Foreign Affairs).

URL: http://itra.esteri.it/.

Summary: The Ministry of Foreign Affairs Database of International Treaties provides access to the text of and information regarding treaties in force in Italy in the fields of judicial cooperation, tax, investment and enforcement of judgments abroad. The information contained in the database is unofficial information, and the Ministry's website suggests that users refer directly to the texts that have been published in the *Gazzetta Ufficiale*.

Note: The interface and content of the database are entirely in Italian.

5 MINISTERO DELLA GIUSTIZIA [MINISTRY OF JUSTICE]

URL: http://www.giustizia.it/giustizia/it/homepage.wp.

Summary: The Ministry of Justice is responsible for the administration of Italy's courts, prisons, and juvenile facilities, and is responsible for implementing government policies. The Ministry's website includes texts of both multilateral conventions and bilateral agreements between Italy and other countries that fall within the competencies of the Ministry of Justice. The database of international agreements can be accessed through the "*Strumenti*" tab, and is searchable by both subject and country. The site also includes the date of entry into force as well as additional information about each treaty.

Diplomatic Documents

6 ARCHIVIO STORICO DIPLOMATICO [ARCHIVES OF DIPLOMATIC HISTORY]
Ministero degli Affari Esteri
http://www.esteri.it/MAE/IT/Ministero/Servizi/Archivi_Biblioteca/Storico _Diplom/.

Summary: The Archives of Diplomatic History is a section of the Ministry of Foreign Affairs and is responsible for the conservation of diplomatic documents created by the Ministry during the course of its activities. The Archives also holds the original copies of international agreements. Access to documents held in the Archives can be arranged upon request and within the limitations of Italian law. Contact information, as well as detailed information regarding the Archives' access policies, are provided on the Archives' website.

7 I DOCUMENTI DIPLOMATICI ITALIANI [ITALIAN DIPLOMATIC DOCUMENTS]
(Rome: Istituto Poligrafico e Zecca dello Stato, 1946–)
URL: http://www.esteri.it/MAE/IT/Ministero/Servizi/Archivi_Biblioteca/Documenti_diplomatici.htm.

Summary: I Documenti Diplomatici Italiani is a collection of diplomatic documents compiled by the Commission for the Restoration and Publication of Italian Diplomatic Documents and published by the State Polygraphic Institute and Mint. It aims to present a historical overview of the evolution of Italian foreign policy, and to provide researchers with the necessary documentation to reconstruct Italy's history with regard to international relations. The editors of each volume of the series select the documents that are to be published. Each volume covers a particular time period in Italy's diplomatic history, and the documents within are arranged chronologically. A list of completed and in-progress volumes is available on the Ministry of Foreign Affairs website.

Note: Volumes published since 2007 are available online in the Virtual Library for Official Publications of the Italian State at http://www.bv.ipzs.it/.

8 POLITICA ESTERA DELL'ITALIA: TESTI E DOCUMENTI [ITALIAN FOREIGN POLICY: TEXTS AND DOCUMENTS]
(Rome: Ufficio Studi, 1972–).

Summary: Annual publication of the Library and Research Office of the Ministry of Foreign Affairs. It contains collected annotated documents that the Office considers to be most relevant to the activities of the administration and to Italy's foreign policy.

Note: A complete list of years in which *Italian Foreign Policy* was published can be seen on the Ministry's website at http://www.esteri.it/MAE/IT/Ministero/Servizi/Archivi_Biblioteca/Biblioteca.htm.

Yearbooks and Digests of State Practice

9 LA PRASSI ITALIANA DI DIRITTO INTERNAZIONALE [THE ITALIAN PRACTICE OF INTERNATIONAL LAW]

Istituto di Studi Giuridici Internazionali (ISGI) del Consiglio Nazionale delle Ricerche (CNR).

URL: http://www.prassi.cnr.it/prassi/.

Summary: The Institute of International Legal Studies of the National Research Council conducts research and studies on the formation and evolution of customary international standards in order to document the development of the international community and of international law over the past century. The Italian Practice of International Law database stores and disseminates the results of this research. It aims to document Italy's contribution to the formation of general rules of international law, and contains over two thousand cases relating to Italian international legal practice during the period between 1919 and 1925.

10 ITALIAN YEARBOOK OF INTERNATIONAL LAW

(Boston: Martinis Nijhoff, 1975–).

Summary: Annual publication that aims to disseminate Italian scholarship and practice in the field of international law among non-Italian speaking scholars and practitioners. Each issue includes peer-reviewed articles; detailed reports on Italian case law, diplomatic and parliamentary practice, legislation, and treaty practice; reports on the practice of the main international courts and tribunals; and a bibliographical index, arranged by subject, of Italian literature in the field of international law that has been published in the past year.

Note: Online subscriptions are also available through HeinOnline and Brill Online.

11 RIVISTA DI DIRITTO INTERNAZIONALE [INTERNATIONAL LAW REVIEW]

(Milan: Giuffrè, 1906–).

Summary: Quarterly journal containing scholarly discussion on issues of public and private international law, with particular attention to those issues that are of the most concern to Italy. Each issue includes several articles, as well as shorter notes that analyze current events in international law.

Note: Also contains reprints of selected EU and Italian jurisprudence addressing questions of international law, Italian legislation relating to international legal issues, and resolutions of the U.N. Security Council.

Japan

Rob Britt

Historical Background

From the time of the first written record, around 57 A.D. when Chinese documents report a tribal king from southern Japan paying tribute to the Chinese emperor,[1] the main islands of Japan (Honshū, Kyushū, Shikoku, and later Hokkaidō and Okinawa) have always remained under the control of ethnically Japanese people, except for the U.S. Occupation period (1945–1952). The Ainu people also lived on the main Japanese islands from a very early time, but the Japanese gradually drove them further and further into northern Honshū, Hokkaidō and islands to the north of that, where they mainly live today.[2] Evidence of continuous residence by ethnic Japanese in the Japanese archipelago is further established by pottery and earth mounds attributed to them that date back to paleolithic times (10,500 B.C.). As early as 240 A.D., the Wei Court in China recognized Himiko as Queen of Japan with a gold seal. Various other Chinese and Korean records provide evidence of the ongoing development of an early Japanese state. By 701 A.D., the Japanese court sent an embassy to the Chinese Tang court, offering a tribute of gold. In the same year, the Japanese rulers also promulgated the 'Taihō Code' [Taihō ritsuryō] (大宝律令), an early civil and penal code. That document and other similar ones that followed were modeled after the Chinese Tang Dynasty legal system[3] and 'basic to the rise of [Japan's] bureaucratic state.'[4] Japan was heavily influenced by China and early Korea, but was nevertheless able to retain control of its territory, and eventually expand it, until the end of World War II, aided in part by geographical barriers, mainly the Japan Sea. Until the mid-nineteenth century, Japan was independent of direct foreign influence, and under the policy of the Tokugawa Bakufu (1603–1868),[5] it had limited

---

1 Delmer M. Brown, *Chronology, in* 1 Cambridge History of Japan, at xxi, xix–xxiii (Delmer M. Brown ed., 1993).

2 J. Edward Kidder, Jr. *The earliest societies in Japan, in* 1 Cambridge History of Japan, 79, 48–107 (Delmer M. Brown ed., 1993).

3 Brown, *supra* note 1, at xix–xxiii.

4 Naoki Kōjirō, *The Nara State, in* 1 Cambridge History of Japan, 221, 221–267 (Delmer M. Brown ed. 1993).

5 The dominant feudal regime that held sway over all the other feudal domains in Japan; Also known as the Tokugawa Shogunate.

 | DOI 10.1163/9789004272224_020

relations with outsiders.[6] In the lead up to the Tokugawa period, the dominant warlord Hideyoshi expelled Portuguese Catholic missionaries in 1587, but he did not abolish foreign trade.[7] Trade continued in a limited way throughout Tokugawa, especially with other Asian countries.[8] For example, the Treaty of Kiyu[9] was concluded in 1609 by Japan and Korea, resolving issues stemming from a war between the two countries in the late 1500s, and setting up conditions for trade.[10]

In 1853, towards the end of a long period of relative isolation, and at time when the long-standing Tokugawa Bakufu's hold on power was beginning to weaken, the U.S. Navy's Commodore Matthew Perry and his 'black ships' steamed into Tokyo Bay brandishing high powered modern weapons. This heavily armed American contingent eventually forced the Japanese to accede to the first of the 'unequal treaties' that Japan was to sign with Western powers. Perry returned the next year, and a treaty was signed in Kanagawa.[11] Between 1858 and 1871, a total of 16 foreign countries signed similar treaties of 'friendship and commerce,' first with the Tokugawa Bakufu and later with the Meiji government,[12] which was established in 1868. The new Meiji government unified the nation under the emperor, and abolished the far-flung 'samurai' war lord-led feudal domains of the Tokugawa Bakufu. The unequal treaties served as incentive for Japanese leaders to re-imagine Japan's relationship to the outside world and to aspire to become players in the Western-dominated international system.[13] The treaties required the Meiji government to give special treatment to westerners within its borders, as its evolving system of government was considered by the West to be primitive, with laws thought to be unfit for application to

6 Although Japan did limit foreign trade and relations during the Tokugawa Period under the policy of national exclusion known as 'sakoku' [鎖国], in fact its isolation was not complete. For one thing, trade was still possible through certain designated ports. *See* for example Ronald P. Toby, State and Diplomacy in Early Modern Japan (1984).

7 Marius B. Jansen, The Making of Modern Japan 66–67 (2000).

8 Id. at 87. Also see Toby, *supra* note 6, at 1–22.

9 Kiyū jōyaku [己酉条約 OR 慶長条約] [Treaty of Kiyu], 1609.

10 Jansen, *supra* note 7, at 69.

11 Peace and amity treaty, U.S.-Japan, Mar. 31, 1854, 11 Stat. 597.
(Known also as the 'Treaty of peace and friendship between Japan and the United States' or 'Treaty of Kanagawa,' and in Japanese as '亜米利加條約' or '亞墨利加條約' [Ameirika jōyaku], and also as '日米和親条約' [Nichi-Bei washin jōyaku], the treaty was concluded between the Tokugawa Shogunate and the United States).

12 Michael R. Auslin, Negotiating with Imperialism: The Unequal Treaties and the Culture of Japanese Diplomacy at Appendix 1 (2004).

13 Id. at 1–3.

westerners. Rankled by these and other treaty provisions, the Japanese government leaders spent much of the early years of the Meiji Era (1868–1912) working towards the development of a fully westernized system of government (and the widespread adoption of aspects of western culture and commerce), with the goal of joining world powers on an equal footing, and ending the system of 'extraterritoriality.'[14] Eventually the unequal treaties were re-negotiated or became irrelevant, and Japan began to operate as a fully vested partner on the world stage, beginning with the Sino-Japanese War (1894–1895). After this war, treaty succession was a much more pertinent issue for Japan and for countries and territories outside its historical borders that for a time Japan controlled.

Issues of Treaty Succession

Japan has occupied the same four main islands since at least the beginning of written history, while at the same time maintaining independence from foreign control. Under those circumstances, issues of treaty succession did not become very relevant until the late nineteenth century, when Japan began to occupy and colonize other Asian jurisdictions, and later when Japan itself was occupied by the United States. Japanese imperial ambitions continued until the disastrous events of World War II finally crushed them. The fall of the Japanese military government, the Occupation by the United States from 1945–1952, and the subsequent re-establishment of an independent Japanese state in 1952 all required wrenching adjustments by the Japanese people, its government and legal system. Many issues stemming from these turbulent decades were finally resolved in the midst of great upheaval. Many other issues remain unresolved today from Japan's perspective and especially from the point of view of its neighbors.

Japan and Taiwan, the Qing Empire and China (1895)

Japan's 1895 victory over the Qing Empire cemented its new world-class status, negating the force of the unequal treaties once and for all, and at the same time setting the stage for many treaty succession issues in the years to come, both for Japan itself and for the populations it annexed or began to control in some degree. The Treaty of Shimonoseki[15] ended the Sino-Japanese War when

---

14 *See*, e.g., John Peter Stern, The Japanese Interpretation of the "Law of Nations," 1854–1874 (1979).

15 Nisshin Ryōkoku Kōwa Jōyaku Oyobi Betsuyaku [日清両国媾和条約及別約] [Treaty of Shimonoseki], Japan-China, Apr. 17, 1895, Kanpō (gōgai), May 13, 1895 at 1.

representatives of China's Qing Empire agreed to cede its possessions Taiwan, the Pescadores islands, and the Liaodung peninsula[16] to Japan.[17] Part of this arrangement was short-lived, as '...within three months, the 'Triple Intervention' (by Russia, Germany and France) forced Japan to retrocede [the Liaodung peninsula] to China which, in turn, was soon forced to lease [it] to Russia...'[18] Russia valued the Liaodung peninsula, which included the vital port of Lüshunkou.[19] Lüshunkou would eventually serve as a railway terminus for Russian railway lines reaching across Asia from Europe and Manchuria[20] (the Trans-Siberian and other lines). Under the circumstances, Japan was obliged to conclude another treaty with the Qing Empire in November 1895, retroceding the peninsula to China.[21] The Japanese were humiliated by the Triple Intervention and other developments, leaving a bitter taste that was to cloud subsequent international relations for many years. In the end, Russia had control of the peninsula, but Japan retained control of Taiwan (and retained it until 1945). Also, Japan's influence in the Korean peninsula was greatly strengthened as a result of the 'diminution of Chinese influence' there.[22] As the loser, the Qing Empire was severely weakened, leaving it vulnerable to Japan and the Western powers.

Japan and Germany, Qingdao and the German Micronesian Islands (1914)

In World War I Japan joined the Allies against Germany, and in 1914 it used the opportunity to expand its colonial empire again. Japan's incentive was

---

16 Known at the time in Chinese as Fengtian Bandao [奉天半島], and pronounced 'Hōten Hantō' [奉天半島] in Japanese. The Chinese name has now changed to Liaodung Bandao [辽东半岛], pronounced 'Ryōtō Hantō' [遼東半島] in Japanese.

17 Mark R. Peattie, *The Japanese colonial empire, 1895–1945, in* 6 Cambridge History of Japan, 1989–1999 217, 225 (Peter Duus ed., 1988).

18 Id., p. 225.

19 Also known as Port Arthur, Lüshunkou [旅顺口] [Ryojunkō in Japanese] is a district at the tip of the Liaodong peninsula, and part of the municipality of Dalian [大连].

20 Historical name for a large region falling mostly in modern Northeast China, but including parts of modern Russia. Also called 'Northeast China,' or 'Dongbei' (东北) in Chinese.

21 Hōten Hantō kanpu ni kansuru jōyaku [奉天半島還付ニ関スル条約] [Treaty for the retrocession of the Liaodung Peninsula], Japan-China, Nov. 8, 1895, 12 Hōrei zensho 307 (Imperial edict [勅令] [chokurei]of Dec. 4, 1895).

22 Peattie, *supra* note 17 at 225.

> ...the tempting German colonial territories in Asia and the Pacific: [Qingdao][23] on the Shantung peninsula and the German island possessions in Micronesia – the Marshalls, the Carolines, and the Marianas (excluding Guam) – all of which were isolated and weakly defended.[24]

Playing its part as one of the Allies, Japan's navy and army captured Qingdao after a battle with German defenders, and proceeded to seize Germany's island possessions without resistance. The Germans had occupied Qingdao since 1898. The Allies were suspicious of Japan's motives at first, and were reluctant to grant Japan's claims to sovereignty over these two possessions. However by the end of World War I Japan was able to make agreements with the parties, and to "...press its claims during the Paris peace negotiations. Subsequently, the League of Nations categorized Japan's claim to these islands as 'Class C mandate,' giving them possession but prohibiting military activities there." [25]

Japan and Russia, the Korean Peninsula, Liaotung Peninsula, Manchuria, and Sakhalin (*1902–1932*)

After success versus China, Japan's influence in East Asia and the world continued to grow, beginning with the Anglo-Japanese Alliance (1902),[26] and continuing to the Russo-Japanese War (1904–1905). Japan's new status as a world power after the Sino-Japanese war ended in 1895 created many challenges and opportunities that were reflected in the documentation of its international relationships that would resonate for many years to come with respect to territorial claims and counter-claims by China, Taiwan, Russia and Korea.

Partly in reaction to Japan's antagonistic relationship with France, Germany and Russia demonstrated by the Triple Intervention, the Japanese and British leaders began to cultivate closer relations as early as 1898.[27] Negotiations between Japan and U.K. representatives on treaty language progressed quickly in 1901, leading up to the completed treaty in 1902, which placed Japan in a

---

23 Also known as Tsingtao, a major Chinese coastal city about half way between Shanghai to the south and Beijing to the north.

24 Peattie, *supra* note 17, at 227.

25 Id., 228.

26 Agreement between the United Kingdom and Japan relative to China and Corea, Gr. Brit.-Japan, Jan. 30, 1902, Gr. Brit. T.S. No.003 (1902) (Cd. 914) (In Japanese, the treaty is known as 'Nichi-Ei Dōmei' [日英同盟])

27 Tatsuji Takeuchi, WAR AND DIPLOMACY IN THE JAPANESE EMPIRE at ch. 11 (1935). Takeuchi gives a detailed account of the activities of Japanese leaders leading up to the treaty with the U.K.

better geo-political position as war with Russia approached. At the same time Japan continued to exert its influence by serving as an 'advisor' to the Korean government and by financing the construction of railways and other projects throughout the Korean peninsula. Meanwhile between 1898 and 1904, Russia also had a strong presence in Korea, furthering tensions. Offers by Japan to Russia of an arrangement whereby Russia would have a free hand in Manchuria in exchange for leaving Korea to Japan (the so-called Man-Kan kōkan [満韓交換]) were rejected.[28] At the same time, the United States was an unknown in many respects to Japan. It was difficult for Japan to make sense of American isolationism and racist immigration policies on the one hand and incursions into the Philippines and activities in China on the other.[29] In this environment, the Russo-Japanese war began in 1904, and fierce fighting ensued on the Liaodong peninsula and also in the Sakhalin islands to the north of Hokkaido. By 1905, Russia had enough, and peace talks began at Portsmouth, New Hampshire in the United States (at the invitation of President Theodore Roosevelt).[30] There are various accounts of the peace negotiations and the reaction of the Japanese public to them. In short, they were very controversial.[31] The treaty that resulted is known as the Treaty of Portsmouth[32] (Portsmouth, New Hampshire, USA).

As noted above, control over the Korean peninsula was one of the major issues at dispute between Japan and Russia in the Russo-Japanese war (1904–1905). The outcome, recorded in the Treaty of Portsmouth, was that Russia was no longer a factor in the area, and Korea "was totally absorbed into the Japanese colonial empire."[33] At first, the Japanese stopped short of outright annexation, but by 1910 Korea was formally annexed, marking the beginning of an occupation that would last until the end of World War II.

In the same negotiations, Japan also acquired the Russian rights and privileges in south Manchuria (the Liaotung Peninsula), and the southern half of Russia's Sakhalin islands (also known as the Kuril Islands), which the Japanese called Karafuto.[34] Karafuto was unpopulated except by a few Ainu people.

---

28 Peattie, *supra* note 17, at 225–226.

29 Richard Storry, JAPAN AND THE DECLINE OF THE WEST IN ASIA 1894–1943 at 33–34 (1979).

30 Takeuchi, *supra* note 27, at ch. 12.

31 *See,* e.g., Peattie, *supra* note 17, at 226–227; and Takeuchi, *supra* note 27, at 149–159.

32 Nichi-Ro ryōkoku kōwa jōyaku oyobi tsuika yakkan [日露両国講和条約及追加約款] [Treaty of Portsmouth], Japan-Russ., Sept. 5, 1905, 10 Hōrei zensho 313 (Imperial edict [勅令] [chokurei] of Oct. 16, 1905).

33 Peattie, *supra* note 17, at 226–227.

34 Id. at 227.

Japan sent colonists there. Since Karafuto had no other native inhabitants, its occupation was less complicated, and the Japanese established a government there with few problems. Japan's claims to these islands however are still disputed today Russia.

Administering the Liaotung peninsula, with interests in southern Manchuria was much more complicated for Japan.[35] However, by 1919 they established a government, plus interests in a rail line in southern Manchuria.[36] By 1922, in the wake of World War I, the Four Power Treaty[37] and the Nine Power Pact[38] were created, largely under the influence of Great Britain and the United States.

> This international order had been organized to protect the interests of the two major victorious powers [in World War I], Great Britain and the United States. The new system led to dissatisfaction among the countries that later turned fascist, such as Germany...Italy and Japan, which, although victorious, felt deprived of adequate rewards.[39]

It wasn't until 1932 that Japan expanded its claims on Manchurian territory beyond those won previously (a rail corridor awarded to Japan by the League of Nations in the early twenties). In March 1932, Japan occupied all of Manchuria, and set up a puppet state there. By 1933, Japan rejected the League of Nations' Lytton Report which was critical of its actions, and "...seceded from the Versailles system..."[40] that the treaties of 1922 had established.

Japan and Republican China (1932–1945)

Having invaded Manchuria, Japan began to colonize it. The military was tempted to invade China-proper partly seeking resources such as iron ore. With China divided between the nationalists and the communists, the situation was ripe for the sabre rattling Japanese military to go even further in fomenting war, sometimes against the expressed wishes of the civilian government back in Tokyo. Gradually the military's influence grew within the

35 Id. at 231.

36 Id. at 231.

37 Insular Possessions and Dominions in the Pacific (Four Power Treaty), U.S.-Fr.-Gr. Brit.-Japan, Dec. 13, 1921 (entered into force Aug. 17, 1923)., 43 Stat. 1646.

38 Principles and Policies Concerning China (Nine-Power Treaty), U.S.-Belg.-China-Fr.-Gr. Brit.-It.-Japan-Neth.-Port., Feb. 6, 1922 (entered into force Aug. 5 1925), 44 Stat. 2113.

39 Peattie, *supra* note 17, at 282.

40 Id. at 297–298.

government, making unilateral decisions by the military more and more possible as time when on.[41] Later, as war dragged on in the 1930s and into the 1940s, the civilian leadership in Japan looked more and more impotent, while at the same time the various military constituencies fought amongst themselves about the causes of their mounting frustration at what they eventually began to realize was a quagmire.[42]

GHQ, Peace Treaties and a Security Treaty (1945–1978)

It is well-known that World War II resulted in Japan's unconditional surrender and occupation in 1945 by U.S. forces. The 'Supreme Commander of the Allied Powers' (known as SCAP) was General Douglas MacArthur, and as such he ruled Japan until 1951, when he was replaced by another U.S. general. The Occupation ended in 1952. The Occupation's headquarters in Tokyo were called General Headquarters, GHQ, which was a bureaucracy operated by several thousand military and civilian administrators. This bureaucracy oversaw the re-building of Japan's infrastructure and political and legal systems.[43]

Leading up to this outcome was a complex web of events ranging from Japan's occupation and military activities in Manchuria and China in the late thirties to its development of a 'Greater East Asian Co-Prosperity Sphere' anchored by its colonies in Taiwan and Korea, and gradually expanding to encompass conquests in China, Polynesia, Indonesia and Southeast Asia. The United States was reluctant to renew its 1911 bilateral 'Treaty of Commerce and Navigation' with Japan,[44] and in 1941 it officially ended the agreement. Japan had committed itself to a very large army and navy spread out over a large swath of Asia and needed oil and other resources to fuel that expanding military-industrial machine. Under Japan's increasingly difficult circumstances, it signed an agreement with Germany and Italy in September 1940,[45] forming the Axis, and cementing the belief in the United States that the coming war

41 Id. at 302–306.

42 Id. at 319–321.

43 Jansen, *supra* note 7, at 666.

44 Treaty of Commerce and Navigation, U.S.-Japan, Feb. 21, 1911, T.S. 558, 1504 (proclaimed Apr. 5, 1911).

45 Nihonkoku, Doitsukoku, Itariakoku-kan sankoku jōyaku [日本国、独逸国及伊太利国間三国条約] [Three-Power Pact Between Germany, Italy, and Japan], Ger., It., Japan, Sept. 27, 1940, Treaty no. 9, 1940, 10 Hōrei zensho 75, 4137 Kanpō 684.
Full text in Japanese from Kanpō (Japan's government gazette) available online at the National Diet Library's 'Online Digital Library': http://dl.ndl.go.jp/info:ndljp/pid/2960635/3.

would be a 'single struggle' with German, Italian and Japanese forces.[46] In fact, coordination between Japan, Italy and Germany during the rest of the war was less than extensive. Japan's surprise attack on Hawaii prompted declarations of war from both sides without much delay. After initial successes, Japan's military fortunes in its far-flung empire grew more and more bleak, and as the early forties wore on, the size and number of territories under the control of Japan shrank inexorably, until by May 1945 not much was left.[47] President Truman's July 26, 1945, Potsdam Declaration demanded Japan's unconditional surrender, but none was offered. The devastation of Hiroshima and Nagasaki (presaged by the firebombing of Tokyo and other large cities) followed. Finally, on September 2, 1945, Japan assented to unconditional surrender.[48] "A Far Eastern Commission made up of the eleven Pacific War allies met in the former Japanese embassy in Washington to make and review policy, and an Allied Council with American, British Commonwealth, Soviet, and Chinese representatives met in Tokyo, theoretically to oversee implementation, but largely in vain."[49] The task of rebuilding Japan was left mainly to the Japanese people and GHQ, with MacArthur in the lead.

Japan's foreign adventures included many ugly episodes in China, Southeast Asia, and Asia in general, involving both the local populations and the Japanese military's prisoners of war from around the world. The body assigned to consider these issues and render judgments was the International Military Tribunal for the Far East (1946–1948).[50] The result was the execution or imprisonment of many of the top leaders of Japan's wartime military and government leadership.

Aspects of the activities of the Japanese military during the 15 years of war ending in 1945 remain issues of dispute today. Issues linger regarding the Imperial Military's activities in China, Korea, Southeast Asia, and also within the Japanese home islands. Unresolved disputes include those regarding slave labor, forced prostitution, experimentation on human subjects, and the treatment of POWs.

The Treaty of San Francisco[51] was concluded between Japan and most of the allies (but not China and the Soviet Union) in September 1951 in San Francisco,

---

46 Jansen, *supra* note 7, at 635.

47 Id., at 647–655.

48 Id., at 659–662.

49 Id., at 666–667.

50 Id., at 673.

51 Treaty of Peace with Japan, Sept. 8, 1951, 3 U.S.T. 3169 (proclaimed by the President of the United States of America Apr. 28, 1952).

signaling the beginning of the end of the Occupation, and restoring sovereignty to Japan, at the price of "…virtually unrestricted use of Japanese territory by the United States."[52] Japan in turn gained the advantages of the protection of the U.S. military at a very minimal price, and access to the largest markets in the world.[53] In 1956, the formal end of a state of war and resumption of diplomatic relations between the U.S.S.R. and Japan came with a joint Soviet–Japanese Declaration. The declaration did not constitute a full and permanent peace treaty.[54] Currently still unresolved issues between Japan and Russia (successor to the U.S.S.R.) are territorial disputes regarding islands to the north of Japan (see above), and a peace treaty has never been concluded.

Provisions in the Treaty of Peace specifically addressed the issue of Japan's defense in a very different way than article 9 of the 1946 "Peace Constitution"[55] does. It left open the possibility of Japan establishing military forces for self-defense, and of Japan entering into a security treaty with the United States. With the recent establishment of the PRC and the beginning of the war in Korea, these issues were seen by U.S. leaders and many other signers of the Treaty of Peace in a very different light than they were immediately following World War II.[56] Not coincidentally, another important treaty was signed on the same day at the San Francisco Peace conference, known in Japan as 'Anpo,' the security treaty with the United States.[57]

> … [T]he necessity of the treaty was a reflection of the changed situation in [East Asia] that had occurred since the end of the war. It is also recognized that Japan was incapable of defending itself in the event of an armed attack. More importantly for Japan, the United States had formally recognized the end of the disarmament period of Japan and was now encouraging Japan to rearm …[58]

The Security Treaty had far-reaching implications both for Japanese domestic politics and international relations.

---

52 Jansen, *supra* note 7, at 701–703.

53 Id., at 703.

54 Id., at 702, and 719.

55 NIHONKOKU KENPŌ (1946) [KENPŌ] [日本国憲法] [CONSTITUTION], art. 9 (Japan).

56 L. Jerold Adams, THEORY, LAW & POLICY OF CONTEMPORARY JAPANESE TREATIES 14–15 (1974), at 89.

57 Security Treaty Between Japan and the United States of America [Nihon to Amerika Gasshūkoku to no aida no anzen hoshō jōyaku] [日本とアメリカ合衆国との間の安全保障條約], U.S.-Japan, Sept. 8, 1951, 3.3 U.S.T. 3329 (entered into force Apr. 28, 1952).

58 Adams, *supra* note 56, at 90.

On April 28, 1952, Japan and the Republic of China (Taiwan) concluded the Japan-ROC Treaty of Taipei.[59] Although Taiwan was led by the generally anti-Japanese Kuomintang (KMT), headed by Jiang Jieshi (Chiang Kai-shek), the KMT government nevertheless negotiated with Japan and concluded the peace treaty. "Sharing both protection from a dominant US and a sense of threat from communism, the Japanese and Taiwanese renewed their contacts and tourism and trade developed."[60]

Of critical importance is the peace treaty Japan signed with the People's Republic of China in 1978.[61] The Japanese eventually negotiated this agreement with PRC in the wake of what seemed to them Nixon's sudden move towards a thaw in U.S.-China relations in 1972. One of the negotiating chips used by President Nixon and Henry Kissinger with China in negotiating that agreement was the threat of Japan re-militarizing in the event of an end to the U.S.-Japan security treaty. Japanese diplomats had to re-think their position under these changed circumstances, which is reflected in their 1978 agreement with China.[62]

Disputed Islands and Airspace (1945–)

In the aftermath of Japan's colonial period and World War II, disputes with neighboring countries regarding the ownership of small islands to the south and west linger today (The northern Sakhalin Islands are also disputed with Russia; see above.) The disputes are partly about patriotic claims in domestic politics that Japan has a right to these islands for historical reasons, but they also concern developing knowledge of a wealth of resources such as oil that have become more evident as scientific research progresses. Three main areas are under dispute currently, with a varying list of interested parties, involving issues that date back many decades. The People's Republic of China and Taiwan both claim possession of the tiny Senkaku[63] islands

59 Nihon to Chūka Minkoku to no Aida no Heiwa Jōyaku [日本国と中華民国との間の平和条約] [Treaty of Peace Between Japan and the Republic of China], Japan-Taiwan, Apr. 28, 1952, 56 JŌYAKUSHŪ 1015 (Japan).

60 Brian Bridges & Chan Che-po, *Looking North: Taiwan's Relations with Japan under Chen Shui-bian*, 81 PACIFIC AFFAIRS 577–596 (2008).

61 Nihon to Chūka Jinmin Kyōwakoku to no aida no Heiwa Yūkō Jōyaku [日本国と中華人民共和国との間の平和友好条約] [Treaty of Peace and Friendship between Japan and the People's Republic of China], Japan-China, Aug. 12, 1978, Treaty no. 19, 1978 NIKOKUKAN JŌYAKU, 323 (Japan).

62 Yukinori Komine, *The 'Japan Card' in the United States Rapprochement with China, 1969–1972*, 20 DIPLOMACY & STATECRAFT 494,508 (2009).

63 Called 'Diaoyu' in Chinese.

located about two hundred kilometers south of the Japanese island of Okinawa. The PRC also claims Okinotori Island, a tiny atoll located 1,740 km south of Tokyo.[64] Also, there is a dispute with South Korea (supported by North Korea) concerning the Liancourt Rocks, known in Japanese as Takeshima and in Korean as Dokdo.[65]

The southern islands of Okinawa, Amami and Ogasawara were under U.S. control according to the Treaty of San Francisco (see above). These islands were eventually returned to Japan: Amami in 1953, Ogasawara in 1969, and finally Okinawa in 1972.[66] In addition to disputes over islands, Japan's claims to airspace in certain areas are in conflict with the claims of South Korea and Russia. Also, airspace around U.S. military bases in Japan is controlled by the United States under treaties, which is the cause of some disputes with Japanese citizens who reside nearby, and others.[67] Currently, under the Security Treaty (see above), the U.S. retains 8 major military bases in Japan and at least 80 facilities of different types in all, stretching from Misawa in northern Honshū, to Kadena and Futenma bases in the southern island of Okinawa.[68]

Treaty Ratification and Implementation

Prior to the era of the unequal treaties, under the authority of the Bakufu, treaties (like all laws) were concluded by the Shogun and his designees with no authorizing constitution, and endorsed perfunctorily by the emperor. In some cases, the Bakufu delegated relations with foreign countries to particular domains, as it did with Korea leading up to the Treaty of Kiyu in 1609, mentioned above, when the Tsushima domain (located across the Japan Sea from Korea) managed negotiations.[69]

64 Alicia P.Q. Wittmeyer, *The Even Smaller Rocks Japan And China Are Fighting Over*, Passport: a Blog by the Editors of FP (Foreign Policy) (Sept. 24, 2012, 1:15 PM), http://blog.foreignpolicy.com/posts/2012/09/24/the_even_smaller_rocks_japan_and_china_are_fighting_over.

65 For the Japanese government perspective, *see* http://www.mofa.go.jp/region/asia-paci/takeshima/position.html ; For the Korean government perspective (Dokdo official website), *see* http://en.dokdo.go.kr/index.do.

66 Koji Furukawa, *Bordering Japan: Towards a Comprehensive Perspective,* 26 Journal of Borderlands Studies 297, 307–310 (2011).

67 Id., at 300–301.

68 United States Forces Japan, http://en.wikipedia.org/wiki/United_States_Forces_Japan.

69 Jansen, *supra* note 7, at 69.

Under the old Meiji Constitution (1889–1945),[70] the Emperor was required to consult with the Privy Council prior to the conclusion of treaties. Also, some exceptions in the wording allowed the cabinet to conclude treaties on its own under certain circumstances.[71] Regardless of legal arrangements, the political environment in Japan including the status of the armed forces vis-à-vis the civilian government changed drastically from 1900 to 1945. During the long lead-up to World War II, military leadership tended more and more towards creating diplomatic policy on its own rather than carrying out the policies of civilian leaders under the Emperor as stipulated in the Meiji Constitution. By 1935, the military was calling most of the shots.[72]

According to article 7 of the modern Japanese constitution of 1946,[73] established during the Occupation period, and written by GHQ, the 'promulgation of…treaties' is to be performed by '…the Emperor, with the advice and approval of the Cabinet.' Article 60, paragraph 2 concerns the budget. It sets a thirty day limit on the time the houses of the legislature (the House of Councilors and the House of Representatives in the Diet) may take to agree on a budget. If there is no agreement between the houses within thirty days of the House of Representative's decision on the budget, the House of Representatives budget becomes law. Article 61 refers to article 60, and provides that the House of Councilors must decide within thirty days whether to approve or reject treaties. If they offer no decision in that time, the decision of the House of Representatives is considered the final decision of the Diet. Articles 65 and 73 state that executive power rests with the Cabinet, and that the Cabinet concludes all treaties. Article 73 further stipulates that the Cabinet must obtain prior consent of the Diet (or under some circumstances after-the-fact consent of the Diet). Finally, article 98 states that the Constitution is the supreme law of the land, and that treaties concluded under the Constitution were established under the rules of international law, and should be faithfully observed.[74] It is not clear under the current constitution or the Meiji constitution whether or not treaties can be considered substantive laws of the state.[75] However, Adams analyzes relevant provisions and court decisions and concludes that

70 DAI NIHONKOKU KENPŌ (1889) [大日本国憲法] [MEIJI KENPŌ] [CONSTITUTION] (Japan).

71 Adams, *supra* note 56, at 18.

72 For example, *see* Ikuhiko Hata, *Continental expansion, 1905–1941 in* 6 CAMBRIDGE HISTORY OF MODERN JAPAN, 293, 271–314 (Peter Duus ed., 1988).

73 NIHONKOKU KENPŌ (1946), *supra* note 54.

74 Adams, *supra* note 56, at 13–14.

75 Id. at 21.

> [b]ased on the above practices and Article 98, paragraph 2 of the Constitution, the domestic courts of Japan can and do apply treaties as a standard of judgment; and it can be concluded further that treaties, excluding non-self-executing treaties, are binding directly upon state organs as well as nationals without special measures of legislation.[76]

A number of domestic Japanese laws are set up to implement international agreements regarding the United Nations, the International Criminal Court, international air and sea laws, and many laws to implement international cooperation with regard to science, technology and commerce. A recent search of the Japanese government's online statutes page found 172 current laws and regulations with 'international' in the title.[77]

Evidence of State Practice

As mentioned above the Constitution of Japan specifies that the Emperor, with the advice and approval of the cabinet is responsible for the promulgation of treaties. The constitution also provides that the Diet (as the Japanese legislature is known in English) must approve or reject treaties in a set period, and must provide any needed funding. The Minister of Foreign Affairs sits on the cabinet, and administers the Ministry of Foreign Affairs (hereafter 'MOFA') bureaucracy which carries out foreign policy. The Prime Minister serves as the lead representative of Japan in dealings with foreign jurisdictions. The Japanese court system, administered by the Supreme Court of Japan, considers treaties and other international agreements in its decisions (for collections of decisions and information about the Japanese court's work in this regard, see below under 'Court Decisions Relevant to Treaties and International Law.')

Annotated Bibliography of Sources

General Treaty Collections

1 JŌYAKUSHŪ [条約集] (TREATY COLLECTION) (Tōkyō : Gaimushō Jōyakukyoku, 1922–1964).

---

76 Id. at 21.

77 http://law.e-gov.go.jp (Hōrei dēta teikyō shisutemu 法令データ提供システム (HŌREI DB) (Ministry of Internal Affairs and Communications Administrative Management Bureau: constitutions, statutes, orders, rules, regulations, and ordinances)).

Summary: From 1965, this publication was split into two parts (see below). It is an authoritative and comprehensive collection of both bilateral and multilateral treaties.

Note: In Japanese (treaties are bilingual or multilingual).

2 JŌYAKUSHŪ. NIKOKUKAN JŌYAKU [条約集. 二国間条約] (TREATY COLLECTION. BILATERAL TREATIES) (Tōkyō : Gaimushō Jōyakukyoku, 1965–).

Summary: This is a comprehensive annual compilation of the bilateral treaties concluded by Japan. It is published by the Ministry of Foreign Affairs Treaty Office.

Index: Each annual volume has a table of contents listing the treaties included.

Note: This annual Ministry of Foreign Affairs (MOFA) treaty compilation is still published in print and available in that format at the National Diet Library and at the U.S. Library of Congress, but since MOFA began to make the contents available online in 2002, few other libraries have print holdings.

Note: In Japanese (treaties are bilingual or multilingual).

3 JŌYAKUSHŪ. TASŪ KOKUKAN JŌYAKU [条約集. 多数国間条約] (TREATY COLLECTION. MULTI-LATERAL TREATIES). (Tōkyō : Gaimushō Jōyakukyoku, 1965–).

Summary: This annual is published by the Ministry of Foreign Affairs Treaty Office, and as such it very is comprehensive and authoritative.

Index: Each annual volume has a table of contents listing the treaties included.

Note: This annual Ministry of Foreign Affairs (MOFA) treaty compilation is still published in print and available in that format at the National Diet Library and at the U.S. Library of Congress, but since MOFA began to make the contents available online in 2002, few other libraries have print holdings.

Note: In Japanese (treaties are bilingual or multilingual).

4 HŌREI ZENSHO [法令全書] (COMPLETE LAWS AND REGULATIONS) (Tōkyō : Naikaku Kanpōkyoku, 1867–).

Summary: This is a monthly that includes all treaties (and other laws and regulations) concluded during the month.

Index: The annual table of contents volume of Hōrei zensho, 'mokuroku' (目録), cites to treaties in both Hōrei zensho itself and in Kanpō (the Government Gazette). If the researcher knows the approximate year that the treaty was concluded, it is therefore possible to use the Hōrei zensho annual table of contents to find treaties in both Kanpō and Hōrei zensho.

Note: In Japanese (treaties bilingual or multilingual).

5 KANPŌ [官報] (GAZETTE)
(Tōkyō : Ōkurashō Insatsukyoku, 1883–).

Summary: This is Japan's comprehensive government gazette. The full text of all treaties is printed in it.

Note: In Japanese (treaties bilingual or multilingual).

Note: Also available online. See below under Internet resources.

Note: During the U.S. Occupation years (1945–1952) Kanpō was also published in an English language version, called 'Official Gazette'. Some libraries hold this English language version, and it is also available online (see entry for 'KINDAI DIGITARU RAIBURARI: KANPŌ', below).

Index: See above under Hōrei zensho. Kanpō is also indexed by the annual publication KANPŌ SŌSAKUIN (COMPLETE INDEX TO KANPŌ), Bunka Tosho, 1988–.

6 SHUSHŌ KANTEI KANPŌ DAIJESUTO [首相官邸官報ダイジェスト]
(PRIME MINISTER'S OFFICE OFFICIAL GAZETTE DIGEST)

Summary: All Japanese treaties are published in Kanpō, the Official gazette (see preceding entry). As a digest, this online resource only allows users to confirm whether or not a given treaty is available in Kanpō on a known date. No keyword searching is available.

Note: In Japanese.

Note: Digest of Kanpō.

Current: http://www.kantei.go.jp/jp/kanpo/digest.html.

Back numbers: http://www.kantei.go.jp/jp/kanpo/digest-bk.html.

7 GAIMUSHŌ JŌYAKU DĒTA KENSAKU [外務省条約データ検索]
(MINISTRY OF FOREIGN AFFAIRS: TREATY DATA SEARCH)
URL: http://www3.mofa.go.jp/mofaj/gaiko/treaty/index.php.

Summary: This MOFA treaties database search page provides access to full-text treaties. It includes treaties approved by the Diet from the 154th session and following (Heisei 14 [2002–]). The treaties are in PDF files, and can be viewed in Japanese and other provided languages. Also included are 'Reference Materials' (Official Text) documents in PDF, the legislative record of the agreement, and explanatory text. Users may search by treaty name or subject keyword. Searches can be narrowed by world region or country, whether bilateral or multi-lateral. Materials available include all modern treaties, plus treaty-related documents, such as 'kōbun' [公文] (public statements).

Note: In Japanese.

8 GAIMUSHŌ JŌYAKU [外務省条約] (MINISTRY OF FOREIGN AFFAIRS: TREATIES)
URL: http://www.mofa.go.jp/mofaj/gaiko/treaty/index.html.

Summary: This page provides a list of links to full-text treaties and related documents in Japanese (along with multilingual texts as available). Documents are listed chronologically, by Diet session. There is no keyword searching.

Note: In Japanese.

9 MINISTRY OF FOREIGN AFFAIRS: TREATY
URL: http://www.mofa.go.jp/policy/treaty/index.html.

Summary: This page is similar to the previous reference, but it has an English interface and English-only treaty text, listed by Diet session. There is no keyword searching.

Note: In English.

Treaty Indexes

Although few usable print stand-alone indexes to Japanese treaties are available, treaty collections do include indexes and tables of contents, as noted above. Online searching of free Japanese government websites also provides good keyword search access to Japanese treaties.

10 GENKŌ JŌYAKU ICHIRAN [現行条約一覧] (CURRENT TREATIES LIST) (Tōkyō : Gaimushō Jōyakukyoku, 1955–1960).

Summary: This publication ceased in 1960, after only a five year run. It listed all current treaties for the period.

11 NIHON HŌREI SAKUIN: TREATY APPROVALS SEARCH PAGE [日本法令索引: 条約承認案件検索] (INDEX TO JAPANESE LAWS AND REGULATIONS: TREATY APPROVALS SEARCH)
URL: http://hourei.ndl.go.jp/SearchSys/frame/jyouyaku_top.jsp.

Summary: This National Diet Library search webpage provides access to treaties concluded in 1947 and following. Many of the treaties are available on the website in full text.

Note: Search for treaties using Japanese keyword and date. Successful results of treaty searches provide a link to full text online version(s) (scanned image files), plus information about whether the treaty is current or abolished.

Note: In Japanese.

12 NIHON HŌREI SAKUIN: ŌDAN KENSAKU [日本法令索引：横断検索] (JAPAN LAWS AND REGULATIONS: CROSS-DATABASE INDEX)
URL: http://hourei.ndl.go.jp/SearchSys/frame/oudan_top.jsp.

Summary: The National Diet Library provides this handy "cross database" search page. The page allows users to search for current and superseded treaties (plus laws and regulations) going back to 1868. It provides a very convenient way to access the full-text scanned repository of the 'Modern Digital Library' (see below) with direct links to that resource in search results. The Modern Digital Library includes the full text of Hōrei zensho (see above), which is the monthly compilation of new laws, regulations and treaties, dating from 1868 to the present.

Note: In Japanese.

13 NIHON HŌREI SAKUIN: JŌYAKU SHŌNIN ANKEN KENSAKU [日本法令索引：条約承認案件検索] (JAPAN LAWS AND REGULATIONS INDEX: TREATY APPROVALS INDEX)
URL: http://hourei.ndl.go.jp/SearchSys/frame/jyouyaku_top.jsp.

Summary: Covers 1947 to current (see details in the preceding entry).

14 KAKKOKU BETSU JŌYAKUSHŪ, JŌYAKU MOKUROKU [各国別条約集・条約目録] (NATIONAL TREATY COLLECTIONS, TREATIES TABLE OF CONTENTS)
URL: http://rnavi.ndl.go.jp/politics/entry/Conventions2.php.

Summary: This is a very useful National Diet Library annotated list of treaty collections available in print and online.

Note: In Japanese.

Topical and Selected Treaty Publications

Historical

15 KINDAI DIGITARU RAIBURARI: KANPŌ [近代デジタルライブラリ：官報] (The Modern Digital Library: Government Gazette) ; Official Gazette (1946–1952)
URL: http://dl.ndl.go.jp/#kanpo.

Summary: This search page for the Japanese government gazette, 'Kanpō' is provided by the National Diet Library, and offers access to full-text treaties concluded between July 30, 1886 April 30, 1952. In addition, it gives valuable full-text access to the English language government gazette, 'Official Gazette' which had an English edition only during the U.S. Occupation years: April 4, 1946 to April 28, 1952.

Note: In Japanese and English.

16 THE JCAR SEARCH PAGE
URL: http://www.jacar.go.jp/english/index.html (English); http://www.jacar.go.jp/index.html (Japanese).

Summary: [See also below under 'Diplomatic Documents'] This English-language search page (also available in Japanese) can be used to access treaties and treaty-related documents covering 1886 and subsequent years. The 'Japan Center for Asian Historical Record' (JACAR) defines 'Asian Historical Records' as "documents possessed by Japanese archival institutions concerning modern Japan and its relations with, among others, neighboring Asian countries."[78] The resource also includes search pages in Chinese and Korean.

17 TREATIES AND CONVENTIONS BETWEEN THE EMPIRE OF JAPAN AND OTHER POWERS = JŌYAKU ISAN [條約彙纂]
(Tōkyō : Printed at the 'Kokubunsha' printing office by order of the Foreign Service, 1884).

Summary: This is a useful source for treaties from the period of the unequal treaties (about 1854–1895), when Japan first began to emerge as a world power.

Note: Microfiche; also available online, in a different edition; see below.

Note: In Japanese.

18 TREATIES AND CONVENTIONS, CONCLUDED BETWEEN EMPIRE OF JAPAN AND FOREIGN NATIONS, 1854–1874
URL: http://dl.ndl.go.jp/info:ndljp/pid/900640.

Summary: This is an online digitization of the print treaty collection noted in the preceding entry. It covers the years 1854–1874, and is available in the online collection 'Kokuritsu Kokkai Toshokan Dejitaru-ka Shiryō' [国立国会図書館デジタル化資料] (National Diet Library Digitized Materials).

Note: The digitized document is in English, but the online viewer controls are in Japanese.

19 JŌYAKU BENRAN: NIKOKUKAN JŌYAKU [条約便覧：二国間条約] (TREATY HANDBOOK: BILATERAL TREATIES)
(Tōkyō : Gaimushō Jōyakukyoku, 1958).

78 ABOUT JCAR (video), http://www.jacar.go.jp/english/jacarmovie/jacarmovie.htm.

(Tōkyō : Nihon Tosho Sentā, 1997) [reprint].

Summary: This 1958 publication of the Ministry of Foreign Affairs (MOFA), Treaty Office includes bilateral treaties concluded between 1854 and 1957.

Note: 1 volume (365 pages).

Note: In Japanese.

20 JŌYAKU BENRAN: TAKOKU KOKUKAN JŌYAKU [条約便覧 : 多国国間条約] (TREATY HANDBOOK: MULTI-LATERAL TREATIES) (Tōkyō : Gaimushō Jōyakukyoku, 1954–1958).

Summary: This 1954–1958 publication of the Ministry of Foreign Affairs (MOFA), Treaty Office includes multilateral treaties concluded between 1854 and 1957.

Note: 3 volume loose-leaf.

Note: In Japanese.

21 KYŪ JŌYAKU ISAN [舊條約彙纂] (COMPILATION OF OLD TREATIES) ([Tokyo]: Gaimushō Jōyakukyoku, 1930–1936).

Summary: This publication of the Ministry of Foreign Affairs includes old bilateral and multilateral treaties, plus a volume of treaties with Korea and the Ryūkyū islands.

Note: In Japanese.

Unequal Treaties

22 JŌYAKU KAISEISHI = HŌKEN KAIFUKU E NO TENBŌ TO NASHONARIZUMU [条約改正史: 法権回復への展望とナショナリズム] (MEIJI TREATY REVISION: THE PROSPECT FOR A UNIFIED JURISDICTION AND NATIONALISM) (Tōkyō : Yūhikaku, 2010).

Summary: The sub-title references Japan's efforts to extract itself from the humiliating unequal treaties in the late nineteenth century.

Note: In Japanese.

The San Francisco Peace Treaty

23 NIHON GAIKŌ BUNSHO. HEIWA JŌYAKU NO TEIKETSU NI KANSURU CHŌSHO [日本外交文書. 平和条約の締結に関する調書] (DOCUMENTS ON JAPANESE FOREIGN POLICY. RECORDS RELATED TO THE CONCLUSION OF TREATY OF PEACE WITH JAPAN) (Tōkyō : Gaimushō, Heisei 14 [2002]).

Summary: This 5 volume set was originally published in 8 volumes of confidential documents by the Gaimushō Jōyakukyoku Hōkika (Foreign Ministry Treaty Office Legal Department) in 1959–1970. Publication of this 2002 edition was followed by the publication of other parts of the collection of San Francisco peace treaty documents. The parts include: Junbi taisaku [準備対策] (Policy preparations), 2006; Taibei kōshō [対米交渉] (Negotiations with the U.S.), 2007; and Chōin, hakkō [調印・発効] (Signed, Entered into Force), 2009.

Note: In Japanese and English.

China

24 CHŪGOKU OYOBI MANSHŪ KANKEI JŌYAKU OYOBI KŌBUNSHŪ [中国及び満洲関係條約及公文集] (PUBLIC DOCUMENTS AND TREATIES CONCERNING CHINA AND MANCHURIA)
(Tōkyō: Ryūkei Shosha, 1993).

Summary: Originally published in 1934, this reprint includes many documents vital to understanding the history of Japan's military and colonial activities in China and Manchuria.

Note: 2 volumes.

Note: Reprint.

Note: In Japanese.

25 NISSHI KANKEI JŌYAKU SŌRAN [日支關係條約總覽] (COMPREHENSIVE LIST OF JAPAN-CHINA TREATIES)
(Tōkyō : Shina Kenkyūsha, 1916).

Summary: Useful for historical research.

Note: 443 pages; Edited by the 'China Research Corporation Editorial Board.'

Note: In Japanese.

26 NISSHI KAN NARABINI SHINA NI KANSURU NIHON OYOBI TAKOKUKAN NO JŌYAKU [日支間竝支那ニ關スル日本及他國間ノ條約] (TREATIES BETWEEN JAPAN AND CHINA, AND TREATIES BETWEEN CHINA, JAPAN AND OTHER COUNTRIES)
(Tōkyō : Nihon Shōkō Kaigishō, 1923?).

Summary: This collection serves as an update to material noted in the previous citation.

Note: 393 pages.

Note: In Japanese.

Korea

27 KOKUSAIHŌ KARA MITA KAN-NICHI REKISHI MONDAI [国際法からみた韓日歴史問題] (LOOKING AT ISSUES OF KOREAN/JAPANESE HISTORY FROM AN INTERNATIONAL LAW PERSPECTIVE)
(Seoul: Tōhokua Rekishi Zaidan, 2008).

Summary: Published in Korea, this work recounts the history of Japan's involvement in the Korean peninsula with reference to international law and treaties.

Note: In Japanese.

28 1905-NEN KANKOKU HOGO JŌYAKU TO SHOKUMINCHI SHIHAI SEKININ
[1905 年韓国保護条約と植民地支配責任] (THE 1905 KOREA PROTECTION TREATY AND THE RESPONSIBILITY TO MANAGE THE COLONY)
(Tōkyō : Sōshisha, 2005).

Summary: This book is an historical study of the treaty between Japan and the Kingdom of Korea concluded after the Russo-Japanese war (1904–1905), the beginning of a 'protectorate' which later became a colonial occupation by Japan that lasted until 1945.

Note: In Japanese.

Russia and the Soviet Union

29 HOPPŌ RYŌDO MONDAI SHIRYŌSHŪ [北方領土問題資料集] (COLLECTION OF DOCUMENTS CONCERNING THE NORTHERN ISLANDS)
(Tōkyō Hoppō Ryōdo Mondai Taisaku Kyōkai 1972).

Summary: This is a convenient set of materials for research on Japan-Russia treaty issues regarding Sakhalin and the Kuril Islands (called 'Karafuto' in Japanese).

Note: In Japanese.

Note: 337 pages.

30 THE RUSSO-JAPANESE TREATIES OF 1907–1916 CONCERNING MANCHURIA AND MONGOLIA
(Baltimore : John Hopkins Press, 1933.)

Summary: This is a convenient collection of treaties concerning Japan's developing interests in Manchuria and Mongolia.

Note: In microfiche; 164 pages.

Note: In English and French.

Germany, Italy and Japan: The Tripartite Pact

31 NIHON GAIKŌ BUNSHO. NICHI-DOKU-I SANGOKU DŌMEI KANKEI CHŌSHOSHŪ [日本外交文書 : 日独伊三国同盟関係調書集] (DOCUMENTS ON JAPANESE FOREIGN POLICY RECORDS RELATED TO

THE CONCLUSION OF THE TRIPARTITE PACT
(JAPAN-GERMANY-ITALY))
(Tōkyō : Gaimushō, 2004).

Summary: This MOFA compilation is a useful collection of treaty-related documents relevant to World War II.

Note: In Japanese.

Note: 593 pages.

Japan-U.S. Security Treaty (Nichi-Bei Anpo Jōyaku)

32 NICHI-BEI ANPO JŌYAKU ZENSHO [日米安保条約全書] (COMPLETE JAPAN-U.S. SECURITY TREATY MATERIALS)
(Tōkyō : Rōdō Junpōsha, 1968).

Summary: This compilation includes the text of the U.S.-Japan Security Treaty (Anpo), plus other documents related to the agreement, and examples of security treaties in various other countries.

Note: In Japanese.

Note: 860 pages.

33 DOKYUMENTO NICHI-BEI ANPO [ドキュメント日米安保] (JAPAN-U.S. SECURITY TREATY DOCUMENTS)
(Tōkyō : Ōzorasha, 1996).

Summary: This book includes many treaty-related diplomatic and other documents, covering the years 1950–1996.

Note: In Japanese.

Note: 6 volumes.

The U.S. Occupation Period (GHQ/SCAP, 1945–1952)

34 TSUIHOBAN OKINAWA MONDAI KIHON SHIRYŌSHŪ [追補版沖縄問題基本資料集] (COLLECTION OF BASIC MATERIALS ON THE OKINAWA PROBLEM, SUPPLEMENTAL EDITION)
(Tōkyō : Nanpō Dōhō Engokai, 1972).

Summary: This is a convenient resource with regard to developments in U.S.-Japan relations concerning Okinawa.

Note: In Japanese.

Note: 973 pages.

Treaty Ratification

35 WAGA KUNI GA MIHIJUN NO KOKUSAI JŌYAKU ICHIRAN : 2009–NEN 1–GATSU GENZAI [わが国が未批准の国際条約一覧: 2009年1月 現在]

(LIST OF INTERNATIONAL CONVENTIONS NOT YET RATIFIED BY JAPAN: AS OF JANUARY 2009)
(Tōkyō : Kokuritsu Kokkai Toshokan Chōsa Oyobi Rippō Chōsa Kyoku, 2009).

Summary: This is a useful list of treaties not ratified by Japan.
Note: In Japanese.
Note: Includes index.

36 JŌYAKU NO KOKUNAI TEKIYŌ KANŌSEI [条約の国内適用可能性] (THE ABILITY TO APPLY TREATIES DOMESTICALLY)
(Tōkyō : Yūhikaku, 1985).

Summary: This work is a treatise on the process of treaty ratification in Japan.
Note: In Japanese.
Note: Includes index.

Court Decisions Relevant to Treaties and International Law

37 NIHON NO SAIBANSHO NI YORU KOKUSAIHŌ HANREI [日本の裁判所による国際法判例] (INTERNATIONAL LAW DECISIONS AND THE JAPANESE COURTS)
(Tōkyō : Sanseidō, 1991).

Summary: Edited by Takeo Sogawa and Shigeru Oda, leading scholars in the area, this work shows how Japanese court decisions have an important bearing on the implementation of international agreements.
Note: In Japanese.
Note: Includes index to cases discussed.

38 KOKUSAI SHIHŌ HANREI HYAKUSEN (DAI 2-HAN.) [国際私法判例百選(第2版)] (ONE HUNDRED SELECTED PRIVATE INTERNATIONAL LAW DECISIONS. 2ND ED.)
(Tōkyō : Yūhikaku, 2012).

Summary: Number 210 in the 'Bessatsu Jurisuto' (Jurist Supplement) series, this is a collection of selected international private law decisions and commentary for quick reference.
Note: In Japanese.
Note: Includes index to cases discussed.

39 KOKUSAI HANREI HYAKUSEN [国際判例百選] (ONE HUNDRED SELECTED INTERNATIONAL LAW DECISIONS)
(Tōkyō : Yūhikaku, 2001).

Summary: Number 156 in the 'Bessatsu Jurisuto' (Jurist Supplement) series, this collection provides decisions and commentary for quick reference.

Note: In Japanese.

Note: Includes index to cases discussed.

Diplomatic Documents

40 GAIMUSHŌ GAIKŌ SHIRYŌKAN [外務省外交資料館] (DIPLOMATIC ARCHIVES OF THE MINISTRY OF FOREIGN AFFAIRS OF JAPAN)
URL: http://www.mofa.go.jp/mofaj/annai/honsho/shiryo/index.html.

Summary: This website has links to information about Japan's diplomatic archives, including FAQs about the contents of the archives and how to use them.

Note: In Japanese.

41 NIHON GAIKŌ BUNSHO [日本外交文書] (JAPAN'S DIPLOMATIC DOCUMENTS)
(Tōkyō : Gaimushō, Heisei 14 [2002]).

Summary: Since 1936, MOFA (Gaimushō) has regularly issued new volumes in this important series of print publications. Selected parts are also published in print and microform by commercial publishers, such as Hara Shobō [原書房]. The publications include topical compilations of diplomatic documents of many types. Some are published as sub-sets on specific topics. Currently, the collection contains about 48,000 files in all.

Note: In Japanese.

Note: Many documents in the series can be viewed online in the "Digital Archive" (see the following entry).

Note: Individual citations for specific issues in this series of particular interest are included elsewhere in this bibliography, under headings beginning with the phrase 'NIHON GAIKŌ BUNSHO'.

Note: A complete list of publications in this series, with detailed information about each is available on the Ministry of Foreign Affairs website, here: http://www.mofa.go.jp/mofaj/annai/honsho/shiryo/bunsho/index.html.

Note: An English page summarizing some of the materials in the series is available here: http://www.mofa.go.jp/about/hq/record/docs.html.

42 NIHON GAIKŌ BUNSHO DEJITARU ĀKAIBU' [日本外交文書デジタルアーカイブ] (JAPAN FOREIGN RELATIONS DIGITAL ARCHIVE)
URL: http://www.mofa.go.jp/mofaj/annai/honsho/shiryo/archives/index.html.

Summary: The contents of this online full-text resource are described in detail in the preceding entry for the print version.

Note: In Japanese.

Note: To use the Digital Archive, users must download and install the provided specialized viewing software 'Djvuビューアー' (Djvu Viewer).

43 THE JCAR SEARCH PAGE
URL: http://www.jacar.go.jp/english/index.html (English); http://www.jacar.go.jp/index.html (Japanese).

Summary: [See also above under 'Topical and Selected Treaty Publications, Historical'.] The 'Japan Center for Asian Historical Record' (JACAR) defines 'Asian Historical Records' as "documents possessed by Japanese archival institutions concerning modern Japan and its relations with, among others, neighboring Asian countries." The resource also includes search pages in Chinese and Korean.

44 GAIMUSHŌ: GAIKŌ SHIRYŌKAN [外務省: 外交資料館] (MOFA: FOREIGN AFFAIRS ARCHIVE)
URL: http://www.mofa.go.jp/about/hq/record/docs.html (English); http://www.mofa.go.jp/mofaj/annai/honsho/shiryo/index.html (Japanese).

Summary: This is the website of the Ministry of Foreign Affairs Foreign Affairs Archive. From the Japanese-language page (link above), there is access to a wealth of documents relating to Japan's foreign affairs, both current and historical. In English, MOFA provides the 'PRINCIPLE HISTORICAL DOCUMENTS' page, which lists and describes five major sets.

45 GAIKŌ KIROKU KŌKAI MOKUROKU (GAIMUSHŌ IKAN FAIRU KENMEI MOKUROKU) [外交記録公開目録(外務省移管ファイル件名目録)] (TABLE OF CONTENTS OF RECORDS OF FOREIGN RELATIONS (TABLE OF CONTENTS OF MOFA FILE NAMES))
URL: http://www.mofa.go.jp/mofaj/annai/honsho/shiryo/shozo/ikan.html.

Summary: This page has links to many PDF file tables that each consist of chronological lists of file names of foreign relations documents available from the Ministry of Foreign Affairs.

Note: In Japanese.

46 GAIMUSHO KIROKU, GAIKŌ KIROKU KŌKAI [公文書管理・外交記録公開] (ARCHIVES MANAGEMENT, RELEASE OF FOREIGN AFFAIRS RECORDS)
URL: http://www.mofa.go.jp/mofaj/public/kiroku_kokai.html.

Summary: Under Japanese law, many foreign affairs-related documents are released to the public after thirty years. This webpage provides links to more information about the Japanese government's document publication policy, and to a searchable index for viewing administrative document files.

Index: Searchable index page: http://files.e-gov.go.jp/servlet/Fsearch

Note: In Japanese.

47 TSŪSHIN ZENRAN AND ZOKU TSŪSHIN ZENRAN [通信全覧, 続通信全覧] (COMPLETE COMMUNICATIONS, CONTINUED COMPLETE COMMUNICATIONS)
(Tōkyō : Yūshōdō, 1983–1988).

Summary: These collections of diplomatic documents are vital to understanding Japan's international relations at the end of the feudal era and the beginning of the modern era. Tsūshin Zenran covers 1859 to 1860, and Zoku Tsūshin Zenran covers 1861–1868 (the last year of the Tokugawa era). The original publication had a total of 1,784 volumes,[79] which are available in a modern reprint in 22 volumes.

Note: In Japanese.

Other Useful Sources

48 JAPANESE LAW TRANSLATION
URL: http://www.japaneselawtranslation.go.jp.

Summary: This website has full-text English translations of Japanese laws. It does NOT include treaties. However, it can be useful for treaty-related research as it include laws and regulations relevant to the implementation of treaties. A keyword search for '条約' [jōyaku] (treaty) yielded 433 hits.

Note: In English.

49 DĒTABĒSU 'SEKAI TO NIHON' [データベース「世界と日本」] ('THE WORLD AND JAPAN' DATABASE)
URL: http://www.ioc.u-tokyo.ac.jp/~worldjpn/front-ENG.shtml (English); http://www.ioc.u-tokyo.ac.jp/~worldjpn/ (Japanese).

Summary: This document database maintained by the Institute for Advanced Studies on Asia at Tokyo University includes sections titled 'Basic Documents of Postwar International Politics' and 'Collection of Multilateral Conventions'. The Japanese language version of the resource includes a searchable interface. (To search, click 'kensaku pēji' [検索ページ] (search page) in the frame to the left).

---

79 *See* MOFA page about these documents, here: http://www.mofa.go.jp/about/hq/record/docs.html.

50 GAIMUSHŌ KOKUSAIHŌ KYOKU [外務省国際法局] (MOFA INTERNATIONAL LEGAL AFFAIRS BUREAU)
URL: http://www.mofa.go.jp/mofaj/annai/honsho/sosiki/joyaku.html.

Summary: This is the main webpage for the Japanese government department responsible for treaties.

Note: In Japanese.

Yearbooks and Digests of State Practice

51 JAPANESE YEARBOOK OF INTERNATIONAL LAW. (PREVIOUS TITLE: THE JAPANESE ANNUAL OF INTERNATIONAL LAW [1957–2007]) (Tokyo: International Law Association of Japan, 1957–).

Summary: This yearbook includes articles by commentators (publicists) on current issues of international law. Each issue also includes relevant decisions of Japanese courts, and new bilateral and multi-lateral treaties.

Note: In English.

Note: An online table of contents for all issues is available here: http://www.ilajapan.org/doc/contents.htm.

Kenya

Victor Essien

Historical Background

Modern day Kenya gained independence from the United Kingdom on December 12, 1963.[1] It had been created out of the East African Protectorate established by the Imperial British government on July 1, 1895.[2] Prior to that date, the area had been administered by the privately financed Imperial British East African Company (IBEAC).[3] British colonial rule had been preceded by the Portuguese explorers who had an uneasy control of the East African coast.[4] After the Portuguese were expelled, the Imam of Oman claimed sovereignty over the coast of East Africa.[5] In the early 1800s the British arrived initially as an ally to the Imam and later as an anti-slaving force.[6] In 1822, the British persuaded the Imam to sign the Moresby Treaty to halt the trafficking of slaves to India or to any Christian State.[7] Slave trafficking persisted, however, up until the mid-1890s.[8] During much of this time neither the British nor any other European power showed an interest in acquiring territory in East Africa.[9] In late 1884, German private interests began the process of German occupation of East Africa. A German nationalist, Karl Peters, managed to get certain local chiefs to sign treaties offering their territories for German colonization.[10] Thereafter, the German Chancellor of the era, Otto von Bismarck, ordered the areas to be under German protection.[11] This German action was met with protests by the locals, especially the Sultan of Zanzibar.[12] The British also recognized that it posed a threat to their influence and trade, which had grown enormously

1 Kenya Independence Order in Council, Statutory Instrument 1963/1968 (U.K.).
2 1 Irving Kaplan, Area Handbook of Kenya 22 (2nd ed. 1976).
3 Id. at 21.
4 Id. at 17.
5 Id. at 18.
6 Id.
7 Id. at 19.
8 Id.
9 Id. at 20.
10 Id. at 21.
11 Id.
12 Id.

 | DOI 10.1163/9789004272224_021

after the Suez Canal was opened in 1869.[13] The Germans and the British entered into an agreement in October 1886 awarding the Sultan of Zanzibar certain coastal islands and another strip of land extending inland about ten miles up to the mouth of the Tana River.[14] The interior behind the coastal strip was divided up into German and British spheres of influence. Two years later, IBEAC was given a royal charter to administer the British sphere.[15]

On July 1, 1890, a new Anglo-German Treaty was signed.[16] The Heligoland-Zanzibar Treaty temporarily settled colonial disputes between Germany and Great Britain. It recognized Tanganyika, present-day Tanzania, as a German colony. In return, the Germans abstained from further encroaching into British Kenya.[17] The Colonial government took over the administration of the territory under British influence from the IBEAC and, in 1895, the territory was formally established as the East African Protectorate.[18] The British government adopted the policy of attracting white settlers to the Protectorate.[19] One problem associated with this policy of attracting white settlers was the question of land titles.[20] IBEAC had signed about one hundred treaties with local leaders but these did not assign land rights.[21] The British Crown Lands Ordinance of 1902 finally made provision for the sale and lease of "waste land and unoccupied land" to white settlers.[22] The issue of land security was a bone of contention during the colonial and immediate post-colonial period.[23]

In 1920, the East African Protectorate became a colony and was officially renamed the Colony of Kenya.[24] The land question undergirded the colonial relations and was central in the African quest for Independence.[25] The latter

13 Id.

14 Id.

15 Id.

16 Id.

17 Agreement between Great Britain and Germany, Respecting Zanzibar, Heligoland, and the Spheres of Influence of the Two Countries in Africa, *reproduced in* German History in Documents and Images: Vol. 5 Wilhemine Germany and the First World War, 1890–1918, *available at* http://germanhistorydocs.ghi-dc.org/chapter.cfm?subsection_id=65.

18 KAPLAN, *supra* note 2 at 22.

19 Simon Coldham, *Colonial Policy and the Highlands of Kenya, 1934–1944*, 23 J. AFRICAN L. 65 (1979).

20 Id.

21 KAPLAN, *supra* note 2 at 25.

22 Id.

23 Kimani, *Kenya's Rocky Road to Independence*, AFRICA TODAY, Dec. 1963, at 4.

24 KAPLAN, *supra* note 2 at 31.

25 Coldham, *supra* note 19.

was often violent and virulent.[26] Ultimately the winds of change blew over Kenya. On June 1, 1963, Kenya was granted internal self-government.[27] Jomo Kenyatta, as leader of the Kenya African National Union (KANU), became Prime Minister and formed the government.[28] On December 12, 1963, Kenya gained full and formal Independence from the United Kingdom.[29]

Issues of Treaty Succession

With independence, the new Kenyan government assumed the conduct of international relations, including treaty relations. Like all newly independent states, Kenya had to contend with issues of succession to colonial treaties.[30] For Kenya, treaty succession has arisen in two contexts. The first is the more common problem that all emergent states face upon independence as to the devolution of treaties signed on their behalf by the colonial powers.[31] The second problem relates to the treatment of treaties entered into between the colonial powers or their surrogates and local chiefs, mostly in relation to territorial acquisition.[32]

Treaties with local chiefs raise a fundamental question of whether those chiefs or their chiefdoms possessed international legal personality to enter into valid treaties.[33] In addition, most of the local chiefs entered into these treaties under duress.[34] Both colonial courts in pre-independent Kenya and post-independent Kenyan courts have had to grapple with the question of the validity of some of these treaties and, in some instances, the issue of succession by independent Kenya. In Ole Njongo & Others v. Attorney-General & Others,[35] the East African Protectorate High Court had to determine the validity of two agreements concluded between the Masai chiefs and His Majesty's Commissioner for the East African Protectorate.[36] The trial Judge, Morris Bonham-Carter, C.J., while

26 KAPLAN, *Supra* note 2 at 33 *et seq.*

27 Id. at 42.

28 Id.

29 *Supra* note 1.

30 D.P. O'Connell, *Independence and Succession to Treaties*, 38 BRITISH Y.B. INT'L LAW 84, *passim* (1962).

31 Okon Udokang, *Succession to Treaties in New States*, 8 CAN Y.B. INT'L L. 123, 142 (1970).

32 M. Mwagiru & R.R. Hunja, *Some Aspects of Treaty Practice in Kenya*, 6 LESOTHO L.J. 7, 9 (1990).

33 Id.

34 Id.

35 1914 E.A.P.L.R. 90.

36 Id.

doubting if the two agreements were valid treaties governed by international law, still held that the agreements must be deemed to be governed by some rules analogous to international law and therefore, worthy of being giving force and effect as treaties.[37] More recently, the validity and effect of treaties entered into by Samburu People and Her Majesty's Government has come up for judicial determination before the Nyeru High Court in Kenya.[38]

Beside the issue of succession to treaties entered into with local chiefs, the main issue remained the succession to treaties entered into between the United Kingdom and other sovereign states prior to Kenya's independence. At independence, Kenya adopted what had been christened the Nyerere doctrine on state succession to colonial treaties.[39] This is different from the approach of other newly Independent Commonwealth countries like Ghana and Nigeria which signed devolution agreements with the departing Colonial power.[40] Kenya, like Tanzania and Uganda before it, submitted a Unilateral Declaration addressed to the Secretary-General of the United Nations and circulated to member states of the United Nations clearly mapping out how Kenya was going to treat multilateral and bilateral treaties that applied to it under the colonial dispensation.[41] The text of the declaration addressed by the Prime Minister of Kenya to the Secretary-General of the United Nations on March 25, 1964 read as follows:

"The Government of Kenya wishes to make the following Declaration to the Members of the United Nations on the subject of Succession to Treaties extended or applied to Kenya by the Government of the United Kingdom and Northern Ireland prior to Independence.

In so far as bilateral treaties concluded by the United Kingdom on behalf of the territory of Kenya or validly applied or extended by the former to the territory of the latter are concerned, the Government of Kenya is willing to be a successor to them subject to the following conditions:

(a) That such treaties shall continue in force for a period of two years from the date of Independence (i.e. until December 12th, 1965);
(b) That such treaties shall be applied on a basis of reciprocity; and
(c) That such treaties may be abrogated or modified by mutual consent of the other contracting party before 12th December, 1965".[42]

---

37 Id.

38 Mwagiru & Hunja, *supra* note 32 at 11.

39 Udokang, *supra* note 31 at 140 *et seq.*

40 Id.

41 Id.

42 Reproduced in Supplement Prepared by the United Nations Secretariat to "Materials on Succession of States" (ST/Leg/Ser.B.14) at 45–46.

The Declaration also stated that after the expiry of the two-year period, the Government of Kenya would consider those treaties which could not be regarded as surviving according to the rules of customary international law as having terminated.[43] The two-year period was intended to afford the interested parties an opportunity to reach satisfactory accord on the continuance or modification or termination of the treaties.[44]

As far as multilateral treaties were concerned, the Government of Kenya intended within two years from the date of Independence, or such later date as may be notified, to indicate to the depositary in each case the step it wished to take in regard to each instrument.[45] It was expected that the Government of Kenya would indicate whether each instrument was to be terminated, succeeded to or acceded to. Meanwhile, any party to a multilateral treaty which applied or extended to Kenya prior to Independence, could on a basis of reciprocity, rely as against Kenya on the terms of such treaty.[46]

Subsequently, on June 4, 1964, the Permanent Representative of the United Kingdom to the United Nations, on behalf of Her Majesty's Government issued a disclaimer contained in a letter addressed to the Secretary-General of the United Nations that as of the date of Kenya's Independence, Her Majesty's Government was no longer responsible for Kenya's international relations.[47]

Treaty Ratification and Implementation

The treaty practice of the newly independent Kenya reflected the United Kingdom treaty practice with its preference for dualism as opposed to monism.[48] Article 23 of the Kenya Independent Constitution vested the treaty-making power in the executive.[49] However, neither the Constitution nor any other law made a clear statement as to who had the authority or power to negotiate treaties in Kenya. The treaty practice, therefore, tended to be rather

---

43 Id.

44 Id.

45 Id.

46 Id.

47 Id.

48 M. Mwagiru, "From Dualism to Monism: The Structure of Revolution in Kenya's Constitutional Treaty Practice" 3 J. LANG TECH & ENTREPRENEURSHIP IN AFRICA 144 (2011).

49 Mwagiru & Hunja, *supra* note 32 at 8.

ad hoc.[50] It was observed that with multilateral treaties, in particular, treaties of a technical and scientific nature, the authority to negotiate vested in the operative department but under the advice of the Ministry of Foreign Affairs.[51] Bilateral treaties, on the other hand, tended to elicit diverse practice although, in general, the Ministry of Foreign Affairs tended to dominate as well.[52] There was no consistent practice regarding co-ordination between the various departments and even on the role of cabinet and, in some cases, that of Parliament in treaty negotiation, ratification and domestication.[53]

In 1990, two Kenya treaty law specialists described emerging Kenya treaty practice as follows.[54] With multilateral treaties, cabinet has to give authority to the responsible Ministry to participate in the multilateral negotiations. At the conclusion of the treaty negotiations, cabinet approval has to be obtained in order for Kenya to express its consent to be bound by the treaty.[55] The consent to be bound by a multilateral treaty should be expressed through ratification, accession or adherence.[56] In the case of bilateral treaties, those that do not import a direct fiscal liability for Kenya should be left within the competence of the operative Ministries and the Ministry of Foreign Affairs to conclude.[57] No further cabinet action is needed.[58] Bilateral treaties with direct fiscal implications for Kenya should require prior cabinet approval before negotiation and conclusion.[59] Consent to be bound by a bilateral treaty with a State may be expressed by signature only on a reciprocal basis. Otherwise, expression of consent to be bound must be contained in the notes exchanged between the parties, confirming that the relevant constitutional procedures have been completed.[60]

The 2010 Constitution revolutionized Kenya treaty practice.[61] To begin with, Article 2(6) of the Constitution proclaimed monism, as opposed to dualism,

50 Id. at 13.
51 Id.
52 Id.
53 Id.
54 Id.
55 Id. at 21–22.
56 Id. at 22.
57 Id.
58 Id.
59 Id.
60 Id.
61 Mwagiru, *supra* note 48 at 144. *See also* Kenya National Commission on Human Rights, Occasional Report-Making the Bill of Rights Operational: Policy, Legal and Administrative Priorities and Considerations 7 (2011).

as the order of the day.[62] Article 2(6) states that "any treaty ratified by Kenya shall form part of the law of Kenya under this Constitution". By this provision, treaties ratified by Kenya, do not have to be domesticated before they apply in Kenya.[63] More importantly, this provision made it imperative for Kenya to clarify and regularize the process of treaty ratification. To this effect, the Kenyan Parliament duly passed the Treaty Making and Ratification Act, 2012.[64] This Act applies to both bilateral and multilateral treaties.[65] The Act makes clear that "a treaty relating to the adjustment, alteration or variation of the present position of Kenya on matters of sovereignty, independence and territorial integrity", however, can only be approved in a referendum organized in accordance with Article 255 of the Constitution.[66]

Article 4(1) of the Act restates that the treaty making power, including the initiation of its ratification process, resides in the national executive.[67] Article 4(2) explains that this executive power may be delegated to a relevant State department.[68]

The Act itemizes the factors the executive or the relevant State department must take into account when deciding to initiate the treaty-making process. These are as follows:

(a) the need that the new treaty is to meet;
(b) the existing legal regime, including the extent of its applicability to the perceived problem;
(c) the probability of reaching the required measure of agreement on the solution aimed for;
(d) any relevant legislative efforts related to the perceived problem;
(e) the optimal form for the proposed treaty;
(f) the likelihood that the proposed treaty shall be accepted by a sufficient number of states, where the treaty is multilateral;
(g) the anticipated time schedule for completing the treaty-making process;
(h) the expected costs of formulating and adopting the treaty to Kenya;

62 The Constitution of Kenya, Art. 2(6) (Nairobi: National Council for Law Reporting, 2010).
63 Kenya National Commission on Human Rights, *supra* note 61 at 7 *et seq.*
64 Act No. 45 of 2012, Laws of Kenya, Kenya Gazette Supplement No. 200.
65 Id.
66 Id. art. 3.
67 Id. art. 4.
68 Id.

(i) in formulating treaties relating to technical or scientific problems; whether extensive scientific studies or research have been carried out to determine the parameters of the problem and the lines of potential solutions.[69]

When the national executive or the relevant State department is satisfied that these conditions are met by the proposed treaty, they shall present a proposal to commence the treaty-making for approval by the national Cabinet.[70] The Cabinet shall consider and approve or disapprove the proposal for treaty-making within a reasonable time.[71]

The Treaty Making and Ratification Act outlines the treaty ratification process.[72] Article 7 describes the steps to be undertaken for Cabinet approval and Article 8 deals with consideration by Parliament. Under Article 7, where the Government intends to ratify a treaty, the Cabinet Secretary of the relevant State department shall, in consultation with the Attorney-General, submit to the Cabinet the treaty and its explanatory memorandum.[73] The memorandum should contain the following information, namely, the objects and subject-matter of the treaty, its constitutional implications, if any, the national interests which may be affected by its ratification, obligations imposed on Kenya by the said treaty and the requirements for implementation of the treaty. In addition, the memorandum must spell out the policy and legislative considerations, the financial implications, ministerial responsibility, implications on matters relating to counties, the summary of the process leading to the adoption of the treaty, its date of signature, the number of State parties and the views of the public on the ratification of the treaty.[74] The memorandum must also state whether the treaty to be ratified admits of reservations, recommendations and/or declarations, and if so, whether there are any proposed reservations.[75]

Upon approval by the Cabinet, the Cabinet Secretary shall lay the proposed treaty and its memorandum before the National Assembly.[76] Depending on its subject-matter, a proposed treaty shall go to one and/or both Houses of Parliament.[77] With regard to treaties subject to the consideration of the two

69 Id.
70 Id. art. 5(3).
71 Id. art. 5(4).
72 Id. arts. 7–12.
73 Id. art. 7.
74 Id. arts 7(a)-(m).
75 Id. arts. 7(n) & (m).
76 Id. art. 8(1).
77 Id. art. 8(2).

Houses of Parliament, both Houses should approve the treaty before further action may be taken on the treaty.[78] Disagreement between the two houses will require a reference to mediation.[79] Where a treaty meets the approval of the two Houses of Parliament, the Cabinet Secretary, at the request of the Cabinet Secretary of the relevant State department, shall prepare the instrument of ratification of the treaty.[80] A treaty may be approved by Parliament, with or without reservations. All instruments of ratification of a treaty shall be signed, sealed and deposited by the Cabinet Secretary at the requisite international body and a copy thereof shall be filed with the Registrar.[81]

The Treaty Making and Ratification Act has established a Registrar of Treaties as a department within the State Department, charged with the responsibility of serving as a depository of all treaties to which Kenya is a party.[82] The Registrar shall maintain a record of all Kenyan treaties and must indicate the status of all such treaties, including whether they are pending ratification or domestication.[83] By the same statute, the Registrar is required to facilitate public access to treaties which Kenya has ratified. The Act further places on the Registrar of Treaties the burden of notifying the general public of Kenya's treaty obligations.[84]

Annotated Bibliography of Sources

General Treaty Collections

1 TREATIES AND AGREEMENTS DATABASE
URL: http://www.kenyalaw.org/treaties/.

Summary: In 2011, with the support of the Financial and Legal Sector Technical Assistance Project (FLSTAP), a Kenyan government project co-funded through a grant from the United Kingdom Department of International Affairs and a credit form the World Bank, the Kenyan National Council for Law Reporting established an on-line database containing the text of multilateral and bilateral treaties to which Kenya is a party or signatory. This database has been christened the National Council for Law Reporting's Treaties and

78 Id. art. 8(6).
79 Id.
80 Id. art. 9(1).
81 Id. art. 10(1).
82 Id. art. 13.
83 Id.
84 Id. art. 15(1).

Agreements Database. In addition, the database provides information on the status of over 500 major multilateral treaties deposited with the Secretary-General of the United Nations, including even those to which Kenya is not a party.[85] The database is supplemented by two finding aids, namely, *Help and How to Guide* and a *Glossary of Terms*. It is user-friendly and affords multiple access points, including the use of general search terms within the text of the treaty, searching within the title and preamble, search by region, by subject and by type of treaty.[86] This database represents a significant improvement in the treaty collection system of Kenya and is better than what obtains in most African countries. The challenge for Kenya will be how to keep this database updated. A researcher for Kenyan treaties may have to supplement the present database with a search of other multi-jurisdictional databases that publish treaties of countries world-wide.

Treaty Index

2 KENYA INTERNATIONAL TREATIES HANDBOOK. VOLUME 1 STRATEGIC INFORMATION AND DEVELOPMENTS
(Washington, D.C.: International Business Publications, 2005–).

Summary: An unofficial publication. It was first published in 2005 with a promise to update it annually. The current print is undated but does not reflect information after 2008. It includes a potpourri of information on the government and political system of Kenya, Kenya's current conditions and challenges ahead and a listing of Kenya's international treaties. The list is poorly organized and does not include citations to the relevant treaties. Clearly, the title of this book is misleading and the book cannot be considered a useful index to treaties to which Kenya is a party.

Topical and Selected Treaty Publications

African Regional Treaties

3 AFRICAN UNION TREATIES
URL: http://www.au.int/en/treaties.

Summary: provides access to treaties, conventions, protocols and charters adopted under the auspices of the African Union (AU) and its predecessor organization, the organization of African Union (OAU). To determine if Kenya has signed a particular instrument, you have to click on the status list button.

---

85 Id.
86 Id.

Colonial and Pre-Colonial Treaties

4 BRITISH AND FOREIGN STATE PAPERS[87]

(London: H.M.S.O., 1815–).

Summary: Includes the text of treaties, diplomatic correspondence, foreign constitutions and laws pertaining mainly to international relations.

Diplomatic Documents

5 FOREIGN AFFAIRS BULLETIN

(Nairobi: Ministry of Foreign Affairs, Press and Public Relations Division, 1998–)

Summary: This bulletin was launched as a monthly publication to serve as a newsletter and a source of state practice in foreign affairs. In reality, its appearance has been spotty and not easily available.

6 INSTITUTE OF DIPLOMACY AND INTERNATIONAL STUDIES. UNIVERSITY OF NAIROBI

URL: http://idis.uonbi.ac.ke.

Summary: This a leading post-graduate training institute based at the University of Nairobi, Kenya. The Institute's faculty and other scholars research and publish on diplomacy and international relations with emphasis on Kenya. While the titles of the publications can be found on the Institute's web site, the text are not available neither are the citations provided.

7 INSTITUTE FOR SECURITY STUDIES

URL: http://www.issafrica.org.

Summary: This is a leading African policy research and training organization based in Pretoria, South Africa with regional offices in Addis Ababa, Ethiopia, Dakar, Senegal and Nairobi, Kenya. Its focus includes conflict prevention and risk analysis, conflict management and peace building and transnational threats and international crime. It provides a forum for the discussion of African foreign policies. In May 2002, it organized a seminar on "Kenya's Foreign Policy and Geostrategic Interests". The report of the seminar is published on the Institute's web site as are other similar reports and research findings. The publications of the Institute are a good source of state practice in international law.

---

87 For more information on this resource, see chapter on "United Kingdom."

Republic of Korea

Jootaek (Juice) Lee

Issues of Treaty Succession

The Constitutional Court of the Republic of Korea (South Korea, *hereinafter* "Korea") defines a treaty as an agreement between more than two states, creating, amending, and expiring rights and duties.[1] Korea did not succeed any treaties concluded before August 15, 1948, when the government of the Republic of Korea was newly established. In 1876 with the unequal *Kwanghwado Treaty* [강화도조약], *Chosun* – a former Korea existed between 1392 and 1897 – opened its door to Japan. Since then, Japanese and Western powers began to demolish a Korean imperial system and its tradition that was over 1500 years old.[2] Finally, by series of illegal treaties, Japan deprived Korea of its diplomatic power in 1905 and ended Korea in 1910. Then, from 1910 until 1945, Korea was devastated under the Japanese rule, and the colonial time ended in 1945 by the loss of Japan in World War II. On September 8, 1951, World War II officially ended, and Japan officially recognized the independence of Korea and renounced all rights and claims to Korea by the San Francisco Treaty of Peace with Japan.[3]

After its new establishment, Korea concluded 2,663 treaties – 2077 multilateral treaties and 586 bilateral treaties – by 2009.[4] The number of treaties increased recently – especially treaties dealing with free trade, prevention of double-taxation, social security, investment protection, extradition, and judicial assistance.[5]

---

1 Constitutional Court [Const. Ct.], 2003 Hun-Ma[헌마]806 at 391(consol.), March 30, 2006 (S. Kor.).

2 Also known as *Japan-Korea Treaty of Amity*. *See* 강화도조약[江華島條約], Doopedia, http://www.doopedia.co.kr.

3 Treaty of Peace with Japan art.2, Sept. 8, 1951, 136 U.N.T.S. 67. The treaty is Japan's to promise to the other 47 nations; neither South Korea and North Korea was not invited to this treaty.

4 *Treaty-Making of Korea* (우리나라의 조약체결), The Ministry of Foreign Affairs of the Republic of Korea, http://www.mofa.go.kr/trade/treatylaw/treatykorea/activities/index.jsp?menu=m_30_50_20&tabmenu=t_1.

5 Id.

 | doi 10.1163/9789004272224_022

Treaty Ratification and Implementation

Treaties are primary sources of law in Korea. Korea signed the 1969 Vienna Convention on the Law of Treaties on November 27, 1969 and later ratified it on April 27, 1977.[6] Article 7 of the 1969 Vienna Convention on the Law of Treaties states that (1) Heads of State, Heads of Government and Ministers for Foreign Affairs can negotiate for a treaty; (2) heads of diplomatic missions can perform all acts relating to a conclusion of treaty; and (3) representatives accredited by States to an international conference or an international organizations can adopt the text of a treaty in that conference or that organizations.[7] Otherwise, a person needs full powers to adopt or authenticate the text of a treaty or to express the consent to be bound by a treaty.[8] In Korea, the President of Korea is the head of state, and ministers are heads of governments. The Minister of Foreign Affairs and Trade is the head of the Ministry of Foreign Affairs and Trade. Korea also sends ambassadors as heads of diplomatic missions to most of countries in the world.

While the President has the ultimate power for foreign relations, the Minister of Foreign Affairs and Trade is mainly responsible for negotiating with foreign governments or international organizations, or signing or initialing treaties according to the Act on the Appointment and Powers of Government Delegates and Special Envoys.[9] The Minister of Foreign Affairs and Trade does not need full powers to sign a treaty. The Bureau (조약과) of the Ministry of Foreign Affairs and Trade does the actual work of negotiating and drafting of a particular treaty.[10]

Under Article 73 of the Constitution of the Republic of Korea (대한민국 헌법; *hereinafter* "Constitution"), the President has the authority to adopt and ratify treaties.[11] Similar to the democratic treaty-making practice of most states, however, this power of the President to ratify is checked by the National

6 Korea also signed 1986 Vienna Convention the Law of treaties between States and International Organizations or between International Organizations, but did not ratify it yet.

7 Vienna Convention on the Law of Treaties art. 7, May 23, 1969, 1155 U.N.T.S. 331.

8 Id.

9 The Act on the Appointment and Powers of Government Delegates and Special Envoys, art. 3.

10 *Treaties*, THE MINISTRY OF FOREIGN AFFAIRS OF THE REPUBLIC OF KOREA http://www.mofa.go.kr/ENG/policy/treaties/treaties/treaty/domestic/index.jsp?menu=m_20_30_10&tabmenu=t_3.

11 DAEHANMINGUK HUNBEOB [대한민국 헌법][Constitution] (Oct. 29, 1987) art. 73 (S. Kor.) [hereinafter S. KOR. CONST.].

Assembly for a democratic purpose. While treaties must be consented to by the National Assembly, under Article 60(1) of the Constitution, the National Assembly's authority to consent to the adoption and ratification is limited to important treaties such as treaties relating to mutual assistance or mutual security, international organizations, friendship, trade and navigation, any restriction in sovereignty, legislative matters, peace treaties, and treaties that give important financial burdens to citizens or Korea.[12]

According to Article 6(1) of the Constitution, treaties are treated as domestic laws of Korea.[13] Unlike the United States which distinguish treaties from executive agreements in terms of the weight of authority, under the Korean Constitution, the Korean treaties which are not subject to the consent to the ratification by the National Assembly are treated same as the treaties which must go through the consent procedure by the National Assembly. This is because Article 6(1) of the Constitution does not break down treaties by its designation and treaty-making process and consider all treaties equally as domestic law. This may raise a concern that the President and the administrative body of the government has a broad, ambiguous, and unregulated authority to make treaties in too many areas of law not enumerated under Article 60(1) of the Constitution. Pursuant to the Case-Zablocki Act,[14] the United States strengthened the oversight by the Congress of the treaty-making process, requiring the Secretary of State to send all executive agreements to the Congress within 60 days from the entry into force. In contrast, Korea has not established such an oversight mechanism yet.[15]

There is no established principle to distinguish self-executing treaties from non-self-executing treaties. If a treaty expressly requires implementing legislation, this triggers the Article 60 procedure which requires the treaty pertaining

---

12 S. Kor. Const. art. 60(1). This limitation of treaties which are subject to the consent by the National Assembly started from the 1948 Constitution while the types of treaties enumerated has been changed. If there is a conflict between the President and the National Assembly regarding what treaties are subject to the consent, the Constitutional Court of the Republic of Korea has the jurisdiction.

13 S. Kor. Const. art. 6(1).

14 1 U.S.C. §112b (2006).

15 A recent bill suggests that the administrative branch of the government report to the National Assembly its beginning of negotiation and conclusion of a treaty. It also suggests that the administrative branch must transmit all the treaties even if those are not subject to the consent by the National Assembly. 조약의 체결 · 비준 동의에 관한 법률안 (Bill regarding the Conclusion and Consent by the National Assembly, no.1900626, The National Assembly of the Republic of Korea (July 11, 2012), http://likms.assembly.go.kr/bill/jsp/BillDetail.jsp?bill_id=PRC_R1B2S0Q7X1B1I1J5J1O8A4S4W7F1K3.

to legislative matters to be consented to by the National Assembly. However, there is no law out there clearly answering whether and when the National Assembly must pass implementing legislation even after giving consent to the treaty. A recent bill in 2012 suggests that the administrative branch report to the National Assembly when it begins negotiation and concludes a treaty. It also suggests that the administrative branch must transmit all the treaties, even if they are not subject to the consent of the National Assembly.

Procedures for concluding treaties are well summarized and visually represented at the website of the Ministry of Foreign Affairs and Trade.[16] Internally, procedures for multilateral treaties and bilateral treaties are distinguished. A bilateral treaty is (1) negotiated by the Bureau of Treaty Affairs (조약국) under the supervision of the Minister of Foreign Affairs; (2) drafted in consultation with the Director-General for Treaties of the Ministry of Foreign Affairs;[17] (3) reviewed by the Ministry of Government Legislation; (4) referred to and deliberated by the State Council;[18] (5) approved by the President with countersignatures by the Prime Minister and the Foreign Minister; (6) signed; (7) approved by the National Assembly if required; (8) ratified and exchanged; (9) Promulgated and published in the official gazette; and (10) registered with the United Nations Secretariat under Article 102 of the United Nations Charter. For a multilateral treaty, the Korean government either makes an accession to the exiting treaty, or participates in the drafting process and adopts the text of the treaty. Unlike bilateral treaties, a multilateral treaty initially reviewed by the Director General for Treaties under the Minister of Foreign Affairs and Trade before being reviewed by the Ministry of Government Legislation and the State Council. Furthermore, unlike bilateral treaties, instruments of ratification, accession, approval, and acceptance pertaining to a multilateral treaty will be deposited in a country or an international organization. Declaration and reservation may be accompanied.

At the request by the Director-General for Treaties, new treaties are published in the official gazette, Gwanbo (관보).[19] In addition to the official gazette, the treaty version(s) in an official language(s) and the Korean texts of

---

16 *Treaties: Treaty Making by the ROK*, THE MINISTRY OF FOREIGN AFFAIRS OF THE REPUBLIC OF KOREA http://www.mofa.go.kr/ENG/policy/treaties/treaties/treaty/domestic/index.jsp?menu=m_20_30_10&tabmenu=t_3.

17 The domestic process of making a treaty begins with the initiation of the Director-General for Treaties who send the agreed text to the Ministry of Government Legislation.

18 S. KOR. CONST. art. 89(3).

19 [*Gwanbo*], [MINISTRY OF PUBLIC ADMINISTRATION AND SECURITY], http://gwanbo.korea.go.kr.

the multilateral treaties are also officially available on the website of the Ministry of Foreign Affairs and Trade.[20] The website covers 2,280 treaties as of 2013. Status information on the recent treaties since 2008 is separately listed in the reverse-chronological order.[21] It provides the date and place of adoption, the date of entry-into-force, depository, the date of publication on the official gazette, the summary of the contents of a treaty, etc.

The Ministry of Government Legislation also provides a treaty database which is included under the general legal database, called Kukga Beobryung Jungbo Center (National Legal Information Center, 국가법령정보센터).[22] In the database, users can browse treaties by clicking the Joyak (treaty, 조약) button or do an advanced search by clicking the Sansegunsaek (advanced search, 상세검색). The advanced search function allows users to choose a country, to search by treaty title, date of entry-into-force and treaty number, and to search full text by key words. The database covers most Korean treaties: 2,090 treaties as of 2013. Instead of official languages, Korean and English versions are available from this database.

Evidence of State Practice

As mentioned before, in Korea, the President of Korea is the head of state, and ministers are heads of governments. The Minister of Foreign Affairs and Trade is the head of the Ministry of Foreign Affairs and Trade. Korea also sends ambassadors as heads of diplomatic missions to most of countries in the world. The powers to negotiate with foreign governments or international organizations, to attend international conferences and important ceremonies held in foreign countries, and to convey the positions and ideas of the government to foreign governments are provided in the Act on the Appointment and Powers of Government Delegates and Special Envoys.[23]

20 *Joyakjungbo* [조약정보], The Ministry of Foreign Affairs of the Republic of Korea, http://www.mofa.go.kr/trade/treatylaw/treatyinformation/multilateral/index.jsp?menu=m_30_50_40&tabmenu=t_2.

21 *Choigeunbalhyojoyak* [최근발효조약], The Ministry of Foreign Affairs of the Republic of Korea, http://www.mofa.go.kr/trade/treatylaw/treatyrecent/index.jsp?mofat=001&menu=m_30_50_30.

22 Kukga Beobryung JungboCenter [국가법령정보센터], The Ministry of Government Legislation , http://www.law.go.kr/main.html.

23 The Act on the Appointment and Powers of Government Delegates and Special Envoys [정부대표 및 특별사절의 임명과 권한에 관한 법률], Act. No. 1081, May 31, 1962,

Korea not only has a civil law system that is influenced by the French and German legal system, but also follows customary law and sound reasoning. Furthermore, American legal principles have affected Korean law since Korea's liberation from Japan by American forces in 1945. Primary sources of law in Korea are its constitution and acts, treaties, emergency executive orders, emergency financial and economic executive orders, presidential decrees, rules of the national assembly, rules of the Supreme Court, rules of the Constitutional Court, rules of the National Election Commission, ordinances of the prime minister and ministries, enforcement decrees, administrative rules, and municipal ordinances and rules. Excellent summaries and graphics of the Korean legislative system, categories of acts and subordinate statutes, and a hierarchy of authorities are provided by the Korea Legislation Research Institute (KLRI) at its *Statutes of the Republic of Korea* web site.[24]

Primary sources of law, including the amendments to the constitution, proposed amendments to the constitution, acts, treaties, decrees, notices, and important government policies are published daily in the *Gwanbo* (Official Gazette, 관보) by the Ministry of Public Administration and Security.[25] The Law Information Service under the Ministry of Government Legislation later compiles and publishes the laws in *Daehanminguk Hyunhaeng Bobryeongjip* [대한민국현행법령집] (Statutes of Current Korean Laws). Treaties are separately published by the Bureau of Treaty Affairs in *Daehanminguk* Joyakjip [대한민국조약집].

Annotated Bibliography of Sources

A more comprehensive list of print publications in English, including *Current Laws of the Republic of Korea* and *Statutes of the Republic of Korea*, and other U.S. and western databases containing Korean primary sources are bibliographically organized in *A Research Guide and a Bibliography for Korean Legal Resources in English*.[26]

---

amended by No. 10308, May 20, 2010, art. 1 (S. Kor.), *translated in* STATUTES OF THE REPUBLIC OF KOREA, *available at* http://elaw.klri.re.kr/eng_service/main.do.

24 *Korea Legislative System and Procedures*, KLRI: KOREA LEGISLATION RESEARCH INST., http://elaw.klri.re.kr/eng_service/struct.do.

25 [*Gwanbo*], [MINISTRY OF PUBLIC ADMINISTRATION AND SECURITY], http://gwanbo.korea.go.kr.

26 Jootaek Lee, *Update: A Research Guide and a Bibliography for Korean Legal Resources in English*, GLOBALEX (Nov./Dec. 2012), *available at* http://www.nyulawglobal.org/globalex/South_Korean_Legal_Resources1.htm.

General Treaty Collections

1 DAEHANMINGUK HYUNHAENG BOBRYEONGJIP [대한민국현행법령집] (Statutes of Current Korean Laws) (Seoul: The Law Information Service [법령정보관리원]: The Ministry of Government Legislation [법제처], 2013)

Summary: This print compilation consists of fifty volumes arranged by (1) types of law, such as the constitution, civil law, criminal law, treaties, and administrative law; (2) institutions, such as courts and the National Assembly; and (3) subjects, such as military, education and scholarship, science and technology, customs, commerce, trade, and industry, labor, etc. As of February 2013, it included 1,287 acts, 1,497 presidential decrees and prime minister decrees, 1,107 ministry decrees, and 317 administrative rules.

Index: Volume 50 provides an alphabetical index and the table of contents of each volume.

Note: In Korean.

Topical and Selected Treaty Collections

2 JOYAKCHEGYEOLGWAJEONGESEOUI GWANGYE JEONGBUGIGWANUI YEOKHWAL MIT BEOBJECHEO JOYAKSIMSA GWANGHWAREUL WIHAN SIMSAMANUAL JEONGRIPE KWANHAN YEONGU [조약체결과정에서의 관계 정부기관의 역할 및 법제처 조약심사 강화를 위한 심사매뉴얼 정립에 관한 연구], JEONG, GABYONG [정갑용] ET AL (Seoul, Ministry of Government Legislation [법제처], 2009).[27]

Summary: This 132 page report by Korean international scholars for the Ministry of Government Legislation comprehensively discusses international treaties, legal basis and issues of the consent to the treaties by the National Assembly, types and number of treaties made, case studies relating to the consent procedure, etc.

Index: Each volume has a table of contents, but does not provide an index.

Note: In Korean.

3 KUKJAEINKWONJOYAKJIP [국제인권조약집], KOREAN NATIONAL COMMISSION FOR UNESCO [유네스코한국위원회] (Seoul: Saramsaenggak [사람생각], 2000).

---

27 *Available at* http://www.moleg.go.kr/news/media/mediaData;jsessionid=ZBFaMUAuX4ZBxm6U40YCXZNsGth9nmg9epZUipJCd8p82CGrHZ2pf91FrlAfNeO9?pstSeq=51031&brdSeq=5&pageIndex=6.

Summary: This book published by the Korean National Commission for UNESCO provides important human rights instruments including the international bill of human rights, treaties relating to protection from discrimination, prevention against torture, children and women's rights, and regional human rights treaties. It is useful to see how Korean texts are translated into English.

Index: It provides a table of contents, but does not provide an index.

Note: In Korean and English.

4 DAEHANMINGUK JOYAKJIP [대한민국조약집 (KOREA TREATY COLLECTION)]: YANGJA JOYAK [양자조약]
(Seoul, The Ministry of Foreign Affairs and Trade [외교통상부], 1978–).

Summary: This is the serial publication published yearly by the Ministry of Foreign Affairs and Trade which officially compiles bilateral treaties to which Korea is a party. This is arranged in the English alphabetical order of the names of the other party. It covers treaties from 1948.

Index: It has the table of contents in the front and does not contain an index.

Note: In Korean and official language.

5 DAEHANMINGUK JOYAKJIP [대한민국조약집 (KOREA TREATY COLLECTION)]: DAJA JOYAK [다자조약]
(Seoul, The Ministry of Foreign Affairs and Trade [외교통상부], 1969–).

Summary: This is the serial published by the Ministry of Foreign Affairs and Trade which officially compiles multilateral treaties to which Korea is a party. It covers treaties from 1948.

Note: In Korean and official language.

6 TREATY LAW AND PRACTICE OF THE REPUBLIC OF KOREA [헌법과 조약체결: 한국의 조약체결 권한과 절차], Bae, JongIn [배종인] (Seoul, Samusa [삼우사], 2009).

Summary: This treatise comprehensive deals with law of treaty, treaty implementation in Korea, various interpretations of Constitutional provisions, and theoretical backgrounds on various aspects of treaty.

Index: It has the table of contents in the front and does not contain an index. An annex in the back provides treaty-related Korean provisions.

Note: In Korean.

7 KOREA LEGISLATION RESEARCH INSTITUTE [KLRI; 한국법제연구원]
URL: http://elaw.klri.re.kr/eng_service/main.do.

Summary: This English website is a government-funded national policy research institute, and it provides a free English legal database, *Statutes of the Republic of Korea*. The *Statutes of the Republic of Korea* allows researchers to search for constitutions, current statutes, old statutes, decrees, and rules by statute name in English.[28] It does not cover treaties.

Note: When users type words in the search box, suggested titles of acts appear under the box. Users can do more advanced searching according to type of law, date, and registration number. Under the "Legal Glossary" menu, users can also search for the statute name by keyword; search results lead to the text of the statute.

Note: In English.

8 LAWNB: THOMSON REUTERS
URL: http://www.lawnb.com.

Summary: This is the most popular, comprehensive commercial database, containing statutes, decrees, rules and ordinances, cases, and treatises in Korean.[29] However, it does not provide English translations and does not cover treaties. LawnB was acquired by Thomson Reuters on March 30, 2012.[30] Westlaw began providing Korean cases, legislation, and law review and journals articles in English from 2013; the *Korea Reports* database covers cases from the Supreme Court, appellate and trial courts from 2000, and the *Korea Legislation* database provides selected legislation including the current Constitution provided by the Korean Ministry of Government Legislation.

Note: LawnB in Korean, Westlaw in English.

Diplomatic Documents

9 JOYAKJUNGBO [조약정보]
The Ministry of Foreign Affairs of the Republic of Korea.
URL: http://www.mofa.go.kr/trade/treatylaw/treatyinformation/multilateral/index.jsp?menu=m_30_50_40&tabmenu=t_2.

Summary: This official treaty database has the most comprehensive treaty collection which covers 2,280 treaties as of 2013. When a conflict happens

---

28 STATUTES OF THE REPUBLIC OF KOREA, *available at* http://elaw.klri.re.kr/eng_service/main.do (registration required for access).

29 LAWnB is a fee-based subscription database that contains approximately 74,000 laws, 150,000 cases, 130,000 administrative materials, 90,000 treaties, articles, and periodicals, 85,000 tax cases, 20,000 lawyers information, 4500 corporations legal information, and 70,000 legal news articles. *See* LAWNB, http://www.lawnb.com/.

30 Kanishk Vergese, *Thomson Reuters Acquires LawnB*, ASIAN LEGAL BUSINESS, *available at* http://asia.legalbusinessonline.com/news/thomson-reuters-acquires-lawnb/108127.

between the database version and the print version, the database version is more reliable because it takes one to two years to correct mistakes in print. Status information on the recent treaties since 2008 is separately listed in the reverse-chronological order.

Note: In Korean and official language.

Yearbooks and Digests of State Practice

10 KOREA YEARBOOK: POLITICS, ECONOMY AND SOCIETY
Rüdiger Frank, James E. Hoare, Patrick Köllner and Susan Pares (Leiden: Brill 2007–).

Summary: Annual compilation containing a chronology of relevant events over the year as well as a number of refereed articles on contemporary Korean affairs in areas of politics, economy and society. Focuses primarily on relations between North and South Korea, but also contains a section on the foreign relations of both jurisdictions.

Note: Selected coverage of volumes available on Google Books: http://books.google.com/books?id=VfdBwWvnLVYC&.

11 KOREAN JOURNAL OF INTERNATIONAL AND COMPARATIVE LAW
(Leiden: Brill, 2013–)

Summary: Semiannual journal which provides analyses of contemporary Asian practice in International Law, and summaries of decisions made by tribunals and both national and international courts.

Mexico

Teresa M. Miguel-Stearns[1]

Issues of Treaty Succession

Estados Unidos Mexicanos[2] is the successor State of Spain in the Northern region of the former Spanish empire in the Americas. Pope Alexander VI issued a papal bull on May 4, 1493, fixing the line of demarcation of conquered territories between the Kings of Spain and Portugal thereby avoiding future conflict; this papal bull in effect granted the then-unexplored territory of what is now Mexico to the Spanish crown. Hernán de Cortes conquered the Aztec empire in 1521 and Spain ruled the territory until Mexican independence in the early 19th century. The territory was called *Nueva España* (New Spain) and its political capital was in what is today Mexico City.[3]

Spanish colonial law was initially a transplantation of Spanish law which at the time of conquest was "a confusing mixture of Roman law, Germanic law, canon law, royal decrees, and administrative practices."[4] In Mexico, Aztec customary law was not completely eliminated by the Spanish crown, especially when it was compatible with Spanish law or the Catholic Church's interests. Some indigenous customs were eventually codified in the *Recopilación de Leyes de los Reynos de las Indias* (1680), the authoritative compilation of laws of the Americas. As evidenced by the *Recopilación*, the laws of Spanish America

1 The author is grateful to the work of several predecessors whose excellent bibliographic publications contributed significantly to the research done into the historical treaty and diplomatic collections. They include: Denys Peter Myers, MANUAL OF COLLECTIONS OF TREATIES AND OF COLLECTIONS RELATING TO TREATIES (Cambridge, Harvard Univ. Press 1922), wholly available on Google Books at: http://books.google.com/books?id=HlQUAAAAIAAJ; John T. Vance and Helen L. Clagett, A GUIDE TO THE LAW AND LEGAL LITERATURE OF MEXICO (Washington D.C., Library of Congress 1945); Helen L. Clagett and David M. Valderrama, A REVISED GUIDE TO THE LAW AND LEGAL LITERATURE OF MEXICO (Washington D.C., Library of Congress 1973).

2 The exact etymology of the Nahua *México* is disputed. One commonly held theory is that México is named for the Aztec people, also called *Mexicas* or *Tenochas*, founders of their capital city, *Mexico-Tenochtitlan*, present day Mexico City.

3 STEPHEN ZAMORA, ET AL, MEXICAN LAW 8 (2005).

4 Id. at 8–9, *citing* GUILLERMO FLORIS MARGADANT, INTRODUCCIÓN A LA HISTORIA DEL DERECHO MEXICANO 28–9 (Mexico, Ed. Esfiage) (8th ed. 1988).

 | DOI 10.1163/9789004272224_023

were developing somewhat independently from the laws of Spain despite a similar political and legal organization.[5]

In 1810, Padre Miguel Hidalgo rang the local church bell in Dolores, Mexico in the first call (known and celebrated as *El Grito de Dolores*) for Mexican independence from Spain. But it wasn't until August 1821 that Agustín de Iturbide successfully negotiated the *Treaty of Cordoba* with the final Spanish viceroy.[6] The *Treaty of Cordoba* contains three guarantees that are represented in the three colors of the Mexican flag: preservation of the Catholic Church (white); absolute independence of Mexico from Spain (green); and the friendly union of Spaniards and Mexicans (red).[7] However, the Treaty was seen as a step backwards towards colonialism and Emperor Iturbide ruled only briefly over the Mexican Empire that included present-day Central America[8] until he was overthrown by revolutionary forces. A Constitutional Congress was convened in 1823 and drafted the first constitution of the new republic, organizing its territories into 19 states.[9]

Shortly after independence, Juan N. Rodriguez de San Miguel, in his effort to clarify what laws, decrees, orders, and treaties were in effect at the time, sorted through the myriad of Spanish and Mexican laws, and pointed to a decree of April 8, 1823 wherein the government declared invalid the *Plan de Iguala*, the *Tratado de Córdoba* , and the *Decreto de 24 de Febrero* that established the government under Agustin de Iturbide. This decree further endorsed the three guarantees of *religión, independencia, and unión* and validated the other plans, treaties, and decrees that were not in opposition to the previous article.[10]

---

5 Angel R. Oquendo, Latin American Law 88–9, 109 (2nd ed. 2011), *citing* John H. Merryman et al, The Civil Law Tradition: Europe, Latin America, and East Asia 362, 366 (1994). *See*, Recopilacion de Leyes de los Reynos de las Indias (Madrid, Julian de Paredes 1681) sec. 2.1.4 and 5.2.22, for example.

6 Zamora, *supra* note 3, at 18, FN 78. *See*, Tratados Celebrados en la Villa de Córdova el 24 de Agosto de 1821 (Treaty of Cordoba) in Colección de Tratados con las Naciones Estranjeras, Leyes, Decretos y Ordenes que Forman el Derecho Internacional Mexicano 1 (Impr. De J.M. Lara, Mexico) (1854).

7 John T. Vance and Helen L. Clagett, Law and Legal Literature of Mexico 5–6 (Library of Congress, Washington) (1945).

8 Central America was part of Mexico when it declared its independence in 1821. In 1823, when the Mexican empire collapsed, the United Provinces of Central America declared independence from Mexico. A treaty was signed wherein Mexico recognized their independence in 1824. Some 15 years later, in 1838, the United Provinces broke up and formed independent countries.

9 Zamora, *supra* note 3, at 19–20.

10 Juan N. Rodríguez de San Miguel, Pandectas Hispano-Megicanas, o sea Codigo General: Comprensive de la Leyes Generales, Utiles y Vivas de Las Siete Partidas,

In other words, Spanish law was still good law unless it supported the Iturbide government.

There is no evidence that the newly formed Mexican State would not or did not honor any treaties previously entered into by Spain that later concerned Mexico. In fact, Mexico demonstrated it would honor treaties concluded by Spain when in 1828 it signed a *Tratado de Limites* (*Boundary Treaty*) with the United States[11] which explicitly provided for Mexico's approval of the *Treaty of Amity, Settlement, and Limits between the United States of America and His Catholic Majesty,* also known as the *Adams-Onís Treaty*.[12] The *Adams-Onis Treaty* was negotiated between Spain and the United States of America settling a border dispute that, shortly thereafter, became Mexico's border with the U.S. upon Mexican independence.[13]

Thus, the 1828 *Boundary Treaty* is a clear example of state succession. Additionally, in the January 8, 1828 *Protocol* to the first conference of the *Boundary Treaty* between the Plenipotentiary of the United States of America and Mexico, both agreed that each was bound by previous treaties with and by Spain:

> The Mexican Plenipotentiaries said that their Government had invariably acted upon the principle that Mexico was bound to respect the Treaties of the Spanish Monarchy prior to the declaration of her Independence, as for instance, Great Britain had acquired rights from Spain within territory of Mexico, (in the bay of Honduras,) which, however inconvenient to the Government, it was proposed not to disturb and

---

RCOPILACION NOVISIMA, LA DE INDIAS, AUTOS Y PROVIDENCIAS CONOCIDAS POR DE MONTEMAYOR Y BELEÑA Y CÉDULAS TOTALMENTE INÚTILES, DE LAS REPETIDAS, Y DE LAS EXPRESAMENTE DEROGADAS (3 Vol.) Vol. III, 2–3 (Mexico, Imp. M. G. Rivera 1839–40). *See also*, RECOPILACIÓN DE LAS LEYES DEL GOBIERNO ESPAÑOL QUE RIGEN EN LA REPUBLICA RESPECTIVAS A LOS AÑOS DE 1788 Y SIGUIENTES. CUARTA PARTE DEL SEMINARIO JUDICIAL (Mexico, Imp. de Galvan 1829).

11 Treaty of Limits, Between the United States of America and the United Mexican States, Jan. 12, 1828, 8 Stat. 372 (ratified and entered into force in 1832). *See also*, DERECHO INTERNACIONAL MEXICANO. TRATADOS Y CONVENCIONES CONCLUIDOS Y RATIFICADOS POR LA REPÚBLICA MEXICANA, DESDE SU INDEPENDENCIA HASTA EL 29 DE ABRIL DE 1876. PRIMERA PARTE. 115–21 (Mexico, Imp. de Gonzalo A. Esteva 1878).

12 Treaty of Amity, Settlement, and Limits between the United States of America and His Catholic Majesty (Adams-Onís Treaty), U.S.–Spain, Feb. 22, 1819, 8 Stat. 252 (ratified by Spain in 1820; ratified by the United States in 1821, a few months before the declaration of Mexican independence).

13 PHILIP COOLIDGE BROOKS, DIPLOMACY AND THE BORDERLANDS: THE ADAMS-ONÍS TREATY OF 1819 191–3 (1939).

> had acknowledged the existence of those rights in the recent Treaty with that Power. The Plenipotentiary of the United States replied that he did not intend to dispute the validity of a Treaty concluded between the United States and Spain at a period when Mexico formed a component part of the Spanish Monarchy; and that it was evident from former conferences and from his note on that subject that he had never controverted this principle.[14]

Similarly and even more explicitly, in the *Protocol* of the second conference of January 10, 1828, it was agreed:

> The limits of the United States of America with the bordering territories of Mexico having been fixed and designated by a solemn treaty concluded and signed at Washington on the 22nd day of February [1819], between the respective Plenipotentiaries of the Government of the United States of America, on the one part, and of that of Spain on the other: and whereas the said treaty having been sanctioned at a period when Mexico constituted a part of the Spanish monarchy, it is deemed necessary now to confirm the validity of the aforesaid treaty of limits, regarding it as still in force and binding between the United States of America and the United Mexican States.[15]

Mexican law, especially Mexican civil law, was virtually indistinguishable from that of Spain long after independence. For some years after independence, the decrees of the *Cortes de España* were collected and published as part of Mexican legislation by order of the Mexican government.[16] Additionally, Spanish legal texts written for Spain's colonies in the Americas, including the *cedulas* of the Council of the Indies, the *Recopilación de Indias,* the *Nueva Recopilación,* varias *Fueros,* the *Siete Partidas,* and the *Novísima Recopilación,* were still an important part of Mexican law well after independence.[17]

---

14 H.R. Doc. No. 42, at 27 (1837). *See also,* Derecho Internacional Mexicano, *supra* note 11, at 112.

15 H.R. Doc. No. 42, at 28 (1837). *See also,* Derecho Internacional Mexicano, *supra* note 11, at 112.

16 For a collection of decrees and orders from the *Cortes* in force at the time of Independence, *see,* Colección de los Decretos y Ordenes de la Cortes de España que se Reputan vigentes en la Republica de los Estados-Unidos Mexicanos (Mexico, Imp. De Galvan 1836).

17 Gustavus Schmidt, The Civil Law of Spain and Mexico 98–100 (New Orleans, Thomas Rea 1851).

However, it is interesting to note that post-independence compilations of treaties published by the Mexican government routinely begin from the date of independence (1821). Indexes and compilations of treaties in force in Mexico beginning at the end of the 19th century also do not include pre-independence treaties that would have been concluded by Spain as ruler of *Nueva España*.

The years that followed Mexican independence were turbulent. Presidents changed quickly and *coups de etats* were commonplace. Slavery was abolished in 1829. Rebellion rose up in what is now Texas, culminating in 1835 with a war of separation from Mexico. Texas declared independence after defeating an unorganized Mexican Army at the Alamo, a Franciscan mission, despite being significantly outnumbered. Some 10 years later, United States support of Texas's secession from Mexico led to armed conflict between Mexico and the United States. In December 1845, Texas was made the 28th state of the United States of America. Mexico refused to accept Texas's accession. In January 1846, the United States army invaded Mexico and fought its way to Mexico City. Mexico eventually surrendered on February 2, 1848, and signed the *Treaty of Guadalupe Hidalgo*[18] at which time Mexico gave up two-fifths of its territory: Texas, New Mexico, Arizona, California, Nevada, and part of Colorado.[19] The U.S.-Mexico borders were further defined in 1853 with the Gadsden Treaty.[20]

From the late 17th century to 1821, Spain made almost 300 land grants to promote development in the frontier lands, reward Spanish subjects, and create a buffer zone between Spanish settlements and Indian tribes. About half of the land grants were awarded to individuals and half to communities (for communal use in perpetuity), including 23 grants to Native American *pueblos*. Most land grants were made in what is today the Southwestern United States. At the time of the land grants, the territory was claimed and controlled by Spain and later by an independent Mexico who continued to recognize the land grants, adhere to the Spanish land policies, and consider the residents Mexican citizens. In accordance with the *Treaty of Guadalupe Hidalgo*, the United States agreed to recognize and protect the property rights of Mexican citizens living in the newly acquired areas.[21]

18 Treaty of Peace, Friendship, Limits, and Settlement (Treaty of Guadalupe Hidalgo), U.S.-Mexico, Feb. 2, 1848, 9 Stat. 922 (ratifications exchanged May 30, 1848; proclaimed July 4, 1848).

19 ZAMORA, *supra* note 3, at 18–21.

20 Treaty of Boundary, Cession of Territory, Transit of Isthmus of Tehuantepec, Etc. (Gadsden Treaty), U.S.-Mexico, Dec. 30, 1853, 1 U.S.T. 1121 (ratifications exchanged and proclaimed June 30, 1854).

21 GOVERNMENT ACCOUNTING OFFICE, TREATY OF GUADALUPE HIDALGO: FINDING AND POSSIBLE OPTIONS REGARDING LONGSTANDING COMMUNITY LAND GRANT CLAIMS IN

Treaty Ratification and Implementation

Mexico signed in 1986 and ratified in 1988 the *Vienna Convention on the Law of Treaties between States and International Organization or between International Organizations*,[22] and applies the definition of treaties set forth in Article 2 of the *Vienna Convention*. Treaty formation in Mexico complies with the *Vienna Convention*.[23]

The Mexican Constitution recognizes treaties as the supreme law of the land.[24] Nonetheless, the role of treaties in Mexican domestic law is a point of controversy. Overturning a 1992 precedent-setting decision that placed treaties on the same plane as federal law, the Mexican Supreme Court in 1999 in plenary session held that international treaties take precedent over domestic federal or state law even when the domestic law is adopted after the international treaty. The Court expressly held that only the Mexican Constitution is superior to international treaties.[25]

Treaty formation and implementation in Mexico is governed principally by three cohesive provisions: the Mexican Constitution; the *Organic Law of the Federal Public Administration* (*LOAPF*);[26] and the *Law of Treaties*.[27] In sum, the President of Mexico or his designees, concludes and signs a treaty and then submits it to the Senate for approval. After Senate approval and after complying with depository and other details, it is published in the *Diario Oficial de la Federación* (*DO*) in accordance with the Federal Civil Code and the *Law of Treaties*.[28]

New Mexico 3–4 (GAO-04–59, 2004), available at http://www.gao.gov/new.items/d0459.pdf. This is the second of two reports created to address a century of grievances by the heirs of land grant holders claiming unfair treatment by the U.S. government.

22 Vienna Convention on the Law of Treaties between States and International Organization or between International Organizations, May 23, 1969, T.S. No. 58, 1155 UNTS 331.

23 Zamora, *supra* note 3, at 90.

24 Constitución Política de los Estados Unidos Mexicanos [C.P.], *as amended*, Art. 133, Diario Oficial de la Federación [DO], 5 de Febrero de 1917 (Mex.), *available at* http://www.diputados.gob.mx/LeyesBiblio/pdf/1.pdf.

25 Zamora, *supra* note 3, at 90, *citing Amparo en Revisión* 1475/98 in Semanario Judicial de la Federación, vol. X 46 (1999).

26 Ley Orgánica de Administración Pública Federal [LOAPF][Federal Public Administrative Law], *as amended*, Diario Oficial de la Federación [DO], 2 de Abril de 2013 (Mex.), *available at* http://www.diputados.gob.mx/LeyesBiblio/pdf/153.pdf.

27 Ley sobre la Celebración de Tratados [Law of Treaties], Diario Oficial de la Federación [DO], 2 de Enero de 1992 (Mex.), *available at* http://www.diputados.gob.mx/LeyesBiblio/pdf/216.pdf.

28 Jorge Palacios Treviño, Tratados: Legislación y Practica en México 55, 78 (Secretaria de Relaciones Exteriores de México, Universidad Iberoamericana 2007).

The Constitution grants power and obligates the President of Mexico to manage foreign affairs and conclude international treaties. Treaty making power includes the ability to enter into, conclude, suspend, modify, and amend treaties; create reservations; and formulate interpretive declarations. While doing so, the President follows the guidelines of: self-determination of the people; non-intervention; peaceful settlement of conflicts; proscription of the threat or use of force in international relations; legal equality of the States; international cooperation for development; and the struggle for peace and international security. The President must submit all such action to the Senate for approval.[29]

The Constitution also grants the Senate exclusive authority to analyze the foreign affairs as developed by the Executive Branch by reviewing annual reports of the President of the Republic and the Secretary of the corresponding office to Congress. Furthermore, the Senate has the power to approve the treaties and diplomatic conventions that the Executive Branch has signed including its decision to end, denounce, suspend, modify, amend, make reservations, and formulate interpretive declarations regarding the same.[30]

The Mexican Constitution, the laws of Congress, and all treaties created in accordance with the Constitution, concluded by the President, and approved by the Senate, are the supreme law of the land. The judges of each State shall abide by this Constitution, laws, and treaties even if they are contrary to the Constitutions or laws of the States.[31] There are other articles that address fine points or restrictive clauses on treaty making power, such as the prohibition for States from entering into treaties with other domestic or foreign States.[32] Still others speak to various types of treaties, such as extradition treaties.[33]

LOAPF charges the *Secretaría de Releaciones Exteriores* (Secretariat of Foreign Affairs) (SRE) with coordinating the foreign affairs of all the entities of the Federal Public Administration including all classes of treaties, conventions, and agreements to which Mexico is a party.[34] By way of other articles, it

---

TRATADOS is a superbly detailed account of treaty-making practice and procedure in Mexico. The *DO* is the official gazette of Mexico. In accordance with the *Código Civil Federal de México*, Art. 3–4 (2000), no law takes effect until three days after it is published in the *DO* unless explicitly stated otherwise in the text of the law. The *Law of Treaties*, Art. 4, also requires publication in the *DO* after Senate approval is reached.

29 Constitución (1917) Art. 89 (x).

30 Constitución (1917) Art. 76 (I).

31 Constitución (1917) Art. 133.

32 Constitución (1917) Art. 117.

33 Constitución (1917) Art. 15.

34 TRATADOS, *supra note 28*, at 73 *citing* LOAPF Art. 28.

grants the entities, or federal agencies, the authority to do the same within each agency's narrow area of expertise and jurisdiction. For example the Secretariat of the Environment and Natural Resources has the power to conclude international treaties on behalf of the SRE in its narrow area of competence.[35]

Additional guidance is provided to the SRE in its handling of treaty affairs through its interior regulations. These regulations mandate, for example, the SRE to provide advisory opinions on the value of signing on to a treaty or participating in treaty negotiations; and to maintain a registry of treaties concluded by Mexico and its agencies.[36]

The *Law of Treaties* distinguishes between two types of international instruments: treaties (*tratados*) and inter-institutional agreements (*acuerdos interinstitutionales*). Article 2 defines a treaty as an international agreement entered into by the government of Mexico that involves one or more subjects pertaining to public international law. Treaties must be approved by the Senate in compliance with Article 76 of the Constitution, and are the supreme law of the land according to the terms of Article 133 of the Constitution. Inter-institutional agreements also deal with matters of public international law. They can be negotiated and entered into by a public administrative agency at the state or municipal level with one or more foreign government agencies or international organizations as long as there is no existing treaty on the matter. The subject-matter of inter-institutional agreements is limited to areas in which the state, municipality, or agency already enjoys exclusive jurisdiction. Inter-institutional agreements are not approved by the Senate, are not published in the *DO*, and are not the supreme law of the land.[37]

Treaty practice in Mexico, as in all countries, differs depending on whether it is a bilateral treaty or a multilateral treaty. With multilateral treaties, the SRE becomes aware of an international conference, for example, either of its own accord or it is brought to the SRE's attention by a relevant federal agency; and the SRE promotes Mexico's participation in the conference. In the case of bilateral treaties, the SRE investigates the efficacy of potential bilateral agreements and then coordinates the necessary parties and steps that might lead to a bilateral agreement.[38]

---

35 TRATADOS, *supra* note 28, at 73–4. *See also*, LAOPF Art. 32 Bis. Sec. IX.

36 Id. at 76. *See also*, Reglamento Interior de la Secretaría de Relaciones Exteriores, *as amended*, Diario Oficial de la Federacion [DO], 4 de Septiembre de 2009 (Mex.), *available at* http://www.ordenjuridico.gob.mx/Federal/Combo/R-280.pdf.

37 *See generally*, TRATADOS, *supra* note 28, at 288–98; *See also*, JORGE VARGAS, MEXICAN LAW: A TREATISE FOR LEGAL PRACTITIONERS AND INTERNATIONAL INVESTORS 22–4 (1998).

38 MONROE LEIGH, ET AL, (ED.), NATIONAL TREATY LAW AND PRACTICE 106 (2003).

For bilateral treaties, if the other State has an embassy or consular office in Mexico, communication generally begins by sending over a representative of the Mexican government who is a specialist in the area of the proposed bilateral treaty to begin discussions. If the initial proposal is positively received and the recipient is interested in pursuing a bilateral treaty, then actual negotiations begin with delegations of both countries meeting to write the text of the treaty. For Mexico, the delegation usually consists of members of the SRE along with experts in the subject matter of the proposed treaty. At times it may be pertinent to consult with private sector interested parties and experts as well. Throughout the process, it is crucial to keep the Mexican Senate abreast of the progress of the negotiations in order to help facilitate Senate consideration after the treaty has been agreed upon by both States. If there is more than one round of negotiations, it is customary to alternate the country hosting the negotiations. It is also not uncommon to meet in a third, neutral country simply for convenience.[39]

When the parties finalize the language of the treaty, an article is created in the treaty indicating as much. To show their consent to the adopted language, the head negotiators sign their initials to the unofficial document. This final document generally consists of a treaty title, preamble, substantive articles, and final clauses. Preambles have been a part of Mexican bilateral treaties since 1857 and customarily contain a Christian invocation, such as the name of God as the ultimate governor of the universe. The preamble also contains the names of the parties or States involved and any designees of the States. Common concepts in the Preamble include friendship between the States, the motives of the treaty, and any previous related treaties.[40] The final sentences contain the legal clauses, obligations, and steps necessary to implement the treaty. It includes how to resolve disagreements that might arise under the treaty. Bilateral treaties are concluded in each of the languages of the parties to the agreement, and each is wholly valid, official, and authentic. Both States sign the identical but linguistically distinct documents.[41]

Bilateral treaties concluded by Mexico are finalized on special paper containing the national seal or coat-of-arms. Although the language is agreed upon, they are often not signed immediately so that the parties can consider further their legal obligations under the treaty. It is generally the Secretary of Foreign Affairs who signs the document in the Federal District of Mexico. If the treaty is signed abroad, it is usually the Mexican Ambassador to that country

39 TRATADOS, *supra* note 28, at 118–9.

40 Id. at 120–21.

41 Id. at 122–23.

who signs the treaty. Despite being signed, all parties know the bilateral treaty is not yet binding as it lacks ratification by the Senate. Nonetheless, after signature, certified copies are made of the original and the original is deposited in the historical archive of the nation.[42]

For both bilateral and multilateral treaties, the Treaty Section of the Legal Advisor's Office of the SRE plays an advisory role throughout the negotiations process. Although a government agency with particular specialization may engage in the actual negotiations for a relevant treaty, the agency is continuously supported by the SRE. The SRE may gather and distribute opinions of affected agencies and entities. As negotiations are underway for both bilateral and multilateral treaties with significant social, political, or economic implications, representatives often appear before Congress to explain the importance and benefits of the treaty. Ultimately, the SRE issues a report at the conclusion of the negotiations that addresses any issues or areas of concern in the treaty including an assessment as to its affect, if any, on domestic law. If the report is not favorable, the SRE's concerns must be addressed and treaty provisions adjusted until the SRE issues a favorable report. Once this occurs, the treaty is ripe for signature.[43]

Once a bilateral or multilateral treaty is signed, it is up to the Executive Power to submit the treaty to the Senate for approval. In practice, the SRE through the Secretary of the Government (SG) submits the treaty to the Senate. The Senate's Commission on Foreign Relations studies the treaty along with relevant specialized standing commissions. Each commission issues a report to the Senate who then performs two readings of the report during which time the senators engage in an article-by-article analysis. At the end, the Chamber of Senators votes on a motion of approval. The Senate must vote and approve reservations, declarations, or understandings at this time as well. If the Senate approves the treaty it issues a decree to the SG and the President.[44]

After the Senate approves the treaty, the President must ratify the treaty before it can become law.[45] For bilateral treaties, the SRE ensures that instruments of ratification are exchanged or, where there are no instruments of ratification, formal notes indicating Senate approval are exchanged. For multilateral treaties, the SRE deposits instruments of ratification as established in the treaty.[46] Note that most multilateral treaties require a certain number of States to ratify a treaty before it has the force of international law.

---

42 Id. at 124–27.

43 National Treaty, *supra* note 38, at 106–7.

44 Id. at 108–9.

45 Constitución (1917), Art. 89 (x)

46 National Treaty, *supra* note 38, at 109; Tratados, *supra* note 28, at 155–58.

After signature, Senate approval, and ratification, the Secretary of the SRE prepares for the President an SRE-endorsed decree which includes the complete text of the treaty. The President orders its publication in the *DO* in accordance with the Federal Civil Code, after which it becomes the supreme law of the land.[47]

The *Law of Treaties* obligates the SRE to maintain a registry of all treaties entered into force in which Mexico is a party. The registry is managed by the Legal Adviser's Office and is available to the public. The SRE also registers all treaties with the United Nations.[48]

The *Law of Treaties* permits agencies of the federal, state, or local governments to enter into international agreements within their limited scope of authority. These agreements are not treaties as they do not require Senate approval or ratification. Nonetheless, agencies entering into international agreements must alert the Department of Foreign Affairs of the intent to enter into international agreements by way of written report. These agreements are negotiated by the local agency with, if desired, the support of the SRE. The Legal Adviser's Office analyzes the draft agreement, consults with relevant and interested parties, and then issues a report through the SRE. The Legal Adviser's Office ensures the agency is not exceeding its jurisdiction or interfering with the interests of the federal government. Like treaties, once concluded all inter-institutional agreements are registered with the SRE.[49]

Evidence of State Practice

Diplomatic Relations of Mexico are controlled by the Executive Power headed by the President and managed by SRE. Evidence of state practice can be seen in the Constitution as well as the stated mission and vision of the Secretariat.[50] The SRE also maintains an extensive website of historical documents.[51]

Both houses of Congress maintain webpages and publish their daily proceedings online and in their respective publications, including full-text laws passed and treaties approved.[52] The national government also publishes a

47 National Treaty, *supra* note 38, at 110.

48 Id.; Ley de Tratados, Art. 6.

49 National Treaty at 111–12; Ley de Tratados, Art. 7–8.

50 For more informtion on the SRE, *see* Secretaría de Relaciones Exteriores, http://www.sre.gob.mx/.

51 Acervo Histórico Diplomático: http://www.sre.gob.mx/acervo/.

52 Senado de la República: http://www.senado.gob.mx/. Cámara de Diputados: http://www.diputados.gob.mx/inicio.htm.

daily *Diario Oficial* wherein all laws, ratified treaties, and other legal documents of interest are published.[53]

Annotated Bibiography of Sources

General Treaty Collections

1 COLECCIÓN DE TRATADOS CON LAS NACIONES ESTRANJERAS, LEYES, DECRETOS Y ORDENES QUE FORMAN EL DERECHO INTERNACIONAL MEXICANO
(Mexico: Impr. De J.M. Lara, 1854).

Summary: A collection of treaties from 1821–1854, beginning with the *Tratado de Córdoba* in 1821. The index is a chronological list of 158 treaties from 1821–1854 plus several additional conventions. Wholly available in Google Books and Hathi Trust at http://hdl.handle.net/2027/umn.31951001873701y.

Index: The index in the back of the volume lists all treaties published in this volume in chronological order just as they appear in this volume.

2 TRATADOS DE MÉXICO: SOBERANÍA Y TERRITORIO 1821–1910
Secretaría de Relaciones Exteriores (Mexico: Secretaría de Relaciones Exteriores, 2000).

Summary: Beautifully illustrated coffee-table style book providing a detailed narrative of how treaties fit into Mexican history during the stated time period.

Note: The appendix has two parts, the first containing reprints of Mexico's treaties involving commerce and the second containing Mexico's boundary treaties with its neighbors.

3 DERECHO INTERNACIONAL MEXICANO. TRATADOS Y CONVENCIONES CONCLUIDOS Y RATIFICADOS POR LA REPÚBLICA MEXICANA, DESDE SU INDEPENDENCIA HASTA EL AÑO ACTUAL, ACOMPAÑADOS DE VARIOS DOCUMENTOS QUE LES SON REFERENTES. PRIMERA PARTE
(Mexico: Imp. de Gonzalo A. Esteva, 1878).

Summary: Volume I contains the treaties and conventions concluded and ratified by Mexico from Independence (1821) to 1877. Wholly available in Google Books at: http://books.google.com/books?id=bscCAAAAYAAJ.

Index: The index in the beginning of this volume lists countries alphabetically then treaties chronologically within each. A second index lists all treaties chronologically.

---

53 Diario Oficial de la Federación: http://www.dof.gob.mx/.

Note: The appendix at the back of the volume reprints a number of documents believed to be interesting and relevant to the study of international relations in Mexico, such as the treaty between the Mexican Empire and the Comanche Nation (1822).

4 DERECHO INTERNACIONAL MEXICANO. TRATADOS Y CONVENCIONES CELEBRADOS Y NO RATIFICADOS POR LA REPÚBLICA MEXICANA: CON UN APENDICE QUE CONTIENE VARIOS DOCUMENTOS IMPORTANTES. SEGUNDA PARTE
(Mexico: Imp. de Gonzalo A. Esteva, 1878).

Summary: This volume contains treaties and conventions concluded but not ratified by Mexico. It was created purely for historical interest and only a small number of copies were printed and distributed. Wholly available in Google Books at: http://books.google.com/books?id=oeHqAAAAMAAJ.

Index: The index in the beginning of this volume lists countries alphabetically then treaties within each. A second index lists all treaties chronologically.

5 DERECHO INTERNACIONAL MEXICANO. LEYES, DECRETOS Y ORDENES QUE FORMAN EL DERECHO INTERNACIONAL MEXICANO O QUE SE RELACIONAN CON EL MISMO. TERCERA PARTE
(Mexico: Tip. Lit. de Filomeno Mata, 1879).

Summary: Volume III contains the laws, decrees, and orders that together form Mexican international law or are related to Mexican international law. Some treaties and conventions are contained in this volume that is organized topically and alphabetically (beginning with *Agentes Comerciales Privados*). Wholly available in Google Books at: http://books.google.com/books?id=baJJAQAAIAAJ.

Index: The index in the back of the volume is organized alphabetically by topic and chronologically within each topic.

6 DERECHO INTERNACIONAL MEXICANO. TRATADOS Y CONVENCIONES CONCLUIDOS Y RATIFICADOS POR LA REPÚBLICA MEXICANA DESDE SU INDEPENDENCIA HASTA EL AÑO 1896, ACOMPAÑADOS DE VARIOS DOCUMENTOS QUE LES SON REFERENTES. SEGUNDA PARTE
(Mexico: Imp. y Lit. de F. Díaz de León Suc., 1896).

Summary: This second *segunda parte* is intended to replace the original *segunda parte* in which a limited number of exemplars were printed and only for historical purposes as those treaties were never ratified. This new *segunda parte* effectually continues the original (and only) *primera parte* by publishing treaties and conventions concluded and ratified by Mexico between December 7, 1877 and March 16, 1896. Bilateral treaties with non-Spanish speaking countries are presented in side-by-side columns in both languages. Multilateral treaties are also reprinted. Wholly available in Hathi Trust at: http://hdl.handle.net/2027/mdp.35112104563954.

Index: The index in the back of the volume lists countries alphabetically then treaties within each chronologically. Multilateral treaties are listed last.

7 TRATADOS Y CONVENCIONES VIGENTES
Secretaría de Relaciones Exteriores (Mexico: J.I. Gerrero y Ca., Sucs. de F. Díaz de León, 1904).

Summary: A collection of treaties in force published by the Department of Foreign Affairs of Mexico, organized chronologically beginning with the *Tratado de Paz, Amistad y Límites, de 2 de Febrero de 1848, con los Estados Unidos de América.* Wholly available in Google Books at: http://books.google.com/books?id=ljooAQAAMAAJ.

Index: There are two indices in the back of the volume: the first is chronological; the second is alphabetical by country.

8 TRATADOS Y CONVENCIONES VIGENTES
Secretaría de Relaciones Exteriores (Mexico: Tip. "Artística," 1909).

Summary: This volume is an appendix to the above collection of treaties and conventions plus an historical sketch of Mexico's treaty relations from the time of independence to 1909. It also includes a chronological list of treaties arranged under each Mexican president. This work is based partly on the 1859 index created by Matías Romero (see no. 13 below).

9 TRATADOS Y CONVENCIONES VIGENTES ENTRE LOS ESTADOS UNIDOS MEXICANOS Y OTROS PAÍSES
Secretaría de Relaciones Exteriores (Mexico: Imp. de la Secretaría de Relaciones Exteriores, 1930–1938).

Summary: A six-volume series of treaties in force in Mexico. Volume I (1930) contains bilateral treaties organized alphabetically by foreign country. Volumes II and III (1931) contain multilateral treaties organized chronologically by date of signature. Volume IV (1938) contains multilateral and bilateral treaties since 1930 and conventions of the International Labor Conference. Volume V contains conventions of the International Labor Conference. Volume VI contains bilateral treaties since 1930.

Index: The indices for volumes I and VI organize the treaties alphabetically by country. The indices for volumes II–V are organized chronologically.

10 DIARIO OFICIAL DE LA FEDERACIÓN
(Mexico, 1917–).

Summary: Daily publication of laws, decrees, treaties and other legal documents. Known simply as *Diario Oficial* from 1917–1986; known by several names from 1722–1917. Available free online at: http://dof.gob.mx/index.php from 1917 (year of current Mexican constitution).

11 TRATADOS CELEBRADOS POR MÉXICO
Senado de La República and Secretaría de Relaciones Exteriores
(Mexico: El Senado, 1993–).

Summary: Annual publication containing the full-text of bilateral and multilateral agreements, and other international instruments from 1823 to the present. Treaties are arranged chronologically by date of signature or conclusion. Treaties can now be found on the website of the SRE: http://www.sre.gob.mx/tratados/ and http://www.ordenjuridico.gob.mx/Publicaciones/CDs2008/CDTratados/cd_tratados.php.

Index: There are several indices: all treaties listed chronologically; bilateral treaties listed alphabetically by foreign country; multilateral treaties listed chronologically; bilateral accords listed chronologically; international instruments of past years adopted this year by Mexico listed chronologically by original date of treaty formation.

Note: Previous title: Tratados Ratificados y Convenios Ejecutivos Celebrados Por Mexico (1973–1993).

12 TRATADOS VIGENTES CELEBRADOS POR MÉXICO (1836–2008)
URL: http://www.ordenjuridico.gob.mx/Publicaciones/CDs2008/CDTratados/cd_tratados.php.

Summary: Interactive website published cooperatively by several government agencies. Contains full-text (unofficial and unauthenticated) pdf documents of all treaties, bilateral and multilateral in force in Mexico, as well as related jurisprudence and national laws pertaining to treaties. Search using interactive map or advanced search. Each treaty contains date of signature, ratification, and entry into force.

Treaty Indexes

13 TABLA SINÓPTICA DE LOS TRATADOS Y CONVENCIONES QUE HAN NEGOCIADO LOS ESTADOS DE MÉXICO CON LAS NACIONES EXTRANGERAS
Matías Romero (Tabasco (Mex.): J.M. Flores, 1859).

Summary: This volume contains a helpful table summarizing all 24 treaties Mexico has signed with foreign countries (including Texas) up to the time of publication (Mexico recognized Texas's independence at this time). The table lists the foreign country, the objective of the treaty, the Mexican and foreign officials involved, the date and place of conclusion, dates of ratification for Mexico and the foreign State, date of publication in Mexico, and duration of the treaty. Additionally, the author details the five types of treaties (friendship, commerce and navigation; conventions; peace; boundaries; alliances; abolition of slavery) and explains the motivation behind each type. The author also summarizes the key points of each of the 24 treaties. There is no index and no full-text reprint of the treaties.

14 MÉXICO: RELACIÓN DE TRATADOS EN VIGOR

Secretaría de Relaciones Exteriores (Mexico: Secretaría de Relaciones Exteriores, 1985–).

Summary: Published sporadically, each issue contains a list of treaties in force in Mexico. Organized in two sections, bilateral (alphabetically by foreign country) and multilateral (alphabetically by subject). Introductory note directs users to the *Coleccion Tratados Ratificados y Convenios Ejecutivos Clebrados Por Mexico* and the *United Nations Treaty Series*(*UNTS*) for full-text. *Consolidated Treaty Series* (*CTS*) and *UNTS* citations given in chart along with dates of adoption, ratification, and entry into force.

15 GUÍA DE TRATADOS PROMULGADOS Y OTROS INSTRUMENTOS INTERNACIONALES VIGENTES SUSCRITOS POR MÉXICO

Secretaría de Gobernación (Mexico: Porrúa, 2005).

Summary: Chronological guide to all treaties and international instruments concluded by Mexico from 1836–2004. Provides dates of signing and promulgation, whether bilateral, multilateral, or international organization, and one or two-word description. Does not indicate current status (whether currently in force). Also available online from the website of the Mexican government agency, *Orden Jurídico Nacional* at http://www.ordenjuridico.gob.mx/Publicaciones/guiia%20de%20tratados2005.pdf.

Topical and Selected Treaty Publications

16 U.S.–MEXICAN TREATIES

Richard A. Westin (Buffalo (NY): Hein, 1996).

Summary: Originally an 11-volume set containing all bilateral and multilateral treaties in force between the United States of America and Mexico, and multilateral treaties to which both countries are signatories, from 1848 (*Treaty*

of Guadalupe Hidalgo) to 1994. Organized chronologically by signing date. Volume 12 is a 1999 Supplement covering 1992 to 1997. Volume 13 is a 2001 Supplement covering 1997 to 2000.

Index: Each volume begins with a chronological index of the treaties contained in each volume, followed by a subject index referencing the appropriate volume. Each treaty entry has a citation to an official or unofficial full-text source. There is also a list of treaties with multiple signing dates. Following the indices is the full-text reprint of the treaties.

17 ARGENTINA-MÉXICO: ACUERDOS BILATERALES, 1912–2000 (Buenos Aires (Arg.): Consejo Argentino para las Relaciones Internacionales, 2002).

Summary: Publication of bilateral treaties, agreements, declarations, acts, and memoranda of understanding between Mexico and Argentina. There is a helpful introduction detailing the history of bilateral agreements between the two countries.

Index: There are two indices: the first lists treaties chronologically by date of signature; the second organizes the agreements topically. Treaties and agreements are reprinted in full in chronological order beginning with their first in 1912.

Diplomatic Documents

18 BOLETÍN OFICIAL DE LA SECRETARÍA DE RELACIONES EXTERIORES Secretaría de Relaciones Exteriores (Mexico: Secretaría de Relaciones Exteriores, 1895–1935).

Summary: Collection of documents published monthly or bimonthly pertaining to the work of the SRE during the course of the year. Includes documents related to treaty negotiations, laws, decrees, circulars, consular reports, legal notices, reports from various departments, and an accounting of finances.

19 INDICE DEL BOLETÍN OFICIAL DE LA SECRETARÍA DE RELACIONES EXTERIORES, 1895–1923 SECRETARÍA DE RELACIONES EXTERIORES (MEXICO: SECRETARÍA DE RELACIONES EXTERIORES, 1924)

Summary: A comprehensive index to the *Boletín* organized topically. References to treaties generally can be found under “Tratados y conveciones”; references to bilateral treaties can be found “Tratados y convenceiones, entre México y” where they are organized further by topic such as “Arbitraje” and “Comercio.”

20 MEMORIA

Secretaría de Relaciones Exteriores (Mexico: Secretaría de Relaciones Exteriores, 1821–).

Summary: Annual publication by the SRE to the Mexican Congress. Contains information about treaties and conventions concluded by Mexico. For example, Vol. (1969–70) contains a section on treaties signed, approved, ratified, and promulgated between Sept. 1, 1969 and August 30, 1970. In this section the treaties are listed chronologically under those four sub-headings. The full-text of some of the listed treaties is reprinted in the appendix of this volume.

Note: There are several government publications entitled Memoria that cover various periods in the 19th c. and focus on unique aspects of the work of the SRE. For a more complete listing, *see*, Denys Peter Myers, *Manual of Collections of Treaties and of Collections Relating to Treaties* (Harvard Univ. Press, Cambridge) (1922).

21 LA DIPLOMACIA MEXICANA

Secretaría de Relaciones Exteriores (Mexico: Tip. "Artistica," 1910).

Summary: A three-volume publication by the Department of Foreign Affairs that primarily includes notes of foreign relations and secondarily includes a selection of relevant treaties concluded by Mexico in conjunction with the activities of the SRE. Organized chronologically beginning in 1821. Not an exhaustive collection of treaties.

22 ARCHIVO HISTÓRICO DIPLOMÁTICO MEXICANO

Secretaría de Relaciones Exteriores (Mexico: Secretaría de Relaciones Exteriores, 1923–1931).

Summary: Collection of numerous volumes each focusing on an historical aspect of Mexico's foreign relations. Contains treaties and other documents. In Vol. 22 (1927), for example, *El Tratado de Paz con España* contains not only the text of the treaty but also all the letters and documents exchanged leading up to the treaty. Many volumes are available as scanned versions of the print volumes, open-access, on the website of the SRE: http://www.sre.gob.mx/acervo/ (go to "Biblioteca Digital de Relaciones Internacionales").

23 COLECCIÓN DEL ARCHIVO HISTÓRICO DIPLOMÁTICO MEXICANO. SERIE TRATADOS

Secretaría de Relaciones Exteriores (Mexico: Secretaría de Relaciones Exteriores, 1974).

Summary: A 13-volume monographic series with each title devoted to a bilateral commercial treaty between Mexico and a foreign country (Switzerland,

France, Belgium/Luxembourg, South Korea, Netherlands, United Arab Emirates, Yugoslavia, Canada, Japan, Italy, El Salvador, Costa Rica, and Greece).

24 ARCHIVO HISTÓRICO DIPLOMÁTICO MEXICANO: CATÁLOGO GENERAL DE PUBLICACIONES, 1923–1991
Secretaría de Relaciones Exteriores (Mexico: Secretaría de Relaciones Exteriores, 1991).

Summary: This catalog lists all publications of the SRE organized into five major time periods, or *epocas*. The *Tercera Epoca* (third period) is from 1973–1980. During this period the government published a series of thirteen treaties, all commercial in nature, and all in 1974. The bibliographic information of few other treaties is also published in this catalog, including several 19th c. treaties published in the 1920s.

Index: There are three indices in the back of the volume where publications are organized alphabetically first by title, then by author, and finally by translator, compiler, and prologue author.

25 POLÍTICA EXTERIOR DE MÉXICO: 175 AÑOS DE HISTORIA
Secretaría de Relaciones Exteriores (Mexico: Secretaría de Relaciones Exteriores, 1985). 4 vols.

Summary: Created and published in commemoration of Mexico's 175th anniversary of the beginning of independence (1810), and 75 years since the Mexican Revolution (1910). Contains three sections: a documentary history of Mexico's foreign relations beginning in the 19th century; an anthology of reflections about Mexico's foreign affairs including difficult times and struggles over the last two centuries; and a collection of essays regarding some of the principle themes that have figured into the agenda of Mexico's foreign affairs in recent times.

Yearbooks and Digests of State Practice

26 ANUARIO MEXICANO DE DERECHO INTERNACIONAL
(Mexico: Universidad Nacional Autónoma de México, Instituto de Investigaciones Jurídicas, 2001–).

Summary: Mostly in Spanish, some English and French. Combines articles from leading scholars, commentaries, summaries of court proceedings, and anaylsis and explanation of state practice. Available full-text online at UNAM's IIJ: http://biblio.juridicas.unam.mx/revista/DerechoInternacional/.

Note: Other title: *Mexican Yearbook of International Law.*

Nigeria

Mary Rumsey

Issues of Treaty Succession

Nigeria gained its independence from the United Kingdom in 1960.[1] Until that time, the United Kingdom conducted Nigeria's foreign affairs, including the negotiation, conclusion, and ratification of treaties. Upon independence, Nigeria issued the following declaration in an exchange of diplomatic letters:

(i) all obligations and responsibilities of the Government of the United Kingdom which arise from any valid international instrument shall henceforth, in so far as such instrument may be held to have application to Nigeria, be assumed by the Government of the Federation of Nigeria;
(ii) the rights and benefits heretofore enjoyed by the Government of the United Kingdom in virtue of the application of any such international instrument to Nigeria shall henceforth be enjoyed by the Government of the Federation of Nigeria.[2]

At independence, Nigeria was bound by at least 334 treaties inherited from the United Kingdom.[3] Despite military coups and other changes in government, Nigeria has adhered to this declaration.[4] The Nigerian Constitution, in its description of the country's "foreign policy objectives", refers to "respect for international law and treaty obligations".[5] The other foreign policy objectives listed in the 1999 Constitution include promotion and protection of the

1 Nigeria Independence Act 1960, 8 & 9 Elizabeth II, c. 55 (Eng.).
2 Nigeria-United Kingdom, Exchange of Letters Constituting an Agreement relative to the Inheritance of International Rights and Obligations by the Government of the Federation of Nigeria, Oct. 1, 1960, 384 U.N.T.S. 207, 208.
3 Babafemi Akinrinade, *Nigeria*, *in* International Law and Domestic Legal Systems: Incorporation, Transformation, and Persuasion 453 (Dinah Shelton ed., 2011). For example, Nigeria's Operational Code of Conduct for Nigerian Forces (Lagos: Federal Republic of Nigeria, 1967) requires compliance with the Geneva Conventions of 1949, which the UK ratified in 1957.
4 Chris Nwachukwu Okeke, The Theory and Practice of International Law in Nigeria 10 (Enugu, Nigeria: Fourth Dimension Publishers, 1986); J.B. Ayala, *Introduction*, *in* 1 Nigeria's Treaties in Force 1970–1990 22 (1990).
5 Nigerian Constitution (1999), § 19(d).

 | DOI 10.1163/9789004272224_024

national interest, promotion of African integration and support for African unity, promotion of international co-operation for the consolidation of universal peace and mutual respect among all nations and elimination of discrimination in all its manifestations, and promotion of a just world economic order.[6]

Nigeria is also active in regional intergovernmental organizations; Nigeria is a member of the African Union and the Economic Community of West African States (ECOWAS).[7] In 2010, Nigeria was ordered by the ECOWAS Community Court of Justice to comply with its international treaty obligations relating to human rights.[8]

Treaty Ratification and Implementation

The Nigerian Constitution gives the federal government complete control over foreign affairs.[9] The Constitution contains no specific treaty-making power,[10] but reserves to the National Assembly the power to implement treaties, including the power to make laws with respect to matters not included on the Exclusive Legislative List.[11] The Executive's power to make treaties is implied.[12] Publication of Nigerian treaties has, unfortunately, been incomplete and sporadic.

Some aspects of treaty ratification and implementation are governed by the Treaties (Making Procedure, etc.) Act, No. 16 of 1993.[13] This Act designates the Federal Ministry of Justice as the depository of all treaties entered into between

---

6 Id.

7 For a useful commentary on ratification of African Union treaties, *see* Tiyanjana Maluwa, *Ratification of African Union Treaties by Member States: Law, Policy and Practice*, 13 MELB. J. INT'L L. 636 (2012). Of the 23 treaties available for ratification by AU members, Nigeria has signed all 23, and has ratified 87% of those 23. Id. at 678.

8 SERAP v. Federal Republic of Nigeria and Universal Basic Education Commission, ECW/CCJ/APP/08/08 (ECOWAS Community Court of Justice, 2010).

9 NIGERIAN CONSTITUTION (1999) [hereinafter NIGERIA CONST.], Second Schedule: Exclusive Legislative List, Item 31 ("Implementation of treaties relating to matters on this list").

10 KEHINDE MOWOE, CONSTITUTIONAL LAW IN NIGERIA 150 (2008).

11 NIGERIA CONST. § 12(2).

12 Mowoe, *supra* note 10, at 151; Christian N. Okeke, *International Law in the Nigerian Legal System*, 27 CAL. W. INT'L J. 311, 337 (1997) (hereinafter Okeke, *International Law*) (discussing language from the 1979 constitution that is identical to language in the 1999 constitution).

13 http://www.placng.org/lawsofnigeria/node/389.

the Federation and any other country.[14] Moreover, the Act classifies treaties into three separate types: First, "law-making treaties, being agreements constituting rules which govern inter-state relationship and co-operation in any area of endeavour and which have the effect of altering or modifying existing legislation or which affects the legislative powers of the National Assembly"; these require enactment into law.[15] Second, "agreements which impose financial, political and social obligations on Nigeria or which are of scientific or technological import";[16] these require ratification.[17] Third, "agreements which deal with mutual exchange of cultural and educational facilities";[18] these "may not need to be ratified".

Nigeria adopts the dualist approach to international law;[19] thus, to become effective, treaties must be incorporated into national legislation. Section 12(1) of the Constitution provides: "No treaty between the Federation and any other country shall have the force of law except to the extent to which any such treaty has been enacted into law by the National Assembly".[20] Nigerian courts have interpreted this provision strictly, "refusing to apply the provisions of unimplemented treaties".[21]

Nigeria has signed many treaties that it has not implemented legislatively.[22] These treaties create obligations for Nigeria vis-à-vis other parties, but do not

---

14 Treaties (Making Procedure, Etc.) Act, §4.

15 Treaties (Making Procedure, Etc.) Act, §3(1)(a). See also Chris Okeke, Speech, *The Contributions of Nigeria to the Progressive Development of International Law in Africa and the World* (Nov. 2010), available at: http://www.thenigerianvoice.com/nvnews/39326/1/the-contributions-of-nigeria-to-the-progressive-de.html.

16 Treaties (Making Procedure, Etc.) Act, §3(1)(b).

17 Ratification is by the executive. Akinrinade, *supra* note 3, at 457–58 n. 74.

18 Treaties (Making Procedure, Etc.) Act, §3(1)(c).

19 A.O. Enabulele, *Implementation of Treaties in Nigeria and the Status Question: Whither Nigerian Courts?*, 17 African J. Int'l & Comp. L. 326, 330, 331(2009).

20 Nigeria Const. § 12(1); Genera Sani Abacha & Others v. Chief Gani Fawehinmi, S.C. 45/1997, [2000] 4 SCNUJ 400, 466 ("no matter how beneficial to the country or citizenry, an international treaty to which Nigeria has become signatory may be, it remains unenforceable, if it is not enacted into the law of the country by the National Assembly").

21 Enabulele, *supra* note 19, at 330. Enabulele offers a detailed examination of how the Nigerian courts have dealt with the implementation of treaties.

22 Enabulele, *supra* note 19, at 326 (stating that "[t]here are a few, perhaps a handful of implemented treaties in Nigeria"). Elizabeth Oji gives the example of the Convention on the Elimination of All Forms of Discrimination against Women, Dec. 18, 1979, 1249 U.N.T.S. 13 (CEDAW), as a treaty to which Nigeria is a party, but which Nigeria has not implemented. Elizabeth A. Oji, *Application of Customary International Law in Nigerian Courts*, 1 NIALS

create enforceable obligations or rights for Nigerian citizens.[23] Nigerian courts have not given clear guidance on the status of "treaties that have not been formally approved as treaties through the constitutional ratification process".[24]

Nigeria[25] has not made a practice of depositing its treaties with the UN. An examination of the UN Treaties database shows only one treaty that was submitted by Nigeria rather than by another treaty party: Nigeria—United Kingdom, Exchange of Letters Constituting an Agreement about the Incorporation of the Northern Cameroons into the Federation of Nigeria, May 29, 1961 (submitted on Sept. 23, 1963). Even treaties concluded with smaller African countries were submitted by those countries; e.g., Nigeria—Republic of Equatorial Guinea, Protocol on implementation of article 6.2 of the Treaty between the Federal Republic of Nigeria and the Republic of Equatorial Guinea concerning their maritime boundary, Apr. 2, 2002 (submitted by Equatorial Guinea); Cameroon—Nigeria, Maroua Declaration, June 1, 1975 (submitted by Cameroon). Of course, other UN members have deposited various bilateral treaties made with Nigeria, covering various subjects such as investment protection, air traffic, and double taxation.[26]

Evidence of State Practice[27]

Nigeria's state practice is characterized by a lack of documentation. As stated earlier, the executive branch has the power to make treaties.[28] Specifically, the

J. Law & Devel. 151, 159 (2011) ("Nigeria has not yet domesticated [CEDAW], making it ineffective within the country").

23 Enabulele, *supra* note 19, at 329 ("the president may well enter into any international obligation as he pleases and create obligations for the country in the international realm, but for such international obligations to translate to national obligations for the citizens, legislative implementation is required").

24 Akinrinade, *supra* note 3, at 454 (describing the status of such treaties as "not quite clear").

25 The UNTS database lists "Nigeria Colony" and "Nigeria Protectorate" but a search on those entities retrieves no documents.

26 Researchers are advised to consult specialized databases to find more such treaties. For example, several Nigerian bilateral investment treaties not in the UNTS database can be found in the UN Conference on Trade and Development (UNCTAD) database (http://www.unctadxi.org). Similarly, the TIARA index lists several Nigerian bilateral treaties not deposited with the Secretary-General.

27 Post-colonial state practice is considered here. Before the colonial era, there is a scarcity of evidence of practice by Nigerian kingdoms. See Okeke, Theory and Practice, *supra* note 4, at 14–21.

28 Okeke, *International Law*, *supra* note 12, at 337.

Ministry of Justice conducts foreign policy on behalf of the country.[29] Earlier versions of the Nigerian constitution allowed some latitude for the individual Nigerian states to act in foreign policy spheres, but beginning with the 1979 Constitution, all such latitude was removed.[30]

Annotated Bibliography of Sources

General Treaty Collections

1 NIGERIA'S TREATIES IN FORCE FOR THE PERIOD 1ST OCTOBER, 1960 TO 30TH JUNE, 1968
(Lagos: Federal Ministry of Information, 1969).

Summary: Contains some treaties enacted between 1965 and 1969. Although the intention was originally to produce annual volumes,[31] the next volume, which appeared in 1969, stated in the Introductory Note that publication of annual volumes "has not been possible because the number of treaties and international agreements concluded since 1965 were so few that it was considered not worthwhile to publish annual volumes".[32]

Note: Contains the full text of only twenty treaties. Part I lists sixty-six bilateral and multilateral treaties recognized as binding on Nigeria by virtue of the United Kingdom's signature or ratification; Part II lists seventy-seven multilateral treaties and seventy-nine bilateral treaties acceded to or concluded since independence. Part III lists thirty-two agreements with international organizations. This volume also includes appendices; Appendix I contains "Trade Agreements", with the full text of some trade agreements; Appendix II contains Air Services Agreements; and Appendix III contains "Multilateral Agreements to which Nigeria is a Party and which are purely of regional interest to Africa".[33] The volume is described as "contain[ing] all Nigeria's Treaties in force as at July 31, 1968".[34]

Note: The 1969 Introductory Note provides the following insight: "In all, there are some 334 conventions and other international agreements deemed

29 Federal Ministry of Justice, International and Comparative Law, http://www.justice.gov.ng/index.php/about-us/departments/international-and-comperative-la/9-uncategorised/203-functions3.

30 OKEKE, THEORY AND PRACTICE, *supra* note 4, at 47–50.

31 *Introductory Note*, NIGERIA'S TREATIES IN FORCE 5 (1969).

32 Id.

33 Table of Contents, NIGERIA'S TREATIES IN FORCE (1969). An example of a treaty classified as "purely of regional interest to Africa" is the Convention Creating the African Groundnut Council.

34 *Introductory Note*, *supra* note 31.

to be binding on Nigeria in virtue of this exchange of Notes. The State practice of Nigeria is to study each treaty or other international agreement with a view to its adoption, with or without modification, or to re-negotiate it with the other contracting party or parties. It is only those agreements that have been so studied and adopted that are incorporated in this edition".

Note: No information about Nigeria's signing, ratification, or accession dates; its ratification process; entry-into-force dates; or other information is included.

2 NIGERIA'S TREATIES IN FORCE FOR THE PERIOD 1ST OCTOBER 1960 TO 30TH JUNE 1970
(Lagos: Federal Ministry of Information, 1971).

Summary: This set is sometimes marked as the third edition of Nigeria's Treaties in Force. Although the few US law libraries that own the set hold from one to three volumes, the full set had three.[35] Part 1 contains a list of treaties and other international agreements which were recognized as binding on Nigeria; Part II contains a list of treaties and other international agreements which Nigeria had acceded to or concluded since independence. Each of these two parts is further subdivided into multilateral and bilateral treaties. Part III contains a list of international agreements concluded with international organizations.

Note: As with the earlier publication, no status or ratification information is included.

3 NIGERIA'S TREATIES IN FORCE

Summary: Most recent attempt dates from 1990, and contains ten volumes.[36] Volume One contains bilateral agreements, 1970–1990. The remaining nine volumes contain multilateral agreements for the same time period. Part of Volume 10 acts as a supplement to the other volumes.

Index: Each volume in the 1970–1990 Treaty Series has a table of contents (i.e., a listing of treaties) that is labeled an "Index".

Treaty Indexes

No index to Nigerian treaties exists. Although the Treaties (Making Procedure, Etc.) Act of 1993 requires the Ministry of Justice to maintain a registry of treaties that shall be open to members of the public,[37] this Register has never been published.

---

35 Preface, NIGERIA'S TREATIES IN FORCE 1970–1990 iv (1990).

36 NIGERIA'S TREATIES IN FORCE 5 (Federal Ministry of Justice [sine loc.], 1990).

37 Treaties (Making Procedure, Etc.) Act §5.

Diplomatic Documentation

No published collection of Nigerian diplomatic documents exists.

4 NIGERIA: BULLETIN ON FOREIGN AFFAIRS
(Lagos: Nigerian Institute of International Affairs, 1971–).

Summary: While not widely available, this serial, published by the Nigerian Institute of International Affairs, serves some of the functions of a digest of state practice and a collection of diplomatic documents.

Note: Monthly, 1971-Jan. 1982; semiannual, June 1986– (designated as "New Series"); quarterly, 2004–. No issues have appeared since 2006.

Note: The *Bulletin* is currently divided into "Events", "Documents", and "Bibliography". Under "Events", the Bulletin reports briefly on Nigerian ministerial and official visits, based largely on news reports. The "Documents" section includes speeches (often from news stories) and press releases. Some protocols of negotiating sessions are also included. Rarely, the text of a treaty also appears.[38] Another section deals with "International Border Questions", and briefly summarizes relevant news stories. The "Bibliography" section primarily contains references to news stories dealing with Nigerian foreign affairs.

Note: Unfortunately, this publication is not indexed. The Hathi Trust Digital Library[39] has scanned numerous issues from 1972–1988; however, the issues are only searchable, not viewable, due to copyright restrictions.

5 NIGERIAN JOURNAL OF INTERNATIONAL AFFAIRS
(Lagos: Nigerian Institute of International Affairs, 1975–).

Summary: Also published by the Nigerian Institute of International Affairs, the editors take a wide variety of articles on international relations, foreign affairs, and international law; on average, one article per issue deals with some aspect of Nigerian foreign policy or other political question.

Note: Annual, 1975–1981; semi-annual, 1982 – present.

Note: This publication is also un-indexed, and no electronic version is available.

6 MINISTRY OF FOREIGN AFFAIRS
URL: http://www.mfa.gov.ng.

---

38 E.g., Nigeria-Pakistan, Agreement on Scientific and Technical Cooperation, vol. 1 (new series), issue #1, June 1986, pp. 25–27; Nigeria-United Kingdom, Bilateral Investment Treaty, vol. 5 (new series), issue #2, pp. 37–45.

39 Hathi Trust Digital Library, http://catalog.hathitrust.org.

Summary: Web site of the Foreign Ministry. Unfortunately, the site lacks much substantive content. A section on "Foreign Policy Issues" remains empty. The researcher can find a few press releases giving Nigerian positions; unfortunately, the site lacks an archive of press releases.

7 MINISTRY OF JUSTICE
URL: http://www.fmj.gov.ng/default.htm

Summary: Web site of the Ministry of Justice. While the site does not publish Nigerian treaties, it includes a section on International and Comparative Law, describing the functions of the International and Comparative Law Department. These functions include "vetting of international agreements between Nigeria and Various Countries, "ratification of international agreements", "ensuring the observance of Nigeria's Treaty obligations by preparing and collating Nigeria's periodic reports and monitoring Nigeria's obligations in respect of certain international organizations", and "ensuring that all treaties entered into by Nigeria are deposited and registered in the Ministry accordance with Section 4 sand 5 of the Treaties (Making Procedure) Act 1993". Other duties, such as representing Nigeria at meetings of international bodies, are also listed.[40]

Yearbooks and Digests of State Practice

No digest of Nigerian state practice in international law exists. As of 2012, only one of the articles in the *African Yearbook of International Law*[41] (indexed in the *Index to Foreign Legal Periodicals*) deals extensively with Nigeria's practice of international law.

In 1976, one volume of the *Nigerian Annual of International Law* appeared (Lagos, Oxford University Press Nigeria, 1976). The Nigerian Society of International Law has a website, but it lacks substantive content.[42]

40 Nigeria Federal Ministry of Justice, International and Comparative Law, http://www.justice.gov.ng/The_Ministry/Departments/International_and_Comparative_Law/.

41 AFRICAN ASSOCIATION OF INTERNATIONAL LAW (Dordrecht; Boston: M. Nijhoff; Norwell, MA, U.S.A.).

42 Nigerian Society of International Law, http://nsil.org.ng.

Norway

Suzanne Thorpe

Issues of Treaty Succession

The modern kingdom of Norway known to us today has existed for a little more than century. Although Norway was recognized by its neighbors as an independent kingdom as early as 1019, from the early 14th Century through the beginning of the 20th Century, Norway was almost continuously united with one or more of its Nordic neighbors. Norway entered into a union with Sweden in 1319, which lasted through 1355, and again with Denmark in 1380. The latter union lasted for more than 400 years. In 1397, the united kingdom of Norway-Denmark joined with Sweden to form the Kalmar Union. During this union, Norway, Denmark, and Sweden maintained a common foreign policy and defense under the rule of the Danish monarch. Sweden left the Kalmar Union in 1523. Norway, however, remained united with Denmark for another three centuries. In 1814, Denmark ceded Norway to Sweden under the Treaty of Kiel.[1] Iceland, Greenland, and the Faroe Islands, previously under Norwegian rule, were retained by Denmark. Internally, Norway and Sweden existed as two self-governing states. Externally, they maintained a common foreign policy under the Swedish monarch. In 1905, the Norwegian *Storting* (Parliament) dissolved the union with Sweden and Sweden granted Norway independence.

Norway's status during its long unions with its neighbors has been well covered in the legal literature.[2] Aside from likely discussions in unpublished diplomatic records, however, there has been little commentary on the continuing force of the treaties concluded during these unions. One dispute arising out of the Treaty of Kiel has received brief attention.[3] Under Article 6 of this treaty, Denmark obligated Norway to pay a proportional share of the entire National

1 Fredstractat mellom Danmark og Sverig, signed at Kiel 14 January 1814, 1 DANSKE TRACTATER EFTER 1800, 1.samling, 60–72 (1877). Norway opposed this union, but after a brief military skirmish, Norway and Sweden passed common legislation recognizing the union of the two states under the Swedish king.

2 *E.g.,* NARVE BJØRGO, ØYSTEIN RAIN, ALF KAARTVEDT, SELVSTENDIGEHET OG UNION: FRA MIDDELALDEREN TIL 1905 (1995); LESTER B. ORFIELD, THE GROWTH OF SCANDINAVIAN LAW (1953); ARNOLD RÆSTAD, DANMARK, NORGE OG FOLKERETTEN (1933); LUDVIG MARIBOE BENJAMIN AUBERT, NORGES FOLKERETSLIGE STILLING (1897).

3 ERNST HERMANN FEILCHENFELD, PUBLIC DEBTS AND STATE SUCCESSION 142-44 (1931); DANIEL PATRICK O'CONNELL, 1 STATE SUCCESSION IN MUNICIPAL LAW AND INTERNATIONAL LAW

 | DOI 10.1163/9789004272224_025

debt of the formerly united Norway-Denmark. The successor state, Norway-Sweden, disputed this obligation. In 1819, Sweden ultimately negotiated another treaty with Denmark that obligated Norway to pay a reduced portion of the amount agreed upon by Denmark in the treaty.[4] In prior state practice, ceded territories had been held proportionally liable for debts incurred before cession, this was the first instance when a ceded territory was held liable for more than a local debt. Additionally, it has been noted in the literature that Norway and Sweden declared their intention to be bound by the treaties concluded during their union when it dissolved in 1905.[5]

Treaty Ratification and Implementation[6]

Although the Norwegian *Grunnlov* (Constitution)[7] does not define the relationship between public international law and Norwegian municipal law, Norway adheres to the dualist approach to international law.[8] International treaties usually become a binding part of Norwegian municipal law through express legislative action of the Norwegian *Storting*. Article 26 of the *Grunnlov* grants the King[9] the right to "conclude and denounce treaties." This article also

---

396 (1967); THEODORE JORGENSEN, 1 NORWAY'S RELATION TO SCANDINAVIAN UNIONISM, 1815–1871, 389–400 (1935).

4 J. H. W. VERZIJL, 7 INTERNATIONAL LAW IN HISTORICAL PERSPECTIVE, PART 7, STATE SUCCESSION 230 (1974).

5 DANIEL PATRICK O'CONNELL, THE LAW OF STATE SUCCESSION 44–45 (1956).

6 For an official government report on Norwegian treaty implementation practices, *see generally* NORGES OFFENTLIGE UTREDNINGER [NOU] 1972:16 Gjennomføring av lovkonvensjoner i norsk rett [government report series] (Nor.).

7 An English language version of the Constitution is available online at http://www.stortinget.no/en/In-English/About-the-Storting/The-Constitution/The-Constitution.

8 NORGES OFFENTLIGE UTREDNINGER [NOU] 1972:16, *supra* note 6, at 32. Since 1992, when Norway became a party to the European Economic Area Treaty, adherence to the dualism principle appears less strict. Norway became a party to this treaty through Article 93 of the *Grunnlov*. Article 93 permits the *Storting* to consent to allowing an international organization to which Norway is a member "to exercise powers which…are normally vested in the authorities of the state." As a result, Norway has recognized many requirements of European Union law. *See* NORGES OFFENTLIGE UTREDNINGER [NOU] 2012: 2. Utenfor og innenfor: Norges avtaler med EU [government report series] (Nor.), at 234.

9 Although the Grunnlov uses the word, King, it is interpreted to mean the King in Council (with the cabinet). MADS T. ANDENÆS & INGEBORG WILBERG, THE CONSTITUTION OF NORWAY: A COMMENTARY 21 (1987).

requires the *Storting* to consent to "treaties on matters of special importance, and, in all cases, treaties whose implementation, according to the Constitution, necessitates a new law or a decision by the *Storting*." In addition, the article requires the *Storting* to approve treaties that involve appropriations and taxation or concern matters of "special importance."

The *Utenriksdepartment* (Ministry of Foreign Affairs) generally negotiates and concludes treaties. However, the *Utenriksdepartement* confers closely with the *Storting's Utvidede Utenriks- og Forsvarskomité* (Enlarged Committee on Foreign Affairs and Defense)[10] while negotiating treaties. Following the conclusion of a treaty, the *Utenriksdepartement* introduces the adopted treaty to the *Storting* for ratification and implementation.[11] The treaty is referred to the *Utenriks- og Forsvarskomité* (Standing Committee on Foreign Affairs and Defense). This committee issues a report on the treaty with a recommendation to the *Storting* on ratification and implementation.[12]

Treaties are typically implemented in Norway through two legislative methods: *inkorporasjon*[13] (incorporation) and *transformasjon*[14] (transformation). When *inkorporasjon* is used, the *Storting* passes a law adopting the treaty text as Norwegian law. This usually is a very brief declaration that appears with other legislation in the first part of the *Norsk Lovtidend*, the official legal gazette.[15] When *transformasjon* is used, the *Storting* amends an existing law, or enacts an entirely new law, to mirror the provisions of the treaty. These legislative changes also appear in the *Norsk Lovtidend*. Infrequently, a third method of implementation known in Norway as "*konstatering av rettsharmoni*"

10 This committee consists of members of the *Utenriks- og Forsvarskomité*, the President and Vice-President of the *Storting*, and other members of the *Storting*.

11 The treaty is introduced as a "*proposisjon*" (proposition) (Prop. S.), and is published with other government bills and reports to the *Storting* in the publication, STORTINGSPROPOSISJONER. Frequently, the text of the treaty is appended to the "*proposisjon*." The full text of propositions from the *Utenriksdepartement* since 1991 can be found on the website of the *Regjeringen* (Government) at http://www.regjeringen.no/nb/dok/regpubl/stprp.html?id=1752. Other information issued by the *Utenriksdepartment* about Norway's foreign policy is available at http://www.regjeringen.no/nb/dep/ud.html?id=833.

12 These committee reports are published in the parliamentary series, INNSTILLINGER TIL STORTINGET (Innst. S.). The full text of reports issued since 1991 from the *Storting's* committees can be found online at http://stortinget.no/no/Saker-og-publikasjoner/Publikasjoner/Innstillinger. Other information and documents from the *Storting* related to foreign policy can be found at http://www.stortinget.no.

13 The term *henvisning* (referencing) is another term used to describe this method.

14 The term *gjengivelse* (reformulating) is another term used to describe this method.

15 Issues of the NORSK LOVTIDEND since 1991 are available online at http://www.lovdata.no/info/lovtidend.html.

(declaring legal harmony) is used.[16] *Konstatering av rettsharmoni* was utilized when Norway implemented the European Convention for the Protection of Human Rights and Fundamental Freedoms, 4 November 1950. When this method is used, the *Utenriksdepartement* issues a position statement indicating to the *Storting* that the provisions in an adopted treaty already exist in Norwegian municipal law and do not require further ratification or implementation.[17] The treaty then becomes effective in Norway.

Once ratified, treaties must be published in the *Norsk Lovtidend*.[18] They are published by the *Utenriksdepartement* a few years after ratification as a separate publication, *Overenskomster med Fremmede Stater*. Article 75 of the *Grunnlov* directs that a report of all treaties concluded and ratified by Norway must be given to the *Storting*. The *Utenriks- og Forsvarskomité* provides this information in the annual "*Traktatforelegget*,"[19] which lists treaties that entered into force during a given year.

Because treaty provisions are carefully compared to existing Norwegian law throughout the treaty negotiation and ratification process, Norwegian municipal law generally conforms to the provisions in the international treaties concluded by Norway. When rare conflicts arise after a treaty is in force, Norwegian courts and administrative agencies presume that the municipal law was intended to conform to the international law.[20]

Annotated Bibliography of Sources

General Treaty Collections

1 OVERENSKOMSTER MED FREMMEDE STATER
(Oslo, 1879–).

16 NORGES OFFENTLIGE UTREDNINGER [NOU] 2004:20 Ny utlendingslov [government report series] (Nor.), at 73.

17 The statement appears as a *proposisjon* (St.Prp.) and is published with other government bills and reports sent to the *Storting* in the series, STORTINGSPROPOSISJONER. The statements issued since 1991 are available online at http://www.regjeringen.no/nb/dok/regpubl/stprp.html?id=1752.

18 NORGES OFFENTLIGE UTREDNINGER [NOU] 1972:16, *supra* note 6, at 48.

19 This report usually appears as Forelegg for Stortinget av overenskomster inngått med fremmede makter. Treaties involving foreign aid appear in a separate report, Forelegg for Stortinget av bistandsavtaler. Both of these reports appear in the series, INNSTILLINGER TIL STORTINGET (Innst. S.), discussed *supra* note 12.

20 This is known as the *presumsjonsprinsippet* (presumption principle). FINN ARNESEN AND ARE STENVIK, INTERNASJONALISERING OG JURIDISK METODE: SÆRLIG OM

Summary: This publication contains treaties concluded 1879–. Treaty texts appear in consecutive order in English, Finnish, French, and German, if an official treaty language, or in Norwegian translation. This work provides references to Storting actions, signature and ratification dates, and includes announcements of new ratifications, accessions, and cessations.

Note: Irregularly supplements *Norsk Lovtidend*, Avd. II.

Note: Issued by Konglige Norske Statsrådssekretariat and Konglige Norske Utenriksdepartement.

Note: Imprint varies: Oslo: Fabritius Strålfors, 1879–1908; Oslo: Grøndahl, 1909–.

Note: Treaties concluded and ratified 1940–1945 were issued in one volume in 1950.

Note: Treaties appearing in this publication since 1992 are available online to subscribers of LovdataOnline, available at http://www.lovdata.no/info/lovdata.html.

Note: Treaties appearing in this publication since 2005 are available online without charge. URL is http://www.lovdata.no/traktater/index.html.

2 NORGES TRAKTATER. KONGLIGE NORSKE UTENRIKSDEPARTEMENT (Oslo: Fabritius Strålfors, 1967–1988). 6 vols.

Summary: Contains selected treaties concluded 1661–1987. Treaties regarding visa requirements and tonnage certificates and temporary treaties are not included. Bd. I: 1661–1944; Bd. II: 1945–1955; Bd. III: 1956–1967; Bd. IV: 1968–1976; Bd. V: 1977–1987. In Bd. I–IV, treaties appear in chronological order in Norwegian, English, French, or German, if used as an official treaty language. Other treaties appear in official Norwegian translations. In Bd. V, treaties appear in one of the official treaty languages, if English, French, or German, and also in Norwegian. Each entry provides the date of signature or the date a treaty was opened for signature, the parties to the treaty, the place of signature, the official number of the treaty, and the full title of the treaty. Amending or supplementing treaties are numbered with the original treaty number, followed by sequential letters indicating the order they appear in the supplementing treaties. Earlier treaties, to which Norway later acceded, are indicated by the original number of the treaty, followed by X or Y.

Index: The *Registerbind* chronologically lists all treaties from 1661–1987 to which Norway is a party. Treaties no longer in force are indicated by brackets.

EØS-RETTENS BETYDNING I NORSK RETT 59 (2009). Another commentator describes this rule as the "municipal effectivation of the norms of international law." Carsten Smith, *International Law in Norwegian Courts*, 12 SCANDINAVIAN STUDIES IN LAW 151, 157 (1968).

Each entry provides the treaty number, date of signing, place of signing, parties, language(s), title in Norwegian and English, citation(s), references to Parliamentary documents, date of entry into force in Norway, references to related treaties. This index also separately lists bilateral treaties by party. Multilateral treaties concluded between the Nordic countries or concluded under the auspices of the Hague Conference on Private International Law or deposited with the Council of Europe, the International Labour Organisation, or the United Nations are listed separately under each of these categories. These lists are arranged chronologically. English and Norwegian subject lists are also provided.

Note: A separate table of contents lists treaties in Bd. I –V by date.

Note: Imprint varies: Bd. I–III: 1967–1968, published in Oslo by Grøndahl; Bd. IV, 1976, published in Oslo by Dataprint.

Note: English title: *The Treaties of Norway.*

Note: In Bd. V, a separate title page and preface appear in English.

3 DANMARK-NORGES TRAKTATER, 1523–1750…MED DERTIL HØRENDE AKTSTYKKER

(Copenhagen: G.E.C. Gad, 1907–1949). 11 vols.

Summary: Although the title indicates treaty coverage through 1750, this work only contains treaties concluded by Denmark-Norway through 1700. Bd. 1: 1523–1560; Bd. 2: 1561–1588; Bd. 3: 1589–1625; Bd. 4:1626–1649; Bd. 5: 1651–1664; Bd. 6: 1665–1675; Bd. 7:1676–1682; Bd. 8: 1683–1689; Bd. 9:1690–1693; Bd. 10: 1694–1698; Bd. 11: 1699–1700. Treaties are arranged in chronological order and appear in Danish, French, Latin, German, or Swedish. Each entry provides the title, signatories, and date and place of signature. Each volume provides a chronological list of treaties, Danish and French alphabetical country lists, and a Danish list of names for the treaties it contains.

Note: Head of title reads *Traités du Danemark et de la Norvège.*

Note: Compilers vary: Bd. 1–9: Laurs Rasmus Laursen; Bd. 10–11: Carl S. Christiansen.

Note: Funded by the Carlsbergfondet.

Note: Microfiche version filmed from the original held by Harvard Law School Library. Zug, Switzerland: Inter Documentation Co., 1986.

4 SVERGES TRAKTATER MED FRÄMMANDE MAGTER JEMTE ANDRA DIT HÖRANDE HANDLINGAR

(Stockholm: RA. Norstedt, 1877–1934). 14 vols.

Summary: Del X–Del XV contain Norwegian treaties concluded 1815–1905. Del X: 1815–1845; Del XI: 1846–1867; Del XII: 1868–1877; Del XIII: 1878–1890; Del XIV: 1891–1899; Del XV: 1900–1905. Treaties appear in chronological order in one of the official treaty languages. Each volume provides a chronological list of treaties, indexes by country in Swedish and French, a geographical index, and a personal name index.

Note: Editors: Del X–Del XI: O.S. Rydberg; Del XII: Oscar Alin; Del XIII-Del XIV: Carl Sandgren; Del XV: Sten Lewenhaupt.

Note: Del X–Del XIV have added title: *Sverges och Norges Traktater med Främmande Magter;* Del XV has title: *Sveriges Traktater med Främmande Makter Jämte Andra Dit Hörande Handlingar*. These volumes are also separately numbered Del I–VI.

5 RECUEIL DES TRAITÉS DE LA NORVÈGE

Norway. Ministère des Affaires Étrangères (Kristiania: Grøndahl, 1907–1926). 2 vols.

Summary: This work was compiled for use by Norwegian diplomats and consuls. Tome 1 contains bilateral and multilateral treaties in force in 1907 and selected diplomatic notes. Tome 2 contains treaties concluded from 1907–1924. Postal, telegraph, telephone, and railroad treaties are excluded. The titles of all treaties are in French, but the texts are in the official treaty languages or in Norwegian translations. Bilateral treaties are arranged chronologically under country. Each bilateral entry provides the treaty title, date of signature, and date of ratification. Multilateral treaties are arranged chronologically. Each multilateral entry provides the treaty title, date of signature, place of signature, parties, and date of ratification. Each volume provides a table of contents.

6 UTVALG AV NORGES OVERENSKOMSTER MED FREMMEDE STATER

(Oslo: Nikolai Olsens Boktrykkeri, 1936). 343 pp.

Summary: Contains 41 annotated treaty texts, 1815–1930. Treaties appear in chronological order. Annotations provide information on parties, implementing documentation, and dates of ratification and entry into force. Texts are in Norwegian. A table of contents is included.

Note: Editor: J.G. Ræder.

Note: Published by the Law School at the University of Oslo.

7 NORGES NÅGJELDENDE OVERENSKOMSTER MED FREMMEDE STATER UNNTATT POST-, TELEGRAF-, TELEFON- OG JERNBANEOVERENSKOMSTER OG ANDRE OVERENSKOMSTER AV ADMINISTRATIV NATUR: FØRT A JOUR 1 SEPTEMBER 1939.

(Oslo, 1939). 33 pp.

Summary: Contains treaties in force in 1939. Postal, telegraph, telephone, and railroad treaties are not included.

Treaty Indexes

8 TRAKTATFORELEGGET

Norway. Storting Utenrikskomité (Oslo: Stortinget, 1814–).

Summary: This annual report contains a list of the treaties that entered into force in Norway each year.

Note: Title varies: *Forelegg for Stortinget av Overenskomster med Fremmede Stater og Internasjonale Organisasjoner…*; *Overenskomster Inngått med Fremmede Stater og Internasjonale Organisasjoner…*; *Innstilling fra Utenrikskomiteen om Overenskomster Inngått med Fremmede Stater og Internasjonale Organisasjoner…*; *Innstilling fra Utenrikskomiteen om Overenskomster Inngått med Fremmede Makter.*

Note: Series title: *Innstillinger til Stortinget.*

Note: Since 1984 the report is available online at http://www.stortinget.no.

9 TRAKTATREGISTERET

NORWAY. KONGLIGE UTENRIKSDEPARTEMENT.

URL: http://www.lovdata.no/traktater/index.html.

Summary: This index covers bilateral and multilateral treaties 1661–, to which Norway is a party. It does not cover treaties involving foreign aid. Treaties are listed by year. Treaty information includes the title (in Norwegian and other languages, if applicable), subject, signing date, place of signing, date of entry into force, ratification date, depository, signing authority, and citations to the introduction of the treaty and reports of committees in the Storting.

Note: The database is searchable by title, subject, date of signing, date of ratification, and date of entry into force.

Note: Searchable full texts of treaties published in *Overenskomster med Fremmede Stater* since 1992 are included.

Topical and Selected Treaty Collections

10 DE NORDISKE KONVENTIONER: ÆGTESKAB, ADOPTION OG VÆRGEMAAL, INDDRIVELSE AF UNDERHOLDSBIDRAG, ANERKENDELSE OG FULDBYRDELSE AF DOMME, KONKURS, ARV OG DØDSBOSKIFTE

(Copenhagen: Ejnar Munksgaard, 1947). 56 pp.

Summary: This source provides the Danish text of five treaties between the Nordic countries on marriage, adoption and guardianship, maintenance, recognition and enforcement of judgments, bankruptcy, and inheritance and succession. These treaties were concluded between 1931 and 1935.

11 OVERENSKOMSTER VEDRØRENDE KRIGENS RETT SOM NORGE STÅR TILSLUTTET

Norway. Konglige Utenriksdepartement (Oslo: Grøndahl, 1961). 406 pp.

Summary: This work contains treaties related to war concluded by Norway. Texts appear in their official language, if English, French, or German, or in Norwegian translation.

Diplomatic Documents

12 UD-INFORMASJON
(Oslo: Konglige Utenriksdepartement, 1966–2001).

Summary: This irregular publication contains speeches of the Foreign Minister, statements of the Foreign Minister in the Parliament, and press releases in English and Norwegian.

Index: Separate indexes cover 1966–1983; 1980–1985.

Note: Since 2001, speeches, articles, and press releases are available online at http://www.regjeringen.no/nb/dep/ud/aktuelt/taler_artikler.html?id=844.

Yearbooks and Digests of State Practice

13 NORSK UTENRIKSPOLITISK ÅRBOK
(Oslo: Norsk Utenrikspolitisk Institutt, 1973–1992).

Summary: Contains articles on Norwegian foreign policy. Excerpts of foreign policy documents and speech are included. An annual bibliography of books, articles, and official publications is provided.

Index: Each volume provides a list of articles, subject index, and personal name index.

Note: Series title: *Norwegian Foreign Policy Studies.*

14 NORDIC JOURNAL OF INTERNATIONAL LAW
(Leiden, Netherlands: Martinus Nijhoff, 2006–).

Summary: Volumes 69–70, 73 and 76 contain articles that digest developments in Norwegian state practice for 1999, 2000, 2001/2003, and 2006.

Imprint varies: Dordrecht: Kluwer Academic Publishers, 1986–2005.

Continues: Nordisk Tidsskrift for International Ret, 1930–1985.

Romania

Dana Neacsu

Historical Background

Though Romanian history is far from linear, it is not hard to grasp. It is also essential for the understanding of the country's practice in international law.[1] Romania, as it is today, has undergone various permutations during its hundreds of years of history. For most of its history it was divided into different political entities, such as the principalities of Moldavia, Wallachia, and Transylvania. In the early sixteenth century, the Romanian principalities recognized Turkish suzerainty, even though they never became Ottoman provinces (or Pashailiks). During the eighteenth century, in the midst of the struggle between the Austrian, Russian and Ottoman empires, the Romanian principalities went through a period of tremendous political crisis. While Moldavia and Wallachia continued to remain under Ottoman suzerainty, Transylvania became part of the Austrian empire. At that time Austria also occupied northwestern Moldavia (Bukovina) in 1775, and Russia annexed eastern Moldavia (Bessarabia) in 1812.

The 19th century brought the union of Wallachia and Moldavia into one political entity: Romania.[2] The political union of 1859 happened under Prince Alexandru Ioan Cuza (1859–1866). He abdicated in 1866, and the throne passed to Prince Carol I, of the German house of Hohenzollern-Sigmaringen, who thus became Romania's "Domn" (leader).[3] However, not until after the Peace Conference in Berlin (1878), which recognized Romania's independence, did modern Romania as an independent, national state emerge. For example, Romania became a monarchy in 1881, and Prince Carol I its king. Romania preserved its form of government until 1947.

The first Romanian Constitution, following the Belgian model, was adopted in 1866.[4] Two more constitutions were adopted before Romania became a

1 For more on Romanian history, *see, e.g.*, Constantin Giurescu and D.C. Giurescu, The Making of the Romanian Unitary State, 1980, A History of Romania, (K. Treptow, ed., 1997); D.C. Giurescu and S. Fisher-Galati, Romania: A Historic Perspective (1998).

2 *See., e.g*, Constantin Giurescu and D.C. Giurescu, The Making of the Romanian Unitary State, 1980.

3 Constitutiounea din 1866, *in* Monitorul –Jurnal Oficial Al Romaniei, Nr. 142 din1/13 iunie 1866, *available at* http://www.rogoveanu.ro/constitutia/const1866.htm, Art.82.

4 Id.

 | doi 10.1163/9789004272224_026

republic: in 1923[5] after the unification of all Romanian provinces, which included Transylvania, had been achieved as a result of the defeat of the Austro-Hungarian Empire in 1918, and in 1938.[6]

World War II brought more territorial disputes between Romania and its neighbors. In 1940 the USSR occupied Bessarabia and northern Bukovina. Romania was also forced to cede northern Transylvania to Hungary and southern Dobrudgea to Bulgaria.[7] Subsequently, in the same year Romania signed the Axis Pact and joined in Germany's attack of the Soviet Union. On August 23, 1944, a Royal coup ousted the fascist regime and Romania joined the Allies against the Axis. An armistice convention was signed in Moscow. One year later, after the Yalta Conference, Romania regained northern Transylvania and entered the Soviet zone of influence.

On February 10, 1947, the Paris Peace Treaty was signed, and thus World War II ended for Romania.[8] The loss of Northern Bukovina and Bessarabia to the Soviet Union was now officially recognized. Ten months later, on December 30, 1947, King Michael was forced to abdicate and Romania was proclaimed a People's Republic.

For the next forty years, three constitutions will record various political changes. The first such Constitution was the one of 1948,[9] followed by the 1952 Constitution.[10] The last so-called socialist constitution was adopted in 1965,[11] and it mirrors the political changes associated with Nicolae Ceauşescu, the last president of the so-called socialist era. The same year the new Constitution

---

5 Constitutiounea din 1923 which was published in Monitorul Oficial Nr. 282 din 29 martie 1923, *available at* http://www.rogoveanu.ro/constitutia/const1923.htm.

6 Constitutiounea din 1938 *available at* http://www.rogoveanu.ro/constitutia/const1938.htm.

7 The text of the secession, "Arbitrajul de la Viena" was published in *Universul*: September 1, 1940, and is *available at* http://www.historia.ro/exclusiv_web/general/articol/textul-arbitrajului-viena-30-august-1940#. For more details, *see, e.g.*, D.C. Giurescu and S. Fisher-Galati, Romania: A Historic Perspective (1998).

8 Treaty of Peace with Romania : February 10, 1947, in Charles I. Bevans, 4 Treaties and Other International Agreements of the United States of America 1776–1949, *available at,* http://avalon.law.yale.edu/20th_century/usmu011.asp.

9 Constitutia Republicii Populare Romane 1948, which was published in Monitorul Oficial, partea I, Nr. 87 bis din 13 aprilie 1948, *available at* http://www.rogoveanu.ro/constitutia/const1948.htm.

10 Constitutia Republicii Populare Romane 1952, which was published in Monitorul Oficial Nr. 87 bis din 13 Aprilie 1948, *available at* http://www.rogoveanu.ro/constitutia/const1952.htm.

11 Constitutia Republicii Socialiste Romania 1965, published in Buletinul Oficial, 22/20 februarie 1968, *available at* http://www.rogoveanu.ro/constitutia/const1965.htm.

was adopted, the official name of the country changed to the Socialist Republic of Romania.

In December 1989, after the demise of Ceauşescu's regime, a provisional council headed by former members of the communist party took control of the country. In December 1991 a new Constitution was adopted according to the standards of parliamentary democracy of Western Europe.[12] On September 28, 1993, at a session of the Parliamentary Assembly of the Council of Europe, Romania was admitted as a member with full rights.[13] In January 1994 Romania became the first former communist country to adhere to the Partnership for Peace initiated by NATO. On February 1, 1995, Romania became an associate member of the European Union, and on July 15, 1997, the European Commission delivered its opinion concerning Romania's application for membership. In conformity with this opinion there is an "Association Partnership",[14] relating to the principles, priorities, intermediate objectives and conditions for Romania's accession.[15] The structural changes required by the EU accession process are also mirrored in the 2003 amendments made to the Romanian constitution.[16] Despite a rocky process,[17] Romania's candidacy to the European Union was successful, and on January 1, 2007 Romania became a EU member.[18]

---

12 CONSTITUTIA ROMANIEI, 1991, *available at* http://www.rogoveanu.ro/constitutia/const1991.htm.

13 Doc. 6901, 1403-15/7/93-2-E, *available at* http://assembly.coe.int/ASP/Doc/XrefViewHTML.asp?FileID=7253&Language=EN.

14 Council Decision 98/261/EC of March 30, 1998.

15 The second Regular Report from the Commission on Progress Towards Accession was issued on Oct. 13, 1999. For more information, *see* http://ec.europa.eu/index_ro.htm. According to the composite report (summarized in IP/99/751), negotiations began on full Romanian membership in 2000.

16 Monitorul Oficial, Partea I Nr. 767 din 31/10/2003, *available at* http://www.rogoveanu.ro/constitutia/const.htm.

17 *See* European Commission, 2004 REGULAR REPORT ON ROMANIA'S PROGRESS TOWARDS ACCESSION 146 (2004), *available at* http://europa.eu.int/comm/enlargement/report_2004/pdf/rr_ro_2004_en.pdf, and for an-in-depth analysis of the accession process see e.g., Neacşu, *Romania, Bulgaria, The United States and the European Union: The Rules of Empowerment at the Outskirts of Europe* 30 BROOKLYN J. INT'L 185 (2004).

18 Treaty Between Member States of the European Union and the Republic of Bulgaria and Romania, Concerning the Accession of the Republic of Bulgaria and Romania to the European Union, April 25, 2005, 2005 O.J. (L 157) 11, and for a discussion of the accession, see, e.g., Ruth J. Lee, *The Stepchildren of the EU: Bulgaria and Romania,* 16 J. TRANSNAT'L L. & POL'Y 361 (2007). On January 1st, 2007, Romania became member of the European Union, and subject to EU law. For a concise overview of the Romania's accession to the EU and its legal implications is available on the site of Romania's Permanent Representation

Issues of Treaty Succession

With so many changes in Romania's territory during its recent history, there are a large number of succession issues. This is especially true because the Republic of Romania is the natural continuation of the Socialist Republic of Romania, within absolutely the same geographical boundaries.

Public international law regards changes in ideology and/or government as leaving statehood unaffected.[19] The changes in government structure can be radical and yet not amount to the creation of a new state. Article 11(1) of the 1991 Constitution stipulates that "the Romanian State pledges to fulfill to the letter and in good faith, its commitments under the treaties to which it is a party".[20] This provision regards both treaties ratified before and after December 1989.[21] However, there are some instances when, after December 1989, Romania has revised its positions about declarations or reservations expressed at the time of ratifying certain multilateral treaties under the communist regime.[22] In 2003, a nation-wide referendum amended the previous constitution.[23] The next section addresses the impact of the 2003 amendments of the Romanian law of treaties, especially that of Article 11 and Article 148.[24]

---

to the European Union at http://ue.mae.ro/index.php?id=33&lang=en&id=1597 (in Romanian) and on the site of the European Commission's Representative Office in Romania, available at http://ec.europa.eu/romania/index_ro.htm.

19 See, e.g., Michael John Volkovitsch, *Righting Wrongs: Towards a New Theory of State Succession to Responsibility for International Delicts*, 92 COLUMBIA L.REV. 2162, 2166 (1992).

20 CONSTITUTIA of December 8, 1991, ratified by Referendum on December 13, 1991, published in MONITORUL OFICIAL, Partea I, Nos. 21 and 23, on December 14, 1991. English version available in V. PECHOTA, 5 CENTRAL AND EASTERN EUROPEAN LEGAL MATERIALS, (1990–).

21 Id., Title VII, Final and Transitory Provisions. Article 150 (Old Law) states that "[l]aws and all other normative acts will remain in effect as long as they are not in conflict with the present Constitution".

22 I.M. Anghel, DREPTUL TRATATELOR (The Law of International Treaties), (1993). In Section VIII, vol. 1, at pp. 629–634, there is a full analysis of all the reservations and declarations that Romania made for political reasons and that were abolished after December 1989.

23 Law No. 429/2003 on the reform of the Constitution, which was published in MONITORUL OFICIAL no. 758 of 29 October 2003. The amended version is available in English on-line at http://www.cdep.ro/pdfs/reviz_constitutie_en.pdf.

24 Lege de Revizuire a Constituţiei României, 18 Sept. 2003, MONITORUL OFICIAL no. 669, 22 Sept. 2003, *available at* http://www.cdep.ro/pdfs/reviz_constitutie.pdf. An English translation is available at http://www.cdep.ro/pdfs/reviz_constitutie_en.pdf. The 2003 Amendments were approved by the Constitutional Court, DDC 356/2003, M.OF. Nr. 686.

Treaty Ratification and Implementation

Before December 1989, according to the 1965 Constitution and its several amendments, treaty making was the responsibility of the General National Assembly (GNA)[25] and its implementation was within the purview of the Council of Ministers.[26] In reality, the highest echelons of the Romanian Communist Party (the Permanent Bureau and the POLEXCO) formulated all aspects of foreign policy and the treaty-making process. Party decisions were channeled through the Central Committee's Directorate for International Affairs to the GNA, which approved them automatically, without any amendment. In principle, the State Council was, according to the Constitution, supposed to exercise the executive function of ratifying or denouncing international treaties and establishing diplomatic relations with other states.[27]

---

30 Sept. 2003, then by a referendum on 18–19 Oct. 2003. There were reports of irregularities in the referendum, including allegations that ballots were collected in ad-hoc, improper places, such as supermarkets and other stores, and that some local officials paid citizens to vote (the compensation said to include free television sets, furniture, soccer tickets and firewood) or threatened them with non-payment of pensions. It was asserted, in particular, that the number of votes collected in the last two hours–which were needed to meet the minimum count for approval–was impossibly large in the absence of fraud. Some stories from the news media, including the Financial Times, MNBC and the BBC, are collected in a "Database of information on the Romanian Referendum to revise the Constitution, 2003", *available at* http://www.geocities.com/romanian_referendum/#14; see also http://www.pressreview.ro/EN/index.cfm?an=2003&luna=10&zi=20. It appears that no prosecutor initiated an investigation into these allegations, so no court ruling on them is anticipated. A challenge to the validity of the referendum was rejected by the Constitutional Court on 22 October 2003, Decision No. 3, CCR, M.OF. Nr. 758, 29 Oct. 2003. The revised Constitution was republished and came into force on 31 October 2003. Law No. 429/2003, M.OF. Nr. 767, 31 Oct. 2003. *See* Peter W. Schroth & Ana Daniela Bostan, *International Constitutional law and Anti-Corruption Measures in the European Union's Accession Negotiations: Romania in Comparative Perspective*, 52 AM. J. COMP. L. 625, 667 (2004).

25 CONSTITUTION OF THE SOCIALIST REPUBLIC OF ROMANIA, published in the BULETINUL OFICIAL AL REPUBLICII SOCIALISTE ROMANIA, Partea I, No. 1, August 21, 1965. An English version can be found in A.P. BLAUSTEIN & G.H. FLANZ, CONSTITUTIONS OF THE COUNTRIES OF THE WORLD: A SERIES OF UPDATED TEXTS, CONSTITUTIONAL CHRONOLOGIES AND ANNOTATED BIBLIOGRAPHIES, permanent edition, (1971–), in the historical section. See Title III, articles 43(10), 43(21), 43(24). Also, the English translation of the consolidated text of the 2003 Romanian Constitution is available in WORLD CONSTITUTIONS ILLUSTRATED.

26 Id., Title IV, art. 9.

27 Id., Title III, art. 63(4).

In fact, for 24 years the head of the state (in Ceausescu's case also the General Secretary of the Party) directly decided in almost any matter related to international treaties.[28] Because decision-making powers resided in the party leadership, the GNA, the Council of Ministers, the Council of State, and the Ministry of Foreign Affairs functioned almost exclusively as administrative agencies.

The current treaty-making authority and mechanism are regulated by the 2003 Constitution[29] and by Law nr. 590/2003 on the conclusion and ratification of treaties.[30] Unlike England and other members of the British Commonwealth, as well as most Latin American countries which do not consider treaties as part of their municipal law, Romania incorporates its international conventions into municipal law. Article 11(2) of the Constitution clearly says that "[T]reaties ratified by Parliament, according to the law, are part of domestic law".[31] Moreover, under Article 20(1) and (2) international treaties in the field of human rights take precedence over contrary municipal law: "Constitutional provisions on the rights and freedoms of citizens shall be interpreted and applied in accordance with the Universal Declaration on Human Rights and with other treaties and pacts to which Romania is a party. If there is disagreement between the pacts and treaties on fundamental rights to which Romania is a party and domestic laws, the international regulations will have priority".[32]

In the conventional international practice of Romania, a predominant part is played, nowadays as it was in the past, by bilateral legal instruments, representing 63 percent of the total number of agreements, conventions and treaties concluded.[33] Most of these instruments are friendship and co-operation

---

28 Id., Title IV, art. 75(13) only says that "the President initiates international treaties in the name of the Socialist Republic of Romania" and represents the country in international relations.

29 The 2003 Constitution was published in MONITORUL OFICIAL, Partea I nr. 767 din 31/10/2003.

30 Law no.590/2003, published in MONITORUL OFICIAL, PARTEA I nr. 23 din 12/01/2004.

31 *See* article 11(2) of the 2003 Constitution.

32 Id., art. 20(1) and 20(2). See also on this subject O. Craiciuc, *The International Rule in Relation With Municipal Law, in* V.1 REVUE ROUMAINE DES SCIENCES JURIDIQUES, Tome V (XXXVIII), 99–136 (1994); G. Antoniu, *Implications des Articles 5 et 6 de la Convention Europeene sur la Loi Processuelle Roumaine* (Implications of Articles 5 and 6 of the European Human Rights Convention on the Romanina Law of Criminal Procedure), ID. 3–11.

33 *See* V. Duculescu, *Romania's Conventional Practice in the Field of International Agreements,* 1 REVUE ROUMAINE DES SCIENCES JURIDIQUES. Tome V (XXXVIII) 180 (1994). Romanian bilateral treaties are published only in Romanian in the Monitorul Oficial, even though

treaties. This is in line with Article 10 of the Constitution: "Romania maintains and develops peaceful relations with all the states, and in this framework, relations of good neighborliness based on the principles and on the other generally recognized norms of international law".[34]

Presidential power in treaty-making is regulated by the Constitution and Law No. 590/2003. Most international treaties need to be submitted to Parliament for ratification.[35] In practice, treaties are negotiated by the government.[36] International agreements signed at the level of the Government are submitted to the Parliament for ratification by the means of law.[37] Denunciations or accessions follow the same rule. The Government briefs the President and the Parliament on any treaty, convention, or any other international agreement concluded that does not require ratification procedures.[38] International conventions that are simply negotiated by the Ministry of Foreign Affairs by the means of reciprocal agreements, exchange of notes or diplomatic letters shall enter into force at the date of their conclusion, without any ratification procedure.[39] Treaty negotiation on behalf of Romania is done, within the limitations of Article No. 17 of Law No.4/1991, by the Ministry of Foreign Affairs. Other governmental departments in cooperation with the Ministry of Foreign Affairs, which is empowered to act as the main authority in this field, may initiate such negotiations.[40] The President, the Prime Minister of the Government, and the Minister of Foreign Affairs may negotiate and sign treaties, agreements, conventions or any other international accords, with no full powers.[41] The ratification or denunciation of treaties concluded on behalf of Romania are to be recorded in the instruments of ratification, accession or denunciation, signed by the President of Romania, invested with the seal of the state, and countersigned by the minister of Foreign Affairs.[42] The above mentioned instruments are then subject to exchange or deposit with the depository agency, in conformity with the rules and the practice of international law.

---

most of them claim that the English version prevails in any dispute. The English version may only be found with the depositary.

34 *See e.g.,* PECHOTA *supra* note 20. *See also,* Art. 10 of the 2003 CONSTITUTION.

35 Id., art. 91, and Law nr. 590/2003, *available at* http://www.dreptonline.ro/legislatie/legea_tratatelor.php#, art. 19.

36 Id., arts. 2 et seq.

37 Id., art. 22.

38 Id., art. 17.

39 Id., art. 20.

40 Id., arts. 18 et seq.

41 Id., art. 25.

42 Id., art. 25(4).

Treaties, conventions and other international instruments concluded at the governmental level have to be transmitted by special notification to the other party, parties or depository by diplomatic channels.[43]

Application and implementation of international treaties and conventions fall within the sphere of Government responsibility. The Government also periodically has to keep the President informed about the progress in the implementation of such international instruments. Whenever there are obstacles or problems they should be solved by the Government in cooperation with the President, in full consensus with the principles of international law and the best interest of Romania.[44]

Laws ratifying treaties and decisions to approve international agreements, as well as the full text of those treaties and agreements, are to be published in Romanian in the *Monitorul Official* (Official Gazette). However, the Parliament, i.e., the Government, may decide not to publish some international treaties and conventions. The Ministry of Foreign Affairs is in charge of publication in the official gazette of all pertinent data and information with regard to changes in the status of those international instruments Romania is a party to, as well as with their registration with the United Nations.[45]

Upon its accession to the European Union,[46] even more attention needs to be given to Article 148 on the *Integration into the European Union.*[47] Accordingly, Romania's accession to the constituent treaties of the European Union, transferred certain powers to community institutions, and started a common exercise with the other member states the abilities stipulated in such treaties. Those duties are to be carried out by means of a law adopted in the joint session of the Chamber of Deputies and the Senate, with a majority of two thirds of the number of deputies and senators.[48] Additionally, as a result of the accession, the provisions of the constituent treaties of the European Union, as well as the other mandatory community regulations, are to take precedence over contrary provisions of the national laws, in compliance with the provisions of the accession act.[49]

---

43 Id., art. 25.

44 Id., art. 37.

45 Id., art. 24(2).

46 James B. Cronon, *Accession to a Surrender of Sovereign Autonomy in Law?: The Effect of the European Union Membership Process upon Romania* 36 GA. J. INT'L & COMP. L. 189 (2007).

47 *See* the English translation of Art.148 *available at* http://www.cdep.ro/pls/dic/site.page?den=act2_2&par1=6.

48 Id.

49 Id.

Paragraph (2) of Article 148 does not identify the mechanism by which EU law is to prevail over domestic law. It only states that EU law will prevail over domestic law.[50] As mentioned earlier, if there is no conflict with existing laws in the national system, the ratified treaty will be the first norm regulating the specific field of law. Furthermore, the clear implication of EU jurisprudence[51] is that every Romanian judge will have and must exercise the power to enforce EU law.

Paragraphs 3 through 5 of Article 148 state that

> (3) The provisions of paragraphs (1) and (2) shall also apply accordingly for the accession to the acts revising the constituent treaties of the European Union.
> (4) The Parliament, the President of Romania, the Government, and the judicial authority shall guarantee that the obligations resulting from the accession act and the provisions of paragraph (2) are implemented.
> (5) The Government shall send to the two Chambers of the Parliament the draft mandatory acts before they are submitted to the European Union institutions for approval.

The constitutionality of Romanian treaties is determined by the Constitutional Court.[52]

Annotated Bibliography of Sources

General Treaty Collections

1 MONITORUL OFICIAL AL ROMANIEI. PARTEA I. LEGI, DECRETE, HOTĂRÎRI ŞI ALTE ACTE NORMATIVE [ROMANIAN OFFICIAL MONITOR. PART I. LAWS, DECREES, DECISIONS, AND OTHER NORMATIVE ACTS] (Bucureşti: Parlamentul Romaniei, Adunarea Deputaţilor, 1989–). URL: http://www.monitoruloficial.ro/

---

50 For a brief review of how EU law prevailed *see, e.g.*, Adam Lazowski. THE APPLICATION OF EU LAW IN THE NEW MEMBER STATES: BRAVE NEW WORLD (2010).

51 *See e.g.,* Case 106/77, Amministrazione delle Finanze dello Stato v. Simmenthal SpA (II), [1978] E.C.R. 629, [1978] 3 C.M.L.R. 263, and its discussion in Peter W. Schroth & Ana Daniela Bostan, *International Constitutional law and Anti-Corruption Measures in the European Union's Accession Negotiations: Romania in Comparative Perspective*, 52 AMJCL 625, 668 et seq. (2004).

52 *See* PECHOTA, *supra* note 20 at 11, art.144. The Constitutional Court is a newly created institution, since traditionally the Curtea de Casatie, following the model of the French Cour de Cassation, had control over international treaties (until 1950). For a discussion of this subject, *see* O. Craiciuc, *supra* note 32 at 123–136.

Summary: Coverage includes, inter alia, treaties and international agreements, 1990–. Text is in Romanian only. Treaties are published together with domestic legislation, in the chronological order of their ratification. The Law approving the ratification of the treaty precedes the full text of the agreement. Each individual issue has a table of contents. This is the only source for Romanian current treaties. There is no running treaty series.

Note: Title succeeded the former *Buletinul Oficial al Republicii Socialiste Romania, Bucureşti, Serviciul Buletinului Oficial Şi al Publicaţiilor Legislative,* 19(?)-1989.

2 LEGISLATIA ROMANIEI [ROMANIAN LEGISLATION]
(Bucureşti: Regia Autonomă Monitorul Oficial, 1991–).

Summary: This is a quarterly publication that reprints in chronological order Romanian bilateral and multilateral treaties together with legislation, Parliamentary decisions, Senate decisions, House of Deputy decisions, Decrees and Presidential pronouncements. Citation to the official gazette is provided for each document.

Index: Each quarterly cummulation has its own chronological and alphabetical index.

Treaties are to be found either by date or by topic. There is no special treaty section.

Note: Head of title reads "Parlamentul Romaniei (Romanian Parliament)".

Note: The publication continues Colectia de Legi, Decrete şi Alte Acte Normative (Collected Legislation, Decrees, and Other Normative Acts), Bucureşti, Sectorul Buletinului Oficial şi al Publicaţiilor Legislative, 1976–1990 and Colecţia de Legi, Decrete şi Dispoziţiuni, Bucureşti, Ministerul Justiţiei, 195?-1975.

Treaty Indexes

3 ANUAR LEGISLATIVE AL ACTELOR NORMATIVE PUBLICATE IN MONITORUL OFICIAL AL ROMANIEI [THE ANNUAL INDEX OF LEGISLATIVE ACTS PUBLISHED IN THE ROMANIAN OFFICIAL MONITOR]
(Bucureşti: Regia Autonomă Monitorul Oficial, 1992–).

Summary: There are two indexes, chronological and alphabetical, covering all the laws and delegated legislation published in the Romanian official gazette. Treaties are to be found in the alphabetical index by subject matter or under the name of the other contracting country.

4 ACORDURILE INTERNATIONAL INCHEIATE DE ROMANIA SAU LA CARE ROMANIA A DEVENIT PARTE [INTERNATIONAL AGREEMENTS CONCLUDED OR ACCEDED TO BY ROMANIA]
Compiled by Adrian Năstase (Bucureşti: Editura Metropol, 1995.) 183 p.

Summary: This compilation covers five years of Romanian treaties, from December 22, 1989, to December 19, 1994. Content is exhaustive. Treaties are cited in Romanian only. The first part (pp. 7–113) is a chronological listing of treaties. The topical index (pp.116–183) makes treaties retrievable by subject matter. In the chronological section, covering more than 530 treaties, the place and date of conclusion are provided for each document, the accession date as well as the Romanian ratification instruments are cited, and a reference to the Romanian official gazette is available. Chapter I covers multilateral treaties ratified by the Parliament; chapter II covers bilateral treaties ratified by the Parliament; chapter III covers multilateral agreements approved by the Government; chapter IV covers bilateral agreements approved by the Government.

5 ROMANIA SPRE STATUL DE DREPT * LA ROUMANIE VERS L'ETAT DE DROIT * ROMANIA TOWARDS THE STATE GOVERNED BY THE RULE OF LAW
(Bucureşti: Editura "Monitorul Oficial", 1993.) 743 p.

Summary: The book includes inter alia a list of the 110 international documents ratified by Romania after the date of December 22, 1989, until February 1, 1993. Documents are listed in chronological order, ratification instruments and their publication date in the Official Gazette of Romania (Monitorul Oficial) are mentioned. Also includes the Romanian Constitution of 1991, in Romanian, French, and English. Includes table of contents, also in Romanian, French, and English.

Note: The volume was compiled by the Technical and Legislative Department of the Chamber of Deputies.

Note: On the first page the editors stipulate that "It must be specified that the only text which shall produce legal effects is the text in the Romanian language."

Topical and Selected Treaty Publications

6 ROMANIA-NATO: TRATATE FUNDAMENTALE: TEXTE, NOTE, COMENTARII SI LEGISLATIE NATIONALA INCIDENTA (ROMANIA-NATO; FUNDAMENTAL TREATIES: TEXTS, NOTES, COMMENTARIES AND NATIONAL LEGISLATION)
Compiled by Teodor Atanasiu (Bucuresti, Editura Militara, 2006).

Historical Treaty Collections

7 COLECTIUNE DE TRATATE SI CONVENTIUNILE ROMANIEI CU PUTERILE STRAINED DE LA ANUL 1368 PANA IN ZILELE NOASTRE [COLLECTED TREATIES AND ROMANIAN CONVENTIONS WITH THE FOREIGN POWERS FROM THE YEAR 1368 TO PRESENT]

M. Mitilineu (Bucuresci: Noua Typographie, 1874.) 365 p.

Summary: This is the first attempt to consolidate a Romanian treaty collection. Obviously, using "Romania" for those agreements signed by Wallachia and Moldavia, as subjects of international law under Ottoman suzerainty is debatable. Treaties are reproduced in their original language. Includes table of contents.

8 TRAITES, CONVENTIONS ET ARRANGEMENTS INTERNATIONAOUX DE LA ROUMANIE ACTUELLEMENT EN EN VIGUEUR. TRACTATE, CONVENTIUNIM INVOIRI INTERNATIONALE ARE ROMANIEI ACTUALMENTE IN VIGUARE [TREATIES, CONVENTIONS AND INTERNATIONAL AGREEMENTS OF ROMANIA IN FORCE]

Trandafir G Djuvara (Bucuresci: A. Degenmann, 1888.) 1013 p.

Summary: This is a comprehensive collection of international treaties and conventions in force at the time of publication, reproduced in the original language of their conclusion and in French and Romanian. Includes alphabetical and chronologic indexes. Table of custom tariffs is also available.

Note: The compilation was published at the request of the Ministry of Foreign Affairs.

Note: Statistical charts in reference to foreign trade and an introduction to the Romanian conventional practice in international law are provided.

9 CODUL GENERAL AL ROMANIEI. CODURILE, LEGILE SI REGULAMENTELE UZUALE IN VIGOARE, 1856–1942 [THE ROMANIAN GENERAL CODE. CODES, LAWS AND USUAL RULES IN FORCE, 1856–1942]

C. Hamangiu (Bucureşti: Alcalay, 1942.) 38 vols.

Summary: This multi-series work initiated by C. Hamangiu covers, inter alia, treaties, conventions and other international agreements. Includes table of contents, alphabetical and chronologic indexes. Cross references are also included.

Note: This is a collective work that has had, in time, as joint editors C. St. Stoicescu and G. Alexianu.

Note: Texts of treaties are in Romanian only.

10 CONDICA TRATATELOR SI A ALTOR LEGEMINTE ARE ROMANIEI, INCEPING DIN ANUL 1354 [CODEX OF TREATIES AND OTHER INTERNATIONAL AGREEMENTS INVOLVING ROMANIA, FROM THE YEAR 1354]
Frederic C. Nano (Bucureşti: 1938–1942.) 3 vols.

Summary: This is a very comprehensive collection of treaties and other international instruments involving the Romanian Principalities under foreign sovereignty as well as the Romanian independent state. Each volume has its own table of contents.

Note: The work was commissioned by the Ministry of Foreign Affairs.

Note: Vols. 1 and 2 cover the historical period from 1354 to 1937. Vol. 3 covers the years 1938–1942 and brings additions to the first two volumes.

11 INTERESELE SI DREPTURILE ROMANIEI IN TEXTE DE DREPT INTERNATIONAL PUBLIC [ROMANIAN INTERESTS AND RIGHTS IN PUBLIC INTERNATIONAL LAW INSTRUMENTS]
Nicolae Daşcovici (Iaşi: A. Terek, 1936.) 686 p.

Summary: This is a selection of the most important bilateral and multilateral treaties of Romania. Text in Romanian. Includes detailed table of contents and chronological list of treaties.

Note: Introduction by N. Daşcovici and a comprehensive bibliography at pp. 657–664.

12 TRATATELE INTERNATIONALE ALE ROMANIEI, 1354–1920: TEXTE REZUMATE, ADNOTARI, BIBLIOGRAFIE [ROMANIAN INTERNATIONAL TREATIES, 1354–1920: ABBREVIATED TEXT, ANNOTATIONS, BIBLIOGRAPHY]
Ion Ionaşcu (Bucureşti: Editura Stiinţifică Si Enciclopedică, 1975.) 527 p.

Summary: Handy collection of abbrievated texts of the most relevant treaties. Very useful annotations. Basic information about each treaty is provided. Text is in Romanian only. *Index:* Includes chronologic and thematic indexes.

Note: Petre Bărbulescu and Gheorghe Gheorghe are listed as co-authors.

Note: Bibliography at pp. 459–464.

13 TRATATELE INTERNATIONALE ALE ROMANIEI, 1921–1939: TEXTE REZUMATE, ADNOTARI, BIBLIOGRAFIE [ROMANIAN INTERNATIONAL TREATIES, 1921–1939: ABBREVIATED TEXT, ANNOTATIONS, BIBLIOGRAPHY]
Gheorghe Gheorghe (Bucureşti: Editura Ştiinţifică Şi Enciclopedică, 1980.) 574 p.

14 TRATATELE INTERNATIONALE ALE ROMANIEI, 1939–1965: TEXTE REZUMATE, ADNOTARI, BIBLIOGRAFIE [ROMANIAN INTERNATIONAL TREATIES, 1939–1965: ABBREVIATED TEXT, ANNOTATIONS, BIBLIOGRAPHY]
Gheorghe Gheorghe (Bucureşti: Editura Stiinţifică şi Enciclopedică, 1983.) 423 p.

15 TRATATELE INTERNATIONALE ALE ROMANIEI, 1965–1975: TEXTE REZUMATE, ADNOTARI, BIBLIOGRAFIE [ROMANIAN INTERNATIONAL TREATIES, 1965–1975: ABBREVIATED TEXT, ANNOTATIONS, BIBLIOGRAPHY]
Gheorghe Gheorghe (Bucureşti: Editura Ştiinţifică Şi Enciclopedică, 1986.) 501 p.

Diplomatic Documents

16 THE FOREIGN POLICY OF ROMANIA, 1918–1939
Frederic C. Nano (Washington, D.C.: 1953.) 205 p.

Summary: Contains diplomatic documents, treaties and other international instruments in English. Includes table of contents.

Note: Microfilm of typescript produced by the Library of Congress Photoduplication Service, 1953.

Note: National Committee for a Free-Europe, Mid-European Center, Research Documents, No. 116.

17 RELATIILE CONSULARE ALE ROMANIEI [ROMANIAN CONSULAR RELATIONS]
Nicolae Ecobescu and Gheorghe Bădescu (Bucureşti: Editura Politică, 1975–77.) 2 vols.

Summary: Vol. 1 contains consular treaties, conventions and agreements. Vol. 2 contains collected domestic legislation in the field. Text in Romanian. Table of treaties and laws in chronological order.

Note: Texts selected by Aurel Bonciog and Vasile Păcurăreţu.

Note: Includes bibliographical references.

18 RELATIILE INTERNATIONALE POSTBELICE: CRONOLOGIE DIPLOMATICA [POST-WAR INTERNATIONAL RELATIONS: DIPLOMATIC CHRONOLOGY]
Petre Bărbulescu et al., eds. (Bucureşti: Editura politică, 1983.) 2 vols.

Summary: Comprehensive collection of the most important documents related to Romanian diplomacy over almost 40 years. Text in Romanian. Chronological list of documents.

19 LEGISLATIE IN ASISTENTA SOCIALA. VOL. 1 REGLEMENTARI INTERNATIONALE. VOL. 2 REGLEMENTARI INTERNE [LEGISLATION ABOUT SOCIAL ASSISTANCE: VOL. 1. INTERNATIONAL REGULATIONS; VOL. 2. DOMESTIC REGULATIONS]

Abraham Pavel (Bucureşti: Editura Natională, 2000).

Summary: This work is structured in two parts. The first part talks about international rules regarding social assistance in light of the current discourse of human rights, and the second part analyzes the domestic legislation and the its compatibility with the existing similar regulations at the international and European level.

20 DREPTUL ROMANESC SI INTEGRAREA ROMANEASCA

(Bucureşti: Editura Tempus, 2004).

Summary: This work is a compilation of the papers presented by the research fellows from the Institute of the Institute for Legal Research of the Romanian Academy during the conference held on March 28th 2003 on the topic of how domestic law reflects the demands imposed by the EU accession process.

21 DREPTUL TRATATELOR [THE LAW OF INTERNATIONAL TREATIES]

Dr. Ion M. Anghel (Bucureşti: Editura Lumina Lex, 1993.) 2 vols.

Summary: Section VIII of this basic treatise in the law of international treaties contains a discussion of Romanian practice in the field of reservations to international treaties. Other sections also discuss aspects of Romanian practice in the field of international law with respect to treaty making and implementation. The book has a table of contents in English.

22 DREPTUL TRATATELOR

Nicolae Ecobescu and Victor Duculescu (Bucureşti: Editura Continent XXI, 1995.) 213 p.

Summary: This is a remarkable monograph, including in Chapter 15 a systematic presentation of the leading treaty collections of the world as well as state practice in international law, current legal practice repertories, and a substantial bibliography of Romanian treaty collections. The book has a table of contents in Romanian.

Note: Head of title reads "Uniunea Juriştilor din Romania (The Union of Romanian Jurists)".

Note: Appendix 1 contains the full Romanian text of the Vienna Convention on the Law of Treaties and Appendix 2 reprints the text of Law No. 4 of January 11, 1991, on the conclusion and ratification of treaties.

23 DREPT INTERNATIONAL PUBLIC [PUBLIC INTERNATIONAL LAW, REVISED AND ENLARGED EDITION]
Dumitra Popescu and Adrian Nastse (Bucureşti: Casa de Editură şi Presă "Sansa", 1997.) 500 p.

Summary: The chapter "Teritoriul de stat in dreptul internaţional" (State territory in International Law) contains a discussion of the legal regime of Danube, and mentions all pertinent agreements ratified by Romania (pp. 160–167). Annex II reprints "Law No.4 of January 11, 1991 on the Conclusion and Ratification of International Treaties" (423–426). Annex III reprints the "Presidential Decree for Ratification of the Peace Partnership and the Additional Protocol of Brussels", June 19, 1995 as well as the "Agreement between the North Atlantic Treaty and the States in the Peace Partnership" (427–456). Annex VII offers a checklist of treaties adopted by the European Council and ratified by Romania (pp. 466–469). In Annex VIII there is a complete list of the United Nations agencies of which Romania is a member (pp. 469–500).

Russia

Joseph Luke

Issues of Treaty Succession

The modern Russian state began its rise as the Mongol rule waned in the latter half of the fifteenth century. The grand principality of Muscovy consolidated its territory and began to expand into both Europe and Asia.

Russia had a continuous international identity from the mid-fifteenth century through the October Revolution in 1917. Within the government there were occasional reorganizations which included the department responsible for diplomacy. Tsar Ivan IV (in power 1547–1584) created a department for foreign affairs early in his reign, the Ambassadorial Department (*Posol'skij Prikaz*).[1] The members of this department produced diplomatic reports (*statejnye spiski*), which contained official reports and personal impressions from many European and Asian kingdoms. Many of these documents still survive in the archives of the Ministry of Foreign Affairs.[2] Tsar Peter I introduced institutional reform into the department in the early part of the 18th century, and by 1720 the department had undergone major changes and become the College, or Collegium, of Foreign Affairs. Finally, in 1802, the department became known as the Ministry of Foreign Affairs.

The question on the succession of states arose with the formation of the Union of Soviet Socialist Republics (USSR) in 1922. As an empire, Russia controlled approximately the same territory (and countries) that later formed the USSR. After the 1917 revolution, there was a brief period when the Bolsheviks consolidated power in Russia and other territories fell away. The Bolshevik government viewed the revolution as a change in governments, not a change of statehood. This is reflected in the government's view on Russia's earlier international obligations. It abrogated only the "secret treaties" of 1917 because they "aimed at giving advantage and privileges to Russian landowners and capitalists, and to retaining and increasing annexations of Great Russians".[3] During this period the Russian Socialist Federative

1 For a more complete description of the development of international law in Russia, *see* V.E. Grabar, The History of International Law in Russia, 1647–1917: A Bio-Bibliographic Study, trans. W.E. Butler (1990).

2 Id., p. 6. Several were published in *Sbornik Imperatorskogo Russkogo istoricheskogo obshchestva* (Saint Petersburg: s.n., 1867–1916).

3 "Decree on Peace", translated and reprinted in W.E. Butler, Russian Law of Treaties 150 (1997). *See also* "Letter of the Soviet Government to the Director of the Institute of

 | DOI 10.1163/9789004272224_027

Soviet Republic (RSFSR) adopted its first Constitution and began to fight its civil war. Several of the governments of the territories began a period of unrest, many governments declared independence, including the three Baltic republics and Finland. In several countries new, soviet governments were created.

On December 30, 1922, a Union Treaty was signed by which the Union of Soviet Socialist Republics (USSR) was founded. Although a federal structure with the RSFSR as a "federal mother'" to the other Soviet governments had been the de facto circumstance at the time of the union's formation,[4] the Bolsheviks organized the USSR formally in a structure where Russia stood equal with the other member republics. (In the beginning there were three other republics; eventually there were 14 others). However, Russia remained preeminent and Moscow, the capital of Russia, remained the capital of the USSR until the union dissolved.[5]

The first USSR constitution came into force January 31, 1924. In a letter to the Director of the Institute of International Law at the Hague, dated April 2, 1924, the Soviet government stated that certain treaties of the former government would have to be renegotiated, given the new political realities, but "[t]he Soviet government has never declared a general renunciation of all treaties concluded by Russia under the Tsarist regime or under the Provisional Government", and confirmed that the financial obligations of the former Russian Governments were unaffected by the changes that had taken place.[6]

The USSR endured for over 70 years. On June 12, 1990, the RSFSR declared its independence and on December 12,1991, renounced the USSR treaty.[7] It subsequently informed all the representatives of foreign governments by diplomatic note that

> [t]he Russian Federation continues to perform the rights and fulfill the obligations following from the international agreements signed by the Union of the Soviet Socialist Republics . . . In accordance with this, the

---

International Law, the Hague" in W.E. Butler, The Law of Treaties in Russia and the Commonwealth of Independent States: Text and Commentary (2002).

4 F.J.M. Feldbrugge, Russian Law: The End of the Soviet System and the Role of Law 93 (1993).

5 Most commentators accept that the Soviet Union was the successor state to imperial Russia without question. See also the brief discussion in Butler (1997), *supra* note 3 at 10–11.

6 Butler (1997), *supra* note 3 at 151–52.

7 Renunciation published in Rossiiskaia Gazeta [Ros. Gaz.] [Official Newspaper] December 17, 1991.

> Ministry (of Foreign Affairs of the Russian Federation) requests that the Russian Federation be looked upon as the party to all international treaties with the Soviet Union which are still in effect.[8]

Although all of the former Soviet Union nations, apart from the three Baltic states, consider themselves successor states to the USSR, Russia termed itself a "continuer" state, implying that although the other nations are successors, it alone is the direct descendant.[9] It has assumed most of the USSR's debt (after an initial treaty dividing the debt, Russia has returned to most of the constituent nations of the USSR to reassume the debt in bilateral agreements[10]), its membership in many international organizations, including the UN, and its embassies. Russia states in its Concluding and Transitional Provisions in the Constitution, that laws of the USSR will "apply in that part which is not contrary to the Constitution of the Russian Federation".[11]

Treaty Ratification and Implementation

By mid-1925 the USSR had adopted the "Decree on the Procedure for the Conclusion of International Treaties of the USSR" and the "Decree on the Procedure for the Submission of International Treaties and Agreements Concluded in the Name of the USSR for Approval, Confirmation and Ratification of the Government of the USSR".[12] The USSR rewrote its constitution in 1936 and again in 1977. With each new constitution the laws for ratification were

---

8 *Diplomaticheskii vestnik*, No. 2–3 (1992), p. 34 (author's translation).

9 *See* BUTLER (2002), *supra* note 3 at 15–19. *See also* Rein Müllerson, *Law and Politics in Succession of States: International Law on Succession of States, in* DISSOLUTION, CONTINUATION AND SUCCESSION IN EASTERN EUROPE 8–32 (Brigitte Stern, ed., 1998). *See generally* MALCOLM N. SHAW, INTERNATIONAL LAW 960–984 (6th ed. 2008).

10 Id. at 11–14. See also BUTLER (1997), *supra* note 3 at 11–12.

11 KONSTITUTSIIA ROSSIISKOI FEDERATSII [KONST. RF] [CONSTITUTION] Second Section no. 2. Reprinted in English in CONSTITUTIONS OF THE COUNTRIES OF THE WORLD (A.P. Blaustein and G.H. Flanz, eds. 1971–).

12 SOBRANIE ZAKONOV I RASPORIAZHENII RABOCHE-KREST'IANSKOGO PRAVITEL'STVA SSSR [SZ SSSR] [Collected Laws and Regulations of the Worker-Peasant Government of the USSR] 1925, No. 35, Item 258 and No. 68, Item 503 respectively. Translations of relevant parts of the Constitutions and laws for Soviet public international law up through the mid-60s can be found in 3 SOVIET STATUTES AND DECISIONS: A JOURNAL OF TRANSLATIONS, no. 4, Summer 1967. The last Constitution of the USSR and the ensuing law on treaties post-date this work's publication. The 1978 law on treaties was officially published in

redrafted, "On the Procedure for the Ratification and Denunciation of International Treaties of the USSR"[13] and "On the Order of Conclusion, Ratification and Denunciation of International Treaties of the USSR"[14] respectively.

The Russian Federation adopted its constitution in 1993. It states that the generally recognized principles and norms of international law and international treaties of the Russian Federation shall be an integral part of its legal system. If rules established by an international treaty of the Russian Federation conflict with those provided for by a law, the rules of the international treaty apply (art. 15 (4)). In describing the federal structure of the Russian Federation, the constitution lists foreign policy, international relations, and international treaties as under the jurisdiction of the Russian Federation (art. 71(j)), as opposed to the jurisdiction of the subordinate subjects of the Russian Federation. The President of the Russian Federation will have the authority to conduct negotiations and sign international treaties and the instruments of ratification (art. 86 (c) and (d)). Federal laws ratifying or denouncing international treaties must be passed by the State Duma and their passage is subject to obligatory review by the Soviet of the Federation (art. 106 (d)). The Constitutional Court may, at the request of the appropriate state authority, decide cases on the conformity to the Russian constitution of international treaties that have not yet entered into effect (art. 125(d)).

On the basis of the 1993 Constitution and the 1969 Vienna Convention on the Law of International Treaties, Russia adopted the Federal Law on International Treaties of the Russian Federation (June 16, 1995).[15] This law applies to international treaties regardless of form, name, or character, including those to

---

Vedomosti Verkhovnogo Soveta SSSR [VVS SSR] [Bulletin of the USSR] 1978, No. 28, Item 439, and was reprinted in translation in W.E. Butler, Documents on the Soviet Legal System 284–292 (1983) as the "Law on the procedure for the conclusion, execution, and denunciation of international treaties of the USSR". The USSR rewrote its constitution in 1936 and again in 1977.

13 VVS SSSR 1938, No. 11.

14 VVS SSSR 1978, No. 28, Item 439. Translated in 17 I.L.M. 1122 (1978).

15 Federal'nyi Zakon RF o Mezhdunarodnykh Dogovorov Rossiiskoi Federatsii, SZ RF 1995, No. 101-FZ, Item 2757. This law was amended in 2007 in connection with the passage of a law creating the State Atomic Energy Corporation "Rosatom". The amendment provided for that the government bodies who are competent to act under the 1995 law may authorize other agencies or bodies to act for them, *see* Federal'nyi Zakon RF o Gosudarstvennoi korporatsii po atomnoi energii "Rosatom" [Federal Law of the Russian Federation on the State Corporation on Atomic Energy "Rosatom"], SZ RF 2007, No. 317-FZ, Item 6079. Useful annotated versions of this law, although predating the 2007 amendment, in English are

which Russia is a party as the State-continuer of the USSR (art. 1). The drafters of the law gave attention to the federative nature of Russia and required that treaties, whose fulfillment falls into the jurisdiction or partial jurisdiction of subjects of the Federation, go through a process that includes the participation of the local governments. It is possible that arts. 4, 9(5), 36(1) and 37(5) read together "in effect give... subjects of the [Russian Federation] the right, with respect to the questions which directly affect the interests of the subject of the [Russian Federation], to veto the conclusion, termination or suspension of an international treaty", although it is unclear, if more than one subject is involved, how their rights are balanced.[16] The federal government must solicit the proposals of the subjects when preparing drafts of such treaties (art. 4). A treaty may fall into one of the following categories: it may be inter-State, i.e., a treaty concluded with a foreign nation or with an international organization in the name of the Russian Federation; intergovernmental, i.e., a treaty in the name of the government of the Russian Federation; or interdepartmental, i.e., a treaty in the name of a federal agency of executive power (art. 3 (2)). This division of treaties results in different requirements in the initial process of negotiation and ratification. As head of state, the President negotiates and signs inter-state treaties. The Chairman of the Russian government or the Minister of Foreign Affairs negotiates and signs inter-governmental treaties. Federal ministers or executive agency directors may negotiate and sign interdepartmental treaties within their competences (art. 13).

Various federal organizations may submit recommendations to the President or Government of Russia concerning the conclusion of a treaty. The organizations empowered to do so include both chambers of the federal assembly, the Supreme Court of the Russian Federation, the Supreme Arbitrazh, Court of General Procuracy, the Central Bank, and the Plenipotentiary of Human Rights (art. 8). The President or Government must reply to a recommendation within one month of its receipt.

Some federal organizations may submit proposals, which are distinguished from recommendations under the law on treaties. Commentators note that a recommendation may be a weaker act than a proposal.[17] The process of recommendation is not described in detail, but proposals must include the treaty's

---

BUTLER (1997), *supra* note 3; BUTLER (2002), *supra* note 3; and in Russian, ZVEKOV ET AL., KOMMENTARII K FEDERAL'NOMU ZAKONU "O MEZHDUNARODNYKH DOGOVORAKH ROSSIISKOI FEDERATSII" (1996).

16 *See* BUTLER (1997), *supra* note 3 at 21–22.

17 *See* ZVEKOV ET AL., *supra* note 15 at 29–30; BUTLER (1997), *supra* note 3 at 40–41.

draft text or basic provisions, a determination of its advisability and conformity to Russia's laws and an assessment of possible economic and financial effects (art. 9(5)).

Depending on the type of treaty, federal bodies must submit proposals either to the President or Government. Proposals concerning the conclusion of interstate treaties shall normally be submitted to the President, but shall be submitted to the Government instead, if their subject matter falls within its jurisdiction. The Ministry of Foreign Affairs shall submit all proposals to the President. Any proposals from other federal agencies must be made through the Ministry or with its agreement. If the Government is required to pass on the treaty preliminarily, adoption of its decision to submit a proposal is by decree (art. 9(1)–(2)).

Proposals relating to inter-governmental treaties must be submitted jointly by the federal agency, whose competency includes the treaty's subject matter, and the Ministry of Foreign Affairs, or by the agency alone with the Ministry's agreement. Analogously, proposals relating to interdepartmental treaties must be submitted by the federal agency whose competency includes the subject matter of the treaty, together with the Ministry of Foreign Affairs, or with its agreement (art. 9 (3)–(4)). The role of the Ministry of Foreign Affairs in foreign policy and treaty-making was clarified by the presidential edict "On the Coordinating Role of the Ministry of Foreign Affairs of the Russian Federation in Conducting the Unified Foreign Policy Line of the Russian Federation".[18] The roles of the subordinate subjects or government agencies vis-à-vis the Ministry was clarified by the presidential decree, "On the Organization and Execution of Functions Relating to Activity Abroad by Federal Organs of Executive Power and by Russian Governmental Departments".[19]

The Ministry of Justice must agree to the submission of any treaty proposals that would establish rules in conflict with existing legislation. It shall also give opinions regarding the questions of conformity to existing law (art. 10). The Constitutional Court decides the constitutionality of treaties not yet in force and settles disputes concerning competencies of federal agencies (art. 34).

Either the President or the Government will make decisions regarding the negotiations and signing of a treaty, depending on the subject matter of the treaty and its importance. In the case of interdepartmental treaties, the federal minister or director of the federal agency concerned may make decisions in agreement with the Ministry of Foreign Affairs (art. 11).

18 SZ RF 1996, No. 12, Item 1061.

19 SZ RF 1997, No. 24, Item 2743.

To express consent to be bound by a treaty, the Russian Federation may affix a signature, exchange documents, ratify, confirm, adopt, agree to accession, or use any method which the parties have stipulated (art. 6). The processes of confirming, adopting, and agreeing to accession are basically the same as for ratification. The method depends on the nature of the treaty. Ratification, which is effectuated in the form of a federal law (art. 14), is necessary for treaties that: require a change in federal laws; change the nation's boundaries, economic zone or continental shelf; affect defense, disarmament or international control over armaments, including peace treaties and treaties on collective security; stipulate by their terms that they must be ratified (art. 15).

After the treaty is signed, the negotiating body submits a proposal for ratification together with a certified copy of the official text of the treaty, a substantiation of its advisability, an opinion as to its conformity with existing law, and an economic and financial evaluation as to its effect. If the treaty has an impact on the federal budget, an opinion of the Government is also required by Section 104 of the Constitution. The Government shall adopt in the form of a decree its decisions to submit a treaty for ratification (art. 16).

If it wishes to ratify the treaty, the State Duma adopts the decision as a federal law. The federal law is then reviewed by the Soviet of the Federation (art. 17). After passage in both chambers, the instrument of ratification is signed by the President and the Minister of Foreign Affairs and the presidential seal is affixed (art. 18). The Minister of Foreign Affairs or his delegated diplomatic representative is responsible for exchanging instruments of ratification or depositing instruments of ratification with the appropriate parties (art. 19).

Russia follows the 1969 Vienna Convention in provisionally applying any treaty to which it anticipates becoming a party. Treaties enter into force according to the dates they specify, but if no term speaks to the date, then upon signature or the exchange of ratification instruments (art. 24). Where there is an official communication pertaining to the entry into force of a treaty, the communication may be published based on the decision of the Ministry of Foreign Affairs. Decisions to ratify a treaty, since they are in the form of a federal law, are to be published upon the recommendation of the Ministry of Foreign Affairs in the *Sobranie zakonadatel'stva Rossiiskoi Federatsii.* International treaties (excluding interdepartmental treaties) are published in the *Biulleten' mezhdunarodnykh dogovorov,* also upon recommendation of the Ministry of Foreign Affairs. Interdepartmental treaties are published upon the recommendation of the corresponding federal agency in its official publication.

The same law that outlines the procedure for ratification also outlines the procedure for termination or suspension of an international treaty. A treaty's termination must conform to international law and any treaty terms pertaining to termination. Those treaties that have been agreed to through the passage of a federal law must be terminated through repeal or amendment of that law. Therefore the Duma and Federal Assembly must decide on termination in these instances (art. 37).

Annotated Bibliography of Sources–Russian Federation

Due to the number of sources for different parts of Russian history, the annotated bibliography for this chapter is divided up into three separate sections: those for the current Russian Federation, the former USSR, and Imperial Russia.

General Treaty Collections

Many of the following collections include diplomatic documents as well as treaties.

1 INTERNATIONAL AGREEMENTS OF THE UNITED STATES AND THE FORMER SOVIET REPUBLICS

Russian Federation. Igor Kavass, comp. (Buffalo: William S. Hein, 1996).

Summary: A loose-leaf service that has the complete bilateral treaties between the United States and Russian Federation since the beginning of 1992 (and three trade agreements made in 1990). The treaties are accessible by four different indexes: numerical (TIAS where available, otherwise Kavass number), alphabetical, chronological, and subject. Also of great use is a list of the bilateral and multilateral agreements with the Russian Federation or the Union of Soviet Socialist Republics, which the United States considers still in force as of January 1, 1995.

2 BIULLETEN' MEZHDUNARODNYKH DOGOVOROV [BULLETIN OF INTERNATIONAL TREATIES]

Administration of the President of the Russian Federation (Moscow: IUridicheskaia literatura, 1993–).

Summary: The title translates as the Bulletin of International Treaties. It is published monthly by the Administration of the President of the Russian Federation. This periodical is one of the official publications for treaties. Treaties that are ratified together with ratification documents are also found in the *Sobranie zakonodatel'sva Rossiiskoi Federatsii,* published weekly since May 1994. It succeeds *Sobranie aktov Prezidenta i pravitel'stva Rosiiskoi Federatsii,* which was issued weekly from July 1, 1992.

Note: Both the *Biulleten' mezhdunarodnykh dogovorov* and the *Sobranie zakonodatel'stva Rossiiskoi Federatsii* are available on the official site: Sobranie zakonodatel'stva Rossiiskoi Federatsii (http://www.szrf.ru/index.phtml). Starting with 2012 downloadable PDF files of documents were included.

3 CONSULTANT PLUS, GARANT, AND KODEKS [COMMERCIAL DATABASES]
URL: Consultant Plus-http://www.consultant.ru/ (Russian); http://www.consultant.ru/sys/english/ (English).
Garant-http://www.garant.ru (Russian); http://english.garant.ru/ (English).
Kodeks-http://www.kodeks.ru (Russian); http://www.kodeks.ru/english.html (English).

Summary: These fee based Russian legal databases contain all current legislation and much relevant legislation from the USSR with limited free access to documents including treaties in Russian.

Note: English version of Kodeks available as a subscription through East View Information Services.

Note: Free access to select documents on Consultant Plus available from 8pm to 12am (Moscow Time, UTC+4) on weekdays as well as all day on weekends.

4 DIPLOMATICHESKII VESTNIK [DIPLOMATIC HERALD]
(Moscow: Mezhdunarodnye otnosheniia 1992–2004).

Summary: The Ministry of Foreign Affairs published this semi-monthly. The Diplomatic Herald printed diplomatic texts, including treaties, official meetings, press briefings, UN and Russian embassy activities. The documents are listed in the table of contents under headings of broad categories.

5 MEZHDUNARODNOE PRAVO [INTERNATIONAL LAW]
URL: http://www.mid.ru/bul_newsite.nsf/kartaflat/02.07.

Summary: The Russian Federation's Ministry of Foreign Affairs provides a list of Russia's bilateral treaties (with full text) and a second list of multilateral treaties (also with full text) for which Russia is a depository. The origin of a document's text is stated. The texts vary in format. Some of the treaties predate the current Russian state and date as far back as mid-1800s, with some in English. Information on whether a convention is still in effect or not is included. The documents are provided for the benefit of the site visitor but are not authenticated or official. In 2012 the bilateral treaties page states that it is still in beta testing.

Note: While most treaties will be in Russian, one may find English texts of bilateral treaties with English speaking countries at their analogous government sites for treaties, e.g., for the USA see the Library of Congress site, http://thomas.loc.gov/home/treaties/treaties.html; for Australia's Department of Foreign Affairs and Trade, see http://www.dfat.gov.au/treaties/.

6 ROSSIISKII EZHEGODNIK MEZHDUNARODNOGO PRAVA [RUSSIAN YEARBOOK OF INTERNATIONAL LAW]
Russian Association of International Law (Saint Petersburg: Russia-Neva, 1994–).

Summary: In 1994 the yearbook for 1992 was published. Each issue has a final section of up to five documents, generally Russian translations of multilateral treaties. The Soviet Yearbook on International Law, of which this is the continuation, had far fewer documents. The table of contents is listed in Russian and English.

7 SBORNIK MEZHDUNARODNYKH DOGOVOROV SSSR I ROSIISKOI FEDERATSII [COLLECTION OF INTERNATIONAL TREATIES OF THE USSR AND RUSSIAN FEDERATION]
(Moscow: Mezhdunarodnaia otnosheniia, 1994–).

Summary: This annual is a continuation of the Soviet one and starts with No. 47. (See *Sbornik deistvuiushchikh dogovorov, soglashenii i konventsii, zakliuchennykh s inostrannymi gosudarstvami*, no. 17 below.) It does not contain interdepartmental treaties and certain other treaties, according to its own description, but does have the majority of the major treaties.

8 VNESHNIAIA POLITIKA ROSSII: SBORNIK DOKUMENTOV [FOREIGN POLITICS OF RUSSIA: A COLLECTION OF DOCUMENTS], 1990–2004
Ministry of Foreign Affairs (Moscow: Mezhdunarodnye otnosheniia [last volume published by Nauchnaya Kniga], 1996–2008).

Summary: With the initial volume that covers 1990–1992, this ongoing publishing project of diplomatic texts offers a collection of diplomatic documents starting from June 12, 1990, when Russia declared its independence, finishing with the year 2004. Each volume contains approximately 200 documents including treaties, diplomatic notes, protocols, official announcements, etc. The documents are arranged chronologically in each volume. An index of countries with page citations to the relevant documents in the collection is included. They may be difficult to find as print runs for each book were 650 copies or fewer.

General Treaty Indexes

9 PERECHEN' MEZHDUNARODNYKH DOGOVOROV ROSSIISKOI FEDERATSII, RATIFITSIROVANNYKH ILI DENONSIROVANNYKH ROSSIISKOI FEDERATSIEI S 1-OGO IANVARIA 1990 GODA PO 31-OGO AVGUSTA 1996 GODA [LIST OF INTERNATIONAL TREATIES OF THE RUSSIAN FEDERATION RATIFIED OR RENOUNCED BY THE RUSSIAN FEDERATION FROM JANUARY 1, 1990, THROUGH AUGUST 1996.]
(Moscow: Izvestiia, 1997). 106 pp.

Summary: This list of international treaties of the Russian Federation, ratified or renounced by the Russian Federation from January 1, 1990, through August 31, 1996, was compiled by the legal department of the Duma and Federal Assembly.

Topical and Selected Treaty Collections

10 PERECHEN' DOGOVOROV ROSSIISKOI FEDERATSII I KITAISKOI NARODNOI RESPUBLIKI, PODPISANNYKH VO VREMIA VISITA PRESIDENTA ROSSIISKOI FEDERATSII B.N. EL'TSINA V KNR: 17–19 DEKABRIA 1992 GODA [LIST OF TREATIES OF THE RUSSIAN FEDERATION AND THE PEOPLE'S REPUBLIC OF CHINA SIGNED DURING THE VISIT OF THE PRESIDENT OF THE RUSSIAN FEDERATION B.N. YELTSIN IN PRC : 17–19 DECEMBER 1992]
G.A. Stepanova and A.V. Skorodumov, eds. (Moscow: s.n., 1993). 120 pp.

Summary: The texts of 17 agreements with some accompanying memoranda and protocols between China and Russia signed by President Yeltsin during his trip to China in 1992.

11 PRAVOVAIA POMOSHCH' PO MEZHDUNARODNYM DOGOVORAM ROSSII SO STRANAMI SNG I BALTII: SBORNIK MEZHDUNARODNYKH DOGOVOROV [LEGAL ASSISTANCE ACCORDING TO INTERNATIONAL TREATIES OF RUSSIA WITH THE CIS COUNTRIES AND THE BALTICS: COLLECTION OF INTERNATIONAL TREATIES]
N.I. Marysheva, comp. (Moscow: De-IUre, 1995). 201 pp.

Summary: A collection of judicial assistance treaties, the parties to which are the Baltic countries and the countries of the Commonwealth of Independent States.

12 SBORNIK MEZHDUNARODNYKH DOGOVOROV ROSSIISKOI FEDERATSII PO USTRANENIIU DVOINOGO NALOGOLOZHENIIA: OBSHCHIE DOGOVORY, MORSKOI TRANSPORT, VOSDUSHNYI TRANSPORT, AVTOMOBIL'NYI TRANSPORT [COLLECTION OF INTERNATIONAL

TREATIES OF THE RUSSIAN FEDERATION ON THE AVOIDANCE OF DOUBLE TAXATION: GENERAL TREATIES, OCEAN TRANSPORT, AIR TRANSPORT, AUTOMOBILE TRANSPORT] (MOSCOW: SPARK, 1995). 511 PP.

Summary: Contains treaties on double taxation and transportation by sea, air and land.

13 SBORNIK MEZHDUNARODNYKH SOGLASHENII MVD ROSSII [COLLECTION OF INTERNATIONAL AGREEMENTS OF THE MINISTRY OF INTERNAL AFFAIRS OF RUSSIA]
T.N. Moskal'kova, N.B. Sliusar', comps. (Moscow: SPARK, 1996). 257 pp.

Summary: International agreements, both multilateral and bilateral, of the Ministry of Internal Affairs with corresponding ministries of other countries regarding law enforcement and judicial assistance. This volume includes some Russian municipal law regarding the treaty-making powers of the Ministry.

14 SBORNIK SPETSIAL'NYKH MEZHDUNARODNYKH DOGOVOROV ROSSIISKOI FEDERATSII PO VOPROSAM PRAVOVOI POMOSHCHI I PRAVOVYKH OTNOSHENII PO GRAZHDANSKIM, SEMEINYM, YGOLOVNYM I INYM DELAM [COLLECTION OF SPECIAL INTERNATIONAL TREATIES OF THE RUSSIAN FEDERATION ON THE ISSUES OF LEGAL ASSISTANCE AND LEGAL RELATIONS REGARDING CIVIL, FAMILY, CRIMINAL AND OTHER MATTERS]
(Moscow: TICO-Poligraf, 2006) 604 pp.

Annotated Bibliography of Sources – USSR

General Treaty Collections

15 STATUTES AND DECISIONS: A JOURNAL OF TRANSLATIONS
(White Plains, NY: International Arts and Sciences Press, 1964–).

Summary: Occasionally an issue will be devoted to treaties. Volume III (Fall 1966–Summer 1967) is of especial interest providing translations not only of select treaties and international agreements, but also excerpts of the earlier Soviet laws pertaining to the ratification of treaties. It predates the last Soviet law on treaties. A translation of that 1978 law may be found in *International Legal Materials.* In 1998 the journal published several of the treaties between the Russian Federation and its subjects.

Note: Title varies: *Soviet Statutes and Decisions: A Journal of Translations*, 1964–1991. The present journal is titled Statutes and Decisions: The Laws of the Soviet Union and its Successor States (Armonk, NY: M.E. Sharpe, 1991–), which has not published any treaties for over 10 years.

16 MEZHDUNARODNYE DOGOVORY I AKTY NOVOGO VREMENI [INTERNATIONAL TREATIES AND ACTS OF THE MODERN ERA]

Evgenii Aleksandrovich Korovin, ed. (Moscow: Gosudarstvennoe izdatel'stvo, 1924). 395 pp.

Summary: The collection arranged the treaties by subject matter and then by chronology. The first three conventions are from the 19th century ("The Epoch of the Three Congresses"). There are also Soviet Russian and USSR laws pertaining to consular or diplomatic matters. In all there are 79 treaties dating through 1924.

17 SBORNIK MEZHDUNARODNYKH DOGOVOROV SSSR I ROSIISKOI FEDERATSII [COLLECTION OF INTERNATIONAL TREATIES OF THE USSR AND THE RUSSIAN FEDERATION].

(Moscow: Mezhdunarodnye otnosheniia, 1921–).

Summary: Annual. This series does not contain interdepartmental treaties or, according to its own description, "certain other treaties". The contents are listed in the front of each volume in three ways, by subject matter (grouped under seven or eight subject headings), by participating party, and by date.

Note: Title varies: *Sbornik deistvuiushchikh dogovorov, soglashenii konventsii, zakliuchennykh R.S.F.S.R.S inostrannymi gosudarstvami*, 1921–1923; *Sbornik deistvuiushchikh dogovorov, soglashenii i konventsii, zakliuchennykh s inostrannymi gosudarstvami*, 1924–79 (nos. 1–35); *Sbornik mezhdunarodnykh dogovorov SSSR*, 1980–92 (nos. 36–46).

Note: Imprint varies: Moscow: R.S.F.S.R. Narodnyi komissariat po inostrannym delam, 1921–1923; Ministertsvo inostrannykh del SSSR. Moscow: Mezhdunarodye otnosheniia, 1924–1979; Moscow: Mezhdunarodnye otnosheniia, 1980–1992.

18 VESTNIK MINISTERSTVA INOSTRANNYKH DEL SSSR

(Moscow: Mezhdunarodnye otnosheniia, 1987–1991).

Summary: Semimonthly compilation of treaties. Continued by *Diplomaticheskii vestnik* (no. 4, above).

Note: Title varies: *Vestnik Ministerstva Vneshnikh Snoshenii SSSR*, Nov. 30–Dec. 30, 1991.

Treaty Indexes

19 A CALENDAR OF SOVIET TREATIES, 1917–1980

George Ginsburgs, ed. (Dordrecht; Boston : Martinus Nijhoff Publishers, 1959–1987). Vol. 1, 530 pp.; vol. 2, 908 pp.; vol. 3, 666 pp.

Summary: This three-volume set attempted to catalogue from all available sources the treaties and other international agreements into which the Soviet government entered from 1917 through 1980. Vol. 1 covers the years 1917–1957. Vol. 2 covers the years 1958–1973. Vol. 3 covers the years 1974–1980. The list is in chronological order. If the authors found the text of the document in more than one place, they cited all sources. The sources are generally cited in the following heirarchy: Soviet official sources, other Soviet sources, official sources of the treaty partner, other sources of the treaty partner, official international sources, any other source. Some entries provide summaries of the content of the treaty.

Note: Editor varies: Vol. 1, edited by Robert M. Slusser and Jan F. Triska; Vol. 2, edited by George Ginsburgs and Robert M. Slusser.

Note: Imprint varies: Vol. 1, Stanford: Stanford University Press, 1959; Vol. 2, Alphen aan den Rijn: Sijthoff & Nordhoff, 1981.

Topical and Selected Treaty Collections

20 ECONOMIC TREATIES AND AGREEMENTS OF THE SOVIET BLOC IN EASTERN EUROPE, 1945–1951, 2ND ED.

(New York: Mid-European Law Project, 1952). 138 pp.

Summary: This work is in three parts: a survey of the treaties; a list of all known treaties and agreements; and translations of selected treaties of the Soviet Union and other Soviet bloc nations with a chronology of treaties of East Germany with Soviet bloc nations. Some treaties were not available from official sources so the editors cited commercially published works.

20 SALT II AGREEMENT, VIENNA, JUNE 18, 1979

(Washington: U.S. Dept. of State, Bureau of Public Affairs, 1979).

Summary: The volume includes some supporting documents for the treaty as well as the text of the treaty.

21 U.S.-SOVIET COMMERCIAL AGREEMENTS, 1972: TEXTS, SUMMARIES, AND SUPPORTING PAPERS

Peter G. Peterson (Washington: U.S. Dept. of Commerce, Bureau of East-West Trade, 1973). 107 pp.

22 MEZHDUNARODNYE SOGLASHENIIA PO MORSKOMU SUDOKHODSTVU, 2ND ED [INTERNATIONAL AGREEMENTS ON MARITIME TRAFFIC]
IUsuf Khazanovich Dzhavad, ed. (Moscow: Transport, 1968). 143 pp.

Summary: Contains maritime treaties.

23 SBORNIK TORGOVYKH DOGOVOROV I SOGLASHENII PO TORGOVO-EKONOMICHESKOMU SOTRUDNICHESTVU SSSR S INOSTRANNYMI GOSUDARSTVAMI NA 1 IANVARIA 1977 GODA [COLLECTION OF TRADE TREATIES AND AGREEMENTS ON TRADE-ECONOMIC COOPERATION OF THE USSR WITH FOREIGN STATES 1 JANUARY 1977]
G.S. Burguchev, ed. (Moscow: Ekonomika, 1977). 2 vols.

Summary: These two volumes were published by the Ministry of Foreign Trade. The treaties are those in effect as of January 1, 1977; none predates 1924. The USSR had treaties with 106 countries at this time and they are all represented in this collection.

Note: An earlier collection, *Sbornik torgovykh dogovorov, torgovykh i platezhnykh soglashenii i dolgosrochnykh torgovykh soglashenii SSSR s inostrannymi gosudarstvami, na 1 ianvaria 1961 goda*, edited by K.K. Bakhtov (Moscow: Vneshtorgizdat, 1961, 623 p)., contains commercial treaties in force as of January 1, 1961. The collection covers treaties concluded between 1924 and 1960, with one addition, a 1907 declaration of Russia and Sweden. The treaties are arranged alphabetically (Cyrillic alphabet) by country and chronologically within each country.

24 SOGLASHENIIA SOVETSKOGO SOIUZA S INOSTRANNYMI GOSUDARSTVAMI PO KONSUL'SKIM VOPROSAM: SBORNIK. [AGREEMENTS OF THE SOVIET UNION WITH FOREIGN GOVERNMENTS ON CONSULAR ISSUES: A COLLECTION]
Grigorii Efimovich Vilkov, Igor' Pavlovich Blishchenko, comps. (Moscow: Instituta mezhdunarordnoi otnoshenii, 1962). 231 pp.

Summary: Along with treaties on questions of consular matters, there are excerpts from municipal laws pertaining to this topic (including the marriage of USSR citizens outside of the USSR). The treaties are arranged chronologically with first two agreements predating the USSR (Soviet Russia is the party to the treaty).

25 TORGOVYE DOGOVORY I SOGLASHENIIA SSSR S INOSTRANNYMI GOSUDARSTVAMI [TRADE TREATIES AND AGREEMENTS OF THE USSR AND FOREIGN STATES]
A.S. Korolenko, ed. (Moscow: Vneshtorgizdat, 1953). 315 pp.

Summary: The first 200 pages of the book are essays on commercial treaties and the USSR. The latter part of the book is an appendix with 20 bilateral commercial treaties in effect at time of publication. Includes bibliographic references.

Bilateral Treaty Collections

26 SOVIET TREATY SERIES: A COLLECTION OF BILATERAL TREATIES, AGREEMENTS AND CONVENTIONS, ETC., CONCLUDED BETWEEN THE SOVIET UNION AND FOREIGN POWERS

Leonard Shapiro, ed. (Washington, D.C.: Georgetown University Press, 1950–55). 2 vols.

Summary: Volume 1 covers 1917–1928; volume 2, 1929–1939. The treaties are in English and compiled in chronological order. Entries include dates of signature and ratification, as well as place of signature. The translations are unofficial and from various sources. There is a separate list of the names of the treaties, a signatory index and a subject index as well as an appendix of alleged secret agreements. Each volume also includes a chronology.

27 TREATY OF PEACE BETWEEN LATVIA AND SOVIET RUSSIA 11. VIII.1920

(Stockholm: Latvian National Foundation, 1985).

Summary: Besides the Peace Treaty there is also the Treaty regarding re-evacuation of refugees between Latvia and the Soviet Union. The peace treaty is in Latvian, Russian, English, German, and French. The re-evacuation treaty is in English and Latvian.

Collections of Bilateral Treaties with Individual Countries

The USSR published collections of diplomatic papers and treaties with individual countries, or specific regions of the world. Usually these were joint projects with the other country and publication was both in Russian (published in Moscow) and in the official or major language of the other country (published in the capital of the other country). The collections consist overwhelmingly of documents such as official announcements, protocols, and congratulatory resolutions of the respective governments. There are generally a few non-commercial treaties included, however. These include treaties on cooperation, foreign aid, cultural exchanges or on specific construction projects. Indexing varies. Some sets have no indexing whatsoever, some include a subject index, name index and list of abbreviations used in the text for the sources upon which the editors relied. The form of the title varies. A selection of these works is given below.

Afghanistan

28 SOVETSKO-AFGANSKIE OTNOSHENIIA, 1919–1969: DOKUMENTY I MATERIALY [SOVIET-AFGHAN RELATIONS, 1919–1969: DOCUMENTS AND MATERIALS]
V.M. Vinogradov et al. (Moscow: Politizdat, 1971). 439 pp.

African Nations

29 SSSR I STRANY AFRIKI, 1946–1962: DOKUMENTY I MATERIALY
[USSR and the Countries of Africa, 1946–1962: Documents and Materials]
V.A. Brykin (Moscow: Politizdat, 1963). 2 vols.

30 SSSR I STRANY AFRIKI, 1963–1970: DOKUMENTY I MATERIALY [USSR AND THE COUNTRIES OF AFRICA, 1963–1970: DOCUMENTS AND MATERIALS]
L.F. Il'ichev, et al, eds. (Moscow: Politizdat, 1982). 2 Parts. Part 1: 1963–1966. Part 2: 1967–1970.
Summary: Includes bibliographical references and index.

31 SSSR I STRANY AFRIKI, 1971–1976: DOKUMENTY I MATERIALY [USSR AND THE COUNTRIES OF AFRICA, 1971–1976: DOCUMENTS AND MATERIALS]
(Moscow: Politizdat, 1985). 2 Parts. Part 1: 1971–1974. Part 2: 1975–1976.
Summary: Includes bibliographical references and index.

Argentina

32 SSSR (ROSSIIA)-ARGENTINA: STRANITSY ISTORII, 1885–1986: DOKUMENTY I MATERIALY [USSR (RUSSIA)-ARGENTINA: PAGES OF HISTORY, 1885–1986: DOCUMENTS AND MATERIALS]
E.A. Shevardnadze et al. (Moscow: Politizdat, 1990). 335 pp.

Arab Nations

33 SSSR I ARABSKIE STRANY 1917–1960: DOKUMENTY I MATERIALY [USSR AND THE ARAB COUNTRIES, 1917–1960: DOCUMENTS AND MATERIALS]
V.IA. Sipols et al, eds. (Moscow: Politizdat, 1961). 854 pp.

Austria

34 SSSR-AVSTRIIA 1938–1979: DOKUMENTY I MATERIALY [USSR-AUSTRIA, 1938 1979: DOCUMENTS AND MATERIALS]
(Moscow: Politizdat, 1980). 159 pp.

Bulgaria

35 SOVETSKO-BOLGARSKIE OTNOSHENIIAI SVIAZI: DOKUMENTY I MATERIALY [SOVIET-BULGARIAN RELATIONS AND COMMUNICATIONS: DOCUMENTS AND MATERIALS]
L.B. Valev et al., eds. (Moscow: Nauka, 1976–). 3 vols.

Summary: List of periodicals, chronology of events and proper name index. Coverage through 1969.

36 SOVETSKO-BOLGARSKIE OTNOSHENIIA 1944–1948: DOKUMENTY I MATERIALY [SOVIET-BULGARIAN RELATIONS 1944–1948: DOCUMENTS AND MATERIALS]
(Moscow: Politzdat, 1969). 508 pp.

37 SOVETSKO-BOLGARSKIE OTNOSHENIIA 1948–1970: DOKUMENTY I MATERIALY [SOVIET-BULGARIAN RELATIONS 1948–1970: DOCUMENTS AND MATERIALS]
(Moscow: Politzdat, 1974). 638 pp.

38 SOVETSKO-BOLGARSKIE OTNOSHENIIA, 1971–1976: DOKUMENTY I MATERIALY [SOVIET-BULGARIAN RELATIONS 1971–1976: DOCUMENTS AND MATERIALS]
N.N. Rodionov et al. (Moscow: Politizdat, 1977). 584 pp.

39 SOVETSKO-BOLGARSKIE OTNOSHENIIA 1977–1982: DOKUMENTY I MATERIALY [SOVIET-BULGARIAN RELATIONS 1977–1982: DOCUMENTS AND MATERIALS]
(Moscow: Politzdat, 1985). 525 pp.

40 SOVETSKO-BOLGARSKIE OTNOSHENIIA 1983–1986: DOKUMENTY I MATERIALY [SOVIET-BULGARIAN RELATIONS 1983–1986: DOCUMENTS AND MATERIALS]
V.P. Loginov et al. (Moscow: Politzdat, 1988). 294 pp.

China

41 SOVETSKO-KITAISKIE OTNOSHENIIA, 1917–1957: SBORNIK DOKUMENTOV [SOVIET-CHINESE RELATIONS, 1917–1957: COLLECTION OF DOCUMENTS]
Ivan Fedorovich Kurdiukov et al., eds. (Moscow: Izdatel'stvo vostochnoi literatury, 1959). 465 pp.

Colombia

42 SSSR-KOLUMBIIA: 50 LET USTANOVLENIIA DIPLOMATICHESKIKH OTNOSHENII, 1935–1985: DOKUMENTY I MATERIALY [USSR-COLUMBIA: 50 YEARS OF THE ESTABLISHMENT OF DIPLOMATIC RELATIONS, 1935–1985: DOCUMENTS AND MATERIALS]
E.A. Shevardnadze et al., eds. (Moscow: Politizdat, 1988). 182 pp.

Czechoslovakia

43 DOKUMENTY I MATERIALY PO ISTORII SOVETSKO-CHEKHOSLOVATSKIKH OTNOSHENII. [DOCUMENTS AND MATERIALS ON THE HISTORY OF SOVIET-CZECHOSLOVAKIAN RELATIONS]
P.N. Pospelov, ed. (Moscow: Nauka, 1973–1988). 5 vols. in 6 books.
Summary: Covers years from 1917 to 1948.

44 SOVETSKO-CHEKHOSLOVATSKIE OTNOSHENIIA, 1945–1960: DOKUMENTY I MATERIALY [SOVIET-CZECHOSLOVAKIAN RELATIONS, 1945–1960: DOCUMENTS AND MATERIALS]
(Moscow: Politizdat, 1972). 556 pp.

45 SOVETSKO-CHEKHOSLOVATSKIE OTNOSHENIIA, 1961–1971: DOKUMENTY I MATERIALY [SOVIET-CZECHOSLOVAKIAN RELATIONS, 1961–1971: DOCUMENTS AND MATERIALS]
(Moscow: Politizdat, 1975). 703 pp.

46 SOVETSKO-CHEKHOSLOVATSKIE OTNOSHENIIA, 1972–1970: DOKUMENTY I MATERIALY [SOVIET-CZECHOSLOVAKIAN RELATIONS, 1961–1971: DOCUMENTS AND MATERIALS]
(Moscow: Politizdat, 1977). 455 pp.

47 SOVETSKO-CHEKHOSLOVATSKIE OTNOSHENIIA, 1977–1982: DOKUMENTY I MATERIALY [SOVIET-CZECHOSLOVAKIAN RELATIONS, 1961–1971: DOCUMENTS AND MATERIALS]
V.F. Mal'tsev et al., eds. (Moscow: Politizdat, 1984). 511 pp.

Finland

48 SOVETSKO-FINLIANDSKIE OTNOSHENIIA, 1948–1983: DOGOVOR 1948 G. O DRUZHBE, SOTRUDNICHESTVE I VZAIMNOI POMOSHCHI V DEISTVII: DOKUMENTY I MATERIALY [SOVIET-FINNISH RELATIONS, 1948–1983: TREATY OF 1948 ON FRIENDSHIP, COOPERATION AND MUTUAL ASSISTANCE IN ACTION: DOCUMENTS AND MATERIALS]
A.G. Kovalev et al. (Moscow: Politizdat, 1983).

France

49 SOVETSKO-FRANTSUZSKIE OTNOSHENIIA VO VREMIA VELIKOI OTECHESTVENNOI VOINY, 1941–1945: DOKUMENTY I MATERIALY [SOVIET-FRENCH RELATIONS DURING THE TIME OF THE GREAT PATRIOTIC WAR, 1941–1945: DOCUMENTS AND MATERIALS]
A.L. Adamishin et al., eds. (Moscow: Politizdat, 1983). 2 vols.

50 SOVETSKO-FRANTSUZSKIE OTNOSHENIIA, 1965–1976: DOKUMENTY I MATERIALY [SOVIET-FRENCH RELATIONS, 1965–1976: DOCUMENTS AND MATERIALS]
(Moscow: Politizdat, 1976). 255 pp.

German Reich (Weimar Republic)

51 SOVETSKO-GERMANSKIE OTNOSHENIIA OT PEREGOVOROV V BREST-LITOVSKE DO PODPISANIIA RAPALL'SKOGO DOGOVORA, 1917–1922: SBORNIK DOKUMENTOV [SOVIET-GERMAN RELATIONS FROM THE NEGOTIATIONS IN BREST-LITOVSK TO THE SIGNING OF THE TREATY OF RAPALLO, 1917–1922: COLLECTION OF DOCUMENTS]
(Moscow: Politizdat, 1968). 2 vols.

52 SOVETSKO-GERMANSKIE OTNOSHENIIA, 1922–1925: DOKUMENTY I MATERIALY [SOVIET-GERMAN RELATIONS, 1922–25: DOCUMENTS AND MATERIALS]
(Moscow: Politizdat, 1977). 2 Parts: Part 1, 408 pp.; Part 2, 383 pp.

German Democratic Republic (East Germany)

53 OTNOSHENIIA SSSR S GDR, 1949–1950: DOKUMENTY I MATERIALY [RELATIONS OF THE USSR WITH GDR, 1949–1950: DOCUMENTS AND MATERIALS]
(Moscow: Politizdat, 1974). 727 pp.

54 SSSR-GDR—30 LET OTNOSHENII, 1949–1979: DOKUMENTY I MATERIALY [USSR-GDR–30 YEARS OF RELATIONS, 1949–1979: DOCUMENTS AND MATERIALS]
Igor' Nikolaevich Zemskov et al., eds. (Moscow: Politizdat, 1981). 754 pp.

Hungary

55 SOVETSKAIA ROSSIIA-VENGERSKAIA SOVETSKAIA RESPUBLIKA 1919: DOKUMENTY I MATERIALY [SOVIET RUSSIA-HUNGARIAN SOVIET REPUBLIC 1919: DOCUMENTS AND MATERIALS]
(Moscow: Mezhdunarodnye otnosheniia, 1990). 328 pp.

56 SOVETSKO-VENGERSKIE OTNOSHENIIA, 1945–48: DOKUMENTY I MATERIALY [SOVIET-HUNGARIAN RELATIONS, 1945–48: DOCUMENTS AND MATERIALS]
L.F. Il'ichev et al., eds. (Moscow: Politizdat, 1969). 356 pp.

57 SOVETSKO-VENGERSKIE OTNOSHENIIA, 1948–1970: DOKUMENTY I MATERIALY [SOVIET-HUNGARIAN RELATIONS, 1948–1970: DOCUMENTS AND MATERIALS]
N.N. Rodionov et al., eds. (Moscow: Politizdat, 1927). 324 pp.

58 SOVETSKO-VENGERSKIE OTNOSHENIIA, 1971–1976: DOKUMENTY I MATERIALY [SOVIET-HUNGARIAN RELATIONS, 1971–1976: DOCUMENTS AND MATERIALS]
V.F. Mal'tsev et al., eds. (Moscow: Politizdat, 1984). 574 pp.

59 SOVETSKO-VENGERSKIE OTNOSHENIIA, 1977–1982: DOKUMENTY I MATERIALY [SOVIET-HUNGARIAN RELATIONS, 1977–1982: DOCUMENTS AND MATERIALS]
V.F. Mal'tsev et al., eds. (Moscow: Politizdat, 1984). 421 pp. Index.

Italy

60 SSSR-ITALIIA: STRANITSY ISTORII, 1917–1984: DOKUMENTY I MATERIALY [USSR-ITALY: PAGES OF HISTORY, 1917–1984: DOCUMENTS AND MATERIALS]
A.A. Gromyko et al., eds. (Moscow: Politizdat, 1985). 293 pp.

Korea (Democratic People's Republic of)

61 OTNOSHENIIA SOVETSKOGO SOIUZA S NARODNOI KOREEI 1945–1980: DOKUMENTY I MATERIALY [RELATIONS OF THE SOVIET UNION WITH THE PEOPLE'S KOREA 1945–1980: DOCUMENTS AND MATERIALS]
(Moscow: Nauka, 1981). 424 pp.

Luxembourg

62 SSSR-LIUKSEMBURG: STRANITSY ISTORII, 1867–1984: DOKUMENTY I MATERIALY [USSR-LUXEMBOURG: PAGES OF HISTORY, 1867–1984: DOCUMENTS AND MATERIALS]
A.A. Gromyko et al., eds. (Moscow: Politizdat, 1985). 271 pp.

Mexico

63 SOVETSKO-MEKSIKANSKIE OTNOSHENIIA, 1917–1980: SBORNIK DOKUMENTOV [SOVIET-MEXICAN RELATIONS, 1917–1980: COLLECTION OF DOCUMENTS]
A.I. Sizonenko, L. Kardenas (Moscow: Mezhdunarodnye otnosheniia, 1981). 111 pp.

Mongolia

64 SOVETSKO-MONGOL'SKIE OTNOSHENIIA, 1921–1966: SBORNIK DOKUMENTOV [SOVIET-MONGOL RELATIONS, 1921–1966: COLLECTION OF DOCUMENTS]
S.D. Dylykov et al., eds. (Moscow: Nauka, 1966). 360 pp.

65 SOVETSKO-MONGOL'SKIE OTNOSHENIIA, 1921–1974: DOKUMENTY I MATERIALY [SOVIET-MONGOL RELATIONS, 1921–1974: DOCUMENTS AND MATERIALS]
F.I. Dolgikh et al, eds. (Moscow: Mezhdunarodnye otnosheniia 1975–1979). 2 vols. in 3 books.

Summary: Vol. 1, 1921–1940; vol. 2, 1940–1974. Includes bibliographical references and indexes.

Norway

66 SOVETSKO-NORVEZHSKIE OTNOSHENIIA 1917–1955: SBORNIK DOKUMENTOV SOVIET-NORWEGIAN RELATIONS, 1917–1955: COLLECTION OF DOCUMENTS]
A.O. Chubar'ian et al., eds. (Moscow: ELIA-ART-O, 1997). 682 pp.

Index: Subject and personal name indexes.

Poland

67 DOKUMENTY I MATERIALY PO ISTORII SOVETSKO-POL'SKIKH OTNOSENII [DOCUMENTS AND MATERIALS ON THE HISTORY OF SOVIET-POLISH RELATIONS]
Ivan Aleksandrovich KHrenov et al., eds. (Moscow: Nauka, 1963–1986). 12 vols, covering 1917–1965.

68 SOVETSKII SOIUZ-NARODNAIA POL'SHA, 1944–1974: DOKUMENTY I MATERIALY [THE SOVIET UNION-PEOPLE'S POLAND 1944–1974: DOCUMENTS AND MATERIALS]
V.P. Loginov et al., eds. (Moscow: Politizdat, 1974). 664 pp.

69 SOVETSKII SOIUZ-NARODNAIA POL'SHA, 1974–1987: DOKUMENTY I MATERIALY [THE SOVIET UNION-PEOPLE'S POLAND 1974–1987: DOCUMENTS AND MATERIALS]
V.P. Loginov et al., eds. (Moscow: Politizdat, 1989). 486 pp.

United Kingdom

70 SOVETSKO-ANGLIISKIE OTNOSHENIIA VO VREMIA VELIKOI OTECHESTVENNOI VOINY, 1941–1945: DOKUMENTY I MATERIALY [SOVIET-ENGLISH RELATIONS DURING THE TIME OF THE GREAT PATRIOTIC WAR, 1941–1945: DOCUMENTS AND MATERIALS]
G.P. Kynin et al., eds. (Moscow: Politizdat, 1983). 2 vols.

United States

71 SOVETSKO-AMERIKANSKIE OTNOSHENIIA VO VREMIA VELIKOI OTECHESTVENNOI VOINY, 1941–1945: DOKUMENTY I MATERIALY V DVUKH TOMAKH [SOVIET-AMERICAN RELATIONS DURING THE TIME OF THE GREAT PATRIOTIC WAR, 1941–1945: DOCUMENTS AND MATERIALS IN 2 VOLUMES]
G.A. Arbatov et al., eds. (Moscow: Politizdat, 1984). 2 vols. Indexes.

Uruguay

72 SSSR-URUGVAI: 60 LET DIPLOMATICHESKIKH OTNOSHENII, 1926–1986: DOKUMENTY I MATERIALY [USSR-URUGUAY: 60 YEARS OF DIPLOMATIC RELATIONS, 1926–1986]
Eduard Amvrosievich Shevernadze et al., eds. (Moscow: Mezhdunarodnye otnosheniia, 1988). 151 pp.

Vietnam

73 SOVETSKII SOIUZ-V'ETNAM: 30 LET OTNOSHENII 1950–1980: DOCUMENTY I MATERIALY [SOVIET UNION-VIETNAM: 30 YEARS OF RELATIONS 1950–1980: DOCUMENTS AND MATERIALS]

N.P. Firubin et al., eds. (Moscow: Politizdat, 1982). 655 pp.

Yugoslavia

74 SOVETSKO-IUGOSLAVSKIE OTNOSHENIIA, 1917–1941: SBORNIK DOKUMENTOV I MATERIALOV [SOVIET-YUGOSLAV RELATIONS, 1917–1941: COLLECTION OF DOCUMENTS AND MATERIALS]

V.V. Zelenin et al., eds. (Moscow: Nauka, 1992). 410 pp. Index.

75 SOVETSKO-IUGOSLAVSKIE OTNOSHENIIA, 1945–56 [SOVIET YUGOSLAV RELATIONS, 1945–1956]

(Novosibirsk: Alpha-Porte, 2010).

Diplomatic Documents

76 DOKUMENTY VNESHNEI POLITIKI SSSR [DOCUMENTS OF THE FOREIGN POLICY OF THE USSR]

(Moscow: Politizdat, 1957–1998). 23 vols.

Summary: The first volume contains official documents pertaining to foreign affairs from November 7, 1917, through December 31, 1918, although generally it does not include treaties. Each ensuing volume covers the specified length of time shown on its title page.

77 MEZHDUNARODNAIA POLITIKA NOVEISHEGO VREMENI V DOGOVORAKH, NOTAKH I DEKLARATSIIAKH [INTERNATIONAL POLITICS OF THE MOST MODERN ERA IN TREATIES, NOTES AND DECLARATIONS]

IU. Kliuchnikov and Andrei Sabanin, eds. (Moscow: Litizdat NKID, 1926). 3 vols.

Summary: The second volume has materials from World War I to the blockade of Soviet Russia. The third volume has materials from the blockade to the 10 year anniversary of the October Revolution: Part I has acts of Soviet diplomats and Part II has acts of the foreign governments. The overwhelming majority of the material is diplomatic documents. Also contains some treaties and treaty excerpts. See no. 78, below.

Annotated Bibliography of Sources – Imperial Russia

This section contains selected collections or indexes of Pre-Soviet Russia from about the mid-1800s. A more detailed and exhaustive handling of Pre-Soviet Russian materials may be found in V.E. Grabar, *The History of International Law in Russia, 1647–1917: A Bio-Bibliographical Study,* translated by W. Butler (Oxford: Clarendon Press, 1989). The English translation adds to the information that Grabar made available in the original Russian edition.

General Treaty Collections

78 MEZHDUNARODNAJA POLITIKA NOVEJSHEGO VREMENI V DOGOVORAKH, NOTAKH I DEKLARATSIJAKH [INTERNATIONAL POLITICS OF THE MOST MODERN ERA IN TREATIES, NOTES AND DECLARATIONS]
IU. Kliuchnikov and Andrei Sabanin, eds. (Moscow: Litizdat NKID, 1926). 3 vols.

Summary: First volume contains materials from the French Revolution to World War I, This work supplies only excerpts of the larger treaties that it contains. It overlaps the Pre-Soviet and Soviet eras. The other two volumes are listed above, no. 77.

79 SBORNIK DIEISTVUIUSHCHIKH TRAKTATOV, KONVENTSII I SOGLASHENII, ZAKLIUCHENNYKH ROSSIEI S DRUGIMI GOSUDARSTVAMI I KASAIUSHCHIKHSIA RAZLICHNYKH VOPROSOV CHASTNOGO MEZHDUNARODNOGO PRAVA [COLLECTION OF TREATIES, CONVENTIONS AND AGREEMENTS IN FORCE CONCLUDED BY RUSSIA WITH OTHER STATES REGARDING VARIOUS ISSUES OF PRIVATE INTERNATIONAL LAW]
(Sankt Peterburg: Tipp. Trenke i Fiusno, 1889–1896). 4 vols.

Summary: This is a general collection of treaties with the third volume (1891) devoted to treaties pertaining to borders. Second editions of the first two volumes were published in 1902–1906. The texts are in Russian and either French or German (depending on the parties, although generally French).

80 SBORNIK DOGOVOROV ROSSII S DRUGIMI GOSUDARSTVAMI: 1856–1917 [COLLECTION OF TREATIES OF RUSSIA WITH OTHER STATES: 1856–1917]
Adamov, ed. (Moscow: Politizdat, 1952). 462 pp.

Summary: This is a collection of 74 important treaties of Imperial Russia, collected as a text for students of history of diplomacy. The treaty texts are from official sources, including Martens, see no. 82 below, and the central government archives.

81 SOBRANIE DIEISTVUIUSHCHIKH DOGOVOROV, ZAKLIUCHENNYKH ROSSIEIU S INOSTRANNYMI DERZHAVAMI [COLLECTION OF PREVAILING TREATIES CONCLUDED BY RUSSIA WITH OTHER FOREIGN POWERS]
Ignatii Aleksandrovich Ivanovskii, ed. (Odessa: Tipp. Odesskago viestnika, 1889–1890). 2 vols.

Summary: Texts are in both Russian and French. The first volume has commercial treaties and conventions on consular matters. The second volume has conventions, declarations and notes of mutual judicial assistance.

82 SOBRANIE TRAKTATOV I KONVENTSII, ZAKLIUCHENNYKH ROSSIEIU S INOSTRANNYMI DERZHAVAMI/RECUEIL DES TRAITÉS ET CONVENTIONS, CONCLUS PAR LA RUSSIE AVEC LES PUISSANCES ÉTRANGÈRES [COLLECTION OF TREATIES AND CONVENTIONS CONCLUDED BY RUSSIA WITH FOREIGN POWERS]
F. Martens, ed. (St. Pétersbourg: Impr. du Ministère des Voies de Communication, 1874–1909) (A. Böhnke). 15 vols.

Summary: Published by order of the Ministry of Foreign Affairs. The treaties are arranged by country: Austria, Germany, England and France in that order. Within each country the treaties are arranged chronologically. The treaties are in two columns of parallel French and Russian text.

Note: Reprinted: Nendeln/Liechtenstein: Kraus Reprint, 1969. Digital copies of the original may be available for free through University of Michigan. Contact hathitrust-help@umich.edu with your request.

83 SOBRANIE TRAKTATOV, KONVENTSII I DRUGIKH AKTOV, ZAKLIUCHENNYKH ROSSIEIU S EVROPEISKIMI I AZIATSKIMI DERZHAVAMI, A TAKZHE I S SEVERO-AMERIKANSKIMI SOEDINENNYMI SHATATAMI [COLLECTION OF TREATIES, CONVENTIONS AND OTHER ACTS CONCLUDED BY RUSSIA WITH EUROPEAN AND ASIAN POWERS, AS WELL AS WITH THE NORTH AMERICAN UNITED STATES]
(Saint Petersburg: V. Morskoi Tipp., 1845).

Summary: This work published by the Ministry of Maritime Affairs is often considered the first treaty collection produced in Russia. It had several supplements, the last in 1874.

84 SOBRANIE VAZHNIEISHIKH TRAKTATOV I KONVENTSII ZAKLIUCHENNYKH ROSSIEI S INOSTRANNYMY DERZHAVAMI, 1774–1906 [COLLECTION OF THE MOST IMPORTANT TREATIES AND CONVENTIONS CONCLUDED BY RUSSIA WITH FOREIGN POWERS, 1774–1906]
Introduction and annotations by V.N. Aleksandrenko (Varshava: Tipp. Varshavskago uchebnyi okrug, 1906).

Summary: The introduction treats the history of publishing treaty collections in Europe. The treaties are divided into 8 subheadings, which include political, commercial, consular, extradition matters and maritime matters.

85 VNESHNIAIA POLITIKA ROSSII XIX-NACHALO XX VEKA: DOKUMENTY ROSSIISKOGO MINISTERSTVA INOSTRANNYKH DEL [FOREIGN POLICY OF RUSSIA NINETEENTH-BEGINNING TWENTIETH CENTURIES: DOCUMENTS OF THE RUSSIAN MINISTRY OF FOREIGN AFFAIRS]
(Moscow: Mezhdunarodye Otnosheniia, 1960–2005) 17 vols.

Summary: This work is an ongoing series starting with documents 1800 and with the last volume published in 2005, going through 1832 so far. It is prepared jointly by the Ministry of Foreign Affairs and Russian Academy of Sciences. Documents are in the original French with Russian translation.

Note: The imprint varies, earlier volumes were published by Gospolitizdat.

Treaty Indexes

86 ARKHIV VNESHNEI POLITIKI ROSSIISKOI IMPERII: PUTEVODITEL [ARCHIVE OF THE FOREIGN POLICY OF IMPERIAL RUSSIA: GUIDE]
Ministerstvo Inostrannykh Del Rossiiskoi Federatsii.
(Minneapolis: East View Publications, 1995). 425 pp. Index.

Summary: The guide to the Ministry of Foreign Affairs' archives. This provides descriptions of the various record groups present in the archives. Generally material dates between 1720 and 1917. Includes references to a few treaties, but mostly to diplomatic correspondence.

87 SBORNIK MOSKOVSKAGO GLAVNAGO ARKHIVA MINISTERSTVA INOSTRANNYKH DIEL [COLLECTION OF MOSCOVITE MAIN ARCHIVE OF THE MINISTRY OF FOREIGN AFFAIRS]
Izdaniia kommissii pechataniia gramot i dogovorov.
(Moscow: Tipografija Obshchestva rasprostr. polezhnykh knig 1880). Nos. 1–7 (1900).

Summary: These contain information on what is held in the archives of the Ministry of Foreign Affairs, but the 1995 work is more thorough. (See no. 86 above.) However, whereas the 1995 work simply lists descriptions of what is found in various collections in the archives, these books contain some scholarly essays.

88 EZHEDGODNIK MINISTERSTVA INNOSTRANYKH DIEL [YEARBOOK OF THE MINISTRY OF FOREIGN AFFAIRS]
(Sankt Peterburg: Russia Ministerstvo innostranykh diel, 1861–1917).

Summary: The initial issues were in French. From 1887 to 1893 they were in a mix of Russian and French. From 1887–1893 there was an alternative title in French. From 1894 to 1917 this title was completely in Russian. The annual had a section devoted to official diplomatic documents. There is an index for documents published in the annual in 1886. From 1894 to 1908 every issue had a cumulative index of the documents. The 1909 issue had a supplement for 1908 and 1909, but all ensuing editions were without an index.

Note: Title varies: *Annuaire diplomatique de l'empire de russie*, 1861–1893; current title was used as alternative title, 1887–1893.

Note: Imprint varies: Petrograd: Russia Ministerstvo innostranykh diel, 1914–1917.

89 UKAZATEL' TRAKTATOV I SNOSHENII ROSSII S 1462 PO 1826. [INDEX OF TREATIES AND RELATIONS OF RUSSIA 1462 THROUGH 1826]
S. Dobroklonskii, ed. (Moscow: s.n., 1838).

Summary: The list of treaties is in Russian (translated sometimes from the original French) and arranged chronologically under the reigns of the various tsars. The citations to other works are in abbreviated form and may require looking through the introduction to understand.

Topical and Selected Treaty Publications

Commercial Treaties Collections

90 SOBRANIE NYNIE DEISTVUIUSHCHYKH TORGOVYKH TRAKTOV ROSSII S INOSTRANNYMI GOSUDARSTVAMI [COLLECTION OF CURRENTLY IN FORCE TRADE TREATIES OF RUSSIA WITH FOREIGN STATES]
Preface by Jean Gratsianskii (St. Petersburg: Tipp. Khromolitografiia i tipografiia V. Gratsianskago, 1877).

Summary: The treaties appear in both Russian and French in parallel columns. The table of contents lists the countries in Cyrillic alphabetical order. Each country has all its entries first listed in Russian and then in French.

91 SBORNIK TORGOVYKH DOGOVOROV I DRUGIKH VYTEKAIUSHCHIKH IZ NIKH SOGLASHENII, ZAKLIUCHENNYKH MEZHDU ROSSIEI I INOSTRANNYMI GOSUDARSTVAMI [COLLECTION OF TRADE TREATIES WITH OTHER SUBORDINATE AGREEMENTS CONCLUDED BETWEEN RUSSIA AND FOREIGN STATES]
(Petrograd: Kirshbaum, 1915).

Summary: A collection of commercial treaties with related documents. The texts appear in both Russian and French.

92 SOBRANIE TORGOVYKH DOGOVOROV, ZAKLIUCHENNYKH ROSSIEIU S INOSTRANNYMI GOSUDARSTVAMI [COLLECTION OF TRADE TREATIES CONCLUDED BY RUSSIA WITH FOREIGN STATES]
(Saint Petersburg: Kirshbaum, 1902).
Summary: This work contains commercial treaties in both Russian and French.

Treaties Concerning the Far East

93 THE RUSSO-JAPANESE TREATIES OF 1907–1916 CONCERNING MANCHURIA AND MONGOLIA
Ernest Batson Price (Baltimore: Johns Hopkins University Press, 1933).
Summary: This is a published dissertation which has as an appendix the French text and English translation of the Sino-Russian treaty of 1896 and the Russo-Japanese treaties of 1912 and 1916. It also has an annotated bibliography.

94 SBORNIK DOGOVOROV I DIPLOMATICHESKIKH DOKUMENTOV PO DIELAM DAL'NIAGO VOSTOKA: 1895–1905 GG. MINISTERSTVO INOSTRANNYKH DIEL [COLLECTION OF TREATIES AND DIPLOMATIC NOTES ON MATTERS OF THE FAR EAST: 1895–1905 MINISTRY OF FOREIGN AFFAIRS]
(Saint Petersburg: Tipp. Mendelevicha, 1906). 763 pp.
Summary: The work contains texts of treaties concluded during this period, some by Russia and some by other European nations that pertain to the Far East (the Asian parties are generally China, Japan or Korea). They are arranged chronologically and the treaties are in Russian and the language of the western party. Where Russia is the Western party, the treaty appears in Russian and French. The work provides the dates of the treaties in the old and new calendars.

95 SBORNIK DOGOVOROV I DRUGIKH DOKUMENTOV PO ISTORII MEZHDUNARODNYKH OTNOSHENII NA DAL'NEM VOSTOKE: 1842–1925 [COLLECTION OF TREATIES AND OTHER DOCUMENTS ON THE HISTORY OF THE INTERNATIONAL RELATIONS IN THE FAR EAST: 1842–1925]
Ervin Davidovich Grimm, ed. (Moscow: Izd. Instituta Vostokovedeniia, 1927). 218 pp.
Summary: A collection of treaties and other documents on diplomatic relations with the countries of the Far East. Grimm's texts have been criticized for having been poorly translated into Russian from French and poorly edited.

96 SBORNIK DOGOVOROV ROSSII S KITAEM, 1689–1881 [COLLECTION OF TREATIES OF RUSSIA WITH CHINA, 1689–1881]
Ministry of Foreign Affairs (Saint Petersburg: Izd. M.I.D., 1889). 270 pp.
Summary: Collection of treaties between China and Russia. The treaties are in parallel languages, Russian and French. Reproductions of documents in Manchurian, Mongolian, Chinese.

97 STARYE I NOVYE DOGOVORY ROSSII S KITAEM. 2D ED [OLD AND NEW TREATIES OF RUSSIA WITH CHINA]
M. Venyukov (Saint Petersburg: Tipp. V. Bezobrazov, 1863). 95 pp.
Summary: A thin volume of treaties and other documents pertaining to relations between Russia and China. The original intent was to provide officials with a reference collection of sections from Sino-Russian treaties. The first edition was in 1861, which quickly sold out, according to the second edition's foreword.

98 SVOD MEZHDUNARODNYKH POSTANOVLENII, OPREDIELIAIUSHCHIKH VZAIMNIA OTNOSHENIIA MEZHDU ROSSIEIU I KITAEM, 1689–1897 [COLLECTION OF INTERNATIONAL REGULATIONS DEFINING THE MUTUAL RELATIONS BETWEEN RUSSIA AND CHINA, 1689–1897]
(Saint Petersburg: Kirshbaum, 1900). 132 pp.
Summary: The clauses of various treaties are presented in digest form, those handling the same subject grouped under individual headings. The collection includes both treaties to which Russia is a party, and to which other European countries are a party, representing an editorial idea of the importance for Russia of these documents for Russia's relationship with China. In Russian and French.

Bilateral Treaty Collections

99 *ROSSIIA PORTUGALIIA:XVIII-NACHALO XX VEKA. TOM 1. 1722–1815*
[RUSSIA-PORTUGAL: EIGHTEENTH–BEGINNING OF THE TWENTIETH CENTURIES. VOL. 1. 1722–1815]
(Moscow: Moskovskaia Typografiia No. 2, 2007)
Summary: This collection contains 462 documents, including treaties, correspondence between courts, etc. A companion volume was issued in Portugal in Portuguese.

Singapore

Evelyn Ma

Issues of Treaty Succession

The Republic of Singapore's status as a sovereign nation responsible for its own international relations, including treaty-making, evolved over time in a series of significant historical developments.

Originally an island inhabited by fishermen of Malay and Chinese descent, Singapore was founded by Sir Thomas Stamford Raffles of the British East India Company in 1819 when he established the island as a trading post. The Anglo-Dutch Treaty of 1824[1] formalized British occupation of Singapore when the Sultan of Johor and Temenggong ceded the island to the British. At the time the British East India Company also possessed Penang and Malacca.[2] The latter was administered by the Bengal Presidency together with Singapore while Penang was governed by a separate Presidency. In 1826, a Royal Charter of Justice[3] was passed to enable the Crown to establish the administration of justice in Singapore and Malacca. It also annexed Singapore and Malacca to Penang, creating a Presidency of the Straits Settlements. In 1829, the British East India Company abolished the Straits Settlements

1 Treaty of Commerce and Exchange with the Netherlands, Mar. 17, 1824, Gr. Brit.-Netherlands, 11 B.S.P. 194.
[hereinafter Anglo-Dutch Treaty of 1824]. It is also known as the London Treaty of 1824. The establishment of the Straits Settlements followed the Anglo-Dutch Treaty of 1824 settling prior trade and territorial disputes between the two nations.

2 The Straits Settlements were formed in 1826 by the amalgamation of the three Settlements of Singapore, Penang and Malacca. The island of Labuan, off the coast of Borneo, was also incorporated into the colony effective 1 January 1907, and become a separate settlement within it in 1912. With the exception of Singapore, Christmas Island, and the Cocos Islands, these territories now form part of Malaysia.

3 "On 20 March 1827, the long-awaited Charter of Justice which was dated 27 November 1826 arrived…The main purpose of the Charter was to extend the jurisdiction of the Recorder's Court at Penang to Malacca, Singapore and all present or future dependencies of the Straits Government." Kevin Y.L. Tan, *A Short Legal and Constitutional History of Singapore, in* Essays in Singapore Legal History 32 (Kevin Y.L. Tan ed., 2005). The full-text of the Charter can be found in Letters Patent, Establishing the Court of Judicature at Prince Of Wales' Island, Singapore, and Malacca, in the East-Indies; Bearing Date the Twenty-Seventh Day of November, in the Seventh Year of the Reign Of George IV, Anno Domini, One Thousand, Eight Hundred And Twenty-Six (1827).

 | DOI 10.1163/9789004272224_028

Presidency.[4] Subsequently in 1830, administration of the Settlements passed to the Bengal Presidency.[5] In 1858, the British East India Company was itself abolished, and the Straits Settlements came under the jurisdiction of the new colonial Indian Government with Singapore being the Settlements' administrative center. The Straits Settlements remained largely under the India Office until 1867.[6]

From 1867–1946, the British administered Singapore as part of the British Crown Colony under the operation of the Straits Settlements, together with Penang, Malacca, Labuan, the Cocos Islands and Christmas Island.[7] With the surrender of the British in 1942 during the Second World War, Singapore came under Japanese military rule until 1945. When the British regained Singapore, the Straits Settlements (Repeal) Act of 1946[8] disbanded the Straits Settlements. The Malayan Union, predecessor to the Federation of Malaya, was formed by Penang and Malacca with nine other Malay states.[9] Singapore became a separate colony with its own Legislative Council and system of Courts.[10]

On August 1st 1958, the British Parliament passed the State of Singapore Act[11] and granted Singapore the right to self-government. By the Singapore Constitution Order in Council 1958,[12] the post of the Governor was abolished. The People's Action Party (PAP) was voted into power in 1959. The new Constitution was established by Proclamation on June 3rd 1959.

---

4 For a brief introduction of the history of the abolition of the Penang Presidency, *See* Tan, *supra* note 3, at 34.

5 Id.

6 Id. *at* 37.

7 The establishment of the Straits Settlements followed the Anglo-Dutch Treaty of 1824 between the United Kingdom and the Netherlands, *supra* note 1. "Only when, as a result of the Anglo-Dutch Treaty of 1824, England took permanent possession of Malacca in 1825, did they plan to establish a regular administration of law, and the following year when Malacca became part of the Straits Settlements, a Royal Charter of Justice extended the jurisdiction of the Court of Judicature of Prince of Wales Island to Malacca and Singapore, introducing the law of England into these settlements." 7 AM. J. COMP. L. 249, 254 (1913).

8 Straits Settlements (Repeal) Act, 1946, 9 & 10 Geo. VI, c. 37 (Eng.)

9 MALAYAN UNION AND SINGAPORE, STATEMENT OF POLICY ON FUTURE CONSTITUTION, Cmd. 6724 (1946); MALAYAN UNION AND SINGAPORE: SUMMARY OF PROPOSED CONSTITUTIONAL ARRANGEMENTS, Cmd. 6749 (1946).

10 See Kevin L. Tan, *The Evolution of Singapore's Modern Constitution: Developments from 1945 to the Present Day*, 1 SING. ACAD.L.J. 1, 6–8 (1989).

11 State of Singapore Act, 1958, 6 & 7 Eliz. II, c. 59 (Eng.)

12 The Singapore (Constitution) Order in Council, 1958, S.I. 1958/1956 (U.K.).

Under the new Constitution, the "self-governing state"[13] of Singapore had control over most internal local matters, while responsibilities relating to Singapore's defense and foreign affairs, including its international treaty making powers and scope of competence, remained with the British government.[14]

The status of Singapore changed in 1963 when it became a member of the Federation of Malaysia. Through the Malaysia Agreement signed by the United Kingdom, Malaya, Singapore and the Borneo States,[15] the United Kingdom relinquished all sovereignty and jurisdiction exercised over Singapore. Under the agreed provisions of the Constitution of the Federation of Malaysia, and the new State Constitution of Singapore, the division of powers between Singapore and the central government of Malaysia was reallocated and Singapore abrogated its jurisdiction over international relations to Malaysia.[16]

Singapore's merger with Malaysia was brief. Due to political differences, Singapore was expelled from the Federation.[17] On August 9th 1965, Singapore seceded from Malaysia through the Independence of Singapore Agreement.[18] For the first time in its history, Singapore assumed all powers, including those relating to international relations, defense and foreign affairs, as a sovereign and independent state.

Treaty succession for the newly independent nation of Singapore was complicated by the fact that it seceded twice: first when it gained independence from the British Crown by joining the Federation of Malaysia in 1963 and subsequently in 1965, when it seceded from the Federation. The separation from Malaysia was accomplished by a series of documents.[19] The Malaysian

13 Tan, *supra* note 10, at 12. The Preamble of the Order states that "it was agreed that it was desirable that Singapore should bear the title "The State of Singapore" and that a new Constitution should be established conferring upon the State of Singapore internal self-government under a Yang di-Pertuan Negara and reserving to the Government of the United Kingdom responsibility for defence and external affairs," Id.

14 *Supra* note 12. Part VIII of the Order delineates (1) the reservation of rights of defence and external affairs to the U.K. Government (2) the delegation of powers relating to the conduct of matters concerning the trade and cultural relations of Singapore with other countries to the Singapore Government (3) the procedure for safeguarding discharge of United Kingdom Government's responsibilities.

15 Agreement relating to Malaysia, Gr. Brit.-Sing.-Malaya, July 9, 1963, 750 U.N.T.S.10760.

16 Id.

17 For a detailed explanation of the history of the period, *see* Tan, *supra* Note 3, at 48–50.

18 Agreement relating to the separation of Singapore from Malaysia as an independent and sovereign State. Sing.-Malay., Aug.7, 1965, 563 U.N.T.S. 8206.

19 Tan, *supra* note 3, at 51.

Parliament enacted the Constitution and the Malaysia (Singapore Amendment) Act[20] thereby transferring all legislative and executive powers by the government of the Federation to the new Singaporean Government. Additionally, the Constitution of Singapore Amendment Act[21] amending the Singapore State Constitution was passed on December 22nd 1965. The Republic of Singapore Independence Act (RSIA) of 1965[22] was passed providing certain provisions in the Malaysian Federal Constitution to be applicable to Singapore. From 1965 to 1979, the Constitution of Singapore was a composite of the three documents and they were consolidated into one single constitutional text "Reprint" on March 31st 1980.[23]

Much of the difficulty relating to treaty succession facing Singapore stemmed from the wording of the Clause 13 of Annex B to the Separation Agreement signed between Malaysia and Singapore.[24] As the clause is an integral part of the Malaysia Agreement, it binds Singapore to succeed international treaties, agreements, conventions as well as decisions of international organizations accepted by the Government of Malaysia prior

---

20 Constitution and the Malaysia (Singapore Amendment) Act, Malaysia Act of Parliament No. 53 of 1965.

21 Constitution of Singapore Amendment Act, Malaysia Act of Parliament, No. 8 of 1965.

22 Republic of Singapore Independence Act (RSIA) of 1965, Malaysia Act of Parliament, No. 9 of 1965. It was passed on December 22nd 1965 and made retrospective to August 9th 1965.

23 Tan, *supra* note 3, at 52. *See also* Tan, *supra* note 10, for a detailed discussion of the series of Amendments, 16–23.

24 *Supra* note 18. *See also* S. Jayakumar, *Singapore and state succession: International relations and internal law, in* SINGAPORE AND INTERNATIONAL LAW: THE EARLY YEARS: ESSAYS IN MEMORY OF S. TIWARI 158, 163–167, (Kevin Y.L. Tan, ed. 2008) for a detailed analysis of the issues of treaty succession facing Singapore in relation to the devolution agreement. Annex B of the Separation Agreement contains a draft statute that Malaysia agreed to enact into law to implement Singapore's secession and independence. The draft statute was enacted in Toto as the Constitution and Malaysia (Singapore Amendment) Act by the Malaysian Parliament on August 9th, 1965. Section 13 of Annex B of the Malaysian Act begins as follows: "13. Any treaty, agreement or convention entered into before Singapore Day between the Yang di-Pertuan Agong or the Government of Malaysia and another country or countries, including those deemed to be so by Article 169 of the Constitution of Malaysia shall in so far as such instruments have application to Singapore, be deemed to be a treaty, agreement or convention between Singapore and that country or countries, and any decision taken by an international organization and accepted before Singapore Day by the Government of Malaysia shall in so far as that decision has application to Singapore be deemed to be a decision of an international organization of which Singapore is a member."

to Singapore Day, August 9th 1965.[25] Technically, it can bind Singapore to treaties and agreements entered into by the Malaysian Government or by the British Government (under Article 169 of the Federal Constitution) "in so far as such instruments have application to Singapore."[26] Additionally, it can bind Singapore to "decisions of international organizations in so far as that decision have application to Singapore."[27] Similar devolution agreements containing language imposing on the successor state obligations and rights of the predecessor state made between the Federation of Malaysia and the British government was also evidenced in an exchange of diplomatic correspondence in 1957.[28]

This situation highlighted the two differing theoretical positions towards treaty succession by newly independent states. The existence of devolution agreements reinforces the notion of universal succession by the new state in that it would succeed wholesale treaty rights and obligations of its predecessor state. However, the validity of devolution agreements has been debated on the ground that such agreements cannot "establish any treaty relation between the Successor State and third States."[29] The other competing position, encapsulated as the "clean slate" principle in Article 16 of the Vienna Convention on Succession of States In Respect of Treaties,[30] postulates that the new state is free to pick and choose which treaties it will succeed.[31] The questions then facing Singapore were: which treaties and agreements it would succeed from the Federation of Malaya and which, from the British Government?

---

25 S. Jayakumar, *supra* note 24, at 166.

26 *Supra* note 18, 563 U.N.T.S. 8206, Annex B, Section 13.

27 Id.

28 Hick Tin Chao, *Singapore And International Law: A Brief Survey Of The Questions Relating To Singapore's Membership Of International Organisations, State Succession And The Law Of The Sea, in* SINGAPORE AND INTERNATIONAL LAW: THE EARLY YEARS: ESSAYS IN MEMORY OF S. TIWARI 189, 196–97 (Kevin Y.L. Tan, ed., 2008).

29 Id. at 197. Chao further notes that Singapore does not view "the devolution clause in the Separation Agreement of 1965 as constituting an obligation on her part to accept all previous treaties which applied to Singapore. In response to the usual letter of inquiry from the UN Secretary-General Singapore did not reply that she considered bound by all previous treaties. Instead she said that Singapore was reviewing her position vis-à-vis multilateral treaties entered into by either the UK or Malaysia and whose application was extended to Singapore at a time when those countries were responsible for the external relations of Singapore." Id. at 198.

30 Vienna Convention on Succession of States In Respect of Treaties, Aug. 23, 1978, 1946 UNTS 3.

31 Chao, *supra* note 28, at 200.

Professor S. Jayakumar, Singapore's Minister of Law, 1988–2008, wrote shortly after Singapore's independence in 1970s, that Singapore could only clearly succeed to three types of treaties: namely (i) those concluded before Malaysia Day by the self-government of the state or Singapore "with the assent of the United Kingdom"; (ii) those concluded or extended by the United Kingdom Government before Malaysia Day after having consulted, or having obtained the consent of, the Singaporean Government; and (iii) those concluded or extended by Malaysia (when Singapore was part of the Federation) after having consulted, or having obtained the consent of the Singaporean Government.[32] In all other cases, it was his view that "the position of the Singaporean Government is that the Separation Agreement has not determined with finality all questions of succession and that Singapore is still entitled to state its position and to express its willingness to succeed or to make reservations."[33]

This has been Singapore's position towards treaty succession since independence.[34] It viewed itself as a newly independent state which should start from a clean slate with respect to its obligations towards prior treaties.[35] As a newly independent state, Singapore was entitled to state its position on its own volition and in accordance with its own national interest as to whether or not to succeed treaties signed by predecessor states and whether or not to make reservations. For example, Singapore rejected Japan's claim of continuance of traffic rights into Singapore even though the right was granted under the 1952 UK-Japan Agreement for Air Services. Instead, Singapore acknowledged this particular treaty obligation to Japan on its own by emphasizing that it had voluntarily assumed the obligations of the British government under the 1952 Agreement.[36]

---

32 Jayakumar, *supra* note 25, at 168.

33 Id.

34 Chao, *supra* note 28, at 200.

35 Id.

36 For a discussion of the series of events, *see Succession of States in Respect of Bilateral Treaties, Second and Third Studies Prepared by the Secretariat*, U.N. Doc. A/CN.4/243, in [1971] 2 Y.B. Int'l L. Comm'n 140-141, available at, http://legal.un.org/ilc/documentation/english/a_cn4_243.pdf. For a sample of agreements Singapore indicated her formal acceptance retrospectively, *see* Chao, *supra* note 28, at 200. They include the following: (i) International Convention to Facilitate the Importation of Commercial Samples and Advertising Materials, 1952 (ii) Convention for the Suppression of Traffic in Women and Children, 1921 (iii) International Agreement for the Suppression of the White Slave Traffic, 1904 and 1949 (iv) Convention concerning Customs Facilities for Touring, 1954.

Treaty Ratification and Implementation

The Constitution of the Republic of Singapore is deemed the supreme law of the land.[37] Similar to other states that operate under a Westminster-style constitution, there is no strict separation of powers between the legislative and executive branches of government, even though the judiciary is independent.[38] However, on matters relating to the sovereign's treaty-making powers with foreign nations, the Constitution is silent. There is no provision in the Constitution delineating the inter-relationship between international law and its domestic order. Nor is there domestic law which expressly defines the practices and procedures of treaty ratification and implementation. There is no formal provision in the Constitution governing the reception of international law or establishing the hierarchical ordering of international and domestic law. The text does not specify which branch of government is involved in the process of treaty-making.[39]

Following British practice, powers to manage foreign affairs and international relations in Singapore are primarily vested in the executive government.[40] Singapore follows the dualist system where international law and domestic law are distinct entities and systems of law; treaties are not self-executing.[41] As such, treaties and international conventions have no domestic legal effect until subsequently incorporated by an Act of Parliament.[42]

The Constitution is similarly silent as to the role played by Parliament in Singapore's treaty-making process. There is no provision requiring the consent of Parliament before an international convention can be ratified. Article 38 of the Constitution of Singapore stipulates that Parliament possesses the law-making power in Singapore.[43] Treaties concluded by the Executive branch have no legal effect until they are incorporated as domestic municipal law by a subsequent Act of Parliament.[44] For international conventions which expressly

---

37 Const. of the Republic of Sing. (1965), art. IV. [hereinafter Sing. Const.]

38 Kevin Y.L. Tan, Constitutional Law in Singapore 31 (2011).

39 Li-ann Thio, *Reception and Resistance: Globalisation, International Law and the Singapore Constitution*, 4 Nat'l Taiwan U. Law Rev. 335, 349 (2010).

40 Id.

41 Tan, *supra* note 38, at 43.

42 Id., at 44.

43 Sing. Const., *supra* note 37, at art. XXXVIII.

44 Simon S.C. Tay, *The Singapore Legal System and International Law: Influence or Interference*, *in* The Singapore Legal System 473 (Kevin Y.L. Tan, ed. 1999). Tay further explains "However, international treaties cannot be incorporated into national law without corresponding national laws. This normally requires the concurrence of the legislature to the

require implementation by way of domestic statute, only Parliament is empowered to translate the required treaty obligations into enforceable legal rights and obligations in the form of national legislation through the legislative process. Parliament can also engage in debates of questions relating to international law, including international treaties to which the Executive wishes to negotiate or accede.[45]

There are two ways that a treaty can be implemented in Singapore: (i) Incorporation by specific legislation and regulations through the legislative process and (ii) Enactment of subsidiary legislation and administrative policies by the executive under general legislation.[46] For example, the Hazardous Wastes (Import, Export and Transit) Act[47] was enacted pursuant to Singapore's accession to the Basel Convention on the Control of Hazardous Wastes and Their Disposal.[48] The Act established a framework for national implementation of international obligations toward compliance with requirements regulating trade of hazardous wastes. The bill was debated and passed by Parliament after the third reading and published in the Gazette effective March 16th 1998.[49] In some cases treaty obligations are implemented through the use of subsidiary legislation and/or administrative policies with the mandate of the executive under general legislation, and do not go through the formal legislative process. For example, the implementation of the Ozone Treaties[50] was effected through enactment of direct subsidiary legislation and administrative

---

new laws. In this way, the primary role of the legislature in law-making is preserved." Id. at 473.

45 *Supra* note 37. "It is accepted that Parliament's consent is not required before the executive branch may bind Singapore by way of treaty. However, the Constitution does not say that Parliament cannot debate questions of international law, including such treaties which the executive branch wishes to negotiate and conclude." Lim Chin Leng, *Singapore And International Law, in* SINGAPORE ACADEMY OF LAW : AN OVERVIEW OF THE SINGAPORE LEGAL SYSTEM, http://www.singaporelaw.sg/content/IntLaw.html (last visited 5/25/2013).

46 Tay, *supra* note 44, at 476.

47 The Hazardous Waste (Control of Export, Import and Transit) Act (1997), No. 13 of 1997 (Sing.).

48 Basel Convention on the Control of Transboundary Movements of Hazardous Wastes and Their Disposal, Mar 22, 1989, 1673 U.N.T.S.126; 28 ILM 657 (1989).

49 Tay, *supra* note 44, at 475.

50 "The 'Ozone Treaties' are a series of environmental agreements that control the international trade and use of substances that deplete the protective ozone layer in the atmosphere. These agreements are the 1985 Vienna Convention; the 1987 Montreal Protocol; and a series of amendments made in London, Copenhagen, and Vienna, to vary and largely to strengthen the regime of obligations." Tay, *supra* note 44, at 477.

regulations regulating and providing aid to industries pursuant to the general legislative powers under the Control of Imports and Exports Act.[51]

Treaties acceded to and ratified by the executive are published in the Singapore Government Gazette Treaties Supplement.

Evidence of State Practice

Powers of administering foreign and international affairs in Singapore are primarily vested in the executive government.[52] Within the Singapore Government, the International Affairs Division of the Attorney General Chambers provides legal advice on all aspects of international law to its subsidiary agencies.[53] It represents Singapore at bilateral or multilateral negotiations, particularly in trade related matters and transnational crimes.[54] It is also involved in the drafting and negotiating of international instruments, as well as the domestic implementation of Singapore's international obligations.[55] When an international convention entails responsibilities that fall under the purview of multiple government ministries or agencies, an Inter-Ministerial Committee is established, as in the case of the Inter-Ministerial Task Force on Anti-Terrorism formed by the Attorney General in conjunction with the Minister for Foreign Affairs subsequent to the terrorist attacks on September 11th 2001.[56]

Singapore will accede to an international convention after systematic review by its Executive Branch and only when the latter deems it in its national interest to do so and when it is fully satisfied that it can give effect to and comply with the provisions of the international conventions.[57] It was noted that there is an operating

---

51 Control of Imports and Exports Act, ch.56 (repealed by Act No. 24 of 1995, Dec. 1, 1995) (Sing.). *See also* Tay, *supra* note 44, at 476–478.

52 Tan, *supra* note 38, at 43.

53 Overview of International Affairs Division (IAD), Attorney General's Chambers, *available at* http://app.agc.gov.sg/What_We_Do/International_Affairs_Division/Overview_of_International_Affairs_Division.aspx.

54 Id.

55 Id.

56 Report to the Counter-Terrorism Committee on Singapore's Implementation of United Nations Security Council Resolution 1373 (2001), *available at* http://www.mfa.gov.sg/content/mfa/overseasmission/newyork/index_report.html.

57 "Such international conventions and treaties are periodically reviewed by the Ministry of Foreign Affairs and other Government Ministries and Agencies. As the Member may know, Singapore became a party to the Convention on the Elimination of Discrimination against Women as well as the Convention on the Rights of the Child in October 1995.

presumption that before Singapore accedes to an international convention, its domestic legal framework is assessed to be sufficient to enable it to perform its international obligations.[58] Singapore acceded to the Basel Convention in 1996,[59] discussed earlier, some four years after the Convention entered into force, preceded by most of its other South East Asian neighboring countries.[60] Prior to Singapore's accession, Singapore established its domestic legal framework for regulating hazardous waste by enacting the Environmental Public Health (Toxic Industrial Waste) Regulations under the Environmental Public Health Act.[61]

Singapore has not frequently exercised its rights for reservations and declarations in its international law practice except in the State's accession to human rights treaties.[62] Singapore acceded to three human rights treaties in 1995: (i) the Convention on the Prevention and Punishment of the Crime of Genocide;[63] (ii) the Convention on the Elimination of All Forms of Discrimination against Women (CEDAW);[64] and (iii) the Convention on the Rights of the Child.[65] In Singapore's accession to CEDAW, two reservations were appended to Article 2 (relating to the methods of ending discrimination) and Article 16 (relating to discrimination in marriage and family matters) respectively.[66] No specific enabling legislation has been passed to provide for protection of child rights or gender equality.[67] Singapore acceded to the Convention against Genocide in 1995 but it was the 2007 Amendment of the Penal Code which provides for

---

Whether we will accede to any other international convention will depend on careful examination of our policies, laws and legal procedures... We take our international obligations seriously and accede to international treaties only when it is in our interest to do and when we are fully satisfied that we can give effect to its provisions." *Comments of Minister of Law, Professor S Jayakumar to a question posed by Mr Simon Tay on Accession to Human Rights Treaties in Written Answers to Question for Oral Answer Not Answered by 1:30 pm*, SINGAPORE PARLIAMENTARY REPORTS (HANSARD), PARLIAMENTARY DEBATES, Parliament No. 9, Session No. 1, Volume No. 69, Sitting No. 3, Sitting Date: 30 June 1998 (LawNet).

58 Thio, *supra* note 39, at 350.

59 *Supra* note 48.

60 Tay, *supra* note 44, at 475–476.

61 Id. at 476.

62 Id. at 479.

63 Convention On The Prevention And Punishment Of The Crime Of Genocide, Dec. 9, 1948, 78 U.N.T.S. 277.

64 Convention on the Elimination of All Forms of Discrimination Against Women, Dec. 18, 1979, 1249 U.N.T.S. 20378 (entered into force Sept. 3, 1981).

65 United Nations Convention on the Rights of the Child, G.A. Res. 44/25, U.N. GAOR, art. 5, Nov. 20, 1989.

66 Thio, *supra* note 39, at 353.

67 Thio, *supra* note 39, at 352.

the prosecution of the crime of genocide.[68] When Singapore ratified the Convention of the Rights of the Child, it stated that this did not imply providing for rights "going beyond the limits"[69] prescribed by the Constitution since the domestic laws of Singapore provided "adequate protection and fundamental rights...in the best interest of the child."[70] In the field of human rights, Singapore's treaty practice evidenced a preference for a soft gradualist approach with issuance of guidelines rather than specific enabling legislation to implementing full treaty obligations.[71]

Under the Constitution, the Singaporean courts are empowered to decide the constitutionality of domestic statutes including the power to interpret and review treaty provisions which have been incorporated into municipal law.[72] The courts have been deferential to the parliamentary executive when it comes to politically sensitive foreign affairs.[73] Ruling on the case of *Civil Aeronautics Administration v. Singapore Airlines Ltd,*[74] the court refused to challenge the position of the executive that Taiwan was not a state and thus could not claim sovereign immunity against civil proceedings. Courts should not "get involved in international relations or reach a conclusion inconsistent with that of the executive."[75]

International law has been considered in ascertaining the scope of legislative power in Public Prosecutor v. Taw Cheng Kong.[76] While the Court of Appeals rejected the notion of an "automatic" application of a rule of customary International law in Singapore, it provided some support for the position

68 Penal Code (Cap 224, 2008 Rev. ed.) ss 130D and 130E (Sing.). *See* Li-ann Thio, *Singapore Human Rights Practice and Legal Policy: Of Pragmatism and principle, Rights, Rhetoric and Realism,* 21 Sing. Acad. L. J. 326, 345 (2009). *See also* Second Reading Speech, Senior Minister of State Ho Peng Kee, Penal Code (Amendment) Bill, Oct. 22, 2007, *available at* http://www.mha.gov.sg/news_details.aspx?nid=MTEzMQ%3D%3D-Fjrp1hVtn40%3D.

69 Para. 3, Instrument of Accession, Oct. 2, 1995. *See also* Thio, *supra* note 39, at 352.

70 Thio, *supra* note 39 at 352.

71 Id. at 351–352. "Particularly in the field of human rights law, the Singapore government has not seen fit to adopt specific enabling legislation, though, reflective of a gradualist approach, amendments to existing laws may and have been made subsequent to accession." Thio, *supra* note 39, at 348.

72 Sing. Const. art. 38. "This executive prerogative to enter into treaties has never been challenged either in Parliament or in the courts of law. However, since treaties and other international obligations are not self-executing, Parliament must legislate to incorporate the treaty obligations and rights into Singapore law since it is only Parliament that has legislative competence." Tan, *supra* note 38, at 44.

73 Thio, *supra* note 39, at 359.

74 Civil Aeronautics Administration v Singapore Airlines Ltd, [2004] 1 S.L.R.(R)) 570; [2004] SGCA 3 (LawNet).

75 Thio, *supra* note 39, at 359.

76 Public Prosecutor v. Taw Cheng Kong, [1998] 2 S.L.R.(R) 489; [1998] SGCA 37 (LawNet).

that the courts will consider those "rules and principles of international law that have been previously received into common law" in construing parliamentary intent in statutory interpretation.[77] The Court recognized an international customary law rule received into the common-law, that is, the presumption against extra-territoriality, and indicated to Parliament its intent to uphold that rule for the purposes of construing a statutory provision.

Annotated Bibliography of Sources

General Treaty Collections

1 SINGAPORE GOVERNMENT GAZETTE. TREATIES SUPPLEMENT
(Singapore: Printed by Government Printing. 1959–).

Summary: The Treaties Supplement, published weekly, contains full-texts of each international convention acceded to by the Singapore executive in separate volumes. In English only.

Note: Continues Colony of Singapore Government Gazette, 1946–59.

2 INTERNATIONAL AGREEMENTS, CONVENTIONS TO WHICH SINGAPORE IS A PARTY
(Singapore: International Organizations' Section, Directorate III, Policy, Planning and Analysis Division, Ministry of Foreign Affairs).

Summary: Compilations with treaties as of June 20th 1982, as of June 1st, 1986, and as of March 2nd 1987 are held in Singapore-Malaysian Collection in C.J. Koh Law Library, National University of Singapore. The compilation is selectively held in U.S. libraries.

Note: The frequency of the compilation cannot be determined.

3 JOINT COMMUNIQUES, MINISTERIAL STATEMENTS AND INTERNATIONAL CONVENTIONS THAT SINGAPORE IS STATE PARTY TO 1995
(Singapore: Public Affairs Directorate, Ministry of Foreign Affairs, Singapore).

Summary: Held by the C.J. Koh Law Library, National University of Singapore.

Index: Yes.

4 SINGAPORE E-GAZETTE
URL: http://www.egazette.com.sg/Welcome.aspx.

---

77 C.L. Lim, "Public International Law Before The Singapore And Malaysian Courts," 8 SING. Y.B. INT'L. L. 243, 253 (2004).

Summary: Electronic version of the Government Gazette. It includes treaty supplements alongside supplements for Bills, Acts, Trademarks, Subsidiary Legislation, Industrial Relations Agreements, and Miscellaneous Information.

Note: Previous 5 days free; archives by subscription.

5 LAWNET TREATIES COLLECTION

URL: http://www.lawnet.com.sg/lnrweb/c/portal/layout?p_l_id=1.

Summary: LawNet originated from the Singapore Statutes Database at the Attorney-General's Chambers and evolved into a Singapore legal research portal. The Legal Workbench module consists of legislation, case law, reference materials, parliamentary reports and treaties. The Singapore Treaties Database contains records of treaties to which Singapore is a party, including exchange of letters, memoranda of understanding, and other agreements regarded as treaties under international law. Key treaties are available in full-text.

6 NATIONAL UNIVERSITY OF SINGAPORE CENTRE FOR INTERNATIONAL LAW CIL TREATY STATUS DATABASE

URL: http://cil.nus.edu.sg/treaty-status-database/.

Summary: The CIL Treaty Status Database is currently in its beta stage. The information is derived from ASEAN's Table of ASEAN Treaties/Agreements and Ratifications (updated as of June 2012).

7 NATIONAL UNIVERSITY OF SINGAPORE CENTRE FOR INTERNATIONAL LAW (CIL) DATABASE OF ASEAN AND INTERNATIONAL LAW DOCUMENTS

URL: http://cil.nus.edu.sg/2009/cil-documents-database/.

Summary: The CIL Documents Database consists of selective ASEAN and International Law Documents. It also includes over 130 selected Southeast Asian Investment documents, including Southeast Asian Investment Treaties and Southeast Asian Arbitration cases. It is intended as a replacement for the official comprehensive ASEAN documents archive maintained by the ASEAN Secretariat. Documents can be searched by subject categories, year and keywords.

8 ASEAN DOCUMENTS AND ARCHIVES

URL: http://www.asean.org/resources/document-archives.

Summary: Includes Table of ASEAN Treaties/Agreements and Ratification from ASEAN Documents Series with full text of the treaties.

Note: The ASEAN website also includes papers, speeches and other diplomatic correspondences relating to the various ASEAN Agreements.

9 SINGAPORE TAX TREATIES/INLAND REVENUE AUTHORITY OF SINGAPORE
URL: http://iras.gov.sg/irasHome/page.aspx?id=812.

Summary: Avoidance of Double Taxation Agreements concluded by Singapore since 1965 are available in full text. It also includes Exchange of Information Arrangements ("EOI Arrangements") for the exchange of information for tax purposes.

10 FTA NETWORK/MINISTRY OF TRADE AND INDUSTRY
URL: http://www.fta.gov.sg/.

Summary: Full texts of Free Trade Agreements (FTAs) concluded between Singapore and other countries.

Note: The portal enables searching agreements which are in force, concluded/signed, undergoing negotiations and pending conclusion.

Diplomatic Documents

11 MALAYSIA AGREEMENT: EXCHANGE OF LETTERS PRESENTED TO THE LEGISLATIVE ASSEMBLY BY THE PRIME MINISTER, ORDERED BY THE ASSEMBLY TO LIE UPON THE TABLE: 26TH JULY, 1963
(Singapore: Government Printing Office, 1963) [28] p.

Series Title: Misc./Singapore Legislative Assembly; Misc. 5 of 1963.

Note: Miscellaneous reports.

12 MALAYSIA AND SINGAPORE IN INTERNATIONAL DIPLOMACY: DOCUMENTS AND COMMENTARIES
P.J. Boyce. (Sydney: Sydney University Press; University Park, Pennsylvania State University Press; New Zealand, Price Milburn; London, Methuen, 1968).

13 PUBLIC INTERNATIONAL LAW CASES FROM MALAYSIA AND SINGAPORE
S. Jayakumar. (Singapore: Singapore University Press, 1974).

14 SINGAPORE AND INTERNATIONAL LAW: THE EARLY YEARS: ESSAYS IN MEMORY OF S. TIWARI
Kevin Tan. (Singapore: Centre for International Law, National University of Singapore, 2011).

15 DEBATES: OFFICIAL REPORT/LEGISLATIVE ASSEMBLY
(SINGAPORE: PARLIAMENT, 1965–).

Summary: Also available in microform and online in LawNet. Verbatim records of the debates and written answers to questions in the Parliament of Singapore are similar in format to the British Hansard. All speeches appear in English, regardless of the language in which they were delivered.

Index: In addition to the index in each volume, there are cumulative indexes for Vols. 1–23 and Vols. 24–41. Index to microform set is entitled: Index to official debates and written answers to questions. 1965–.

Note: Alternate title is "Parliamentary Debates. Singapore. Official Report."

Note: Few copies of the debates are available for public distribution since print runs are small.

16 ASEAN DOCUMENTS SERIES
(Jakarta: ASEAN Secretariat, [1967]–).

Summary: Print versions of ASEAN Documents and Archives at ASEAN official website. Compilation of agreements, communiques, press releases and declarations of ASEAN.

Note: Alternate title is "ASEAN Regional Forum documents series."

Yearbooks and Digests of State Practice

17 SINGAPORE YEAR BOOK OF INTERNATIONAL LAW
(Singapore: Faculty of Law, National University of Singapore, [1997]–).

Summary: Contains scholarly articles and special reports/sections on Singapore's state practice in international law and at times state practice of neighboring countries in South East Asia.

Note: In 1977, Malaya Law Review commenced a regular section with the aim of recording Singapore's growing state practice in international law. A South-East Asian section was subsequently included with a focus on South-East Asian practice. It was renamed the Singapore Journal of Legal Studies in 1991.

Note: In 1997, the Singapore Journal of International & Comparative Law started publication with a focus on international law articles and regular sections on international law state practice.

Beginning with Volume 8 of 2004, the Singapore Year Book of International Law succeeded the Singapore Journal of International and Comparative Law. Intermittent issues contain special reports entitled "Public International Law before the Singapore and Malaysian Courts" reviewing significant decisions on public international law rendered by the Singapore Courts. The final issue of the Singapore Year Book published was Volume 12 of 2008.

Note: From 2010, the Asian Journal of International Law succeeds the Singapore Year Book.

18 ASIAN JOURNAL OF INTERNATIONAL LAW
(Cambridge: Cambridge University Press, 2011–).

Summary: The Asian Journal of International Law (AsianJIL) publishes peer-reviewed scholarly articles and book reviews on public and private international law. It is an official publication of the Asian Society of International Law produced by the National University of Singapore Faculty of Law.

Note: The journal succeeds the Singapore Year Book of International Law.

19 ASIAN YEARBOOK OF INTERNATIONAL LAW
Foundation for the Development of International Law in Asia. (Dordrecht; Boston: Martinus Nijhoff,1993–).

Summary: Consists of scholarly articles on Asian countries' engagement with public international law and regular sections entitled "State Practice of Asian countries in the field of International Law" and "Participation in Multilateral Treaties."

Note: Volumes 1–12 (1992–2006) was published by Brill/Nijhoff. Volumes 13 (2007) – are published by Routledge. The latest issue published is Volume 15 (2009). It is the flagship publication of the Foundation for the Development of International Law in Asia (DILA).

20 ASIA-PACIFIC CONSTITUTIONAL YEARBOOK
(Melbourne, Australia: University of Melbourne Law School, Centre for Comparative Constitutional Studies. 1995–1999).

Summary: Annual reviews of constitutional developments in Asian countries including Singapore and major decisions with constitutional significance, some of which are related to public international law.

21 SINGAPORE'S NATIONAL REPORT FOR THE 1992 UN CONFERENCE ON ENVIRONMENT AND DEVELOPMENT PREPARATORY COMMITTEE
(Singapore: Inter-Ministry Committee for the UNCED Preparatory Committee. 1991). 70 p.

Summary: The report outlines the policy measures that Singapore has adopted in ensuring a balance between development and environment. Its 11 chapters cover topics on environmental problem areas of Singapore; past and present capacity building initiatives; recommendations and priorities on environment and development; environmentally sound technologies; international expectations; and expectations from UNCED.

Republic of South Africa

Ralph F. Gaebler

Issues of Treaty Succession

The Union of South Africa achieved Dominion status within the British Empire in 1910, under a Constitution unifying the Cape of Good Hope, Natal, the Orange Free State and Transvaal.[1] South Africa acquired a legislature under this Constitution, and therefore a measure of self-government. However, the conduct of foreign relations and the negotiation, conclusion and ratification of treaties applicable to the territory of South Africa remained in the hands of the British government.[2]

Together with the other five Dominions, South Africa obtained the formal status of a sovereign state with independent, international legal personality at some point before the adoption of the Balfour Declaration of 1926.[3] Milestones along the way included independent membership in the League of Nations in 1919,[4] and recognition in the Resolution of the Imperial Conference of 1923 that the South African government could not be committed to the acceptance of active obligations except with the definite assent of its own government. In more positive terms, the government was recognized as possessing the authority both to appoint representatives with full powers to negotiate bilateral and multilateral treaties on its behalf and to ratify the results.[5] In theory, the only limitation on this power arose from the fact that South Africa shared the same

1 South Africa Act, 1909, 9 Edw. 8, c 9 (Eng.).

2 The international status of the Dominions at this time is discussed in M.M. Lewis, *The International Status of the British Self-governing Dominions*, 3 BRIT. Y.B. INT'L L. 21 (1922–23). Dominion status between the wars is summarized in Sir Robert Jennings and Sir Arthur Watts, *Oppenheim's International Law*, vol. 1, *Peace*, 9th ed., pp. 256–60 (Harlow: Longmans, 1992).

3 *Report of the Inter-Imperial Relations Committee of the Imperial Conference*, 1926. Cmd. 2768, reprinted in 21 AM. J. IN'TL L. SUPP. 21–38 (1927). The Conference was attended by representatives of Great Britain, Canada, Newfoundland, Australia, New Zealand, India, Irish Free State and South Africa.

4 The legal significance of membership in the League of Nations is discussed in M. Friedlander, *The Admission of States to the League of Nations*, 9 BRIT. Y.B. INT'L L. 84 (1928).

5 Jan Smuts, one of the South African delegates to the Paris Conference, played a particularly significant role in the drafting of the Covenant of the League of Nations. Many of its provisions were based upon his pamphlet, *The League of Nations: A Practical Suggestion* (1918). *See* F.P. WALTERS, 1 A HISTORY OF THE LEAGUE OF NATIONS 27–30 (1952). Smuts' own summary

 | DOI 10.1163/9789004272224_029

head of state with Great Britain and the other Dominions. As a result of this unity, it was not possible to engage in treaty relations with other members of the Empire.[6] In fact, despite formal recognition of South Africa's independence, the Balfour Declaration "frankly recognized" that in the spheres of foreign relations and defense, "the major share of responsibility rests now, and must for some time continue to rest, with His Majesty's Government in Great Britain."

Despite the external independence recognized formally in the Balfour Declaration, internal independence of the Dominions was still circumscribed by the Colonial Validity Act, which barred colonial legislatures from passing legislation repugnant to Acts of Parliament or other forms of legislation applicable to the colonies.[7] Internal independence and equal status of the Dominions with Great Britain were granted by the Statute of Westminster, 1931,[8] which repealed the Colonial Laws Validity Act for Canada, South Africa, and Eire. From this time onward, the Union of South Africa enjoyed both internal and external sovereignty.

Prior to the emergence of the Union of South Africa as an independent state, The Cape of Good Hope and Natal remained dependencies of the British crown, both as independent colonies and as members of the Union. However, the other two eventual members of the Union, the Orange Free State and Transvaal, had enjoyed extensive periods of independence prior to the Boer War of 1899–1902. The British crown abandoned claims to the

---

of his pamphlet is reprinted in THE LEAGUE OF NATIONS AND THE NEW INTERNATIONAL LAW 61–65 (1921). The Dominions were full members of the League Assembly, they served on the League Council, and South Africa was appointed mandatory over South West Africa. Moreover, South Africa was appointed directly by the League Secretariat rather than through the British imperial government.

6 Balfour Declaration (reprinted in 21 AM. J. INT'L L. SUPP. 31 (1927)) According to D.P. O'Connell, this *inter se* doctrine was nothing more than a rule of treaty construction, and proved ephemeral in any case. D.P. O'CONNELL, 1 STATE SUCCESSION IN MUNICIPAL LAW AND INTERNATIONAL LAW 47 (1967).

7 28 & 29 Vict., c. 63, 1865. Limitations imposed by the Colonial Laws Validity Act were reinforced by the customary bar on colonial enactment of laws with extra-territorial application.

8 22 Geo. 5, c. 4. The Statute of Westminster took effect in Australia, New Zealand, and Newfoundland only upon adoption of their respective legislatures. Section 2 of the statute granted the power to adopt legislation repugnant to acts of Parliament, empowered Dominion legislatures to repeal imperial legislation, and provided that no British act of Parliament could be extended to a Dominion without its consent. Section 3 of the statute repealed the limitation on adoption of legislation with extra-territorial application.

Orange River Territory in 1854. This was confirmed by the Bloemfontein Convention, which guaranteed the territory henceforth a "free and independent government."[9] Shortly thereafter, the Orange Free State adopted a Constitution. It is thus beyond dispute that the Orange Free State was a fully independent and sovereign state up to the time of the Boer War, and "[t]hat it had concluded [t]reaties with foreign [p]owers on an equal footing and without any interference or intervention on the part of the British Government."[10] As a result of the support given by the Orange Free State to Transvaal in the Boer war, Great Britain annexed it in 1900, and renamed it the Orange River Colony. This annexation was ratified in international law by the 1902 Treaty of Vereeniging.

The area north of the Vaal River also existed for some time as an independent state. Independence was obtained by the Transvaal in the Sand River Convention of 1852. However, economic and political instability led the British to declare the area once again a British colony in 1877. In response to Boer unrest, the Convention of Pretoria (1881) granted "complete self-government subject to the suzerainty of Her Majesty." Self-government was purely of an internal nature, since British control of Transvaal's foreign affairs and treaty-making power were guaranteed by Article 2 of the Convention. The Pretoria Convention was superseded by the London Convention (1884), which expunged the term "suzerainty," but preserved British control of treaty-making power for the area comprising Transvaal. Thus, at the outbreak of the Boer War in 1899, Transvaal was a self-governing colony, rather than an independent state.[11] During the war (1900) the British annexed Transvaal, as it did the Orange Free State, and this annexation was confirmed by the Treaty of Vereeniging in 1902.

Issues of treaty succession arise in relation to treaties concluded by the Orange Free State between 1854 and 1900, as well as to those concluded by the

---

9 The Bloemfontein Convention is cited and discussed in JACQUELINE A. KALLEY, SOUTH AFRICA'S TREATIES IN THEORY AND PRACTICE, 1806–1998 29–43 (2001). The historical background is also discussed in JOHN DUGARD, INTERNATIONAL LAW: A SOUTH AFRICAN PERSPECTIVE 14–23 (1994).

10 Report of the Law Officers to the Colonial Office, 5 February 1900, reprinted in A.D. MCNAIR, THE LAW OF TREATIES 706–710 (1961).

11 Some contemporary and later commentators argued that the Pretoria Convention and London Convention did not fully strip Transvaal of its sovereignty, but left it a "semi-sovereign" state. Until it annexed Transvaal and the Orange Free State in 1900, Great Britain regarded itself as being at war with sovereign foreign states. *See* DUGARD, *supra* note 9, at 15–16 and especially footnote 13.

South African Republic (Transvaal) between 1852 and 1881.[12] Great Britain adhered at the time to the clean slate theory of treaty succession. Thus, in response to inquiries from the Belgian and Italian governments, Lord Lansdowne replied that treaties of commerce and extradition concluded by the formerly independent states were no longer in effect, but that these colonies were now bound by British treaties on the same subjects.[13] In 1901 the Law Officers of the Foreign Office issued an advisory opinion that even a commercial treaty concluded by Transvaal with Portugal, during the period in which Transvaal was a self-governing colony, was no longer in effect, despite the fact that it was concluded under the terms of the London Convention.[14]

Several other treaty succession issues remain. When the Union of South Africa was created in 1910 from the four previously independent colonies, Section 148(1) of the South Africa Act carried over their separate treaty obligations to the Union. The language of the statute makes plain that it applied to all conventions concluded by the formerly independent colonies, those of a political nature as well as treaties of commerce, extradition, etc. However, it is ambiguous as to whether those treaties were to extend in application to the entire territory of the Union, or merely to the territory comprising what was the relevant former colony.[15]

In 1961 South Africa became a republic.[16] This admittedly important change in government had no effect on South Africa's juristic personality in international law.[17] Nevertheless, Section 112 of the Republic of South Africa Act reconfirmed that pre-Union treaties incorporated in the Union at its creation, and still in force immediately prior to enactment of the present statute, continued to be in force for the Republic. On the same principle, Section 112 confirmed that in-force treaties concluded by the Union prior to 1961 continued to be in force for the Republic.

Drastic political change occurred once again when South Africa jettisoned apartheid and broadened its democracy. Under Section 231(1) of the Republic

---

12 The treaty activities of both the Orange Free State and the South African Republic (Transvaal) are discussed in detail in KALLEY, *supra* note 9, at 29–61.

13 *See* O'CONNELL, *supra* note 6, at 35–36.

14 Opinion of 16 February 1901, Foreign Office Confidential Papers (7763), no. 30. Cited in O'CONNELL, *supra* note 6, at 35.

15 According to JENNINGS AND WATTS, *supra* note 2, the current practice is to exclude survival of political treaties in cases of state succession by merger, to accept the survival of non-political treaties, but possibly to limit their application to the territory of the formerly independent component of the newly merged state. See p. 212.

16 Republic of South Africa Act 32 of 1961.

17 This general principle is summarized by JENNINGS AND WATTS, *supra* note 2, at 1253.

of South Africa Constitution Act of 1993, all in-force treaties continued in force, subject to repudiation by act of Parliament.[18] The final constitution provides under Section 231(5) that "the Republic is bound by international agreements which were binding on the Republic when this Constitution took effect."[19]

Treaty Ratification and Implementation

The treaty-making process is governed by Section 231 of the Constitution of 1996, which refers to treaties as "international agreements." Under Section 231(1), the power to negotiate and sign international agreements rests with the national executive. However, Section 231(2) requires that Parliament approve international agreements. Parliamentary approval is expressed in a resolution adopted by both chambers of Parliament, namely the National Assembly and the National Council of Provinces. This represents a departure from the law prior to adoption of the interim constitution in 1993. Before that time, treaty-making was exclusively an executive function.

Section 231(3) establishes two classes of agreements for which Parliamentary approval is not required. The first class includes agreements "of a technical, administrative, or executive nature[.]" According to the *Manual on Executive Acts of the President of the Republic of South Africa*, this phrase does not refer to three distinct types of agreement, but in general to department-specific

---

18 Constitution of the Republic of South Africa Act 200 of 1993. The text is freely available at http://www.info.gov.za/documents/constitution/93cons.htm. It is also available in HeinOnline's World Constitutions Illustrated. Provision for unilateral termination by act of Parliament was criticized as contrary to Articles 54 and 56 of the 1969 Vienna Convention on the Law of Treaties. *See generally* MATTHEW CHASKALSON ET AL., CONSTITUTIONAL LAW OF SOUTH AFRICA (1996 –), Section 13.2(f) and sources cited therein.

19 Constitution of the Republic of South Africa Act 108 of 1996. The text of the 1996 constitution, as amended, is freely available at http://www.info.gov.za/documents/constitution/1996/index.htm . It is also available in HeinOnline's World Constitutions Illustrated and in Oceana's Constitutions of the Countries of the World. However, neither of the commercial databases includes the latest amendment. According to one commentator, this provision requires determination of whether pre-1993 treaties, and treaties concluded under the Interim Constitution, were binding "in terms of the then-operative dispensation[.]" It they were, they remain so under the 1996 Constitution, subject to termination. See Botha Neville, *National Treaty Law and Practice: South Africa, in* NATIONAL TREATY LAW AND PRACTICE: CANADA, EGYPT, ISRAEL, MEXICO, RUSSIA, SOUTH AFRICA 215 (Washington Monroe Leigh et al. eds., 2003). *See also* id at 210 for a discussion of the uncertainties surrounding the termination procedure.

agreements, agreements without major political significance and agreements that have no financial consequences and do not affect municipal law.[20] The second class includes agreements that by their terms do not require ratification.[21] These classifications are disjunctive, not conjunctive. Thus, a technical treaty requiring ratification does not require Parliamentary approval. Parliamentary approval is required only for agreements that require ratification or accession (usually multilateral agreements) and that are not technical, administrative or executive. Agreements that do not require Parliamentary approval must nevertheless "be tabled in the Assembly and the Council within a reasonable time." Under current practice, the minister in whose jurisdiction the subject matter of a proposed agreement falls must determine whether or not the proposed agreement requires Parliamentary approval. This decision is made in consultation with the law advisors of the Departments of Justice and International Relations and Cooperation. Executive authority to conclude the agreement is granted either by Presidential Minute or by Cabinet Memorandum. The latter form of authorization is used if the subject matter of the proposed agreement is routine, or not department-specific.

Under Section 231(4), "[a]ny international agreement becomes law in the Republic when it is enacted into law by national legislation[.]" Thus, South Africa employs a dualist approach to the incorporation of international law into municipal law, in accordance with pre-1993 practice. During the period in which the interim constitution was in effect, former Section 231(3) stated that a treaty became law upon ratification, "provided Parliament expressly so provides." According to one commentator, this represented a move in the direction of the monist position.[22] However, it is debatable whether this formulation represented much of an inroad on the dualist position. Though it dispensed with the requirement of statutory incorporation, it did so only if Parliamentary intention to incorporate was otherwise expressly manifested in an admittedly more streamlined fashion. Former Section 231 did not contain separate provisions for non-ratification treaties or treaties of a technical, administrative or executive nature, i.e., treaties that currently fall under Section 231(3) and do

---

20 *See* Neville, *supra* note 19, at 200–207 for a discussion of section 231(2) and 231(3). The *Manual* is the primary source of current practice under section 231, but it has not been published for general dissemination.

21 South African case law has recognized the supplementary principle that ratification is not required "where an intention to dispense with ratification can be inferred from the nature of the treaty and the manner in which it was negotiated." *See* S v. Eliasov 1967 (4) SA 583 (A), cited in CHASKALSON ET AL., *supra* note 18, at section 13.2(c).

22 CHASKALSON ET AL., *supra* note18, at section Section 13.2(d).

not require Parliamentary approval. This no doubt explains the different, non-statutory procedure it set out for incorporation of treaty provisions that effected a change in municipal law.[23] The revival of an explicitly dualist approach to incorporation in the permanent constitution reinforces the conclusion that the interim constitution continued the dualist approach, albeit in less explicit terms.[24]

Current Section 231(4) does contain one exception to the dualist form of incorporation. A "self-executing provision of an agreement that has been approved by Parliament is law in the Republic unless it is inconsistent with the Constitution or an Act of Parliament." By its terms, this clause does not apply to Section 231(3) treaties, since they do not require Parliamentary approval. Therefore, it seems clear that any treaty containing self-executing provisions would necessarily fall within the ambit of Section 231(2). This inference is also supported by the *Manual of Executive Acts* directive that Section 231(3) applies to treaties that do not affect municipal law. As a final note of interest, it may be pointed out that Section 231(4) does not provide any definition of what it means for a treaty to be "self-executing," a question that must therefore be left to future South African case law to decide.

Publication of South African treaties was unsatisfactory until recently. In 2003 Neville conceded that "there is simply no general public access to the treaties to which the Republic is a party."[25] The *South African Treaty Series* was published until 1975, and sporadically thereafter until 1990, but no title dedicated to the publication of treaties ever took its place. Treaties that have been incorporated into South African law are typically printed in the Government Gazette (see no. 4, below), and commercially reproduced in *Juta's Statutes of South Africa* (see no. 5, below). But this represents only a small percentage of all treaties ratified. However, in 2012 the Treaty Section of the Office of the Chief State Law Advisor within the Department of International Relations and Cooperation began providing access to recent treaties in its online South African Treaty Register (see no. 1, below). This welcome development has greatly improved access to treaties.

---

23 According to Neville, *supra* note 19, at footnote 3, the rate of treaty-conclusion has risen dramatically since South Africa overcame its diplomatic isolation. Whereas the rate stood at 14 per year in the period immediately before the end of apartheid, it climbed to 70 per year in the decade of the 1990s, and now stands at approximately 90 per year.

24 *See generally* S. Woolman, M. Bishop, J. Brickhill, et al., Constitutional Law of South Africa 30–7 – 30–11 (2d ed. 2002–) (chapter by H. Strydon and K. Hopkins).

25 *See* Neville, *supra* note 19, at 212.

There is some confusion about publication of South African treaties in the *United Nations Treaty Series*. Although South Africa was a charter member of the United Nations, it registered treaties with the Secretariat pursuant to Article 102 of the Charter for only part of the period comprising the years of the apartheid regime. Neville states that South Africa was at some point "precluded" from doing so, but this is not correct.[26] As a UN member, South Africa

---

26 Id. at 211. It is true that South Africa was precluded from participation in the General Assembly beginning with the 29th session (1974). As it had on several previous occasions, the General Assembly rejected the credentials of the South African delegation on moral and political, though legally impermissible grounds. See Resolution 3206(XXIX), 30 September 1974. On 12 November 1974 the Assembly President, Mr. Bouteflika of Algeria, officially interpreted Resolution 3206 as refusal to allow the South African delegation to participate in the work of the 29th session, rather than as "merely a procedural method of expressing [the Assembly's] rejection of the policy of apartheid." See UN Doc. A/PV.2281, pp. 72–76. The actions of the General Assembly relative to South Africa at the 29th session are summarized in the 1974 UN Y.B. 106–18.

Mr. Bouteflika's ruling overturned the 1970 ruling by former Assembly President Hambro of Norway that rejection of credentials "cannot affect the rights and privileges of membership of South Africa." See Records of the 1901st meeting of the General Assembly, 11 November 1970. Mr. Hambro's decision is summarized in the 1970 UN Y.B. 145. Mr. Hambro was acting on the advice of United Nations Legal Counsel that even permissible rejection of credentials under Article 27 does not meet the requirements of Article 5 for suspension of the rights and privileges of membership by the General Assembly, that such suspension violates the Charter, and is therefore ultra vires. See 1970 UN Y.B. 144–45.

The South African delegation made several further attempts to participate in the activities of the General Assembly, both at the 33rd session (1979) and the 35th session (1981), when the question of South West Africa/Namibia came up for debate. In each case, the credentials of the South African delegation were rejected and South Africa was excluded from the General Assembly's debate. Thus, South Africa was effectively precluded from participation in the General Assembly for 20 years, from 1974 until 1994, when post-apartheid South Africa was welcomed back. *See* A/RES/48/258 (23 June 1994) and A/RES/50/83 (15 December 1995). However, South Africa never terminated its membership in the United Nations, and the Security Council explicitly declined to expel it from the Organization. *See* General Assembly Resolution 3207(XXIX) calling upon the Security Council to review the relationship between South Africa and the United Nations in light of its human rights record, and summary of the Security Council's rejection of a draft resolution to expel South Africa, in 1974 UN Y.B. 115–18. Thus, South Africa continued to have an obligation under Article 102 to register treaties as a member of the United Nations, and was not "precluded" from doing so. The entire history of South Africa's illegal exclusion from the General Assembly is summarized and analyzed in JAN C. HEUNIS, UNITED NATIONS VERSUS SOUTH AFRICA (1986). *See also* DUGARD, *supra* note 9, at 298.

was never relieved of its Article 102 obligation to register treaties, and in fact a fair amount of South African treaty activity continued to be reflected in the registry throughout the apartheid period.[27] Since 1994 South Africa has begun to register its apartheid-era treaties retrospectively.[28] But given the size of South Africa's treaty backlog, and the *United Nations Treaty Series*' notorious lack of timeliness in publication, it appears inevitable that that source will for the foreseeable future remain an incomplete source of South African treaties.

Annotated Bibliography of Sources

General Treaty Collections

1 SOUTH AFRICAN TREATY REGISTER

URL: http://www.dfa.gov.za/chiefstatelawadvicer/treatysection.html.

Summary: The Treaty Register is maintained by the Treaty Section of the Office of the Chief State Law Advisor in the Department of International Relations and Cooperation. According to the *Practical Guide and Procedures for the Conclusion of Agreements, 3rd ed.* (http://www.dfa.gov.za/chiefstatelawadvicer/documents/conclusionofagreements3rd.pdf), "the Treaty Section is the depositary of all international agreements and keeps custody of the South African Treaty Collection. There are approximately 2800 agreements deposited with the Treaty Section. The South African Treaty Register is the official record of all bilateral and multilateral agreements that the Republic of South Africa is a party to."

The Registry permits the user to search entries by country-party, date of signature, date of entry into force for South Africa, title keyword, and type (bilateral or multilateral). Entries also provide citation(s) to amending treaties. Entries are included for treaties going back to 1654, with PDF images of the treaties themselves available from 1995 onward.

There are several significant limitations to the Treaty Register. First, it only includes entries for treaties currently in force. Terminated treaties are not included. Second, there are no plans to add PDF images for pre-1995 treaties

27 South Africa ceased registering bilateral treaties in 1968, but its treaty activity continued to be recorded in several ways. First, there are many post-1968 South African bilateral treaties that were registered by the country of opposite party. Second, there were some 35 *ex officio* registrations from 1974–1994 of formalities by South Africa, i.e., signatures, accessions, and ratifications, with respect to multilateral conventions that were deposited with the Secretary General.

28 Neville, *supra* note 19, at 212. The South African Treaty Section is working forward from 1968 by year, and backward from the most recent agreements.

still in force. As a result, there is a period of time, from 1990–1994, for which treaties are completely unavailable, either electronically in the Treaty Register or in the printed Treaty Series (see no.3, below).

Note: The Treaty Section web site provides access to the *Practical Guide*, mentioned above, which includes a useful summary of the treaty ratification process.

2 DEPARTMENT OF INTERNATIONAL RELATIONS AND COOPERATION

URL is http://www.dfa.gov.za/.

Summary: The landing page of the Department of International Relations and Cooperation (formerly Department of Foreign Affairs) provides links to extensive information on South African foreign relations. Most important are summaries of bilateral relations, organized alphabetically by country (http://www.dfa.gov.za/foreign/bilateral/index.htm). For each there is a summary detailing the history of bilateral relations, as well as current developments. A similar set of summaries is provided for multilateral relations, organized by international organization and treaty, convention, and declaration (http://www.dfa.gov.za/foreign/Multilateral/inter/index.html). There are also Regional and Multilateral Summaries (http://www.dfa.gov.za/foreign/Multilateral/profiles/index.html), organized by topic, explaining the current position of the South African government on such topics as debt relief, participation in international peace missions, relations with the European Union, etc. Summaries provide a useful introduction to South African diplomatic activity since introduction of the new constitution in 1994.

Note: The Department web site links to several other sources of lesser interest. The *South Africa Yearbook*, 2001 – (http://www.gcis.gov.za/content/resource-centre/sa-info/yearbook), includes a chapter summarizing the activities of the Department of Foreign Affairs during the previous year. The Department's Annual Report (http://www.dfa.gov.za/department/report/index.htm), Strategic Plan (http://www.dfa.gov.za/department/strategic_plan_2012–2017/index.htm), various press releases (http://www.dfa.gov.za/docs/index.html), speeches (http://www.dfa.gov.za/docs/speeches/index.htm), and cabinet meeting statements (http://www.gcis.gov.za/content/newsroom/media-releases/cabinet-statements) also are available.

3 TREATY SERIES/VERDRAGREEKS

Republic of South Africa (Pretoria: Government Printer, 1931–1952, 1957–1975, 1986–1990).

Summary: This was the official source of publication of South African treaties before the advent of the South African Treaty Register (see no.1, above). It is organized by year and by numbered fascicule. The Treaty Series was suspended in 1975 due to budgetary constraints, then briefly revived in 1986 to publish retrospectively treaties concluded during the preceding 11 years. It was then suspended again in 1990. In English and Afrikaans. There are very limited holdings in libraries outside South Africa.

Note: Afrikaans title precedes English on some numbers.

Index: Indexed by Jacqueline A. Kalley, *South Africa by Treaty, 1806–1986: A Chronological and Subject Index* (Johannesburg: South African Institute of International Affairs, 1987, 513 pp.) This index supersedes earlier titles by Kalley, including *Index to the Union of South Africa Treaty Series, 1926–1960* (1978), *Index to the Republic of South Africa Treaty Series, 1961–1975* (1976), and *Index to the Republic of South Africa Treaty Series, 1961–1979* (1980). (See no.6, below.)

4 REPUBLIC OF SOUTH AFRICA GOVERNMENT GAZETTE
(Pretoria: state library, 1910–).

Summary: This title is the official source for statutes and regulations. According to the *Practical Guide and Procedures for the Conclusion of Agreements, 3rd ed.* (see no. 1, above), "[i]t is recommended, but not constitutionally prescribed that the texts of agreements ratified are [*sic*] published in the Government Gazette." Thus one cannot rely upon the *Gazette* for the text of most treaties in force for South Africa. However, the *Gazette* does include some treaties. Most important, it includes treaties attached as schedules to statutes incorporating them into South African municipal law. This represents only a small percentage of treaties. However, according to the Treaty Section, some additional types of treaties do now make their way into the Gazette as well, i.e., extradition treaties, treaties recognizing privileges or immunities, which are published together with a Minister's Note in compliance with the Diplomatic Immunities and Privileges Act 37 of 2001, and double taxation treaties, which must be published in compliance with the Customs and Excise Act 91 of 1964.

Note: The *Gazette* is published weekly, and also is available in microfiche.

Note: Title varies: *Union of South Africa Gazette*, 1910–1961. The *Gazette* is published also in Afrikaans as *Staatskoerant van die Republike van Suid-Afrika*.

Index: Indexed by *Juta's State Library Index to the Government Gazettes of South Africa*, which is available via the Internet, on CD-ROM or in print.

Note: Sabinet Online provides subscription-based access to the *Gazette* via the Internet. Electronic access to gazetted statutes since 1993 is also available electronically from the South African government web site, at http://www.info.gov.za/documents/acts/index.htm. This version reproduces pages from the Gazette in PDF format.

5 JUTA'S STATUTES OF SOUTH AFRICA

Rae Dalton, senior ed., Nadia Dhansay, ed. (Lansdowne: Juta, 1991–).

Summary: This is an annually re-published compilation of statutes currently in force. It contains a section entitled "International Law," which includes statutes incorporating treaties into South African municipal law. This title is also available by electronic subscription.

Index: Includes index volume. Also, each section has table of contents.

Note: Statutes are also available in *Butterworth's Statutes of South Africa*, a multivolume looseleaf publication. *Butterworth's* is available as a stand-alone electronic subscription, or via Lexis/Nexis.

Note: Neither Juta's nor Butterworth's provides citation to the *Government Gazette* (see no. 4, above). However, citation to the *Government Gazette* is provided by the statute database accessible at the South African government web site.

Treaty Indexes

6 SOUTH AFRICA'S TREATIES IN THEORY AND PRACTICE 1806–1998

Jacqueline A. Kalley (Lanham: Scarecrow Press, 2001). 859 pp.

Summary: Part 2 contains comprehensive chronological listings of treaties concluded by various states responsible for and affecting the territory of the current Republic of South Africa. Chapter 5 includes treaties of the British colonies, namely Cape Colony and Natal. Chapter 6 includes listings of treaties conclude by the Boer Republics, namely Orange Free State and the South African Republic (Transvaal). Chapter 7 includes treaties concluded on behalf of and by the Union of South Africa. Chapter 8 includes treaties concluded by the Republic of South Africa, 1961–1998. Each entry includes a treaty number (chapters are numbered separately), date signed (also separate date of South African signature, if applicable), date of entry into force, date of ratification, place of signature, title of treaty, reference to source of publication, information concerning subsequent amendment, extensions, addenda, etc., and current status. Part 2 also contains an alphabetical index to the treaties, with entries listed by country of opposite party as well as by subject.

Part 1 includes a useful introduction to the development of treaty-making powers in the various states and colonies, as well as a detailed summary of South Africa's treaty activities since 1910, organized by subject.

Note: Supersedes earlier editions, *Index to the Union of South Africa Treaty Series 1942–1960* (1978) and *Index to the Republic of South Africa Treaty Series 1961–1979* (1980). Both of these titles covered only treaties published in the *South African Treaty Series*. Also supersedes *South Africa By Treaty, 1806–1986,* except that this earlier title also indexes the homeland treaties of Transkei, Ciskei, Bophuthatswana, and Venda.

Diplomatic Documentation

7 SOUTH AFRICA DIGEST
Department of Information (Pretoria: Dagbreek (H. & G.) on behalf of the Government Printer, 1954–1988).

Summary: This is a biweekly summary of cultural and political events. Contents taken from newspapers and other popular media "representing diverse views" as well as supplied by publication staff. Issues typically include a section summarizing international events sponsored by or otherwise relevant to South Africa. To some extent a propaganda vehicle focused on ephemeral events, this title is nevertheless a useful record of contemporary views. Issues often contain statements relevant to South African views on international affairs during the apartheid regime, issued by the President of the Republic and other high-ranking officials, and presumably not available elsewhere. Not indexed; therefore, the researcher must already know the approximate dates of interest in order to use the *Digest* effectively.

Note: Title varies. Published under the title *Monthly Digest of South African Affairs*, 1954–1955; *Fortnightly Digest of South African Affairs*, 1955–1962; *South African Digest*, 1962–1988.

Note: Frequency varies. Monthly, 1954–1955; Biweekly 1955–1962; Weekly, 1962–1987; Biweekly, 1987–1988.

Yearbooks and Digests of State Practice

8 SOUTH AFRICAN YEARBOOK OF INTERNATIONAL LAW.
SUD-ARIKAANSE JAARBOEK VIR VOLKEREG VerLoren Van Themaat Centre for Public Law Studies.
University of South Africa (Pretoria: 1975–).

Summary: This title includes articles and shorter notes reviewing international legal issues in relation to South Africa. It also includes discussion of leading South African judicial decisions relevant to international law, as well as a synopsis of South African foreign relations activities, detailed outline of international events relevant to South Africa, and list of international agreements concluded. It no longer includes a summary of South African participation in international organizations, but lists URLs of relevant organizations where documentation can be located in electronic format. Similarly, in reliance upon electronic access to parliamentary debates, excerpts relevant to foreign relations are no longer reproduced as a documentary annex to section on South African foreign relations activities. Electronic access to these documents is available primarily at the web site of the Department of International Relations (see no. 2, above), or through the South African Government Online at http://www.gov.za/documents/index.html.

Note: Publisher varies. Vols. 1–15 (1975–1989/90) carry imprint, The VerLoren van Themaat Centre for International Law. University of South Africa.

Spain

Ryan Harrington

Issues of Treaty Succession

Spain's history can be divided into several distinct periods, but for the purposes of this chapter, Spain's legal system is derived from the integration of laws of kingdoms such as Castile and Aragon, which began in 1492.[1] Spain's first Constitution did not appear until 1812, and the first Spanish Civil Code was approved in 1889.[2] Because this period shaped the Spanish legal system, Spain does not have any issues of internal treaty succession. A complete history of Spain's legal system can best be read studying a title such as *Manual de Historia del Derecho Español*.[3]

Succession issues have arisen, however, with regard to Spain's adhesion to the European Union. The documents concerning Spain's accession to the European Communities specifically required Spain to be bound by all treaties and acts previously concluded by the Communities.[4] These treaties included the Treaty establishing the European Coal and Steel Community, the Treaty establishing the European Economic Community, and the Treaty establishing the European Atomic Energy Community.[5] By joining the European Union, Spain forfeited sovereignty over these matters, which jeopardized the supremacy of Spain's own Constitution.[6] Spain resolved the tension by passing the Law of Bases for Delegation to the Government for the Application of the Law of the European Community immediately thereafter.[7] This law incorporated the European Community's international law into Spanish domestic law.[8]

Treaty Ratification and Implementation

Spain is a parliamentary monarchy with a representative bicameral parliament known as the *Cortes Generales*. The *Cortes Generales* consists of the

1 Elena Merino-Blanco, Spanish Law and the Legal System 9 (2006).
2 Id. at 17–21.
3 Francisco Tomás y Valiente, Manual de Historia del Derecho Español (5th ed. 1992).
4 1985 O.J. (L 302) 23.
5 Id.
6 *See* Charlotte Villiers, The Spanish Legal Tradition 144 (1999).
7 B.O.E. n. 47, Dec. 27, 1985 (incorporating the European Community's international law into Spanish domestic law).
8 Id.

 | DOI 10.1163/9789004272224_030

Congress of Deputies and the Senate, and the Congress of Deputies is responsible for appointing the President.[9] In 1978, after an approval in referendum, the *Cortes Generales* approved the Spanish Constitution, which was then sanctioned by the King.[10]

The Constitution of 1978 contains provisions governing Spanish treaty-making process, which can be found in the section of Part III entitled "De Los Tratados Internacionales."[11] The section identifies three types of international treaties, and the requirements for ratification depend on the content of the treaty. There are treaties that confer some of the powers of the state onto an international organization; political treaties that may affect fundamental rights and liberties or create financial obligations on the state; and other types of treaties. The approval process for each type of treaty varies greatly, so it is important to determine at the outset the type of treaty being considered.

Article 93 governs the type of treaty that confers powers of the state onto an international organization. These treaties may not be signed without an organic act (*ley orgánica*) authorizing the signature.[12] Organic acts relate to the implementation of fundamental rights and public freedoms. They differ from ordinary laws in that they require an absolute majority of the Congress in a final vote on the act as a whole.[13] Instances when these types of laws are required are specified throughout the Constitution.

To take one example, Spain acceded to the European Union in 1986 after a prolonged process.[14] Because the European Union required Spain to transfer the exercise of certain state powers, accession invoked article 93. The *ley orgánica* that authorized Spain's accession to the EU can be found LO 10/1985 of August 2, authorizing the ratification of the Treaty of Accession to the European Communities, Lisbon and Madrid, June 12, 1985.[15] International

9 Under article 62, the King proposes the candidate elected by the Congress. This is more of a formality than a duty because the King does not appoint or elect the President.

10 Elena Merino-Blanco, Spanish Law and the Legal System 24 (2006). Note the sanctioning of Laws by the King is a formality and it is not an option. Under art. 91 the King has the obligation to sign the laws that shall be published.

11 Art. 93–96 C.E.

12 Information surrounding the process for a *ley orgánica* can be found in Article 81 of the Constitution.

13 Art. 81.2. More information surrounding the legislative process of organic acts, including timelines on votes between chambers and how the acts are introduced, can be found in Bittner, page 348–349.

14 *See* Charlotte Villiers, The Spanish Legal Tradition 141 (1999) (describing the political details surrounding accession to the European Union).

15 B.O.E. 1985, 189.

treaties signed by the European Union are incorporated into the national system once signed, ratified, and published in the official state gazette.

The second type of treaty is described in Article 94. This article enumerates instances where treaties require prior authorization by both chambers of parliament at the request of the executive. Prior authorization (though not an organic act) is required for: a) Treaties of a political nature; b) Treaties or agreements of a military nature; c) Treaties or agreements affecting the territorial integrity of the State or the fundamental rights and duties established in Part I of the Constitution; d) Treaties or agreements which imply financial liabilities for the Public Treasury; and e) Treaties or agreements which involve amendment or repeal of some law or require legislative measures for their execution. While the *Cortes* have some influence on the contents of the treaties, they are limited to requesting renegotiations or forming reservations and declarations.[16] The *Cortes* can refuse authorization of a previous draft, which would require renegotiations.[17] A renegotiation would require the entire treaty process to begin anew, with the executive again coordinating the terms of the treaty and submitting it for authorization.[18] Similarly, the *Cortes* can refuse authorization of a treaty under article 94.1 if the *Cortes* believes the treaty properly falls under article 93 (i.e. the treaty confers powers onto an international organizations).[19] The *Cortes* raised this argument when Spain wished to accede to the North Atlantic Treaty Organization.[20]

The executive may sign and ratify any other treaty and is required merely to notify Parliament following ratification.[21] Any tension created between a treaty and the Constitution will not be valid without a prior Constitutional revision.[22] This places the Constitution in a position of primacy over any other agreement or law. Should there be a question as to whether a contradiction exists, article 95 permits the House or the Government to petition the Constitutional Court, which has the authority to declare that a treaty or a part of a treaty does not comply with the Constitution and is therefore inapplicable.[23]

In contrast to some jurisdictions, Spain does not require any further implementing legislation to confer binding force on an international agreement.

---

16 Jan Willem Bittner, The Treaty Making Power in Spain, 1967–1984: Theory and Practice: A Development Through Transition 372 (1992).

17 Id.

18 Id.

19 Id. at 367.

20 Id.

21 Art. 94.2 C.E.

22 Art. 95.1 C.E.

23 Art. 95.3 C.E.

Once properly ratified, treaties are incorporated directly into Spanish law.[24] Validly concluded international treaties, once officially published in the *Boletín*, shall be part of the internal legal system.[25] The sole requirement for binding force is that the treaty be properly published in the Official State Gazette (*Boletín Official del Estado*). Therefore an unpublished treaty will have no domestic force, even if the treaty has taken effect internationally.[26] The date of entry into validity should be stated in the *Boletín*. This date usually follows the date after publications, but there are instance in which a different date is stated.

Once validly entered, the provisions of a treaty must be respected and can only be repealed, altered or amended in the manner provided in the treaty itself or in accordance with international law.[27] The procedure for denouncing treaties is the same procedure to be used for ratifying them.[28]

Evidence of State Practice

The King is the highest representative of Spain in international relations.[29] The Constitution bestows upon the King a number of international responsibilities, such as the responsibility to express the nation's assent to treaties[30] and to accredit ambassadors and other diplomatic representatives.[31] The Constitution does not provide the King with authority to make decisions on behalf of the country. In fact, Article 56 requires his acts to be countersigned, and stipulates that the acts not be valid without a countersignature.[32] Liability for acts falls on the person countersigning them, not on the King.[33] There are several instances in which the King requires prior authorization to act. For example, the King serves to declare war and to make peace, but the

24 Charlotte Villiers, The Spanish Legal Tradition 50 (1999).

25 Art. 96.1 C.E.

26 The publication of a law approved by Congress is a constitutional obligation under art. 91 and a constitutional right under art. 9.3, so it is only theoretically possible that a law might not be published. The published version is binding, and should there be wording mistakes or other errors, an amendment should be sought to correct it.

27 Art. 96.1 C.E.

28 Art. 96.2 C.E.

29 Art. 56.1 C.E.

30 Art. 63.2 C.E.

31 Art. 63.1 C.E.

32 Art. 56.3 C.E.

33 Art. 64.2 C.E.

Constitution specifies this be done "following authorization from the *Cortes Generales*."[34]

Other state actors include those in the Government, which is charged with conducting domestic and foreign policy, civil and military administration, and the defense of the state.[35] The government is comprised of the President, Vice-Presidents, and a Council of Ministers.[36] Ministers specifically charged with obligations that might affect state practice include The Minister for Foreign Affairs and Cooperation, the Minister for Defense, and the Minister for Home Affairs.[37] Each of the ministries maintains websites that provide access to news and press releases.[38] The English version of the Ministry for Foreign Affairs and Cooperation's website includes access to official statements, interviews, and even ministry reports.[39] The Ministry of Defense maintains a documentation center with free access to the 'Spanish Defense Magazine'[40] and a publications center that catalogs all of the Ministry's official publications.[41]

The Spanish Yearbook of International Law is an excellent resource to locate materials relating to state practice.[42] The Yearbook is published by the Spanish Association of Professors of International Law and International Relations.[43] It contains articles and literature about Spain with foreign and international imputations. It also compiles treaties, municipal legislation, and Spanish judicial decisions relating to private and public international law.

Annotated Bibliography of Sources

General Treaty Collections

1 BOLETÍN OFFICIAL DEL ESTADO [OFFICIAL STATE GAZETTE] (Madrid: Agencia Estatal Boletín Oficial del Estado, 1936–).

---

34 Art. 63.3 C.E.

35 Art. 97 C.E.

36 Art. 98.1 C.E.

37 The Constitution allows for additional posts to be created by law. Id.

38 A portal for the various websites can be located at GOBIERNO, http://www.lamoncloa.gob.es/Gobierno/index.htm.

39 http://www.exteriores.gob.es/Portal/en/Paginas/inicio.aspx. More information might be found on the Spanish version: MINISTERIOS DE ASUNTOS EXTERIORES Y DE COOPERACION, http://www.exteriores.gob.es/Portal/es/Paginas/inicio.aspx.

40 REVISTA ESPAÑOLA DE DEFENSA.

41 DOCUMENTATION AND PUBLICATIONS, http://www.defensa.gob.es/en/documentacion/.

42 THE SPANISH YEARBOOK OF INTERNATIONAL LAW (1974–).

43 Id.

Summary: Spain's official gazette and the official source for the text of treaties and international conventions. The *Boletín* publishes all authorizing statutes, including organic laws, laws and royal laws. It also publishes the full text of the treaty, any reservations or declarations, and the date of entry into force. Published daily, except Sunday.

Index: Includes weekly subject indexes. Monthly chronological and numerical indexes are also provided.

Note: Title and Imprint vary from the gazette's origin in the seventeenth century. An explanatory chart is available on the *Boletín*'s website: http://www.boe.es/buscar/ayudas/gazeta_ayuda.php.

Note: The publication of laws in the *Boletín* complies with the constitutional requirement to provide everyone access to the laws, but a more efficient search might use a commercial database such as Aranzadi. Nonetheless, only the text published in the *Boletín* is the authentic version of the law.

Treaty Indexes

2 ÍNDICES GENERALES DE LOS TRATADOS, CONVENIOS Y OTROS DOCUMENTOS DE CARACTER INTERNACIONAL FIRMADOS POR ESPAÑA DESDE 1801 A 1897 INCLUSIVES: ÍNDICES CRONÓLOGICOS Y POR MATERIAS
(Madrid: T. Minuesa de los Ríos 1900).

Summary: 440 pages of various indexes describing treaties and other international documents chronologically and thematically.

3 CENSO DE TRATADOS INTERNACIONALES SUSCRITOS POR ESPAÑA
(Madrid: Ministerio de Asuntos Exteriores, 1976).

Summary: Spanning the period from 1125 to 1975. First volume collection contains bilateral treaties, second volume contains multilateral treaties from May 1, 1323-August 1, 1975.

Topical and Selected Treaty Publications

4 COLECCION DE LOS TRATADOS DE PAZ, ALIANZA, NEUTRALIDAD, GARANTIA, PROTECCION, TREGUA, MEDIACCION, ACCESION, REGLAMENTO DE LIMITES, COMERCIO, NAVEGACION & C. HECHOS POR LOS PUEBLOS, REYES, PRINCIPES, REPUBLICAS, Y DEMAS POTENCIAS DE EUROPA, Y OTROS PARTES DEL MUNDO; Y ENTRE SI MISMOS, Y CON SUS RESPECTIVOS ADVERSARIOS: Y JUNTAMENTE DE LOS HECHOS DIRECTA, O INDIRECTAMENTE CONTRA ELLA, DESDE ANTES DEL ESTABLECIMIENTO DE LA

MONARCHIA GOTICA, HASTA EL FELIZ REYNADO DEL REY N.S.D. PHELIPE V
Jose Antonio Abreu y Bertodano (Madrid: Diego Peralta, Antonio Marin, y Juan de Zuniga, 1740–1752). 12 vols.

Summary: Collection of treaties from Phelipe III (1598–1621. Divided into three parts plus a supplement); Phelipe IV (1621–65. Divided into ten parts); and Carlos II (1665–1700. Divided into three parts).

Index: Three indexes of the materials contained in respective parts, in alphabetical order.

5 COLECCIÓN DE LOS TRATADOS DE PAZ, ALIANZA, COMERCIO, &C., AJUSTADOS POR LA CORONA DE ESPAÑA CON LAS POTENCIAS EXTRANGERAS DESDE EL REYNADO DEL SEÑOR DON FELIPE QUINTO HASTA EL PRESENTE
Antonio de Capmany y Montpalau (Madrid : Imprenta real, 1796–1801). 3 vol.

Summary: Collection of treaties spanning the time of Felipe V until 1801. Vol. I : 1701–1716. Vol. II : 1718–1749. Vol. III : 1753–1801. In Spanish with selected texts in Italian, French and Latin.

6 COLECCIÓN DE LOS TRATADOS, CONVENIOS Y DOCUMENTOS INTERNACIONALES CELEBRADOS POR NUESTROS GOBIERNOS CON LOS ESTADOS EXTRANJEROS DESDE EL REINADO DE DONA ISABEL II HASTA NUESTROS DIAS, ACOMPANADOS DE NOTAS HISTORICO-CRITICAS SOBRE SU NEGOCIACION Y CUMPLIMIENTO Y COTEJADOS CON LOS TEXTOS ORIGINALES
Ramon de Dalnau y de Olivart (Madrid: El Progresso Editorial 1890–1911). 14 Vols.

Summary: Broken into fourteen volumes, this collection contains treaties and other international documents, as well as annotations from proceedings during the negotiations. The documentation spans the reigns of Isabel II, Alfonso XII, Maria Christina, and the first three years of Alfonso XIII. Vol. I: 1834–48. Vol. II: 1849–58. Vol. III: 1859–62. Vol. IV: 1863–68. Vol. VI: 1868–74. Vol. VII: 1875–79. Vol. VIII: 1880–85. Vol. IX: 1885–90. Vol. X: 1891–93. Vol. XI: 1894–96. Vol. XII: 1897–99. Vol. XIII: 1900–02. Vol. XIV: 1902–1904.

7 TRATADOS DE ESPAÑA. DOCUMENTOS INTERNACIONALES DEL REINADO DE DOÑA ISABEL II, DESDE 1842 A 1868
Florencio Janer (Madrid : Imprenta de Miguel Ginesta, 1869).

Summary: Collection of publications related to international relations of the Spanish crown over a brief span.

Index: Chronological index appears from page 472–81. Alphabetical index from 483–94.

8 TRATADOS Y DOCUMENTOS INTERNACIONALES DE ESPAÑA PUBLICADOS EN LA REVISTA DE DERECHO INTERNACIONAL Y POLÍTICA EXTERIOR

Ramon de Dalnau y de Olivart (Madrid : Los hijos de R. Alvarez, 1905–1912). 4 vol.

Summary: Vol. I: 1900–1905. Vol. II: 1904–1906. Vol. III: 1902–1907. Vol. IV: 1908–1910.

Volume I contains 15 treaties; Volume II contains 31; Volume III contains 15; and Volume IX contains 33.

Index: Each contain a chronological and alphabetical index as well as supplements.

Diplomatic Documents

9 BOLETÍN OFICIAL DEL MINISTERIO DE ASUNTOS EXTERIORES Y DE COOPERACIÓN

(Madrid: Ministerio de Asuntos Exteriores y de Cooperación, 1891–).

Summary: The official gazette of the foreign affairs office is a continuation of a series dating back to 1891 with slight title changes reflecting the changes in the ministry's title.

10 ACTIVIDADES, TEXTOS Y DOCUMENTOS DE LA POLITICA EXTERIOR ESPAÑOLA

(Madrid : Ministerio de Asuntos Exteriores, Oficina de Información Diplomática, 1981-).

Summary: Serial publication that contains speeches and declarations regarding foreign relations from the King, the President, and the Ministry of Foreign Affairs and Cooperation. Also includes parliamentary activity and written responses to inquiries.

Index: Alphabetic

11 MIRADAS AL EXTERIOR: REVISTA DE INFORMACION DIPLOMATICA DEL MINISTERIO DE ASUNTOS EXTERIORES Y DE COOPERACIÓN

(Madrid: Ministerio de Asuntos Exteriores y de Cooperación, 2006–).

Summary: A window into international events with special attention to Spanish diplomatic activity.

12 MEMORIAS DIPLOMÁTICAS Y CONSULARES É INFORMACIONES
(Madrid: Ministerio de Estado, 1902–1929).

Summary: Serial publication containing information from foreign councils and diplomatic notes.

Note: Continuation of Memorias Consulares e Informaciones (1900–1902).

Yearbooks and Digests of State Practice

13 ANUARIO ESPAÑOL DE DERECHO INTERNACIONAL [SPANISH YEARBOOK OF INTERNATIONAL LAW]
(Pamplona: University of Navarra, 1974–).

Summary: Annual publication relating to international law. Contains doctrinal articles and other notes. Also useful for annual summaries of Spanish jurisprudence pertaining to international law.

Index: Annual index describing documentation from nations in alphabetical order.

Note: Volumes 1–21 contain bear the imprint "Anuario de Derecho Internacional."

Sweden

Suzanne Thorpe

Issues of Treaty Succession

Sweden has been recognized as a kingdom since the 10th Century, although it has existed within its current borders only since 1905. From the early 14th Century through the beginning of the 20th Century, Sweden was continuously united with one or more of its Nordic neighbors. Sweden formed a union with Norway that lasted from 1319 to 1355. In 1323, much of current day Finland became a colony of Sweden and remained so until 1809. In 1397, Sweden joined the then united kingdom of Norway-Denmark to form the Kalmar Union. During this union, Sweden, Norway, and Denmark maintained a common foreign policy under the rule of the Danish monarch until Sweden left the union in 1523. In 1814, Denmark ceded Norway to Sweden under the Treaty of Kiel.[1] After the treaty was signed, Sweden and Norway agreed to operate internally as two self-governing states, but with a joint foreign policy under the rule of the Swedish monarch. In 1905, Norway dissolved the union with Sweden and Sweden granted Norway independence.

Sweden's various unions with its neighbors are well documented by historians and legal scholars.[2] Aside from probable discussions in unpublished diplomatic records, few writers have commented on the continuing force of the treaties concluded during these unions. Limited discussion surrounds a succession dispute arising out of the Treaty of Kiel.[3] Article 6 of this treaty obligated Norway, upon dissolution of the union with Denmark, to pay a proportional share of Denmark's national debt. The successor state, the united kingdom of Sweden-Norway, disputed this obligation. This debt issue was resolved in 1819, when Sweden negotiated another treaty with Denmark and

---

1 Fredstractat mellom Danmark og Sverig, signed at Kiel 14 January 1814, 1 Danske Tractater efter 1800, 1.samling, 60–72 (1877). Norway opposed this union but, after a brief military skirmish, Norway and Sweden passed common legislation recognizing the union of the two states under the Swedish king.

2 *E.g.*, Lester B. Orfield, The Growth of Scandinavian Law (1953); Carl A. Reuterskiöld, Folkrätt Särskildt Såsom Svensk Publik Internationell Rätt (1928); Den Svenska Utrikespolitikens Historia (Nils Ahnlund et al., eds., 1951–1961).

3 Ernst Hermann Feilchenfeld, Public Debts and State Succession 142–44 (1931); Daniel Patrick O'Connell, 1 State Succession in Municipal Law and International Law 396 (1967); Theodore Jorgensen, 1 Norway's Relation to Scandinavian Unionism, 1815–1871 389–400 (1935).

 | DOI 10.1163/9789004272224_031

Norway agreed to pay a reduced portion of the amount stipulated in the 1814 treaty.[4] Although, in prior state practice, ceded territories had been held proportionately liable for debts incurred before cession, this was the first instance when a ceded territory was held liable for more than a local debt. Additionally, it has been noted in the literature that Norway and Sweden declared their intention to be bound by the treaties concluded during their union when it dissolved in 1905.[5]

Treaty Ratification and Implementation[6]

Although the Swedish Constitution does not generally define the relationship between public international law and Swedish municipal law, Sweden adheres to the dualist approach to international law.[7] To become a binding part of Swedish municipal law, international treaties usually require express legislative action of the Swedish Parliament. Chapter 10, Article 1 of the Swedish *Regeringsform* (Instrument of Government) grants the *Regering* (Government) the power to conduct foreign relations, but Article 3 of this chapter requires the *Riksdag* (Parliament) to grant prior approval to any treaty that "requires the amendment or abrogation of an act of law or the enactment of a new act of law, or...concerns a matter to be decided by the *Riksdag* In addition, this article requires the *Riksdag* to approve agreements of "major importance."

Under Chapter 10, Articles 11–12 of the *Regeringsform*, the *Utrikesdepartment* (Ministry of Foreign Affairs)[8] is required to confer closely with the *Riksdag's Utrikesnämnd* (Advisory Council on Foreign Affairs) on foreign policy matters. This council consists of the Head of State, the Speaker of the *Riksdag*, and nine other members of the *Riksdag*. Following the conclusion of a treaty, the

4 J.H.W. Verzijl, 7 International Law in Historical Perspective, Part 7, State Succession 230 (1974).

5 Daniel Patrick O'Connell, The Law of State Succession 44–45 (1956).

6 For background on Swedish treaty implementation practices, *see generally* Statens Offentliga Utredningar [SOU] 1974:100 Internationella överenskommelser och svensk rätt [government report series] (Swed.).; Iain Cameron, *Swedish Parliamentary Participation in the Making and Implementation of Treaties*, 74 Nordic J. Int'l L. 429 (2005).

7 Göran Melander, *The Effect of Treaty Provisions in Swedish Law*, 53 Nordisk Tidsskrift Int'l Ret, no. 4, 1984, at 63; Swedish Law: A Survey 58 (Hugo Tiberg et al. eds., 1994); Joakim Nergelius, Swedish Constitutional Law 22 (2011); Cameron *supra* note 6, at 441.

8 The website of the Utrikesdepartement at http://www.regeringen.se/sb/d/1475 provides information about treaty proposals submitted to the Riksdag, news bulletins, press releases, speeches, articles, and other publications related to Sweden's official foreign policy.

Utrikesdepartement introduces the adopted treaty to the Riksdag for ratification and implementation.[9] The treaty is referred to the *Riksdag's Utrikesutskott* (Standing Committee on Foreign Affairs). This committee issues a report with recommendations on ratification and implementation to the *Riksdag*.[10]

Treaties are usually implemented in Sweden through one of two legislative methods: *inkorporering* (incorporation) and *transformering* (transformation).[11] When *inkorporering* is used, the *Riksdag* passes a law adopting the treaty text as Swedish law. This is usually a brief declaration that appears with other legislation in the *Svensk Författningssamling*, the official legal gazette.[12] The treaty text is appended to the declaration, usually in one of the official languages of the treaty and sometimes in an unofficial Swedish translation, if Swedish is not one of the official languages.[13] When *transformering* is used, the *Riksdag* amends an existing law or enacts a new law to mirror the provisions of the treaty. These legislative changes also appear in the *Svensk Författningssamling*. This method is usually used when a treaty text needs further clarification or when there are conflicts between existing Swedish law and a treaty's provisions. Transformation is the most common method of treaty implementation in Sweden.[14] Infrequently, a third method of implementation that is known in Sweden as "*konstatering av normharmoni*" (declaring legal harmony) is also used. This was utilized when Sweden implemented Protocol No. 1 of the European Convention for the Protection of Human Rights and Fundamental Freedoms.[15] With "*konstatering av normharmoni*," the Ministry

---

9 The website of the *Regering* at http://www.regeringen.se/sb/d/108 provides texts of treaties concluded and submitted to the Riksdag for ratification since 1994. A treaty is introduced as a "*proposition*." It is then published with other proposed bills and writings presented to the Riksdag in the parliamentary publication, PROPOSITIONER OCH SKRIVELSER. Treaty proposals received since 1971 are available at http://www.riksdagen.se/sv/Dokument-Lagar/Forslag/Propositioner-och-skrivelser.

10 This report is published with reports and statements from other committees in the parliamentary publication, BETÄNKANDEN OCH YTTRANDEN (committee reports and utterances). The website of the *Riksdag* at http://www.riksdagen.se provides access to the reports of the *Utrikesutskott* since 1971, and debates and decisions of the Riksdag related to treaty ratification and implementation.

11 DEPARTEMENTSSERIEN [Ds] 2007:25 Riktlinjer för handläggningen av ärenden om internationella överenskommelser [government report series] (Swed.), 11–12.

12 SVENSK FÖRFATTNINGSSAMLING, the gazette containing laws since 1736 as initially enacted, is available online *at* http://www.riksdagen.se/sv/Dokument-Lagar.

13 STATENS OFFENTLIGA UTREDNINGAR [SOU] 1974:100, *supra* note 6, at 57.

14 Id. at 49.

15 Michael Bogdan, *Application of Public International Law by Swedish Courts*, 63 NORDIC J. INT'L L 3, 11; Göran Melander, *supra* note 7, at 63.

of Foreign Affairs issues a position statement in a proposition indicating to the *Riksdag* that the language of the treaty is already reflected in Swedish municipal law. The treaty then becomes effective in Sweden without either incorporation or transformation.

Once ratified, treaties must be published in the official Swedish treaty series, *Sveriges Internationella Överenskommelser*.[16] They appear in this publication 2–3 years after ratification. Before 1912, ratified treaties were published in the *Svensk Författningssamling.*

Because treaty provisions are carefully compared with existing Swedish law throughout the treaty negotiation and ratification process, Swedish municipal law generally conforms to the provisions in the international treaties concluded by Sweden. When rare conflicts arise after a treaty is in force, Swedish courts and administrative agencies presume that the municipal law was intended to conform to the international law.[17]

Annotated Bibliography of Sources

General Treaty Collections

1 SVERIGES INTERNATIONELLA ÖVERENSKOMMELSER
Sweden. Utrikesdepartementet (Stockholm: Kungliga Boktryckeriet, P.A. Norstedt, 1912–).

Summary: Treaties are published as separate fascicles with consecutive numbering for each year. Each entry provides the treaty number, title, place of signature, dates of signature, ratification, effectiveness, and parties. Treaty texts are in Swedish and, usually, at least one other official treaty language. Includes annual chronological table of treaties.

Index: Cumulative tables of contents list treaties by date and by party: 1912–1925, 1926–1930, 1931–1936, 1937–1940, 1941–1946. Cumulative subject index: 1912–1940.

Note: Title varies: *Sveriges Överenskommelser med Främmande Makter*: 1912–1990.

16 For an official government report discussing the publication of Swedish treaties, *see* DEPARTEMENTSSERIE [Ds] 1990:13 Regler om publicering av sveriges internationella överenskommelser [government report series] (Swed.). §8 RÄTTSINFORMATIONSFÖRORDNING (SVENSK FÖRFATTNINGSSAMLING [SFS]1999:175) (Swed.) requires ratified treaties in Sveriges internationella överenskommelser to be published on the Regering's website at http://www.regeringen.se/sb/d/3305.

17 Bogdan, *supra* note 15, at 5.

Note: 1913–1918, 1926–1928, 1929–1930, 1931–1932, 1933–1934, 1935–1936, 1941–1945 are issued in combined volumes.

Note: Appendices in some volumes contain official notices related to selected treaties.

Note: Treaties appearing in this publication 1999– are available in PDF format at http://www.regeringen.se/sb/d/3305.

2 SVERGES TRAKTATER MED FRÄMMANDE MAGTER: JEMTE ANDRA DIT HÖRANDE HANDLINGAR

(Stockholm: P.A. Norstedt, 1877–1934). 14 vols.

Summary: Contains treaties concluded by Sweden from 822–1905. Del. I: 822–1335; Del II: 1336–1408; Del III: 1409–1520; Del IV: 1521–1571; Del V, Bd. 1: 1572–1632; Del V, Bd. 2 1632–1645; Del VI: 1646–1648; Del VII: 1649–1722; Del VIII: 1723–1771; Del IX [unpublished]; Del X: 1815–1845; Del XI: 1846–1867; Del XII: 1868–1877; Del XIII: 1878–1890; Del XIV: 1891–1899; Del XV: 1900–1905. Del X–Del XV contain Norwegian treaties concluded from 1815–1905. Treaties appear in chronological order in one of the official treaty languages. Each volume provides a chronological list of treaties, indexes by country in Swedish and French, a geographical index and a personal name index.

Note: Editors: Del I–Del IV: O.S. Rydberg; Del V, Bd. 1: O.S. Rydberg & C. Hallendorff; Del V, Bd. 2–Del VII: C Hallendorff; Del VIII: B. Boëthius; Del X–Del XI: O.S. Rydberg; Del XII: Oscar Alin; Del XIII–Del XIV: Carl Sandgren; Del XV: Sten Lewenhaupt.

Note: Del X–Del XIV have added title: *Sverges och Norges Traktater med Främmande Magter*; Del XV has title: *Sveriges Traktater med Främmande Makter Jämte Andra Dit Hörande Handlingar.* These volumes are also numbered Del I–Del VI.

3 RECUEIL DES TRAITÉS, CONVENTIONS ET AUTRES ACTES DIPLOMATIQUES DE LA SUÈDE: ENTIÈREMENT OU PARTIELLEMENT EN VIGUEUR AU 1ER JANVIER 1910

(Stockholm: P.A. Norstedt, 1910). xx, 1038 pp.

Summary: Contains 355 treaties and international acts concluded 1654–1909 that were in force on January 1, 1910. Treaty texts appear in chronological order in the official treaty languages. Postal, telegraph, and telephone treaties are not included. An alphabetical list of parties is provided.

Note: Editor: Carl Sandgren.

4 RECUEIL DES TRAITÉS, CONVENTIONS ET AUTRES ACTES DIPLOMATIQUES DE LA SUÈDE CONCLUS PENDANT LES ANNÉES 1910 ET 1911

(Stockholm: P.A. Norstedt, 1913). v, 278 pp.

Summary: This source contains multilateral treaties concluded 1906–1910 and bilateral treaties concluded 1907–1911. Texts are in the official treaty languages. It includes an alphabetical list of treaties by country.

Note: Editor: Carl Sandgren.

5 RECUEIL DES TRAITÉS, CONVENTIONS ET AUTRES ACTES DIPLOMATIQUES DE LA SUÈDE: ENTIÈREMENT OU PARTIELLEMENT EN VIGUEUR AU 1ER JANVIER 1926

(Stockholm: P.A. Norstedt, 1926–1927). 2 vols.

Summary: Contains treaties concluded 1780–1925 that were in force on January 1, 1926. Tome 1 contains 108 multilateral treaties arranged in chronological order and includes a chronological list of these treaties. Tome 2 contains 435 bilateral treaties arranged chronologically under each country and includes a chronological list of these treaties. For each treaty, the title and place and date of signature are provided.

Note: Editor: Sten Mauritz Carl Lewenhaupt.

Treaty Indexes

6 REGISTER ÖVER SVERIGES INTERNATIONELLA ÖVERENSKOMMELSER

Sweden. Utrikesdepartementet

(Stockholm: Utrikesdepartementet, Fritzes Kundtjänst, 1972–1998).

Summary: Biennial index covering treaties concluded 1972–1997. Bilateral treaties are listed by country or intergovernmental organization. Multilateral treaties are arranged with separate listings for Nordic treaties, European Union treaties, and other treaties. Special treaties are arranged by intergovernmental organization. Treaties which have not yet been ratified or are not yet in force are included. Each entry provides the date of entry by Sweden, full title, and citation to the official treaty in *Sveriges Internationella Överenskommelser* or *Sveriges Överenskommelser med Främmande Makter. Series: Aktstycken Utgivna av Utrikesdepartementet*; Ny Serie I:E.

Note: Title varies: *Register över Sveriges Överenskommelser med Främmande Makter*: 1972–1990.

Note: Spine title: *Register över SÖ.*

Note: Imprint varies: Allmänna Förlaget: 1972–1990.

Indexes: Cumulative subject indexes were issued with 1978–1994 indexes.

7 UTRIKESDEPARTEMENTETS KALENDER
(Stockholm: Allmänna Förlaget, Fritzes Kundtjänst 1870–).
Summary: Bilateral treaties are listed by party; multilateral treaties are listed chronologically.
Note: Title varies: *Kungl. Utrikesdepartement Kalender:* 1870–1974.
Note: Did not appear 1939–1945, 1947–1950, 1952–54, 1956, 1958, 1960, 1962–63, 1965, 1967–68, 1970–71, 1977.

8 TRAKTATÖVERSIKT: FRÄMMANDE MAKTERS STÄLLNING TILL FÖR SVERIGE BINDANDE INTERNATIONELLA AVTAL
(Stockholm: Kungliga Boktryckeriet. P.A. Norstedt, 1948). ix, 188 pp.
Summary: This work provides a chronological list of treaties concluded 1815–1947. Each entry provides the treaty title, parties, and dates of signature and ratification.
Note: Compiler: Sten Mauritz Carl Lewenhaupt.

9 FÖRTECKNING UPPÅ ALLA KONGL. PLACATER, FÖRORDNINGAR, PÅBUD, RESOLUTIONER, PRIVELEGIER, MANIFESTER, FREDSFÖRDRAGER, ETC
(Stockholm: Hist. Regni Tryckerie, 1754). 547 pp.
Summary: Contains listings of 39 peace treaties concluded 1522–1750. Treaties appear by date with laws, regulations, and other materials. Treaties are listed in the index under heading: "fredsfördrag
Note: Editor: Johan Pehr Höppener.

Topical and Selected Treaty Collections

10 DE NORDISKE KONVENTIONER: ÆGTESKAB, ADOPTION OG VÆRGEMAAL, INDDRIVELSE AF UNDERHOLDSBIDRAG, ANERKENDELSE OG FULDBYRDELSE AF DOMME, KONKURS, ARV OG DØDSBOSKIFTE
(Copenhagen: Ejnar Munksgaard, 1947). 56 pp.
Summary: This work provides the Danish text of five treaties between the Nordic countries on marriage, adoption and guardianship, maintenance, recognition and enforcement of judgments, bankruptcy, and inheritance and succession. These treaties were concluded 1931–1935.

Diplomatic Documents

11 UTRIKESFRÅGOR: OFFENTLIGA DOKUMENT M.M. RÖRANDE VIKTIGARE SVENSKA UTRIKESFRÅGOR
Sweden. Utrikesdepartementet (Stockholm: Utrikesdepartementet, Fritzes Kundtjänst, 1950/51–2000).

Summary: This is an annual compilation of selected official statements, speeches, and documents on Sweden's foreign affairs. General foreign policy statements and speeches appear at the beginning of each volume, followed by chapters on specific foreign policy matters. Each chapter provides a list of the statements, speeches, and documents included in it. Most volumes include lists of recent Swedish agreements with foreign powers and official state visits and bibliographical references to the periodicals, monographs, official reports, and internal manuals of the Foreign Ministry.

Series: Aktstycken Utgivna av Utrikesdepartementet, Ny serie 1:C.

Index: Cumulative subject indexes: 1961–1970 issued with 1970 volume.

Note: Imprint varies: Allmänna Förlaget: 1985–1993.

Note: English language version: *Documents on Swedish Foreign Policy,* published 1950/51–1993 by Allmänna Förlaget. Cumulative subject index: 1950–1959 issued with 1959.

Note: Compilations for 1997–2000 are available online in PDF format at http://www.regeringen.se/sb/d/108.

Diplomatic Documents

12 UD INFO

(Stockholm: Utrikesdepartementet, 1997–).

Summary: This is an irregularly issued compilation of official commentaries on foreign policy topics.

Note: Title varies: *UD-Informerar*: 1977–1997.

Note: Issued as unnumbered, separately titled booklets, 1986–1997.

13 BRIEFING FRÅN UTRIKESDEPARTEMENTET: UTRIKESFRÅGOR, HANDEL, BISTÅND, MIGRATION

Sweden. Utrikesdepartementet (Stockholm: Fritzes Kundtjänst, 1992–2003).

Summary: This is a bimonthly periodical covering developments in Swedish foreign policy and trade.

Note: Previously issued as two separate titles: *Aktuellt i Handelspolitiken*: 1971–1992; *Biståndsnytt från UD:s U-Avdelning*: 1990–1992.

Yearbooks and Digests of State Practice

14 NORDIC JOURNAL OF INTERNATIONAL LAW

(Leiden, Netherlands: Martinus Nijhoff, 2006–)

Summary: Volumes 65, 67–70, 72, 74 and 75 contain articles that digest developments in Swedish state practice for 1995, 1997, 1998, 1999, 2000, 2001, 2003, and 2004/2005.

Imprint varies: Dordrecht: Kluwer Academic Publishers, 1986–2005

Continues: Nordisk Tidsskrift for International Ret, 1930–1985.

Swiss Confederation

Ralph F. Gaebler

Issues of Treaty Succession

Issues of treaty succession do not loom large in the international relations of Switzerland, which has enjoyed relative stability since its neutrality was guaranteed following the Congress of Vienna.[1] But such questions are not entirely absent. In 1848 Switzerland achieved the political form that it retains essentially today. In that year a new constitution was adopted, which solidified the authority of the central government in foreign affairs.[2] Previously the cantons had stood in a loose confederal relationship to one another, and enjoyed a wide power to conclude treaties on their own. With the adoption of the new constitution in 1848 there thus arose a question as to the continued vitality of these treaties.

For the most part the pre-1848 treaties were considered to be still in force.[3] However, as of 1967 only a few of these treaties were still in force, with France and Germany.[4]

Treaty Ratification and Implementation

The process of treaty-making and treaty implementation in Switzerland reflects the unique nature of its government and political culture, which emphasizes local autonomy and consensual decision-making. The national government is composed of a Federal Assembly (*Bundesversammlung* or *Assemblée Fédérale*) and a Federal Council (*Bundesrat* or *Conseil Fédéral*). The

1 Act accompanying the Definitive Treaty of Peace between Austria, Great Britain, Prussia and Russia and France, Nov. 20, 1815, 17 PARL. PAPERS 157 (1816), reprinted in 65 Consol. T.S. 299. Also printed in 3 B.S.P. 359 (1815–1816), reproduced electronically in Google Books.

2 Bundesverfassung, Constitution fédérale, May 29, 1874, AS 1, RO 1 art. 90, para. 8 granted the Federal Council jurisdiction over foreign affairs. Article 74, paragraph 5, granted the Federal Assembly power to approve both federal and cantonal treaties. The text of the 1848 Constitution is reprinted in 47 B.S.P. 1245 (1866), and reproduced electronically from the print edition in HeinOnline's World Constitutions Illustrated database. It is also available in various versions in Google Books.

3 For a discussion of the reasons for this conclusion, *see* D.P. O'CONNELL, 2 STATE SUCCESSION IN MUNICIPAL LAW AND INTERNATIONAL LAW 61 (1967), and sources cited therein.

4 Id.

 | DOI 10.1163/9789004272224_032

former is the legislature, comprising the National Council (*Nationalrat* or *Conseil National*), elected on the basis of population, and the State Council (*Ständerat* or *Conseil des Etats*), representing the cantons. The latter is a seven-member executive. The government is not a true parliament. Thus, the National Council is elected for a fixed term quite independent of the Federal Council, and members of the Federal Council may not serve in the Federal Assembly, nor do they direct its activities. The government is best viewed as a hybrid, and possibly sui generis system combining elements of both traditional parliamentary democracy and American-style separation of powers with unique elements of its own.

The current 1999 Constitution of the Swiss Federal Republic draws functional distinctions between the roles played in the treaty-making process by the different branches of government.[5] Under Article 54, paragraph one, the conduct of foreign relations is a "federal matter". This carries on the tradition of the Constitution of 1848, which also granted jurisdiction over foreign affairs to the federal government, despite the strongly confederal nature of the republic. However, responsibility for the conduct of foreign relations is split between the Federal Assembly, which "participate[s] in shaping foreign policy" and "supervises foreign relations" under Article 166, paragraph one, and the Federal Council, which "shall conduct foreign relations" under Article 184, paragraph one. As the executive arm of federal government, the Federal Council represents Switzerland on the international level, and therefore enjoys the power to initiate and negotiate treaties. It is empowered specifically by Article 184, paragraph two, to sign and ratify treaties. Under article 54, subject matter jurisdiction of the Federal Council is plenary, although its power is subject to procedural requirements of consultation when proposed treaties impinge on areas within the scope of cantonal jurisdiction. (See below.) Under article 166, paragraph two, the role of the Federal Assembly is to "approve federal treaties, except where by statute or international treaty the Federal Council alone is competent". General practice calls for approval between signature and ratification. Despite some commentary asserting the contrary,[6] this practice reveals

5 Bundesverfassung [BV] [Constitution] Apr. 18, 1999, SR 101 [hereinafter Switz. Const.] The 1999 Constitution is available electronically in HeinOnline's World Constitutions Illustrated, as well as in Oceana's Constitutions of the Countries of the World database. It is also available in English, as well as in the four official languages of Switzerland at the web site of the Federal Authorities of the Swiss confederation, at http://www.admin.ch/org/polit/00083/index.html?lang=en. However, the English-language version is unofficial.

6 Bernhard Ehrenzeller, Legislative Gewalt und Aussenpolitik. Eine Rechtsvergleichende Studie zu den Parlamentarischen Entscheidungskompetenzen des

that Federal Assembly approval is approval to ratify, rather than legislation incorporating international agreements into municipal law. Thus, Switzerland has a monistic, rather than dualist, doctrine of treaty incorporation.[7] However, as in other monistic jurisdictions, such as the United States, treaty rejection is a real possibility, given that the Federal Assembly is not a parliamentary body directed by the executive.

Specifics of the relationship between the Federal Assembly and Federal Council in treaty-making are governed by the Statute on the Federal Assembly (*Bundesgesetz über die Bundesversammlung* or *Loi sur l'Assemblée Fédérale*), originally adopted in 1991.[8] Article 152 of this statute imposes a comprehensive duty on the Federal Council regularly to inform the foreign affairs committees of the Federal Assembly, as well as the presidents of each chamber, on developments in foreign affairs. It also requires the Federal Council to consult with the relevant committees concerning "important" treaty negotiations as they progress, as well as before provisionally applying treaty provisions requiring Federal Assembly approval. Finally, article 152, paragraph 5, grants the relevant committees of the Federal Assembly an affirmative power to request information from, or consultations with, the Federal Council on foreign affairs matters at any time. Despite the comprehensive nature of inter-agency communications established by this statute, the statute does not grant the Federal Assembly any

---

BUNDESTAGES, DES AMERIKANISCHEN KONGRESSES UND DER SCHWEIZERISCHEN BUNDESVERSAMMLUNG IM AUSWÄRTIGEN BEREICH 462–463 (1993).

7 This is the official position of the Swiss Department of Foreign Affairs, as described at the web site of the Directorate of International Law, at http://www.eda.admin.ch/eda/en/home/topics/intla/cintla/natint.html. *See also* the chapter on Switzerland, by Luzius Wildhaber Adrian Scheidegger, and Marac D. Schinzel, *in* NATIONAL TREATY LAW AND PRACTICE 627, 659 (D. Hollis, et.al. eds., 2005). Wildhaber et. al. assert the view that "the notion of 'legislation' includes the power to determine not only whether a norm should be enacted, but also the content of a norm. Since the Federal Assembly lacks power to influence the content of a treaty submitted for approval..., the power to approve is not the same as the power to legislate". Wildhaber et al. provide the most comprehensive and up-to-date English-language discussion of Swiss treaty-making. See also L. Wildhaber, *Parliamentary Paarticipation in Treaty-making, Report on Swiss Law, in* PARLIAMENTARY PARTICIPATION IN THE MAKING AND OPERATION OF TREATIES. A COMPARATIVE STUDY (S. Riesenfeld and F.M. Abott, eds., 1994); L. Wildhaber, *Conclusion and Implementation of Treaties in Switzerland, in* SWISS REPORTS: PRESENTED AT THE THIRTEENTH INTERNATIONAL CONGRESS OF COMPARATIVE LAW (Montreal, August 19–24, 1990); and L. Wildhaber, *Switzerland, in* FEDERALISM AND INTERNATIONAL RELATIONS: THE ROLE OF SUBNATIONAL UNITS (H.J. Michelmann and P. Soldatos, eds., 1990).

8 SR 171.10, AS 2003 3545, available in English at the web site of the Federal Authorities of the Swiss Confederation, at http://www.admin.ch/ch/e/rs/c171_10.html, and reprinted in part in Wildhaber et al, *supra* note 7, at 677.

direct role in treaty-making, in addition to its power to approve or disapprove completed treaties; therefore it preserves the functional separation of powers outlined in the constitution.

It should also be noted that more than half the international agreements that enter into force for Switzerland do so without Federal Assembly approval.[9] This follows from the provisions of the 1997 Federal Statute on the Organization of the Government and the Administration (*Regierungs – und Verwaltungsorganisationsgesetz* or *Loi sur l'Organisation du Gouvernement et de l'Administration*), which partly codified long-standing practice.[10] Article 7a of this statute grants to the Federal Council power to conclude executive agreements without approval of the Federal Assembly when they have been authorized beforehand, implicitly or explicitly, either by statute or international treaty. This accounts for the vast majority of such agreements. Article 7a also defines minor agreements (*Bagatellverträge* or *traités internationaux de portée mineure*), which the Federal Council is authorized to conclude without Federal Assembly approval.[11]

In addition to the requirement of consultation imposed on the Federal Council by the Statute on the Federal Assembly, a further duty to consult more widely at the cantonal level and among political parties and interest groups is imposed by the Federal Statute on Consultation (*Bundesgesetz über das Vernehmlassungsverfahren* or *Loi Fédérale sur la Procédure de Consultation*).[12] Under article 3, this wider consultation procedure is triggered by treaties subject to approval by referendum (see below), by treaties that affect essential interests of the cantons, or by treaties of political, financial, economic, ecological, social, or cultural significance, the administration of which would be carried out by agencies outside the federal administration.

The participation of the cantons in treaty-making is anchored by article 55 of the 1999 constitution, which guarantees the cantons a right to participate in making foreign policy decisions that affect their essential interests, and even guarantees them a right to participate in international negotiations of treaties

---

9 *See* Wildhaber et al., *supra* note 7, at 648.

10 SR 172.010, AS 1997 2002, available in English at the web site of the Federal Authroities of the Swiss Confederation, at http://www.admin.ch/ch/e/rs/c172_010.html, and reprinted in part in Wildhaber et al., *supra* note 7, 678.

11 The categories of treaties not requiring Federal Assembly approval are currently set out in a regulation adopted in 1987, 51 VPN 58, available electronically from an official archival database of pre-2007 regulations, at http://www.vpb.admin.ch/deutsch/doc/51/51.58 .html.

12 SR 172.061, AS 2005 4099, available in English at the web site of the Federal Authorities of the Swiss Confederation, at http://www.admin.ch/ch/e/rs/c172_061.html.

relating to matters within their jurisdiction. Thus, in addition to the Federal Statute on Consultation, articles 4 and 5 of the Federal Statute on the Participation of the Cantons in the Foreign Policy of the Confederation (*Bundesgesetz über die Mitwirkung der Kantone in der Aussenpolitik des Bundes* or *Loi Fédérale du 22 Décembre 1999 sur la Participation des Cantons à la Politique Extérieure de la Confédération*) also place specific requirements on the Federal Council to consult the cantons and include them in treaty negotiations when their jurisdiction is affected.[13]

The most notable and distinctive feature of Swiss treaty-making involves the referendum, entrenched in articles 140 and 141 of the 1999 Constitution. Article 140 deals with the mandatory referendum (*obligatorisches Referendum* or *Référendum obligatoire*), which requires approval by popular vote in cases involving adherence to organizations of collective security or to supranational organizations. Mandatory referenda require approval by a majority of voters and a majority of cantons, under article 142. This more stringent requirement reflects Switzerland's long tradition of neutrality. Article 141 deals with the optional referendum (*fakultatives Referendum* or *Référendum facultative*). Triggered by the request of 50,000 voters or eight cantons within 100 days of official publication, this referendum applies, under article 141, paragraph 1(d), to treaties that are of unlimited duration and may not be terminated, provide for accession to an international organization, contain important legislative provisions, or whose implementation requires the enactment of federal legislation. In this case, approval requires only a majority of voters.

Both the mandatory and optional referenda have existed in their present form only since 2003,[14] but have deep roots in Swiss popular democracy. The constitution of 1874 was amended by popular initiative in 1921 to include the optional referendum. Under the terms of then article 89, all federal statutes and decrees were subject to popular referendum if 30,000 voters or eight cantons so requested. In addition, the popular referendum extended to any treaty of indeterminate or more than 15 years' duration.[15] Article 89 was amended again in 1977 to apply more broadly to the same classes of treaties now covered

---

13 SR 138.1, AS 2000 1477, available in the official languages at the web site of the Federal Authorities of the Swiss Confederation, at http://www.admin.ch/ch/d/sr/c138_1.html, and reprinted in part in English in Wildhaber et al., in *National Treaty Law and Practice*, supra note 7, p. 680.

14 AS 2003 1949 1953, available in the official languages at the web site of the Federal Authorities of the Swiss Confederation, at http://www.admin.ch/ch/d/as/2003/indexo_27.html.

15 RO 37 304.

by article 141, except that instead of applying to treaties containing important legislative provisions, they applied more narrowly to treaties contemplating multilateral unification of law only.[16] It is interesting to note that the cantons did not successfully take advantage of their power to initiate a referendum until 2003. Nevertheless, a total of 153 referenda were held between 1874 and 2004.[17]

The mandatory treaty referendum dates from 1920, when the Federal Assembly subjected accession to the League of Nations to a mandatory referendum, analogizing from the then-existing provision for subjecting constitutional amendments to the same requirement. However, it was formally added to the constitution only in 1977.[18]

Given the confederal nature of the Swiss state, it is not surprising that cantons possess a limited right to conclude treaties on their own. Under Article 48 of the constitution of 1999, they may conclude agreements among one another and "create common organizations and institutions". In particular, they may "join forces to undertake tasks of regional interest". Inter-cantonal institutions may themselves legislate and involve participation by the Confederation. More important, the cantons enjoy the right under Article 56, paragraph one, to "conclude treaties with foreign states within the scope of their competences".[19] However, though cantons may deal directly with lower ranking foreign officials, "in other cases the Confederation shall conduct relations with foreign

16 RO 1977 807. All versions of the optional treaty provision in the 1874 constitution are available electronically in French in HeinOnline's World Constitutions Illustrated.

17 See Wildhaber et al., *supra* note 7, at 631–32. Of course, the majority of the 153 referenda involved statutes rather than treaties. Between 1921 and 1977 there were three treaty referenda, and from 1977 to 2004 an additional two. Id. at 653, 655. According to one commentator, the referendum provision was "easy to evade and make of no effect". See Christopher Hughes, The Federal Constitution of Switzerland 102 (1954). For a more complete description of the referendum regime before the changes of 2003, *see* F. Dessemontet and T. Ansay, Introduction to Swiss Law (3d ed. 2004). Procedures governing referenda are set out in the Federal Statute on Political Rights (*Bundesgesetz über die Politischen Rechte* or *Loi Fédérale sur les Droits Politiques*), SR 161.1, AS 1978 688, available in the official languages at the web site of the Federal Authorities of the Swiss Confederation, at http://www.admin.ch/ch/d/sr/c161_1.html.

18 *See supra* note 16.

19 The language of the 1999 constitution actually broadens the cantonal right to conclude treaties. Under the old, 1874 constitution, Article 9 only granted cantons the right to conclude treaties with foreign states "concerning matters of public economy, neighborly relations and police". *See supra* note 16. The broader scope of the 1999 constitution reflects what some commentators felt was the spirit, if not the letter, of the former provision.

states on behalf of a Canton". Moreover, cantons must inform the Confederation before concluding a treaty, and under Article 186 the Federal Council may "raise objections to treaties" concluded among the cantons or between cantons and foreign countries. If such objections are raised, the Federal Assembly has the discretionary power under Article 172 to decide whether to approve the treaty in question. These provisions track similar provisions in the 1874 constitution, and it is perhaps worth noting that in many instances cantonal treaties under the old constitution were never actually approved.

Of much greater importance is the fact that cantonal treaties may not conflict with federal law, and are subject to federal legislative supremacy under Article 49. Since the federal treaty-making power extends to all subject areas, this means in practice that "there is room for the conclusion of cantonal agreements only insofar as they are compatible with federal treaties".[20] Unfortunately, many cantonal treaties have never been published and therefore are difficult to obtain.

Publication of treaties is governed by the Federal Statute on Collections of Statutes and the Federal Gazette (*Bundesgesetz über die Sammlungen des Bundesrechts und das Bundesblatt* or *Loi Fédérale sur les Recueils du Droit Fédéral et la Feuille Fédérale*), which came into force on 1 January 2005.[21] Under Article 3, treaties must appear in the weekly Amtliche Sammlung (AS)/Recueil Official (RO) (see no. 3, below) if they were subject to the referendum procedure, enact law or confer legislative powers. Article 3 also requires publication of any decisions taken by treaty-based international organizations that either enact law or confer legislative powers. Treaties that will be in force for less than six months, or are considered minor, are excluded from publication. However, the Federal Council has discretion to make exceptions to this exclusion, and may authorize publication of non-law-making treaties as well.

Under Article 4, treaties between the federal government and cantons that enact law or confer legislative powers must be published in the AS/RO. Like article 3, article 4 authorizes the Federal Council to publish other cantonal treaties at its discretion.

Article 5 authorizes publication of title and citation only to treaties that affect a small number of people, are of a purely technical nature, or for technical reasons must be published in another format. In addition, treaties may also be published by title and citation only if their full publication in alternative

20 Wildhaber et al., *supra* note 7, at 666.

21 SR 170.512, AS 2004 4929, available in English and in the official languages at the web site of the Federal Authorities of the Swiss Confederation, at http://www.admin.ch/ch/d/sr/c170_512.html.

sources has been authorized by federal statute or regulation, or otherwise have been published in an official source available in Switzerland.

Article 6 establishes an exception, under which secret security treaties are not to be published in the AS.

Under Article 7, article 3 and article 4, treaties must be published in the AS at least five days before coming into force, or directly upon the in-force date becoming known, when the in-force date is not known at the time of ratification. Under Article 8 treaties can create legal obligations only upon publication, and under Article 9 the version published in the printed edition of the AS is authoritative, and if published only by title and citation, then the source cited is authoritative.

Finally, under Article 13, Article 3 treaties subject to optional or mandatory referendum must be published in the Official Gazette (*Bundesblatt/Feuille Fédérale*) before being subjected to a vote. In addition, Article 17 of the Regulation concerning Collections of Federal law and the Federal Gazette (*Verordnung über die Sammlungen des Bundesrechts und das Bundesblatt* or *Ordonnance sur les Recueils du Droit Fédéral et la Feuille Fédérale*) requires publication in the Official Gazette of the text of all other Article 3 treaties supplied to it by the Federal Council.[22]

Annotated Bibliography of Sources

General Treaty Collections

1 BUNDESBLATT DER SCHWEIZERISCHEN EIDGENOSSENSCHAFT (Bern: Bundeskanzlei, 1848–).

Summary: Official gazette. Includes the text of all treaties that are subject to either the optional or obligatory referendum procedure, and the text of any other treaties supplied to the Federal Assembly by the Federal Council as part of the approval process. Messages from the Federal Council requesting treaty approval provide detailed summaries of treaties in question, even if not the text of the treaties themselves. Published weekly. Available electronically. (See no. 4, below.)

Note: Published also in French as *Feuille Fédérale de la Confederation Suisse.*

Note: Published also in Italian as *Foglio Federale.*

Note: Title varies. *Schweizerisches Bundesblatt,* 1849–1919.

Note: Also available on microfilm.

---

22 RS 170.512.1, AS 2004 4937, available in the official languages at the web site of the Federal Authorities of the Swiss Confederation, at http://www.admin.ch/ch/d/sr/c170_512_1.html.

2 SYSTEMATISCHE SAMMLUNG DES BUNDESRECHTS
(Bern: Bundeskanzlei, 1970–).

Summary: Looseleaf. Systematic arrangement of federal Swiss law published in the *Amtliche Sammlung* (see no. 3, below) and currently in force. Separate sub-series of binders contains treaties, and follows roughly the same systematic arrangement as the statute volumes. Treaty collection includes most treaties ratified since 12 September 1848 and still in force. Some treaties never repealed, but no longer of practical effect, have been excluded, without implications for their continuing status. Federal Assembly approvals including some form of condition (e.g., reservation or declaration) are also reprinted. Updated quarterly. For discussion of electronic access, see no. 4, below. Not legally binding evidence of the law.

Note: For more detailed description, see the web site of the Federal Authorities of the Swiss Confederation at http://www.admin.ch/ch/d/sr/sr.html.

Note: Published also in French under the title, Recueil Systematique du Droit Fédéral: Nouveau Recueil Systématique des Lois et Ordonnances de la Confédération, mis à Jour et Etabli par Matiêres.

Note: Supersedes the Bereinigte Sammlung (BS), 1848–1947.

Note: Available in CD-ROM version, 1999–.

Index: See no. 6 below.

3 AMTLICHE SAMMLUNG DES BUNDESRECHTS
(Bern: s.n., 1848–).

Summary: Weekly compilation of laws adopted by the federal government of Switzerland. Begins with the year 1848, and includes treaties. For discussion of electronic access, see no. 4, below.

Index: See no. 6 below.

Note: Title varies: *Offizielle Sammlung der das Schweizerische Staatsrecht Betreffenden Aktenstücke, Bundesgesetze, Verträge und Verordnungen* (1848–1850, one volume); *Amtliche Sammlung der Bundesgesetze und Verordnungen der Schweizerishcen Eidgenossenschaft* (published in two series, vols. 2–11, 1851–1874, new series vols. 1–42, 1875–1926); *Eidgenössische Gesetzsammlung, Neue Folge* (vols. 43–63, 1927–1947); *Sammlung der Eidgenössischen Gesetze* (40 vols., 1948–1987).

Note: Published also in French: *Recueil Officiel des Pièces Concernant le Droit Public de la Suisse, des Lois Fédérales, Traités, Décrets et Arrêtés depuis l'Introduction de la Nouvelle Constitution Fédérale du 12 Septembre 1848* (1848–1850, one volume); *Recueil Officiel des Lois et Ordonnances de la Confédération Suisse* (published in two series, vols. 2–10, 1851–1874, new series in 19 volumes, 1875–1904); *Recueil des Lois Fédérales* (1904–1914, 1920–1987); *Recueil des Lois Suisses* (1915–1919), *Recueil Officiel des Lois Fédérales*, (1988–).

Note: Published also in Italian: *Raccolta Officiale delle Leggi Federali, Decreti e Regolamenti della Confederazione Svizzera* (1851–1873); *Raccolta Officiale della Leggi ed Ordinanze della Confederazione Svizzera* (1874–1891); *Raccolta Officiale delle Leggi e Decreti della Confederazione Svizzera* (1892–1904), *Raccolta delle Leggi Federali* (1904–1987), *Raccolta Ufficiale delle Leggi Federali* (1988–).

Note: Imprint varies: Bern: Staempfli, 1850; Bern: C. Fischer, 1850–1856; Bern: R. Jenni, 1857–1866; Bern: C.J. Wyss, 1867–1904; Bern: K.J. Wyss, 1904–1964; Bern: C.J. Wyss, 1965–.

Note: Pre-1848 treaties can be found in *Recueil Officiel des Pièces Concernant le Droit Public de la Suisse, des Décrets et Arrêtés de la Diète et des Concordats en Vigueur, ainsi que des Traités Conclus entre la Confédération Suisse et d'autres Etats* (Berne: ?, 1832–1849, 3 vols.).

4 SCHWEIZERISCHE EIGGENOSSENSCHAFT
Die Bundesbehörden der Schweizerischen Eidgenossenschaft.
URL: http://www.admin.ch/index.html?lang=de.

Summary: This web site provides access to *Datenbank Staatsverträge* (http://www.eda.admin.ch/eda/de/home/topics/intla/intrea/dbstv.html), an index of treaties currently in force, with links to the full text of each treaty as it appears in the *Systematische Sammlung des Bundesrechts* (no. 2, above). Treaty entries are divided by category into bilateral treaties (then listed alphabetically by country of opposite party), bilateral treaties with international organizations (then listed alphabetically by organization), and multilateral treaties organized by topic. All treaty entries are arranged by *Systematische Sammlung* classification number. Information varies by entry, but includes treaty title (usually in multiple languages), subject area, dates of signature, ratification, and entry into force, name of agency responsible for carrying out obligations under the treaty, citation to publication in the *Amtliche Sammlung* (no. 3 above), and a link to the full text as published in the *Systematische Sammlung*. Entries for multilateral treaties also include place of signature, depositary, list of official languages, as well as date of signature, ratification, and entry into force for Switzerland. Multilateral treaty entries also include a list of parties together with dates of ratification and entry into force for each.

This web site also provides access to the *Bundesblatt der Schweizerischen Eidgenossenschaft* (no. 1 above), *Systematische Sammlung des Bundesrechts* (no. 2 above), and the *Amtliche Sammlung des Bundesrechts* (no. 3 above). The link to the Bundesblatt (http://www.admin.ch/ch/d/ff/index.html) is searchable by year, 1849 -. Each year includes a detailed table of contents, in which treaties are usually listed under the name of the country of opposite party. There is also an advanced search interface that supports Boolean keyword searches and date range searches.

The link to the *Systematische Sammlung* (SR) (http://www.admin.ch/ch/d/sr/sr.html) permits researchers to search for treaties currently in force in a variety of useful ways, e.g., by subject term, through a systematic table of contents, and by date of entry into force. It is also possible to search via the advanced search interface described above. For each text, there is a wealth of supplementary information (*zusätzliche Informationen*), including links to the full texts in the *Amtliche Sammlung*, a list of amendments with links to the full texts in *the Amtliche Sammlung*, a chronology with links to the full texts in the *Amtliche Sammlung*, and PDFs of all versions. In each case, pre-1998 references are to AS citations only. There is also a *Sprachenvergleich* utility that presents article-by-article comparison of Italian, German, and French versions of document texts. Finally, the SR indexes repealed provisions by date of repeal and date of conclusion. However, repealed provisions are not available in full text, since the *Systematische Sammlung* is a collection of in-force texts only.

The link to the *Amtliche Sammlung* (http://www.admin.ch/ch/d/as/index.html) permits researchers to search individual issues of the AS back to the beginning of 1998, using AS citation (year and page number) to retrieve the desired text. If the citation is unknown, the researcher can obtain it by looking up the desired text in the *Systematische Sammlung* first. It is also possible to search the *Amtliche Sammlung* via the advanced search interface described above. Publicatiion of treaties in the *Amtliche Sammlung* is usually delayed until several months after ratification.

In general, treaty retrieval is simplest via the *Datenbank Staatsverträge*, as long as the desired treaty is still in force. However, the *Systematische Sammlung* is the best source of treaty information is the researcher requires earlier versions of a treaty. Finally, the researcher will have to use the printed *Amtliche Sammlung* if the treaty text required is either no longer in force or if the version required is pre-1998.

This web site also provides access to treaties concluded between the Swiss Confederation and the European Union at http://www.admin.ch/ch/d/eur/search.html.

Note: Since 2007 the Official Publications Center (*Kompetenzzentrum Amtliche Veräffentlichungen*) has begun creating an English-language version of the Systemataische Sammlung at http://www.admin.ch/ch/e/rs/rs.html. According to the accompanying description, "[n]ew translations will also be regularly added to the compilation, but there is no plan to translate all Swiss legislation into English."

5 DIE SCHWEIZERISCHE BUNDESGESETZGEBUNG. NACH MATERIEN GEORDNETE SAMMLUNG DER GESETZE, BESCHLÜSSE, VERORDNUNGEN, UND STAATSVERTRÄGE DER SCHWEIZERISCHEN EIDGENOSSENSCHAFT, SOWIE DER KONKORDATE. 2ND ED
P. Wolf, ed.
(Basel: Kreis, 1905–1909). 4 vols.

Summary: This title includes the text of all treaties concluded by Switzerland up to the time of publication.

6 OFFIZIELLE SAMMLUNG DER DAS SCHWEIZERISCHE STAATSRECHT BETREFFENDEN ALTENSTÜCKE, DER IN KRAFT BESTEHENDEN EIDGENOSSISCHEN BESCHLÜSSE, VERORDNUNGEN, UND CONCORDATE, UND DER ZWISCHEN DER EIDGENOSSENSCHAFT UND DEN BENACHBARTEN STAATEN ABGESCHLOSSENEN BESONDERN VERTRÄGE
(Zurich: Orell, Fussli, 1820–1849). Bd. I 407 pp., Bd. II 612 pp.; Bd. III 368 pp.

Summary: In three volumes. Vol. I includes the *Bundesvertrag zwichen den XXII Cantonen*, the *Acte Portant Reconaissance et Garantie de la Neutralité Perpétuelle de la Suisse et de l'Inviolabilité de son Territorie*, as well as a number of other agreements emanating from the 1815 Congress of Vienna, relating to the status of Switzerland. Many of the agreements are in French, with German translations, others are in German only. Vol. I also includes a variety of agreements between the cantons relating to the internal organization of the Confederation, touching upon such subjects as justice, police, military service, and the conduct of diplomatic affairs. Vol. I also includes a collection of "special" treaties between the Confederation and foreign powers. Vol. II updates the categories of inter-cantonal agreements relating to the internal organization of the Confederation, and that of "special" treaties, in this case organized by country of opposite party. Vol. III includes a section of inter-cantonal agreements perfecting arrangements made by foreign powers relating to the Confederation, an updated section of inter-cantonal agreements relating to internal organization of the Confederation, and an updated section of "special" treaties, in this case organized principally by treaty category, e.g., commercial treaties, treaties relating to freedom of movement, extradition treaties, etc.

7 CH.CH
Die Bundesbehörden der Schweizerishcen Eidgenossenschaft.
URL: http://www.ch.ch/verzeichnis/index.html?lang=de&viewpage=kanton.

Summary: This web site is part of the *Schweizerische Eidgenossenschaft* collection of web sites, and provides clearinghouse access to cantonal treaties housed at the individual cantonal web sites. (See no. 4, above.) Cantonal treaties are included in systematic collections of in-force legislation, published primarily in loose-leaf format. These include, for example, the *Zürcher Gesetzessammlung* (ZH-Lex), the *Bernische Systematische Gesetzessammlung* (BSG), the *Recueil Systématique Genevois* (RSG). Electronic versions typically also include legislation no longer in force. Most cantonal web sites also provide access to official gazettes, though some on subscription basis only (e.g., Basel-Stadt).

Note: In German, French or Italian only, depending on canton.

Note: Navigation is not uniform across all cantonal web sites. Therefore, listed below are links to the systematic collections of in-force legislation of some of the more important cantons:

Bern: http://www.sta.be.ch/belex/d/default.asp.

Fribourg: http://bdlf.fr.ch/.

Geneve: http://www.ge.ch/legislation/.

Glarus: http://www.gl.ch/xml_1/internet/de/application/d1256/d41/f343.cfm.

Grabünden: http://www.gr-lex.gr.ch/?locale=de.

Neuchâtel: http://www.ne.ch/neat/site/jsp/rubrique/rubrique.jsp?StyleType=bleu&CatId=2151.

Schwyz: http://www.sz.ch/xml_1/internet/de/application/d999/d2522/d24457/p477.cfm.

Uri: http://ur.lexspider.com/uri/page/search?execution=e1s1.

8 LEXFIND

University of Fribourg Institute of Federalism.

URL: http://www.lexfind.ch/.

Summary: The Institute of Federalism maintains a database of federated cantonal legislation, LexFind, which includes information about cantonal treaties. This database is based upon the systematic, looseleaf collections of laws currently in force, made available electronically through each of the cantons' web portals (see no. 7, above). In effect, this database makes it possible to search all such loose-leaf collections simultaneously, and to retrieve copies of legally binding instruments (including treaties) in full-text. The search interface permits searches by systematic number or title. Documents are in German, French, or Italian, although the Institute's search engine is available in English.

9 RECUEIL DES ACCORDS INTERNATIONAUX CONCLUS PAR LES CANTONS SUISSES: EN VIGUEUR AU 1 JANVIER 1980

Yves Lejeune, ed.,

(Bern: P. Lang, 1982). 495 pp.

Summary: This title contains the text of treaties concluded by the Swiss cantons, and in force as of 1 January 1980. The collection is not exhaustive, but representative of the kinds of treaties the cantons have concluded, and continue to conclude. The oldest treaty dates from 1756, but the collection includes 40 treaties concluded since World War II as well. Treaties are organized by canton, and within each canton by subject. Each treaty includes a brief annotation, noting its official source, dates of ratification by relevant bodies, date of commencement, addition of new parties, presence of compromissory clauses and relationship to subsequent federal treaties. Treaties are reproduced primarily in French, but some in German, when no official French text was available. Includes outline subject classification, index by canton and subject index. Also includes helpful introductory section, summarizing the constitutional status of cantonal treaty-making since 1803 and indicating criteria of inclusion in the collection.

Note: According to the preface, the majority of cantonal treaties have not been published in the cantons' session laws.

Series title: *Schriften des Forschungsinstituts für Föderalismus und Regierungsstrukturen*, Nr. 8.

Treaty Indexes

10 AMTLICHE SAMMLUNG DES BUNDESRECHTS UND SYSTEMATISCHE SAMMLUNG DES BUNDESRECHTS. INHALTSVERZEICHNIS

(Bern: Bundeskanzlei, 1970–).

Summary: Annual index of Swiss law. This title is published in conjunction with the *Amtliche Sammlung des Bundesrechts* (see no. 3 above); it also serves as an index to the *Systematische Sammlung des Bundesrechts* (see no. 2 above).

Note: Title varies: *Amtliche Sammlung und Systematische Sammlung des Bundesrechts. Inhaltsverzeichnis*, 1970–1972; *Sammlung der Eidgenossischen Gesetze und Systemataische Sammlung des Bundesrechts*, 1973–1986.

Note: Published also in French, as *Recueil des Lois Fédérales et Recueil Systématique du Droit Fédéral. Table des Matières* (1973–1986), *Recueil Officiel des Lois Fédérales et Recueil Systematique du Droit Federal. Table des Matieres* (1987–).

11 BUNDESVERFASSUNGSRECHT. STAATSVERTRÄGE. SONDERHEFT ZUR ZEITSCHRIFT FÜR SCHWEIZERISCHES RECHT

Hans-Urs Wili and Laurenz Rotach

(Basel: Helbing & Lichtenhahn, 1989–?).

Summary: Published as an annual, unnumbered supplement to *Zeitschrift für Schweizerisches Recht*. It is in two sections, one of which covers treaty developments for the previous year (1989 issue covers 1987 and 1988). Entries provide information about source of publication, and status of treaty, i.e., whether signed, ratified, or entered into force. Each entry also indicates whether the treaty was summarized in the *Zeitschrift für Schweizerisches Recht*. Published for the years 1987–1990. Apparently no longer published.

12 SYSTEMATISCHES REGISTER ZU DEN GELTENDEN STAATSVERTRÄGEN DER SCHWEIZERISCHEN EIDGENOSSENSCHFT UND DER KANTONE MIT DEM AUSLAND

Schweizerische Justiz – und Polizeidepartement, per Paul Marx (Zurich: Orell, Fussli, 1918). 414 pp.

Summary: This title contains an index to treaties concluded by Switzerland, as well as by individual cantons, and in force as of the date of publication. Treaty entries are grouped into nine basic areas, and into sub-topics as needed. Multilateral treaties are listed first, followed by bilateral treaties, organized first by country of opposite party, and then according to the topic outline. Information regarding date of signature and date of effect is given, together with citations to major print sources. Multilateral treaty entries include a list of parties. Following each treaty entry, individual articles and clauses are indexed within the topical scheme. The title includes a fold-out table listing extradition treaties, and the crimes covered within each, together with references to the relevant clauses. Not an official publication, although compiled in cooperation with the Swiss Department of Justice.

Note: Also published in French, as *Répertoire Systématique des Traités en Vigueur entre la Confédération Suisse ou les Cantons et l'Etranger*.

Topical and Selected Treaty Collections

13 ABKOMMEN SCHWEIZ-EWG

Texte und Kommentare des Freihändelsabkommens und anderer Abkommen der Schweiz mit der EWG oder anderen Europäischen Institutionen (Zurich: [ ], 1973–1983). 7 vols.

Summary: Looseleaf. Contains the text of treaties concluded by Switzerland and various European institutions, especially the European Economic Community. Includes the treaty on free trade.

14 SAMMLUNG DER HANDELS-, NIEDERLASSUNGS – UND KONSULAR-VERTRÄGE DER SCHWEIZ MIT DEM AUSLANDE, IMBEGRIFFEN DIE VERTRÄGE ÜBER DEN SCHUTZ DES GEISTIGEN EIGENTHUMS

A. Eichmann

(Zurich: Orell Fussli, 1885). 351 pp.

Summary: Collection of treaties related to commerce, residence and consular relations, in force at the time of publication. This title also includes treaties related to intellectual property. Each treaty is reproduced in full, and preceded by a note indicating the date of signature, the date of coming-into-force for Switzerland, citations to the official source of publication (*Bundesblatt* or *Amtliche Sammlung*) and citations to accompanying reports of the National Commission. Excerpts from the reports are reproduced as well, in those instances where they are essential to an understanding of treaty language. This title includes a table of contents, organized by country of opposite party, a chronological table of treaties in force and a table of treaties no longer in force, organized by jurisdiction. Also includes a subject index.

Note: Series title: *Schweizerische Rechtsbücher.*

Note: Published also in French as *Traités de Commerce et d'Etablissement, Conventions Concernant les Attributions Consulaires ainsi que la Propriété Industrielle, Littéraire et Artistique en Vigueur le 1er Juillet 1886 entre la Suisse et les Pays Etrangers* (Berne: Impr. Stampfli, Lack, Scheim and Cie, 1886).

Diplomatic Documents

15 DIPLOMATISCHE DOKUMENTE DER SCHWEIZ: 1848–1945
Nationale Kommission für die Veröffentlichung Diplomatischer Dokumente der Schweiz.
Various publishers, 1979–.

Summary: This is a major, continuing series of volumes documenting Swiss practice in foreign relations, 1848–. Documents are selected because they "reveal a general orientation of Swiss foreign policy" or because "they have had a lasting effect on this orientation at a particular time".

Volumes reproduce documents concerning the foreign relations of Switzerland, derived principally from the Swiss Federal Archives. Documents include diplomatic correspondence, as well as documents from the files of all federal departments involved in the formation and implementation of foreign policy. Documents are arranged in chronological order, reproduced in the original language and mostly in full, with some well marked deletions. The editorial gloss is spare, but includes important identifying information. Footnotes provide cross-references to other related documents in the collection, and document appendices reproduce documents mentioned in the body of the text.

The set includes an extremely helpful thematic index, which organizes the documents by topic and provides document summaries. It also includes indexes of personal and place names, as well as various useful appendices, such as an organizational chart and list of diplomatic and consular personnel.

The first series is complete in 15 volumes, covering the period 1848–1945. The second series, commencing in 1997 and to be completed in 2020, will cover the period 1945–1989, known as the "Petitpierre era", in recognition of the dominant influence of Max Petitpierre, Federal Councillor responsible for Swiss diplomacy during that entire time. Vols. 16–24 have been published to date, covering the period through December, 1966.

The entire first and second series are accompanied by the DoDiS database, available at the web site of the National Commission for the Publication of Diplomatic Documents (http://db.dodis.ch/dodis?_l=de), which reproduces in full both the first and second series. This database includes photographic archive, presently covering the years 1945–1973 (http://dodis.ch/de/node/292), and a collection of helpful, thematically organized, documents not included in the printed version of the set (http://dodis.ch/de/services/dokumentationen). There is an excellent user guide at http://www.dodis.ch/de/faq.

The DoDiS database also includes an extremely useful bibliography of books and articles on Swiss diplomacy, organized by topic. This bibliography is housed at http://dodis.ch/de/services/bibliographie.

Note: Alternate titles for first series: *Documents Diplomatiques Suisses: 1848–1945*, and *Documenti Diplomatici Svizzeri, 1848–1945*. Similarly for second series.

Note: Publisher varies. Bern: Benteli, 1979–1996; Zurich: Chronos, Locarno: Armando Dado, Geneva: Editions Zoe, 1997–.

Note: This important set is summarized, in German, in Wikipedia, at: http://de.wikipedia.org/wiki/Diplomatische_Dokumente_der_Schweiz#cite_note-2.

16 SWISS FEDERAL ARCHIVE
URL: http://www.bar.admin.ch/dokumentation/00445/index.html?lang=de.

Summary: The Swiss Federal Archive maintains a list of print titles published in several different series of essays, reports and archival documents, related to various topics in Swiss history and contemporary events. Some titles are issued by the Federal Archive itself, others by other agencies, such as the Swiss Department of Foreign Affairs. Some are published as government documents, others by commercial publishers, notably Chronos Verlag. Some titles have individual authors, others do not. Some titles are available in full text at the Federal Archive web site, others are represented by tables of contents and/or introductions, links to publishers' descriptions, etc., while yet others are only very briefly summarized.

From the point of view of Swiss practice in international affairs and international law, the most important series is that entitled *Inventare*, which comprises about 20 titles issued since the late 1970s. Representative examples of this series include the following. *Schweiz—Naher Osten von der Nachkriegsszeit bis zu den 1990er Jahren* (Chronos: 2004) includes a listing of 15,000 documents related to Swiss relations with nations of the Middle East since 1945, organized by topic. It also includes a selection of significant documents in full-text and a detailed historical introduction to Swiss practice in this area during the time span covered by the documents themselves. It also includes a CD-ROM.

Two other series cataloged at the Federal Archive web site are *Studien und Quellen*, and *Dossiers*. The former are issued as a numbered series, and include essays by experts on a variety of topics related to Swiss foreign relations. The latter have thematic volume titles, such as *Die Verwaltung der Schweizerischen Aussenpolitik, 1914–1978* (Chronos: 2002).

PDFs listing all titles currently in print for all series are available at the department's web site, listed above.

17 EIDGENÖSSISCHES DEPARTEMENT FÜR AUSWÄRTIGE ANGELEGENHEITEN
URL: http://www.eda.admin.ch/eda/de/home.html.

Summary: A component of the *Schweizerische Eidgenossenschaft* family of web sites (see nos. 4 and 7, above), the web site of the Department für Auswärtigen Angelegenheiten (Department of Foreign Affairs) includes reports and summaries of *Vernehmlassungen* (consultations) on subjects related to international relations, undertaken under both Article 152 of the Statute on the Federal Assembly and Article 3 of the Federal Statute on Consultation (see the section on Treaty Implementation, above). Reports are included for both current and completed consultations, and there is an agenda of planned consultations as well. See the Department's web site, at http://www.admin.ch/aktuell/vernehmlassung/index.html?lang=de.

18 TEXTE ZUR SCHWEIZER SICHERHEITSPOLITIK, 1960–1990
Jurg Stussi-Lauterburg und Pierre Baur, eds.
(Brugg, Schweiz: Effingerhof, 1991).

Summary: This series reprints diplomatic documents related to Swiss military and political security. Texts are primarily in German, with one text in French.

19 DOKUMENTE ZUR SCHWEIZERISCHEN NEUTRALITÄT SEIT 1945: BERICHTE UND STELLUNGNAHMEN DER SCHWEIZERISCHEN BUNDESBEHÖRDEN ZU FRAGEN DER NEUTRALITÄT, 1945–1983
Dietrich Schindler et al., eds.
(Bern: P. Haupt, 1984). 481 pp.

Summary: This title contains documents related to Swiss neutrality. Documents are organized into topical chapters, dealing with such topics as neutrality and the United Nations, neutrality and European and other regional organizations, armed neutrality and so on. Documents are derived from a number of official sources, and each is introduced by a brief note indicating both the source and the context in which it was issued. Many documents are excerpted. Mostly in German, but some documents are in French as well. The title includes a detailed table of contents and a subject index.

Series title: *Schriftenreihe der Schweizerischen Gesellschaft für Aussenpolitik*, Bd. 9.

Yearbooks and Digests of State Practice

20 SCHWEIZERISCHE ZEITSCHRIFT FÜR INTERNATIONALES UND EUROPÄISCHES RECHT

Schweizerische Vereinigung für Internationales Recht.
(Zürich: Schulthess Polygraphischer Verlag, 1991–).

Summary: Published four to five times per year (three to four times per year, 1991–1992), this title includes annual updates of Swiss practice in a variety of areas, including sources of international law, relations between international and municipal law, state territory, subjects of international law, state succession, diplomatic and consular protection, the law of international organizations, international responsibility, collective security and the pacific settlement of disputes, law of armed conflict and the law of neutrality.

Note: Supersedes the *Schweizerisches Jahrbuch für Internationales Recht/Annuaire Suisse de Droit International*, published in 47 vols, from 1944–1990.

Note: French title is *Revue Suisse de Droit International et de Droit Européen*. Italian title is *Rivista Svizzera di Diritto Internazionale e di Diritto Europeo*. Also has English title: *Swiss Review of International and European Law*, but articles are primarily in French and German.

United Kingdom

Maria I. Smolka Day

Treaty Ratification and Implementation

In the United Kingdom legal system, treaty-making power was traditionally vested in the Crown as part of the Royal prerogative. The Queen, however, according to British constitutional practice, has exercised this power only on the advice of Her Ministers. This means that actual responsibility for concluding treaties lies with the Secretary of State for Foreign and Commonwealth Affairs, who, if needed, may consult with other Departments of Government. The Foreign and Commonwealth Office (FCO) Legal Advisers and the FCO Treaty Section must always be given the opportunity to comment on the drafts of all treaties under negotiation to ensure that they are drafted in accordance with correct international practice.

The United Kingdom does not have a written constitution, and until recently, the rules on conclusion and ratification of treaties resulted from custom and usage. There was no constitutional or even a legislative requirement for Parliamentary approval of treaties. However, after 1924 but before 2010, treaties subject to ratification or equivalent action (with limited exceptions[1]) were laid before the Parliament for 21 sitting days according to the Ponsonby Rule. This gave Members of Parliament a chance to hold hearings, ask questions, or in any other way effect a treaty ratification, but this practice was treated as a constitutional convention only and did not result in any formal sanction. The position of Parliament was substantially strengthened when Part 2, "Ratification of Treaties," of the *Constitutional Reform and Governance Act (CraG) 2010 (C. 25)* entered into force on November 11, 2010. The Act changed previous governmental practice into a legislative requirement prescribing more precisely the actions which the Government and both Houses of Parliament have to follow. The Government has to lay a copy of the treaty before both Houses of Parliament and wait for 21 sitting days. Although no positive action on the part of Parliament is required for ratification of a treaty, its negative opinion cannot be ignored anymore, and, in the case of the

1 Although now superceded by the CraG Act, a description of exceptions from the Ponsonby Rule can be found in the "Note on the Ponsonby Rule" *available at* http://www.publications.parliament.uk/pa/ld200506/ldselect/ldconst/236/23612.htm.

 DOI 10.1163/9789004272224_033

House of Commons, it triggers a prolonged and complicated additional procedure.[2]

Under the law of the United Kingdom treaties are not self-executing and do not become part of the internal legal system upon entry into force. According to British constitutional law, rights and obligations under a treaty are incorporated into the national legal order by an act of Parliament or other official act. The following categories of treaties require legislative action for their implementation:

1. treaties requiring for their execution and application in the United Kingdom a modification of or an addition to existing common law or statute;
2. treaties requiring for their execution in the United Kingdom that the Crown receives some new powers not already possessed by it;
3. treaties affecting private rights;
4. treaties creating a direct or contingent financial obligation upon the United Kingdom;
5. treaties providing for an increase in the powers of the European Parliament.[3]

Additionally, on the basis of constitutional practice, any treaty involving the cession of British territory is approved by the Parliament in the form of a statute.[4] The legislative action incorporating treaty obligations into the British legal system is usually taken before ratification. If the need for such an action was not anticipated and taken before the conclusion of a treaty, the proper steps have to be taken immediately thereafter to bring UK law into the compliance with it. Such a situation may result, for example, from the decision of an international court.

Treaties subject to ratification and laid before the Parliament are published as *Command Papers* in the *Miscellaneous, Country*, or *European Communities* series. Since 1997 each treaty must also be accompanied by an Explanatory Memorandum, which describes the subject matter of the treaty, presents reasons why the Government proposes its ratification, and explains the benefits and burdens for the United Kingdom which might result from participation in the treaty.

2 *See* Jill Barrett, *The United Kingdom and Parliamentary Scrutiny of Treaties: Recent Reforms*, 60 INT'L & COMP. L. Q. 225-245 (2011).

3 *See* Sir Ian Sinclair & Susan J. Dickson, *United Kingdom, in* NATIONAL TREATY LAW AND PRACTICE: FRANCE, GERMANY, INDIA, SWITZERLAND, THAILAND, UNITED KINGDOM 320 (Monroe Leigh & Merritt R. Blakeslee eds., 1995).

4 Id.

All treaties binding upon the United Kingdom are published in the *Treaty Series* of *Command Papers*. There are no "classified agreements" unavailable to the public. Confidential arrangements between governments cannot have the form of legally binding instruments, since all such instruments are subject to publication and registration with the United Nations in accordance with Article 102 of the UN Charter.

British official language differentiates between a treaty and a so-called Memorandum of Understanding (MOU). This term is used for an international agreement not legally binding in nature. Its form and wording, different from that of a treaty, should clearly express such an intention of the parties.[5] MOUs are used, among other purposes, to specify agreements in matters of defense or technology where there is a need for such documents to be classified.[6] They are not published. A note of caution, however: a treaty may nonetheless be called a "Memorandum of Understanding" and such a treaty, like any other treaty, is a legally binding instrument.

Annotated Bibliography of Sources

General Treaty Collections

1 TREATY SERIES

(London, Her Majesty's Stationary Office (HMSO), 1892–).

Summary: Commonly known as *United Kingdom Treaty Series*, this is a sub-series in the parliamentary series *Papers by Command*. Every treaty has both a command paper number (in the lower left corner) and a *Treaty Series* number. Issues of *Treaty Series* contain the official text of all treaties ratified by the United Kingdom. A text of the same treaty before ratification may appear with only a command number in one of the other sub-series of the *Papers by Command* as mentioned above. The link to such earlier publication is indicated by a note in the upper left corner of the final publication. Unlike command papers, which are numbered consecutively in an ongoing series, the numbering of *Treaty Series* begins each year with no. 1.

Index: There is an annual *Index to Treaty Series*, which includes a numerical list of all treaties published during the year, subject and country indexes. Three

5 Suggested terminology to be used in the drafting of MOUs is included in *Treaties and MOUs: Guidance on Practice and Procedures*, 2nd ed. April 2000, revised April 2012 and available at: https://www.gov.uk/government/publications/treaties-and-mous-guidance-on-practice-and-procedures.

6 Id., p. 1.

or four *Supplementary Lists of Ratifications, Accessions, Withdrawals, etc.* are also published each year. Each consecutive *List* supplements, but does not cumulate, information from the previous *List*. Exchanges of Notes which extend the duration of an earlier agreement are printed only in the *Supplementary Lists*, and not in the *Index*. Therefore all lists should be retained. The HMSO used to publish every 3 years a *General Index to Treaty Series*, but the most recent of these, covering the years 1977–1979, appeared in 1983.

Note: Digital versions of *Command Papers* containing the text of treaties published in one of the four series (*Country, Miscellaneous, European*, or *Treaty Series*) as well as indexes published in those series are available in Chadwyck-Healey's database "House of Commons Parliamentary Papers" available by subscription.

Note: UK Treaties Online (http://treaties.fco.gov.uk/treaties/treaty.htm) is a web page maintained by the Foreign and Commonwealth Office of the British Government. It contains information on 14,000 treaties, but in many cases it does not provide direct access to their texts. Paradoxically, it tends to include older texts, but treaties from the years 2002–2012 may be found on the archival page of the Foreign and Commonwealth Office at: http://webarchive.nationalarchives.gov.uk/20121212135632/http://www.fco.gov.uk/en/publications-and-documents/treaties/.

Note: Information on current treaty actions may be found in the monthly *Bulletin* available online since 2013 at: https://www.gov.uk/government/collections/uk-treaty-action-bulletins. The Foreign and Commonwealth Office has prepared a document, *UK Treaties: Guidence to The Treaties to Which the UK is, or has been, a Party*, available at: https://www.gov.uk/uk-treaties. At this time it is the best place for starting online research.

Note: The full text of British legislation from 1988 on, including acts implementing international treaties, is available in *UK Public General Acts*, on the HMSO home page at http://www.legislation.gov.uk/ukpga. There is also partial coverage for the years 1801–1987.

Note: Treaty information is also available on The Stationary Office page, www.tsoshop.co.uk, where a text of the treaty may be ordered for a fee.

Treaty Indexes

2 AN INDEX OF BRITISH TREATIES....

Clive Perry and Charity Hopkins. (London: HMSO, 1970–1991). 4 vols.

Summary: Contains a comprehensive index of all treaties concluded by England or the United Kingdom from 1101 to 1988. Main entries, organized in *Chronological List of Treaties* are included in vol. 2 (1101–1925), vol. 3

(1926–1968), and vol. 4 (1969–1988). Additionally, vol. 4, published in 1991, contains information updating the entries in vols. 2 and 3. The following information is provided: title, parties, place of signature, date of signature, entry into force, source of printed publication, information on duration, modifications, and cessation (where applicable), and languages of authentic texts. Entries for multilateral treaties include also information on the place where the treaty and documents of ratification or accession are deposited as well as dates of entry into force for individual parties.

Index: Vol. 1 includes subject indexes of multilateral treaties and bilateral treaties, as well as an index of bilateral treaties arranged by country and then by subject.

Note: Vols. 1–3, *An Index to British Treaties, 1101–1968* compiled and annotated under the auspices of the International Law Fund and the British Institute of International and Comparative Law. Vol. 4, covering the period 1969–1988, compiled and annotated under the auspices of the University of Nottingham Treaty Centre by D. J. Harris and J. A. Shepherd.

Topical and Selected Treaty Publications

3 HERTSLET'S COMMERCIAL TREATIES

Compiled from authentic documents by Lewis Hertslet. (London : Butterworth, 1840–1925). 31 vols.

Summary: This series contains the texts of multilateral and bilateral treaties of the United Kingdom dealing with commerce and navigation, broadly understood, including issues of slavery, extradition, nationality, copyright, postal matters, etc. Vol . 29 (1923) contains a "special collection of documents relating to peace settlement." The selection covers treaties dated from 1354 to 1921. Multilingual, but mostly in English.

Index: "General index" in v. 3–10. "General index. Countries. Subjects," in v. 11, 18. "Index of subjects, vol. i-xii," in v. 12. "Chronological [and] General index" in v. 13, 15, 17, 19, 20. "General index arranged in order of countries and subjects ... vol. i-xv ... by Sir Edward Hertslet," in v. 16. "General index, arranged in order of countries and subjects ... vols. 1–21. With notes. Compiled by H.W. Brant." in v. 22. "Chronological and General index to the treaties, laws and other documents contained in vols. xxiii-xxx. Compiled by C.S. Nicoll and W.L. Berrow." in v. 31.

Note: Compilers: Lewis Hertslet, v. 1–11, 1840–64.–Sir Edward Hertslet, v. 12–19, 1871–95. –Edward C. Hertslet, v. 17–19, 1890–95. –Augustus H. Oakes, v. 20, 21, 23, 1898–1905. –Frederick H.T. Streatfeild, v. 20, 1898. –Richard W. Brant, v. 21–25, 1901–10. –Godfrey E.P. Hertslet, v. 24–26, 1907–13. –Edward Parkes, v. 26–27, 1913–17. –W.L. Berrow, v. 27–31, 1917–25. –C.S. Nicoll, v. 28–31, 1922–25.

Note: Title varies. v. 1–24: A complete collection of the treaties and conventions, and reciprocal regulations, at present subsisting between Great Britain & foreign powers, and of the laws, decrees and orders in council, concerning the same.

Note: Title varies slightly in v. 25–31: "Hertslet's commerical treaties..."

Note: Volumes 2, 4–7, 11–12, 20–31 published by HMSO.

Note: Ceased as a separate publication with v. 31, being incorporated with *British and Foreign State Papers*, of the Foreign office, beginning with v. 116. (see no. 4 below)

Note: Digitized and partially available on Google Books.

4 BRITISH AND FOREIGN STATE PAPERS

Compiled by the Librarian and Keeper of the Papers, Foreign Office. (London: James Ridgway and Sons, 1841–1977). 170 vols.

Summary: Includes among other documents the texts of international treaties. Volumes for 1922–1950 incorporate *Hertslet's Commercial Treaties*. (see no. 3 above). For a full description of the set, see no. 7 below.

5 HERTSLET'S CHINA TREATIES

TREATIES, &C. BETWEEN GREAT BRITAIN AND CHINA; AND BETWEEN CHINA AND FOREIGN POWERS; AND ORDERS IN COUNCIL, RULES, REGULATIONS, ACTS OF PARLIAMENT, DECREES, &C. AFFECTING BRITISH INTERESTS IN CHINA IN FORCE ON THE 1ST JANUARY, 1908.

Rev. under the superintendence of the librarian of the Foreign Office, by Godfrey E. P. Hertslet, with the assistance of Edward Parkes. (London, Printed for HMSO, by Harrison and Sons, 1908). 2 vols.

Summary: Includes treaties not only between China and the United Kingdom but also between China and other countries, but those with Britain predominate. One of the British publications emphasizing British treaty relations with individual countries. For a full listing of such publications, which are mostly of historic significance, see: *Manual of Collections of Treaties and Collections Relating to Treaties*.[7]

Note: Digitized by Google Books.

6 A COLLECTION OF TREATIES, ENGAGEMENTS, AND SANADS RELATING TO INDIA AND NEIGHBOURING COUNTRIES

---

7 Denys Peter Myers. (Cambridge: Harvard University Press, 1922).

Compiled by C.U. Aitchison. Rev. and continued up to 1929. (Calcutta : Government of India Central Publication Branch, 1929–1933). 14 vols.

Summary: Collection of treaties of Indian subcontinent and other parts of Asia during the British colonial time. Contents: v. 1. Punjab, Punjab states, and Delhi. v. 2. United provinces of Agra & Oudh, Bengal, Bihar, Orissa & the Central Provinces. v. 3. Rajputana. v. 4. Central India Agency, Bhopal Agency & southern states of Central & Malwa Agency. v. 5. Central India (Bhundelkhand & Baghelkhand & Gwalior). v. 6. Western India states & Baroda.. v. 7–8. Bombay. v. 9. Hyderabad, Mysore & Coorg. v. 10. Madras & the Madras States. v. 11. Aden & the south western coast of Arabia, the Arab principalities in the Persian Gulf, Muscat (Oman), Baluchistan & the North West Frontier Province. v. 12. Jammu & Kashmir, Sikkim, Assam & Burma. v. 13. Persia & Afghanistan. v. 14. Eastern Turkistan, Tibet, Nepal, Bhutan & Siam. Includes indexes.

Note: Reprinted in 1983 under the imprint: Delhi: Mittal Publishers.

Note: Digitized by Google Books.

Diplomatic Documents

7 BRITISH AND FOREIGN STATE PAPERS

Compiled by the Librarian and Keeper of the Papers, Foreign Office. (London: James Ridgway and Sons, 1841–1977). 170 vols.

Summary: From Volume 1: “This publication is intended to comprise the principal Documents which have been made public, relating to the Political and Commercial Affairs of Nations, and to their Relations with each other, from the termination of the War in 1814 to the latest Period.” The source covers the years 1812–1968, containing texts of international treaties and other diplomatic documents such as statements, speeches, declarations, communiques, etc. from the UK and other countries, relevant for international relations and practice of international law. Text of treaties in English and in language(s) of co-signatories. Also includes information on treaty actions.

Index: Each volume includes chronological and alphabetical (subject) indexes of documents included in the volume as well as those affected by them. The cumulative indexes are published as follows: index for vols. 1–20 (1812–1833) issued as v. 21, pt. 1; vols. 1–42 (1812–1853) issued as v. 43 (covers 1373–1853); vols. 1–63 (1812–1873) issued as v. 64 (covers 1373–1873); vols. 65–79 (1873–1888) issued as v. 80; vols. 65–92 (1873–1900) issued as v. 93; vols. 94–114 (1900–1921) issued as v. 115; vols. 116–137 (1922–1934) issued as v. 138; vols. 139–164 (1935–1960) issued as v. 165; vols. 166–169 (1961–1968) issued as v. 170.

Note: Vols. for 1812/14–1961/62 issued by Great Britain. Foreign Office; 1963/64–1976/68 by Great Britain: Foreign and Commonwealth Office.

Note: Vols. 41–170 published by HMSO.

Note: Incorporates *Hertslet's Commercial Treaties*, 1922–1950 (see no. 3 above).

Note: Digitized and partially available from Google Books.

8 DOCUMENTS ON BRITISH FOREIGN POLICY, 1919–1939

Edited by E.L. Woodward and Rohan Butler. (London: HMSO, 1946–).

Summary: Selected documents from the Archives of the Foreign Office relating to British foreign policy between 1919 and 1939. Issued in four series consisting of 65 vols.: First series, 1919–1929 (27 vols.); Series 1A, 1925–1929 (7 vols.); Second series, 1930–1938 (21 vols.); Third series, 1938–1939 (10 vols.). Each volume contains an analytical table of contents.

Index: Third Series, Vol. 10, *Index* includes reference tables of sovereigns and holders of office arranged by country, as well as an index of persons and a subject index.

Note: Continued by: *Documents on British policy overseas* (see no. 9 below).

Note: Digitized by Google Books.

9 DOCUMENTS ON BRITISH POLICY OVERSEAS

Edited by Rohan Butler and M.E. Pelly, assisted by H. J. Yasamee. (London: HMSO, 1984–).

Summary: Selected documents, largely from Foreign and Commonwealth Office, starting after WWII. Series I: 1945–1950: v. 1. Conference at Potsdam July-August 1945; v. 2. Conferences and conversations 1945: London, Washington, and Moscow; v. 3. Britain and America, negotiation of the United States loan, 3 August-7 December 1945; v. 4. Britain and America: atomic energy, bases and food, 12 December 1945–31 July 1946; v. 5. Germany and Western Europe, 11 August-31 December 1945; v. 6. Eastern Europe, August 1945-April 1946; v. 7. United Nations: Iran, Cold War and world organization, 1946–1947; v. 8. Britain and China 1945–1950. Series II: v. 1. The Schuman Plan, the Council of Europe and Western European integration, May 1950-December 1952; v. 2. The London conferences, Anglo-American relations and Cold War strategy, January-June 1950; v. 3. German rearmament, September-December 1950; v. 4. Korea, 1950–1951. Series III: v. 1. Britain and the Soviet Union, 1968–1972; v. 2. Conference on security and Cooperation in Europe, 1972–1975; v. 3. Detente in Europe, 1972–1976; v. 4. The year of Europe : America, Europe and the energy crisis, 1972–1974; v. 5. The Southern flank in crisis, 1973–1976; v. 6. Berlin in the Cold War, 1948–1990; v. 7. German unification 1989–1990; v. 8. The invasion of Afghanistan and UK-Soviet relations, 1979–1982.

Note: Most volumes include an index. Some volumes in Series III are accompanied by CD-ROMs with "fully-searchable facsimile documents, [some] of which are otherwise unavailable to researchers."--P. [4] of cover, Ser. III, v. 4.

Note: Continues: *Documents on British foreign policy, 1919–1939* (see no. 8 above).

Note: Series III: v. 3 published by Frank Cass; v. 4 – by Whitehall History Publishing; v. 6 – by Routledge.

Note: Digitized by Google Books. Database, *Documents on British Policy Overseas: Diplomacy in the Twentieth Century*, produced by Chadwyck-Healey / ProQuest in cooperation with Foreign and Commonwealth Office is available by subscription.

10 BRITISH DOCUMENTS ON FOREIGN AFFAIRS
Reports and Papers from the Foreign Office Confidential Print. (Frederick, Md.: University Publications of America, 1983–).

Summary: Compilation of diplomatic reports, dispatches, and telegrams printed since circa 1850 for limited circulation within the British government. Only a portion of these papers survived, and parts are made available to the public, edited by English scholars. The completed publication will consist of 425 volumes divided into seven geographic series and four topical series. Part I: From the mid-nineteenth century to the First World War: Series A, Russia, 1859–1914; Series B, The Near and Middle East, 1856–1914; Series C, North America, 1837–1914; Series D, Latin America, 1845–1914; Series E, Asia, 1860–1914; Series F, Europe, 1848–1914; Series G, Africa, 1848–1914. Part II: From the First to the Second World War: Series A, the Soviet Union, 1917–1939; Series B, Turkey, Iran, and the Middle East, 1918–1939; Series C, North America, 1919–1939; Series D, Latin America, 1914–1939; Series E, Asia, 1914–1939; Series F, Europe, 1919–1939; Series G, Africa, 1914–1939; Series H, The First World War, 1914–1918; Series I, The Paris Peace Conference of 1919; Series J, The League of Nations, 1918–11941; Series K, Economic affairs, Cultural propaganda, and the reform of the Foreign Office, 1910–1939. Part III: From 1940 through 1945: Series A, The Soviet Union and Finland; Series B, Near and Middle East; Series C, North America; Series D, Latin America; Series E, Asia; Series F, Europe; Series G, Africa; Series L, World War II and general. Part IV: From 1945–1950: Series A, The Soviet Union and Finland; Series B, Near and Middle East; Series C, North America; Series D, Latin America; Series E, Asia; Series F, Europe; Series G, Africa; Series M, International Organizations, Commonwealth Affairs, and General.

Index: Each volume contains an introduction and a chronological table important to the series. A detailed table of contents identifies each document by type, author, date, and subject.

Note: Digitized and partially available from Google Books.

Yearbooks and Other Digests of Practice in International Law

11 BRITISH YEAR BOOK OF INTERNATIONAL LAW

(London: H. Frowde: Hodder and Stoughton, 1921–).

Summary: This annual publication includes, in addition to scholarly articles and notes, permanent and systematic sections digesting each year's decisions of the British courts involving questions of public and private international law, of the European Court of Justice as well as decisions on the European Convention on Human Rights. The last part, "*United Kingdom Materials on International Law*" (UKMIL), published regularly since 1978, includes materials arranged on the basis of the *Model Plan for the Classification of Documents Concerning State Practice in the Field of Public International Law* adopted by the Committee of Ministers of the Council of Europe in 1968, and amended in 1997. These are excerpts from various published sources, such as *Hansard* (Parliamentary Debates), Command Papers, and UN & EU publications as well as texts provided by the Foreign and Commonwealth Office, many of which might not be easily available. Appendices to UKMIL include lists of multilateral, European Community, and bilateral agreements signed by the UK in the given year and UK legislation concerning matters of international law passed during the year.

Indexes: Each volume includes a table of cases and an index for the volume. Cumulative indexes: Vol. 1–10 (1920–1929) in vol. 10; vol. 11–20 (1930–1939) in v. 20, and vol. 1–36 (1920–1960) in separate volume.

Note: Publication suspended 1940–1943. 1955/1956, 1965/1966, 1968/1969, 1972/1973, 1974/1975 and 1976/1977 are issued in two-year compilations.

Note: Vol. 1–46 (1920/21–1972/73) published under the auspices of the Royal Institute of International Affairs (called, until 1927, the British Institute of International Affairs).

Note: Online subscribers have an access to back volumes from 1996. HeinOnline provides access to v. 1–46 (1920–1973).

12 BRITISH DIGEST OF INTERNATIONAL LAW: COMPILED PRINCIPALLY FROM THE ARCHIVES OF FOREIGN OFFICE

Edited by Clive Parry; consulting editor, Sir Gerald Fitzmaurice. (London: Stevens, 1965–1967).

Summary: Based on both published and unpublished sources, this unfinished work was planned to be published in two phases; Phase One, 1860–1914 in 10 volumes and Phase Two, 1914–1960 in 5 volumes. Only the following volumes of Phase One were published: v. 2b, pt. III. Territory; v. 5–6, pt. VI. The individual in international law; v. 7–8, pt. VII. Organs of state. Each volume includes a table of cases, a table of statutes, and an index. Lists of Secretaries of State for Foreign Affairs and Law Officers of the Crown whose reports were utilized in the Digest are also included.

Note: Published under the auspices of the International Law Fund.

13 BRITISH PRACTICE OF INTERNATIONAL LAW

Edited by E. Lauterpacht with the assistance of Gillian White. (London: British Institute of International and Comparative Law, 1962–1971). 6 vols.

Summary: Arranged by subjects, this survey of British practice is based on published British official documents, records of the UN principal organs, and information obtained directly from the Foreign Office. It covers the period from January 1962 to December 1967 on a semiannual and, since 1966, on an annual basis. Each volume includes a table of cases and an index.

Note: Published under the auspices of the International Law Fund and the British Institute of International and Comparative Law.

Note: Two parts covering 1962 were published under the title *The Contemporary practice of the United Kingdom in the field of international law.*

Note: Continues a feature entitled "The Contemporary practice of the United Kingdom in the field of international law – survey and comment" by E. Lauterpacht, published irregularly in *International and Comparative Law Quarterly*. Nine parts, covering period from February 16, 1956 to December 31, 1959, were published in vols. 5 (1956)-10 (1961).

14 BRITISH INTERNATIONAL LAW CASES: A COLLECTION OF DECISIONS OF COURTS IN THE BRITISH ISLES ON POINTS OF INTERNATIONAL LAW

Prepared under the auspices of the International Law Fund and British Institute of International and Comparative Law. (London: Stevens, 1964–1973). 9 vols.

Summary: Reports of decisions of courts sitting within the British Isles, including the Judicial Committee of the Privy Council, dealing with matters of international law. Contents include: v. 1–2. States as international persons; v. 2. State territory; v. 3. Jurisdiction; v. 4–5. The individual in international law; v. 5. Aliens, extradition, fugitive offenders; v. 6. Diplomatic and consular agents, treaties, addendum; v. 7. Supplementary volume, 1951–1960; v. 8. Supplementary volume, 1960–1965; v. 9. Supplement, 1966–1970. Includes indexes.

Note: Vols. 7 & 8 edited by Clive Parry, vol. 9 edited by Clive Parry & J.A. Hopkins.

United States

Marci Hoffman

Issues of Treaty Succession

It is generally accepted that the United States did not succeed to any treaty obligations of Great Britain.[1] In *United States v. Curtiss-Wright Export Corporation*, Justice Sutherland of the United States Supreme Court stated: "[a]s a result of the separation from Great Britain by the colonies, acting as a unit, the powers of external sovereignty passed from the Crown not to the colonies severally, but to the colonies in their collective and corporate capacity as the United States of America. Even before the Declaration, the colonies were a unit in foreign affairs, acting through a common agency—namely, the Continental Congress, composed of delegates from the thirteen colonies".[2] When the United States became a sovereign nation, it acquired the inherent authority to enter into international agreements with other nations.

The issue of entering into treaties with other nations was considered during the Continental Congress in 1776. For a thorough historical examination of treaty-making, see S.B. Crandall, *Treaties, Their Making and Enforcement*, 2nd revised ed. (Boston: Little, Brown and Company, 1916). This work describes the history of independence and treaty-making in the United States. The first sections describe the treaty-making power of a state generally. Chapters II through V provide for the history of treaties in the United States prior to the Constitution. This includes an examination of the negotiations and ratifications of the first treaties with France. These chapters contain detailed information on treaties prior to the Articles of Confederation through the adoption of the Constitution. Chapters VI through X focus on the development of the making of treaties. The remainder of this work examines the execution and enforcement of treaties. There are detailed footnotes throughout the volume.

For further reading on the history of treaty-making in the United States, see C.H. Butler, *The Treaty Making Power of the United States* (New York: Banks Law Book Co., 1902). Part 2 of this two-volume work provides a historical review of the treaty-making power of the United States. The researcher may also wish to consult H.S.G Tucker, *Limitations on the Treaty-Making*

1 Lord McNair, The Law of Treaties 60 (Oxford: Clarendon Press, 1986).

2 *United States v. Curtiss-Wright Export Corporation*, 299 US 304, 316, 57 S.Ct. 216, 219 (1936).

 | DOI 10.1163/9789004272224_034

Power under the Constitution of the United States (Boston: Little, Brown, and Company, 1915).[3]

Treaty Ratification and Implementation

"Domestically, treaties to which the United States is a party are equivalent in status to Federal legislation, forming part of what the Constitution calls 'the supreme Law of the Land'. However, the word treaty does not have the same meaning in the United States and in international law".[4] The Vienna Convention on the Law of Treaties defines a treaty as "an international agreement concluded between States in written form and governed by international law, whether embodied in a single instrument or in two or more related instruments and whatever its particular designation".[5] Under United States law, however, there is a distinction made between the terms *treaty* and *executive agreement*. "In the United States, the word treaty is reserved for an agreement that is made 'by and with the Advice and Consent of the Senate' (Article II, section 2, clause 2 of the Constitution). International agreements not submitted to the Senate are known as 'executive agreements' in the United States".[6] Generally, a treaty is a binding international agreement and an executive agreement applies in domestic law only. Under international law, however, both types of agreements are considered binding. Regardless of whether an international agreement is called a convention, agreement, protocol, accord, etc.; if it is submitted to the Senate for advice and consent, it is considered a treaty under United States law.

When conducting US treaty research, it is critical to understand the ratification and implementation process. Negotiation of treaties and international agreements is the responsibility of the Executive Branch. The US Department of State provides the Foreign Service with detailed instructions for the negotiation and conclusion of treaties and international agreements. These

---

3 Also available on *The Making of Modern Law*, http://galenet.galegroup.com/servlet/MOML, and *HeinOnline*, http://www.heinonline.org.

4 Congressional Research Service, Treaties and Other International Agreements: The Role of the United States Senate: A Study, S. PRT No. 106–71, at 1 (2001), http://www.gpo.gov/fdsys/pkg/CPRT-106SPRT66922/pdf/CPRT-106SPRT66922.pdf.

5 Vienna Convention on the Law of Treaties, art. 2, s 1(a), May 23, 1969, 1155 U.N.T.S. 331, 333.

6 Treaties and Other International Agreements: The Role of the United States Senate: A Study, *supra* note 4.

instructions are part of the *Foreign Affairs Manual*, Circular 175.[7] Circular 175 summarizes the constitutional requirements for determining whether an international agreement should be considered a treaty or an agreement. It outlines the general procedures for negotiation, signature, publication, and registration of treaties and international agreements.

In *Parliamentary Participation in the Making and Operation of Treaties: A Comparative Study*, S.A. Riesenfeld and F.M. Abbott, eds. (Dordrecht; Boston: M. Nijhoff, 1994), pp. 205–382, several chapters explore the role of the United States Senate in the making and operation of treaties. Specifically, the chapters on the US focus on the role of the Senate in "self-executing" and "non-self-executing" treaties; the constitutional power of the US Senate; and the scope of the Senate's control over the conclusion and operation of treaties.

Many scholars have explored the allocation of treaty power in the United States and the role of treaties and international agreements in domestic law. For further readings, see M. Glennon, *Constitutional Diplomacy* (Princeton, NJ: Princeton University Press, 1990), and L. Henkin, *Foreign Affairs and the Constitution*, 2nd edition (Oxford: Clarendon Press; New York: Oxford University Press, 1996). One of the standard treatises in this area is C.C. Hyde, *International Law Chiefly as Interpreted and Applied by the United States*, 2nd revised edition (Boston: Little, Brown, 1945). This three-volume set provides a thorough analysis of international law and how it relates to the law of the United States. The *Restatement (Third) of the Law of Foreign Relations* (Washington, DC: American Law Institute, 1987–) is an important work for understanding how the law of foreign relations is applied in United States courts.

An excellent study of the treaty-making provisions of the Constitution, as well as the international and domestic law on treaties and other international agreements, is *Treaties and Other International Agreements: The Role of the United States Senate: A Study*, prepared for the Committee on Foreign Relations, United States Senate, Senate Print 106–71 (Washington, DC: US Government Printing Office, 2001). This slim volume (a revision of the 1984 and 1993 editions) delves into the treaty-making process, indicates how treaties and international agreements are amended, modified, or terminated, and explains the congressional role of overseer in regard to international agreements. It provides background information on the Senate's role concerning treaties and international agreements. An extremely valuable (and handy) portion of this work is the appendices. For example, there is an annotated bibliography of treaty sources and related materials; the Case-Zablocki Act on the transmittal

7 11 US Department of State, Foreign Affairs Manual, §§ 720 – 727 (2006), http://www.state.gov/m/a/dir/regs/fam/11fam/700/index.htm.

of international agreements to Congress; Circular 175; the Vienna Convention on the Law of Treaties; and a glossary of treaty terminology. In addition, this work contains several useful charts, including charts that outline the steps in the making of a treaty and an executive agreement, and another chart listing the publications that provide information on US treaties throughout the treaty-making process.

If this volume is not enough, there are several other useful sources that discuss the process and the relevant documentation. See J. Zwirn, "United States Treaties" (Chapter 11), *Congressional Publications and Proceedings: Research on Legislation, Budgets, and Treaties*, 2nd edition (Englewood, CO: Libraries Unlimited, Inc., 1988), pp. 222–254. For a concise review of the process and the documentation, see R.E. Dalton, "United States" in *National Treaty Law and Practice: Dedicated to the Memory of Monroe Leigh* (Leiden; Boston: Martinus Nijhoff Publishers, 2005), pp. 765–822. A very brief but informative report is available from CRS (No. 98–384), see V. Heitshusen, *Senate Consideration of Treaties* (2012).[8]

Many more executive agreements than treaties are concluded each year.[9] There are three types of such agreements: 1) congressional-executive agreements, agreements concluded by the President when Congress has previously or retroactively authorized an agreement; 2) executive agreements made pursuant to an earlier treaty; and 3) sole executive agreements, an agreement made pursuant to the President's constitutional authority and does not require any congressional authorization.[10] For an examination of executive agreements, see R.J. Erickson, "The Making of Executive Agreements by the United States Department of Defense: An Agenda for Progress," in *Boston University International Law Journal*, Volume 13, Spring 1995, pp. 45–139, This article is not limited to describing the role of the Department of Defense; it also discusses the organizational framework, and explores all phases of the negotiation process as it relates to executive agreements generally. The capacity of the United States to enter into executive agreements is discussed by M.M. Whiteman, "Executive Agreements," in *Digest of International Law*,

---

8 Available at https://opencrs.com/document/98-384/.

9 Michael John Garcia, Cong. Research Serv., RL32528, International Law and Agreements: Their Effect Upon US Law 3 (2010), http://www.fas.org/sgp/crs/misc/RL32528.pdf. For the statistical data on treaties and international agreements concluded during 1986–2003, see R.E. Dalton, *United States, in* National Treaty Law and Practice: Dedicated to the Memory of Monroe Leigh 820 (Leiden; Boston: Martinus Nijhoff Publishers, 2005).

10 For a good outline of the steps used in the making of an executive agreement, *see* Treaties and Other International Agreements, *supra* note 4, at 10.

Volume 14, 1970, pp. 193–255.[11] An in-depth investigation of executive agreements is contained in a 1984 historical study by L.K. Johnson, *The Making of International Agreements: Congress Confronts the Executive* (New York: New York University Press, 1984). In 2008, Oona A. Hathaway published an extensive examination of US treaties and international agreements using empirical, comparative, historical, and policy frameworks; see *Treaties End: The Past, Present, and the Future of International Lawmaking in the United States*, 117 Yale L.J. 1236 (2008).

An excellent compilation of works on the many issues facing the treaty researcher, both in the US and beyond, is now available; edited by D. B. Hollis, *The Oxford Guide to Treaties* (Oxford, U.K.: Oxford University Press, 2012). This large volume (804 pages) contains the work of many of the leading international treaty scholars and covers numerous treaty-related topics, such as formation, application, and interpretation.[12]

A note on citation formats. US treaties are referred to by the name or title of the agreement (the title is usually created from general terms relating to subject matter). A complete citation includes: title of the treaty or agreement, date of signing, parties (if 3 or fewer), and references to the main sources of publication. See Rule 21.4 et seq., *The Bluebook: A Uniform System of Citation*, 19th edition (Cambridge, MA: Published and distributed by the Harvard Law Review Association,), pp. 187–191.

Annotated Bibliography of Sources

General Treaty Collections

While the United States has quite an extensive treaty documentation system, it is also quite a maze of documents and systems. For a good discussion of historical treaty collections, see D.P. Myers, *Manual of Collections of Treaties and of Collections Relating to Treaties* (Cambridge, MA: Harvard University Press, 1922), pp. 342–362;[13] and United Nations, Codification Division, *List of Treaty Collections* (New York: United Nations, 1956), pp. 150–161.[14] Since these two volumes do such an excellent job of covering the major sources from

11 Also available on *HeinOnline*, http://www.heinonline.org.

12 THE OXFORD GUIDE TO TREATIES (Duncan B. Hollis ed., Oxford, U.K.: Oxford University Press, 2012).

13 Also available on *HeinOnline*, http://www.heinonline.org, and *The Making of Modern Law*, http://galenet.galegroup.com/servlet/MOML.

14 Also available on *HeinOnline*, http://www.heinonline.org.

1776 through the early 1950s, this chapter will not provide exhaustive coverage of these same collections. Rather, it will focus on some of the primary historical and official collections, as well as many of the contemporary sources.

1 UNITED STATES TREATIES AND OTHER INTERNATIONAL AGREEMENTS (UST)
(Washington, DC: US Government Printing Office, 1950–).

Summary: This is the cumulative collection of TIAS pamphlets (see no. 2, below) and is the current official collection of US treaties and agreements. The bound volumes are arranged by the TIAS number. Several volumes used to appear annually, but nothing has been published since 1984. The texts are in English and in the other official languages of the agreement and include a chronology. Commences with TIAS no. 2010, January 27, 1950 and ends with TIAS no. 11,059, April 5, 1984.

Index: Each volume contains a subject and country index which covers that volume only. There are several cumulative indexes produced by W.S. Hein; *United States Treaties and Other International Agreements Cumulative Index, 1950–1970*, compiled by Igor Kavass and Adolf Sprudzs (Buffalo, NY: W.S. Hein & Co., 1975, 4 vols.: vol. 1, 437 pp.; vol 2, 762 pp.; vol. 3, 466 pp.; vol. 4, 488 pp.); *United States Treaties and Other International Agreements Cumulative Index, Supplements*, compiled by Igor Kavass and Adolf Sprudzs (Buffalo, NY: W.S. Hein & Co., 1977, 2 vols.: vol. 1, 593 pp.; vol. 2, 840 pp.); *UST Cumulative Indexing Service: Current Supplement*, compiled by Igor Kavass and Adolf Sprudzs (Buffalo, NY: W.S. Hein & Co., 1978–); and *United States Treaty Index: 1776– Consolidation*, compiled and edited by Igor Kavass (Buffalo, NY: W.S. Hein & Co., 1991–).

Note: Available on microfiche through Law Library Microform Consortium, Honolulu, Hawaii.

Note: Due to the publication lag time, more recent agreements are available on the US Department of State, Treaty Affairs website from 2005-present, http://www.state.gov/s/l/treaty/caseact/index.htm (see no. 3, below).

Note: UST is available on Lexis.com (USTRTY), Westlaw Classic (USTREATIES) and WestlawNext (see Federal Administrative Decisions & Guidance, Department of State, United States Treaties and Other International Agreements) from 1778 to present.

Note: Available on *HeinOnline*, US Treaties and Other International Agreements, http://www.heinonline.org/ (Treaties and Agreements Library).

Note: Available on *LLMC Digital*, http://www.llmc-digital.org.

2 TREATIES AND OTHER INTERNATIONAL ACTS SERIES (TIAS) (Washington, DC: US Government Printing Office, 1946–).

Summary: This series provides the first official publication of new treaties and agreements. Numbering in this series begins with 1501.[15] Agreements are numbered consecutively and arranged by the effective date of the agreement (which means that they are not in chronological order). This series prints the English and the other official languages of the agreement, and also includes the dates of its development and approval, the president's proclamation, and any correspondence or supplemental agreements which affect the content of the treaty. Final acts of international conferences are also included. TIAS is considered the slip copy for the bound volumes of the *United States Treaties and Other International Agreements* (UST), see no. 1, above. Due to the extremely long publication lag time, since 2002, treaties and non-treaty acts have a new numbering system. The number is derived from the entry into force date of the agreement. For example, a document with the number 12–208 means that this is a 2012 treaty that came into force on February 8, 2012.

Index: While there is no index included as part of this series, many other indexes can be used to access the relevant TIAS numbers for treaties and agreements. See *Treaties in Force* and other cumulative indexes listed in *General Treaty Indexes* section of this chapter.

Note: These pamphlets combine and continue *Treaty Series* and *Executive Agreement Series*, see nos. 4 and 5, below.

Note: Available on microfiche through Law Library Microform Consortium, Honolulu, Hawaii.

Note: Available on the US Department of State, Treaty Affairs website from 1996 to present, http://www.state.gov/s/l/treaty/tias/index.htm.

Note: Available on *HeinOnline,* TIAS Agreements, TIAS 11,060 to present (1982–), http://www.heinonline.org/ (Treaties and Agreements Library).

Note: TIAS No. 10,979 forward is available on Westlaw (USTREATIES) and WestlawNext, see Federal Administrative Decisions & Guidance, Department of State, United States Treaties and Other International Agreements.

---

15 This number was derived by combining the total number of treaties from TS (994) and the total number of agreements from EAS (506). TREATIES AND OTHER INTERNATIONAL AGREEMENTS: THE ROLE OF THE UNITED STATES SENATE: A STUDY, *supra* note 4, 343.

3 UNITED STATES DEPARTMENT OF STATE, TREATY AFFAIRS

Office of the Assistant Legal Adviser for Treaty Affairs.

URL: http://www.state.gov/s/l/treaty.

Summary: The treaty office is the principle US government repository for treaties and other international agreements. The website provides access to the full-text of treaties and agreements, including those not yet published in the official sources (UST and TIAS, see nos. 1 and 2, above). In addition to the documents, it also contains *Treaties in Force* (see no. 26, below), treaties pending in the Senate, multilateral treaties for which the US is the depositary, treaty actions, and other documents and information.

4 TREATY SERIES (TS)

(Washington, DC: US Government Printing Office, 1908–1946).

Summary: This set is a series of pamphlets containing the texts of treaties. After October 1929, it contained only treaties submitted to the Senate and not executive agreements. All of the treaties are available in all of the original languages. Arranged alphabetically by country, then chronologically.

Index: See separate index under the title *Subject Index of the Treaty Series and the Executive Agreement Series* (Washington DC; US Government Printing Office, 1932), 214 pp.

Note: The publication of this series, in its present form, was commenced by the Dept. of State in January 1908, with Treaty Series no. 489. Prints issued prior to no. 489 bear no numbers.

Note: Merged with *Executive Agreement Series* (see no. 5, below) to form *Treaties and Other International Acts Series* (TIAS), see no. 2, above.

Note: Treaty Series 491-A, 668–892 are available on *HeinOnline*, http://www.heinonline.org/ (Treaties and Agreements Library).

5 EXECUTIVE AGREEMENT SERIES (EAS)

(Washington, DC: US Government Printing Office, 1929–1946).

Summary: First official version of international executive agreements from October 1, 1929 to March 16, 1946. The agreements were numbered consecutively and separately published in pamphlet form in the original languages.

Index: See separate index under the title *Subject Index of the Treaty Series and the Executive Agreement Series* (Washington DC: US Government Printing Office, 1932). 214 pp.

Note: Merged with *Treaty Series* (see no. 4, above) to form *Treaties and Other International Acts Series* (TIAS), see no. 2, above.

Note: Prior to October 1, 1929, executive agreements were usually included in the *Treaty Series*, see no. 4, above.

Note: Available on microform from Law Library Microform Consortium, Honolulu, Hawaii.

Note: Available on *HeinOnline*, http://www.heinonline.org/ (Treaties and Agreements Library).

6 UNITED STATES STATUTES AT LARGE (STAT)
(Washington, DC: US Government Printing Office, 1789–).

Summary: Prom 1776–1950, treaties and international agreements were published in *Statutes at Large* in parts 2 or 3. Volume 8 contains all treaties between the US and other nations from 1778–1845. Volume 64, part 3 contains a cumulative list of all treaties and agreements included in volumes 1–64. The treaties and agreements are arranged alphabetically by country and then by topic.

Index: Annual Index.

Note: After 1950, *United States Treaties and Other International Agreements* (UST) became the official publication, 64 Stat. 980 (1950), see no. 1, above. The *Statutes at Large* are considered the official collection for treaties and agreements before *United States Treaties and Other International Agreements* (UST).

Note: Imprint varies. Publication began in 1845 by Little, Brown and Company under authority granted by a joint resolution of Congress. In 1874 Congress transferred the authority to publish the title to the US Government Printing Office.

Note: Available from the Library of Congress, *American Memory Project: A Century of Lawmaking*, http://memory.loc.gov/ammem/amlaw/lawhome.html.

Note: Available on *HeinOnline*, http://www.heinonline.org/ (US Statutes at Large Collection).

7 TREATIES AND OTHER INTERNATIONAL AGREEMENTS OF THE UNITED STATES OF AMERICA, 1776–1949
Charles L Bevans, comp. (Washington, DC: US Government Printing Office, 1968–1976). 13 vols.

Summary: Thirteen-volume set containing all treaties and executive agreements from 1776 to 1949 with some commentary. Volumes 1–4 contain the texts of multilateral treaties and agreements in chronological order by date of signature. Volumes 5–12 contain bilateral treaties and agreements in alphabetical order by country This set is considered the most comprehensive retrospective collection of treaties and agreements.

Index: Each volume has an index, and volume 13 has a cumulative country and subject index for the entire set.

Index: See also *United States Treaties and Other International Agreements Cumulative Index 1776–1949: Cumulative Index to United States Treaties and Other International Agreements 1776–1949 as Published in Statutes at Large, Malloy, Miller, Bevans, and Other Relevant Sources,* compiled by Igor I. Kavass and Mark A. Michael (Buffalo, NY: W.S. Hein & Co., 1975), 4 vols.; vol. 1, 363 pp.; vol. 2, 615 pp.; vol. 3, 325 pp.; vol. 4, 278 pp.

Note: US Department of State Publication Series Nos. 8407, 8441, 8484, 8521, 8543, 8549, 8566, 8590, 8615, 8642, 8728, 8761, and 8830.

Note: This compilation includes all of the documents that were originally printed in *Statutes at Large,* the *Treaty Series,* and the *Executive Agreement Series* from 1776 to 1949.

Note: This set is commonly referred to as *Bevans* and supersedes the compilations by Malloy and Miller. (See nos. 8 and 9, below).

Note: Available on microfiche from Law Library Microforms Consortium, Honolulu, Hawaii.

Note: Available on *HeinOnline,* http://www.heinonline.org/ (Treaties and Agreements Library).

Note: Available on *LLMC Digitial,* http://www.llmc-digital.org/.

8 TREATIES AND OTHER INTERNATIONAL ACTS OF THE UNITED STATES OF AMERICA

Edited by Hunter Miller (Washington, DC: US Government Printing Office, 1931–1948). 8 vols.

Summary: Contains the full text of treaties concluded 1776–1863. Volume 1 sets out the organization of the compilation including a cumulative list of documents and tables. Volumes 2 through 8 contain the texts of the treaties and agreements in chronological order in the official languages. This set also includes legislative history information and commentary.

Index: While there is no index to this set, volume 1 may be used for assistance in locating a treaty through a cumulative list of documents and a list of treaties by country.

Index: See also *United States Treaties and Other International Agreements Cumulative Index 1776–1949: Cumulative Index to United States Treaties and Other International Agreements 1776–1949 as Published in Statutes at Large, Malloy, Miller, Bevans, and Other Relevant Sources,* compiled by Igor I. Kavass and Mark A. Michael (Buffalo, NY: W.S. Hein & Co., 1975), 4 vols.: vol. 1, 363 pp.; vol 2, 615 pp.; vol. 3, 325 pp.; vol. 4, 278 pp.

Note: US Department of State Publication Series Nos. 175, 453, 645, 1017, 1719, 1791, and 3141.

Note: Commonly referred to as *Miller.* Superseded by *Bevans,* see no. 7, above.

Note: Available on *HeinOnline*, http://www.heinonline.org/ (Treaties and Agreements Library).

Note: Available on *LLMC Digital*, http://www.llmc-digital.org/.

9 TREATIES, CONVENTIONS, INTERNATIONAL ACTS, PROTOCOLS, AND AGREEMENTS BETWEEN THE UNITED STATES OF AMERICA AND OTHER POWERS

Edited by William M. Malloy (Washington, DC: US Government Printing Office, 1910–1938). 4 vols., 5775 pp.

Summary: Four volume set contains the texts of treaties and agreements from 1776 to 1937 with annotations. Volumes 1 and 2 cover 1776–1909; volume 3 supplements the first two volumes and covers 1910–1932; volume four supplements the other volumes and covers 1923–1937. Bilateral treaties and agreements are arranged alphabetically by country, followed by multilateral treaties and agreements arranged chronologically.

Index: Volume 4 contains a cumulative index and a numerical list of treaties that provide relevant citations to *Statutes at Large.*

Index: See also *United States Treaties and Other International Agreements Cumulative Index 1776–1949: Cumulative Index to United States Treaties and Other International Agreements 1776–1949 as Published in Statutes at Large, Malloy, Miller, Bevans, and Other Relevant Sources*, compiled by Igor L Kavass and Mark A. Michael (Buffalo, NY: W.S. Hein & Co., 1975), 4 vols.: vol. 1, 363 pp.; vol. 2, 615 pp.; vol. 3, 325 pp.; vol. 4, 278 pp.

Note: Commonly referred to as *Malloy*, Superseded by *Bevans*, see no. 7, above.

Note: Prepared under the direction of the Committee on Foreign Relations, United States Senate. Volumes 1 and 2 compiled by William M. Malloy and issued as Senate Doc. 357, 61st Congress, 2d. session; volume 3, 1910–1923, issued as Senate Doc. 348, 67th Congress, 4th session, Denys P. Myers, co-editor; and volume 4, 1923–1937, issued as Senate Doc. 134, 75th Congress, 3d session.

Note: Available on microfilm from University Microfilms, Ann Arbor, Michigan and on microfiche from Law Library Microforms Consortium, Honolulu, Hawaii.

Note: Available on *HeinOnline*, http://www.heinonline.org/ (Treaties and Agreements Library).

10 CONSOLIDATED TREATIES AND INTERNATIONAL AGREEMENTS CURRENT DOCUMENT SERVICE: UNITED STATES

(Dobbs Ferry, NY: Oceana Publications 1990–).

Summary: This is a continuation of the set called *Consolidated Treaty Series 1648–1918* (C. Perry, ed., Dobbs Ferry, NY: Oceana Publications, 1969–1986). This set reprints bilateral and multilateral treaties and international agreements within ninety days of release from the State Department or ratification. Since the treaties and agreements collected in this set are recent, they do not have any official TIAS number assigned by the State Department. All agreements are assigned an internal State Department number which begins with the last two digits of the year and then numbered consecutively and designated as DOS 90–101, etc. Additionally, the editor of this set assigns an internal Consolidated Treaties & International Agreement (CTIA) number to these agreements. This set covers treaties since 1990 (DOS No. 90–1).

Index: Each volume contains a *Table of Contents* listing the treaties in their numerical sequence in that particular volume. Also included is a country index which uses the same topics as *Treaties in Force.* Other finding tools include a list of multilateral agreements with references to the CTIA numbers, a topical index, a list of treaties cited in subsequent treaties, an unpublished treaties list, and a list of treaties cited in the volume that have been published in the set.

Note: See also *Index to International Treaties & Agreements,* compiled and edited by Erwin C. Surrency (Dobbs Ferry, NY: Oceana Publications, 1994–1998), no. 36, below.

Note: Available as part of the *Treaties and International Agreements Online,* http://www. oceanalaw.com/. See no. 12, below.

Note: Now published by Oxford University Press.

11 HEIN'S UNITED STATES TREATIES AND OTHER INTERNATIONAL AGREEMENTS: CURRENT MICROFICHE SERVICE
(Buffalo, NY: W.S. Hein & Co., 1991–).

Summary: Bimonthly microfiche installments containing treaties and international agreements that have been recently ratified. The fiche is arranged by KAV number (an internal numbering system developed by the original editor, Igor I. Kavass, since these documents do not yet have TIAS numbers). Good for locating recent treaties as well as older treaties. Coverage begins with 1957 to present.

Index: Cumulative subject index (issued in print and microfiche), a list of TIAS numbers, and a list of KAV numbers (internal numbering scheme).

Note: See also the other Hein treaty indexes: *Current Treaty Index, Kavass's Guide to the United States Treaties in Force,* and the *United States Treaty Index: 1776– Consolidation,* all described in the *Treaty Indexes* section of this chapter below.

Note: Available on *HeinOnline,* KAV Agreements (1987 – present), http://www.heinonline.org/ (Treaties and Agreements Library).

12 TREATIES AND INTERNATIONAL AGREEMENTS ONLINE [1999–]
URL: http://www.oceanalaw.com.

Summary: This database contains the text of over 18,000 treaties and agreements that are in force as of January 1, 1988. The earliest treaty dates back to 1783, the Treaty of Paris. It also includes *Senate Treaty Documents* from no. 96–1 through the current Congress, and US Department of State documents from DOS 86–1 to present. The advanced search mechanism allows for searching by title, text, subject, country, and citation. The complete text of the treaty or agreement is included as well as amendments, modifications and protocols. In many cases, the source document is available in PDF.

Note: Originally issued as a CD-ROM: *Treaties and Other International Agreements Researchers Archive* (TIARA) (Dobbs Ferry, NY: Oceana Publications, 1993).

Note: The print equivalent is *Consolidated Treaties & International Agreements: United States Current Document Service* (see no. 10, above).

Note: Database discontinued as of March 2014.

13 SENATE TREATY DOCUMENTS
(Washington, DC: US Government Printing Office, 1981–).

Summary: From the 97th Congress to present, proposed treaties, along with other documentation, are transmitted to the Senate Committee on Foreign Relations from the President. This "transmittal package" is then printed as a *Senate Treaty Document.* These documents are numbered consecutively through the Congressional session, e.g., S. Treaty Doc. 105–1. Generally, this is the first available source for the text of the treaty. These documents contain the text of the treaty before the Senate committee mark-up.

Index: *Monthly Catalog, CIS Index* (1970–present), *Congressional Universe,* and. CCH *Congressional Index* cites these documents.

Note: Replaces *Senate Executive Documents,* see no. 23, below.

Note: *Senate Treaty Documents* became part of the *Congressional Serial Set* beginning with the 96th Congress.

Note: Available on *Thomas, Treaties,* http://thomas.loc.gov/home/treaties/treaties.html.

Covers treaty information from the 90th Congress to the present and links to the text of the treaty from 104th Congress to present (text is from GPO). Information is available for just a few treaties from the 81st through the 89th Congresses. Legislative actions are also included.

Note: Senate Treaty Documents are available through *ProQuest Congressional* and *CIS Microfiche.*

Note: Available on Westlaw (USTREATIES).

Note: Available on the *FDsys: GPO's Federal Digital System*, 99th Congress to present, http://www.gpo.gov/fdsys/.

Note: Available on US Senate Committee on Foreign Relations website from 107th Congress to present, http://www.foreign.senate.gov/treaties/. Executive Reports are also included.

Note: Available on *HeinOnline*, No. 97–1 through current, http://www.heinonline.org (Treaties and Agreements Library).

14 SENATE EXECUTIVE REPORTS

(Washington DC: US Government Printing Office, n.d.).

Summary: These reports are issued by the Senate Foreign Relations Committee and contain the Committee's analysis and recommendations concerning proposed treaties. They are a valuable source for treaty interpretation.

Index: CIS Index to US Senate Executive Documents & Reports, the *Monthly Catalog*, the *CIS/Index* (1970 to present), and *ProQuest Congressional.* The CCH *Congressional Index* also cites these documents.

Note: Electronic access is available from *FDSys: GPO's Federal Digital System* from 104th Congress to present, http://www.gpo.gov/fdsys/.

Note: Also Available on the *ProQuest Congressional.*

Note: Reports from 1917 to 1969 appear in *CIS Senate Executive Documents and Reports* [*and Microfiche*], see no. 23, below.

Note: Senate Executive Reports became part of the *Congressional Serial Set* beginning with the 96th Congress. See no. 22, below.

15 US TREATIES

Available through Lexis.com (USTRTY).

Summary: Collection of US treaties and international agreements in force from 1776 to present. Provides the text of the treaty or agreement as well as some notes and citation information to the primary treaty collections.

Note: Treaties are not yet available on Lexis Advance.

16 US TREATIES

Available through Westlaw Classic (USTREATIES).

Summary: This Westlaw database contains the full texts of treaties and international agreements from 1778 to present. It also contains *Senate Treaty Documents* from the 103rd Congress (1993/1994) to date and US Department of State documents from DOS 90–1. If the treaty is in force, the text is from TIAS or Senate Treaty Document. If there is no TIAS number available, the KAV number is used from *United States Treaty Index.*

Note: The source of the information is the US Senate or the US Department of State.

Note: Treaties are available on WestlawNext, see Federal Administrative Decisions & Guidance, Department of State, United States Treaties and Other International Agreements.

17 CIS/INDEX TO PUBLICATIONS OF THE UNITED STATES CONGRESS [AND MICROFICHE]

(Bethesda, MD: Congressional Information Service, Inc., 1970–).

Summary: This set is composed of Index and Abstract volumes and the full text of the documents on microfiche. It provides access to congressional publications, including *Senate Treaty Documents, Senate Executive Reports*, and relevant hearings and other documents. Access to the microfiche is through the Index and Abstract volumes. Issues are published monthly, with quarterly, annual and multi-year cumulations. Treaties and agreements are indexed under the relevant subject, the title of the treaty or agreement, or under the heading "treaties and conventions". *Treaty Documents* and *Executive Reports* are listed by number in the "Index to Report and Document Numbers". Abstracts are arranged by Committee and then by form of publication. The abstracts provide bibliographic information for locating the publication. Both the Index and Abstract provide a CIS accession number to enable access to the microfiche set where the full text of the document is available. Treaties included in this set are in draft (i.e., pre-ratified) form.

Index: Chronological index arranged alphabetically by subject. Supplemental indexes include documents number indexes. Indexes are issued monthly, annually, and in multiple year cumulative indexes.

Note: The microfiche, finding tools and website have been produced and hosted by various publishers over the years: Congressional Information Service, LexisNexis and ProQuest. The electronic product has also gone through several name changes: *Congressional Masterfile 1* (*1789–1969*) and *Congressional Masterfile 2* (*1970–1998*) on CD-ROM, *Congressional Universe, LexisNexis Congressional*, and now *ProQuest Congressional.*

Note: Access is also available on *ProQuest Congressional*, http://congressional.proquest.com. This service provides access to CIS index and abstract access tools, as well as online access to the full text of related government documents and publications.

18 CONGRESSIONAL RECORD: PROCEEDINGS AND DEBATES OF THE... CONGRESS
(Washington, DC: US Government Printing Office, 1874–).

Summary: The texts of proposed treaties often appear under the date that debate and consideration first begins on the floor of the Senate.

Index: Annual index, search under the heading "treaties" as well as under the subject and title of the treaty.

Index: The Thomas website provides access from the 101st Congress to the present, http://thomas.loc.gov/home/thomas.php.

Note: ProQuest also makes the *Congressional Record* available on microfiche.

Note: Available on *FDsys: GPO's Federal Digital System*, from 1994 to present, http://www.gpo.gov/fdsys/.

Note: The *Congressional Record* was preceded by the *Annals of Congress*, *Register of Debates*, and *Congressional Globe*, all available on the Library of Congress, *American Memory Project: A Century of Lawmaking*, http://memory.loc.gov/ammem/amlaw/lwac.html.

Note: Available from 1985 to present on Westlaw (CR) and WestlawNext and Lexis.com (CONGREC).

Note: Available on *HeinOnline*, http://www.heinonline.org (US Congressional Documents Collection).

Note: ProQuest Congressional provides the Congressional Record Bound edition (and its predecessors) from 1789–2001, and the Daily Edition from 1985 – present.

19 COMPILATION OF PRESIDENTIAL DOCUMENTS
URL: http://www.gpo.gov/fdsys/.

Summary: This publication contains statements, messages, and other Presidential materials released by the White House during the preceding week. Compiles the letters of transmittal sent to the Senate about proposed treaties as well as proclamations for ratified treaties. However, the *FDsys: GPO's Federal Digital System* does not include the text of the treaty in the Compilation of Presidential Documents. Coverage is from January 11, 1993 to the present.

Note: Formerly called *Weekly Compilation of Presidential Documents*. This publication ceased in January 2009. For historical research, consult the quarterly, semiannual, and annual indexes. Each issue carries a cumulative index to prior issues. Locate relevant pages under the specific country, region or subject. Also indexed by *Public Affairs Information Service Bulletin* and *Public Papers of the Presidents of the United States.*

Note: Available on Lexis.com (PRESDC) and Lexis Advance from March 24, 1979 through February 2, 2011; on Westlaw Classic from January 2000 (WCPD) and WestlawNext beginning with 1984.

Note: Available on *HeinOnline*, http://www.heinonline.org, 1965 to present (US Presidential Library).

20 LEGISLATION ON FOREIGN RELATIONS THROUGH...[YEAR] (Washington, DC: US Government Printing Office, 1977–).

Summary: An annual five-volume set of legislation and related materials which are frequently referred to by the House Committee on International Relations and the Senate Committee on Foreign Affairs. Amended to date and annotated to show relevant history and cross-references. The first four volumes contain legislation and related materials, such as executive orders, code sections, and State Department delegations. Volume five contains treaties and related international documents. Volume five is not necessarily revised every year.

Note: Continues *Legislation on Foreign Relations, with Explanatory Notes* (Washington, DC: US Government Printing Office, 1957–1976).

Note: This set is available on *FDsys: GPO's Federal Digital System*, http://www.gpo.gov/fdsys and from 1999 to present at http://democrats.foreignaffairs.house.gov/about.asp?sec=documents.

21 INTERNATIONAL LEGAL MATERIALS (ILM) (Washington, DC: American Society of International Law, 1962–).

Summary: Bimonthly publication reprints the texts of selected treaties and agreements. Background notes are often included with the text of the document.

Index: Each year, the November volume contains the index for that year. There are also decennial indexes.

Index: Listed in ABC *POL SCI: A Bibliography of Contents: Political Science and Government; IBZ-International Bibliography of Periodical Literature*; and *PAIS International.*

Note: ILM is also available on Lexis.com (ILM) from 1962 to date; on Westlaw Classic (ILM) from 1980 to date; on JSTOR from 1962–present; and on *HeinOnline*, http://heinonline.org (Law Journal Library), from 1962–present.

Note: The tables of contents are available from 1999 to present on the ASIL website, http://www.asil.org/ilm.cfm.

Note: Available on microfiche from W.S. Hein & Co., Buffalo, New York.

22 UNITED STATES CONGRESSIONAL SERIAL SET
(Washington DC: US Government Printing Office, 1817–).

Summary: Contains reports and documents from Congressional committees. *Senate Treaty Documents and Senate Executive Reports* became part of the Congressional Serial Set beginning with the 96th Congress (1979).

Index: CIS US Serial Set Index 1789–1969 (Washington, DC: Congressional Information Service, Inc., 1975–). See also the *Monthly Catalog, CIS/Index,* and *ProQuest Congressional.*

Note: Available on microfiche from the US Government Printing Office. The complete collection on microfiche is also available from Congressional Information Service, *CIS US Serial Set on Microfiche.*

Note: Some documents that are part of the Serial Set are available on *FDSys: GPO's Federal Digital System* from 104th Congress to present, http://www.gpo.gov/fdsys/.

Note: A portion of the Serial Set (23rd, 25th, 27th, 30th–64th Congresses) is available on the Library of Congress, *American Memory Project: A Century of Lawmaking,* http://memory.loc.gov/ammem/amlaw/lwss.html.

Note: Available from 1789 to present on *ProQuest Congressional,* http://congressional.proquest.com.

23 CIS SENATE EXECUTIVE DOCUMENTS AND REPORTS [AND MICROFICHE]
(Bethesda, MD: Congressional Information Service, Inc., 1987).

Summary: Microfiche collection of treaty documents and reports from 1817 to 1969 which were never printed in the *US Congressional Serial Set.* The documents are arranged by CIS accession numbers.

Index: See two-volume publication *CIS Index to US Senate Executive Documents & Reports* (Bethesda, MD, Congressional Information Service, Inc., 1987, 2 vols.: vol. 1, 352 pp.; vol. 2, 229 pp.). Volume 1 contains an alphabetical subject index which provides the CIS accession numbers. Volume 2 is the Reference Bibliography section containing bibliographic information about documents and brief annotations. This section is arranged by Congress and then numerically by report and document numbers.

Note: CIS Index to US Senate Executive Documents & Reports was also available on *Congressional Masterfile I* (*1789–1969*) on CD-ROM.

Note: Available on *Proquest Congressional,* http://congressional.proquest.com.

24 SENATE EXECUTIVE DOCUMENTS
(Washington, DC: US Government Printing Office, 1798–1981).

Summary: Senate Executive Documents contains the texts of proposed treaties that are transmitted to the Senate Committee on Foreign Relations from the Executive Branch, along with any other documentation to support ratification.

Index: CIS Index to US Senate Executive Documents & Reports, the *Monthly Catalog* (since 1977 when these documents became depository items), the *CIS/Index* (1970 to date). CCH *Congressional Index* also cites these documents.

Note: With the 97th Congress, these documents were replaced with *Senate Treaty Documents*, see no. 13, above.

Note: Reports from 1917–1969 appear in *CIS Senate Executive Documents and Reports* [*and Microfiche*], see no. 23, above.

Note: Available on *Proquest Congressional*, http://congressional.proquest.com.

25 UNPERFECTED TREATIES OF THE UNITED STATES OF AMERICA, 1776–1976
Christian L. Wiktor, ed. (Dobbs Ferry, NY: Oceana Publications, 1976–1994).

Summary: Six-volume set includes treaties and agreements concluded by the US between 1776 and 1976 which, for whatever reason, never entered into force. The introduction states that "[t]he term 'unperfected' refers to treaties which have been signed on the part of the United States, or have been submitted to the Senate, but which have, for one reason or another, definitely failed to go into force". Arranged chronologically by the date of signature and includes information on when submitted to the Senate, printed text citations, and notes.

Index: Each volume has an index for that volume, and the last volume contains a general subject index for the entire set.

Treaty Indexes

Locating the current status of treaties and agreements can be challenging for the researcher. Many of the indexes and finding tools mentioned below aid the researcher in this process. Unlike Congressional bills, treaties do not die at the end of the congressional session. Therefore, it is often important to determine where a treaty is in the ratification and implementation process.

26 TREATIES IN FORCE: A LIST OF TREATIES AND OTHER INTERNATIONAL AGREEMENTS OF THE UNITED STATES IN FORCE AS OF JANUARY 1,...(TIF)
(Washington DC: US Government Printing Office, 1929–).

Summary: Official index and source for status information. Contains information on all international agreements to which the US is a party and which are still in force. Treaties which have been officially terminated are not included. The first section of TIF lists bilateral treaties arranged alphabetically by country and then by subject, and the second section lists multilateral treaties by subject and then by country.

Note: Available on the US Department of State, Office of the Legal Adviser, Treaty Affairs website, http://www.state.gov/s/l/treaty/tif/index.htm. The information contained in *Treaties in Force* can be updated with *Treaty Actions* (see no. 37, below.)

Note: Archived volumes, 1929 on, are available on *HeinOnline*, http://www.heinonline.org/ (Treaties and Agreements Library).

27 KAVASS'S GUIDE TO THE UNITED STATES TREATIES IN FORCE
Igor I. Kavass and Adolf Sprudzs, comp. (Buffalo, NY: W.S. Hein & Co., 2009–).

Summary: This index is to be used in conjunction with *Treaties in Force* (TIF), see no. 26, above. It is designed to supplement the information in TIF, not replace it. The *Guide* is issued in three parts: part I contains numerical lists for both bilateral and multilateral agreements; part II provides access to treaties and agreements by subject and provides a geographic checklist; and part III contains a chronological index of multilateral treaties and a list of countries and international organizations. Each entry contains the treaty number (TS, TIAS, KAV, etc.), country information, TIF subject, title or description of the agreement, citation, in-force information, and notes on amendments or limitations. The *Guide* is issued annually as new editions of TIF appear. The *Guide* indicates if the text of the treaty is available in *Hein's United States Treaties and Other International Agreements: Current Microfiche Service* (see no. 11, above).

Note: This tool is further enhanced by the *Guide to the United States Treaties in Force: Current Treaty Action Supplement.* This supplement contains information about actions that have occurred since the cut-off date of the latest edition of TIF.

Note: Included in *Hein's United States Treaty Index on CD-ROM*, see no. 30, below.

Note: Previous title was *A Guide to the United States Treaties in Force* (1982–2008).

Note: Available on *HeinOnline*, http://www.heinonline.org (Treaties and Agreements Library).

28 UNITED STATES TREATY INDEX: 1776 – CONSOLIDATION

Igor I. Kavass, comp. and ed. (Buffalo, NY: W.S. Hein & Co. Inc., 1991–).

Summary: This set indexes treaties and international agreements since 1776. Includes bibliographic information about treaties that are still in force and about treaties that are no longer in force. It is supplemented with the annual *Current Treaty Index*, a two-volume supplement. The introduction to this work states that the purpose is to make the treaties and other international agreements the United States enters into with other countries more accessible to the public. Access to these documents is provided in a number of ways: chronologically, by country, by international organization, by subject, numerically, and by a geographic-subject combination. Entries include the treaty number, subject, country, short title, description, signing date, source(s), amending information, in force information, and legislative histories. This index indicates which documents are available in *Hein's United States Treaties and Other International Agreements: Current Microfiche Service.* If there is no TIAS number available, an internal KAV number is assigned to the treaty (the same numbers that are used in *A Guide to the United States Treaties in Force* and *Current Treaty Index*).

Note: This Consolidation replaces many volumes and publications published by Hein from 1973 through 1980 in the *UST Indexing Service.* These titles include: *United States Treaties and Other International Agreements Cumulative Index, 1776–1949*, compiled by Igor Kavass and Mark A. Michael {Buffalo, NY: W.S. Hein & Co., 1975, 4 vols: vol. 1, 363 pp.; vol. 2, 615 pp.; vol. 3, 325 pp.; vol. 4, 278 pp.); *United States Treaties and Other International Agreements Cumulative Index, 1950–1970*, compiled by Igor Kavass and Adolf Sprudzs (Buffalo, NY; W.S. Hein & Co., 1975, 4 vols.: vol. 1, 437 pp.; vol. 2, 762 pp.; vol. 3, 466 pp.; vol. 4, 488 pp.); *United States Treaties and Other International Agreements Cumulative Index, Supplements*, compiled by Igor Kavass and Adolf Sprudzs (Buffalo, NY: W.S. Hein & Co., 1977, 2 vols.: vol. 1, 593 pp.; vol. 2, 840 pp.); *UST Cumulative Indexing Service; Current Supplement*, compiled by Igor Kavass and Adolf Sprudzs (Buffalo, NY: W.S. Hein & Co., 1978–); and, compiled by Igor Kavass and Adolf Sprudzs, annual volumes from 1986 to 1989 (Buffalo, NY: W.S. Hein & Co., 1987–1989), 4 vols.: vol. 1, 498 pp.; vol. 2, 593 pp.; vol. 3, 584 pp.; vol 4, 642 pp.).

Note: Periodically reconsolidated. The *Consolidation* was originally published in 1991 with a 1995 revision. With the 1998 revision, the first three volumes are completely updated and replace the original three volumes. The other ten volumes are from the 1995 revision. 2001 reconsolidation currently in progress.

Note: Available on *Hein's United States Treaty Index on CD-ROM,* see no. 30, below.

29 KAVASS'S CURRENT TREATY INDEX

Igor I. Kavass and Adolf Sprudzs, comp. (Buffalo, NY: W.S. Hein & Co., 1982–).

Summary: This index is a supplement to the *United States Treaty Index: 1776 – Consolidation* (see no. 28, above). It is published twice a year and contains information on current treaty actions by the US The information comes from treaties and agreements published in TIAS as well as those entered into by the US and publicized by the State Department but not yet published. The *Index* contains a numerical index, a chronological index, a country index, and a subject index. There are numerous conversion tables (i.e. TIAS to KAV) and a list of the documents available in *Hein's United States Treaties and Other International Agreements: Current Microfiche Service* and available on *HeinOnline.* Like the other Kavass materials, it utilizes the KAV internal numbering system. Starting with the 1990–1991 edition, this index contains information on treaties and agreements that have entered into force by the US since 1990 but are not yet published in TIAS series nor assigned a TIAS number.

Note: Included in *Hein's United States Treaty Index on CD-ROM,* see no. 30, below.

Note: The information contained in *Unpublished and Unnumbered Treaties Index,* compiled by Igor I. Kavass and Adolf Sprudzs (Buffalo, NY: W.S. Hein & Co., 1987–1989, 4 vols.: vol. 1, 498 pp.; vol. 2, 593 pp.; vol. 3, 584 pp.; vol. 4, 642 pp.) now appears in *Current Treaty Index.*

Note: Available on *HeinOnline,* http://www.heinonline.org (Treaties and Agreements Library).

30 HEIN'S UNITED STATES TREATY INDEX ON CD-ROM

(Buffalo, NY: W.S. Hein & Co., 1991–).

Summary: Brings together the information on treaties and agreements entered into by the United States since 1776 to present. This set provides comprehensive indexing through a number of indexes: numerical, chronological, country, subject, and geographical. Citations to all official treaty series are included. New discs are issued semiannually.

Note: The print equivalents are *Current Treaty Index, A Guide to the United States Treaties in Force,* and the *United States Treaty Index: 1776– Consolidation,* nos. 27, 28 and 29, above.

31 CCH CONGRESSIONAL INDEX
(Chicago, IL: Commerce Clearing House, Inc., 1937–).

Summary: Two-volume set issued for each new Congressional session. The Senate volume of this set contains a section on treaties pending before the Senate. It provides information on the status of these treaties. The treaties are listed chronologically by the session of Congress in which they were introduced and include the Treaty Document number and a brief summary. The summary includes references to *Senate Treaty Documents, Senate Executive Reports,* hearings and ratifications. Covers the 75th Congress to present.

32 EXECUTIVE CALENDAR OF THE SENATE, TREATIES
(Washington, DC: US Government Printing Office, 1987–).

Summary: This section identifies Treaties submitted by the President to the Senate for ratification, placed on the Executive Calendar with a sequentially assigned calendar number and ready for Senate floor consideration. It includes the Treaty Document Number, the subject, and the Senate Executive Report number.

Note: Calendars from 1996-present, http://www.senate.gov/pagelayout/legislative/one_item_and_teasers/exec_calendar_page.htm.

33 CATALOG OF US GOVERNMENT PUBLICATIONS (CGP)
URL: http://catalog.gpo.gov/.

Summary: The Catalog of US Government Publications (CGP) is the finding tool for electronic and print publications from the legislative, executive, and judicial branches of the US government. The CGP contains descriptive records for historical and current publications and provides direct links to those that are available online.

Note: The CGP was originally the online counterpart of the *Monthly Catalog of United States Government Publications,* however, the print version of the *Monthly Catalog* was discontinued with the December 2004 edition. For publications issued prior to 1976, the printed *Monthly Catalog* should be consulted (see no. 34, below).

34 MONTHLY CATALOG OF THE UNITED STATES GOVERNMENT PUBLICATIONS
(Washington, DC: US Government Printing Office, 1895–2004).

Summary: This is a comprehensive index of US government publications, including both depository and non-depository materials. The user can locate treaties, agreements, documents, and hearings. Use the subject entry, "US Treaties, etc". or search by title or subject.

Note: The *Monthly Catalog* has changed its name many times and has modified its format as well.

Note: For current coverage, see the *Catalog of US Government Publications* (CGP), no. 32, above.

35 AMERICAN FOREIGN POLICY AND TREATY INDEX (AFPTI) [AND MICROFICHE]

(Bethesda, MD: Congressional Information Service, Inc., 1993–1999).

Summary: AFPTI indexes and abstracts treaties and international agreements to which the US is a party, including implementing legislation and other ratification documents. Each issue consists of an abstracts volume and an index volume. The abstracts volume contains bibliographic information for all of the publications listed and a summary of the content.

An AFPTI-assigned number is given to each document, and the abstracts are arranged in ascending order. The index volume contains five separate sections: index by subjects and names, index by titles, index by agency report numbers, index by congressional bill numbers, and index by Superintendent of Documents numbers. All of the indexes refer to the AFPTI-assigned number for use in the abstracts volume or to retrieve the publication from the microfiche collection.

Note: Former title was *American Foreign Policy Index: a Guide to Foreign Policy and Foreign Relations Publications of the US Government* (*AFPI*) (Bethesda, MD: Congressional Information Service, Inc., 1993–1995).

Note: Many of the documents included in this microfiche set are available from US depository libraries; however, the AFPTI microfiche contains many non-depository documents as well as publications that are only issued in electronic form.

Note: Since this source is no longer updated, it is useful for historical research only.

36 INDEX TO INTERNATIONAL TREATIES AND AGREEMENTS

Erwin C. Surrency, comp. and ed. (Dobbs Ferry, NY: Oceana Publications, 1994–1998).

Summary: This index covers in force treaties and agreements from 1783 until it ceased in print. The first part of the index is a country index under which treaties are listed based on subject. The next section is the subject index with a list of each country under the topic. With a few exceptions, the topics are the same as the ones used in TIF. The last section is a date signed index. There is also a citation table which provides the parallel citations (if available) for CTIA number, DOS number, TIAS, UST, Bevans, and UKTS.

Note: This information is available in electronic format as part of *Treaties and International Agreements Online*, see no. 12, above.

Note: Since this source is no longer updated, it is useful for historical research only.

37 TREATY ACTIONS

US Department of State, Office of the Legal Advisor.

URL: http://www.state.gov/s/l/treaty/c3428.htm.

Summary: A record of actions taken by States in regard to treaties and agreements. Issued monthly, the document is divided into bilateral and multilateral treaties and agreements. Provides signature, conclusion and entry into force dates, as applicable.

Note: This publication can be irregular.

Note: An archive is available back to 1997.

38 US SENATE

URL: http://www.senate.gov/pagelayout/legislative/d_three_sections_with_teasers/treaties.htm

Summary: This page provides access to the following information; 1) list of treaties received from the President, 2) list of treaties on the Executive Calendar, 3) list of treaties approved by the Senate, and 4) listings of other recent treaty status actions, including treaties which were rejected by the Senate or withdrawn by the President during the current Congress. Each entry provides the treaty document number, the treaty type (extradition, arms control, etc.), and the name or brief description of the treaty. Under treaties approved by the Senate, there is a link to the text of the treaty ratification resolution.

39 CIS/INDEX TO PUBLICATIONS OF THE UNITED STATES CONGRESS

(Bethesda, MD: Congressional Information Service, Inc., 1970–).

Summary: For description, see no. 17, above.

40 TREATIES SUBMITTED TO THE UNITED STATES SENATE: LEGISLATIVE HISTORY, 1989–2004

Christian L. Wiktor (Leiden; Boston: Martinus Nijhoff, 2006).

Summary: While not strictly an index, this volume covers the legislative history of treaties submitted to the Senate from 101st to the 108th Congress (329 treaties in all). Each entry contains the exact title of the treaty; a summary of the legislative history of the Senate's consideration of the treaty, including information related to reservations, understandings, declarations, or other conditions; information regarding implementing legislation; information concerning any subsequent actions taken by the Executive to bring the treaty into force; and other annotations, such as references to previous related treaties. All entries are arranged by the date of conclusion of the treaty. Citations to treaty documents, U.N.T.S. and other sources are included. The forward by Robert E. Dalton indicates that another volume is forthcoming, covering 1789–1988.

Topical and Selected Treaty Collections

There are many compilations of treaties and international agreements by topic, especially in the areas of taxation, trade, environment, and human rights. Listed below are some of the more readily accessible collections, arranged alphabetically by name of collection or website. For the most part, multilateral treaty collections are not included.

41 COMPACTS OF FREE ASSOCIATION: PACIFIC ISLANDS TREATIES AND AGREEMENTS WITH THE UNITED STATES

Igor I. Kavass, comp. (Buffalo, NY: W.S. Hein & Co., 1998–).

Summary: Two volume looseleaf containing the initial compacts and subsidiary agreements between the US and the federated States of Micronesia, Palau and the Republic of Marshall Islands. The agreements are in chronological order with a separate section for each of the three countries. Each section has its own finding tables and indexes. There is also an alphabetical table of titles and a numerical index.

Note: This set has not been updated for quite some time.

42 CUSTOMS LAW & ADMINISTRATION: TREATIES, 3RD EDITION

Ruth F Sturm, ed. (Dobbs Ferry, NY: Oceana Publications, 1997–).

Summary: Five volume looseleaf provides bilateral and multilateral customs treaties between the U.S and other countries. Arranged alphabetically by topic, it includes the text of the agreements, name of the agreement, date signed, and the date entered into force. Exchange of letters, notes, annexes, and attachments are included. The finding tools include parallel citation table, a list of treaties by date, and a list of bilateral treaties by date.

Note: West took over publishing this title in 2011–2012.

43 ENVIRONMENTAL LAW TREATIES OF THE UNITED STATES

Nicholas A. Robinson, comp. and ed. (Dobbs Ferry, NY: Oceana Publications, 1997). 2 vols. Vol. 1, 958 pp.; vol. 2, 831 pp.

Summary: This two-volume set is comprised of environmental treaties between the US and other countries in the following areas: transboundary environmental impact assessment, transboundary hazardous wastes, air pollution, protection of the ozone, climate, armed conflict, world heritage, wetlands, and biological diversity.

Note: Since this source has not been updated, it is useful for historical research only.

44 EXTRADITION LAWS AND TREATIES, UNITED STATES

Igor L Kavass and Adolf Sprudzs, comp.
(Buffalo, NY: W.S. Hein & Co., 1989–).

Summary: This five volume work contains all operative extradition treaties of the US, including legislative provisions. Arranged alphabetically by country. The texts of treaties were taken from *Treaties and Other International Agreements of the United States of America, 1776–1949* and *United States Treaties and Other International Agreements.* Each document provides some brief legislative history information and official citations.

45 FEDERAL TAXATION—US TREATIES AND CONVENTIONS

Westlaw Classic (FTX-TREATIES).

Summary: Contains tax agreements between the U.S. and foreign governments released by the IRS and published in the *Internal Revenue Bulletin.* Coverage begins in 1844.

46 FEDERAL TRADE COMMISSION, INTERNATIONAL COMPETITION AND CONSUMER PROTECTION COOPERATION AGREEMENTS

URL: http://www.ftc.gov/policy/international/international-cooperation-agreements.

Summary: A collection of agreements on competition (antitrust) and consumer protection.

47 INTERNATIONAL AGREEMENTS OF THE UNITED STATES AND THE FORMER SOVIET REPUBLICS

Igor L Kavass, comp. (Buffalo, NY: W.S. Hein & Co., 1996).

Summary: This set contains multilateral and bilateral treaties arranged by KAV number, an internal numbering system used by Hein. Each treaty provides the name of the treaty, signing date, entry into force date, and citation to official US sources. There is a chronological and subject index.

Note: Although initially intended as a looseleaf set, it was never updated. This source is useful for historical research only.

Note: Available on *HeinOnline*, http://www.heinonline.org (Treaties and Agreements Library).

48 INTERNATIONAL HUMAN RIGHTS INSTRUMENTS: A COMPILATION OF TREATIES, AGREEMENTS AND DECLARATIONS OF ESPECIAL INTEREST TO THE UNITED STATES. 2ND EDITION

Richard B. Lillich (Buffalo, NY: WS. Hein & Co., 1990–).

Summary: This volume contains 48 international human rights instruments concluded under the auspices of the United Nations, the Organization of American States, the International Labor Organization, and other international bodies and conferences. They are considered "especial" to the US because the US is a party to them, or can become a party Some instruments are included due to the fact that they are considered norms of customary international law. Besides the text of the instrument, reservations and declarations made by states parties are included.

Note: Available on *HeinOnline*, http://www.heinonline.org (Treaties and Agreements Library).

Note: Has not been updated in quite sometime.

49 PRIVATE INTERNATIONAL LAW

US, Department of State, Assistant Legal Advisor for Private International Law.

URL: http://www.state.gov/s/l/c3452.htm.

Summary: Provides access to treaties in force for the US in the area of private international law, such as wills, trusts and estates; family law; judicial assistance; and commercial law. This site also includes other international instruments (model laws) and information on current negotiations and projects in this area.

50 RHOADES AND LANGER US INTERNATIONAL TAXATION AND TAX TREATIES

Rufus von Thülen Rhoades and Marshall J. Langer (New York: Matthew Bender, 1971–).

Summary: Part V, Appendix A of this set contain US tax treaties and agreements arranged in alphabetical order, by country, including income tax, estate and gift tax, transportation, social security, and exchange of information treaties. Each country is introduced by a status page that lists all of the treaties and other agreements in existence. There is also extensive analysis and commentary Along with the text of the agreements, the set provides citation information, entry into force dates, and citations to related documents.

Index: Volume 6 contains an index and table of treaties.

Note: Available as an e-book and on CD-ROM.

Note: Available on Lexis.com (INTTXT) and Lexis Advance.

51 SOCIAL SECURITY AGREEMENTS

US Social Security Administration.

URL: http://www.ssa.gov/international/totalization_agreements.html.

Summary: A collection of 24 bilateral social security agreements, including a status table.

52 TAX RESEARCH PLATFORM, TREATIES

International Bureau of Fiscal Documentation (IFBD).

URL: http://www.ibfd.org.

Summary: Database containing tax treaties between the US and other countries on tax (including double taxation), social security, transport, inheritance and gift, and other related subjects; includes protocols and amendments, supplementary agreements and exchanges of notes to these treaties. Conclusion and entry into force dates are provided as well as status and effective dates.

53 TAX TREATIES

(Chicago, IL: Commerce Clearing House, Inc., 1952–).

Summary: Seven – volume looseleaf set provides all of the income and estate tax treaties into which the US has entered with other countries for the alleviation of double taxation and the prevention of fiscal evasion. The agreements are arranged alphabetically by country. In addition to the text of the treaty, the set includes US regulations relating to the treaty, reports of the US Department of State, the Senate Foreign Relations Committee, and the Treasury Department, as well as pertinent administrative rulings and court decisions. Older treaties and model treaties are also included.

Index: Volume 1 contains a topical index and volume 7 has a cumulative index.

Note: Available on CCH *Intelliconnect*, http://intelliconnect.cch.com.

54 TRADE AGREEMENTS

Office of the United States Trade Representative.

http://www.ustr.gov/trade-agreements.

Summary: This site contains a variety of agreements on trade and related issues negotiated by the United States Trade Representative, including WTO, free trade agreements, trade and investment framework agreements, bilateral investment treaties (BITs), and other documents.

55 TRADE AGREEMENTS

Trade Compliance Center, US Dept. of Commerce.

http://tcc.export.gov/Trade_Agreements/index.asp.

Summary: The Trade Compliance Center of the Department of Commerce provides access to trade and related agreements, including intellectual property rights agreements and bilateral investment treaties. The database contains the texts of most trade agreements to which the United States is a party and related documents that are important to business. Access to the documents is available by agreement name or through the search engine on the site.

56 TRADE AGREEMENTS AND NEGOTIATIONS
United States Department of Agriculture, Foreign Agricultural Service.
http://www.fas.usda.gov/itp/agreements.asp.
Summary: A collection of agreements related to agricultural trade issue.

57 UNDER SECRETARY FOR ARMS CONTROL AND INTERNATIONAL SECURITY
US Department of State, Under Secretary for Arms Control and International Security.
http://www.state.gov/t/index.htm.
Summary: Contains collections of treaties and agreements for two bureaus: arms control, verification and compliance and international security and nonproliferation, The text of the treaty is provided along with some narrative information. Signing and entry into force dates are also included as well as any additional protocols or memorandums.
Note: This organization used to be called Arms Control and Disarmament Agency; it was abolished in 1998 and its functions were transferred to the Secretary of State.[16]

58 UNITED STATES INCOME TAX TREATIES
The Internal Revenue Service, Office of Tax Administration Advisory Services.
http://www.irs.gov/Businesses/International-Businesses/United-States-Income-Tax-Treaties---A-to-Z.
Summary: Provides access to the texts of income tax treaties between the US and other countries.

16 For information on the history of agency changes, see *History of Agency Organizational Changes: Federal Agencies Terminated, Transferred, or Changes in Name Subsequent to March 4, 1933*, *in* The United States Government Manual, http://www.gpo.gov/fdsys/browse/collection.action?collectionCode=GOVMAN.

59 US BILATERAL INVESTMENT TREATIES

US Department of State, Office of Investment Affairs.
http://www.state.gov/e/eb/ifd/bit/117402.htm.

Summary: List of bilateral treaties with links to some full-text documents in PDF. Also includes the signature and entry into force dates.

60 US INCOME TAX TREATIES AND TIEAS

US Department of the Treasury
http://www.treasury.gov/resource-center/tax-policy/treaties/Pages/treaties.aspx.

Summary: Access to the texts of recently signed US income tax treaties and tax information exchange agreements (TIEAs) and the accompanying Treasury Department tax treaty technical explanations as they become publicly available, as well as the US Model Income Tax Convention. Please note that treaty and TIEA documents are posted on this site upon signature and prior to ratification and entry into force.

61 US-MEXICAN TREATIES

Richard Westin, comp. (Buffalo, NY: W.S. Hein & Co., 1996). 13 vols.

Summary: This thirteen-volume set is a compilation of bilateral treaties between the US and Mexico. It includes only treaties in force. The treaties are arranged chronologically by signing date. Each treaty provides a reference to at least one traditional source (TIAS, UST, ILM, etc.). Many of the documents included in the set were obtained from Lexis and Westlaw.

Index: Chronological and subject index which provides the signing date, short title, treaty number, and location in the set.

Note: Available on *HeinOnline*, http://www.heinonline.org (Treaties and Agreements Library).

Note: Last update was in 2001.

62 US TAX TREATIES IN FORCE

RIA Checkpoint.
https://checkpoint.riag.com/.

Summary: In-depth analysis and full official text of every treaty, protocol, and agreement between the United States and foreign countries relating to income, gift, and estate tax, shipping and transportation, exchange of information, and social security. Also includes Treasury Technical Explanations, Senate Committee Reports, Reports of the Secretary of State, and other related documents. Includes the latest cases and rulings, along with the status and content of new treaties and protocols.

Note: Available on Westlaw (RIA-TREATIES).

63 WORLDWIDE TAX TREATIES
Tax Analysts, Inc.
http://www.taxanalysts.com.

Summary: A database with more than 9,000 treaties. Coverage includes income tax treaties, estate and gift tax treaties, transportation treaties, administrative assistance treaties, and model tax treaties. Includes in-force, pending, terminated and unperfected treaties. Also includes a collection of the legislative histories of all US tax treaties.

Note: Available on Lexis.com (WWTRTY), Lexis Advance and Westlaw Classic (RIA-TAXT).

Diplomatic Documents

The United States publishes more documents and information related to the negotiation, ratification, and implementation of treaties and agreements than probably any other nation. In addition to the sources mentioned above, there is a great deal of documentation relating to US foreign policy. These documents emanate from the President, the Congress, the Department of State, various other Executive Branch agencies, and other federal agencies and departments. Some of the collections mentioned in the sections below are compilations of declassified information and the rules governing declassified US information are contained in several Executive Orders.[17] Other materials are collected through the Freedom of Information Act (FOIA).[18]

Many of the most important collections of documents regarding foreign policy and foreign relations are outlined in this section on *Diplomatic Documents* as well as the following section on *Other Documentation of External Relations*. For more information on the many sources not included in these sections, the researcher should consult *American Foreign Relations since 1600:*

---

17 Executive Order 13,526 (3 C.F.R. 298 (2010)), available at http://www.gpo.gov/fdsys/pkg/CFR-2010-title3-vol1/pdf/CFR-2010-title3-vol1-eo13526.pdf, is the latest in a series of Executive Orders outlining how classified documents and information should be handled. This EO establishes the principle that no records may remain classified indefinitely and provides enforceable deadlines for information to be reviewed for declassification at 25 years. For more information, see the Department of State's Freedom of Information Act website, http://www.state.gov/m/a/ips/.

18 The Freedom of Information Act (FOIA), 5 U.S.C. §552 (2009).

A Guide to the Literature, Robert L. Beisner ed. (2d ed., Santa Barbara, Calif.: ABC-Clio, 2003); E. Plischke, *US Foreign Relations: A Guide to Information Sources* (Detroit, Mich.: Gale Research Co., 1980); and *Foreign Affairs 50-Year Bibliography: New Evaluations of Significant Books on International Relations 1920–1970*, B. Dexter ed. (New York: Published for the Council on Foreign Relations by R.R. Bowker Co., 1972).

For more information on federal government publications, see J. Morehead, *Introduction to United States Government Sources*, 6th ed, (Englewood, CO: Libraries Unlimited, Inc., 1999) and E. Herman, *Locating United States Government Information: A Guide to Sources*, 2nd ed. (Buffalo, NY: W.S. Hein & Co., 1997). While these books are a bit dated, they do an excellent job of highlighting the kinds of documents and publications issued by government agencies. The information about the documents and publications has remained the same and many of the materials are now available on *FDsys: GPO's Federal Digital System*, http://www.gpo.gov/fdsys/.

64 FOREIGN RELATIONS OF THE UNITED STATES
Department of State (Washington DC: US Government Printing Office, 1861–).

Summary: This series provides the official, documentary, historical record of major US foreign policy decisions and significant diplomatic activity. Preparation of the series is guided by statute (Department of State's Basic Authorities Act of 1956, 22 USC 4351 et seq. (1994)). The Advisory Committee on Historical Diplomatic Documentation, established under this statute, reviews records, advises, and makes recommendations concerning the Foreign Relations series. Documents included are from the Department of State, Department of Defense, National Security Council, White House, Central Intelligence Agency, Agency for International Development, and other agencies involved in foreign affairs. Volumes since 1952 are arranged chronologically into sub-series according to Presidential administrations and geographically and topically within each sub-series. The documents in each section are numbered sequentially, and footnotes provide the source of the document and other events or facts. Each volume preface outlines the sources used for the series, the editorial methodology, and the declassification review. There is also a detailed section on sources.

Index: An index is included at the end of the volume for the particular time period.

Index: See also the separate publications *General Index to the Published Volumes of the Diplomatic Correspondence and Foreign Relations of the United States, 1861–1899* (Washington, DC: US Government Printing Office, 1902, 945 pp.),

Papers Relating to the Foreign Relations of the United States: General Index, 1900–1918 (Washington DC: US Government Printing Office, 1941, 507 pp.), and *The Cumulated Index to the US Department of State Papers Relating to the Foreign Relations of the United States 1939–1945* (Millwood, NY: Kraus International, 1980, 1031 pp).

Note: Some of the print volumes are accompanied by microfiche supplements and printed guides. The guides contain lists of sources, abbreviations and persons; summary of the relevant print volumes; and document lists.

Note: Volumes appeared in various editions and under varying titles until 1870, for example *Papers Relating to Foreign Affairs (1861–1869)*. In 1870, the series became known as *Papers Relating to the Foreign Relations of the United States.* In 1947 (volumes for 1932), the series became *Foreign Relations of the United States: Diplomatic Papers.* In 1969 (volumes for 1946) the title was shortened to its present form.

Note: Available from *US Department of State, Office of the Historian,* http://history.state.gov/historicaldocuments. Collection begins with begins with 1945–1950. Site is searchable by title of administration or by keyword within the volumes.

Note: Available on *HeinOnline,* http://heinonline.org/ (Foreign Relations of the United States (FRUS) Collection).

Note: Some volumes available from the *HathiTrust Digital Library,* http://catalog.hathitrust.org/.

65 INDEX TO UNITED STATES DOCUMENTS RELATING TO FOREIGN AFFAIRS, 1828–1861

Adelaide R. Hasse (Washington, DC: Carnegie Institution of Washington, 1914–1921). 3 vols., 1980 pp.

Summary: A three-volume index to published records, documents, papers, correspondence, legislation, and other primary sources related to foreign affairs. Arranged alphabetically by names of individuals and subjects.

Note: Reprint available from Kraus Reprint Co., New York, 1971. Also available on microfilm from Library of Congress, Photoduplication Service, 1955.

66 AMERICAN FOREIGN POLICY CURRENT DOCUMENTS

US Department of State (Washington, DC: US Government Printing Office, 1959–1991).

Summary: This annual one-volume set of documents contains public foreign policy messages, addresses, statements, interviews, press briefings and conferences, and congressional testimony by the executive branch. The focus of this material is the "contemporary public expression of US foreign policy". Some of the documents may have appeared in other official publications and some appear in these volumes for the first time. All of the documents are public in nature and no internal working documents are included. The editors select what they consider to be the most important documents. The first chapters cover some of the more general areas (general principles of American foreign policy, national security policy, arms control, foreign economic policy, the United Nations, etc.). The other chapters are divided into broad geographical areas and then subdivided by country. The Table of Contents provides a list of documents contained in the volume by chapter and a list of abbreviations. Each document is numbered and the text follows thereafter. There is a footnote which indicates the source of the document. Other footnotes contain information and editorial comments to clarify events or provide cross-references to other documents.

Index: Each volume contains a topical index.

Note: The State Department has published various sets of documents on American foreign policy: *A Decade of American Foreign Policy: Basic Documents 1941–1949* (see no. 67, below) and the subsequent publication *American Foreign Policy, 1950–1955: Basic Documents* (Washington, DC; US Government Printing Office, 1957, 2 vols., 3244 pp.). The series continued with *American Foreign Policy: Current Documents,* with annual volumes for 1956–1967, There was an interruption and the series began again in 1983 with *American Foreign Policy: Basic Documents 1977–1980.* The title then returned to *Current Documents* for volumes 1981 forward.

Note: Since 1981, an annual microfiche supplement has been published which contains a much larger and more complete selection of documents than what appears in the printed volumes. A document list accompanies the microfiche supplement.

Note: 1981–1991 is available on *HeinOnline,* http://www.heinonline.org (Foreign Relations of the United States (FRUS) Collection).

67 A DECADE OF AMERICAN FOREIGN POLICY: BASIC DOCUMENTS 1941–1949

Department of State (Washington, DC: US Government Printing Office, 1950). 1381 pp.

Summary: Basic collection of public documents on US foreign policy for the time period. The documents are arranged chronologically by topic. Includes policy statements, addresses, treaties and agreements, communiqués, etc. Includes bibliographical references and an index.

Note: A revised edition of this volume was published in 1985. The revised edition contains about 90 percent of the documents from the original edition, and the order of the documents was reorganized. A *Decade of American Foreign Policy: Basic Documents, 1941–1949*, rev. ed. (Washington DC: US Government Printing Office, 1985). 969 pp.

Note: Followed by *American Foreign Policy, 1950–1955: Basic Documents* (Washington, DC: US Government Printing Office, 1957). 2 vols., 3244 pp.

68 UNITED STATES DEPARTMENT OF STATE PRESS RELEASES
US Department of State.

Summary: Information about new treaties and agreements as well as other diplomatic actions.

Notes: Daily Press Briefings are available from 2009 to present on the current site, http://www.state.gov/r/pa/prs/dpb/index.htm. An archive is also available from 2001–2009, http://2001-2009.state.gov/r/pa/prs/.

69 UNITED STATES DEPARTMENT OF STATE, FREEDOM OF INFORMATION ACT (FOIA)
US Department of State, Under Secretary for Management, Bureau of Administration.
http://www.state.gov/m/a/ips/index.htm.

Summary: This site provides access to many records controlled by the State Department. Information about FOIA requests is also available.

70 JOURNAL OF THE EXECUTIVE PROCEEDINGS OF THE SENATE OF THE UNITED STATES OF AMERICA
US Congress. Senate (Washington, DC: US Government Printing Office, [1828]–).

Summary: This is the official record of proceedings of the executive sessions of the Senate. Includes votes on treaties, list of treaties received during a session, fist of executive reports, a list of treaties pending from earlier sessions, and contains the resolutions of ratification. One volume issued per session of Congress.

Note: Volume 1 covers 1789/1805–.

Note: Available on *LLMC Digital*, 1828–2005, http://www.llmcdigital.org/.

Note: Available on the Library of Congress, *American Memory Project: A Century of Lawmaking*, 1789–1875, http://memory.loc.gov/ammem/amlaw/lwej.html.

71 UNITED STATES DEPARTMENT OF STATE DISPATCH

(Washington, DC: US Government Printing Office, 1939–1999).

Summary: This publication has gone through a number of changes in names and frequency. The former title is *Bulletin* which began publication and 1939 and ceased publication in December 1989. In 1990, the *Dispatch* became a weekly newsletter. Each issue has a section called "Treaty Actions" which includes current information on multilateral and bilateral treaties. Where possible, it provides Senate Treaty Document number, ratification and signature and entry into force dates, recent accessions, and TIAS numbers where appropriate.

Index: Semi-annual and annual indexes.

Index: See also *US Government Periodicals Index* (Bethesda, MD: Congressional Information Service, Inc., 1994–) and *A Reader's Guide to Periodicals Literature* (New York: H.W. Wilson & Co., 1902–).

Note: Replaced the *United States Department of State Bulletin*, 1939–1989.

Note: Available on Lexis.com (DSTATE), Westlaw Classic (USDPTSTDIS).

Note: For some archived editions of the *Dispatch*, see the Department of State Foreign Affairs Network (DOSFAN), contains an archive of documents produced by the State Department from 1990–1997, http://dosfan.lib.uic.edu/ERC/index.html. See also the archives from 1998 to January 20, 2001, http://1997-2001.state.gov/, and from January 20, 2001 to January 20, 2009, http://2001-2009.state.gov/. The materials include speeches, statements, and testimony by the President, Secretary of State, and other senior department officials; along with many other publications which have traditionally been provided to depository libraries, including the *Dispatch*, Background Notes, other official publications, and congressional reports.

Note: Available on *HeinOnline*, http://www.heinonline.org/ (Treaties and Agreements Library).

72 FOREIGN POLICY BULLETIN: THE DOCUMENTARY RECORD OF UNITED STATES FOREIGN POLICY

P. Auerswald, ed. (The Hague: Kluwer Law International, 1990–).

Summary: Published bimonthly. Contains background information on selected treaties and agreements.

Note: Starting with February 2005, vol. 15, no. 1-, publication moved to Cambridge University Press.

Note: Available on *Cambridge Journals Online*, http://journals.cambridge.org/, from volume 1 (1990) to present.

73 AMERICAN STATE PAPERS: DOCUMENTS, LEGISLATIVE AND EXECUTIVE, OF THE CONGRESS OF THE UNITED STATES
Walter Lowrie and Mathew St. C. Clarke, eds. (Washington, DC: Gales & Seaton, 1832–1861). 38 vols.

Summary: Published under the direction of Congress, these volumes contain documentary materials from the early history of the United States (1789–1838). The six-volume sub-series, Class I: Foreign Relations, is the most relevant set of volumes. Other subs-series may also be of interest, see Class IV: Commerce and Navigation or Class V: Military Affairs. Each volume has a table of contents and index.

Note: Reprint available from W.S. Hein & Co., Buffalo, NY, 1998.

Note: Available on *HeinOnline*, http://heinonline.org/ (US Congressional Documents Collection).

Note: Available on the Library of Congress, *American Memory Project: A Century of Lawmaking*, http://memory.loc.gov/ammem/amlaw/lwsp.html.

Note: Available on the Readex database, http://infoweb.newsbank.com.

74 AMERICAN FOREIGN RELATIONS: A DOCUMENTARY RECORD
(New York: New York University Press for Council on Foreign Relations, 1931–1978). 40 vols.

Summary: Covers the period 1931–1978. Eight volumes covering 1971–1978 provide a condensed historical narrative and a selection of documents reflecting the salient aspects of US foreign relations. The format includes two parts: part one provides a detailed historical essay which reviews the main foreign policy developments, and part two contains the documentary materials. Both sections provide footnotes to the relevant sources. The appendix provides a list of the documents referred to in each volume. An index is included at the end of each volume.

Note: Title and imprint vary: *The United States in World Affairs; An Account of American Foreign Relations* (New York: Simon and Schuster for the Council on Foreign Relations, 1931–1971, 32 vols.).

75 THE DECLASSIFIED DOCUMENTS CATALOG [AND MICROFICHE]
(Woodbridge, CT: Primary Source Microfilm, 1986–).

Summary: Bimonthly catalog of declassified documents from the CIA, Department of State, Department of Defense, and documents from Presidential libraries. The types of documents include correspondence, telegrams, reports, minutes of meetings, etc. These documents do not duplicate what is available in *Foreign Relations of the United States* (see no. 64, above), other documents in wide public dissemination, or microfiche collections from NASA or NTIS. The catalog contains three parts: 1) an annual cumulative subject index, 2) a bimonthly catalog of document abstracts and subject index, and 3) a microfiche set containing the full texts of the documents. The catalog provides the full description of each document and the number for locating it on microfiche.

Index: The index and abstracts are available on CD-ROM.

Note: Continues *The Declassified Documents Quarterly Catalog* (Washington: Carrollton Press, 1975–1985, 11 volumes).

Note: A subset of the microfiche documents are available on the DDRS (*Declassified Documents Reference System*) database, see no. 76, below.

76 DDRS (DECLASSIFIED DOCUMENTS REFERENCE SYSTEM)
(Primary Source Media (Gale), 1998–).
http://galenet.galegroup.com.

Summary: These collections of documents are from presidential libraries, the CIA, the FBI, and many other federal agencies from post-World War II. The collection contains more than 75,000 documents, including Cabinet meeting minutes, National Security Council policy statements, State Department political analysis, dispatches, memoranda, and many other types of materials. The documents can be searched full-text or by search fields.

Note: Declassified Documents Reference System is also available on microfiche. The collection is available from 1974 onward. Printed abstracts and indexes to facilitate bibliographic access are available.

Note: Formerly under the title *Declassified Documents Retrospective Collection or DDRS.*

77 DOCUMENTS ON AMERICAN FOREIGN RELATIONS
(Boston: World Peace Foundation, 1939–1970).

Summary: The purpose of this collection was to provide a documentary record of US foreign relations during the previous year. Included government documents and papers that have given direction to foreign relations. Arranged by topic with footnotes to the source documents. Excerpts from the actual documents are often included with a note as to the source of the document.

Index: Each volume contains cumulative index for the preceding five years.

Note: Published 1938/1939–1943/1944 in Boston by the World Peace Foundation; 1944/45–1951 in Princeton, N.J. by the Princeton University Press for the World Peace Foundation; 1952–1970 for the Council on Foreign Relations.

Note: Available on microfiche, Buffalo, NY, W.S. Hein & Co.

78 THE NATIONAL STATE PAPERS OF THE UNITED STATES 1789–1817: TEXTS OF DOCUMENTS

Martin P. Claussen, ed. (Wilmington, Del.: Michael Glazier Inc., 1980).

Summary: 35 volumes cover the administration of George Washington and 24 volumes cover the administration of John Adams. Contains the full text of extant bills, legislative resolutions, amendments, petitions, presidential messages, Senate and House committee reports, and other supplementary materials in chronological order. These documents are pre-Serial Set (see no. 22, above). The set does not provide an index, but the documents are listed in the table of contents.

79 PUBLIC PAPERS OF THE PRESIDENTS OF THE UNITED STATES

(Washington, DC: US Government Printing Office, [1956–]).

Summary: These volumes constitute an official compilation of the public messages, speeches, joint statements with leaders of foreign governments, and press statements of the Presidents. The documents are in chronological order by the date of the document or event. The many appendices include a digest of other White House announcements, nominations, a checklist of White House press releases, proclamations and executive orders, subject and name indexes, and a documents categories list.

Index: Indexes for each administration under the title *The Cumulated Indexes to the Public Papers of the Presidents of the United States* (Millwood, NY: KTO, 1977–).

Note: Beginning with the volumes on President Carter, this series expanded coverage to include all materials printed in the *Compilation of Presidential Documents* (see no. 19, above).

Note: Available on Lexis.com (PRESDC) and Lexis Advance from March 24, 1979 through February 2, 2011, Westlaw Classic (PRES) and WeslawNext (see Administrative Decisions & Guidance, Federal Administrative Decisions & Guidance, Executive Office of the President) from 1984 to present.

Note: Available on *FDsys: GPO's Federal Digital System*, George H.W. Bush, 1991 to present, http://www.gpo.gov/fdsys/.

80 COMPILATION OF REPORTS OF COMMITTEE…1789–1901

United States, Congress, Senate. Committee on Foreign Relations (Washington DC: US Government Printing Office, 1901).

Summary: Volumes 1–7 compile the reports from the Committee on Foreign Relations from 1789 to 1901.

Index: Volume 8.

81 STATE PAPERS AND PUBLICK DOCUMENTS OF THE UNITED STATES, FROM THE ACCESSION OF GEORGE WASHINGTON TO THE PRESIDENCY, EXHIBITING A COMPLETE VIEW OF OUR FOREIGN RELATIONS SINCE THAT TIME. 3RD ED

(Boston: Thomas B. Wait, 1819).

Summary: Twelve volumes which cover the period 1789–1815. General chronological arrangement.

Note: Includes confidential documents first published in the second edition of this work.

82 UNITED STATES CONGRESSIONAL COMMITTEE HEARINGS

(Washington, DC: US Government Printing Office, [n.d.]).

Summary: Many congressional committees hold hearings on treaties and agreements, especially the Senate Committee on Foreign Relations. The hearings may be explanatory or investigatory and offer testimony and information about the topic.

Index: The most accessible indexes are the CIS publications, see *CIS US Congressional Committee Hearings Index* (Bethesda MD: Congressional Information Service, 1981–). This index and its microfiche text covers titles from the 1830s through 1969. Coverage after 1969 is through the *CIS/Index to Publications of the United States Congress* [*and Microfiche*] (Bethesda, MD: Congressional Information Service, Inc, 1970–). As with other CIS indexes, treaties and agreements are indexed under the relevant subject, the title of the treaty or agreement, or under the heading "treaties and conventions".

Note: Unpublished hearings for both the House and the Senate, with companion microfiche, are published in an on-going series providing coverage since the 1830s to date, see *CIS Index to Unpublished US House of Representatives Committee Hearings* (Bethesda, MD: Congressional Information Service, 1988–) and *CIS Index to Unpublished US Senate Committee Hearings* (Bethesda, Md.: Congressional Information Service, 1986–).

Note: Many hearings transcripts are available on Lexis.com (HEARNG) and Westlaw Classic (USTESTIMONY and CONGTMY).

Note: Available on *ProQuest Congressional*, http://congressional.proquest.com.

83 FOREIGN POLICY BULLETIN: THE DOCUMENTARY RECORD OF UNITED STATES FOREIGN POLICY

P. Auerswald, ed. (The Hague: Kluwer Law International, 1990–).

Summary: For description, see no. 72, above.

84 UNIVERSITY PUBLICATIONS OF AMERICA RESEARCH COLLECTIONS (Bethesda, MD: Congressional Research Service, 1974–).

Summary: Since 1974, University Publications of America (UPA) has been publishing documentary research collections. Some of the collections include the *Confidential US State Department Central and Special Files, National Security Files,* and *Presidential Papers and Documents.* These documents are microfilmed from the original documents in the National Archives, with little editorial intervention. The collections include complete reel, subject and correspondent indexes, as well as guidebooks to the collections which include introductory material highlighting important parts of the collection and placing the material in its historical context.

Note: For more information on these document collections, see the ProQuest website, http://cisupa.ProQuest.com/.

Note: UPA was an imprint of Congressional Information Service, part of the LexisNexis company and is now part of ProQuest.

85 NATIONAL ARCHIVES AND RECORDS ADMINISTRATION (NARA)

Summary: The National Archives holds the federal records and publications emanating from the executive, legislative and judicial branches of government dating from pre-federal times to the present. Presidential documents constitute the largest portion of NARA's holdings. Many State Department documents are also available at the National Archives. These documents include the following series: *Records Relating to Political Relations Between the United States and...; Records Relating to Internal Affairs of...; Notes from the... Legation in the United States;* and *Diplomatic Instructions.* Other relevant sets of documents include diplomatic dispatches, notes to foreign missions, communications from heads of state, and records of various offices within the State Department. In addition, the records of the Senate Foreign Relations Committee are available, including treaty files, committee papers and minutes, reports, presidential messages and communications, and other records.

Many of these collections of documents are made available on microfilm (National Archives Microfilm Publications series). To locate these microform collections, see the Archival Research Catalog (ARC), http://www.archives.gov/research/search/. The catalog provides the name of each set of microfilm, the dates of coverage, and the number of reels.

Index: See *The Guide to Federal Records in the National Archives of the United States 2nd ed.* (Washington, DC: National Archives and Records Administration, 1998, 3 vols., n.p.). This descriptive guide contains information about the federal records held in the Archives and is intended to help researchers locate relevant materials in the record groups. The 1995 edition of this publication is available on the NARA website, http://www.archives.gov/research/guide-fed-records/.

Index: Other printed guides include *Guide to the Records of the United States Senate at the National Archives, 1789–1989* (Bicentennial edition, Washington, DC: National Archives and Records Administration, 1990, 365 pp.), *Diplomatic Records: A Select Catalog of National Archives Microform Publications,* by John J. Hedges (Washington, DC: National Archives and Records Administration, 1986, 245 pp.), and *A Reference Guide to United States Department of State Special Files,* by Gerald Haines (Westport, CT: Greenwood Press, 1985, 393 pp.).

Note: Another tool for locating records at various archives is the Archive Finder, a directory which describes over 220,000 collections of primary source material housed in thousands of repositories across the United States, published by Chadwyck Healey, http://archives.chadwyck.com/home.do.

Note: For more information about the National Archives and its collections, see the NARA website, http://www.archives.gov/index.html.

86 NATIONAL SECURITY ARCHIVE COLLECTIONS

Summary: The National Security Archive[19] has produced a series of large microform collections of documents on US foreign policy. These collections consist of over 94,000 pages of documents released through the Freedom of Information Act (FOIA) and other governmental processes, accompanied by finding aids – indices, catalogs, chronologies, glossaries, bibliographies and introductory essays. These documents contain information on the development of US foreign policy since World War II.

Index: Printed indexes and guides are available for each document collection. See also the *National Security Archive Index on CD-ROM* (Washington, DC: National Security Archive, 1994) which combines the printed indexes and guides for the twelve titles included in the *Making of US Policy* series.

Note: Twelve of these collections (Afghanistan, Berlin Crisis 1958–1962, Cuban Missile Crisis, El Salvador, Iran-Contra Affair, Intelligence Community, Iran Revolution, Military Uses of Space, Nicaragua, Nuclear Non-Proliferation, Philippines, and South Africa) are available on the web in the Digital National Security Archive through ProQuest, http://nsarchive.chadwyck.com/home.do.

---

19 National Security Archive was founded in 1985 as an independent non-governmental research institute and library. The Archive's collections and published declassified documents are acquired through Freedom of Information Act (FOIA) requests. The Archive is located at George Washington University in Washington DC. For more information about the National Security Archive, see its website, http://www.gwu.edu/~nsarchiv/.

Contains over 94,000 declassified documents that led to critical policy decisions. More collections will be added in the future.

Note: The National Security Archive also maintains its own website which provides information about its mission and collections, http://www.gwu.edu/~nsarchiv/. At this site there is information on the Archive's microform collections, books by the Archive Staff, and the electronic briefing books, http://www.gwu.edu/~nsarchiv/publications/index.html.

Note: Formerly produced by Chadwyck-Healey.

Yearbooks and Digests of State Practice

87 DIGEST OF PUBLISHED OPINIONS OF THE ATTORNEYS-GENERAL, AND OF THE LEADING DECISIONS OF THE FEDERAL COURTS, WITH REFERENCES TO INTERNATIONAL LAW, TREATIES, AND KINDRED SUBJECTS

John L. Cadwalader, comp. (Washington, DC; US Government Printing Office, 1877). 290 pp.

Summary: The first of many series of official digests of US state practice arranged alphabetically by topic.

Note: Available on *HeinOnline,* http://www.heinonline.org (Foreign & International Law Resources Database).

88 DIGEST OF THE INTERNATIONAL LAW OF THE UNITED STATES, TAKEN FROM DOCUMENTS ISSUED BY PRESIDENTS AND SECRETARIES OF STATE, AND FROM DECISIONS OF FEDERAL COURTS AND OPINIONS OF ATTORNEYS-GENERAL, 2ND ED

Francis Wharton, ed. (Washington, DC: US Government Printing Office, 1887). 3 vols. Vol. 1, 825 pp.; vol 2, 832 pp.; vol. 3, 1003 pp.

Summary: Three-volume set arranged under broad subject headings. Includes an index.

Note: Follows the Cadwalader digest, see no. 87, above.

Note: Available on *HeinOnline,* http://www.heinonline.org/ (Foreign & International Law Resources Database).

89 A DIGEST OF INTERNATIONAL LAW

John B. Moore, comp. (Washington DC; US Government Printing Office, 1906).

Summary: This eight-volume set contains commentary and documentary sources of US state practice twenty years after the first publication of Wharton's Digest. The sources include diplomatic discussions, treaties, and court decisions, as well as Presidential documents and Department of State materials.

Index: Volume 8 is an index organized by international law topics.

Note: This digest supersedes the Cadwalader and Wharton digests, see nos. 87 and 88, above.

Note: Available on *HeinOnline*, http://www.heinonline.org/ (Foreign & International Law Resources Database).

90 DIGEST OF INTERNATIONAL LAW

Green H. Hackworth, comp. (Washington, DC: US Government Printing Office, 1940–1944).

Summary: This eight-volume set succeeds Moore's digest and covers 1906 through 1939. The general outline follows the Moore and Wharton digests. Like its predecessor, this digest contains commentary, extracts from diplomatic communications, treaties and agreements, and citations to relevant sources from Department of State records and other sources.

Index: Volume 8.

Note: This digest supersedes Moore's digest, see no. 89, above.

Note: Available on *HeinOnline*, http://www.heinonline.org/ (Foreign & International Law Resources Database).

91 DIGEST OF INTERNATIONAL LAW

Prepared by and under the direction of Marjorie Whiteman (Washington, DC: US Government Printing Office, 1963–1973).

Summary: This fifteen-volume work covers 1940 through 1960. While an effort was made to follow the content and format of the earlier digests, this work contains many new topics. There is a cross-reference to corresponding chapters of the predecessor digests at the beginning of each chapter.

Index: Volume 15.

Note: This digest is the successor to the Hackworth digest, see no. 90, above.

Note: Available on *HeinOnline*, http://www.heinonline.org/ (Foreign & International Law Resources Database).

92 DIGEST OF UNITED STATES PRACTICE IN INTERNATIONAL LAW

Compiled by the Department of State (Washington, DC: Office of the Legal Adviser, Dept. of State, 1974–1986).

Summary: This series marks a departure from the earlier sets of digests. With this set, the State Department decided to publish an annual volume of US practice. The material included in each annual volume was selected based on "its importance in the development of international law, or its role in confirming international legal precedent, or for purposes of simply noting the record in vital areas of international law". The types of materials covered include treaties, executive agreements, domestic legislation, federal regulations, federal case law, diplomatic notes, correspondence, statements, etc. There is a brief summary of contents followed by a detailed table of contents. Under each topical section, there is a statement of the practice of the US on that topic for the time period. Each statement is followed by the source of the information. Covers the time period 1973–1980.

Index: Each volume contains a topical index. There is a cumulative index which covers all of the volumes under the separate title, *Cumulative Index, Digest of United States Practice in International Law, 1972–1980* (Washington, DC; Office of the Legal Advisors, Department of State, US Government Printing Office, 1989, 367 pp.). The cumulation is an extensive revision of the individual indexes.

Note: This set follows the Whiteman digest, see no. 91, above.

Note: Available on *HeinOnline*, http://www.heininline.org/ (Foreign & International Law Resources Database).

93 CUMULATIVE DIGEST OF UNITED STATES PRACTICE IN INTERNATIONAL LAW

Marjorie L. Nash, comp. (Washington, DC: Office of the Legal Adviser, Dept. of State, US Government Printing Office, 1993). 3 vols., 3845 pp.

Summary: This three-volume set provides a cumulative overview of US state practice 1981–1988. It contains background information, interpretation, and trends from the Department of State sources.

Index: A subject index is contained in volume 3.

Note: Continues *Digest of United States Practice in International Law.*

Note: Updated by the monthly column "Contemporary Practice of the United States Relating to International Law," *American Journal of International Law*, see no. 95, below.

94 DIGEST OF UNITED STATES PRACTICE IN INTERNATIONAL LAW

Compiled by the Department of State (Washington, DC: International Law Institute, 2001–).

Summary: After a hiatus, the Digest resumed publication covering the year 2000. Since then, annual volumes for 2000 through 2010, a two-volume set covering 1991–1999, and a volume for 1989–1990 have been published on-line and in hard copy. A cumulative index for the years 1989–2008 was released in the spring of 2010. The focus remains the same as the earlier digests, but the format changed to rely on the text of relevant documents introduced by short explanatory notes to provide the reader with some background for understanding the significance of the items included. In order to assist readers in locating the full text of documents which are excerpted in the 2000 Digest but readily accessible elsewhere, the volume includes citations to websites or other public sources. This listing has been created for documents that are not readily available

Note: Also available on the State Department website, http://www.state.gov/s/l/c8183.htm, 1989–present. Beginning with the 2011 Digest, the official version of the Digest is published exclusively on-line.

Note: The Digest volumes covering 1989–2010 were published under a co-publishing agreement between the International Law Institute and Oxford University Press.

95 AMERICAN JOURNAL OF INTERNATIONAL LAW (AJIL)
(Washington, DC: American Society of International Law, 1921–).

Summary: Each quarterly issue of AJIL contains a section on US state practice, arranged by topic, with footnotes to the relevant documents. Entitled "Contemporary Practice of the United States Relating to International Law," this section on state practice updates the Cumulative Digest of United States Practice.

Index: AJIL is indexed in a number of periodical indexes (ABC POL. SCI: A Bibliography of Contents: Political Science and Government; Current Law Index; International Bibliography of Book Reviews and Scholarly Literature; International Bibliography of Periodical Literature; Index to Foreign Legal Periodicals; Index to Legal Periodicals; International Political Science Abstracts; Public International Law: A Current Bibliography of Books and Articles; and Social Sciences Index).

Note: AJIL is available on Lexis.com (AJIL) and Lexis Advance from 1980, Westlaw (AMJIL), and WestlawNext from 1982.

Note: Available from volume 1 on JSTOR, http://www.jstor.org/ and *HeinOnline*, http://www.heinonline.org/ (Law Journal Library).

96 SEAN D. MURPHY, UNITED STATES PRACTICE IN INTERNATIONAL LAW
(Cambridge; New York: Cambridge University Press, 2002–).

Summary: Aimed at being a current source for US practice in international law. This series set out to provide a more comprehensive view of state practice by including actions by the executive, legislative, and judicial braches of the US government.

Index: Each volume contains an index.

Note: Thus far, only two volumes have been published: vol. 1 (covers 1999–2001) and vol. 2 (covers 2002–2004).

Note: Also available as an ebook on *Cambridge Books Online,* http://ebooks.cambridge.org/.

97 HISTORIC DOCUMENTS OF...[YEAR]
(Washington, DC: Congressional Quarterly, 1972–).

Summary: These annual volumes provide convenient access to documents on public affairs, including foreign relations. Documents are arranged in chronological order. There is an introduction to each topical section and document summary and, in some cases, the full text of a particular document. The sources include presidential statements, committee reports, speeches, and other documents.

Index: Separate cumulative indexes have been published over the years, *Historic Documents Index*, 1972–1989, for example. Each volume also contains a cumulative five year index.

Note: Available on the *CQ Press Electronic Library* database, http://library.cqpress.com/historicdocuments/.

98 RESTATEMENT OF THE LAW, THIRD, FOREIGN RELATIONS LAW
(Washington, DC: American Law Institute, 1987–).

Summary: As with all Restatements, this one is not an official document on foreign relations from the United States government. However, it is considered an authoritative work on the general common law of foreign relations. The introduction states that foreign relations law of the United States "consists of (a) international law as it applies to the United States; and (b) domestic law that has substantial significance for the foreign relations of the United States or has other substantial international consequences".

This two-volume set is arranged by chapters, and each chapter covers a topic within foreign relations. The chapters are divided into sections, and each section deals with a general principle of law, followed by comments and reporters' notes. The notes contain citations to cases, treaties, law reviews and other materials. The second volume also contains several tables: cases, statutes, international agreements, parallel tables for the second and third restatements and a cross reference table to the digest system and ALR annotations.

Index: Alphabetical index at the end of volume 2.

Note: There is a cumulative annual supplement reporting cases that cite the Restatement of the Law, Second and Third of Foreign Relations.

Note: Available in electronic form on Lexis.com (FORREL), Lexis Advance, Westlaw Classic (REST-FOREL) and WestlawNext.

Note: Drafts and earlier editions are available on *HeinOnline,* http://heinonline.org (American Law Institute Library).